THE STATE IN MYANMAR

'... ultimately, Leviathan had to learn that enduring empires are not built on common sense. When Leviathan endeavours to organise society for production he forgets that man cannot live by bread alone. But in this he is fighting against human nature and in the long run, for all his tale of martyrs, Leviathan himself must fail unless he can adapt himself to human nature. Fashioned by Art, he must be born again by grace beyond the reach of art.'

J.S. Furnivall, 'The Fashioning of the Leviathan', in *Journal of the Burma Research Society*, vol. XXIX, no. 3 (1939), p. 137.

ROBERT H. TAYLOR

The State in Myanmar

University of Hawai`i Press
Honolulu

First published in the United Kingdom by
HURST Publishers Ltd
41 Great Russell Street, London, WC1B 3PL

Published in North America by
University of Hawaii Press
2840 Kolowalu Street
Honolulu, HI 96822
www.uhpress.hawaii.edu

Library of Congress Cataloging-in-Publication Data

Taylor, Robert H., 1943-
  The state in Myanmar / Robert H. Taylor. — Expanded and updated ed.
    p. cm.
  Previously published as: The state in Burma. London : C. Hurst & Co, c1987.
  Includes bibliographical references and index.
  ISBN 978-0-8248-3362-6 (pbk. : alk. paper)
  1. Burma—Politics and government. I. Taylor, Robert H., 1943- State in Burma.
II. Title.
  JQ751.A58T39 2008
  320.9591—dc22
                                      2008037855

Printed in India

CONTENTS

v

CONTENTS

MAPS

TABLES

vii

GLOSSARY

Ahmu-dan	Persons living on royal lands and owing immediate obligation to the crown; crown servicemen
Akhin wun	Centrally appointed revenue supervisors under the precolonial state
Amyotha Huttaw	Nationalities Legislative Assembly
Ana de	To be restrained for fear of offending
Asiayon	Organisation; association; body
Athi	Persons living at a distance from the court and owing the state primarily tax obligations
Atwin-wun	An Interior minister or member of the *bye-daik*
Baho	Central (as in central government)
Bayin	Autonomous provincial governors before the Toungoo reforms
Bo	An officer; name given to local strongmen and political bosses during the 1950s
Bodhissatta	Emergent Buddha; occasional claim about kings
Bu athin	Village peasant organisations in the 1920s and 1930s that opposed paying taxes and rent
Bye-daik	King's privy council
Cakkravatti	Aspect of kingship; universal monarch or world conqueror
Chettiars	Caste of moneylenders from Madras
Dhamma	Law
Dhammakatika	Buddhist monks who toured villagers and organised peasants in the 1920s
Dhammaraja	Aspect of kingship; lord of law
Do Bama Asiayon	'Our Burma' or 'We Burmans' Association; political organisation of the *thakin* in the 1930s
Gaung	Subordinate to headmen during the colonial period who served as a police officer and assisted with tax collection
Hluttaw	Council of ministers of the pre-colonial court

ix

Hkitsan	Modern
Hpayahlaung	Burmese for *bodhissatta*
Hpon	Innate power or glory; as in *pongyi*; 'great power', the title of Buddhist monks
Hsinyeitha	Poor man or proletarian; name of Dr Ba Maw's political party in the 1930s
Htan-ta-bin sa-nit	One palm tree system of economic analysis
Kamma	Burmese for *karma*
Karma	Buddhist notion of fate as determined by deeds done in previous existences
khamauk	Peasants' hat; symbol given by Electoral Commission to the NLD in the 1990 election
Kin-wun	Minister responsible for crown service men or *ahmudan* population
Ko Min Ko Chin	One's Own King—One's Own Kind; name of the political party formed by *Thakin* for the 1936 election
Kutho	Merit as earned by a Buddhist devotee
Kyedangyi	A subordinate to a village headman with responsibilities for taxation
Let-yon	Force; military power
Lon htein	Riot police
Maha Bama	Greater Burma; Second World War period political organisation
Maistry	Labour recruiters from India who brought workmen to Burma
Ma lok, ma shot, ma pyot	Don't do any work, don't get implicated and don't get fired
Min	King or monarch
Myei-daing	Assistant to *thu-gyi* with special responsibilities for property and taxation
Myo	Township or town in pre-colonial administration
Myochit	Patriot or lover of one's country; political party founded by U Saw in the 1930s
Myo-ok	Township officer appointed under the British
Myo-sa	Appenage holder
Myo-thu-gyi	Village headman
Myo-wun	Provincial governors appointed by the Toungoo and Konbaung kings

GLOSSARY

Naingngan (naingngantaw) Current usage for the state; previously implied area conquered by the state; also can refer to nation; *taw* implies religious or state power and sanctity

Nat Animistic beings thought to people part of the conceptual world of many villagers

Pongyi Buddhist monk

Pongyi kyaung Monastery; centre of monastic education

Pyihtaungsu Hluttaw Union Legislative Assembly; two houses of 2008 Constitution sitting together

Pyithu Hluttaw People's Assembly

Sangha Collective term for the Buddhist monkhood

Sasana Buddhist monkhood and its institutions

Sawbwa Normally a hereditary ruler of a large or medium size area in what are now referred to as the Shan and Kayah states

Sayadaw Senior monk, head of a monastery

Sibwayei athin Economy organisation; village organisations in the 1920s and 1930s similar to the *wunthanu athin*

Sit-ke Military officers assigned by the monarchical court to supervise local administrations, especially in the Shan areas, and to direct military and police arrangements

Taik Township in the pre-colonial period; the term implies a less settled community than a *myo*

Tatmadaw military, armed forces

Thakin Literally master; used as equivalent to *sahib* by the British and taken as their own title by Myanmar nationalists in the 1930s

Thathameda Head tax

Thathanabaing Head of the Buddhist monkhood appointed by the king

Thu-gyi Headmen of villages

Thuriya Sun; name of first Yangon nationalist newspaper

Vinaya Rules of obligation of a Buddhist monk

Wun-gyi Minister or member of the *Hluttaw*

Wunthanu athin Village nationalist organisations in the 1920s and 1930s

Yazawut King's business; eventually criminal law

Ywa Village

ABBREVIATIONS

ABPO	All Burma Peasants' Organisation
ABSDF	All Burma Students' Democratic Front
ABSU	All Burma Students' Union
ADB	Asian Development Bank
AFO	Anti-Fascist Organisation
AFPFL	Anti-Fascist People's Freedom League
ASEAN	Association of South East Asian Nations
BCP	Burma Communist Party, White Flag
BIA	Burma Independence Army
BIMSTEC	Bangladesh-India-Myanmar-Sri Lanka-Thailand Economic Community
BNA	Burma National Army
BPF	Burma Patriotic Forces
BSPP	Burma Socialist Programme Party
CAS(B)	Civil Affairs Service (Burma)
CP(B)	Communist Party (Burma), Red Flag
CRDB	Committee for the Restoration of Democracy in Burma
CRPP	Committee to Represent the People's Parliament
DAB	Democratic Alliance of Burma
DBANRDA	Ministry for the Development of Border Areas and National Races and Development Affairs
DDS(I)	Directorate of Defence Services (Intelligence)
DKBA	Democratic Kayin Buddhist Army
DPNS	Democratic Party for New Society
DSA	Defence Services Academy
DSI	Defence Services Institute
ENSCC	Ethnic Nationalities Solidarity and Cooperation Committee
FBC	Free Burma Coalition
FDB	Forum for Democracy in Burma
FTU(B)	Federations of Trade Unions (Burma)
GAD	General Administration Department
GCBA	General Council of Burmese Associations

ABBREVIATIONS

GCSS	General Council of Sangha Sammeggi
ICRC	International Committee of the Red Cross
ILO	International Labour Organisation
IMF	International Monetary Fund
FCO	Karen Central Organisation
KHRG	Karen Human Rights Group
KIA	Kachin Independence Army
KIO	Kachin Independence Organisation
KMT	Chinese Nationalist Party; Kuomintang
KNDO	Karen National Defence Organisation
KNLA	Karen National Liberation Army
KNU	Karen National Union
LDP	League for Democracy and Peace
MFF	Myanmar Fisheries Federation
MNDA	Myanmar National Democratic Alliance
NCGUB	National Coalition Government of the Union of Burma
NCUB	National Council of the Union of Burma
NDD	Network for Democracy and Development
NDF	National Democratic Front
NED	National Endowment for Democracy
NLD	National League for Democracy
NLD-LA	National League for Democracy—Liberated Areas
NMSP	New Mon State Party
NUF	National United Front
NUP	National Unity Party
OSS	Office of Strategic Services
OTS	Officers Training School
PVO	People's Volunteer Organisation
SAARC	South Asia Association for Regional Cooperation
SAB	State Agricultural Bank
SAC	Security and Administration Committee
SAMB	State Agricultural Marking Board
SLORC	State Law and Order Restoration Council
SNLD	Shan Nationalities League for Democracy
SPDC	State Peace and Development Council
SWAN	Shan Women's Action Network
TUC-B	Trades Union Council-Burma
UMFCCI	Union of Myanmar Federation of Chambers of Commerce
UNDP	Union National Democracy Party
UNHCHR	United Nations High Commission for Human Rights
USDA	Union Solidarity and Development Association

YASU	Yangon Arts and Science University
YIT	Yangon Institute of Technology
YMBA	Young Men's Buddhist Association

PREFACE AND ACKNOWLEDGEMENTS TO

The State in Myanmar

The State in Myanmar is an extended version of *The State in Burma*. The latter was written in 1985/86 and published in 1987. It has been revised to reflect the results of what research has been undertaken on relevant subjects since it first appeared. Less than a year after *The State in Burma* was published, the state faced another of the great challenges that have tested its institutions, and the sagacity and tenacity of its leaders, over the centuries. The new material in this edition attempts to describe that crisis and the efforts of the state's managers to rebuild from its consequences, and of their critics and opponents to wrest control from them. While it was being written, preparations were underway for drafting a new basic charter and holding a referendum to ratify the third constitution of independent Myanmar. After the failure to find a way of governing the country satisfactorily in the past, another attempt was about to be made.

The State in Burma did not predict and I did not anticipate the dramatic events of 1988. Some reviewers and critics were happy to draw attention to that point. Whether their prediction skills were and are more acute than mine is for others to decide. While some reviewers wrote reasonably favourably about the book and some even understood its purpose, many seemed exasperated, if not rather angry about it. The ability of the original book to generate antagonism apparently carries on, as I was abruptly reminded a few years ago. I sat at a cafeteria table during a break at an international meeting on Myanmar and introduced myself to a young postgraduate student who was also attending. When I told her who I was, she immediately announced that she hated me. Since we had never met, I was puzzled. How could reading my tedious prose evoke such strong emotions? She could not explain except to suggest incoherently that I was responsible for Myanmar not being the liberal, prosperous country she thought it should be. If only books and their authors had such powers!

Within Myanmar, *The State in Burma* evoked slight interest. It was neither reviewed nor translated into Burmese, although it was translated into Thai, and published in Bangkok, in 2006. I did once chance upon a pirated copy in a bookstall in Yangon. The late General Ne Win had one hundred copies printed for distribution to the inner circles of his government, party, and army in 1987. No one in a position of authority, to my knowledge, has ever admitted to having read it. I know of no evidence that its existence has changed the politics of Myanmar, for good or ill, in any way. Like *The State in Burma*, *The State in Myanmar* is not a book that predicts the future. It describes and tries to make sense of the past by attempting to develop a coherent picture of the evolution of the state as the dominant institution in Myanmar.

Some reviewers of *The State in Burma* criticised the book for its alleged reification of the state. Perhaps they were right, but who has written a book about the history of a government, country or nation who has not done the same? Whether we like it or not, and whether or not the reader is willing to share the author's usually unstated proposition that people, singularly and collectively, make the decisions of state, there is an institution in the life of almost every human being on the earth today which has a predominant influence on their life. Most of the time, that is the state that has jurisdiction over where they live.

If I am asked now to predict the future of Myanmar, little would be certain beyond the fact that the rainy season will be followed by the cool season, which in turn will be succeeded by the hot season, before the cycle resumes. Beyond that, accident, contingency, ignorance, wisdom, and other uncertain and unknown variables will have their sway. The law of unintended consequences will continue to apply. The vagaries of the weather are also outside the ken of a mere scribbler.

The conditions under which the *State in Myanmar* was written were different from those of its predecessor. Despite endless reports that every year conditions in Myanmar were worse than before, for foreign scholars conducting research in the country, conditions are much easier than they were when I lived in Yangon in the 1970s and 1980s. People, including some government officials, are much more open and accessible, and information is more easily available through the internet and other sources. Travel outside the main cities is now feasible and one can explore most of the country relatively freely. The validity of what one hears and reads, of course, always has to be tested against its plausibility. Whereas when the first book was written interest in Myanmar was minimal and the publishers took a gamble issuing a book on a subject about which most of the world had little concern, now there appears to be a great deal of interest, though much of it ill informed. While there are more news reports, there are not necessarily more facts or cogent analyses of what little is known. Finding accurate statistics and unbiased analysis remains a major problem.

If conditions in Myanmar have changed, so has the author. He is older, not necessarily wiser. He no longer is employed in academic life with all of its expectations and requirements. More important, he has lived through the events that are described in chapter 6 and has spent much more time in Myanmar than was previously possible. He also met a number of the prominent figures who have participated in the life of the state in Myanmar during the past 20 years. Before reviewers and critics jump to conclusions, they should note that, just as he never met General Ne Win, he never met Senior General Than Shwe or most of the key members of the government. Nor has he met Daw Aung Suu Kyi since their last encounter on the morning in July 1989 when she was placed under house arrest for the first time. However, he has witnessed some of the events and discussed with knowledgeable people in and out of Myanmar much of what is described in the new chapter.

Having lived with the state in Myanmar for the past twenty years, and being now freed from the fetters of university life, 'academic freedom' and political correctness, I have felt less compelled to footnote every aspect of what is written. To do so would make an already lengthy chapter even more tedious for the reader. The supplementary bibliography appended provides more than ample sources for testing the validity of my contentions. If errors are found, the fault is mine.

A number of individuals and institutions have assisted me in preparing this volume. Some would prefer to remain unidentified but they know of my sincere thanks and appreciation for sharing their thoughts, time, and country with me. Dr Kyaw Yin Hlaing of the City University of Hong Kong has been especially helpful and I have learned much by reading his many works and travelling Myanmar in his wake. Myanmar political studies are now on much firmer ground thanks to him and other scholars of his generation, especially Dr Aung Myoe and Dr Ardeth Maung Thawng-mung. Their like did not exist in Myanmar before 1988. Professor Ian

Brown, the Dean of Arts and Humanities at the School of Oriental and African Studies, University of London, kindly read the final draft of chapter 6 and encouraged the author to press on. It is customary in thanking various persons who assisted an author to mention one's family. In my case I can safely say they contributed absolutely nothing to what follows other than an occasional cheerful exultation to get busy and extract digit.

For other sustenance, I pay thanks to Danubyu Daw Soe Yee who, like so many others who are now gone from the scene but of whom there are frequent reminders, also unknowingly sustained me in researching the first book. I would also like to thank the exalted but informal society of postcard sellers and street urchins of Padeban Township, Yangon Division. Its members taught me much about the kinds of trust that exists in Myanmar as well as how to keep life in perspective. They were a daily reminder while I was writing most of the new chapter that the state is as important for people without power as for those with it. Those with power could learn from them. Trust can be developed in the most abject circumstances. Dignity can be found in helping and sharing.

Special thanks are also due to the various students, young and not so young, whom I have had the privilege to teach in Myanmar since I left formally employed academic life. Their enthusiasm and will to learn, their desire to understand and explain, in the face of numerous obstacles, convinced me that retirement is not an option. The British Academy Research Committee on South East Asia provided me with an air fare from London to Myanmar in 2002 that encouraged me to get back to writing this volume. I am also grateful to Premier Oil which briefly employed me as a consultant on Myanmar affairs and facilitated two trips to Myanmar during that time. Otherwise, funding for the research for this book has been unsubsidised. Special thanks are due to the team at Hurst and Co. who put the manuscript into book form efficiently and well.

To many other friends and acquaintances, including critics and detractors, in Myanmar, the United Kingdom, Germany, Japan, Thailand, the United States, Singapore, Australia and elsewhere who have assisted me in my understanding of Myanmar, I give my sincere thanks, heartfelt if unspoken. We share the same world. For those who may be enraged by reading this volume, I commend Matthew chapter 18, verse 9. No, on second thoughts, just put the book down. Apoplexy is never a pretty sight.

Yangon and London, May 2008   *R.H.Taylor*

PREFACE AND ACKNOWLEDGMENTS TO

The State in Burma

In 1982 I wrote a short monograph reviewing the development of the study of modern Burma's politics.[1] In it I argued that students of the subject had failed to pursue a line of inquiry first pointed out by John S. Furnivall in his long article "The Fashioning of the Leviathan", published in 1939 in the new defunct *Journal of the Burma Research Society*.[2] Furnivall drew attention explicitly to the development of the British colonial state by tracing its origins back to the first British administration in Tenasserim. In his classic work *Colonial Policy and Practice*,[3] Furnivall demonstrated the consequences of the politics of the colonial state upon Burmese society. This volume, which was written at the request of the British publisher Christopher Hurst, is an attempt to follow Furnivall's notion through a study of the development of the state and its relationship with civil society from the time of the first early modern monarchic state through the colonial period. I seek to explain the contemporary state in Burma by comparing it with previous ones, and to suggest the social and economic consequences of different state formations.

Each of the five substantive chapters that follow looks at the nature of the state and its politics in different periods, attempting to draw out the most important parallels and contrasts of different state forms. Each has had to rely on different sources, and I have been dependent upon the schol-

---

1   Robert H. Taylor, *An Undeveloped State: The Study of Modern Burma's Politics*. Melbourne: Monash University Centre of Southeast Asian Studies Working Paper no. 28, 1983.

2   John S. Furnivall, 'The Fashioning of the Leviathan', *Journal of the Burma Research Society*, Rangoon, vol. XXIX, 3 (1939), pp. 1-138.

3   John S. Furnivall, *Colonial Policy and Practice* (Cambridge University Press, 1948; New York University Press, 1956).

arship of others in large sections of the book. In Chapter I, I am indebted to the work of Victor B. Lieberman and Michael Aung-Thwin: I owe special thanks to Lieberman for reading the draft of the manuscript and making significant improvements in it. The second chapter is, in inspiration and argument, derived from Furnivall's *Colonial Policy and Practice*. Parts of Chapter II and most of Chapter III draw upon my own unpublished PhD dissertation. Chapter IV owes a great deal to the numerous secondary sources cited in the notes. The 1950s saw a boom in Burma studies, especially in the United States, and I have profited from the work done then. However, it is almost certain that the scholars of that generation will disagree with many of my judgements. The final chapter is based upon secondary accounts as well as government documents. I was fortunate to have been able to live and study in Burma in 1978 and in 1982, and the experiences of those extended stays are reflected in my judgements.

In many ways, this book is premature. Too little is firmly known about important aspects of the state in Burma, both historically and contemporaneously, to make hard and fast judgements about what is being discussed. Therefore, I am at one with Michael Faraday, holding my theories on the tips of my fingers in order to allow them to be blown away by the first puff of fact. Perhaps the suggestions made in these pages will encourage others to unearth these facts.

ACKNOWLEDGEMENTS

In addition to Victor Lieberman, I have received help, directly or indirectly, from many people during the preparation of this volume. My appreciation of Burma's history and politics stems from my undergraduate studies at Ohio University with John F. Cady, one of the best teachers one could hope for. At Cornell University I had the privilege of studying Burma's history with D.G.E. Hall. I thus had the benefit of hearing of explanations of Burma's past from leading American and British historians of their generation. Subsequently, I have studied Burma from a variety of other perspectives, and have profited from lengthy discussions with scholars in Burma, especially in the Department of History and the Institute of Economics at Rangoon University. Many others have unwittingly taught me about the administrative and political system of Burma.

In conducting the research that has made this book possible, I have received a great deal of assistance. In 1978 I was an Australian exchange

student under the Colombo Plan scheme, and benefited from the help of
the Foreign Economic Relations Department of the Ministry of Planning
and Finance of the government of Burma, and the Burmese Language Department at Rangoon University. In 1982, I received a British Academy
Leverhulme South East Asian Studies Fellowship that allowed me to work
in the Department of History and the Universities' Central Library in Rangoon. At that time, the Ministry of Education kindly arranged for me to
tour much of central Burma for several weeks and to visit various economic
development projects. Friends in various parts of Burma, including those
on state farms and in factories, as well as universities and research centres,
were very helpful in explaining to me the nature and purpose of their work.
Thanks to a grant from the Nuffield Foundation, I was able to spend several
weeks in Rangoon in 1984 learning more about the workings of the court
system and of local government. Other trips to Burma since 1975 have
been made possible through financial assistance from the University of
Sydney, the Australian Academy of Social Science and the Research Committee of the School of Oriental and African Studies, London.

It would be invidious to single out individuals in Burma for thanks, but
they, I believe, know of my gratitude. Overworked as the staff of the universities and libraries are, they were always unfailingly cooperative. My colleagues in the Department of Economic and Political Studies at the School
of Oriental and African Studies allowed me to test some of my preliminary
thoughts upon them. I am especially grateful to David Taylor and Richard
Boyd for their comments on my tentative and less than fully formed ideas.
Students in my South East Asian politics seminar in 1985-6 were sufficiently tolerant to let me talk through the book with them. Michael Dwyer
of C. Hurst & Co. has been a most helpful and careful editor.

London, April 1987					R.H.T.

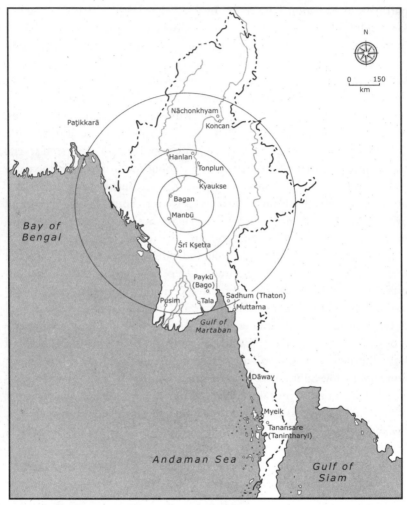

Map 1. Myanmar and the Kingdom of Bagan.
Adapted with permission from *Pagan: The Origins of Modern Buma*, by Michael Aung-Thwin, © 1985 by the University pf Hawaii Press.

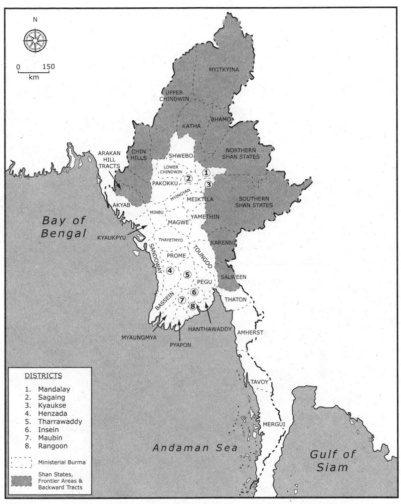

DISTRICTS

1. Mandalay
2. Sagaing
3. Kyaukse
4. Henzada
5. Tharrawaddy
6. Insein
7. Maubin
8. Rangoon

Ministerial Burma

Shan States,
Frontier Areas &
Backward Tracts

Map 2. Major Administrative divisions of British Burma circa 1937.
Adapted from *Burma Parliamentary Companion*, compiled by Ganga Singh,
Rangoon: British Burma Press (Rangoon Gazette Limited), 1940.

Map 3. Major Administrative divisions of Burma circa 1974.

Map 4. Major Administrative divisions of Myanmar, circa 25 May 2008.

INTRODUCTION

This book is an essay on the kinds of politics that have appeared in Myanmar, generally known in the English-speaking world as Burma before 1989, during the past few hundred years and the reasons for their development. The principal issue that it addresses centres on the relationship between the state and society within the country. Burma's political history since the late sixteenth century can be conveniently divided into three or four obvious periods, distinguishable by the prevailing style of state-society relationship: the time of the kings, between the founding of the Restored Toungoo dynasty in 1597 and the deposition of King Thibaw in 1885; the period of British colonial rule, cut off by the Japanese invasion of 1942 but not terminating until Burma's attainment of sovereignty and membership of the comity of nations in 1948; and independent government and politics to the present day. The latter period can be divided, at 1962, between the predominantly civilian government that preceded that date and subsequent military dominance. The nature of military rule changed fundamentally in 1988 as the socialist party that the army had created collapsed. It is the nature of the state and its personnel that provide meaning to these historical periods, for it is the state that has been the dominant institution in shaping economic, social and other opportunities for the population. In turn, the way that the state has created and maintained order in society, and the way that it has directed economic activities and permitted or denied the existence of rival institutions, have varied according to the conditions in which it has existed, as well as the manner in which the state's leading personnel interpreted the opportunities these conditions provided.

It is important to remember, when discussing the state, that it is an institution composed of a number of actors, both corporate agents and prominent individuals. How they relate with each other, how they are seen individually and collectively depending on circumstances, often determines how they are judged. How they are judged often defines how they respond

1

to demands and requirements. The contest over the control of the state, and its assets, often shapes the nature of the state as it exists and evolves.

The official name for the institution known to the English-speaking world as the state of Burma between 1974 and 1988 was *Pyihtaungsu Hsoshelit Thammata Myanma Naingngantaw*, or the Socialist Republic of the Union of Burma. The word 'state' did not appear in the official English translation of the title. However, in the Burmese version, the final word, *Naingngantaw*, is the current term used to describe the institution that is recognised as the state. *Naingngantaw* is apparently derived from the verb *naing*, which carries the meaning of 'to prevail, conquer, overcome' and 'to be competent to perform, or to be prevalent', combined with the verb *ngan*, meaning 'to be enough' or 'sufficient'. The suffix *taw* connotes the notion of royalty or of religious sanctity, and lends the term a degree of dignity. *Naingngan* was used over a thousand years ago to denote the periphery of the kingdom of Bagan. In the nineteenth century, the term was accepted as meaning a kingdom or a country under one jurisdiction or government; or an authority of power; or, figuratively, a domain. In the mid-twentieth century, *naingngan* came to mean 'nation', and thus in contemporary Burma state and nation have been linked conceptually.

Prior to that time, the state was referred to by other terms, indicating both its nature and the ideas of its controllers had about its relationship with society. During the British colonial period, the ruling institution was referred to as the *asoya*, which was translated, in the style of the nineteenth and twentieth century, as 'the government'. *Aso* comes from the verb *so*, 'to rule over', and with *ya*, which is a verb affix implying necessity, *asoya* has the meaning of 'to have authority over'. Before colonisation and the destruction of the monarchy, which made it necessary to develop neologisms for sovereign authority, what is thought as the state referred to the monarch, for whom there were a variety of titles: *ngado ashin*, our lord; *bawa shin*, lord of life; *yei-myei thahkin*, master of water and earth; or *maha dama yaza*, lord of the law. The basic and most simple words for the king were *buyin* or *min*.[1]

The development during the past two hundred years of new terms to denote the state suggests that there is possibly little or no continuity between the state in Myanmar at the beginning of the twenty-first century and the state in the seventeenth or nineteenth centuries. However, such a possibility

---

1   Hla Pe, *Burma: Literature, Historiography, Scholarship, Language, Life and Buddhism* (Singapore: Institute of Southeast Asian Studies, 1985), p. 119.

INTRODUCTION

is belied by several factors, including the state's very title. The contemporary state, in its modern guise, includes the use of the neologism *pyihtaungsu* (group of countries gathered together) to mean union, and previously included the transliterated English term *hsoshelit* (socialist) in its title, as well as the term *thammata* ('elect' or 'chosen') to convey the notion of a repub- lic. *Thammata*, however, stems from Buddhist philosophy, in which the first king was elected to protect man from his own base nature, but was also elected as a superior man trusted to curb his own nature in the interests of others. The first king was the *thammata*. The title also includes the term *Myanmar*, denoting the idea of the Myanmar people as a group of persons distinct from all the rest of humanity and who live under this state.

Thus, the adjectives that have been used to modify *naingngantaw* have brought together both ancient and modern notions. It represents the classical myth of the need for control, for their own benefit, over humanity's behaviour in society. It represents several nineteenth century myths that were introduced to South East Asia with colonial rule. One of these was that Myanmar is composed of many 'races', and that these must be brought together in a federation like that of England, Scotland and Wales (or Yugoslavia), under the mythical sovereign power of a recognised institution which has uniform authority throughout a territory depicted on a map. It also represents the dominant organisation notion of the globe for the past few centuries, namely that groups of people defined as nations should be separately identified in a community of such nations and recognised by distinctive ethnic labels. Furthermore, it conveys the idea that this institution not only has an obligation to control the behaviour of the people who live within the demarcated territory, but should also assist them in improving their condition by organising production and distribution so as to benefit the entire population.

This accretion of modifiers to the word for 'state' suggests the manner in which the state has evolved in the past two hundred years or so. In this process, the state has accumulated new roles and responsibilities, but none of its leading personnel, be they Burmese kings, British soldiers and civil servants, or Burmese politicians or army officers, have ever sought to deny the lineage of the institution that they controlled and that the population has accepted as the putative ruling authority in their lives. Equally, other institutions in society have recognised the salience of the state and its leading personnel as possessing the ability, and usually the right, to determine the parameters of their own existence. Through its various guises, there has

3

been a continuity to the state, but the personnel and context of the state have changed and this has forced the state to alter society in ways that have created new or rival personnel and established new contexts.

The analytical problem involved in the study of the state in Burma centres primarily on describing the characteristics of the state and analysing its relationships with other institutions in society. In that way, it is possible to see how it has changed over time and what the consequences of these changes have been for society. What we are attempting to understand is the state which is given a capital 'S' when it is considered to be more than just a human institution, to have a life and spirit of its own, separate from, if not superior to the individuals who compose it. As Anderson has written:

> The state has to be understood as an institution, of the same species as the Church, the university, and the modern corporation. Like them, it ingests and excretes personnel in a continuous, steady process, often over long periods of time. It is characteristic of such institutions that 'they' have precise rules for entry -- at least age, often sex, education, etc., and, no less important, for exit. . . . the state not only has its own memory but harbors self-preserving and self-aggrandising impulses, which at any given moment are 'expressed' through its living members, but which cannot be reduced to their passing personal ambitions.[2]

There is an alternative analytical approach that suggests it is more appropriate to examine the relationship between regimes or governments with counter-institutions, such as evolving property relations or developing ideological constructions. Clearly, what Perlin refers to as 'non-official aspects of the economy and society', suggesting that they need a broader analytical discussion in order to treat them appropriately, cannot be ignored.[3] However, in the approach taken in this volume, it is the interaction of the official state and non-official institutions that is being examined, and it is argued that, to judge from the evidence, most of the time it is the state which is expected to be, and is, the determining partner in such relationships. In this sense the state, through its 'continuous administrative, legal, bureaucratic and coercive systems', shapes the relationship between itself and civil society, but also shapes the structure of 'many crucial relationships within civil society as well.'[4] The state is thus normally able to determine

2   Benedict R. O'G. Anderson, 'Old State, New Society: Indonesia's New Order in Comparative Historical Perspective', *Journal of Asian Studies*, XLII, 3 (May 1983), p. 478.

3   Frank Perlin, 'State Formation Reconsidered', *Modern Asian Studies*, 19, 3 (July 1985), pp. 451-2.

4   Alfred Stephan, *State and Society: Peru in Comparative Perspective* (Princeton

what is a political issue and what is not capable of political solution, as it limits the growth of institutions that can express official or private political opinions and options.[5]

In those rare historical periods when the state is not the dominant institution over society, but must compete with a variety of other groups that are mobilising against it and attempt to usurp it, individuals or corporate groups whose careers are linked to the state will take action to attempt to reassert its domination. Even if the primary means they have to achieve this initially weaken the state, that is a price to be paid. This allows an elite group, such as the officer corps of the Burma army in 1962 or in 1988, free from obligations to other institutions in society, to launch an act of destruction and simultaneous reconstruction in order to adopt a new pattern for the development of the state and its relationship with society.

This conclusion is based on the assumption that the contemporary state in Myanmar cannot be understood other than through appreciation of the nature of the early modern precolonial state. Both the colonial state and the contemporary state developed and functioned in the same geographical and ecological condition as the precolonial state, and there are significant cultural continuities between the periods of the state's existence. In these periods, the leading personnel of the state reshaped it and ruled through altered structures and with different ideas of the proper relationship of the state to the individual and society.

The nature of the postcolonial state has made obvious the linkage between the contemporary state and its colonial predecessors throughout South East Asia; its bureaucratic and military organisations are readily apparent as descendants of the colonial state. This linkage, which results from the fact that many contemporary states such as Indonesia, the Philippines and Malaysia were creations of foreign imperialists, should not obscure the fact that for the mainland states of South East Asia the core of the contemporary state predates European imperialism. In terms of the state's basic functions to maintain social order, control economic distribution, and ensure state and elite perpetuation, the modern state in Myanmar, like those in Vietnam and Thailand, has a historical linkage that goes back 600 to 1,000 years.

University Press, 1978), p. xii, quoted in Theda Skocpol, 'Bringing the State Bank In: Current Research', in Peter B. Evans, Dietrich Rueschemeyer and Theda Skocpol (eds), *Bringing the State Back In* (Cambridge University Press, 1985), p. 7.

5 Ibid., p. 21.

The period before colonisation saw the emergence of most of the major factors that have shaped the context of the formation of the contemporary state in Myanmar. Before the arrival of the British, as a result of monarchical, political and administrative reforms from the beginning of the seventeenth century, the power of the state relative to society increased because of more effective taxation and greater military strength; increased and centralised military strength was also a consequence of advances in technology, together with an altered external political and economic environment, the result of increasingly rapid changes in Europe and in neighbouring areas. These factors led those who controlled the state in Myanmar and those who challenged that control—for reasons of political opportunity and survival—to develop patterns of control, authority, and resistance not unlike those found later under the colonial state and, later still, after independence. However, the environment of the contemporary state is obviously differ in some regards from that of the precolonial state. The relationship between the state and the world economic and political system is much closer now than it was two hundred years ago. The globalisation of the nineteenth century European state system significantly altered the external environment of the South East Asian state, but not its essential functions and purpose.

There are now available many alternative models of the state and the means by which it can achieve its aims. It is now also assumed that the state has many more obligations to society than merely the maintenance of order. Contemporary state managers tend to think in terms of the utility of borrowing from experiences different from their own, and they assume that the state must conduct industrial, research, planning and other economic functions that either did not exist or were carried out by other institutions in the past.

Analysing the contemporary South East Asian state solely in terms of its colonial predecessors has cut off comparative study from the literature on the development and perpetuation of the state in Europe. However, comparable experiences in the formation and perpetuation of the state in mainland South East Asia and Europe are apparent. For example, it has been argued by Charles Tilly that 'the most general conditions' of state-formation and survival in European experience were:

(1) the availability of extractable resources; (2) a relatively protected position in time and space; (3) a continuous supply of political entrepreneurs; (4) success in war; (5) homogeneity (and homogenization) of subject populations; (6) strong coa-

litions of the central power with major segments of the landed elite. A high standing on one of these factors can make up for a low standing on another.[6]

These general conditions for state-making and survival existed in Myanmar from the late sixteenth century onwards, and the success of Myanmar's state-makers since then has depended upon their ability to control them. The external forces which created the colonial state briefly altered these conditions by increasing the physical force of the state vis-à-vis civil society through greater organisational coherence at the core, demarcated borders on the periphery, and in particular the use of externally-derived sources of coercion. The increased coercive capacity of the colonial state was necessary for its maintenance because of its diminished legitimacy in the eyes of the populace.

From the Bagan dynasty (c.849-1287) onwards, the twin resource bases of the state have primarily been its expropriation of the economic surplus produced in the rice growing heartland of the central Ayeyawady valley and its control of foreign trade. The tax-base of the colonial state was founded on these same resources, as are the financial resources of the contemporary state. The size of this surplus and the methods of expropriation have changed over time in response to the capacity of the state to assist or control agricultural production. With sparsely populated mountains on three sides and the sea on the fourth, Myanmar's relative isolation provided both time and space with which to develop a state before new, mechanised forms of travel, communications and warfare made for easier penetration of these natural barriers.

Warfare has been a feature of the state's activities from Bagan times, and so have the state's efforts, through the Buddhist religion, and later education and ideology, to create a homogeneous population from ecologically and culturally variable human settlements. It could be argued that success in warfare, more continuous from the early seventeenth century to the early nineteenth than before, was greater than success in homogenisation of the population, for it was the expansion of the state's domain in the late eighteenth and early nineteenth centuries and the consequent incorporation of non-homogenised populations and rival power centres on its peripheries that led to the first military defeat at the hands of the British-Indian empire

---

6   Charles Tilly, 'Reflections on the History of European State-Making', in Charles Tilly (ed.), *The Formation of National States in Western Europe* (Princeton University Press, 1975), p. 40.

in 1826. Nonetheless, from the seventeenth to the nineteenth centuries, homogenising of the population was a key feature of Myanmar's history.

Domestically, the power of precolonial central state rulers was a function of their ability to form alliances of interest and loyalty with the local gentry through patron-client ties. After colonisation, such a system began to re-emerge, though too feebly to form a basis for the state's perpetuation. There is in Myanmar a clear divergence from European experience where economic differentiation was allowed to develop and the rulers permitted the expansion of interests not tied to the state. Land surpluses, manpower shortages and particular traditions of land usufruct and sumptuary laws have led to different but no less crucial questions for the architects and maintainers of the state in precolonial and postcolonial Burma.

From the time of the Bagan kings and their competition with the Buddhist monkhood for the control of agricultural land and labour, we can see in Myanmar a struggle between the state and potential rival institutional interests over economic rights. This factor in the development of the state manifested itself in different forms in later periods. The rulers of the Restored Toungoo (1597-1752) and Konbaung (1752-1885) dynasties were, during the seventeenth and eighteenth centuries, continually attempting to limit the power of the local gentry and provincial governors in order to strengthen that of the central state. Throughout the colonial period, the state was determined to ensure that there was no economic or social mobilisation outside its control.

In contrast to the era of monarchical rule, during the colonial period the externally buttressed state was sufficiently strong to delegate some of its authority to landlords and moneylenders, through they remained dependent upon the state's legal system for their positions. This was made possible by the vastly increased surplus created by new economic conditions and policies at the expense of the precolonial gentry and, eventually, of the peasantry. In a sense, the colonial state destroyed the self-perpetuating and integrated social networks created by the monarchical state and replaced them with the bureaucratised networks of 'a business concern'.[7] During the post-1962 socialist period the state, by the resumption of all landownership and a monopolistic claim to all surpluses, attempted to re-establish the dominance of the state and in so doing gain the support of the peasantry at

---

7   The imagery comes from J.S. Furnivall, 'South Asia and the World Today', in Phillips Talbot (ed.), *South Asia in the World Today* (University of Chicago Press, 1950), p. 7.

the expense of the landowners, moneylenders, and urban and/or foreign-oriented commercial interests which arose during the colonial period. Since 1988, an effort to create new state dependent agents, indigenous entrepreneurs, has been attempted as a buttress to state power. A similar situation has developed in the relationship between the central state and political authorities and economic elites in the more peripheral areas of the state's domain. At all times the interests of the state, of course, have been held by its controllers to be paramount, for its interests are their interests.

In Myanmar, as in Europe, there has been a close relationship between state domination and perpetuation and the expansion of the armed forces, increases in taxation and consequent popular rebellions. This relationship is not just a colonial and postcolonial phenomenon; the outward manifestations of these activities until the colonial period were often different from the European experience. But the political dynamics underlying these activities were and still are the same. So, too, are the basic issues that face the state. However, even with differences in style, the analytical generalisations that Tilly draws for Europe are points that can be seen in Myanmar, and perhaps in much of the remainder of South East Asia:

> The state-makers only imposed their wills on the populace through centuries of ruthless efforts. The effect took many forms: creating distinct staffs dependent on the crown and loyal to it; making those staffs (armies and bureaucrats alike) reliable, effective instruments of policy; blending coercion, co-optation, and legitimization as means of guaranteeing the acquiescence of different segments of the population; acquiring sound information about the country, its people and its resources; promoting economic activities which would free or create resources for the use of the state. In all these efforts and more, the state-makers frequently found the traditional authorities allied with the people against them. Thus it became a game of shifting coalitions; kings rallying popular support by offering guarantees against cruel and arbitrary local magnates or by challenging their claims to goods, money or services, but not hesitating to crush rebellion when the people were divided or sufficient military forces was a hand; magnates parading as defending local liberties against royal oppression, not hesitating to bargain with the crown when it appeared advantageous. Ultimately, the people paid.[8]

What kind of institution is the state? What sets it apart from other institutions that claim to regulate aspects of social life? Tilly suggests that 'an organization which controls the population occupying a defined territory is a state *in so far as* (1) it is differentiated from other organizations operating in the same territory; (2) it is autonomous; (3) it is centralized; and (4) its

---

8   Tilly, 'Reflections on the History of European State-Making', p. 24.

divisions are formally coordinated with one another.'⁹ It is necessary to add to this definition that the state is the only institution expected to determine its relationship with other bodies and to determine for other institutions in civil society their relationship with each other. Some would argue that this is to claim too much for the domination of the state in pre-colonial Myanmar. However, essentially it is differences of degree that are seen between the early modern state in Myanmar and the European state, especially in their early modern forms.

For example, precolonial mainland South East Asian states did not have a 'population occupying a defined territory' in the sense of a territory demarcated by externally as well as internally recognised and reasonably precise borders. In such circumstances, the concept of 'foreign affairs' would not have had the same sense as in Europe. The differences between the European and the mainland South East Asian state should not be overstated, however. European borders were often imprecise and much contested until relatively recent times, while South East Asian rulers knew what territory they were able to control and tax, and their subjects knew to whom they owned taxes and service, if not always allegiance. Indeed, crude equivalents to demarcated borders did exist before the arrival of European concepts of statecraft.

Another significant comparison can be made between Europe and South East Asia concerning nationalism. In Myanmar, as in Europe, mass nationalism is a phenomenon that developed subsequent to the formation of the modern state. In terms of historical evolution, elite or intellectual nationalism in Europe was a force from the early eighteenth century onwards, but its impact on the political elite in Myanmar only occurred towards the beginning of the twentieth century, after the dissolution of the monarchical state, although its precursors could be seen from the middle of the nineteenth century. Indeed, proto-nationalism in the form of attachment to the crown and the Buddhist faith predates the modern state.

However, when considered as a mass political phenomenon, the emergence of nationalism as a significant political force, one able to shake not only the foundations of the state but the stability of the state's external environment, occurred in Myanmar within twenty years of its near universal impact in Europe. The First World War led to the spread of nationalism to the general populace of Asia and Europe. The political consequences of that war included the stimulation of a common belief among the broad mass of European people and many of the colonised peoples of Asia that

9   Ibid., p. 70, emphasis in the original.

mass action, interpreted as national action, could change the leadership and the behaviour, if not the ultimate nature, of the state. In Myanmar, as in other Asian countries, nationalist sentiment was constructed upon the institutions of the precolonial state and society, particularly the old governing class and religion

The development of mass nationalism and its corollary, the belief that the state should belong to the people, present one of the potential differences in the nature of the state in the premodern and modern periods. Though embedded in society and highly dependent upon it, the precolonial state in Myanmar was largely autonomous. There was no notion that the king was 'responsible' to the people in any other than a general moral sense for their well-being; still less was there any idea that the state's officials 'represented' the people. However, the growth of the democratic idea and the increasing competitiveness of other institutions threatened to limit the autonomy of the state. This often develops as a consequence of the growth in the power and autonomy of rival institutions, making the state an arena of conflict rather than an arbiter of conflict and allocator of resources.[10] In the case of Myanmar, it was the collapse of the state after 1942, and the simultaneous growth of mass mobilisation movements, especially those of peasants and others deprived of influence under the colonial state, which overwhelmed the state and severely limited its autonomy. However, these mobilisation movements were not themselves highly institutionalised and the collapse of the state resulted in a power vacuum in society which no rival could fill.

The reassertion of the state's predominant position after 1948 was attempted initially by recreating the pattern of the colonial state and increasing its representative quality. Because of the weakness of the state in these circumstances it could not easily penetrate society and regain control over rival institutions. In reality, few states, including authoritarian ones, are able to penetrate directly to such a degree as to determine all of these relationships. However, dominant states are able to structure social relations so as to ensure that no threats to their stability and perpetuation can develop, as the state is the ultimate arbiter of societal conflicts. The establishment of state hegemony and the state's consequent ability to set the limits of acceptable political, economic and social behaviour are only possible when

---

10   Dietrich Rueschemeyer and Peter B. Evans, 'The State and Economic Transformation: Toward an Analysis of the Conditions underlying Effective Intervention,' in P.B. Evans et al. (eds), *Bringing the State Back In*, p. 49.

the state is accepted as legitimate and no other institution can effectively deny its dictates.

For state managers in Myanmar in 1962, and again in 1988, such a condition was far removed from existing circumstances. For the first 14 years after independence was regained in 1948, the state had been displaced from the apex of society to a position where it was merely the most important competitor for public support and obedience. After the army seized power for the second time in 1962, it attempted to recreate the state in order to reassert its primary authority through socialism. The failure of that attempt led to the near bankruptcy of both state and society in 1988, leading to a third attempt by the military, as the ultimate force in the state, to regenerate the state's dominance. To those who felt a primary obligation to the perpetuation of the state and whose personal careers were directly linked to its prospects, in both 1962 and again in 1988, the state seemed unable to defend itself against other institutions and the classes or groups that led them.

Theoretically, in the post-independence period of most states in Asia and Africa, individuals wishing to resurrect the dominance of a state have two options before them. One is to open society to external institutions and forces such as the world economy and military alliances with more powerful states. In that way the state, as the institution through which other states and foreign capital must operate in order to penetrate society and the economy, is able to use outside resources to establish its position within the country. However, this is at the cost of abandoning a degree of state autonomy to other states and institutions whose interests cannot be identical with those of the state itself.

The alternative is to force the state upon the remainder of society with the few weapons at its disposal. Given the state's lack of positive inducements because of its impecunious nature, this requires eliminating its rivals through the power of the law while ensuring that the institutions permitted to exist are dependent upon the state, either through their personnel or their finances, and are therefore unable to organise effective opposition to it. Such an attempt is extremely difficult, and in the end many compromises have to be made between the ideal of state autonomy and dominance and the political, economic and social conditions within which the state and its leading personnel must function. In Myanmar, the second strategy was chosen by the leaders of the 1962 military coup, and forced, as a consequence of economic sanctions, upon their successors following the 1988 reassertion of military dominance. This was only to be expected given their own corporate experiences since before independence as well as the relatively benign strategic position of Myanmar in world politics and economics in the 1950s and 1960s and after the end of the Cold War.

It was tempting but facile to conclude that the state in Myanmar by the 21st century had returned in character and nature to that of the precolonial state, and thus to see the colonial period as a brief and ultimately unimportant episode in the history of the country. Such a return to the past is impossible because too many conditions surrounding the state have changed. Moreover, the managers of the state and the people they govern, as well as the rest of the world, expect a great deal more of the state now than was the case two hundred years ago.

The failure to create the economic growth and social betterment that the modern state is now expected to provide led again to the near collapse of the state in 1988. During the next two decades the army, the only state institution to have developed a viable independent existence since the Second World War, as it dealt with the vicissitudes of independence in the modern world sought once more to redefine the state and its relationship with society. The contested nature of that effort remains unresolved and provides some of the issues that will shape the future of the state in Myanmar. Whether future state managers, and their domestic and international interlocutors, learn from and heed the lessons of their predecessors will determine how successful they will be in fulfilling their responsibilities. Just as when the first version of this volume was published, approximately half of the population of Myanmar now have little personal memory of the issues the state has attempted to address in the past two decades. Will they, like their predecessors, want to remake the relationship between state and society again, seemingly *de novo*, as occurred in 1988? Or will the state and society in Myanmar develop a positive mutual relationship, allowing both to grow without threatening either?

1

THE PRECOLONIAL STATE

The evolution of the precolonial state

The first millennium of the state in Myanmar, between the founding of the kingdom of Bagan around AD849 and the fall of the last Konbaung king in 1885, is conveniently divided between the classical Bagan period ending in 1287, a 300-year interregnum with several rival state centres, and the founding of the early modern state of the Restored Toungoo (1587-1752) and Konbaung (1752-1885) dynasties. The reason for ending this period in 1885 is obvious: no event in the history of Myanmar was as complete and as traumatic to Myanmar's civilisation as the loss to the British-Indian empire of the monarchical state and the Buddhist order it upheld. But this political and cultural watershed should not obscure the fact that the precolonial period itself was not, in terms of the structure and nature of the state, one long, uninterrupted, unchanging seamless pattern.

Two significant forces caused the nature of the precolonial state to change. One was the force of internally and externally sanctioned economic and technological change. This recast the environment in which the state functioned, especially in the early modern period at the beginning of the seventeenth century. The other force was the evolution of the scale of the state as a consequence of its territorial expansion, some modest population growth,[1] and the accumulated experience of the ruling strata. Throughout the precolonial period, the nature and behaviour of the state in its relation-

---

1   By the middle of the eighteenth century, the best estimates suggest that the state in Myanmar controlled a population of between 2 and 2.5 million persons. William J. Koenig, 'The Early Kon-baung Polity, 1752-1819: A Study of Politics, Administration and Social Organisation in Burma' (PhD, University of London, 1978), pp. 97-8.

ship with important socio-economic institutions in society were far from stagnant, and the evolving relationship of the state with society during the last two dynasties shaped the capabilities the ruling elites possessed to cope with internal and external challenges to their power and authority.

However, there were significant aspects of continuity between classical Bagan and the early modern periods. Clearly the fulcrum of the state throughout the precolonial period was the monarch. Strong, charismatic kings, usually the founders or early monarchs of new dynasties, put their personal stamp on their reigns. To the popular mind the monarchy, and often the monarch himself, was seen as the state. Notions of kingship and statecraft derived from classical Indian Buddhist thought persisted throughout the period. Territorial control was seen as the consequence of the king's possession of a full treasury and a strong army, and it was the exercise of that territorial control that made possible the taxation of labour and agriculture which filled the treasury and fed the army.[2]

Throughout the era of the precolonial state, and in the present day, parallel to the state stood the institutional form of the Buddhist faith, the *sangha* or monkhood, usually in a subordinate relationship, but when the state was weak a challenging one. Being closer to the people and in a less obviously exploitative coercive posture, the monkhood survived dynastic changes to provide society in central Myanmar with a cultural unity that was little questioned and more rarely tested until the rise of the colonial state and mass nationalism during the late nineteenth and early twentieth centuries. The outward manifestations of the institutions of the Buddhist faith, which were remarkably uniform from the fifteenth century onwards, provided the only important, albeit narrow, avenue of social mobility for those who were young and ambitious until the colonial period, and gave the populace a shared experience and social expectations that both explained and justified the vicissitudes of life and the state.

Complementing the order which Buddhist institutions gave to society were 'the hereditary local chieftains', as Furnivall labelled the village (*ywa*) and township (*myo* or *taik*) authorities who regulated the day-to-day lives of most of the population and were the main administrative link between the central state and its subjects. These authorities who constituted the gentry class, together with the monkhood, survived 'through intervals of anarchy'

---

2   S.J. Tambiah, *World Conqueror and World Renouncer* (Cambridge University Press, 1976), pp. 52-3, describes the analogous Thai state during the same period.

when the power of the state was being contested, 'and it was from them that society grew up anew, but on old lines, when order was restored'.[3] Furnivall should not mislead us though, for while it is true that at the base of society the re-establishment of central authority by the state made possible the recreation of order and stability, allowing the annual agricultural and cultural cycles of most of the population to continue essentially unaltered, from the early 1600s onwards the state gradually expanded and adapted its response to its changing environment. The precolonial state rested upon a society which had a fundamental stability grounded in agriculture and religion which it was little able, or willing, to alter. The problem for the controllers of the state was how to direct and use these societal institutions for their own purposes, while rivals in the *sangha*, and especially the local gentry, championed the institutional power of religion and the rights of the village and town in the name of ideals and interests which were sometimes at odds with those of the king and the central state.

In the terminology of comparative Weberian sociology, the precolonial state is best described as 'patrimonial'.[4] It contained within it strong centrifugal forces constantly tugging at the authority of the monarch and his central institutions which, in turn, rested on the shifting ties of patron-client dyadic relationships. These patron-client ties ran from the royal and court-appointed central officials down to the township and village gentry class. Princes, ministers, provincial officials and village and township headmen, as well as rival power centres on the periphery of the state's domain, were continually seeking opportunities to organise sufficient power to keep wealth and authority in their own hands. The central state had to struggle constantly to regroup and control the resources provided by agriculture and trade, and the king's influence over the institutions of the Buddhist religion made the aggrandisement of the state easier by clothing it with the mantle of legitimacy.

The nature of the administrative and power controls at the king's disposal made for a constant battle between the centre and the extremities of the state. Michael Adas has referred to this form of state structure as a 'contest state', noting that,

---

3   J.S. Furnivall, *Colonial Policy and Practice: A Comparative Study of Burma and Netherlands India* (New York: New York University Press, 1956), p. 17.

4   Max Weber, *Economy and Society* (edited by Guenther Roth and Claus Wittich) (New York: Bedminster Press, 1968), vol. III, pp. 1010-38.

central to this form of political organization is the rule by a king or emperor who claims a monopoly of power and authority in a given society but whose effective control is in reality severely restricted by rival power centres among the elite, by weaknesses in administrative organization and institutional commitment on the part of state officials, by poor communications, and by a low population-to-land ratio, that places a premium on manpower retention and regulation.[5]

Adas draws attention to the significant gap between the theory of the all-powerful and all-knowing monarch and the practice of the precolonial state in regard to the lives of the peasantry and other non-official sectors of society. Nonetheless, the state's presence was always felt—or else the insecurity caused by its absence—and because of its singular ability to amass power and other resources of rule, the wielders of the state's authority were generally in a commanding position.

The widely held assumption by an earlier generation of scholars that the controllers of the state in Myanmar learned nothing from the failures of their precursors suggested that until the coming of colonial rule the state rose and fell in an inevitable and futile cycle. This is the perception of the state and Myanmar's rulers conveyed in the first works on the history of the country by foreigners.[6] We know, however, that rulers elsewhere, like their political opponents and rivals, learned from their predecessors' failures. The history of the state in Myanmar between 1597 and 1885 also reveals a process of accumulation of political and administrative skills. The defeat of the controllers of the state in the face of the British challenge demonstrates that the wielders of state power were unable to create sufficient strength quickly enough to cope with all the new external forces they faced, while continuing to deal with ceaseless domestic political forces. That the reforms and diplomacy of the penultimate king, Mindon, proved to be too little and were introduced too late does not alter the fact that he was well aware of the need for adaptation, as were many of his ministers and advisers who continued in office after him.[7] His Restored Toungoo predecessors, facing less radical external challenges, had had more success in adjusting to internal challenges by using externally derived resources.

---

5   Michael Adas, 'From Avoidance to Confrontation: Peasant Protest in Precolo-
     nial and Colonial Southeast Asia', *Comparative Studies in Society and History,*
     vol. 23, no. 2 (April 1981), p. 218.

6   A tradition of interpretation best exemplified by G.E. Harvey, *History of Burma*
     (London: Frank Cass, 1925, repr. 1967).

7   John F. Cady, *A History of Modern Burma* (Ithaca and London: Cornell Univer-
     sity Press, 1958), pp. 99-116.

With the formation of the Toungoo dynasty, the post-Bagan political order of Myanmar was destroyed and a unity was created in the central core that has not been broken since, except for the years between 1825 and 1885 when the British governed Rakhine and Tanintharyi and, subsequently, southern Myanmar, separately from the king at Innwa or Mandalay. As Lieberman has argued, before the early 1600s only the Bagan empire was able to create this political unity (though within a more limited area).[8] The Bagan state system fell, as Aung Thwin has shown,[9] not only for reasons of the central state's inability to control the wealth of the monkhood and its institutions, but also because of external factors threatening central Myanmar. These included pressure from the Tai-speaking peoples and the Mongols as well as the growth of Chinese and Indian Ocean trade, which encouraged the formation of a rival kingdom situated on the southern coast away from Bagan.[10] For both internal and external reasons, from the early seventeenth century onwards the state in Myanmar changed its nature and structural relationships, as well as its bases of stability and power, so that the last two dynasties were 'more stable and militarily more powerful than their Pagan or Avan predecessors'.[11] New commercial patterns, the use of European firearms and mercenaries, the growth of domestic agriculture and population, and the state's greater ability in controlling the internal wealth of its domains made this possible. In turn, the growing power of the state led to longer periods of internal peace and expanded productivity which further strengthened the central state.

But if this is true, why did the penultimate dynasty, the Restored Toungoo, fall in 1752, to be replaced by the Konbaung dynasty? Lieberman's

8   Victor B. Lieberman, 'Continuity and Change in Burmese History: Some Preliminary Observations', unpubl. paper, p. 12.

9   Michael Aung Thwin, 'The Role of *Sasana* Reform in Burmese History: Economic Dimensions of a Religious Purification', *Journal of Asian Studies*, XXXVIII, 4 (Aug. 1979), p. 673; see also the same author's 'Divinity, Spirit and Human: Conceptions of Classical Burmese Kingship', in Lorraine Gesick, ed., *Centers, Symbols and Hierarchies: Essays on the Classical State of Southeast Asia* (New Haven: Yale University Southeast Asian Studies Series no. 26, 1983), p. 46; and 'Jampudipa: Classical Burma's Camelot', in *Contributions to Asian Studies*, vol. 16, 'Essays on Burma', edited by John P. Ferguson (London: E.J. Brill, 1981), pp. 38-41; and *Pagan: The Origins of Modern Burma* (Honolulu: University of Hawaii Press, 1985).

10   Victor B. Lieberman, 'The Political Significance of Religious Wealth in Burma History: Some Further Thoughts', *Journal of Asian Studies*, XXXIX, 4 (Aug. 1980), p. 756.

11   Ibid., p. 766.

analysis of the political dynamics of the Restored Toungoo period in his *Burmese Administrative Cycles* shows why.[12] The continual interaction of three factors—elite autonomy, popular evasions of state authority and requirements, and royal demands—similar to those which tested the control of the early modern European state, brought an end to the Toungoo dynastic line when its rivals managed to construct a coalition of gentry and peasants against it. The state itself, however, was not dissolved with the end of the old dynasty as had occurred in pre-Toungoo times; rather, the new rulers reinvigorated the existing state structures. But the political rivalries and administrative weaknesses which had brought down the final Toungoo ruler did not cease with the decline of his dynasty. Rather, Alaungpaya, the first Konbaung king, having successfully exploited the laxity of the regime to rise to power himself, had in turn to quell his extra-state allies with the power of the state he captured. He understood the weaknesses of the political and administrative policies of his predecessors and thus knew what to do to ensure that no one wrest power from him. As the state continued as an ongoing institution, he and his successors by and large followed Toungoo 'political organization' with only minor modifications until the mid-nineteenth century'.[13] The, organisational and technological devices borrowed from abroad were introduced at the centre, allowing for a further extension and regularisation of central supervision over peripheral political authorities.

The final failure of the Konbaung dynasty would seem to contradict the argument that the state had strengthened itself as a consequence of the changes introduced after 1597. During the final 133 years of the precolonial state the kings attempted to control elite autonomy, but the urge for power on the part of rivals continued to provide an incentive for the gentry class to devise new means of avoiding central controls. The centre attempted to reduce popular evasion of state demands for manpower and taxes, but to do so usually required the formation of an alliance with a set of local power-holders or incipient elites, which in turn led to increasing dissatisfaction among other groups, especially the peasantry. The peasants sought to evade state demands, but giving way to popular protests or evasive actions would have weakened the state at the expense of greater power accruing to its temporary gentry allies and subordinate state officials. The

---

12   Victor B. Lieberman, *Burmese Administrative Cycles: Anarchy and Conquest, c. 1580-1760* (Princeton University Press, 1984).

13   Frank N. Trager and William J. Koenig (eds), *Burmese Sit-tans 1764-1826, Records of Rural Life and Administration* (Tucson: University of Arizona Press for the Association for Asian Studies, 1979), p. 19.

coming of the British-Indian empire to challenge the king's control of the state and its resources proved too great a burden for the central institutions. Nonetheless, that the idea of the precolonial state proved attractive as a nationalist symbol fifty years after the demise of the last monarch demonstrates the strong image that it had created for itself in the minds of the people, perhaps in part because the weaknesses of the precolonial state had provided a means for local interests to defend themselves against the central rulers, while still maintaining overall political and social order.

Underlying the stability and greater coherence of the state in Myanmar from the early 1600s onwards were many crucial factors. One of the most important was that the most astute kings sought and found alternative sources of power such as foreign trade and technology to help them control internal political rivalries. Thus they were not solely dependent on internal expropriation of the surpluses of the gentry and peasantry, which led to the spread of popular evasion, political tensions and weakened central control. 'Rulers from Nyaungyan Min (r. 1587-1606) through Alaungpaya (r. 1752-60) [as well as Mindon Min (r. 1853-78)] showed an appreciation of the military and political value of maritime contacts, and frequently sought to widen these channels.'[14] Perhaps because the last two dynasties were increasingly able to concentrate power in the central state, political rivalries and conflicts in the king's court escalated, making the Konbaung dynasty particularly prone to factionalism. But throughout this period of some 280 years the kingdom as a whole enjoyed a remarkable degree of internal order and stability, except at the very end of the Restored Toungoo period. As in Siam during the same time, there was 'a long-term trend toward centralization',[15] giving this period a unique place as a 'coherent unit in the institutional and administrative history' of Myanmar.[16]

The territorial organisation of the precolonial state

In the behaviour as well as in the study of the state, theory and practice have to be distinguished. In theory the king was a universal monarch who allowed others the use of his land; they received the benevolence of his tolerance and thus enjoyed the order he bestowed on the populace and their institutions, especially the Buddhist religion. In reality, the monarch was

---

14   Lieberman, *Burmese Administrative Cycles*, p. 277.

15   Ibid., p. 14.

16   Lieberman, 'Continuity and Change', pp. 20-2.

caught in a web of internal rivalries and external threats to the security of his throne, to the wealth of his treasury, and to the power of his state. In theory the kingdom 'was minutely regulated. The whole kingdom ... was governed by the pen,'[17] and indeed there was a plethora of official regulations limiting the mobility of the population and the consumption or investment of wealth. Because of this, then as now, a great deal of the people's time and ingenuity was devoted to avoiding the bureaucratic strictures and requirements of the state—nullifying theory in practice.

In territorial terms, the structure of the precolonial state evolved from the form established by the founders of the Bagan state to that developed by the Restored Toungoo and Konbaung dynasties. Neither the Bagan nor later administrative systems during the Innwan interregnum were stagnant, but rather they changed gradually, as indicated by the coinage of a new administrative terminology. Bagan consisted of four different territorial categories: 1. the nucleus, 2. secondary settlements, 3. strategic stockades, 4. conquered 'foreign' areas. The nucleus was the core of the state's territory from which, by controlling its irrigation system, it derived the bulk of its manpower and revenue and had the greatest control over its subjects' occupations. The secondary settlements on the state's western frontier were probably of little economic value, although some trade may have been conducted there. The relatively undefended nature of the secondary settlement zone suggests that the rulers perceived the area as posing little threat. Threats were perceived to come from the north and east, where the state created a string of forty-six stockades under control of the king's army. As an indication of the restricted area of the Bagan state in comparison with its seventeenth- and eighteenth-century successor, the so-called conquered territories (*naingngan*) lay mainly to the south of the nucleus zone in what became the heart of the state's domain in the last period of the precolonial state. Depending upon the power of the centre in any given period, this domain included areas such as Pyi, the Ayeyawardy delta, and the Kra isthmus. The conquered territories also included what is now referred to as the Shan State, from whence came the rulers who replaced the Bagan dynasty during the Innwan interregnum.[18]

---

17   Furnivall, *Colonial Policy and Practice*, p. 15.

18   Michael Aung Thwin, 'Kingship, the *Sangha*, and Society in Pagan', in Kenneth R. Hall and John K. Whitmore (eds), *Explorations in Early Southeast Asian History: The Origins of Southeast Asian Statecraft* (Ann Arbor: Michigan Papers on South and Southeast Asia, no. 11, 1976), pp. 218-20.

The territorial structure of the early modern state in its final form was simpler as well as more powerful and centralised than its Bagan precursor. Rather than possessing four different types of administrative zones, the Restored Toungoo and Konbaung state had only three.[19] The nuclear zone, the most important, was in some respects similar to, though much larger than, the nucleus of the Bagan state. Here in the central plains the king ruled directly through his ministers, maintained many of his political supporters and royal relatives through appanage grants, provisioned his most concentrated military forces and recruited the bulk of his officials.

The other two zones were removed from the king's direct control, but increasingly came under the supervision and authority of his administration as the organisers of the Restored Toungoo dynasty and the reformers of the state during the later years of the Konbaung dynasty augmented their powers. In the second zone, which Lieberman refers to as the zone of dependent provinces, authority was placed in the hands of centrally appointed officials known as *myo-wun,* whose staff, also centrally appointed, represented the king in provincial capitals. Unlike their predecessors in the Bagan and Innwa periods, the *myo-wun* were agents of the king, not deputies who possessed power in their own right.

Further from the king's supervision lay the third zone, that of the tributaries. Here, hereditary rulers from a variety of cultural and ethnic backgrounds exercised immediate authority. These rulers, Shan *sawbwa,* Kachin *duwa,* Kayin and Chin chiefs, etc., paid allegiance to the central court through tribute missions, marriage alliances, military forces and similar non-permanent, non-bureaucratic displays of obligation. When these tributaries posed no serious threat to the central state, kings allowed them to conduct their affairs undisturbed. Their economic surplus was so marginal that, until their minerals and timber because valuable in the nineteenth century, security was the king's only concern. Their rulers were permitted to maintain the symbols of office and legitimacy in their own courts as if they were lesser versions of the central state. However, from the middle of the nineteenth century onwards the central state imposed greater control through the stationing of military officers at the larger local courts and through the requisition of regular payments to the central treasury.[20]

---

19   Lieberman, *Burmese Administrative Cycles,* pp. 54-5.

20   After 1868, when the *thathameda* tax—a village lump-sum assessment used in central Burma—began to be extended into the Shan States during the reign of King Mindon, continuing the process of regularising state institutions between the two areas, the 'chief activity of the Burmese political agents was to collect

23

Various means were used to achieve greater centralisation, particularly in the zone of dependent provinces, during the final 280 years of the pre-colonial state. The first Restored Toungoo kings began the process of re-moving the 'aura of independent sovereignty outlying centres had once enjoyed' by taking away the local authorities' symbols of office, replacing the independent *bayin* (provincial governors) with *myo-wun*, and requiring princes holding distant appanages to reside at the capital.

On a more practical level, Ava [Innwa, the Restored Toungoo capital] expanded its control over subordinate officials within each lowland province; official spies, military commissioners, treasurers, and so on were now selected by the capital, whereas in earlier periods deputies had usually been appointed by the local governor.[21]

Furthermore, the court concentrated professional soldiers more in the capital area, removing from local princes, other appanage holders and officials forces with which to challenge the centre, while monopolising the import and distribution of firearms. All in all, the central state 'trimmed the self-sufficiency of provincial governors' in the most important zones from what had been the practice during the Bagan and Innwa periods.[22]

Nonetheless, the provinces south of the capital did apparently possess a greater degree of administrative independence than did the provinces lying immediate adjacent to the court. If for no other reason, a degree of provincial administrative autonomy existed because of the slow means of communication of the period; but the frequent rotation of key officials by the king's ministers indicates a significant degree of central supervision. The state's dependence upon the agricultural and demographic resources of the southern areas, as well as the ports through which cash revenue and firearms flowed to the centre, made these provinces immensely important to maintaining the resources of the central authority, and the reforms and policies of the Restored Toungoo monarchs reflected their awareness of this.[23] In comparison with the Bagan and Innwa kingdoms, from the early

the Thathameda tax for the treasury at Mandalay'. Saimong Mangrai, *The Shan State and the British Annexation* (Ithaca: Cornell University Southeast Asian Program Data Paper no. 57, 1965), pp. 58 and 103.

21 Lieberman, 'Continuity and Change', pp. 15-16.

22 Lieberman, *Burmese Administrative Cycles*, p. 64.

23 Ibid., p. 130. The southern area least under the control of the central state lay in the trans-Sittang river littoral and the central lowlands below Pakangyi and Yamethin (areas which have been the most difficult for the contemporary state to control since 1948). Here, from the Restored Toungoo kings until 1885, the administration of the area resembled that of the nuclear and dependent

seventeenth century onwards the state controlled a larger territory under firmer administrative restraint. As a consequence, 'lowland provincial rebellions' led by princely challengers of the sort that had plagued the monarchs in the period between the Bagan and the Restored Toungoo dynasties 'were short lived and infrequent' [24]

The gradual transformation of the residents' ethnic affinities in the expanded nuclear zone indicates both the greater power of the state as well as its greater ability to affect the identity of its subjects. The permanence and power of the state, and its identification with monarchs who were considered to be ethnically and culturally Bamar, led communities and individuals to accept the state's definition of their cultural orientation. As in Europe at the same time, the process of homogenisation of personal identity with the state was taking place. The distinctive identity of being a Mon, which had marked the south in earlier eras, was disappearing,[25] and a proto-national cultural and ethnic formation was being created through the Ayeyawady river valley.

The central state's control of the tributary zones also increased during this time as strategic or economic reasons for undertaking political and administrative reforms became more salient. Initially, the Restored Toungoo kings had seen the highlands primarily as military recruitment grounds and the source of highly prized luxury goods (in addition to serving as the trade route to Yunnan).[26] Those tributaries nearest the capital, especially in the western Shan or Tai areas and the southern Kachin zone where minor Shan sawbwa-ships were recognised, were more carefully superintended by the king's officers. Not until the nineteenth century was systematic reform undertaken which began to transform the Shan tributaries into dependent provinces.[27] In these areas, however, the process of homogenisation of ethnic and cultural identities had not advanced as rapidly, and economic

zones. 'However, … distance, economic regionalism, and traditions of local sovereignty combined to pose challenges to central authority that were quite unknown in the nuclear zone proper.' Ibid., p. 113.

24 Lieberman, 'Continuity and Change', p. 21.
25 Ibid., p. 36.
26 Lieberman, *Burmese Administrative Cycles*, p. 131.
27 Robert H. Taylor, 'British Policy and the Shan States, 1886-1942', in Prakai Nontawasee (ed.), *Changes in Northern Thailand and the Shan States, 1886-1940* (Singapore: Southeast Asian Studies Program, Institute of Southeast Asian Studies, Report No 1, 1988), pp. 13-62.

exchanges with the plains remained infrequent and largely unintegrated with the state's central economy.

Authority relations in the precolonial state

The pattern of authority relations in the precolonial state, like its territorial organisation, was hierarchical, with the king at the centre/top and the most distant hill-peoples and their tributary rulers at the periphery/bottom. The dominant religious and cosmological ideas of the precolonial world provided a justification for these relations,[28] and the political and economic reality of the precolonial state and the administrative devices at its disposal made such relations possible and perhaps inevitable. According to Aung Thwin, throughout the history of the classical state the 'essence of social and administrative organization' was its structuring along patron-client lines through a form of 'cellular' organisation.[29] The king stood at the apex of a society in which the bulk of the population was attached to specific organic communities, tied to him through a network of interlocking relationships which provided the warp and woof of state and society. In practice, the king's ability to control the behaviour of his subjects was limited, as his authority was mediated through a chain of subordinate authorities of varying kinds. The king's clients had their own interests to pursue and their own sources of extra-state personal authority as well as state-sanctioned power. As the monarch made little differentiation between his property and that of the state, so his subordinates made scant distinction between their official responsibilities and their private interests. And when they did so, private interest often took primary place in their calculus of duty. 'The fact that despite the Restored Toungoo reforms, the imperial administration was loosely integrated both vertically and horizontally, and power was diffuse'[30] meant that central commands and requirements were still of limited effectiveness in the early modern period.

In the lower levels of the administrative and political hierarchy prestige diminished, as did access to direct royal authority. The further from the centre the more difficult it was for officials to convince their subordinates of the state's sanction for their demands. Although in traditional society

---

28   The classic statement of the cosmological underpinnings of the precolonial state is Robert Heine-Geldern, 'Conceptions of State and Kingship in Southeast Asia', *The Far Eastern Quarterly* (2 Nov. 1942), pp. 15-30.

29   Aung Thwin, 'Divinity, Spirit, and Human', p. 46.

30   Lieberman, *Burmese Administrative Cycles*, p. 137.

the prestige gained from the high status of government service provided a good deal of personal authority for the incumbent, the threat of coercion was often necessary when making demands for payments in kind, labour or coin. Tax collectors and other such appointees, including military officers—especially when they exceeded accepted norms of required contributions—were the cause of much of the political discontent and conflict within the precolonial social and political order.

Below the king in the hierarchy stood the princes of the blood, often rivals of the incumbent who became co-rivals on his demise. There were principles of succession, but these were often challenged by the sons, uncles and brothers of the king. From the perspective of the incumbent, the princes were a threat to his security, but if carefully supervised they were an asset, for more than any other group in society they saw their personal interests directly linked with the perpetuation of the state upon which their livelihoods and status depended. Furthermore, their elite education in the royal court and monasteries gave them administrative skills and a level of literacy found only among the most privileged, leisured groups. Thus, before the Restored Toungoo reforms, the princes proved very useful as administrators and provincial governors, the king providing for the addition to their incomes through the assignment of appanages.

The holder of an appanage was known as a *myo-sa*, literally 'the eater of the town'. In order to expropriate their share of the revenues of their fiefs, the *myo-sa* assigned agents to collect on their behalf. Even after the replacement of princely *bayin* with *myo-wun* following the Restored Toungoo reforms, the monarchs continued to assign appanages to royalty in order to ensure their political support. Except for its expansion under the first Konbaung kings, no changes in this system were made until well into the nineteenth century.[31] The appanage system was not allowed to develop into a feudal system, for no proprietary rights were assigned with the grant, no military service was necessarily required, and no grant was made in perpetuity.[32] Herein lay not only one of the fundamental differences between the early modern European state and its counterpart in Myanmar, but also a key source of the centralising and dominating power of the early modern state in Myanmar. The kings developed a system intended to ensure that no permanently independent bases of provincial power could arise to challenge their dominant position.

31   Koenig, 'Early Kon-baung Polity', p. 249.
32   Lieberman, 'Political Significance of Religious Wealth', p. 758.

Below the royal princes in the political and social hierarchy stood the state's appointed officials. During the Restored Toungoo and Konbaung dynasties, this group grew in size relative to the princely coterie, as the king appointed an increasing number of provincial officials directly dependent upon him while requiring the princes to reside at the capital where they could be watched and prevented from raising provincial revolts. These court-appointed officials became the crucial intermediaries between the court and the hereditary village and town headmen who had direct control over the manpower and resources of the kingdom.

The king, at the centre of the state, was in theory, and often in practice, involved in the details of the state's administration. All edicts were promulgated in the monarch's name, and while he probably had little involvement in their drafting, he had a clear supervisory role. 'Policymaking' in the contemporary sense was not a major activity, as the kings were concerned with the achievement of established goals rather than with the formulation of new ones.[33] Thus, active monarchs were personally involved in what in policy-oriented bureaucracies might seem trivial matters of administration and organisation, including the appointment of officials. However, in the precolonial state, personnel appointments were far from trivial and the image of an active, knowledgeable monarch who had not only the power but also the ability to check on any of his subordinates was a key to the effective use of authority. Through the network of administrators, princes and spies, information about the affairs of state was conveyed to the king, through doubtless distorted in the process by the interest and perceptions of its sources.[34] The early monarchs of a new dynasty or outsiders within the princely group were probably better equipped to judge the value of information than those who had spent their formative years cosseted in the royal palace. The inability of the last Restored Toungoo monarchs as well as the last Konbaung king, Thibaw, to adequately assess their informants' reports may have been a contributory factor in their downfall.

Despite the king's theoretically all-powerful position, the officials who surrounded him, as well as his cultural and political milieu, placed other limitations on the effectiveness of his authority. Growing bureaucratic tendencies in the administration 'restrained him from having a free hand'. There are documented cases of the most powerful Konbaung kings, Bodawpaya, Bagyidaw and Mindon, bowing to the requirements of their administrative

33   Koenig, 'Early Kon-baung Polity', p. 218.
34   Lieberman, *Burmese Administrative Cycles,* p. 74.

advisers, and it would be safe to assume that if records were available similar examples from the Restored Toungoo period could be found.[35]

The strengthening of central power made the capital and central administration the focus of politics in the early modern state in Myanmar. As noted above, the Restored Toungoo and Konbaung monarchs increased their control over the administration by requiring the royal appanage holders to reside at the court. They supervised their rivals' daily activities and hindered the development of power bases outside the capital. As a consequence, the princes were in closer contact with the centrally appointed court functionaries and state administrators who carried out the king's bidding, and as administrators became attached to the princes, rivalry among individuals in these groups sometimes developed.[36]

In theory, all royal princes and court officials were committed to supporting the monarch. In practice, the linchpin in the system of monarchical controls of the administrators stemmed from the king's position as chief patron of the court. It was he who had the final word over the dispersal of appanage grants, rewards and punishments, promotions and demotions. In the day-to-day operations of the court, even the most ambitious princes were aware of their dependence upon the monarch. Only a brave or foolhardy man would challenge a powerful king unless he was certain of the support of many other princes and officials. The king's ability to control his subordinates was further strengthened by 'an elaborate duplication and fragmentation of authority' which allowed him to keep a firm hand through what would now be called 'checks and balances'. The effect may been less efficient administrative procedures than a more rationalised bureaucratic system would have produced, but the monarch had a greater degree of information and leverage over his subordinates and thereby enhanced his political control.[37]

As Lieberman writes, at the beginning of a dynasty the central and regional elites 'were tied to the throne by a sense of personal obligation for royal patronage, by fear of offending successful warriors, by the desire to associate themselves with kings of obvious religious merit, and by a practi-

35   Khin Maung Kyi and Tin Tin, *Administrative Patterns in Historical Burma* (Singapore: Institute of Southeast Asian Studies, Southeast Asian Perspectives, no. 1, 1973), p. 56.

36   Trager and Koenig, *Burmese Sit-tans*, p. 19.

37   Lieberman, *Burmese Administrative Cycles*, pp. 85-6.

cal recognition of the benefits that strong government conferred.'[38] While subsequent monarchs often did not possess the charismatic and dominating qualities of the founders of the final two dynasties, these factors continued to operate to ensure the loyalty to the throne of the majority of officials most of the time. The fact that no appointments were permanent (they could be recalled by the monarch) made jockeying for position by administrators a constant factor of central government.

The non-royal officials in the administration had the least secure positions and therefore were of the greatest use to the king. Being ambitious men without the prestige that came with royal birth, they sought to advance by gaining the king's or another patron's favour. All 'were selected on a personal basis', but 'qualification or efficiency were given due consideration.' Appointees to high office in the capital were men who had become skilled in the administration and had worked their way up. Entrance into the administrative corps of the precolonial state remained informal and non-rationalised until the mid-nineteenth century, when King Mindon introduced monastic *pahtamabyan* examinations—intended for testing the skills of members of the *sangha*—as a means of determining the suitability of candidates for admission to government service.[39] Until then nothing had been done to alter the patron-client basis of gaining appointment to the royal service.

The monarchs of the Restored Toungoo and Konbaung dynasties divided the affairs of the central state into two different administrative units, though here, as elsewhere in the system, there was some overlap of duties and functions designed to ensure political reliability. Public affairs of state were primarily the responsibility of the Council of Ministers or *hluttaw*, while the Privy Council, or *bye-daik*, saw to the affairs of the king's court and to private matters. This division of responsibilities persisted unchanged throughout the last two dynasties, and its continuity is indicative of the reliability of the system from the crown's political perspective.[40] Like most administrative agencies, the *hluttaw* and the *bye-daik* with their respective subordinate staff were expected to be the instruments of whoever held power. They also provided continuity to the state when the monarch died, even though in theory there was no legal

---

38   Ibid., p. 11.
39   Khin Maung Kyi and Tin Tin, *Administrative Patterns*, pp. 50-1.
40   Lieberman, *Burmese Administrative Cycles*, pp. 86-7.

continuity and occasionally in practice there were significant personnel changes, especially at times of crisis in the regime.

The activities of the *bye-daik* were the focus of the court's administration, as it had ready access to the monarch and was in a superior position to the Council of Ministers. All written communications to the monarch went through its machinery, supervised by the four Interior ministers, or *atwin-wun*. Not only were the *atwin-wun* able to censor much of the official information which reached the monarch, they also had access to the workings of the Council of Ministers which the *hluttaw* members did not have in regard to the Privy Council.[41]

Despite its inferior position in terms of access to the monarch, the Council of Ministers was higher in ceremonial rank than the Privy Council—suggesting that symbolically, the affairs of state were more important than the affairs of the king. Normally composed of four chief ministers, or *wun-gyi*, the *hluttaw*, like the *bye-daik*, operated its decision making process on a collegial basis. This had the effect of limiting the ability of ambitious individuals to rise in authority over their equals, as did the practice of plural appointments to office.[42]

The Council of Ministers, like the Privy Council, posed little political threat to the monarch, and although it did occasionally have a hand in the selection of a new king when princely factionalism made a purely dynastic succession impossible, or dominate the throne towards the end of a dynastic line. Officials never attempted to take the throne themselves. There were various reasons for this. One was their non-royal antecedents; another was the fact that ministers lacked a clear corporate identity. Being of equal rank, they were generally unwilling to concede the advancement of one of their number over themselves. The competition between the officials of the Privy Council and the Council of Ministers meant that the monarch had the opportunity to play one group of officials off against another, as well as one individual off against another, especially given the absence of clearly-defined responsibilities. The monarch's access to information, or at least gossip, was thus greatly enhanced.

Within the central administrative service, younger officials keen for promotion often conspired with members of the royal family to unseat an incumbent and thus solidify their utility to a prospective king. Royal intrigues led to administrative duplicity but also to political control of

41   Ibid., p. 89.
42   Ibid., p. 87.

ministers and other officials by the royalty as a ruling group.[43] One consequence of the limitations on princes' administrative power brought about
by the Restored Toungoo reforms was an increase in the autonomous
power of the king's ministers. In certain regards, the kings became dependent upon the ministers because of their superior knowledge of affairs
of state.[44] While the central administration of the precolonial state did not
approximate the Weberian rational-bureaucratic, ideal-typical, modern
state,[45] it would be wrong to conclude that many European states at this
time were significantly different at the level of court politics. Indeed, an
interesting comparison can be drawn from the fact that at the beginning
of the development of the modern state in both Europe and Myanmar
there arose powerful ministers as key advisers to the monarch in the place
of princes and other hereditary figures.

Beneath the *hluttaw* in the central organisation, administrative functions were divided between two types of departments. Territorial agencies
supervised and organised the activities of the geographical zone under their
authority regardless of the social categories resident therein. Departmental
agencies, on the other hand, were concerned with administration of the affairs of particular population groups regardless of their place of residence.[46]
This overlapping system provided another check from the centre on the
activities of officials and limited their ability to control affairs to the monarch's detriment.

The population of the nuclear zone and the zone of dependent provinces,
under obligation to serve the state, was divided into two different categories under the territorial and geographical agencies of the *hluttaw*. Another
population category, slaves or debt bondsmen, did not come directly under
the authority of the state, as their labour was the resource of their lay or
monastic masters. Those men in service of the crown (*ahmu-dan*) and the
free servicemen (*athi*) were the state's greatest resource, and it was in their
control that the state's greatest efforts lay. These manpower categories stood
in a hierarchical relationship with each other and with the state.

43   Ibid., pp. 140-1.
44   Victor B. Lieberman, 'Provincial Reforms in Taung-ngu Burma', *Bulletin of the School of Oriental and African Studies,* XLIII, 3 (1980), p. 566.
45   See Reinhard Bendix, *Max Weber* (Garden City, NY: Anchor Books, 1960), pp. 423-30.
46   Lieberman, *Burmese Administrative Cycles,* pp. 87-8.

The higher *ahmu-dan* group 'provided the crown with labour on a fixed, rotational basis'.[47] Its members tended to live nearest the capital and received grants of land and villages sites directly from the central state. *Athi* stood in a more independent posture vis-à-vis the capital. They were less likely to reside in the irrigated areas of the centre but were found on the periphery of the nuclear zone and the most distant provinces. In contrast to the *ahmu-dan* communities' dependence on the state-maintained irrigation and distribution systems, the villages and fields of the *athi* were primarily the result of their own efforts to develop new agricultural zones.[48] Exempted from regular military service which the *ahmu-dan* were required to provide, the *athi* were subject to a higher level of taxation but received fewer benefits from the state. Both groups were required to provide corvee labour as demanded by the king's officials. Though the *ahmu-dan* were the permanent core of the state's armed forces, in times of need the *athi* could be required to serve the state as military auxiliaries.[49] *Ahmu-dan* were generally administered by the departmental and *athi* by the territorial agencies.

From this it can be seen that the *ahmu-dan* villages were the most important cellular groups for the power and stability of the throne, and were consequently under the supervision of the *hluttaw* through the service gentry and the departmental officials. In theory their headmen had less autonomy than those of the *athi* communities. The court attempted to control the hereditary taxpayers and servicemen through a system of quotas and censuses. This highly complex system was actually too elaborate for the meagre administrative resources of the monarchical state to maintain, and over time these groups tended to become lost to the court as individuals drifted into slavery, debt-bondage, vagabondage or dacoity.[50] This would necessitate a particular effort to regroup these persons back under central control, and therefore the *hluttaw* was continually seeking to strengthen its control over these groups.[51]

In practice, the officials appointed directly by the king were usually too few in number to maintain effective control over these manpower resources,

---

47 Ibid., p. 97.

48 Ibid., p. 105.

49 Ibid., pp. 106-7.

50 Normally these persons were not a serious drain on state resources, but at times of crisis they more easily escaped the state's authority and were thus lost to the crown's power-base when most needed. Koenig, 'Early Kon-baung Polity', pp. 128-32.

51 Lieberman, *Burmese Administrative Cycles*, p. 12.

THE STATE IN MYANMAR

and the state had to rely on the cooperation of the gentry who were in direct contact with the local communities. As these members of the gentry were not mainly appointed by the court, but were hereditary officials, the court had limited powers of supervision and dismissal over the state's lowest level agents.[52] The officials in charge of territorial administration, because of the multifaceted aspects of their posts, were in a position to expand their wealth and power by squeezing taxes and manpower resources from their residents without passing the proceeds on to the central state. This not only weakened the power of the centre in an immediate way, but also tended to create long-term economic and political problems for the state as people migrated or otherwise developed techniques for avoiding the exactions of their rulers.[53]

To obviate these problems, the Restored Toungoo monarchs instituted additional reforms intended to increase central control over manpower and other resources. By raising the proportion of hereditary servicemen in the capital zone from roughly 20 to 45 per cent, the centre had a distinct advantage over the other zones which were unable to muster the same level of well-equipped military forces. To the south of the nuclear zone, the Restored Toungoo monarchs expanded control over subordinate officials and removed some of their intermediary functions in relation to village headmen. 'The principal significance of these reforms, which remained in place after the fall of the Toungoo Dynasty (1752) well into the nineteenth century, was that they permitted a more efficient integration of dry zone and coastal resources than at any previous time in Burmese history.'[54]

Until the Restored Toungoo and Konbaung kings, the key centrally appointed provincial administrators were the *myo-wun*. A *myo-wun* was assisted by a clerk who often served as his deputy. In addition, most districts had assigned by the king's ministers a *sit-ke* who oversaw military and police matters, and a revenue officer or *ahkin-wun*, together with a monarchical representative or spy. These officials, especially the *myo-wun*, worked with the township or village headmen and other local hereditary officials, the chiefs of the crown service units and any local agent of the ap-

---

52   Ibid., p. 112.
53   Ibid., p. 91.
54   Lieberman, 'Continuity and Change', pp. 15-16. The exceptions were the Kayin communities around Kayah, the Sittaung valley and the Ayeyawady delta. See Koenig, 'Early Kon-baung Polity', pp. 106-8.

panage holder in carrying out the state's wishes.[55] Several of these officers, in particular a *sit-ke* and an *ahkin-wun*, were assigned to the major Shan sawbwas' administrations in the eighteenth and nineteenth centuries. The interesting point about such an administrative system at the local level is that while the state did not have the bureaucratic machinery of the colonial state, the early modern state's architects had thought through the problems of political and economic control over resources and maintenance of order. They had done this in such a way as to elaborate a complex system of checks over local power holders in order to limit their ability to evade central demands, and to make it extraordinarily difficult for them to create any institutionalised power which might threaten the central state and its interests. Such a system obviously made for less efficient administration, with many opportunities for lines of authority to become crossed and connivance at misdemeanours to take place. It did mean, though, that by judicious rotation of officials, the centre could keep extant reliable sources of intelligence on local political activities and problems. This was at the cost, however, of condoning a large measure of what would now be referred to as peculation or corruption.

Given the relative inefficiency of the provincial administration in such a system, the enduring strength of the economic and social order rested on the local hereditary officials (the gentry) who manned the lowest level of the governmental system.[56] The hereditary headmen were essentially of two types: heads of townships (*myo* or *taik*) and heads of villages (*ywa*). During the Restored Toungoo period, at the core of the state there were more than fifty townships, each containing 12 to 145 villages.[57] The heads of townships were normally title *myo-* (or *taik*) *thu-gyi* and their subordinate villages were called *ywa-thu-gyi*, although there was some variation in the titles used. *Thu-gyi* were often assisted by another official known as a *myei-daing*, who 'in his narrowest definition was responsible for arranging and recording the sale of all immovable property in his jurisdiction and took a commission on the sale price'.[58] Most probably, however, the *myei-daing* served as an assistant to the *thu-gyi*, as he had access to many of the important records of the village and thus was able to assist in levying taxes.

55   Trager and Koenig, *Burmese Sit-tans,* p. 38.
56   Lieberman, *Burmese Administrative Cycles,* pp. 92-3; Trager and Koenig, *Burmese Sit-tans,* p. 38.
57   Lieberman, *Burmese Administrative Cycles,* p. 93.
58   Trager and Koenig, *Burmese Sit-tans,* p. 40.

The *myo-thy-gyi* and *thu-gyi* were the pillars of the precolonial state's administration. It was they who gathered the revenue and manpower from the villagers. They were 'the pivotal intermediaries between the state and the mass of the peasantry'[59] and, because of their hereditary status, had both personal power and authority derived from their positions as patrons, which was denied the transient appointees of the king who supervised their activities.

The *myo-thu-gyi* and *thu-gyi* were probably the descendants of the headmen of occupational groups in the pre-Bagan period. A headman controlled the social unit 'by the power of personality and the personal loyalty given him by his followers'.[60] However, unlike the headmen of the Bagan and Avan eras, the *thu-gyi* of the *athi* villages in the early modern period all owed their appointment to the crown rather than to the provincial appanage holder or the *myo-wun*. Nonetheless, membership in the gentry was mainly inherited; their authority over the residents in their communities was derived from their recognised status in society. This contradiction is suggestive of the nature of the political and administrative problems that the late early modern state faced in implementing centralising reforms. The gap between theory and practice, between ideal political control and the need to work with historically developed customs, meant that old practices often lived on in new guises.

Myo-thu-gyi and *thu-gyi* incomes came primarily from taking a percentage of tax collections, most of which they were obliged to pass on to the king's provincial administrators and any appanage holder. Their incomes were augmented by gifts given in exchange for protection and by favours such as reduced tax and labour demands. These men, who took a long-term perspective on their positions, were loath to invoke extortionate demands on the population, and thus stood in a protective stance vis-à-vis their transient superiors who sometimes tried to quickly amass a personal fortune.[61] Thus the interests of the king and the central state at the top and the headmen at the bottom coincided. Both sought to increase the manpower and resources at their disposal so as to maintain ongoing personal, familial and institutional interests. In contrast, the layer of ambitious court-appointed provincial officials and royal appanage holders sought to maximise their earnings with less regard to the long-term consequences for the viability of the state. The lack of fixed salaries for state officials made such a situation

59   Adas, 'From Avoidance to Confrontation', p. 22.
60   Aung Thwin, 'Kingship, the *Sangha*', p. 111.
61   Lieberman, *Burmese Administrative Cycles*, p. 93.

inevitable. This was one of the key weaknesses of the precolonial administrative system; not only was it inefficient, it also tended to generate peasant antagonism towards the state.

In addition to levying taxes in kind, the *myo-thu-gyi* and *thu-gyi* were responsible for the allocation of corvee labour demands, military service requirements and the maintenance of order. They were also responsible for maintaining detailed census records of all the inhabitants of their jurisdiction, including each person's name, age, date of birth and service affiliation, if applicable. The *myo-thu-gyi* were in charge of local judicial administration and personally adjudicated petty civil and criminal cases. Given the manifold nature of their duties and their access to the wealth of an entire township or village, the headmen were substantially better off than the average peasant cultivator.[62] Their wealth, allied with their hereditary and state-sanctioned status, allowed them to publicly display their importance and authority. Their housing and mode of transport set them clearly apart from the rest of local society and outwardly connected them with the power of the state.

The authority relationship of the state to the people living on the periphery of the nuclear and dependent province zones was different from that of the central core, and varied from place to place depending on the nature of settlement under various ecological conditions. The relationship of most concern to the centre was with the rulers of the Tai population groups in the Shan plateau. The relationship of the monarch to these groups was analogous to that of the *athi* population in terms of corvee labour, military service and taxation obligations. Politically, the rulers of the Tai communities, the sawbwa, had a different relationship with the central state, somewhere between that of the village headman in the nuclear or dependent province zones and that of the semi-independent appanage holders and officials in the lowlands (before the Restored Toungoo administrative reforms). As Lieberman writes, the Tai tributaries' 'prestige in many cases equalled that of Burman princes, [but] in terms of association with the throne and political autonomy, they were analogous to lowland headmen.'[63]

Regarding control over the more sparsely populated, swidden agricultural areas of the surrounding hills, the power of the centre was mainly derived from military, not administrative strength. These areas had only a small economic surplus for expropriation by the state because of their

62   Trager and Koenig, *Burmese Sit-tans*, p. 39.
63   Lieberman, *Burmese Administrative Cycles*, p. 137.

meagre populations and difficult agricultural conditions. In addition, the administrative weaknesses of the state, as well as poor communications, made control difficult. Nevertheless, the military threat posed by these peripheral areas required that they be kept under central suzerainty.[64] Because administrative reform outside the nuclear and dependent province zones was put off until late in the Konbaung period and was not an early priority of its colonial successors, the administrative and political system of the precolonial state persisted there to a large extent into the twentieth century.

Financing the precolonial state

The state treasury during the precolonial period rested upon an economy that was not, by comparison with either the later European feudal economy or the colonial economy of Burma, a dynamic one. The agricultural technology of the period and the relatively modest population base of the state made economic expansion difficult. In order to increase output of agricultural and other products, monarchs sought to increase their populations through the expansion of their domain and the capture of skilled artisans in war. The administrative systems also limited the state's ability to tap fully the local production surplus.

That the precolonial economy can be characterised as essentially a subsistence economy should not, however, obscure the fact that it did provide a sufficient surplus to support an expensive state structure which demonstrated its power through conspicuous consumption, a sizeable standing army relative to the size of the population, heavy expenditure on religious edifices, and the support of a proportionately large Buddhist *sangha*. During the period of the Restored Toungoo and Konbaung monarchs, as part of their effort to strengthen administrative controls over provincial political and economic power, the state relied increasingly on revenue from trade through southern seaports. Moreover, the relatively long era of stability during the final two dynasties meant that there was a slow but steady increase in domestic production that tended to benefit the state coffers. The spiral of reinforcing factors during this period indicates a strengthening financial basis for the state prior to colonisation.

Why, then, did the state not undertake a fuller rationalisation of its revenue and tax system in order to increase the proportion of economic surplus going to its treasury by introducing institutions similar to those

64   Ibid., p. 199.

of the modern bureaucratic state? The reason was essentially political. The experience of the monarchical system in Myanmar was such as to convince kings that they would be unable to control the private power that would probably have resulted from economic expansion and rationalisation, even if this caused an increase the overall resource base of society and ultimately the state. Besides, full-scale rationalisation was then beyond the technical capacity of the state and, given the delicate balance of interests in the political system, the method of indirect revenue collection, coupled with direct taxation upon trade, provided a system that was easy to operate and lucrative in the short term, as well as being a source of political stability. Reform of the existing system, as the events of the final years of the Konbaung dynasty eventually demonstrated, could have resulted in an unmanageable degree of political opposition.

The subsistence aspects of the economy were, moreover, advantageous to the state's controllers inasmuch as they tended to limit the economic aspirations of the bulk of the population; demands by society on the state for economic improvements were rare. Avoidance of the state, not reliance upon it, was the norm. Aware as they were of how small an individual surplus they actually produced, and knowing of their governors' conspicuous consumption patterns, the peasantry attempted to evade tax payments. The religious and cosmological justifications for giving financial support to the state were too ephemeral to induce voluntary contributions. Thus, a variety of means to evade state demands were developed, and the inability of the central state's administrative system to penetrate the village beyond the *thu-gyi* made this all the easier. The decentralised nature of the state's accounting and revenue assessment systems ensured that the central authorities' knowledge of the real resource base of the state was only as great as the honesty of village officials who felt a certain, but limited, sense of personal obligation to the central state. Inasmuch as the provincial administrators and tax collectors were dependent on the reporting of the *myo-thu-gyi* and *thu-gyi* of each township and village for an assessment of taxable resources, these men were in a key position to limit the state's revenue while protecting their populations and increasing the proportion of wealth that could be retained within their areas for their own and their communities' benefit.[65]

---

65   See Koenig, 'Early Kon-baung Polity', for an excellent description of the Konbaung fiscal system.

The fact that the economy lacked any standard coinage until the reign of King Mindon in the mid-nineteenth century[66] made any system of standard accounting impossible, as well as preventing any significant rationalisation of the taxation system. Nonetheless, there was an apparent tendency towards greater reliance on coin and commercial taxes in the early modern period, though taxes in kind or as corvee labour remained the norm until near the time of the formation of the colonial state. The greater strength of the European state at the end of the feudal period rested upon its development of an effective, centralised tax system. The absence of such a system in Myanmar was the consequence not only of various administrative problems but also of the political and ideological principles of the precolonial state.

The wealth of administrators and local gentry gave them distinct advantages because their access to economic surpluses through the power of the state enabled them (as noted above) to be among the few to have more than a subsistence income. This permitted them to increase their non-state income also. As a consequence of an expansion in agricultural production, money lending became an important aspect of the agrarian economy in the nuclear zone, and the most important lenders to the peasantry were state officials, including both administrators and army commanders together with members of the gentry.[67]

The primary basis of the state's finances was taxation of produce. With regard to land tax, by tradition the king could lay claim to one-tenth of all production which 'was ... viewed as a return for tenancy',[68] thus making no distinction between land rent and land tax. Scholarly authorities differ in their interpretations as to the legal and actual relationship of the peasant to the land he tilled. Examining the legal theory, Koenig and Trager conclude that though the monarch was the 'owner of all land', land could nevertheless 'be owned privately, alienated, mortgaged and inherited'.[69] This view is supported by Hla Aung.[70] Khin Maung Kyi and Tin Tin con-

---

66   Trager and Koenig, *Burmese Sit-tans,* p. 50; M. Robinson and L.A. Shaw, *The Coins and Banknotes of Burma* (Manchester: published by the authors, 1980), pp. 82-102.

67   Lieberman, *Burmese Administrative Cycles,* pp. 161-3; Ono Toru, 'Konbaung Hkit Kyeitow Ywa Ngweihkyei Sanit' (The village money lending system of the Konbaung era), *Myawati,* March 1976, pp. 37-42.

68   Trager and Koenig, *Burmese Sit-tans,* p. 45.

69   Ibid.

70   Hla Aung, 'The Effect of Anglo-Indian Legislation on Burmese Customary Law', in David C. Buxbaum (ed.), *Family Law and Customary Law in Asia: a*

tend, however, that usufruct did not give peasants the legal right of title suggested in theory. Rather, because land 'revenue formed an important basis of the king's finances, various orders and edicts were issued to confine the cultivator to his land.' Especially for the lowest segments of society, the traditional social order had some characteristics of a caste system with little social mobility; an individual was sometimes 'permanently shackled to his order'.[71] Rather than the peasant controlling the use of the land, the state used the land to control the peasant.

Theory and practice differ here, and in reality the system described by Khin Maung Kyi and Tin Tin probably predominated in central areas. Such a system was maintained not because of its economic desirability in terms of increasing production, but because of its political utility in controlling manpower. Given the shortage of labour, the absence of technological innovations and the surplus of land, manpower mobility and land trading were regulated in order to avoid the destruction of customary social relations upon which the king's power and the state's perpetuation depended.[72] The observations of the first British administrator to govern a part of Myanmar shed some light on this problem in southern areas. Colonel Maingy, the Commissioner of Tenasserim (Tanintharyi), wrote in October 1825:

Land Tenures. Land is of no value in the Province of Mergui: it was allowed to be cleared indiscriminately by anyone, and held by no title deeds of any kind, nor could I discover that any of the lands so cleared were ever registered or account kept of them, yet they constitute clear and distinct private property, some of them ancient, and were never interfered with unless owing to those arbitrary measures under the late absolute and despotic Government. Every landholder is allowed to dispose of his property either by sale or gift, and it regularly descends to his family. It sometimes happens but very rarely, that in the transfer of some lands, bills of sale were drawn out but being written on black tablets in general use among the Burmese might be defaced or altered at pleasure.

Any person quitting his land for a season and leaving no one in charge of it could not on his return claim it, or turn off the actual possessor, without an order from one of the Members of Government, and this could alone be affected by bribery.[73]

Contemporary Legal Perspective (The Hague: Martinus Nijhoff, 1968), p. 78.

71   Khin Maung Kyi and Tin Tin, *Administrative Patterns*, p. 38.

72   Ibid., p. 27.

73   A.D. Maingy, 12 Oct. 1825, in *Selected Correspondence of Letters from and Received in the Office of the Commissioner Tenasserim Division from the years 1825-26 to 1842-43* (Rangoon: Government Printing and Stationery, Burma, 1929), p. 9.

41

Maingy's account provides a clue to the situation in regard to land own-ership and its legal status, although the fact that the area he describes was on the periphery of the state doubtless affects the nature of his account, particularly in regard to land clearance. Nearer the capital, and in particular on *ahmu-dan* lands, the state was much more careful in its regulation of land usage.

In general terms, land usufruct was of three kinds. First there was gov-ernment land, cultivated by the *ahmu-dan* population on behalf of the state. Private land, the second kind, belonging ancestrally to a family, clan or village, was rarely taxed by the state until the late nineteenth century when a head tax or *thathameda* became the normal method of taxing the *athi* population. Religious lands, which had been donated by individuals and the monarch for the support of the Buddhist *sangha*, were semi-perma-nent endowments. This third type was worked by pagoda slaves and others for the benefit of the religious institutions and was not taxed. During the Restored Toungoo and Konbaung dynasties, alienation of state land to monastic control was relatively unimportant because of the state's firmer control over the monastic order as well as the generally greater wealth avail-able to the state by then.[74]

In practice, the system of government land regulation appears to have been this: land was in theory owned by the king, and therefore his officials had the right, in his name, to determine use and settlement patterns if their authority was appealed to in cases of disputed usufruct. However, in practice, the overwhelming bulk of land was regulated by customary understandings among the villagers under the supervisory authority of the *thu-gyi*. The commonly accepted understandings of the village on land use gave little leverage for the state to interfere in the community and thus helped fend off the intrusion of the king's officials in local affairs. The state was forced to tolerate such a disjuncture between theory and practice in land ownership and usage because it did not have the political power, ad-ministrative means, or economic necessity to change it; moreover there was no incentive for the development of state-sanctioned legal concepts of property rights as developed in European feudalism.[75]

Unable to administer land in practice, the precolonial state attempted to regulate the people who cultivated the fields and allowed them to de-

<hr>

74   Lieberman, *Burmese Administrative Cycles*, pp. 278-9.
75   See Douglas C. North and Robert Paul Thomas, *The Rise of the Western World, A New Economic History* (Cambridge University Press, 1973), pp. 19-24.

termine usage. However, the authority of the state always lay behind the customary arrangements, and when these were disputed by a segment of the community, the king's fictive ownership gave his officials the right to determine the outcome. Politically this arrangement proved beneficial to maintenance of the monarch's monopoly of power by limiting the growth of independent centres of wealth. Any potential for appanage holders or other wealthy individuals to amass large tracts of private land was blocked, and thereby the possible development of a decentralised state was obviated. The price the kings of Myanmar paid for their centralised power was the opportunity for a more dynamic and production-oriented internal economy to emerge, based upon private property, contract, and the security of investment and trade.

In addition to taxes on land and population, taxes on commerce and trade were increasingly important sources of revenue. The equivalents of customs posts were established to control internal and external trade on the reasonably well developed network of cart and high roads and the rivers which connected the major towns,[76] as well as to perform certain police functions involving the movement of population. These posts were manned by crown service men from the *ahmu-dan* population and were supervised by a minister known as the *kin-wun*. During the Konbaung period there were about thirty such posts in the nuclear and dependent province zones and another seventeen or so in the Tai-populated areas east and north of the capital area.[77] The revenue raised by these customs posts was increased by the fact that goods travelling from one region to another as well as those leaving or entering as 'foreign' trade were liable to taxation.

Though trade grew in importance for the finances of the central state, land tax or rent, as well as non-sanctioned forms of emolument, remained the basis of most of the income of the state's intermediate officials and of the hereditary gentry. As only a slight proportion of land revenue was actually passed on to the central court, state projects of a military or economic nature depended greatly on the ability of the king's officials to control manpower. Here, corvee or compulsory labour was a key to the state's capacity to carry out its functions.

Men of all classes, even village ... headmen, were called upon to afford their labour towards the execution of any public work, and towards the defence of the territory.

---

76   Koenig, 'Early Kon-baung Polity', p. 134.

77   Trager and Koenig, *Burmese Sit-tans,* p. 49.

... These compulsory labourers received no remuneration, although rarely, a small proportion of grain.[78]

The most important use of corvee labour was in building and maintaining the irrigation systems of the central dry zone that formed the original core of the state. The economic vitality of this zone, with its elaborate expenditure on pagodas and state buildings, was crucial to the state's ability to maintain and provision its elite military forces as well as the central court and administrative cadre. Thus it can be seen 'that the aim of the Burmese revenue system was to extract agricultural surplus value to maintain the growing administrative system which was a result of the irrigation system.'[79] The irrigation system itself, however, was apparently not managed by the central state's officers but by local authorities.

As noted above, the system of customs posts served both resource gathering and economic and social control functions. Khin Maung Kyi and Tin Tin stress the secondary purpose of this system (control) over the first, for it was intended, they argue, 'to inhibit any spontaneous growth of commerce.'[80] According to this view, the state attempted consciously to preserve the original agrarian basis of society, and the economic relations therein, from the competition that would have evolved from the growth of free trade and private capital formation and the classes that these would have spawned. While the customs revenue system, like the land revenue system and sumptuary laws, doubtless had this effect, it is arguable whether the king and his ministers perceived this as their purpose. Aware of their immediate problems of revenue and political control, and perhaps aware of the inhibiting effect of their policies on the economic potential of the country, they used the land and customs systems as ways of gaining revenue and of ensuring the perpetuation of the state. Customs checks provided a means of monitoring centrally the flow of manpower and other resources in a way no other institution could in such a diffuse administrative system.

It is difficult to estimate what proportion of the economy's surplus reached the state's coffers. The nominally prescribed and religiously sanc-

---

78   A.D. Maingy, 1 May 1827, in *Correspondence for the Years 1825-26 to 1842-43 in the Office of the Commissioner Tenasserim Division* (Rangoon: Office of the Superintendent, Government Printing, Burma, 1929), p. 62.

79   Khin Maung Kyi and Tin Tin, *Administrative Patterns*, p. 39.

80   Ibid., p. 38. One of the authors subsequently explained that the publication was written in part as a critique of the socialist policies of the government of Burma at the time it was written in 1973. (Conversation with the author, Singapore, 1989.) How much this skewed their analysis is unclear.

tioned rate of 10 per cent *ad valorem* taxation was avoided by practices established to reduce the officially recorded value of goods. Misrepresentation and false reporting, as well as deduction of commissions by headmen, tax collectors and appanage holders, meant that probably only about one-third of tax revenue actually got through the system to the central state institutions.[81] The level of actual taxation must have varied according to the rapacity of the local collectors as well as the demands of the state. According to a British account of 1825, the previous court-appointed *myo-wun* in Taninthayi had set the rates quite arbitrarily, though at reasonably low levels.[82] The rate probably went up in times of war or other regime crises and this, rather than the weakness of the state *per se*, hastened the decline of dynasties as they were forced to exact more and more revenue from a shrinking resource base.[83]

Given the patron-client nature of most authority relationships in the precolonial state, heavy taxation almost inevitably led to a declining tax base. This was because individuals sought to transfer their residence and/or clientage to an area with headmen, appanage holders and officials who were less demanding, or to abandon settled occupations for vagabondage or dacoity. As the size of the state's institutions grew after the founding of the Restored Toungoo dynasty, and as its demands for revenue consequently increased owing to its enlarged political patronage as well as continuing religious patronage obligations, so the court attempted to tap more of the resources of those most immediately under its control.

Myanmar's increasing involvement in Indian Ocean trade from the late sixteenth century onwards undermined the traditional reliance of the state on agrarian-based sources of revenue and provided the financial means for implementing provincial reforms. It also assisted in the amendment and consolidation of the appanage system under the central court.[84] Lieberman points out three important ways in which this economic changed assisted state consolidation:

It assisted economic integration and thus helped indirectly to erode regional loyalties that, by definition, were inimical to central authority; it provided Ava with a

81   Oliver B. Pollack, *Empires in Collusion: Anglo-Burmese Relations in the Mid-Nineteenth Century* (Westport, CT: Greenwood Press, 1979), p. 117.

82   A.D. Maingy, 12 Oct. 1835, *Selected Correspondence*, p. 12.

83   Thus also increasing transaction costs and causing greater financial losses to the state. North and Thomas, *Rise of the Western World*, p. 87.

84   Lieberman, *Burmese Administrative Cycles*, p. 124.

major source of cash income needed for political patronage and military expeditions; and it furnished the crown with firearms, which afforded a reliable advantage over more traditionally equipped rebels.[85]

The importance of trade with the Indian Ocean and the taxes derived therefrom can be seen from the fact that by the late eighteenth century, cash revenue from trade through the port of Yangon was greater than cash revenue from the traditional Kyaukse irrigated agricultural zone of central Myanmar.[86] The total wealth of the economy grew as a result of this trade. The increased strength of the state which followed led in turn to longer periods of tranquillity under the Restored Toungoo and Konbaung kings, permitting some modest expansion of agricultural production and internal trade.[87] Even if the early modern state did not develop the capacity to mobilise resources for the state's benefit to the same degree as the colonial, increased economic productivity resulting from the state's enhanced power laid the basis, by the seventeenth century, for the growth of a more centralised administrative system. The economic reforms, including the initial countrywide monetisation introduced by Mindon in the nineteenth century, were the forerunners of the production- and trade-oriented state of the late nineteenth and early twentieth centuries.[88]

The agencies of the precolonial state

The hierarchical territorial organisation and authority relations that provided the order of the precolonial state were designed to enable the rulers to carry out their primary duties of control, security and resource accumulation. The elite identified the interests of the state with their own interests. Therefore, the perpetuation of the state was a matter not merely of abstract problems of government, but of the actual continuity of the traditional ruling strata of royalty, officialdom and gentry. The leaders used military, economic, religious and legal instruments to perpetuate themselves and the state.

During the precolonial period the activities of the central state would have seemed less obvious and obtrusive to the populace than such activities would seem today, for far more of the regulatory aspects of people's lives

---

85   Ibid., p. 117.
86   Koenig, 'Early Kon-baung Polity', pp. 240-2.
87   Lieberman, 'Continuity and Change', p. 18.
88   See Pollack, *Empires in Collision*, pp. 113-36.

were controlled by the patron-client system in the cellular organisation of traditional society. Members of different population categories, *ahmu-dan, athi,* slave, Tai, or swidden agriculturists, knew what the state expected of them and their patron's tasks were normally carried out without the need to invoke the structures of the state or the use of physical coercion. In any event, the weakness of the state's coercive instruments limited the latter option, and this allowed the people to have some degree of self-protection in their relations with officialdom.

As the areas of settled agriculture and concentrated population slowly grew or shifted, the kings sought to increase the effective power base of the state. In order to ensure an adequate economic surplus to maintain the state, new land settlements, expansion of settled agricultural lands and development of irrigation systems in the dry zone of central Myanmar were initiated. In particular, the kings sought to increase the proportion of the population classified as *ahmu-dan,* as it was these who owed the most direct royal service and were the most reliable taxpayers. The obverse side of this effort was to ensure that as few persons as possible were classified as slaves to monastic or lay masters and thus lost to the resources of the state. It was the responsibility of the king's officials, both appointed and hereditary, to ensure that these manpower controls were maintained to the state's benefit, and when, instead, the officials used their centrally sanctioned power for their personal benefit, it was the monarch's task to reimpose control over them. Given the diffuse nature of power in the precolonial state, the maintenance of central control was extremely difficult, and organisation and force alone were insufficient. Of great importance to the state were the charisma of the monarch and the ratification of the state's legitimacy created by customary religious beliefs and practices.

Nevertheless, the coercive and defensive power provided by the king's army was the key to maintenance of the precolonial state's control. This was the force with which the court defended itself against external enemies and maintained its dominance over internal rivals. Any decline in the military capacity of the centre, as at the end of the Restored Toungoo dynasty, made possible the raising of a provincial rebellion and the toppling of the incumbent monarch. The standing army of the classical state was based on the *ahmu-dan* population's obligation to provide military service on a rotational basis. *Athi* could be called upon at times to war to assist the state's standing army and recruits to the king's service were sought through

47

the capture of prisoners in battle and from the peoples residing among the tributary groups in the hills.

What distinguished the Restored Toungoo and Konbaung dynasties from their predecessors in this regard, giving the early modern period one of its unique aspects, was the apparent fact that the standing army was both more concentrated and larger than in previous periods. By 1862 the standing army was estimated to number about 56,130 men, perhaps slightly more than 1 per cent of the population,[89] compared to about 0.5 per cent of the population in the mid-1980s. The enhanced military power of the centre had a consequent deterrent effect, limiting the need for the state to use the army for suppressing frequent internal revolts and forestalling external assaults on its domains. This allowed time for the development of a more effective administrative system to control the population. Unlike the First Toungoo dynasty which had 'no internal administrative structure per se' and therefore relied on punitive expeditions as 'the principal means of maintaining order',[90] the Restored Toungoo and Konbaung dynasties used primarily administrative mechanisms to maintain order, security and population control.

In comparison with the organisation of the modern army, the military force of the precolonial state was not rationally organised; nor did it have clear command structures from the political centre downward. Rather, the army reflected the pattern of political relations that existed in society. It was hierarchical, but the effectiveness of command rested not upon the impersonal authority of rank but upon patron-client loyalties. Commanders of platoons were more like patrons than commanding officers as understood today. They were open to persuasion through gifts, and sought to maintain the strength of their units by offering material inducements such as high status or reduced taxes to men to serve under them. The link between the platoon commanders and their superiors in the court and *hluttaw* was also based upon patron-client ties.[91]

The army of the precolonial state in its later periods was in some ways comparable to the military organisation of the early modern European state where military commanders operated much more like private entrepreneurs rather than state officials. European kings used indentured companies, then foreign mercenaries and finally *corps entretenus* to form the backbone of

89   Ibid., p. 119.

90   Lieberman, 'Political Significance of Religious Wealth', p. 763.

91   Lieberman, *Burmese Administrative Cycles*, pp. 102-5.

their fighting forces. 'The common assumption was that the king would commission a gentleman to raise, equip, officer and lead a given force of men: the king paid him, he for his part did the rest, and if any money stuck to his fingers, this was after all his livelihood.'[92] As indeed it was for the commanders of the king of Myanmar's platoons who were members of the gentry class or court officials. Men sought to rise into elite military units, for it was upon these that the king disposed his largesse most generously. Some of the king's forces may have actually been spared the drudgery of growing their own food on land assigned to them by the court, as they were paid cash salaries instead.[93] It is not possible to determine to what degree the kings of Myanmar encroached upon the powers and independence of the platoon commanders during the final years of the precolonial state as they sought to increase their direct control over the state's army, although it is known that the army became fully salaried in 1872.[94]

That cash payments had begun to be important in the organisation and maintenance of the Myanmar army during the late classical period suggests that the power of the centre to regulate the armed forces was increasing. The reforms introduced by the Restored Toungoo dynasty, and the hiring of foreign military advisers in the nineteenth century, also demonstrate that the rationalisation of the armed forced commenced before colonisation. It is often forgotten that the great European armies of the twentieth century were distinctly the products of that century. In Europe, 'wholly native armies were a product of the nineteenth century',[95] but this was never the case among the military forces of the European empires in Asia, even in the twentieth century. Native armies are the consequence of nationalism, a political force which was not to touch upon military organisation in Myanmar or most of the old world until the last century.

The increasing rationalisation of the king's army towards the end of the early modern period was a factor behind the growing reliance of the state on cash and the taxation of internal commerce, as well as foreign trade. This same pattern had developed in Europe as well, and the experience of other mainland South East Asian states was probably the same. Until more

---

92   Samuel E. Finer, 'State- and Nation-Building in Europe: The Role of the Military', in Charles Tilly (ed.), *Formation of National States in Europe* (Princeton University Press, 1975), pp. 100-1.

93   Lieberman, *Burmese Administrative Cycles*, p. 102.

94   Pollack, *Empires in Collusion*, p. 119.

95   Finer, 'State- and Nation-Building', p. 101.

research is concluded on the political role and nature of the army in the precolonial state and its relationship with the economy and local authority, little more can be confidently said.

The state's perception of the threats to its power from secular economic forces, provincial officials and local gentry has been outlined above. The problem of religious power in the history of Myanmar during the precolonial period is a much documented feature of the political order and shows most clearly how the state used certain nominally extra-state agencies for its perpetuation. Here, of course, the monarchs were in part over-reacting, for the rival power of the institutions of the Buddhist religion was dependent upon the state and cyclical in nature; it waxed and waned, and could always be brought to heel under the dominance of the state, whereas bureaucratic or feudal power, as European monarchs learned, tended to grow unilinerally and therefore required the increasing growth of centralised power in order to keep control of the autonomous individuals and institutions that private trade makes possible. For the kings of Myanmar, the growth of autonomous religious power posed a similar continual political concern, though one of a smaller magnitude.

Because 'the relationship between secular and religious pressures was probably reciprocal rather than lineal and sequential' in Myanmar's precolonial political system,[96] as the power of religious institutions grew the state was proportionately weakened, and therefore not only did the ruler's ability to control religious institutions decline, but so also did his ability to control secular society. Private and personal wealth then tended to increase, further weakening the state in a process which, if not halted, would have made the king and his state merely *primus inter pares* among the institutions of society. The state's ability to control the political and economic system would then have declined and Myanmar, without the centralising force of an integrated economy, would have once more been broken up into a number of petty principalities, as during the Innwa interregnum. Had the state, as a consequence of the Restored Toungoo reforms, not been able to centralise political power in the Ayeyawady valley, then perhaps a form of feudalism would have emerged, but this was precluded by the power of the central monarchs.

From the perspective of the king, the state had to intervene in the affairs of the Buddhist *sangha* to curb religious institutional autonomy. In the process, the state also curbed secular independent wealth by stopping the drift of re-

---

96   Lieberman, 'Political Significance of Religious Wealth', p. 756.

ligious wealth into secular hands. This action, furthermore, re-sacralised the monarch, and thus regained both the faith's political support and a secular and religious economic surplus for the central state. Aung Thwin's description of *sangha* reform in the classical period aptly describes this:

> Burmese kings initiated *sasana* reform, or purification of the *sangha*, to regain some of this wealth in a legal and socially acceptable manner. A rich *sangha* meant of course, that the monks were no longer living according to the rules of the *Vinaya*: therefore, reform was ideologically justifiable. *Sasana* reform had the material effect of reducing the size of the *sangha* (and so the tax-free sector), and the ideological effect of purifying it. The reform also enabled the state to regain both cultivable land and labour resources subject to its corvee, and to impose per capita taxes on previously exempt categories. Purifying the Order eliminated sanctuaries for rebel leaders, pretenders to the throne, and other political opponents to the rulers. The entire process returned usable resources and political security to the state, giving it a new 'lease on life'. Once the *sangha* was purified, however, it began to attract greater public patronage, for the quality of individual merit was contingent on the purity of the monks one supported. The *sangha* also began once more to incur royal favour, since doctrine held the king to be protector and perpetuator of the Religion. Public and royal patronage culminating in monastic landlordism eventually recurred -- and once more the state had to intervene to reform the *sangha* -- the cycle continued.[97]

It was the inability of the last Bagan dynasty kings to implement *sasana* reform effectively that apparently led to its 'internal decay and fall' in 1287[98] and created major problems for the First Toungoo dynasty as late as the 1590s.[99]

The situation was more complex in the time of the Restored Toungoo dynasty. The phenomenon of *sasana* reform indicates not the autonomous power of the *sangha* even when at its most powerful, if corrupt, but rather its ultimately dependent relationship with the state. In the longer term institutional interest of the religious, its purification and control by the state was necessary, and the senior leaders of the monkhood, including the chief abbot or *thathanabaing* who was appointed by the king, were doubtless aware of this. The dependence of the monkhood on the state was solidified by reforms carried out in the time of the Restored Toungoo dynasty. The disintegration of the religion during the Innwa period gave the newly centralised state the justification to require that monastic lands be

---

97   Aung Thwin, 'Role of *Sasana* Reform', pp. 672-3.
98   Aung Thwin, 'Kingship, the *Sangha*', p. 206.
99   Lieberman, *Burmese Administrative Cycles*, pp. 109-10.

cultivated by crown servicemen and taxpayers, rather than pagoda slaves, and therefore their economic surplus beyond the subsistence needs of the tilling peasants and the income requirements of the local monastery were now taxable by the state.[100]

Some scholars have gone so far as to argue that state encouragement of the Theravada form of Buddhism with its requirement for 'the *sangha* to ignore all worldly gains, money and economics' was a direct consequence of the early kings' desire to maintain control of the country's wealth; and that consequently later kings ensured that Buddhism was the only recognised and encouraged religious form in the country.[101] Whatever the original intention, the effect was the same. The control of the *sangha* was to the advantage of the state and the purity the state could impose upon the *sangha* was to the advantage of the religion. The king always had the final say as to whether monastic practices were legitimate, and he maintained this power through his ability to grant 'tax-exempt status or royal endorsement and approval' through patronage of those institutions and practices which were legitimate *'as interpreted by the king'*.[102]

The relations between the state and religion in pre-colonial Myanmar were similar in some broad respects to those between the monarch and the clerical orders in early modern Europe. Like the kings of Myanmar, European kings involved in the formation of the early modern state 'had little autonomous creative power' at their disposal, and hence 'clerics were useful partners' in both an administrative and a legitimising sense. Religious organisations in Europe and Myanmar—Christian orders and the Theravada Buddhist *sangha*—were dissimilar, especially as the pre-national Christian churches had in Rome a supra-state authority to which to appeal. But from the perspective of the state, they both had the advantage of having on the one hand large, wealthy and respected organisations, but on the other a disadvantage—compared with soldiers, landlords and the gentry class— in converting 'state resources under their control into transmissible private property. They were also less apt to build their own rival dynasties.'[103] The celibacy of the monkhood made it easier for the state to remain the dominant partner in their reciprocal relationship, while its kingdom-wide

100   Lieberman, 'Continuity and Change', p. 19.
101   Khin Maung Kyi and Tin Tin, *Administrative Patterns*, p. 45.
102   Aung Thwin, 'Role of *Sasana* Reform, p. 681, emphasis in the original.
103   Charles Tilly, 'Reflections on the History of European State-Making', in Tilly (ed.), *Formation of National States in Western Europe*, p. 63.

institutions provided a useful means of communications when the secular administrative order failed to respond to central edicts.

One of the most important indicators of the differences between the precolonial state in Burma and the early modern state in Europe is the absence of an articulated, countrywide and centrally administered legal and court system. Herein lay a political strength for the monarch and the perpetuation of the state's monopoly of power, but an administrative weakness and a hindrance to the development of a more integrated political system. The kings of the Restored Toungoo and Konbaung dynasties, until late in the nineteenth century, made few if any attempts to modify the system of administration of justice that they inherited from the Bagan kingdom. In the main, the state's judicial system rested on the principle that village, township and provincial officials could settle most cases at the local level by arbitration. Law and custom were little distinguished and legal codes were intended more as guides to moral conduct than as principles of decision and right. The general concept of law was radically different from that in the modern European state. Viewed like the laws of nature, laws were 'a statement of cause and effect', and decisions were to be based upon 'reasonableness' more than 'legality' as found in codified law.[104] The most important law codes, based upon the Indian-derived Code of Manu, were intended to provide 'a compilation of easy-to-read Burmese that judges could understand.'[105]

There was a formal procedure from the lower courts to the *hluttaw* with ultimate appeals from its decisions to the king himself, and more formal judge's courts were established in the capital and major towns.[106] However, there was little effort to distinguish between the state's executive officers and its judicial officers or functions, and the judicial system was marked by a high degree of personalised behaviour, with little procedure other than prevailing notions of status and etiquette. Indeed, until reforms were introduced during the reign of King Thibaw, most courts were conducted in the private residences of officials.[107] The inability of the central state to provide more than a mere guide to the laws meant that there was a distinct absence

---

104 Hla Aung, 'Effect of Anglo-Indian Legislation', p. 75.

105 Lieberman, *Burmese Administrative Cycles,* p. 263.

106 Alan Gledhill, 'Burma', in John Gilissen (ed.), *Bibliographical Introduction to Legal History and Ethnology,* vol. E, no. 7 (Brussels: Éditions de l'Institute de Sociologie, Universite Libre de Bruxelles, 1970), p. 10.

107 Khin Maung Kyi and Tin Tin, *Administrative Patterns,* p. 53.

of uniform decisions throughout the kingdom and local customs generally provided individuals with notions of their rights and obligations.

A rationalised judicial system would have speeded centralisation of the state and homogenisation of the population. However, such a system would have been dependent on codes of law which would have established more clearly not only the rights of individuals in civil law vis-à-vis one another, but also the subject's rights in relationship to the state. The question of legal protection of private property would have arisen and the state's ability to monopolise wealth would probably have diminished. Obscure, moralistic codes allowed for the continuity of local customs and ideas of ownership and usufruct, but also provided no bar to state intervention in the distribution and use of secular or religious land, labour and other economic resources. The codes also created no notions of legal equality of individuals in the eyes of the state, and thus helped preserve the hierarchical, patron-client structures of society. Informal law meant that informal bonds of protection were necessary for the weak. In the precolonial state law, like the army, the administrative system and the economic order and the religious institutions, was used for the maintenance of royal authority upon which the monarchs depended for the perpetuation of their state.

The legitimacy of the precolonial state

Throughout the precolonial period, doubtless the strongest basis for the perpetuation of the state was its clear and largely unchallenged claims to be acting in accordance with the cosmological order. Today we might call this the basis of the state's legitimacy. In the intellectual climate of a traditional society,[108] it appears that the idea of progress and cumulative linear change coupled with a notion of the separation of society from the state did not exist. It was thus natural to accept the inevitability of the existing political order. That order was buttressed by both religious doctrine and customary beliefs, and was rarely brought into question until the arrival of rival religions and ideologies from Europe in the early modern period. The king, as the centre of the state, was the focus of the state's legitimising ideology. The king's claim to be the lord of all life and resources within his kingdom was the basis of the power of his officers, from the *hluttaw* to the *thu-gyi*,

---

108   This is a subject that has yet fully to be studied. See Koenig, 'Early Kon-baung Polity', ch. 3, 'The State I. -- Kingship and Political Thought', pp. 158-217, for the best available guide. See also Donald Eugene Smith, *Religion and Politics in Burma* (Princeton University Press, 1965), pp. 12-37.

to demand taxes, labour and military service from his subjects. In so doing, the king accepted a reciprocal obligation to his subjects to maintain social order so as to guard both their economic and physical security and their religious salvation. This in turn justified the economic system of the state as well as the state's intimate involvement in supervision and management of the institutions of the Buddhist *sangha*.

The apparent continuity of legitimising ideology of the classical state has a partial parallel in the development of the modern European state. Even though, as mentioned earlier, the actual functioning of the administrative and political system of the state in Myanmar was altered during the final two dynasties, there was no obvious change in its justifying ideology. Just as some state-makers in modern Europe justified their actions on the basis of the tradition of Roman law stretching back for more than 700 years through European tradition,[109] so also did the kings of Myanmar rely on the doctrines of the Bagan kingdom to justify their rule. The crucial difference between Europe and Myanmar was in the nature of the classical tradition. In Europe this was a set of legal codes and practices guaranteeing the protection of property and profit from the monopolistic desires of the state, whereas in Myanmar tradition upheld the state's claim to all wealth and power.

Within the structure of beliefs of classical Myanmar, the legitimacy of the state rested upon the monarch's alleged descent from the first king of the earthly world, Mahasmmat (*thammata*). He had been 'elected' by the people in exchange for a share of their resources so as to create order out of the natural anarchy of man's condition. Man was inherently greedy and lustful, and these human failings caused him to seek to gain advantage over his fellows that, while to his short-term material advantage, was to his long-term spiritual disadvantage. The king was 'elect' in two senses. First, he was chosen by the people; secondly, and more importantly, he was morally superior to them, and therefore it was safe and wise to entrust all power to him. In this conception of the social contract, man abandoned all of his rights to the state in exchange for total protection. There was no notion of society (man in relationship with his fellows) having any collective rights vis-à-vis the state.[110] The consequent unequal division of rights between

---

109   Tilly, 'Reflections on the History of European State-Making', p. 25.

110   Lieberman, *Burmese Administrative Cycles*, p. 65; Aung Thwin, 'Divinity, Spirit, and Human', p. 52; Tambiah, *World Conqueror and World Renouncer*, pp. 13-14; a modern Burmese version is found in Aung Hsan, 'Naingnganyei Amyomyo', *Dagun Maggazin* ('Kinds of Politics', *Dagon Magazine*), No. 234, pp. 61-70.

the king and the populace provided the justification for the social status system, including the 'distinction between the common man and the royal *ahmudan* class, the rights and privileges of the people were divided according to their office'.[111]

The ideology of classical kingship had many elements. All were interrelated and sanctioned by the teachings of Theravada Buddhism or by folk beliefs about local and regional gods known as *nats*. Individuals throughout society were taught these doctrines through the life cycle of Buddhist institutions and through village drama. The ideology also found support in the political history of the precolonial state, for the historical memory of the social disorder and personal insecurity that occurred when there was no powerful king remained strong. While the state could be an evil force in the life of man, demanding, perhaps unfairly, wealth and labour and even life itself, it, like other evils of existence such as fire and flood, was also necessary and had to be borne for the benefits it granted.

The classical Myanmar concept of kingship contained within it several notions of the nature of the monarch himself. He was first of all a human, a man, albeit a superior one. The ruler was obliged to create order primarily by his moral example and the powers of persuasion that his moral superiority provided him. When these failed he was able to use force to gain his ends, although the ultimate purpose of his actions had to be for the good of the religion. Thus he had justification for violating the Buddhist doctrines about the evil of war and killing.[112] On this basis was developed the system of criminal law, *yazawut*, or king's business, which made murder, theft, arson and rebellion crimes against him and the state. His role as *dhammaraja* or lord of the law also made him responsible for the physical wellbeing of his subjects, and this provided the ideological justification for the state's economic system.[113] There existed a dialectic in this notion of kingship which posed severe problems for the legitimacy of the monarch. His power was justified by his ability to maintain order and welfare and to uphold the *dhamma* (law), and if he failed to do so his legitimacy was in doubt and therefore rebellion against the state was potentially sanctioned.[114] Hence his need to resort to force to maintain order; but an excessive reliance upon

111 Khin Maung Kyi and Tin Tin, *Administrative Patterns*, pp. 46-7.
112 Aung Thwin, 'Divinity, Spirit and Human', pp. 52-3.
113 Ibid., p. 54.
114 Lieberman, *Burmese Administrative Cycles,* pp. 67-8.

coercion rather than example would begin to create doubts in the people's minds about his moral superiority.

It was his role as *dhammaraja* which give the king the power to purify the *sangha*. Law, understood by the term *dhamma*, was the norm of correct behaviour as comprehended in Buddhist thought and custom. In practice, for the purposes of the monkhood, the law is explained in the rules of monastic conduct known as the *vinaya*. The *vinaya* enjoins members of the *sangha* to abstain from sexual acts or other lustful behaviour, from the possession and enjoyment of wealth and property, and from involvement in the mundane pleasures of entertainment by lay society. Although it was normally self-regulating, when monks violated these norms and the *sangha* was unable to expel lax members or reform its institutional practices, it was the right, even the duty, of the king to intervene and purify the membership and practices of the religious order.[115] Indeed, a king who successfully carried out purification of the monkhood enhanced his own legitimacy by demonstrating to both lay and religious subjects the strength of his commitment to the upholding of the *dhamma*. While himself subject to the requirements of the law, he was the law's protector, and his unquestionable power, if used righteously, could not be questioned and, indeed, had to be honoured.

'Technically separate from but conceptually related' to the idea of the *dhammaraja* is the notion of the king as being a *cakkavatti*, a universal monarch or world conqueror.[116] As a *cakkavatti* the king laid claim to being the supreme ruler on earth, and from this claim stemmed the obligation of all humans to obey him. It was, in a sense, the source of his and the state's claim to sovereignty, but in a form quite different from the idea of sovereignty that developed in European monarchical traditions. This difference resulted in a significant divergence in the development of the state's notions of political order in Europe and Myanmar, and was one of the ideological hindrances to political unity in the classical states of Myanmar and other parts of South East Asia. As a universal monarch, not just one of several equally sovereign monarchs within separate territories, the Myanmar king was obliged to ensure that within his domain other, lesser monarchs were allowed to exist.[117] As long as these minor monarchs possessed neither the wealth nor the power to challenge his supremacy, and their domains possessed no important sources of wealth that his state could easily tap, he had

---

115   Aung Thwin, 'Divinity, Spirit, and Human', p. 54.

116   Ibid., p. 55.

117   Tambiah, *World Conqueror and World Redeemer*, pp. 46-7.

no justification for their elimination or the incorporation of their subjects under his direct authority. There was thus an ideological justification for maintaining the notion of political and perhaps even ethnic pluralism under the single supreme monarch. It was for this reason that the tributary states of the Shan plateau and states further from the nuclear and dependent province zones were not absorbed more rapidly into the administrative system of the state. The king had to demonstrate his universal conquering powers by a continual display of military victory, but he was constrained from pushing his conquests to their administrative conclusion by destroying local authorities at the end of the kingdom.

The strength of the king's earthly claims to legitimacy was reinforced by the power of his image as a semi-divine figure. The king was popularly thought of and often self-described as an emergent Buddha or *bodhissatta* (*hpayalaung* in Bamar). As Aung Thwin writes,

Although Theravada Buddhist doctrine teaches that each person is ultimately responsible for his or her salvation, in a living community where reciprocity and redistribution were expressions of social concern, and in which those having more merit [as demonstrated by their superior status] shared with those having less, salvation was in practice, the responsibility of the economically endowed. When kings shared their abundant store of merit with their subjects, the latter's chances for salvation by a better rebirth were significantly enhanced. In effect then, the king was like a personal saviour, resembling the compassionate Mahayanist *bodhistva*, filling the void left by the Theravada *pacceka buddha* who sought salvation only for himself.[118]

In other words the king, through his display of wealth and solace for the less well off, filled a psychological void in the practice of ascetic Buddhist salvation techniques. The theoretical remoteness and selfishness of the monk who sought his personal salvation with the support of society was countered by the supreme monarch, who, though himself capable of gaining Buddhist enlightenment, *nirvana*, and of leaving the toil and travail of the mundane world, held back in order to help in the salvation of those less endowed with merit than himself. The king sacrificed himself for the benefit of man and of religion by his protection of the religion and the maintenance of order.

The religious element of the basis of the king's legitimacy should not, however, be over-emphasised, for kings and the government in Myanmar, like elsewhere, were seen by most people, most of the time, not as deities

118   Aung Thwin, 'Divinity, Spirit, and Human', pp. 56-7.

on earth but as human rulers.[119] The ideological complex that provided the legitimacy of the Buddhist state in the classical period was much more intricate than these Buddhist-derived theories would imply. Important in this web of ideas was the monarch's incorporation of various forms of religious and customary beliefs in Myanmar, most especially the propitiation and support of the cult of the thirty-seven *nats*. This cult was particularly important for its unifying aspect, binding together distinct parts of the country in a commonly accepted belief about the unity of the kingdom by integrating provincial and local gods into a kingdom-wide hierarchical pantheon under the king. It also tied the present with the past through ceremonies that contained significant aspects of ancestor worship linking the present king to the putative first king of the realm and to his ancestors.[120]

However individuals in different periods interpreted the reasons for the legitimacy of the monarch, the ultimate basis of the monarchy stemmed from the notion of *karma*. In Burmese Buddhist thought, as Lieberman nicely puts it, 'The Burmese never asked, "Why is there no necessary correlation between reward and virtue?", for in the Buddhist view the correlation was perfect.'[121] To a Burmese Buddhist, the doctrine of *karma* explains one's present status and existence as being the result of merit (*kutho*) that one has earned through virtuous behaviour in previous incarnations. High or low status, power or slavery are not the consequences of current behaviour and labour. These are the consequences of previous action and there is nothing one can do to alter one's situation. One can only live virtuously in the expectation that one's position will improve in the next life. Therefore, if one was born or became king, it was because his *karma* was the best of any in the land. Merit causes glory in the logic of Theravada Buddhism.[122]

In contemporary parlance, a king's *hpon* (charismatic glory, innate power), *let-yon* (force, especially military force) and *a-na* (domination, authority) were proportional to the maturity of his Perfections and to his accumulation of good *karma*. These in turn were the keys of Omniscience.[123]

---

119   Ibid., pp. 59, 71-2.
120   Ibid., p. 64; Lieberman, 'Continuity and Change', pp. 7-8.
121   Lieberman, *Burmese Administrative Cycles*, p. 71; see also Aung Thwin, 'Divinity, Spirit, and Human', p. 69.
122   Aung Thwin, 'Divinity, Spirit, and Human', p. 40; Melford E. Spiro, *Buddhism and Society: A Great Tradition and Its Burmese Vicissitudes* (New York: Harper and Row, 1972), pp. 442-4.
123   Lieberman, *Burmese Administrative Cycles*, p. 72.

If legitimacy stemmed from the monarch's *karma*, then illegitimacy and the justification for rebellion against the monarch had to stem from the bad *karma* of the incumbent. Despite the conservative nature of much Buddhist thought as applied to politics, it was not a doctrine that made rebellion impossible. When an unjust or ineffective king was overthrown, the interpretation was that his *karma* was insufficient to maintain the throne. In fact, the very act of his removal from office was proof not only of this but also of the fact that his successor, the leader of the revolt against him, possessed superior *karma* and therefore rightly deserved the throne.[124] However, the fundamental conservatism of the legitimacy principles of the classical state, justified by the Buddhist theory of the nature of man, is revealed in this. It was not contemplated that a different form of government other than a monarchy might ever replace the existing institutional order; nor that a new monarch had to do more than rule justly in order to demonstrate his *karma*.

Politics under the precolonial state

The usual image of politics in the precolonial period of Myanmar's history is that of dynastic politics. The idea of the rise and fall of dynastic lines as a consequence of the inability of kings to create self-perpetuating ruling institutions separate from their own person has been uncritically accepted by several generations of students of Myanmar. These is a degree of truth in this image, but as has been suggested in the work of Lieberman, and reiterated in this chapter, politics at least during the last two dynasties was more institutionalised, centralised and complex than previously understood. Going further than Lieberman, it has been argued here that in fact the seeds of the contemporary state are found in the reforms instituted by the Restored Toungoo and Konbaung monarchs as they came to grips with the opportunities and challenges that changing economic and social conditions posed for them.

A more probing examination of politics and society during the early modern period requires a study not only of court politics, but also of the relations of provincial officials and the local gentry with the central state and each other, as well as the ways in which the peasantry, the bulk of the population, responded politically to the requirements of their distant or immediate superiors. In examining the relations of the court, officialdom

---

124   Ibid., p. 75.

and the gentry, and the peasants with the state, one has to remember that the aims of the state were perceived differently by these elements of the polity. For royalty, the state was the means to perpetuate their privileged place in society. For officialdom and the gentry, it was a set of mechanisms that allowed them to support their different hereditary or appointed positions in the state's intermediary administrative structure. In many ways theirs were the most difficult political roles to play, but the financial and personal benefits were sufficiently greater than those that could be derived from tilling the soil, and no one gave up a position easily. For the peasantry, the state was probably more a burden than a blessing most of the time, but there were few long-term choices available given the tyranny of chaos that would emerge without the order that the state provided. Exploitative as the state was, it provided a modest degree of security to most of its subjects most of the time, while safeguarding the maintenance of the religion which provided the individual solace necessary at other times.

This review of politics during the precolonial period has also shown a general gap between theory and practice in the nature of the state and its relationship with society. The 'lord of life' monarch, in fact, had only tenuous control over his subjects through a set of institutions that often operated more for the benefit of the state's intermediary functionaries than of the king. As the kings of Myanmar eventually learned to their disadvantage, however, this was a phenomenon not unique to their form of political and military organisation.[125] The divorce between theory and practice made monarchs aware of the political problems they faced. The strongest of them, or rather those faced with the greatest challenges, undertook various reforms to reintegrate practice with theory in order to strengthen the state, and when that proved impossible, to amend theory where ideologically possible in order to justify new practices.

The final Konbaung dynasty's efforts in this regard are suggestive of the political problems involved. Alaungpaya, who founded the dynasty in 1752, carried out reforms in keeping with the maintenance and perpetuation of the state in an internal and external environment little changed from that which the founder of the Restored Toungoo dynasty faced:

He halted the 'wastage' of manpower to private service and debt-slavery; enlarged the royal service and *athi* populations that in the late Toungoo era had suffered serious attrition; reasserted control over the refractory gentry class; and created a unified system of ministerial patronage whose strength derived from the intense

---

125   Pollack, *Empires in Collision*, p. 95.

personal attachment of leading officials to the king. Private power centers were restricted, and the formal structure again approximated the actual distribution of authority between the king and his chief ministers.[126]

His successors strove constantly to ensure that his reforms were maintained in order to keep alive the strength of the central state institutions. Succeeding kings 'issued reams of edicts and conducted kingdom-wide cadastral, revenue and population surveys in 1765, 1783 and 1802 in the teeth of local opposition' as part of this effort.[127]

Local opposition to the centre, however, stemmed not from any desire to abolish the state or the monarchy. Rather the intent was to weaken its ability to remove from the hands of local communities and intermediary officials the wealth that they were able to amass from agricultural labour or the taxation of other people's labour. Indeed, there was on their part 'an ardent desire to improve their standing within the socio-political hierarchy of which the king was apex and guarantor.'[128] The nature of precolonial society worked against the development of ideas of class-consciousness, and when peasants rebelled it was

not to effect fundamental changes in a socio-political order, which they accepted as legitimate and divinely ordained, but to back a lord or faction against rivals, to express displeasure with excessive demands of a particular lord or, in times of dynastic collapse, to influence the outcome of contests that would determine which family and factions of the nobility would control the throne.[129]

Consequently, ' despite its long-term centralising trend, the Burmese monarchy to end remained less bureaucratic than patrimonial.'[130]

Nonetheless, at this point, to discontinue an analysis of the early modern state's potential for further reform and rationalisation would be to underestimate the significance of its centralisation. A brief examination of how the Konbaung dynasty responded to the final threat posed to it by the British-Indian empire in the nineteenth century suggests at least the possibility that the precolonial state system could have adopted further centralisation and rationalisation measures in order to defend itself.[131] However, the nature of

126 Lieberman, *Burmese Administrative Cycles*, p. 270.
127 Trager and Koenig, *Burmese Sit-tans*, p. 28.
128 Lieberman, *Burmese Administrative Cycles*, p. 112.
129 Adas, 'From Avoidance to Confrontation', p. 228.
130 Lieberman, 'Continuity and Change', p. 27.
131 See the discussion in Pollack, *Empires in Collision*, ch. 6, 'Burmese Modernization: Administration and Economy (1853-1866)', pp. 113-36; also Myo

the British-Indian challenge was of such a fundamentally different quality than those faced by earlier monarchs that it proved impossible for the necessary reforms to be carried out in time to save the kingdom. Their ultimate failure needs to be assessed not only within the context of an examination of the nature of the external challenge posed by the British, but also in terms of the internal political system which militated against sufficiently rapid reforms.[132]

At the time of the defeat of the Myanmar army following the 1824-6 Anglo-Burmese war, the state was little prepared to defend itself against the superior military technology and manpower of the British East India Company. The king not only under-emphasised the power of the British but was also over-confident of his own resources. It has been estimated that by 1820 the crown had lost to independent secular authorities the service of perhaps 25 per cent of its *ahmu-dan* and *athi* population, compared with the situation in 1783.[133] The defeat in 1852 stemmed not only from the inferior power of the state, but also from faulty intelligence, which misunderstood the belligerent nature of the British-Indian commanders, in contrast to the seemingly pacific desires of the civilian governments in London and Calcutta.[134] The defeat of the Myanmar troops in the second Anglo-Burmese war of 1852 led to more significant political and administrative changes than the first defeat. The post-war settlement, which included the annexation of the Lower Ayeyawady Delta, directly weakened the economic resources of the state and suggested the possible eventual collapse of the monarchy.

The removal from the throne of the king, Bagan Min, at the time of the second war was the result of several economic and political factors which factions at the court were able to use in order to replace him with their favourite, Mindon Min. In particular, the loss of the rice surplus produced in southern Myanmar as a result of the British blockade drove up prices at a time when many members of the *ahmu-dan* population were involved in the military campaign in the south.[135] Also, the loss of revenue from

Myint, 'The Politics of Survival: Diplomacy and Statecraft in the Reign of King Mindon, 1853-1878'. PhD dissertation, Cornell University, 1987.

132   As Pollack, *Empires in Collision*, emphasises, although in a more balanced manner than earlier standard sources such as Cady, *History of Modern Burma*.

133   Lieberman, 'Political Significance of Religious Wealth', pp. 764-5.

134   Pollack, *Empires in Collusion*, p. 95.

135   Ibid., p. 103.

trade through the southern ports weakened the financial basis of the state. The link between the vitality of the state and its control of the entirety of Myanmar's agricultural and trade revenues could not be more clearly demonstrated.

Mindon Min launched a series of reforms by centralising political decision-making designed to strengthen the state and ensure the loyalty of the population. It was deemed necessary to bolster central control over provincial officials; for the conclusion was drawn at the capital that a major cause of the second Anglo-Burmese war was that Bagan Min's ministers at Yangon had been more uncooperative with the British than central policy had intended. Mindon also 'attempted to expand the use of cash taxes in both lowlands and hills, to develop a variety of commercial monopolies, and to rationalize military affairs and communications along Western lines.'[136] But as Myo Myint has shown, Mindon Min also paid close attention to the indigenous basis of his and his state's legitimacy, the institutions and practices of the Buddhist faith, to which a large proportion of the state's revenues were devoted.[137]

Facing a crisis that threatened the continued independence of the state, Mindon become a policy-oriented ruler. One of his first policies was to try to bring down the price of rice following the southern blockade. The political significance of the high rice price cannot be overemphasised, for with the price at the capital three times the price at Pyi near the frontier with British held territory, there was a significant incentive for people to move out of the king's domain to areas of cheaper food and greater opportunities. In response to this, Mindon both imported rice from British Burma and purchased all the available rice within his kingdom. This was in turn sold at subsidised prices, but as there was an insufficient quantity to supply demand, a black market quickly developed and prices again rose.[138] Doubtless those closely connected with the court or who had liquid assets found it easier to purchase the state-price rice and resell it at a profit. The longer term solution to the food crisis the state faced was to be found in increased production in the remaining domains, and Mindon's officers devoted a great deal of time and money to repairing and expanding the dry zone irrigation systems.

---

136   Lieberman, 'Continuity and Change', p. 23.
137   Myo Myint, 'Politics of Survival'.
138   Pollock, *Empires in Collision*, pp. 123-4.

The rationalisation measures implemented by the king were designed not only to increase administrative control over provincial officials, but also to increase state revenue. The costs of providing food subsidies, public works and administrative and political reforms were very heavy in comparison to the quantity and quality of projects the state had previously undertaken, and had to be carried out with declining resources. The effect of the reforms, including the introduction of salaries for officials, was to increase the tax revenue available, but not sufficiently to pay for the additional patronage the king had to dispense in order to keep his political supporters behind him. The reforms did, however, greatly strengthen central control, and 'local officials, now more than ever, were agents for the centre rather than autonomous commanders.'[139] The same is true of the leadership of the *sangha*.[140] The need for extra income to finance these operations, however, finally spelled the end of the precolonial state.

The dilemma facing the controllers of the early modern state in its final years can be summarised as follows. First, they needed to rationalise the state's administrative and political structures in order to increase revenue. But rationalisation meant increasing political patronage in order to buy off political discontent among officials who were losing their independent sources of income. The loss of trade revenues to the south meant that alternative revenues also had to be found through other forms of trade, and here the easiest course to take was to grant timber concessions to foreign, mainly British, firms. This in turn created greater pressures, political and economic, on the centre, for the foreign concessionaires were always seeking reduced rates, and political opponents of the ministers could accuse them of selling out the interests of the country to the foreigners. The intrigues that surrounded Mindon's demise and the placing of Thibaw on the throne were the product of these political and economic dilemmas.

While involved in these immediate and in the end most crucial problems, the state still had to contend with the basic political problems that all rulers of Myanmar have had to face: the need to expropriate as much revenue as possible from an agrarian population which sought to avoid losing control of its product; the need to control the wealth and influence of the Buddhist *sangha* and other, secular, centres of power and influence; and

---

139   Ibid., p. 118.
140   E. Michael Mendelson, *Sangha and State in Burma, A Study of Monastic Sectarianism and Leadership* (edited by John P. Ferguson, Ithaca and London: Cornell University Press, 1975), pp. 113-4.

the need to ensure the security of the state from the loss of control of areas on its periphery. This was enough to challenge the most firmly established states and rulers, and ultimately too much for the young and inexperienced Thibaw. His ignominious dethronement in 1885 by the British Indian army marked the end of the independence of the state in Myanmar for the next 63 years.[141]

---

141 Thant Myint-U in *The Making of Modern Burma* (Cambridge University Press, 2001) assesses the pressures on the last indigenous state and the resulting chaos from its inability to reform itself in the face of the challenges posed by British India.

2

THE RATIONALISATION OF
THE STATE, 1825-1942

Introduction

How rulers perceive their roles in the manifold forces that shape the societies they govern is an important indicator of the nature of the state they wish to create and perpetuate. Their concepts of the state's duties provide them with the reasons for administering the institutions of social control and economic production in the particular manner that they choose. For the kings and ministers of the precolonial state in Myanmar, the maintenance of order and security required them to be involved intimately in the symbolic, spiritual, and customary life of the society and the regulation of economic affairs. Any distinction between the public and private spheres of life was alien to their conception of the relationship of state to society.

The colonial rulers, however, viewed their roles and obligations very differently. They were detached from society not merely because they were foreigners, but because their ideas of rule presumed a distinction between the public and private aspects of life. The rationality of the modern state was a force separate from the liberty of personal choice, even though it was its guarantor. The ideological justifications of nineteenth century European liberalism not only provided them with a moral justification for colonialism, but also allowed them to interpret the political and social consequences of the policies they implemented and the institutions they created to carry these out as an integral and necessary consequence of the evolution of the modern world.

From the arrival of the first British officials to govern what they called Arakan (Rakhine) and Tenasserim (Tanintharyi) in 1825 until the last of them walked out of the country before the advancing Japanese imperial army in 1942, they believed that they colonial state was 'a benevolent but impartial umpire'[1] which freed the economy of Myanmar from the precolonial state's restrictions on trade and commerce, and thus liberated the individual from the fetters of custom and the extortion of an exploitative ruling class.[2] By the twentieth century the élite of the bureaucracy, the officers of the Indian Civil Service (ICS), saw themselves as 'holding the ring' for the political and economic life of Burma in order that the people who resided there, indigenous and foreign, might conduct their political and economic affairs in a safe and peaceful manner.

As the ultimate arbiters and guides of Burma, the British civil servants saw no contradiction between their powers to rule an alien land and their preaching about creating self-government in that country. Recognising no form of self-government in existence upon their arrival, but only an outdated form of oriental despotism, they saw themselves as the midwives of the modern world in backward Asia. If there was any contradiction between the freedom and prosperity of Burma, which they governed, and Britain, for whom they governed, it could and would be resolved by their abilities to see the 'true' interests of all sides and to govern in the name of fairness, efficiency, and the long-term welfare of all concerned. If the people they governed did not view the state they created and the policies they pursued in this way, this was because they did not as yet understand the intricacies of statecraft in the modern world. In that sense the British who managed the colonial state were like their indigenous predecessors who also believed that their methods of rule were the most appropriate for the maintenance of society, even if occasionally resisted by those they governed.

Transforming the structures of the state

What distinguishes the early modern state from the colonial state is neither the political problems with which it had to contend, nor even the basic

---

1   J. S. Furnivall, *Colonial Policy and Practice: A Comparative Study of Burma and Netherlands India* (Cambridge University Press, 1948; reprinted New York: New York University Press, 1956), p. 64.

2   The demonisation of Thibaw Min and his teenage queen, Supayalat, by colonial historians was part of the propaganda campaign the early colonial rulers mounted to justify the revolution they imposed on Myanmar. See, for example, E.C.V. Foucar, *They Reigned in Mandalay* (London: Dennis Dobson, 1946). Also H. Fielding[-Hall], *Thibaw's Queen* (New York and London: Harper and Brothers, 1899).

functions it had to perform to ensure its perpetuation. Despite its different outward purposes, the raison d'être of the state remained the maintenance of order, thus allowing its persistence and ensuring the smoothing functioning of the society that provided the state with its resources. What most distinguished the colonial state from its predecessor was that it was self-consciously imposed by a powerful foreign empire that operated under radically different notions about the relationship of the state to society, to the economy, and to the individual than those that informed the political and administrative instruments of the Myanmar monarchy. In the early years of British rule the state did little to alter the terminology and basic local institutions of the precolonial state, but nonetheless, as in India at the same time, fundamental alterations were taking place in the nature of both the state and society in Myanmar.[3]

The colonial state was an instrument intended to create and free wealth as efficiently as possible, in the context of a larger set of external imperial, economic, political and strategic interests. The domestic political and social consequences of such a purpose, which no indigenous government could have ignored, were little considered by the British state until the 20th century. Thus, the colonial state had an artificial quality that a genuinely independent state would never have. This major difference existed between the colonial state and that which preceded it, as well as between the colonial state and the independent state that succeeded it.

Outwardly, the most obvious contrast between the precolonial state and the colonial state was the degree of formal centralisation. The colonial state was able to intervene more in the institutions of local government and the lives of the people and direct them more effectively than the early modern state had been able to do. There is a strange paradox in this. The increasing centralisation of power meant a greater *decentralisation* of the state's means of access into the society, particularly allowing institutions and agencies that were only partially and indirectly instruments of the state to carry out a number of state functions. The 'central instruments of rule and exploitation' perfected by the colonial state, 'measurement and calculation, involvement in the various occasions of survey and in the distribution of tax burdens within villages ... ', led to the full flowering of a capitalist economy, with dramatic effects on the distribution of power and wealth

---

3   Frank Perlin, 'State Formation Reconsidered', *Modern Asian Studies*, 19, 3 (July 1985), p. 475. See also Burton Stein's stimulating essay 'State Formation and Economy Reconsidered', pp. 387-414, in the same issue of *Modern Asian Studies*.

in Myanmar society. While the growth of the use of money allowed for greater state intervention in society, it also created new social and economic skills, 'and the means of participation among the population at large', thus increasing the rate of social mobility to rates unknown in the precolonial period. For those able to take advantage of these new opportunities, the colonial state created greater personal autonomy and economic advantages.[4] But the distribution of these opportunities was not uniform throughout society and the minority who were most tied to the colonial state, or who already possessed the necessary skills to take advantage of the new conditions, benefited to a greater extent than the majority could. As will be made clear by the end of this chapter, the majority of the Myanmar population were not the main beneficiaries of the changes effected by the colonial state.

The primary reason for this was that from its inception in 1825 until eleven years before independence in 1948, Burma was in the eyes of the imperial government merely a distant provincial appendage of the Indian empire. Even after separation from India on 1 April 1937, the major parameters of economic and security policies in Burma were shaped in the interests of governments in London and New Delhi, and even Tokyo and Washington, as much as the state's own capital, Rangoon. Although as early as 1923 the colonial rulers were impelled to create formal mechanisms for the encouragement of self-governing but truncated national institutions (including political parties, elections and a legislature), the colonial state, because of its external resources, especially the British-Indian army, remained so powerful that it could relatively easily suppress major expressions of discontent. The colonial state was much more remote from the political and economic developments in the country, at least until the 1920s, than the precolonial state had ever been, and this was the basis of its initial strength and ability to rationalise the political, administrative and economic orders. But its remoteness was also the cause of its ultimate collapse, for it could not survive without external support.

Within Burma what made the colonial state seem so different from its predecessor was not, initially, the fact that it was managed by foreigners, nor even the way in which it functioned, including its reliance upon a Western-derived concept of law and impersonal, bureaucratic authority relationships. Rather, it was the new rulers' concern with the growth of trade that set it apart from the government of the kings. This was the core feature of its internal rationality, reflecting the nature of its parent, the British East

---

4   Perlin, 'State Formation Reconsidered', p. 476.

India Company. The precolonial state grew and expanded organically in response to internal political ideas, pressures and challenges until near its demise. The colonial state was not only imposed by the world's then greatest trading empire, it also sought to remake the country in its own image and thus had the will to reshape internal social and economic structures to suit its own interests. In consequence, the colonial state in time became more efficient and comprehensive than the precolonial state in the eyes of foreign observers, the British-Indian civil servants who constructed it, and, ultimately, the Burmese political elite who inherited it.

When the British first began to construct their state in the southern periphery of the Myanmar king's domains they found little in the way of the systematic order which they had been taught to recognise as the early modern state, at least in its Indian guise. The Myanmar administrative structure was to them 'so lacking in uniformity that they experienced great difficulty in understanding it'.[5] That the existing system had a logic of its own, and was perhaps even preferable to their own schemes for many of their Myanmar subjects, they little knew nor cared. For the British officials, the crucial task was to develop, as quickly as possible the means to pay for the more elaborate administrative institutions that were the prerequisites for expansion of trade and production.[6] In this way the state took on new roles while creating additional resources with which to rule. As a consequence the social structure of Myanmar as well as the nature of the domestic economy was altered, giving rise to new class and ethnic structures, new ideologies, and more organised and systematic forms of anti-state political action in the twentieth century.

Retrospectively, this transformation seems to have taken place rapidly and to a pre-designed plan. In fact, of course, from the perspective of its participants and subjects, the process was gradual and piecemeal. In many ways, the pervasive impact of the rationalisation of the state during the colonial period was not reached until well into the twentieth century, by

---

5   F. S. V. Donnison, *Public Administration in Burma: A Study of Development During the British Connexion* (London: Royal Institute of International Affairs, 1953), p. 13.

6   While their political masters at the centre of the empire may, for political and strategic reasons, have seen advantages in the growth of British power, the administrators who actually had to manage the empire were much less keen. Thus the Chief Commissioner of British Burma opposed the final annexation of Burma in 1885 because the administrative and military costs would outweigh the increase in revenues. Ni Ni Myint, *Burma's Struggle Against British Imperialism (1885-1895)* (Rangoon: Universities Press, 1983), p. 29.

which time the basis of its destruction at the hands of rising political forces had already begun. In terms of the lives of most of the population of Myanmar, the impact of the British-induced changes came only after 1886, when the colonial government removed the last Myanmar monarch, demobilised the indigenous military forces, ignored indigenous social and status distinctions, and abandoned constraints on economic growth, besides denigrating the social role of Buddhism. In the place of these core agencies of the precolonial state, the British built a state based upon a bureaucratic administration backed by a foreign army and justified by Western capitalist conceptions of justice, law and economic rationality. The abandonment of the golden palaces of the kings at Mandalay as the centre of the state for the great utilitarian pile of Victorian brick in Rangoon known as the Secretariat provides a visual symbol of this transformation.

It has been argued by students of the classical period's history and of the colonial period's political economy that the imposition of the colonial state resulted in the *only* fundamental change in Myanmar society from the creation of the Bagan kingdom until the regaining of independence.[7] Their argument is based upon a set of linked contentions concerning the degree of change wrought by the British in regard to the political and administrative structures of the state, the nature of the domestic economy, and the concepts of law and justice that prevailed in both politics and economics. There is a good deal of truth in this position, although, as developed in Chapter I, whether the precolonial period was as stagnant as often asserted, and whether the transformations of the nineteenth century were the result solely of the imposition of British rule, can be doubted. The problem needs to be examined from both ends of the historical spectrum. Trends evident well before 1886 suggest that the development of some of these phenomena under monarchical auspices was already taking place, and the consequences of these changes are not always as clear or unilinear as often assumed. It should not be forgotten that the British ruled Burma in its entirety for less than 65 years, and the impact of the period on the basic societal values and political concepts was less than the impact on institutions and economic structures.

---

7   As explicitly argued by Michael Aung Thwin, 'Divinity, Spirit and Human: Conceptions of Classical Burmese Kingship', in Lorraine Gesick (ed.), *Centres, Symbols and Hierarchies: Essays on the Classical States of Southeast Asia* (New Haven: Yale University Southeast Asian Studies Series no. 26, 1983), pp. 45-86, esp. p. 47; and implicitly by Furnivall, *Colonial Policy and Practice*, pp. 23-30.

The soul of the precolonial state was the king, who was obliged to guard the customary legal concepts of the Buddhist law of cause and effect. The mind of the colonial state was the civil servant, who was constrained by British legal concepts of precise bounds of authority, rigid rules of procedure and the protection of life and property. The king in the precolonial state was not above the law, he was the fount of law, and from this stemmed both his personal strength and the administrative weakness of his state. But, as Furnivall wrote, the colonial state, the new Leviathan, was different:

Leviathan was a creature of the Law; it is by the law he lives, and laws and regulations are both the substance of his being and the basis of his power. The strong man, like some Burman rulers of the past, can build up an empire, but unless the framework be fashioned out of law his empire will last no longer than his strength. It is not sufficient for him to enforce the law; he must also submit to it, offer himself a willing sacrifice to Leviathan.[8]

The centralising and perpetuating power of the precolonial state stemmed from the king's ability to shape the law in order to control the economic resources of his kingdom and thus prevent the rise of rival centres of wealth and power. The economic and administrative rationality of the colonial state stemmed from its normal obligation to bend to the law and thus maintain a distinction between public power and private wealth.

But Furnivall claims too much for the law-bound nature of the colonial state. It was legal in the Weberian sense of concepts of state supremacy and it was legalistic in its careful attention to rules of procedure and protection of life and property. However, when political forces threatened its monopoly of control, it was able to find laws to ensure its perpetuation in the hands of its creators or their designated successors. And when economic power became sufficiently great to create forces to undermine social stability, it was able to use the law to control those forces too. The colonial Leviathan was a servant of the law, as Furnivall wrote, but it was also the custodian and author of that same law. The most radical difference in the nature of law in the monarchical state and the colonial state is the assumption in the colonial law of the legal equality of all subjects, including officialdom. The abolition of the customary status distinctions of the precolonial state and the patrimonialism it created was a key aspect of the revolution that the colonial state forced upon Myanmar.

---

8   J.S. Furnivall, 'The Fashioning of Leviathan', *The Journal of the Burma Research Society*, XXIX, 3 (1939), p. 18.

The implications of the principle of legal equality would not have been in the forefront of the minds of the founders of the colonial state. They had a job to do in difficult and largely unknown circumstances, and had to fashion a state out of the ideas and materials at their disposal as inexpensively as possible. Perhaps no clearer statement of the initial intentions of the colonial state can be found than the first pronouncement of the Commissioner of Tenasserim, Mr Maingy, to his new adult male subjects on 30 September 1825:

Proclamation to the inhabitants of Mergui:

Rest assured that your wives and children shall be defended against all foreign and domestic enemies. That life and property shall enjoy full liberty and protection, and that your religions shall be respected and your Priests and religious edifices secured from every insult and injury. Proper measures shall be immediately adopted for administering justice for you, according to your own established laws as far as they do not militate against the principles of humanity and natural equity. In respect of revenue and all other subjects your own customs and local usages will be taken into consideration; but the most free and unrestricted internal and external commerce will be established and promoted. All that is required from you is to aid me toward giving you peace, order and happiness by each inhabitant returning to his usual occupation, by your respecting and cheerfully obeying all such as may be placed in authority over you, and by your discountenancing and pointing out wherever necessary, the seditious and evil disposed enemies of the British Government. Lastly, I wish it to be clearly understood, that access at all hours and at all places will be afforded by me to any, even the poorest inhabitants, who may desire to see me upon business.[9]

Doubtless to Maingy this proclamation seemed an innocuous statement which would reassure the inhabitants of the new British territory that their rulers would do nothing to harm the customs and practices held most dear by them, but would ensure the creation of a better, more equitable, egalitarian society. Little did he realise that the two aims of maintaining tradition and establishing an egalitarian, commercially-oriented society would prove, even in the short run, impossible. The liberal ideology which was the root of his assumptions ran counter to the ideological basis of Myanmar tradition. The practices of an economy geared to free trade and the free

---

9   In *Selected Correspondence of Letters Issued from and Received in the Office of the Commissioner Tenasserim Division for the Years 1825-26 to 1842-43* (Rangoon: Government Printing and Stationery, Burma, 1928), p. 16.

THE RATIONALISATION OF THE STATE, 1825-1942

flow of capital and labour made erosion of customary practices inevitable, and the promise of open and equitable government proved impossible to maintain in the face of the demands placed upon it. The liberal umpire could not be unbiased towards the traditional practices that stood in the way of economic and administrative efficiency, and an authoritarian bureaucracy was installed in the name of progress.

There are a variety of criteria that can be used to divide the stages of development of the colonial state in Burma. Viewed in terms of the degree and nature of the authority of the highest executive and legislative officials of the state, the period can be divided into five segments.[10] From the first Anglo-Burmese war until 1834, Tenasserim was governed from Penang, and Arakan was made a part of the Presidency of Bengal. From 1834 to 1862, both were extensions of the Bengal administration located in Calcutta, as was Pegu province, also called Lower Burma, after its annexation in 1852. This period ended with the creation of a Chief Commissioner for British Burma in 1862, when the country became a province in its own right, directly under the Governor-General of India. It was during this second period of 35 years, which ended in 1897, that the major structures of the colonial bureaucracy, the framework of the central administrative organisations in Rangoon and the local government institutions, were completed. During both these periods the government in Burma possessed no legislative powers and the rules and regulations it followed were those drawn up by and for the government of India.

However, during the third period, from 1897 to 1923, an appointed Legislative Council was established in Rangoon to advise the Lieutenant-Governor in drafting legislation applicable to Burma. This advisory body grew from nine to thirty members, the majority representing commercial interests, mainly foreign. This development 'tended to increase the preponderance of capitalist interests in the direction of affairs, and reflected their growing importance in the economic life of Burma.'[11] The head of the government was referred to as the governor from 1923 onwards, when a partially elected assembly was created under the so-called dyarchy constitution (which placed some authority in the hands of non-officials, including two elected indigenous ministers responsible for education, local government, public health, agriculture and forests). This period, the fourth, ended with the formal separation of Burma from India in 1937 and the establish-

---

10   Donnison, *Public Administration*, p. 2.
11   Furnivall, *Colonial Policy and Practice*, p. 72.

ment at that time of a constitutional order which contained provisions for a significant degree of self-government through a cabinet responsible to a fully elected legislature under the supervision and ultimate veto of the governor, who remained responsible for defence, foreign relations, finance, and the peripheral regions of the state, now called the Frontier Areas and the Shan States.

One can also conceptualise the periods of British rule from the perspective of the policies that the imperial authorities pursued.[12] Here, three periods can be distinguished. From the formation of the initial colonial authority in 1825 until 1879, *laissez-faire* predominated. The state, responsible mainly for maintaining order through the police and courts and collecting taxes to pay for these, made little effort to guide economic forces in the semi-frontier conditions of the southern regions. After 1880, until 1923, the state slowly became more concerned with enhancing the economic efficiency of the society and began to devote resources to the development of communications, schools and rudimentary health and agriculture services in order to support the more rapid development of the country's resources, both human and material. During this period there was a marked improvement in rail and water-borne communications throughout the country, especially after 1886 when the north became integrated into the expanding colonial economy of the export-oriented south.[13]

After the establishment of state policies directed towards progress and welfare, the focus of government policy then turned to the development of liberal democratic political institutions, in particular participatory bodies through which the state might gain legitimacy in the eyes of the populace. This was in response primarily to changing political conditions in India and only secondarily to political demands in Burma.[14] It was during this period that organised Myanmar political nationalism developed rapidly in opposition to colonial rule.

For the purposes of this book, it is appropriate to divide the colonial era into just two periods, pre- and post-First World War. The choice of the First World War as a dividing point is not made because the war had

---

12   The basic and classic source is Furnivall's *Colonial Policy and Practice*, chs. II-VI.

13   Shein, *Burma's Transport and Foreign Trade (1885-1914)* (Rangoon: Department of Economics, University of Rangoon, 1964), chs. II-III.

14   Robert H. Taylor, 'The Relationship Between Burmese Social Classes and British-Indian Policy on the Behaviour of the Burmese Political Elite, 1937-1942' (PhD, Cornell University, 1974), ch. 2.

many direct effects upon Burma, but because it was from about this time that the political nature of the state and the popular response to it changed most dramatically. Before then, most forms of political action found in the country would have been easily recognisable to anyone who had been familiar with the precolonial state. Land was still relatively plentiful and cheap, labour was still scarce and—by Indian standards—well paid, and people's expectations of the government were few. The political impact of the state was most strongly felt in the newly developed cities, especially Rangoon, Bassein, Akyab (Sittwe), and Moulmein, located on the edge of rural society. These were essentially foreign trading enclaves with increasing numbers of migrant labourers and entrepreneurs serving to expedite the growing export of rice and other commodities and the importation of manufactured goods. After the First World War, however, the economic and political interests of the cities, and the external economic interests they served, tended increasingly to affect the lives and livelihoods of the peasantry directly in more obvious ways, especially in the delta areas of southern Burma. In parallel with the development of the modern political state, political interests and expectations developed that mobilised both demands on the state and new political elites to found and control institutions articulating their demands.

The development of the colonial state involved rationalising of the procedures of the state as it attempted to maintain itself in the face of the political and other conditions that it inherited from its predecessor. However, in the process of achieving its larger imperial functions as an appendage of the British-Indian empire, as it evolved the colonial state also created new social structures and interests in Burma. The promise of the first Commissioner to the people of Mergui in 1825 (see above, p. 74) was partially fulfilled. 'The most free and unrestricted internal and external commerce' was largely established and not only did agricultural production dramatically increase, leading to the export of a large surplus of rice as well as timber and eventually rubber and minerals, it also allowed for the importation of large quantities of foreign made consumer goods and even food. Further, to add to the labour available in the country, the immigration of foreign labour, primarily from India but also from China, was encouraged. Foreign capital, mainly British and Indian, flowed in as investments and flowed out as profits and central Indian government revenues; Burma became firmly linked to the world economy. In effect, the colonial government willed the abandonment of the economic and social stability that the precolonial state had maintained as the basis of its political power for the more dynamic but unstable fluctuations of world trade and social change.

In the early years of this development, conditions were such that there was sufficient land, employment and profit for everyone, so that while there was rapid economic growth, there was little social mobilisation. Unlike the experience of early modern European societies where the state maintained stricter control over economic development and social change, the colonial state was sufficiently powerful to feel that it could ignore the political consequences of change until the 1920s. In Burma, mainly Indian migrant labour filled the new employment roles in the urban and commercial sectors of the economy, while indigenous labour remained wedded to the agricultural sector. Those in the minority who benefited most significantly from the new opportunities created naturally supported the state. The result of these changes was to create not the integrated society that the early modern state in Europe forced into being, but what Furnivall aptly named the 'plural society'.[15]

In the plural society in Burma, Europeans, Indians and Chinese lived side by side with the indigenous Burmese in a 'medley of peoples', for as Furnivall wrote at the end of the colonial period,

they mix but do not combine. Each group holds by its own religion, its own culture and language, its own ideas and ways. As individuals they meet, but only in the market-place, in buying and selling. There is a plural society, with different segments of the community living side by side, but separately, within the same political unit.[16]

Politically, Furnivall said, the plural society had 'three characteristic features: The society as a whole comprises separate racial groups; each section as an aggregate of individuals rather than a corporate or organic whole; and as individuals their social life is incomplete.'[17] Thus, he argued, not only was the plural society composed of three communities that only met in the market-place, but even within these communities individuals did not identify with others in the same group. Composed of a partially uprooted indigenous population along with transient immigrant labourers, few of whom intended to settle in the country, and equally uncommitted foreign businessmen and officials, the society lacked the social and cultural bonding of a settled, integrated political unit or nation. This lack of cohesion

---

15   Furnivall, *Colonial Policy and Practice*, pp. 303-12.

16   Ibid., p. 304.

17   Ibid., p. 306.

created a society that had no political will to control the economic forces of capitalist production, as its individual members felt no motive of self-sacrifice for the good of the whole. Social demand, the controls that integrated societies imposed upon economic forces through loyalty and shared concern for mutual welfare, was lacking. Price rather than value became the determining factor in decision-making by individuals, for it was only for his or her material wants that they became involved in society.[18] Thus:

A plural society is broken into groups of isolated individuals, and the disintegration of social will is reflected in a corresponding disorganisation of social demand. Even in a matter so vital to the whole community as defence against aggression, the people are reluctant to pay the necessary price. In religion and the arts, in the graces and ornaments of life, there are no standards common to all sections of the community, and standards deteriorate to such a level as all have in common. And because each section is merely an aggregate of individuals, those social wants that man can satisfy only as members of a community remained unsatisfied. Just as the life of an individual in a plural society is incomplete, so his demand tends to be frustrated. Civilisation is the process of learning to live a common social life, but in a plural society men are decivilised. All wants that all men want in common are those which they share in common with the animal creations; on a comprehensive survey of mankind from China to Peru these material wants, essential to the sustenance of life, represent the highest common factor of demand. In the plural society the highest common factor is the economic factor, and the only test that all apply in common is the test of cheapness. In such a society the disorganisation of social demand allows the economic process of natural selection by the survival of the cheapest to prevail.[19]

In Furnivall's view, the new colonial Leviathan created in Burma had only partially achieved for mankind release from the conditions of Hobbes's pre-Leviathan state of nature: life might not necessarily be poor or short, but it most certainly remained solitary, nasty, and brutish; and therefore the colonial state had not fulfilled its promise to the people made by Maingy in 1825. Indeed, one cannot imagine a greater distinction than that between the anomic, economy-ridden, Darwinian plural society of colonial Burma and the integrated, religiously-rooted communal-traditional society that the precolonial state had maintained, with its patronage of the arts and regulation of economic self-advancement. Despite Furnivall's romanticisation of traditional society, especially at the village level, it is nonetheless true that the changes in society that the new policies and struc-

18   Ibid., pp. 308-9.
19   Ibid., p. 310.

tures of the state allowed caused the destruction of the cohesion of Burma's precolonial social life.

Furnivall's ideas of the plural society provide a graphic metaphor for the results of the colonial state's mode of government in Burma. But it is a stagnant image: a society that was acted upon, but which could not respond to the economic and other external forces that were imposed upon it. By analysing the political workings of the plural society, it may be possible to grasp more fully the dynamic characteristics of Burma's society during the period in which the plural society and the bureaucratic state were created. Thus it may be possible to better understand what has followed since. But before we can turn to study the relationship of the state to society in contemporary Myanmar, it is necessary to examine what kind of state it was that created the plural society and what kinds of class formations and politics existed within it. This Chapter is devoted to the first of these questions, the next to the second.

The territorial organisation of the state

The rationalisation of the state was partially a consequence of the territorial revisions made by the British. These were important both conceptually and administratively. Administratively, they further simplified the divisions of the state from the three types of territory recognised in the early modern state to two. These were 'Burma proper', which incorporated both the nuclear and the dependent province zones of the early modern period, and the 'excluded' or 'frontier areas' of the surrounding hills. Conceptually, they introduced the idea of firm territorial divisions of authority. It is beyond the scope of this volume to explore fully the implications of the development of firm borders with neighbouring states—China, French Indo-China, Siam, and British India—but this too was part of the general process. In a sense, the colonial state did not just rationalise the map of Myanmar, it drew it, though incompletely.

The territorial pattern developed in the 1820s for the governance of Tenasserim and Arakan, borrowed from the British-Indian model, set the mould for the later development of the British state. British officials directly ruled all of Tenasserim from the time of the annexation, whereas in Arakan the practice was established of dividing the plains and hill areas into zones with different administrative patterns. While direct rule was implemented in the plains, in the hills a system of indirect rule relying on the recognition of traditional chiefs was deemed appropriate. The British Raj merely replaced the king of Burma as the suzerain to whom the chiefs paid allegiance through tribute. The Karen population residing in the hills of Tenasserim, however, was immediately placed under direct British control. Tenasserim set the pattern for Burma proper. It was divided into three districts, each under the supervision of a British Deputy Commissioner.[20] This figure was the linchpin between the British-dominated central administration and the largely indigenous local government officials throughout the colonial period.

The first Commissioner of Tenasserim began, albeit gradually, the process of disrupting the traditional pattern of local government. The hereditary *myo-thu-gyi* and *thu-gyi* were confirmed in their positions, but the concept of their responsibilities and obligations was fundamentally altered from a personal, patron-client relationship to a territorial and impersonal one. The old Burmese township, the *myo* or *taik*, seen erroneously by the British as the same as the Indian village tract or circle, was redefined as a geographical unit in which all the residents were under identical obligations to the headman.[21] Ignored were any distinctions between *athi* and *ahmu-dan* population categories living in proximity but with their own headmen. From the beginning the British instructed headmen to draw the territorial boundaries of their 'circles' as if these administrative units were geographical concepts considered meaningful to the local population.[22] The precise demarcation of administrative boundaries, a key aspect of the concept of the rationalised state, was being imposed in place of the complex non-territorial administrative divisions of the lowlands that the pre-colonial state's control of manpower had necessitated. Similar practices were followed in Arakan, but in the hill areas where the amount of revenue that could be raised from local taxes was too small to justify more than 'light administration' (one of the code phrases of the period), the British did nothing to change the responsibilities of the local chiefs. Here, until the twentieth century, the British seemed by and large to consider precisely drawn administrative maps as unimportant.

After the annexation of Bago, the British extended the territorial organisation established in Tenasserim and lowland Arakan to their new ter-

---

20   Ibid., p. 36.

21   Ibid., p. 37.

22   *Correspondence for the Years 1825-26 to 1842-43 in the Office of the Commissioner Tenasserim Division* (Rangoon: Government Printing and Stationery, Burma, 1929), p. 19.

ritory. The province was divided into five districts, each under a Deputy Commissioner with the same powers as counterparts in the other areas of southern Burma. In 1862 the different terminology and adjustments that had developed in the practice of local government were systematised. The districts were divided into administrative townships under a *myo-ok* or township officer who was a junior version of a Deputy Commissioner.[23] Each township was in turn composed of a number of *myo* under a headman who administered one or more villages within his territory or circle.

The pattern of territorial administration in Burma proper was thus established before the completion of the British restructuring in 1886. The structure was a tiered set of administrative relationships headed by a Chief Commissioner, later Governor, under whom served the Commissioners of what would eventually be seven Divisions. The latter in turn supervised the activities of the Deputy Commissioners or District Officers, usually called the 'DC', who administered the affairs of the township officers or *myo-ok*. The interface between the township and the district was where the colonial state had the most immediate initial impact on the rural population, for the District Officers were the men who ensured that central policy was carried out at the local level, and who controlled the appointment of subordinate officials and magistrates.

The colonial territorial redivision did not begin to affect the lives of the people to any significant extent until the period of so-called 'pacification' (1886-96), when order was restored through military and administrative methods following the rebellions that broke out after the deposition of King Thibaw. At this time a Village Act was passed under martial law regulations which had the purpose of breaking up the *myo/taik* administrative level, thus further enhancing the role of the new-style township and placing greater responsibilities on the village headman.[24] Before 1886, the British government had seen fit only to alter the traditional *taik* and *myo* jurisdictions by amalgamating or splitting them for reasons of administrative convenience and territorial rationality on a case-by-base basis. Now, under the Village Act, the government went further and abolished the *myo*, only to re-amalgamate villages later in some cases for reasons of financial viability.[25] The traditional social unit of the *myo* was obliterated and replaced

---

23   Donnison, *Public Administration*, pp. 23-4.
24   Ibid., pp. 31-2.
25   This process began in 1886 and apparently reached its peak in 1919 when 593 headman posts were abolished. In all, between 1909 and 1919 over 2,000 head-

by a non-organic administrative village which itself was 'little more that a cogwheel in the machinery of maintaining order and collecting revenue'.[26] The anomie of the indigenous sector of Burma's twentieth-century plural society had its roots in these territorial administrative policies.

In the hills, territorial adjustments did little to break down the traditional, organic social units. After 1886 the British state gained additional responsibilities as it assumed suzerainty over the extensive hill areas of northern Myanmar. This territory amounted to about half of the land area received from the Myanmar king. Here the British followed the pattern established in Arakan of administering areas indirectly and leaving essentially untouched the pattern of relations they found. However, the existing units recognised, or in some cases created, were never considered intrinsically important and the government, especially in the twentieth century, was willing to redefine them for administrative reasons, even though this often meant altering or ignoring promises given to the ancestors of the local authorities.

The rationalisation of authority relations

The colonial state imposed a formal bureaucratic structure on society which, while not completely abolishing the system of personal patron-client ties which had been the basis of the precolonial *myo*-centred order, complicated, amended, or ignored it by creating a pattern of systematic 'line of command' procedural relationships and obligations. The very language used to describe this change indicates its nature, for the rationalisation of the state meant creating a 'sphere of government' separate from society and more clearly differentiated from other, less obviously coercive, aspects of social control. The process of this transformation was gradual in Arakan and Tenasserim but more rapid in Pegu. The policies pursued after 1886 speeded the process even more, so that by the turn of the century the relationship of the state with society through its local territorial and functional officials had been rationalised in a form similar to that of the modern European state of the same period. This transformation of authority relationships was a natural corollary of rationalisation of the colonial state's territorial structure.

---

men were removed from their positions as villages were amalgamated on the criteria of sufficient size to provide an adequate financial base to pay the headman out of his revenue collections, but not too large as to make the exercise of his duties impossible. Furnivall, *Colonial Policy and Practice*, pp. 74-5.

26   Ibid., p. 75.

The first Commissioner of Tenasserim, Mr Maingy, and his three Deputies attempted to establish their notions of proper authority relationships quickly, but soon had to bend to local practices as they had neither the manpower nor the money to enforce rapid changes. They primarily confined themselves to tasks of administrative reorganisation and tax collection, although they also assumed judicial responsibilities. Initially they were left to their own devices in determining how to carry out their tasks. However, like their counterparts in Arakan, they were required after 1832 to justify their actions to higher authorities in Calcutta in terms of the practice of the British Indian empire's bureaucratic regulations.[27]

Despite the desire to reform the government, Maingy recognised the utility of employing cooperative officials who had served the precolonial state and who, because of their hereditary positions, had personal influence over the local population. But he sought immediately to amend their personal authority so that it became more formal and under his control.[28] In his eyes, the old system was merely one of plunder and extortion which, even when regularised by placing officials in salaried positions, was still open to bribery and corruption as defined in his code of official conduct.[29] In the face of rising disorder, particularly what he called 'crime', Maingy was forced to 'swear in and employ as constables' sixteen of the old headmen on a fixed salary.[30] As the headmen were turned into salaried officials of the new state, they were no longer seen 'as local representatives but as government officials to be transferred from one charge to another as the convenience of administrative might dictate'.[31]

The destruction of the headmen's personal authority and their ability to intercede between the demands of higher officials and the wishes of their former patrons started a decline in their ability to govern without significant amounts of coercion. Thus, although the reinstatement in government service of the king's *thu-gyi* was intended to reduce the rate of crime, its effect was to increase the level of disorder as the traditional social bonds that had checked anti-social behaviour in the past were sapped of their vitality. The system, in some respects, nonetheless slipped back into practices of the past, but without the social conditions that had made them effec-

27   Ibid., p. 36.
28   *Selected Correspondence Tenasserim Division,* p. 2.
29   Ibid., pp. 3-4.
30   Ibid., p. 40.
31   Furnivall, 'The Fashioning of Leviathan', p. 46.

tive means of social control. Bribery, corruption and force were replacing patron-clientage ties. While the old system may not have been as extortion-ate as Maingy believed, the system created by the British took on aspects of organised and state-sanctioned plunder by imposed officials.

Until the 1860s, and in most areas the 1880s, officials of the British state above the level of *myo-* and *taik thu gyi* were seldom able to penetrate directly into the villages. Poor communications, limited resources and the bureaucratic inertia caused by perpetuation of the old but debilitated sys-tem of maintaining order and collecting revenue in the conditions of an expanding economy provided little incentive for thoroughgoing reform. 'The system, though in theory one of direct rule, was in effect a system of indirect rule through the circle headmen.'[32] In a sense, the early colonial state sat upon the traditional local administrative system in a more exploit-ative manner than the precolonial state had done, only interfering with its personnel recruitment and posting patterns.

Nonetheless, the territorial revisions and introduction of the township officer after 1862 began to transform the quality of local government au-thority relations to a further degree. The *myo-ok* was a new kind of official administering an additional bureaucratic tier. Some of the first recruited were *myo-* and *taik-thu-gyi*.[33] Those who got on best with the new regime learned English. The *myo-ok* became the link between the British army officer or civilian who was Deputy Commissioner of the District and the *myo-* or *taik*-headman who administered the circle. Subordinate to the headmen were appointed police officers or *gaung* who also assisted in rev-enue collection. Subordinate to these officials were the village officers, the old *kyedangyi*, or largest taxpayers, who had had similar responsibilities un-der the kings but were often now no longer men of personal influence. They were responsible for maintenance of law and order and collection of revenue in their villages.[34]

During the 1860s the personal authority of the headmen was further undermined by a variety of new regulations intended to raise the level of administrative skills of local officials. By the mid-1860s, headmen had all their original powers removed except for the collection of revenue, and many of their police powers were assumed by a new, centrally directed, force under a British officer. In 1867 it was ordered that headmen had

32   Furnivall, *Colonial Policy and Practice*, p. 42.
33   Donnison, *Public Administration*, pp. 23-4.
34   Furnivall, *Colonial Policy and Practice*, pp. 39-40.

THE STATE IN MYANMAR

to be qualified land surveyors, and twelve years later a system of qualify-
ing examinations for village headmanship was established, similar to that
which was already applied to township officers. Surveying, accounting, and
knowledge of revenue law now became matters considered in making appointments of headmen in addition to 'hereditary claims, local influence,
intelligence, and good character'. 'Impersonalization, specialization, and
division of roles' now became the hallmark of the government system at all
levels in Burma proper.[35]

The changes in the territorial structure of local administration, which
the abolition of the *myo* and *taik* level of government in favour of direct
control of the village unit introduced after 1886, had a profound impact
upon the relationship of the peasantry with the state. The effect of these
changes in terms of authority relationships was essentially to abolish any
remaining notions of local self-government and replace them with a system
of tightly centralised district administration under the rigorous control of
the District Commissioner.[36] Whereas previously the *myo-* and *taik-thu-gyi*,
even with his diminished powers, had been able to serve as an intermediary,
mediating the demands of central authority for his community in an informal manner, the new act placed directly upon the villagers collectively,
through an emasculated village headman, the obligation to obey the law
or suffer collective penal sanctions enforced by the armed and mounted
'punitive' police of the central administration. The effect of this legislation
was to abolish 'self-government over any unit larger than the village and,
by converting the village from a social and residential unit into an administrative unit', it cut 'at the root of organised social life within the village',
destroying the solidarity of the traditional community which was based
on the *myo*. The position of the *myo-* or *taik-thu-gyi* was abolished and the
village headman became the instrument through which the central government worked directly in the villages on a sustained basis.[37]

Implementation of this change was gradual, but by 1891 the old order
was effectively gone. In its place the British instituted officially nominated
bureaucratic local bodies that were largely ignored by both the people and

35   J.A. Mills, 'Burmese Peasant Response to British Provincial Rule, 1825-1885',
      in D.B. Miller (ed.), *Peasants and Politics* (Melbourne: Edward Arnold Aus-
      tralia, 1978), p. 94.

36   Hugh Tinker, *Foundations of Local Self-Government in India, Pakistan, and
      Burma* (Bombay: Lavani, 1957), pp. 56-7.

37   Donnison, *Public Administration*, pp. 31-2; John F. Cady, *A History of Modern
      Burma* (Ithaca: Cornell University Press, 1958), pp. 141-4.

the civil servants. Know as circle boards, they were seen primarily as another mechanism for raising government revenue through their cess funds, half of which was used for the payment of the police.[38]

The precolonial system of patron-client ties and hereditary authority was now destroyed and replaced by a system of salaried, appointed headmen who, though usually men from the local area, were appointed more for their knowledge of British procedures than for their vigilance in protecting local interests. Not only were they seen as cogs in the wheel of a regularised bureaucratic state; they were very minor cogs at that, for many of the positive and less coercive functions of the state were soon assumed by specialist officials from the central administration. The development of agriculture, education, sanitation and health departments and other functionally specific country-wide government services meant that each of these bureaucracies had their own personnel to carry out their own policies—though in ignorance of local conditions. These subordinate central government officials, given specialised tasks to perform, now involved themselves directly in the lives of the peasantry. Despite their welfare-type activities, many 'were regarded as agents of oppression, to be propitiated by petty bribes,'[39] for the village headmen were unable to intercede in opposition to their schemes.

The headmen were no longer the natural leaders of their communities, able to defend their clients interests against a rapacious state, but the salaried tax-collectors of that state providing the funds for the policies, police and courts which most of the people neither wanted nor believed to be for their benefit. In Burma, as in much of the rest of South East Asia, the colonial state undermined communities that had controlled their own internal affairs for generations. The efficiency that rationalisation brought was at the cost of decivilising the village; however, turning the village into a revenue raising and administrative unit created systematic order and facilitated agricultural production. The rationalisation of village administration became a central political cause of the growth of anti-state sentiments among the peasantry throughout the colonial period, and no amount of subsequent tinkering with its form could either recreate the old order or cause satisfaction with the new.

Among the peoples living in the hill territories that first fell under British control, the new officials were little capable or desirous of imposing their new system of authority relationships. Here, in a sense, the patterns

38   Tinker, *Foundations of Local Self-Government*, p. 54.
39   Furnivall, *Colonial Policy and Practice*, p. 77.

of authority seemed to have been frozen from the early nineteenth century until the middle of the twentieth. However, as will be shown subsequently, changes with great political significance for the state in the middle of the twentieth century were underway. Initially, the British Commissioner in Tenasserim felt he knew too little about the people living in the hills, collectively referred to as Karens (and sometimes in the earliest years as Malays), to attempt 'to reduce them to any system' of rule.[40] Nothing was done to interfere with existing patterns of relations between these hill peoples and the lowland state authorities until the twentieth century, although there was a drift of people out of the hills to more prosperous and settled areas in the lowlands. It was from this pool of people living in the Karen hills, as well as from people in the plains who identified themselves as Karen, that the early conversions to Christianity were made by American Baptist missionaries. Many converts then became attached to the institutions of the British state.[41]

In Arakan, where the system of separate administrative patterns for the hills was established, the British did little to tamper with the so-called traditional authority structures they found. However, before formally guaranteeing the authority of an individual who was put forward, or more likely put himself forward, as the local leader, they ensured that he was amenable to overall control.[42] It was not until 1871 that any alterations were made to the governing and taxation system the British found upon their arrival. Greater control was then introduced first by increasing the size of the police presence. Control of the population had to precede other efforts to 'reduce them to any system'. Following the establishment of police control, the system of tributary payments by chiefs was abolished and 'a uniform rate of one rupee for each hill clearing, and one rupee a house was imposed on all tribes alike'.[43] Rationalisation inevitably meant monetisation, and greater state intervention meant less authority for tribal chiefs. Prior to these changes, the British administration had been represented by only a Superintendent over the chiefs who had 'administered [the law] in the simplest and most paternal form' and encouraged the

40   Selected Correspondence Tenasserim Division, p. 7.
41   Cady, History of Modern Burma, pp. 137-41.
42   British Burma Political Department, Report on the Administration of Hill Tracts, Northern Arakan, 1870-71 (Rangoon: Secretariat Press, 1872).
43   Report on the Progress of Arakan Under British Rule from 1826 to 1875 (Rangoon: Government Press, 1876), pp. 14-15.

growth of trade between the hills and plains.[44] In later years, especially after the annexation of northern Burma, the development of interaction between the hills and plains was discouraged for military and political reasons. Moreover the divide between Burma proper and the frontier areas become much more marked administratively and politically, with important consequences after independence.

More than administrative reform, it was the relative peace that British rule brought to the hill areas that caused political change there. Internecine conflicts between villages and tribes were largely halted by the threat of punishment of offenders by British-Indian troops and, later, the frontier force. Periodic flag marches by the colonial armed forces, the only significant evidence of the power of the state in many regions, nonetheless led in time to a weakening of the power of the tribal chiefs. Their power was based on the need of isolated cultivators to gather together for security. Once relative order was created in an area, it was more advantageous for people to live nearer their fields, and they tended to drift away from the larger village settlements and the control of the traditional leaders.[45] The decline of the local leaders' authority in turn led to the development of the idea of Chin, Kachin and other local ethnic identities, as local elites sought to create a separate identity for their people (and were encouraged to do so by the amateur anthropologists of the British-Indian army).

Financing the rationalised state

The method of financing the precolonial state—passing upward through the chain of patron-client ties and appanage arrangements of a proportion of revenue collected from villages, usually in kind and rarely audited, in addition to corvee labour provided for public works—was largely rejected by the colonial state in the plains areas.[46] As far as the first British administrators were concerned, there was no effective financial system in the traditional Myanmar order. When, for example, Maingy in Tenasserim attempted to find out the means by which local government officials were paid under the kings, he 'could not discover that they received any other re-

44   Ibid., p. 19.

45   Kyin Mya, 'The Impact of Traditional Culture and Environmental Forces on the Development of the Kachins, a Sub-Cultural Group of Burma' (PhD, University of Maryland, 1961), p. 51.

46   Although Maingy continued to demand corvee in the early years in Tenasserim.

muneration besides the liberty of plundering and extorting from the lower classes'.[47] One of his first acts, therefore, was to attempt to rationalise the revenue collection system in order to raise auditable funds with which to pay a salaried class of government servants. He order that collectors of land revenues should be appointed and that they should collect one-tenth of the grain produced.[48] This was in fact only a partial reorganisation and reallocation of the tax burden of the previous system, for the Commissioner abandoned earlier levies on fruit trees and similar non-grain crops because, at that time, they were too difficult to assess. In fact the new state probably reduced the overall level of taxation, thus perhaps lessening the proclivity of the recently colonised people to organise resistance to their new rulers. It was made clear, however, that this low rate of taxation would not be allowed to persist, and the peasants were repeatedly warned that the rate would increase in the future.[49] The abolition of traditional controls on economic activity and the free export of rice at highly profitable prices, combined with the grain taxes, led to a substantial increase in the local price of grain in the towns. This, in turn, was one of the causes of increasing rates of taxation, as the servants of the government had to pay more for food and therefore had to receive higher salaries derived from local revenue.

The Commissioner's belief that he would be able to reduce taxes was partially based upon his liberal assumptions that a more rationalised system, operating in a free market, would result, as production increased, in larger revenue for the state at a lower unit cost to the peasant. Indeed, the state's revenue did increase because senior officials had a more complete knowledge of what was taxable, although in time the rate of taxation on the peasants, both direct and indirect, also rose. By appointing the *thu-gyi* on a salaried basis, the Commissioner believed that he would get accurate information about the amount of grain available to be taxed.[50] What he clearly failed to take into account was that bribery and corruption would continue to ensure that headmen under-reported the resources of their villages, despite repeated threats to remove them for involvement in pecuniary malpractice.[51] In fact, the failure of the early colonial state to establish a completely rationalised system of taxation meant that soon there was 'a

47   *Selected Correspondence Tenasserim Division*, p. 10.
48   Ibid., p. 2.
49   Ibid., pp. 51-2.
50   Ibid., p. 40.
51   *Correspondence for the Years 1825-26 to 1842-43*, p. 18.

return ... to the Burman custom of paying [headmen] by a commission of their revenue collections'.[52] It was not until the introduction of a province-wide cadastral survey in the 1870s that it was possible effectively to make headmen salaried officials. When this was done, it was believed, land revenue receipts doubled.[53]

If the first British-appointed headmen were still able to keep land revenue that was legally supposed to be passed on to the coffers of the state, they were less successful in regard to the capitation or head tax, which, at least in Arakan, was properly administered from the perspective of British officials.[54] The introduction of such reforms was believed for many years to be one of the major achievements of the British state. The system of extortion and plunder that the first Commissioner of Tenasserim complained of was supposed to have been replaced by an impartial and incorruptible administration. The gap between theory and practice was great, for an 'incorruptible administration remained very largely an ideal through the British connexion'.[55] Bribery and corruption, the new name of the clientage aspects of local administration, now became a major administrative 'problem' for the state, as well as an additional financial burden upon the peasantry. It also became one of the practices that kept the system of local government from becoming more oppressive than it was.

Despite the fact that a large proportion of state revenues continued to remain in or flow into private hands during the British period, the government was more effective in taxing the land and people than the precolonial state had been. Increases in revenue were also due in part to the increased level of production. In Arakan, for example, between 1830-1 and 1868-9, before the boom in Burma's exports to Europe, the acreage devoted to paddy cultivation increased 139 per cent and the revenue on this land increased 213 per cent. During the same period the amount of garden and orchard land on which taxes had to be paid increased by over 1,000 per cent and revenue went up more than 500 per cent. In all, total land revenue during the period increased 324 per cent. While the level of capitation tax was actually reduced, because 99 per cent more people were paying it in 1869 than in 1830, revenue increased 54 per cent, but the greatest

---

52   Ibid., p. 1.

53   Ibid., p. 93.

54   'Report on the Progress Made in the Arakan Division from 1865-66 to 1874-75', in *Report on the Progress of Arakan*, p. 2.

55   Donnison, *Public Administration*, p. 50.

increases in revenue were in new excise duties on spirits, toddy, and opium shops, which increased 96 per cent during the period.[56]

Nonetheless, financing the colonial state was never an easy matter. Its costs continued to rise as it assumed greater administrative and service responsibilities. The fact that the civil service elite was paid at European salary levels added significantly to the wage bill. Basic research on the finances of the colonial state remains to be done; it has been shown, however, that the country would have developed economically more rapidly had the colonial government not been an appendage of the Indian empire. From the earliest days, the government of India insisted that Burma must be financially self-supporting and no funds would be authorised from the central Indian treasury for its development.[57] However, when it did become a financially viable province of India following the development of the rice export industry, there was always a shortage of funds for the development of roads and other infrastructure because of the system of 'provincial contracts' that existed until separation in 1937.[58] Even then, Burma had to assume a debt to India and continue to pay for Indian troops stationed in Burma.

The Shan States under the British

To illustrate a few of the points made earlier and to explain more fully the colonial state's organisational development, an examination of the relationship of the colonial state with what came to be called the Shan States will prove useful here. Such an example is also illuminating for in this area, as in the other 'excluded' areas, the British were less intent upon introducing a rationalised administrative system. In the Shan States the colonial government initially followed the pattern of political organisation established near the end of the precolonial period at the lower levels of the political-administrative hierarchy, but it also began a process of rationalising the administrative system from the centre which gradually permeated down to affect the lives of more and more of the population. In the case of the plains-dwelling peasantry this process, after a slow beginning in Arakan

56   *Report on the Progress of Arakan*, pp. 40-2.
57   Furnivall, 'The Fashioning of Leviathan', p. 16.
58   Shein, *Burma's Transport and Foreign Trade*, p. 89; for an analysis of the provincial contract system and its impact on the finances of Burma, see Shein, Myint Myint Thant and Tin Tin Sein, '"Provincial Contract System" of the British Indian Empire, in Relations to Burma -- A Case of Fiscal Exploitation', *The Journal of the Burma Research Society*, LII (Dec. 1969), pp. 1-26.

and Tenasserim, developed rapidly after 1886, so that by the time of the First World War few peasants had not been affected by these changes. In the hill areas, which the British governed by a separate system of 'indirect rule' and whereby they 'professed "to administer the chiefs rather than the people"',[59] this process was much more gradual. And in the case of the peoples living in the Chin and Kachin designated areas, obvious administrative change did not occur until after independence.

For several reasons, this process was well underway before the Second World War in the Shan areas, as well as in the juridically similar but administratively separate Kayah zone. One reason was that the British government shared the same concerns as the Burmese kings: that the Shan plateau and the mountains beyond posed the major strategic threat to the state, for historically, it was through or from these regions that invading armies had attacked the Ayeyawady basin. A second reason was that the Shan States were, to use the language of the colonial state, the 'most politically advanced' of the hill areas. That is to say, they possessed an obvious class structure and had been governed in a more complex manner, on a larger geographical scale, than the so-called tribal communities of the Chin and Kachin regions, as well as those among the Karens. As discussed in Chapter I, in the Shan States the sawbwas stood in a position comparable both to an independent sovereign paying tribute to the king at Ava, and to a *thugyi* under the administrative control of the centre. Therefore it was easier to organise the region indirectly through the use of indigenous authorities than elsewhere in either the plains or the frontier areas. Finally, although it proved impossible to make the administration of the Shan States self-financing, it was thought possible to do so if the region was economically developed, because it possessed valuable teak reserves, potential mineral deposits and trade routes to the fabled markets of China. Thus the developmental potential of the Shan States, coupled with the financial drain of their administration that the British inherited from the monarchy, created the belief that rationalisation of their administration carried the promise of beneficial rewards for the state in trade, taxation, and improved security.

But the economic potential of the region became exploitable only in the twentieth century. Initially the British, like the kings, sought to control the area and its people as cheaply as possible through the utilisation of the ex-

---

59   Ba Thann Win, 'Administration of Shan States from the Panglong Conference to the Cessation of the Powers of the Saophas 1847-1959' (MA, Rangoon Arts and Sciences University, nd), p. 5.

isting political authorities, the sawbwas. Little was done to change this until new economic opportunities emerged. The British little understood the
complexities of the Shan and other hill ecological zones they inherited. The
simplistic pseudo-anthropology of the colonial world easily classified peoples
and practices in an abstract and reifying manner, thus creating political problems of ethnicity and group relations for later generations. When taking over
a new region, the British tended to accept and implement the advice they
received from the existing local authorities who were most cooperative with
them, and these figures, arguing their alleged historical grievances against the
Myanmar monarchs and by extension the Bamar people, became the rulers
recognised by the colonial state as the legitimate exercisers of authority in a
particular region.[60]

In 1886 the British authorities sent letters to the sawbwas explaining
the principles that guided their policy. The chiefs 'were assured that these
was no desire to interfere in the internal affairs of the State' which they
governed, but they had to acknowledge British supremacy, maintain peace
and not oppress their subjects. In exchange for the sawbwas accepting these
conditions and paying an annual tribute to the government of India's treasury, 'the British Government undertook to recognise the sawbwas who
were in effective possession, to uphold their rights, and to give freedom and
open the way for commerce'.[61] In subsequent years, the descendants of the
sawbwas ruling in 1886 referred back to these undertakings to justify claims
to semi-sovereign powers and privileges. However, British insistence on fair
treatment of the rulers' subjects and the opening of the states to free commerce gave the central state a pretext for increasing external interference in
the states' internal affairs. Between 1886 and 1895 the sawbwas pledged
their allegiance to the British crown, and after being forced to abandon any
claim to control the borders of their domains, they were placed under the
supervision of British Assistant Superintendents.

From the beginning, the colonial state attempted to limit the powers of
the sawbwas, just as the nineteenth-century Burmese kings had done by
insisting that the tribute levied upon their domains must be calculated on
the basis of the *thathameda* or household tax, levied under the supervision
of central inspectors since Mindon's time. The sawbwas wished to revert to

60   Robert H. Taylor, 'Perceptions of Ethnicity in the Politics of Burma', *Southeast Asian Journal of Social Science*, 10, 1 (1982), p. 12.
61   Charles Crosthwaite, *The Pacification of Burma* (London: Frank Cass, 1968; 1st published 1912), p. 147.

an earlier system whereby they themselves determined the taxable resources of their states, thus allowing them to keep a larger proportion of revenue within those states. This was unacceptable to British.[62] However, in effect, but not in law, the sawbwas were recognised as the heads of 'native states, with much the same status as the native states of India, and were placed under the personal supervision of the Chief Commissioner as Agent of the Governor-General [of India]'.[63] In law, the chiefs were British administrative agents permitted to maintain juridical and other rights over their subjects. Thus, despite some administrative rationalisation, the egalitarian consequences of rationalised law were not to reach the Shan States until the 1950s.

Like the precolonial state, the colonial state denied the *sawbwa*s control over the forests, mines and mineral resources of their domains, but asserted proprietary control much more effectively through the granting of exploitation contracts (mainly to British firms). The towns that developed in the region during this period were also removed from the control of the sawbwas and placed under local councils controlled by expatriates. The newly appointed Superintendents of the Northern and Southern Shan States who resided in their respective areas gradually increased their supervisory powers 'and there was a trend in the direction of extending to the Shan States the regulations which were in force in Upper Burma'.[64] This was because of the central state's desire that the sawbwas 'adopt more orderly methods of government and more effective means of raising revenue.' The regulation of criminal and other law was increasingly standardised following the promulgation of 'a set of rules, modelled on the Indian penal and procedural codes in a form adopted to a primitive people'.[65] *The Shan State Manual* came to supplement the customary law of the region as the guide to judicial behaviour for the sawbwa (who remained the administrator of the law under the supervision of the Resident).[66] There was, however, no uniformity imposed

62   J. George Scott and J. P. Hardiman, *Gazetteer of Upper Burma and the Shan States* (Rangoon: Government Printing and Stationery, Burma, 1900), pt. I, vol. I, p. 300.

63   *A Study of Social and Economic History of Burma (The British Period)*, pt. V: 'Burma Under the Chief Commissioners, 1886-87 to 1896-97' (Rangoon: Economic and Social Board, Officer of the Prime Minister, roneoed, 1957), p. 6.

64   Ibid., p. 12.

65   Scott and Hardiman, *Gazetteer of Upper Burma and the Shan States*, pt. I, vol. I, p. 398; see also *Materials for the Study (British Period)*, pt. BV, p. 1.

66   Interview with Saw Khun Khio, former *Sawbwa* of Mongmit, Cambridge,

on the region at that time.[67] The Superintendents also began to encourage the sawbwas to regularise the management of their governments by having them 'submit rough budgets of proposed receipts and expenditures'.[68]

Although a few of the bureaucratic procedures of the rationalised state were imposed on the sawbwas in the 1890s, little major change was attempted until the early 1920s, when political events elsewhere in British India and Burma necessitated new administrative arrangements. The colonial government maintained its control over the sawbwas through the threat of dismissal from their tenure or the abolition of their state if they did not comply with the Superintendent's requirements. In fact, fourteen states were abolished through amalgamation by not maintaining sawbwaships, thus making for large, more efficient administrative units.[69]

Although the intention of the British was not to change the sawbwas' traditional relationship with their subjects, in time the colonial administration 'tended to make the Chiefs think more and more of their own interests and less and less of their subjects who [could] no longer drive them out if found unsatisfactory or oppressive' because they were backed by the superior armed force of the colonial state.[70] For the sawbwas, colonial rule made their task easier as long as they obeyed the British, but for their subjects the weight of the state became greater. This was especially the case as the more settled conditions created by the colonial regime led the sawbwas, few of whom were really wealthy, to attempt to increase their tax revenues—which, in areas where the people were not well-integrated into the traditional domain, led to rebellion. By the mid-1900s, several sawbwas' expenditure had outrun their income and they had to be removed or disciplined by the Superintendents for debt or extravagance. The monetisation of the economy following increased taxation also led to a growth

---

England, Jan. 1983.

67   Scott and Hardiman, *Gazetteer of Upper Burma and the Shan States*, pt. I, vol. I, pp. 316-8.

68   *Materials for Studying (British Period)*, pt. V, pp. 11-12; Scott and Hardiman, *Gazetteer of Upper Burma and the Shan States*, pt. I, vol. I, p. 311.

69   Changes are noted in *The Shan States Manual* (Rangoon: Government Printing and Stationery, Burma, 1933), pp. I-ii. See also Minutes of the 5th Meeting of the Committee on Scheduled Areas Held on the 15th Dec. 1942 in BOF M/4/2803 and Minute Paper Bo. 761/38, Burma Office: Proposed Amalgamation of two lesser Shan States, by R.M.J. Harris, 11 Feb. 1938, in BOF 1506/37.

70   Minutes of the 5th Meeting of the Committee on Scheduled Areas held on the 15th Dec. 1942. BOF M/4/2803.

in crime that caused some states to expand their police forces and to build better prisons.[71]

The formal administrative entity known as the Shan States was not created until the early 1920s. The decision to introduce the dyarchy system of partially responsible government into central Burma made it necessary, in the eyes of the British, to establish a Shan States Federation in order to protect the sawbwas from the effects of the more democratic government and of Myanmar nationalism. The aim was to remove the Shan States from the legislative jurisdiction of the soon to be formed Indian central and Burma provincial legislatures. Also, it was hoped that the creation of the Federation would ensure that 'in the course of time' the Shan States would not be a financial drain on the revenues of the central Burma state. This was because the introduction of elections in Burma proper would mean that the voting taxpayers there would have to subsidise the Shan States over which elected ministers would have no control. But the federation was far from a genuine federal government. It merely established a Council of sawbwas to advise the Commissioner while simultaneously giving the British administration greater control over the financial affairs and economic development of the sawbwas' states. Matters such as road construction and other public works were removed from the control of the states, though education remained their responsibility.[72] At the same time, a separate civilian administrative cadre known as the Burma Frontier Service was established to administer the Shan States as well as the other excluded areas.[73] Clearly, the establishment of the Shan States Federation was not intended to enhance the powers or status of the sawbwas, but rather had the effect of bringing their areas under tighter British administrative control and further from political control by democratically elected politicians.

Despite the effect of British policy, which was to subsume the sawbwas within a larger federation and to impose the strictures of the rationalised state on them, the local rulers never gave up their desire to be recognised as the hereditary rulers of sovereign states under British protection. The final decade and a half before the Japanese invasion in 1942 saw the sawbwas fight a rearguard action against the British to preserve and enlarge what had

---

71   *Materials for Studying (British Period)*, pt VI, p. 1.

72   'Preliminary Proposals for the Future Administration of the Shan States', by T. Lister, 6 March 1920. IOF L/PS/10/145. A copy is also found in BOF P&J(B) 396.

73   Letter, R. Lewisohn, Chief Secretary, Government of Burma, to Political Secretary, Government of India, 25 Aug. 1920. IOF L/PS/10/1073.

now come to be defined by them as their traditional and historic rights as independent monarchs. The sawbwas were concerned about losing control of the internal affairs of their states as well as being absorbed into the larger political and administrative system of the central state. Both they and the British recognised that they were anomalies in the rationalised, formally democratic, and egalitarian structures of the central state. Financially, they were unable to fend for themselves either singly—except for those states with extensively developed teak and mineral resources—or in a Federation, and thus remained dependent on finance from Rangoon. Various compromises were reached between the sawbwas and the government during the 1930s, but the sawbwas never achieved their desire to be recognised as independent sovereigns like the Malay sultans and the Indian princes. Aware as they were of the nationalist demands of politicians in Burma proper, as well as some of their own subjects who had been educated in Rangoon, for incorporation of the Shan States into a democratic and independent Burma, they sought to demonstrate their loyalty to the British before the war by organising their own military forces for the defence of the country (a measure which also provided them with their own security forces).[74] At the same time they sought to ensure that the British would do nothing to alter their status after the war.[75]

The consequences of the Second World War on the nature of state power in the Shan States will be discussed in a subsequent chapter. After the impact of nationalism reached the Shan States and began undermining the authority of the sawbwas, the process of incorporating the states—along with the remainder of the frontier areas—into the unified and uniform structures of the central state accelerated. But had the post-colonial authorities not changed the shape of the distribution of power and the relationship of the Shan States with Burma proper during and after the Second World War, the British would have done so in any case. The British spent the war years planning how to consolidate the Shan States, reduce their number, make their government less autocratic, and link them to a federal Burma, thus completing the rationalisation of their administration begun sixty years earlier.[76] The intent of these plans was to truncate the independence of Burma, but the effect would

---

74   Burma Defence Bureau Intelligence Summary no. 10, 28 Oct. 1939. BOF I 358.

75   Text of proposals of Representatives of Shan Chiefs to the Governor, 14 March 1941. BOF 1505/37.

76   See correspondence in BOF M/4/2803.

have been to further undermine the powers of the sawbwas. No matter who won the war, no matter who took control of the central state of Burma, the imperatives of the modern state meant that the Shan States would in time become egalitarian and more firmly integrated into the political and administrative system of Burma proper.

Rationalising and expanding the functions of the state

The changes in authority relations resulting from the new territorial and bureaucratic nature of the colonial state were not merely a function of foreign rule coupled with administrative rationalisation. These changes were also a consequence of two other factors. First, the colonial state faced greater physical resistance to its authority which required it to develop stronger instruments of suppression and social control, and secondly, the social changes consequent to economic change, urbanisation, population growth and new class formations demanded that the state assume greater responsibilities in such fields as education, agriculture and public health. Ironically the British, who came with a pledge to free the people of Burma from the shackles of a state that denied a distinction between the public and private spheres of life, did the contrary by ensuring that the private sphere could be controlled and manipulated more directly and immediately by the public sphere. The shackles of custom were replaced by the fetters of regulation of personal choice by police, courts, and the beginning of the modern state's control of private choice in education, occupation and lifestyle. The initial increase in the range of personal options that were apparent in the nineteenth century soon gave way to tighter regulation and growing resentment in the twentieth.

State security and public order. The security of the colonial state rested primarily on the army, although by the close of the British period the government had developed more complex instruments of social and political control by the police, including an intelligence capacity which allowed it to monitor the plans of anti-state and anti-British movements and individuals. Such activities were, however, minor in the overall maintenance of the state. The army on which the colonial state depended was that of the Indian empire; it was this army which had won the three British victories over the kings in the nineteenth century and supplied the personnel which established most of the initial colonial administration.

One of the reasons advanced in 1885 for the final annexation of northern Myanmar was the external threat to the security of India and British Burma which would be posed if France or some other power gained control of the upper Ayeyawady valley and the Shan plateau. However, after the 1893 agreement between France and Britain to neutralise the Chao Phraya valley in neighbouring Siam, there was no longer an obvious external threat to India and Burma from the east until the early 1940s. With China weakened by internal disorder and external penetration, Laos and Vietnam under French control, Siam for all practical purposes within the British sphere of influence, and India part of the same empire, few in Burma or elsewhere in the British empire felt there was any threat to the external security of the colony even after the rise of Japanese militarism and expansionism in the 1930s.

Therefore, 'the primary role of the Army in Burma' was 'Internal Security'.[77] After each defeat of the king's forces, troops from the British-Indian army were retained in Burma to garrison the towns and maintain control until civilian administrators could take over their tasks. When after the 1852 annexation of Bago, and more especially after the 1886 deposition of Thibaw, there was widespread disorder and rebellion against the new rulers, additional troops were brought in to restore order.[78] During the twentieth century both regular British and Indian troops were always stationed in the country. In 1938 there were a total of 4,713 British soldiers plus 358 officers in the country, and 5,922 Indian army or Burma army troops, of which more than half were Indian. The core of the British Burma army—created only on 1 April 1937 by transferring units of the Indian army to the command of Governor of Burma—was the Burma Company of Sappers and Miners. This was made up of British officers and NCOs with 380 other ranks drawn entirely from the plains dwelling population, and the Battalion of the Burma Rifles composed of British and indigenous officers and 715 indigenous other ranks, all of whom came from the hill areas.[79]

From 1887 until near the end of the British period, except briefly during the First World War, it was army policy not to recruit and train infantrymen from the plains and delta because, it was argued, they were too expensive to maintain in comparison to Indian troops and less prepared

---

77   Notes on the Land Forces of Burma, app. III (n. d. [1938]), typescript, IOF L/WS/1/276.

78   See ch. III, pp. 157-161.

79   Notes on the Land Forces of Burma, p. 2.

to accept the methods of discipline and training of the Indian army. Also, as a matter of political policy, it was thought imprudent to train and arm a large number of Bamar because they had only been conquered in the previous century and, being in the terminology of the British-Indian army a 'martial race', would perhaps be more of a hindrance than an asset to the maintenance of British rule.[80] Even after the rapid expansion of the Burma army between 1939 and 1941 when it was felt necessary to raise forces following the outbreak of the Second World War in Europe, and in the face of feared Japanese aggression in Asia, only 1,893 of the troops of the regular Burma army were classified as Burmans, in comparison to 2,797 Karens, 852 Kachins, 1,258 Chins, 32 Yunnanese, 330 Chinese, 137 others, and 2,578 Indians. Even the Territorial Army, a sort of home guard that was expanded most rapidly, contained after two years of recruitment only 1,189 Burmans compared to 939 Karens and 940 Shans out of a total of 3,272.[81] Myanmar nationalists interpreted the unwillingness of the army to recruit men from Burma proper as part of the 'divide and rule' strategy of the imperialists. The British government undoubtedly viewed using Indian and hill area-recruited troops as the safest method of controlling nationalist opposition in central Burma, for there was less likelihood that they would side with demonstrators or rebels they were sent to put down.

The regular Burma army as well as the British and regular Indian army were held as a reserve and only called out 'in aid of the Civil Power' at times of severe public disorder such as riots and major rebellions. The largest of these, the Hsaya San peasant rebellion in 1930-2, required more than 3,500 additional regular Indian army troops to be brought into the province from central India.[82] For the normal maintenance of internal security the British government relied primarily upon the Military Police, which had been created from units of the Indian army after the suppression of the disorders following the 1852 annexation, and expanded in the same manner after 1886. After the separation of Burma from India, the Military Police was divided into two units, one primarily for use in central Burma and under the control of the elected Burmese Home Minister, and the other, renamed the Burma Frontier Force, for use in the excluded areas (but avail-

---

80   Furnivall, *Colonial Policy and Practice*, pp. 178-83.

81   Statement Showing by Class [i. e., ethnicity] the Strength (other than officers) of the Burmese Army and the Frontier Force on the 30th April 1941. BOF 66/41.

82   Cady, *History of Modern Burma*, p. 316.

able for deployment in Burma proper) under the control of the Governor. The troops of the Military Police, numbering 4,294 men in 1941, were almost entirely Indian and were under the command of British and Indian officers seconded from the Indian army. At that time, the 10,073-strong Frontier Force was composed of 7,376 Indians and the remainder coming primarily from the hill areas of Burma.[83]

The development of the Military Police, also referred to in the blunt language of the colonial state as the 'punitive police' because of its use in punishing entire villages for alleged acts of crime, followed from the inability of the unarmed civil police force to maintain order in the villages and towns. Initially, the British attempted to develop a local police service from the officials they inherited from the precolonial system. The *kyedangyi*, the largest taxpayer who assisted the *thu-gyi* in revenue collection and policing, was enlisted an as unarmed village constable. By the 1880s, if not earlier, these men were no longer figures of influence in their communities and the British found it ever more difficult to recruit men for those posts, even after increasing the salary which went with the job.[84] The bulk of the unarmed civil police were recruited in Burma proper and in 1938 nearly 71 per cent were Bamar. However, nearly 11.5 per cent were Indians and another 8.7 were Karens, which indicated the state's continued reliance on minority and foreign personnel for maintaining law and order. Reflecting the largely Indian nature of Rangoon, only about 26 per cent of the police in the capital were Bamar while over 67 per cent were Indians.[85] The senior police officers and most urban sergeants were British, often Scottish or Irish.

From the 1880s onwards the British devoted a larger and larger effort to maintaining and expanding the police force in a vain effort to control the growing social unrest and the high rate of crime, including murder, in the country. Between 1871-5 and 1933-8 the rates of crime committed and reported to the police rose dramatically. Dacoity increased 41 per cent and the rate of murder 53 per cent.[86] Increases in crime in a district often led to the imposition of extra police, including Karen levies and punitive police forces, which were paid for out of taxes added to the villagers' normal land

83   State Showing by Class the Strength (other than officers) of the Burmese Army and the Frontier Force on the 30th April 1941. BOF 66/41.

84   Mills, 'Burmese Peasant Response', p. 95.

85   Notes on the Land Forces of Burma.

86   G.E. Harvey, *British Rule in Burma 1824-1942* (London: Faber and Faber, 1946), p. 40.

rates.[87] While in the early years of British rule it could have been fairly claimed that life and property were safer than under the kings' rule,[88] this was doubtful by the end of the colonial period.

In summarising the role of the police in maintaining internal security during the colonial period, one can do little better than cite the experiences of Tharrawaddy district in the reasonably quiet period between 1900 and 1912. When, in 1907, there developed 'another severe storm of crime ... the regular police force was increased by 117 men and a punitive police force of 263 men was imposed ... at a cost ... which was recovered from the local inhabitants by a ten per cent cess upon land revenue.' This increase was on top of an earlier increase in the size of both police forces, so that by 1905 there was a ratio of one policeman for every 760 head of population, compared one per 876 five years earlier. As a former Deputy Commissioner of Tharrawaddy wrote in retrospect,

a marked feature of the modern history of the district is the frequency with which punitive police forces have been imposed; in the late nineties they were a regular institution in most of the townships. The increase in crime in 1906 and the repeated effect of an increased police force in diminishing crime suggest nothing so much as a spring compressed by the police and expanding at the slightest relaxation of pressure.[89]

Courts and the law. The strong arm of the colonial state, the force provided by the military and the police, was justified in the name of the preservation of a system of law which was felt by the British to be more fair and just than that which they had found upon their arrival in Myanmar. The administration of law and the courts were important to the colonial state, and the consequences of this change were crucial in shaping the relationship of the individual to the state during the colonial period. The growing depersonalisation of the legal system, its increasingly complex and rule-bound nature, and its tendency to rely less and less on Myanmar customary law and more and more on British-Indian codified law meant not only a more expensive and less understandable legal system for the mass of the population, but also an increase in crime and litigation as the customary bonds of society were replaced with what seemed arbitrary and unjust dictates from the foreign-controlled state.

---

87   S.G. Grantham, *Studies in the History of Tharrawaddy* (Cambridge University Press [for private circulation], 1920), pp. 17-18.

88   Furnivall, *Colonial Policy and Practice*, p. 53.

89   Grantham, *Studies in the History of Tharrawaddy*, p. 24.

With the establishment of British rule in Tenasserim, the Commissioner began the introduction of the British-Indian system. British Burma's legal system remained under the supervision of courts in Calcutta until 1871. Under this system the executive officer of the government was responsible for all judicial functions including both prosecution and adjudication in civil and criminal cases.[90] Initially, the Commissioner in Tenasserim instructed his subordinates to apply Myanmar customary law 'as far as possible', and gave them wide discretion in this.[91] It had been his original intention to re-establish Myanmar courts, but he found their structure and principles 'so complicated' that to him the traditional courts were incapable of dispensing justice but were merely institutions of official extortion and arbitrary decision-making not untainted by bribery. It was therefore necessary for him 'to draw up a Code of Regulations for the Administration of Justice' making the Commissioner, or his deputy or assistant, the sole judge in all courts.[92] Nonetheless, these courts were to be advised, as he wrote at the time, by 'a person ... skilled in the Burman laws and usages and well acquainted with the decisions that would have been given by the late Judges in cases similar to those that may be brought before the Commissioner, according to whose statement a judgement will be given so long as it be not cruel or does not militate against natural justice'.[93] In order to ensure that justice was done in the eyes of the Burmese as well as the British, the first courts used local juries. But when the British judges in Calcutta reviewed some of these decisions and found them unacceptable, as being too much in the nature of Myanmar arbitration and accommodation, as well as improvisation, rather than being based upon a search for 'evidence and truth', the jury system was abandoned.[94]

It was through the courts as well as the gaols and police buildings that the British state first became permanently visible to most of the people.[95] Still, until the 1870s, most disputes between villagers and even villages were settled through the traditional system of arbitration conducted by the

---

90   Alan Gledhill, 'Burma', in vol. E. no 7 of John Gilissen (ed.), *Bibliographical Introduction to Legal History and Ethnology* (Brussels: Editions de l'Institut de Sociologie, Université Libre de Bruxelles, 1970), p. 10,
91   *Selected Correspondence Tenasserim Division*, pp. 1-2.
92   Ibid., pp. 9-10.
93   Ibid., p. 11.
94   Furnivall, 'The Fashioning of Leviathan', p. 24.
95   *Report on the Progress of Arakan*, p. 9.

myo-thu-gyi. At the same time, however, the British appointed indigenous judicial officers to apply British-Indian law in the villagers. Few of these law advisers were familiar with the English that was the language of this law and many did not even have copies of the laws they were expected to interpret. In such circumstances, one can safely assume that in most cases Myanmar practices in the courts, as well as the tradition of avoiding the courts altogether, continued, especially in civil cases.[96] However, once the colonial authorities decided that it was necessary to maintain law and order more systematically throughout their jurisdictions, they appointed the legal officers needed to carry out the management of a full judicial system as then found in India.

In 1872 a Judicial Commissioner was appointed for Lower Burma 'who exercised most of the powers of the Indian High Court and for some purposes sat with the Recorder of Rangoon to form a Special Court'.[97] The involvement in judicial administration by the Chief Commissioner, until then the highest appeals officer in British Burma, had been scant, receiving no more than twelve appeals per year. The full-time Judicial Commissioner, having no other duties, managed by 1875 to generate 225 appeals and called on his own initiative 1,613 other cases to review. The effect of this typical bureaucratic behaviour was to weaken the authority of the lower courts. In time, 'almost no order was looked upon as final' because every decision was potentially open to review.[98] This was particularly the case after 1891, when a British Judicial Commissioner set aside a *myo-thu-gyi's* decision for being contrary to indigenous law.[99]

The elaboration of the judiciary grew apace with the growth of the state in the twentieth century. A Judicial Commissioner was appointed for Upper Burma in 1890 and a new judicial service was formed in 1905 to relieve the Deputy Commissioner of all civil and some criminal cases.[100] The office of the Recorder at Rangoon was merged with that of the Lower Burma Judicial Commissioner in 1900 and a Chief Court of Lower Burma was formed with appeal and revision powers throughout the southern regions. In 1923 a court with jurisdiction throughout Burma proper was set up when the Rangoon High Court assumed the duties of Chief Court of Low-

---

96   Furnivall, *Colonial Policy and Practice*, pp. 38-9.

97   Gledhill, 'Burma', p. 10.

98   Dennison, *Public Administration*, p. 36.

99   Furnivall, *Colonial Policy and Practice*, pp. 75-6.

100   Ibid., p. 72.

er Burma and the Judicial Commissioner of Upper Burma. At the lower levels, as well, the judicial system became more elaborate and separate from the executive officers of government. Magistrates tried lesser crimes and Sessions Courts dealt with the more serious, as well as serving as the first court of appeal. The Sessions judges were also in charge of the new system of district courts that relieved Deputy Commissioners of judicial tasks in most areas of Burma proper.[101] However, this modern judicial system did not extend to the frontier areas.[102] There the traditional rulers, under the supervision of the British Superintendent, applied simplified British-Indian law or modified customary law as interpreted through the minds of British-trained officials.

The changes in the judicial system introduced by the colonial state led not only to growing litigation and crime, but also to a weakening of the authority of local government officials, both indigenous and foreign. The replacement of customary law with the British-Indian codified law became one of the most important grievances that Myanmar nationalist politicians could cite in developing popular arguments for their movements. As one Myanmar scholar of the subject has written, 'in Burma … under British rule, the judicial system became more and more the apparatus of a foreign government. . there was a wide gap between law and life and to the common man the "rule of law" came to be almost synonymous with caprice.'[103] As that 'capricious' law was used as an instrument to remove peasants from their lands in the twentieth century, the strength of negative feeling toward it cannot be underestimated.

Nonetheless, the usefulness of colonial law and its institutions and consequences justified its use for many Myanmar as well as the state. The growth of the indigenous legal profession is one indicator of this. The development of a more complex economy and society which followed the imposition of the rationalised state made property laws and procedural rules and norms vital for controlling the new social forces which were coming to dominate Burma's political economy. Increasingly, for many urban and propertied segments of society, the law came to be seen as a tool rather than as a moral

---

101   Gledhill, 'Burma', pp. 10-11.

102   Donnison, *Public Administration*, p. 55.

103   Hla Aung, 'The Effect of Anglo-Indian Legislation on Burmese Customary Law', in David C. Buxbaum (ed.), *Family Law and Customary Law in Asia: A Contemporary Legal Perspective* (The Hague: Martinus Nijhoff, 1968), p. 80. A similar assessment of judicial changes under the British is given in Cady, *History of Modern Burma*, pp. 144-8, and Harvey, *British Rule in Burma*, pp. 33-7.

norm, a blessing if you could use it to advantage, a curse when you could not. Even peasants came to use the law when they were unable to gain protection or redress through more direct methods. The old proverb that 'a Tharrawaddy man comes to you with a law-book in one hand and a *dah* [common knife] in the other'[104] soon became true of most of the population of Burma proper.

State and economy. Under the prevailing liberal economic doctrine of *laissez-faire*, the economic functions of the colonial state were to have been kept to a minimum. Particularly during the nineteenth century, when the state assumed few economic responsibilities, Myanmar's traditional subsistence economy was transformed into an export-oriented, rice-production-based economy. Not assuming responsibilities, however, did not meant that the state lacked a keen interest in the trends of economic change and did not act to encourage those aspects that it saw as politically and economically desirable from the perspective of its interests and external links. Measurement of economic growth became almost a fetish of the rationalised state. The consequences of the economic changes allowed by the colonial state were, in terms of the development of contemporary Burma's social and political order, as important as the changes introduced by the state itself.

The key to the colonial government's economic policies in the nineteenth century was the encouragement of trade between Burma and India and further afield. Thirty years before the annexation of Rakhine and Tanintharyi, the Governor-General of India saw Myanmar as a potential market for British and Indian goods. Other British observers, sent to Myanmar in the first half of the nineteenth century, saw the Ayeyawady delta as a potential source of additional food for India in time of famine, and as a 'safety-valve' for the overcrowded and famine-threatened masses of the subcontinent.[105] Indeed, after the annexation of Bago, the government of India encouraged the migration of Indian labour to Burma to open up the sparsely settled delta. For ten years after 1876 the government subsidised the migration of labourers recruited by agents in India to travel to Burma,[106] but this scheme

---

104   Grantham, *Studies in the History of Tharrawaddy*, p. 21.

105   Michael Adas, *The Burma Delta, Economic Development and Social Change on an Asian Rice Frontier, 1852-1941* (Madison: University of Wisconsin Press, 1974), pp. 28-9.

106   N.R. Chakravarti, *The Indian Minority in Burma: The Rise and Decline of an Immigrant Community* (London: Oxford University Press for the Institute of Race Relations, 1971), pp. 8-9.

was abandoned, to leave it to the 'laws of the economy' to provide sufficient incentive for the flow of labour from Bengal and southern India to Burma throughout the remainder of the nineteenth and the first four decades of the twentieth century.[107] This business expanded and became so lucrative that the interests behind it lobbied long and hard to try to ensure that Burma remained a province of India and did not become closed to Indian labour by immigration restrictions.

It was in the period between the final annexation in 1885 and the outbreak of the First World War in Europe that the economic structure of modern Burma came into being. Until then the British to the south and the kings in the north and central regions continued to preside over an economy that had only loose ties with the larger world trade system. As was discussed in the previous chapter, Mindon and his officials were as keenly aware of the benefits of foreign trade and increased production for the strength of the state as their predecessors in the Toungoo and early Konbaung dynasties had been, and they had also been made aware of the advantages of economic reform in order to free resources for increased domestic production. However, the political environment in which they operated had made radical changes to the traditional system slow and difficult. Even in southern Burma, where none of these political inhibitions existed, the speed of change was not great and was limited to small areas and a few trade items (except perhaps in Arakan, which became closely tied to the more active trading zone of the Bay of Bengal). An indication of the slow rate of change in the economy until the final three decades of the nineteenth century was the apparent fact that there was no money-based exchange economy of countrywide proportions until the 1880s. The late impact of an exchange economy on Burma was one of the factors determining the consequences, in class and ethnic terms, of economic development during the next seventy years.[108]

When the British first arrived in Burma, they perceived the traditional economy to be sluggish and the people to be insufficiently oriented to trade and commerce. It was the intention of the new rulers to change these conditions, for the wealth and security of their empire depended upon the lively development of trade and the state revenue it would provide to pay for their ruling institutions. As Mr Maingy, the first Commissioner for Tenasserim,

---

107   In Bengali literature written during this period, Burma loomed as a frontier 'wild west' land of opportunity. I owe this insight to Dr. Sudipta Kaviraj.

108   Shein, *Burma's Transport and Foreign Trade*, p. 8.

wrote less than a year after taking charge of his domain, the king's discouragement of unofficial exports was now abolished and his government had been able to open up a small but important trade between Tenasserim and Malaya, whence Chinese merchants were coming to purchase sapan wood. Maingy, in a tone of self-congratulation, noted, 'This may be considered as the first decided instance of the Burmese shaking off that indifference they have hitherto evinced about money, and it has been my utmost endeavour to encourage this feeling so that it may be extended to other branches of labour.'[109] He was the first of many with this ambition.

Aware as Maingy was of the importance of trade for the development of his domain, he was not able to ignore the political necessity of controlling food supplies for his population, any more than the kings of Myanmar had been. Having abolished the king's prohibition on exports of all kinds of goods, he was forced to impose control of rice exports from Tavoy to avoid political unrest in Mergui. Under the kings, Mergui had been a rice deficit region and had depended upon imports from Tavoy to feed the population. However, rice exports under Maingy's liberal regime received 'such a spur from the large and unknown profits of a free foreign trade in grain that the love of gain was in danger of running away with a due regard to [the people's] own wants'. He then had to impose limits on this trade after determining first the supply and demand situation in his territories. 'In the balance of good and evil,' he wrote, 'I preferred a deviation from Political Maxim [à la Adam Smith] to the misery of a starving population which seemed evident in the rage of exportation.'[110] This was the colonial state's first act of intervention in the free flow of commerce for the benefit of the stability of society and the state.

After the annexation of the Ayeyawady delta, the state faced fewer such problems. The delta region was underpopulated when the British took control and its agricultural potential was thought to be very promising. What was most lacking was manpower to develop it, and this need was the reason both for the government's encouragement of migration from India and, most important, for the migration of peasants from central to southern Myanmar, which provided the bulk of the labour to open the frontier. The state provided very few inputs into this development, although there was some expenditure on the development of bunds and flood prevention devices to ensure the protection of lands from salination. The rapid growth

109   *Selected Correspondence Tenasserim Division*, p. 43.
110   Ibid., pp. 48-9.

of rice production in the delta meant that from 1851 till the 1920s, despite two or three periods of depressed prices, particularly in the 1890s and the first decade of the 20th century, the migrant cultivators of the region were, in comparison with what was to follow, relatively prosperous. There was plenty of land for development with little or no initial capital investment, and the international price of rice and the level of demand were both normally high. The quick profits to be made in the region attracted not only peasant cultivators but also indigenous land speculators and moneylenders who took advantage of the new protection of ownership and loan repayment that British law provided. Speculation in land and usurious interest rates provided easier profits than tilling the new paddy fields.

The phenomenal growth of the delta economy can be seen by comparing the total land under cultivation at the beginning of the period and at the end. According to the best available estimates, the delta region, also the granary of Konbaung Myanmar, contained over 662,000 acres of cultivated land in 1856-7. By correcting these figures and adjusting for other factors, Adas has concluded that at least 700,000 to 800,000 acres were under cultivation at that time. However, as little as fifteen years later, in 1871-2, 1,146,000 acres were under cultivation, and this was a mere fraction of the total reached by the mid-1930s, 8,702,000 acres.[111]

The inflow of internal labour into the delta to open the fields to cultivation left only one major obstacle to the full development of Burma as a rice-exporting nation. This was the lack of cheap and reliable means of getting the harvest from the fields and villages to the ports. It was in this area that the government first assumed major responsibilities by encouraging and sometimes financing, either directly or through subsidies and contracts, the development of modern communications infrastructure. Until then the costs of transport made profitable rice exports nearly impossible, at least on a large scale. In 1874, for example, the price of rice at Rangoon was three times what it was in Toungoo and other remote rice growing areas, and the significant gap in prices between 'the growing and exporting centres discouraged any extension of cultivation.'[112] Only along the Irrawaddy, where the new steam powered boats of the Irrawaddy Flotilla Company operated with a form of hidden state subsidy, were transport prices low enough to justify export production. The cost of transporting grain from areas far

111   Adas, *Burma Delta*, p. 22.

112   Shein, *Burma's Transport and Foreign Trade*, p. 40.

from the river by slow bullock carts thwarted the development of new fields in these areas until the 1870s.

Therefore the development of roads and, more importantly, railways, was crucial for the expansion of the export trade. Internal security was the major reason for the government's desire to improve transport, thus allowing troops to be moved more rapidly and cheaply to areas of disturbance and lowering garrison costs. Ultimately, the economic impact of the railways was to prove of greater significance.[113] The government saw the need to develop roads to lower transport costs, but was constrained by budgetary considerations as they had to be built out of current revenue. By 1870 there were only 709 miles of roads in British Burma and three years later there were still only 815 miles.[114] Railways, however, could be built with funds raised in capital markets and were thus easier for the government to finance. Between 1877 and 1886, 333 miles of railways were built in British Burma and by 1914 there were 1,599 miles in operation.[115] Though crucial for the development of southern Burma, the expansion of the road and railway network in central Burma had less effect on agricultural production. There the roads and railways were also built primarily for military purposes, subsequently becoming important for the export of minerals from the surrounding hills and imports of foreign goods as well as rice from the south. By the end of the 1930s, Burma was served by 4,100 miles of roads and 2,060 miles of railways, all built and maintained by the state.[116]

The development of new state functions. While the maintenance of internal security and the encouragement of trade and agriculture through *laissez-faire* policies remained the essence of the colonial state's responsibilities from the turn of the century until the First World War, the government developed other functions designed to improve the living standards of the population and raise the level of economic production and efficiency. The liberal reforms of the European world were then being extended to Burma and much of the rest of colonial South East Asia. Most of these new functions took their outward form in the shape of new government agencies and ministries.[117] Their impact on the nature of authority relationships in

113   Ibid., pp. 61-4.
114   Ibid., p. 37.
115   Ibid., pp. 41-2.
116   Harvey, *British Rule in Burma*, p. 7.
117   Cady, *History of Modern Burma*, pp. 148-50.

the countryside was discussed earlier. The development of a fuller and more modern system of medical provision and public health began in 1899 when the prison administration was separated from the hospitals. A central administration for land settlement and cadastral survey was developed after 1900. Government concern for credit began in 1904 with the creation of the Cooperative Credit Department. A Forest Department, first begun in the 1860s, reached its full form in 1905,[118] and an Agriculture Department came into being in 1906 along with a Veterinary Department and a Fisheries Department. The Public Health Department emerged from the work of the Sanitary Commissioner who was first appointed in 1908.[119] These, along with the Public Works Department which was responsible for roads, canals, the construction and maintenance of public buildings and the government-owned railways, were little affected in future years by the political and social changes around them.

The introduction after 1923 of the dyarchy system of government, which gave elected Myanmar ministers executive authority over most of these departments, had little effect on their purposes or modes of operation. Most departments were staffed by British and Indian officials at the upper levels and tended to become preserves of certain minority communities at the lower levels. For example, the medical service was staffed predominantly by Indians and the railways by Indians and Anglo-Burmans. Among the elite administrative services, including the Burma Agricultural Service (Class I), the Burma Forestry Service (I), the Indian Medical Service, the Burma Veterinary Service (I), the top administrative personnel of the Education Service (I), the Public Works Department, the Railways and the Post and Telegraphs Department, in the late 1930s non-Europeans held only about 25 per cent of all posts.[120] According to the 1931 census, although 87.9 per cent of the total participants in the country's labour force were indigenous by birth, only 62.9 per cent of those involved in public administration were locally born and only 47.2 per cent of those working in the police and other security agencies were indigenous. In comparison, 28.9 per cent of those involved in public administration were Indian (2.3 per cent born in

118   Raymond Bryant, *The Political Ecology of Forestry in Burma, 1824-1994*, (London: Hurst, 1997).

119   Furnivall, *Colonial Policy and Practice*, pp. 71-3; Donnison, *Public Administration*, pp. 42-3.

120   European and Non-European Strength of the Civil Departments of Burma (carbon typescript), 25 March 1943. Clague Papers in the India Office Archives and Library, London.

Burma) and 45.5 per cent of those in security work were Indian (2.0 per cent born in Burma).[121] The rationalised state was largely a foreign institution in the eyes of most of the population.

Despite the growth of its functional agencies, the bulk of the state's expenses until the end of the colonial period were directed at administrative costs. The rationalised state was expensive compared to its predecessor and importation of the Indian system made it difficult to lower these costs. As late as 1938-9, only 24.3 per cent of all government expenditure was on health, education, and economic development activities, while the remaining 75.5 per cent was spent on 'purely administrative services'.[122] Efficient as it was in increasing revenue, the rationalised state consumed most of its funds simply to maintain itself. And, unlike the precolonial state, its perpetuation was not deemed to depend on maintaining and enriching the cultural and spiritual life of the community.

Education. It was in the field of education that the colonial state had its most dramatic impact upon the culture of the people as well as their political responses to rationalisation. The precolonial education system had been designed to provide the rudiments of literacy to boys through the decentralised agency of the village monastery or *pongyi kyaung*. Higher education was also provided through the monkhood, and the educational responsibilities of the religious institutions were part of their hold on the community and their usefulness to the monarchical state. The British, however, first saw education less as a prop for the state and an agency of cultural continuity than as an instrument for the training of English-speaking clerks to fill government offices and provide skilled labour for the trading offices of foreign firms. As Vernon Donnison, once Chief Secretary of the colonial government, wrote, the education provided in government schools 'was an alien affair imposed from above, not an indigenous growth developed to meet modern needs'. The kind of knowledge imparted was largely 'artificial' and 'did not grow out of the experience and inheritance of the people'.[123] Nonetheless, the opportunities for well paid and comfort-

---

121   Taylor, 'Relationship Between Burmese Social Classes and British-Indian Policy', table 8, p. 45, based on *Census of Burma 1931*.

122   *Fiscal Enquiry Committee Report, Second Report* (Rangoon: Government Printing and Stationery, Burma, 1938), p. 1; statistical breakdown on p. 16.

123   Donnison, *Public Administration*, pp. 46-7. A similar assessment was made by an American teacher at Judson College in the 1930s. See John F. Cady, *Contacts with Burma, 1935-1949: A Personal Account* (Athens, Ohio: Ohio University Centre for International Studies, Southeast Asia Program, 1983), pp. 1-37, pas-

able employment provided by an English education made such schools highly popular among those few who could gain access to them for by the 1870s their graduates 'would be worth Rs. 150 to Rs. 200 a month in a merchant's or Government office' in Arakan.[124]

Western education was initially provided primarily in missionary schools in Tenasserim and Arakan, and later in Pegu. Following the development of the province of British Burma, the government began to take a more direct role in education and a Department of Education was established in Rangoon in 1866. At first, the government attempted to use the pongyi kyaung as a medium for the introduction of Western learning to Myanmar youth, but the monkhood was by and large uncooperative and the government then concentrated its efforts on developing government schools and facilitating the activities of missionary schools. In 1891-2 there were 4,324 government recognised monastic schools but still only 890 secular schools. Less than thirty years later, in 1917-18, there were 4,650 secular schools and only 2,977 monastic schools. A major cause of the decline in the number of monastic schools was the belief by parents that their children would get a better education in the secular institutions.[125]

Most of the secular schools were privately owned and elite institutions were directly under government or missionary management. In the 1930s there were 5,582 secular schools teaching in the Bamar medium, of which 5,440 were privately run under the lax supervision of local education authorities. The standards of these schools were not high and the requirements for employment as a teacher were minimal. Nepotism rather than knowledge was often important in gaining a post.[126] Advanced education necessary for the gaining of government and commercial employment, including teaching of English, was provided in the English-medium and Anglo-vernacular (that is, joint English-Bamar medium) schools found in the towns and cities. The growth of the numbers of students in these schools and in college-level institutions in the twentieth century was dramatic.

---

sim.

124   *Report on Progress of Arakan*, p. 10.

125   Cady, *History of Modern Burma*, p. 179.

126   *Report of the Education Reconstruction Committee* (Rangoon: Government Printing and Stationery, Burma, 1947), pp. 4-5.

The tremendous growth in the enrolment of students in secondary and university education is indicative of the changing society of the first four decades of the twentieth century. Whereas in 1900 there were 27,401 students in government-recognised secondary schools, by 1940 there were 233,543 students, almost an eightfold increase. In college and university education the increase was even more dramatic, the figure rising from 115 students in 1900 to 2,365 students in 1940, an almost twenty-fold increase. However, the growth of enrolment in colleges and universities did not mean that the Myanmar population was reaping comparable benefits in terms of gaining the knowledge, skills and wealth that such education was intended to provide. As in other areas of change induced by the colonial state, communities not indigenous to Myanmar gained disproportionate benefits.[127]

While the overwhelming majority of secondary students were undoubtedly indigenous, this was not true of university students. The percentage of indigenous students in colleges between 1900 and 1925 fluctuated around 55 to 65 per cent. By 1940, however, in all institutions of higher education in Burma, Bamar and Kayin students were only a bare majority, 1,298 students out of 2,465. In University College at Rangoon University, the most important college in Burma, the proportion of indigenous students never reached two-thirds of the student body, and sank to a bare majority during the peak of the depression in the early 1930s.[128] Increased opportunities for education in Burma commenced with the founding of Rangoon University in 1920 and the later founding of a medical college, a teacher training college, an intermediate college at Mandalay and an agricultural institute at Pyinmana, as well as the Baptist Judson College affiliated to Rangoon University. These new institutions not only increased the opportunities for Myanmar students to gain higher education, but also increased the likelihood that Indian and other non-indigenous youths would stay in Burma for their education and subsequent careers. Thus, to the educated Myanmar people, the expansion of educational opportunities, like the development of other opportunities for careers in administration, the professions and commerce, also

---

127 Taylor, 'Relationship Between Burmese Social Classes and British Indian Policy', table 10, p. 57, based on *Reports* and *Quinquennial Reports on Public Instruction in Burma*.

128 Ibid., table 11, p. 58, based on *Education Reports, 1900 and 1925*; table 12, p. 58, based on *Education Reports, 1940*; table 13, p. 59, based on *Education Reports, 1927, 1937, 1940*. (All official government documents.)

increased the number of Indians who could successfully compete with them for such posts.

State 'legitimacy' and constitutional policy

As noted earlier, the great strength of the colonial state was its external sources of military power gained from Britain and India. The great weakness of the colonial state was its inability to sustain support, either active or passive, from the indigenous population. The precolonial state had persisted with relatively few physical coercive instruments because it it was supported by a vast range of religious and customary norms; these created an environment where questioning its legitimacy or purpose was not only not encouraged, but rarely encountered. Dissatisfaction, when it arose among villagers or officials, was directed towards a particular set of superiors or particular ruler, including the king himself *in extremis*, but not at the system. Such a culture made government easier than it would have been had there existed countervailing intellectual and political currents. On the other hand, one of the key sources of the precolonial state's physical weakness was its inability to mobilise support, except in times of great peril and then often too late to be of assistance. The second and third defeats in the nineteenth century at the hands of the British-Indian empire concluded with a *post-hoc* rising of popular sentiments around the symbols and institutions of Burmese monarchical government, the Buddhist religion and local autonomy. But the kings themselves had few mechanisms for mobilising such popular support, as the only instruments at this disposal were the *ahmu-dan* population and the patron-client system that allowed them to use these relatively uncoordinated forces for their defence.

For the British, however, the question of legitimacy did not arise in the same way. It was, of course, impossible for them to assume the mantle of the kings and the carapace of authority that enshrouded them. The possibility of retaining the monarchy after the third Anglo-Burmese war was briefly considered but soon abandoned for direct rule as already practised in British Burma. The lack of reliable Burmese princes to put on the throne and the economic efficiency of the new system in the south made the abolition of the monarchy an easy decision. Otherwise, the British might have introduced into Myanmar something similar to the two-part administrative system which the French installed in Vietnam, retaining a powerless monarch in the north while directly managing a more internationally oriented colony in the south. The degree of ethnic homogeneity that Burma proper had attained by the 1870s would have made the justification of such a division difficult, but perhaps not impossible.

Initially, in a world that had yet to experience mass nationalism, the colonial authorities felt confident that the new economic and personal freedoms created by their state and its laws would be sufficient to ensure the loyalty and support of the indigenous population. This would result not merely from the economic prosperity they believed would be created, but also from the 'character' of the people. As Maingy wrote soon after taking control of Tenasserim, 'The Burmese of Mergui are a lively, good natured and tractable race. . . little trouble will, I think, be required to strengthen the sentiments of respect and confidence they already entertain towards our Government'.[129] In fact, in the small and isolated provinces of Tenasserim and Arakan, during most of the nineteenth century, the British faced little opposition to their rule. Perhaps this was because the new state did little to interfere directly in the lives of the people, and perhaps also because the symbolic continuity of the monarchical state and its support for traditional culture still continued in prestigious splendour across the permeable border between the British territories and the Myanmar state. In addition, these two provinces had only relatively recently been subjected to the centralising schemes of the precolonial state.

However, following the annexation of Bago and the increasing power of the colonial state to intervene in the lives of the people, growing discontent with foreign rule became apparent and the British began to institute reforms designed to build political support for the colonial order. The few Burmese who actively cooperated with the colonial authorities by serving the government were primarily from the minority communities, such as the Kayin; from migrant communities, such as the Indians; and from what the British throughout the colonial period called the 'respectable classes', the wealthier minority of townspeople who benefited from the economic and career opportunities that the colonial state created. But it was obvious to the governors of British Burma by the 1880s that the 'majority did not set much store by British law and order', and the recalcitrant attitude of the peasant majority was the reason for introducing the punitive police force at that time. As J.A. Mills has written, 'It seems hard to escape the conclusion that by the 1880s the British government must have been regarded as even

---

129   *Select Correspondence Tenasserim Division*, p. 14.

greater evil than a Burmese government, with most of its vices but few of its virtues'.[130]

Besides increasing its repressive power in the face of both active and passive resistance, the British state began the introduction of participatory institutions with which to gain the cooperation and collaboration of the prosperous minority of the population whose interests were wedded to those of the colonial state. Initially, steps were taken to establish institutions of urban self-government. As early as 1883, two-thirds of the Rangoon municipal government was elected. Its composition is indicative of those interests that the British felt to be on their side and therefore amenable to collaboration with the colonial order. Of the seventeen members elected to the city council, only five were Bamar and one was Kayin, while of the remainder, five were British, two were Chinese, two were Hindus, and three were Muslims, while one was a representative from the British-run Chamber of Commerce.[131] The plural society was now recognised officially. The extension of elected and appointed municipal and district boards designed to establish the rudiments of local self-government outside the capital was even less successful than the efforts in Rangoon. 'People could barely be persuaded to accept membership of municipal boards in Burma, feeling that Government was "getting at them in some way".'[132]

At the central state level in Burma proper, the British did little to introduce institutions designed to mobilise support for, or increase the legitimacy of, the state until the 1920s. The advisory Legislative Council created in 1897 was composed entirely of British officials except for two other Europeans representing business interests. Following the expansion of this body to 15 members in 1909, four Myanmar, one Indian, and one Chinese were appointed by the Chief Commissioner. Its size had been increased to 30 members by 1920, of whom ten were indigenous, two Indian and one Chinese. Business and government held the other positions.[133] This body had no impact on the political life of the country. Because none of its members were elected, and as it had no power, it remained what it was intended to be, a means of ensuring that the governor consulted the economically and administratively influential members of the colonial society's recognised élite.

130   Mills, 'Burmese Peasant Response', pp. 96-7.
131   Tinker, *Local Self-Government in India, Pakistan and Burma*, p. 49.
132   Ibid., p. 51.
133   Cady, *History of Modern Burma*, p. 152.

The absence of serious and effective institutions to ensure that the colonial state developed some semblance of legitimacy in the eyes of the Myanmar population before 1923 does not mean that the government was unaware of the problem posed by its lack of popular support. The breaking of the connection between the state and the Buddhist faith and the growth of new forces and classes convinced leading British officials that there was a need to create positive feelings toward the colonial state. Intellectual and political trends abroad also influenced the thinking of many officials who were aware of the politically unsettling impact of nationalism, and later socialism, on the political stability and legitimacy of the remainder of Asia, as well as of Europe, around the time of the First World War. Perhaps the most imaginative of such attempts to counter these intellectual and political trends was the appointment by Governor Sir Harcourt Butler in July 1916 of a 'Committee to Ascertain and Advise How the Imperial Idea May Be Inculcated and Fostered in the Schools and Colleges of Burma'. The committee, composed of either leading British administrators, four missionary educators, and two Myanmar, 'was charged with devising means of realising through the schools and colleges a spirit of justice, co-operation, and sacrifice in the interest of national development, coupled with a sense of personal loyalty to the king-emperor and an appreciation of the imperial idea.'[134] The committee was to come up with a means to create both 'sentiments of national patriotism and imperial loyalty' by showing how 'Burma for the Burmans within the Empire' was the only effective means of developing the country. The conclusion drawn by one civil servant as to how this seemingly impossible goal was to be achieved reveals that the ideas of legitimacy of the colonial state, in the eyes of the colonial rulers, had changed little between 1826 and 1916. He wrote that the student

should be taught to regard his people as a conquered nation but to understand that England had assumed the task of education and government of his country not as a tyrant but as a trustee for civilisation in order to . . build up those conditions of liberty and opportunity of the individual in which the people can learn to govern themselves.

Textbooks published by the colonial government conveyed much the same message. *Burma Under Colonial Rule* by S.W. Cocks,[135] a standard set

---

134   The following discussion is based upon ibid., pp. 195-9, from which the quotations are also taken.

135   S.W. Cocks, *Burma Under Colonial Rule* (Bombay: K. & J. Cooper, 1ˢᵗ edn., n. d.).

history book throughout the late colonial period, emphasised the despotic nature of the Burmese kings and their thwarting of economic and personal liberty in contrast to the prosperous and free equality of life allegedly created by the colonial state.

From about 1915 onwards, British imperial pronouncements made the repeated promise that the burden of the colonial task in India was not merely trade, commerce and profit, but the creation of conditions for the development of self-government and democracy under British tutelage; by the 1920s these ideas had to be applied to Burma as well. The irony of the situation is that by the late 1930s, Burma had been granted a constitutional form that provided a greater degree of internal self-government than India or indeed almost any other Asian or African British colony had received by that time. But in the early 1920s, it was not believed that Burma was as 'prepared for self-government' as India. It was the logic of British policy towards India that unintentionally determined British policy toward Burma. For the sake of political expediency it was necessary to make it seem that Burma was being treated on an equal footing with India.

From 1919 it had been the avowed purpose of British policy towards India to make the colony a fully equal self-governing member of the British Commonwealth at some unspecified future date. This promise of eventual dominion status was made most unequivocally in 1929 by the Viceroy, Lord Irwin (later Lord Halifax), in his remark that the natural issue of British policy in India, as implied in the preamble to the Government of India Act 1919, was dominion status. But when the 1919 Act was passed by the British Parliament, its provisions for establishment of the dyarchy system of tutelary democracy were not applied to Burma. The dyarchy system had been recommended by the Viceroy, Lord Chelmsford, and the Secretary of State for India, Edwin Montagu. No one concerned with the preparation of the Montagu-Chelmsford reforms visited Burma, and at that time no serving member on the executive council of the Viceroy had had any experience of Burma.[136] Several Burmese politicians did travel to see Montagu while he was on a visit to India. He 'summed up the Burman leaders who came to see him as "nice, simple-minded people with beautiful clothes. Complete loyalty; no sign of political unrest".'[137] The Montagu-Chelmsford report contended that there was no demand or need for political reforms in Burma and implied that the Burmese were politi-

136   Tinker, *Local Self-Government in India, Pakistan and Burma*, p. 112.
137   Ibid.

cally 'less advanced' than Indians.[138] The report thus gave rise to the belief among Burmese leaders that Britain intended to treat Burma less liberally than India. This idea was not without foundation, and was not put to rest until independence.[139]

In lieu of dyarchy the Governor of Burma, Sir Reginald Craddock, prepared his own scheme of constitutional change with an emphasis upon Burma's fiscal autonomy from India. These plans were complex, and proved unacceptable not only to the Burmese nationalist leaders but to the governments of India and Britain as well.[140] Whereas the Burmese nationalists viewed them as reactionary, since all power remained in the office of the governor, the government of India opposed them because they would have lessened its financial and legal control of Burma. Soon after the slights of the Montagu-Chelmsford report and the Craddock schemes became known, the nationalist movement began its first sustained campaign. While directed initially at problems of education rather than governmental reform, the countrywide student strike of 1920 demonstrated to the British government that there was political activity in Burma that required institutional outlets. Political pongyi under the leadership of U Ottama, including many younger monks who were subsequently involved in the General Council of Sangha Sammeggi (GCSS), toured Burma encouraging the populace to resist the British.[141] London was so unaware of political attitudes in Burma that these demonstrations came as a surprise.

When news of the widespread political agitation reached Whitehall, preceded by two delegations of Burmese politicians to argue for the inclusion of Burma in the Indian constitutional reforms, the Secretary of State relented. In 1921 Parliament voted to extend dyarchy to Burma and a Burma Reforms Committee was sent to work out the details of the changes. The special significance of this committee is that it was sent not as an agent of

---

138   Great Britain, House of Commons, *Sessional Papers*, vol. VIII for 1918 (Cmd. 9109), p. 198, in Cady, *History of Modern Burma*, p. 201.

139   Later, when separation of Burma from India was being supported both by the British government in London and Rangoon and British business interests in Burma (but opposed by Indian economic interests with involvement in Burma), many Burmese believed their support for separation was an effort to hold back the constitutional advance of Burma relative to that of other provinces of India. Similar fears were expressed after the Second World War as India's independence became imminent.

140   Cady, *History of Modern Burma*, pp. 199-212, for details.

141   Ibid., pp. 213-42, gives the details. These points are taken up again in ch. III below.

the government of India but as an instrument of Parliament, even though there were no MPs on it. Never again would London consider policy towards India without giving thought to the consequences for Burma. The episode also shattered the imperial illusion that the colonial state was self-perpetuating because of its fairness and efficiency and the alleged passivity of the Burmese. The relative political stability of Burma after the mid-1890s ended in 1920 and was never restored again under the British.

Five years after the introduction of dyarchy into Burma, the British appointed a commission under Sir John Simon to investigate the operation of this experiment in democratic 'tutelage' in India. In regard to Burma, the Simon Commission had not only to consider whether further extensions of self-government should be applied to Burma if granted to India, but also whether Burma should remain an Indian province. The government was not to make the same mistake it had made ten years earlier and ignore the effects of change in India's state structure on the political future of Burma. The government of Burma, through the Governor and his officials, was asked to comment on the possibility of separating Burma from India and extending representative institutional and Burmese control to the central government. While the officials would not officially recommend for or against separation (they had no public objections to greater democracy), they clearly favoured separation for administrative, constitutional and political reasons. Separation, they thought, would better involve Burmese politicians in the management of the state and allow the civil servants of Burma to get out from under the domination of the central Indian administration. Other reasons for separation included the relative national unity of Burma in comparison with India; the fact that the economic interests of Burma were divergent from those of India, especially as the Indian tariffs designed to protect Indian nascent industries drove up prices in Burma; and the drain on the revenues of Burma resulting from the attachment to India. The reasons for keeping Burma as part of India were essentially military, most notably reliance for internal security and defence on the Indian army. There were financial reasons, all of which could be overcome by administrative arrangements.[142]

In addition to the memoranda of the government of Burma, the Simon Commission also received a report from a committee of conservative

---

142   'Secret Memorandum on the Separation of Burma from British India [by the Government of Burma to the Indian Statutory Commission]', 7 Jan. 1929, Clague Papers.

and cooperative members of the legislative assembly.[143] All members of the committee favoured separation except for one, an Indian member who demanded immediate dominion status. The majority's reasons for advocating separation were similar to those of the government but emphasised factors of greater concern to the indigenous population. Political groups unwilling to cooperate with the Simon Commission would have made the same points but more forcefully. First, the connection of Burma to India had always been 'unnatural' as it had been achieved by armed force and maintained merely for reasons of administrative convenience. Secondly, attachment to India was detrimental to the development of the economy of Burma. Thirdly, there was apprehension that continued attachment would destroy the traditional composition of Burma by the continued influx of Indians. As the Burma Committee summarised the latter two points: 'Burma's political subservience to India has seriously jeopardised her financial and economic interests and even threatens to denationalise her.'[144]

The Simon Commission recommended the separation of Burma from India. This was vigorously opposed by the government of India and Indian economic interests in Burma who believed that loss of the province would mean creation of a separate state that would be able to control the flow of labour and capital across its borders. The complex politics of the ensuing five years demonstrated the economic and political power of the Indian community and the civil servants' need to limit their preferences in order to meet nationalist political pressures.[145] Despite election results in 1932 that could have been interpreted to mean that the Burmese electorate and politicians did not desire Burma's separation from India, the actual situation was the reverse. Along with opposition to the colonial state that had developed because of the increasing interference in the lives of the people, there were the economic and national consequences of the country's integration into the capital and labour markets of India. Separation, it was thought, would halt and perhaps reverse this trend, although the superior economic and political power of India in the empire meant that Burma

---

143   'Report of the Burma Committee', *Report of the Indian Statutory Commission*, vol. III, pp. 509-25, Cmd. 3568. As the major nationalist parties boycotted the visit of the Simon Commission, the Committee was composed of members of the minor and minority parties in the legislative council.

144   Ibid., p. 510.

145   Details are provided in Taylor, 'Relationship Between Burmese Social Classes and British-Indian Policy', pp. 102-49.

would have had to delay the full implementation of separate powers to regulate trade and immigration for several years.

The Government of Burma Act, 1935, which came into effect on 1 April 1937, was a significant document in the development of the modern state in Burma. Not only did it establish a system of parliamentary government similar in form to that of the Westminster model of British cabinet government, providing a means for Burmese politicians to involve themselves in the management of the central state. It further legitimised in the eyes of many Burmese politicians the electoral institutions of the dyarchy government, including political parties. The rise of a stratum of politicians who were willing to cooperate with the British led in turn to the further development of organised nationalist opposition to cooperation with the colonial state.[146] Try as the twentieth-century colonial state might to create democratic modes of legitimacy through a policy of progressively extending self-government, the contradictions between the British veto and national self-government, and the domination of external economic and military forces over a recalcitrant population, meant that the colonial state was never able to achieve the acceptance its precolonial predecessor had. Until the end of British rule, people could always hark back, via selective historical memory, to the not too distant past when the king's state apparently demanded less of the people and they lived lives unaffected by international price fluctuations, foreign labour competition, alien landlords, large debts and a punitive police force.

New class and ethnic formations

The most obvious impact of the colonial state upon Burma's social structure during the late nineteenth and early twentieth century was the development of new class and ethnic formations and interests, as a consequence of the economic and administrative changes introduced or encouraged by the British. The social structure of the precolonial state, with its clear correlation of power with status and wealth, was replaced in the twentieth century and the political reforms held out the promise of political power within the state to the new classes. Most dramatically, the colonial era saw the creation and rise to the centre of indigenous political life of a new class, a Burmese middle class, which became the main force behind the development of modern Burmese political nationalism. This class was largely urban

---

146   To be discussed in ch. III.

and had grown out of the opportunities for Burmese to leave the villages and take advantages of the economic, educational and career opportunities created by the colonial order. It was this sector of society that became mobilised both as a prop for the new state and as a rival to British and Indian interests which also benefited, disproportionately, from the new order.

From the 1870s and 1880s onward, the speed of economic and political change provided opportunities for this new class to evolve; but it did so in conditions which worked against its developing into a fully independent class. By the 1930s, however, the class structure had evolved into its most complex form, and it was from this form that the class conflicts of post-independence Burma's politics were fought in the 1940s and 1950s. The class structure of the 1930s can be visualised as a three tiered pyramid. At the apex was a very small group of British government officials and the managers of the major European trade, mineral extraction, and banking firms. Included in this group was a significant proportion of the Eurasian population that, for financial and psychological reasons, was dependent on the British for its position in society. This top group was of less importance for the internal politics of the colonial period than has been generally assumed. The second tier of the class structure was composed of the middle class. For purposes of analysis, the middle class can be divided into three sectors. First, there was the landowning sector; secondly, the commercial and trade sectors, which together were in some ways comparable to the European bourgeoisie; third, independent professionals and government employees—what might be considered in Western terms the 'white collar' middle class. The Burmese middle class, over a period running from about 1907 to 1930 or 1935, became increasingly urban and 'white collar'. Whereas in the 1880s there developed a prosperous class of Burmese traders, landowners, moneylenders, mill owners and the like, over time, as a result of several interrelated problems of the internal and external economy of Burma, Indians began supplanting Burmese in these roles. Burmese in the middle class were losing their sources of independent wealth and were increasingly dependent on government or Indian financiers for their incomes. Even the expansion of university education in the 1920s and 1930s, as discussed above, did not imply an increasingly strong and vigorous middle class relative to the Indian middle class. This was because Indians were settling permanently in Burma in increasing numbers and were using the expanded educational facilities to maintain their relative competitive advantages over the Burmese.

Thus by the 1920s and 1930s the emerging Burmese middle class was already facing a crisis which was encouraged and compounded by the problems of the Burmese peasant population. Because of the exigencies of agricultural production, especially during the depression of the 1930s, the number of landless labourers and insecure tenant cultivators was rapidly increasing. With the growing shortage of new rice lands in the delta and the growing labour surplus in the countryside, more Burmese were competing with Indian workers in the cities and towns for jobs in trade, manufacturing and transport. At the same time as Burmese were seeking unskilled urban employment, more Indians were remaining in Burma to compete for skilled positions in industry that until that time had generally been the prerogative of the Burmese. The result of these pressures was seen in the increase in urban and rural communal tension and violence in the 1930s.

The economic and administrative policies of the colonial state during the period up to the First World War created the conditions for emergence of this class structure and its attendant ethnic characteristic: the plural society. Not only was colonial Burma's society divided by various ethnic communities which remained isolated from each other except for purposes of the market; this horizontal division was further complicated by vertical divisions within each community between those who had superior skills and higher status, or controlled significant quantities of capital, and those who possessed neither of these advantages in the rationalised economy and commercially oriented society. In such a society it was the middle class, Burmese and Indian, as well as the top group of Europeans that served as the communicators among the ethnic communities. The bottom of the social pyramid contained the overwhelming majority of the population, but it remained powerless to affect state policies in any positive manner, composed as it was of agricultural workers and a much smaller but strategically important group of industrial and transport workers largely confined to their own communities. The colonial state was dependent upon the middle class to control and direct these elements.

Within each of the two main tiers of the class structure there was a variety of religious, ethnic, occupational, educational and geographic divisions, but these were sufficiently congruent that they can be discussed in terms of ethnic divisions. Indeed, because of the increasing hold on the most important economic positions by Indians, and the consequent retreat of the Burmese middle class to 'white collar' positions, the main political questions in late colonial Burma was usually articulated in terms of ethnicity rather than class. For analytical purposes, however, it is necessary to combine class and ethnic categories in order to understand the social dynamics of the period. (As the changes in the class and ethnic structures of areas apart from the most economically dynamic areas were slight during the colonial period, they are omitted from the following analysis of colonial Burma's social structure.)

The migration of Indian labour into Burma from the 1870s onwards had the most visible effect in creating the plural society. The size of the Indian population grew proportionally larger from the 1870s to the 1930s. Although it has been estimated that the Indian percentage of the total population declined to 5.4 per cent in the 1941 census because of the effects of the depression in the early 1930s and the anti-Indian demonstrations, riots and legislation in the late 1930s,[147] it is clear that the Indian population grew both in absolute and relative terms into the 1930s.[148]

The Indian population was concentrated in southern Burma; it first became significant in Arakan before spreading later to the other divisions. In the three remaining divisions of southern Burma the Indian population expanded and stabilised most rapidly in Pegu—that is, the Irrawaddy delta—but was continuing to grow in Irrawaddy and Tenasserim. In Arakan, the Indian population was proportionately the largest of any division. It also

---

147   Chakravati, *Indian Minority in Burma*, p. 18. The 1941 census was never published as almost all of its records were destroyed during the Second World War.

148   Chakravarti argues, as did the Baxter Report on Indian Immigration (*Report on Indian Immigration* [Rangoon: Government Printing and Stationery, 1941]), that for most purposes it is fairer and more appropriate to remove Arakan division from any analysis of the size and growth of the Indian population, because of the land connection between Arakan and Bengal and the earlier conquest of Arakan by the British. Chakravarti goes further and argues that the Indian proportion of the total population was much smaller because, at any one time, probably half of the Indians in Burma were temporary residents seeking work and returning to India with their savings. By excluding Arakanese Muslims and an additional 150,000 Indians from the total, which Chakravarti considers the minimum number of temporary residents, the Indian proportion of the population is reduced to 4.8 per cent in 1911 to 3.5 per cent, from 5.5 per cent in 1921 to 4.3 per cent, from 5.8 per cent in 1931 to 5.4 per cent, and from 4.3 per cent to 3.3 per cent in 1941. (Chakravarti, *Indian Minority*, table 2.3, p. 18 and table 2.6, p. 22). While Chakravarti's figures are no doubt correct, they in no way lessen the size of the Indian population that was seeking work in Burma. In fact, because there were more single males in the Indian population in proportion to the total Indian population than among the indigenous population, the Indian labourers took more jobs from Burmese than a permanently settled population of the same size but with a normal age and sex distribution would have done.

127

had the most Burma-born, with less than one quarter of the Indian population born in India, whereas in the rest of Burma this figure was slightly over 72 per cent.[149]

By 1931 over half of the population of Rangoon, the commercial and administrative capital, was Indian;[150] it seemed more an Indian city than a Burmese or South East Asian city.[151] The population remained in great flux into the 1930s. Having grown rapidly from a small port during the colonial period, Rangoon never became a settled city during the colonial period, and as late as 1931 only 35 per cent of the population had been born there.[152]

There was almost an inverse relationship between the size of the various ethnic groups and their hold on political and economic power during the late colonial period. The inclusion of the Burma colonial state in the British-Indian empire was the cause of this. Because it entered Burma in the form and personnel of the government of India, the colonial state relied heavily not only on British but also on Indian and Anglo-Indian personnel. Also, the early economic development of British Burma, except for agriculture, was chiefly undertaken with Indian labour, with British and Indian capital, and with a smaller proportion of Chinese finance.[153] (Table 2.1. sets forth in gross terms the possession of political and economic power in pre-war Burma; it gives the population of Burma at the 1931 census by ethnic classification and should be read from the bottom up.) The five non-indigenous groups, or key elements of them, despite being a small proportion of the total population dominated external trade, all banking except for petty finance, and police and military and the judicial system. The Europeans, mainly the British, with their closely allied groups, the Anglo-Indians and the Anglo-Burmese, dominated the legal, military, police and administrative positions. From a small proportion of the Indian population and a large proportion of the Chinese population came the groups that tended to dominate internal banking, trade and land ownership. The Europeans and Indians shared the external trade of Burma to the almost total exclusion of other groups. The ownership of industrial, min-

149   *Report on Indian Immigration*, p. 16.
150   Chakravarti, *Indian Minority*, table 2.4, p. 19.
151   B.R. Pearn, *History of Rangoon* (Rangoon: A.B.M. Press, 1939).
152   *Report on Indian Immigration*, p. 22.
153   D.G.E. Hall, *History of South East Asia* (London: Macmillan, 3rd edn., 1968), p. 786.

ing, timber, refining, and other modern industrial operations was shared, albeit unequally, by the Indian and European groups. The bulk of the labour in these modern concerns and in internal and external transport was Indian. The key positions in both the administration and the economy of pre-war Burma were held by non-Burmese.

While the Burmans—meaning the majority of residents of the delta and central plains—and other indigenous peoples were at a disadvantage relative to the alien groups in political and economic terms, they were not powerless. Members of the Burman and other indigenous groups, especially the Mon and Karen, were traders and moneylenders, landowners, lawyers and other professionals, and held important positions in the administration and police. More important, however, for the power of the Burmese 'middle class' politicians was the inability of the alien groups to govern and trade without the compliance, if not the support, of the indigenous population.

In a multi-ethnic society such as colonial Burma, the *lingua franca* was the language of the dominant group. Knowledge of English was a key determinant of one's status in society and place in the economy. It was also crucial for contacts in trade and politics outside Burma. The relative positions of the various ethnic groups can be further gauged by examination of levels of literacy in English. Europeans, Anglo-Indians and Anglo-Burmans, along with other tiny minorities, were the most literate groups in English. With over 43 per cent of the males and 71 per cent of females literate in English, these groups, most closely tied in culture and sentiment as well as economic interests with Britain, far surpassed the next most literate group, Indians other than Hindus and Muslims. This group, probably mainly Christians, was also closely tied with the European group. Within the larger population groups, Indian Hindus were the most literate in English, followed by

2.1.   Population of Burma by Ethnicity, 1931

Ethnic categories	
Indigenous[a]	12,680,052
Indian	1,017,825
Chinese	193,589
Indo-Burman	182,166
European and Anglo-Indian	30,851
Others	3,039
Total	14,647,756

(*a*) Burma group 9,267,196; Mon 336,728; Karen 1,367,673; others 1,888,455.

Source: Government of Burma, *Burma Handbook* (Simla: Government of India Press, 1944), Table A, p. 6.

the Chinese population and Indian Muslims. The Burmans and other indigenous peoples were the least literate in English, neither group achieving the national average of 1.9 per cent literate in English. In absolute terms, however, the Burmese had the largest number literate in English of any group in the country.[154]

The relationship between class and ethnicity in gross terms is further demonstrated by examining the occupational structure of Burma towards the end of the colonial period. Table 2.2 gives the participation of ethnic groups in different categories of employment. The Burman and other indigenous groups made up over 87 per cent of the total work force. However, only in agriculture for the other indigenous peoples, and only in agriculture, industry, trade and the professional and liberal arts for Burmans, did they match or exceed their proportion of the total labour force. If the professional and liberal arts categories are used in the Western sense of the term, then Burmans and other indigenous people's percentages are inflated, as the classification includes pongyi and other members of religious orders. The table shows the size of the alien hold on the modern sectors of the state and economy. Only in farming, industry, trade, public administration, and the professional and liberal arts did all the indigenous people combined have more than half of the positions in the country. Even in these occupations, the hold of the indigenous people was weakening and their relative economic standing declining during the period between the First and the Second World War.

Other gross indicators of class and ethnicity in pre-war Burma's social structure are found in the figures for the payment of taxes on trade and commerce and the use of the port of Rangoon. These are useful as they show the strength of the various communities in the most modern and highly monetised sectors of the economy. Table 2.3 indicates the relative size of the European, Indian, Chinese and Burmese involvement in trade and commerce, especially as the table omits tax paid by non-Chettiar Indians paying income taxes outside Rangoon. These figures do not include tax on income derived from property and therefore probably underestimate Burmese earnings from rents, but for the same reason they probably also understate the earnings of Indian population, especially the Chettiars.[155] In any case, it is extraordinary that less than one per cent of the income tax

---

154   *Burma Handbook* (Simla: Government of India Press, 1944), table I, p. 12.

155   The Chettiars were a banking caste from Madras and will be discussed more fully in on pp.143-145.

2.2. Labour Force Participants by Ethnicity and Occupation, 1931

Occupations	Burmans	Other indigenous	Chinese	Indians born in Burma	Indians out of Burma	Indo-Burman	European	Anglo-Indian	Other
All	55.8	32.1	1.5	1.6	7.9	0.9	0.1	0.1	0.1
Agriculture & forestry	56.7	38.0	0.5	1.6	2.5	0.7	0.0	0.0	0.0
Mining	33.5	15.0	9.8	1.0	36.3	0.3	1.4	0.4	0.0
Industry	56.7	24.1	2.3	1.1	14.7	0.9	0.1	0.1	0.0
Transport	40.5	8.3	2.6	2.5	43.2	1.5	0.6	0.6	0.1
Trade	59.2	14.1	6.9	1.6	15.6	2.2	0.1	0.1	0.1
Military & Police	31.3	15.9	0.3	2.0	43.4	0.8	5.8	0.5	0.0
Public administration	37.4	25.5	1.3	2.3	26.6	1.9	0.8	1.7	0.1
Professional & liberal arts	67.1	24.8	0.7	0.8	4.4	0.8	0.5	0.6	0.1

Source: Adapted from Moshe Lissak, 'The Class Structure of Burma: Continuity and Change', *Journal of Southeast Asian Studies*, 1, 1 (March 1970) p. 61, who takes the table from Surider K. Mehta, 'The Labour Force of Urban Burma and Rangoon, 1953, A Comparative Study, (unpub. Ph.D. diss., University of Chicago, 1959), p. 52. Mehta has prepared the percentages from the table on p. 134 of the 1931 *Census of Burma*.

2.3.   Ethnicity and Income/Supertax Payment in Rangoon, 1931-2

Ethnic group	Total tax paid %
Burmese	0.52
Indians (non-Chettiar)	10.70
Chettiars (urban)	2.70
Chettiars (rural)	12.09
Chinese	3.49
Europeans	70.35
Others	0.23

Source: Appendix to Letter, R.G. McDowall, Reforms Secretary, Government of Burma, to D.T. Monteath, Assistant Under-Secretary of State, India Office, 16 Nov. 1933. BOF P&J(B) 15, part 1.

and supertax paid in Rangoon on commercial incomes was paid by Burmese, whereas Indians paid over 25 per cent and Europeans 70 per cent of these taxes.

The strength of Indian interests in the economy of Burma affected the position of the peasant and 'middle class' Burmese population more than did the interests of British and other traders and investors. In addition to mere size there were two other reasons for this state of affairs. First, Indians were more involved than the other foreigners in the daily operations of the economy. This was particularly true in the retail trade and the provision of rural credit, though some Chinese were also active in these sectors. In these and other economic spheres they were in direct competition with Burmese interests. Second, the largest European firms were rarely in competition with Burmese firms. The former were part of the international economy that was beyond the control of either Indians or Burmese. Even if Burma had at that time been politically sovereign like Siam, the European firms, like the multinational corporations and banks of the present day, would still have determined prices and conditions in those sectors of the international economy in which they operated, especially in the rice trade and the timber markets. The European-dominated world economy of the nineteenth and twentieth centuries set the overall conditions within which the Burmese and other Asian middle classes developed.

At this point it is appropriate to examine in greater detail the characteristics of the class formations that developed in Burma between the 1870s and the 1930s. Not only were they the creations of the colonial state, but several of them were major factors in the conflicts of the 1940s, 1950s and 1960s over dominance in the postcolonial state. The tiny but powerful top group of Europeans, mainly English and Scots, accounting for less than 0.002 per cent of the total population in 1931,[156] may be considered briefly. While the British had dominated the upper echelons of the colonial state from its formation, it was the intention of the imperial government after about 1920 that their positions in the civil service, military and police would ultimately be taken by Burmese. By the late 1930s, non-Europeans including non-Burmese had been admitted to positions at all levels in the civil service, and to a few lower-ranking military and police officerships, but not to any extent into the top management and direction of the largest financial, trade, timber, and mineral-extraction firms, like the exclusive British clubs of Rangoon, remained closed to the Burmese until the end of the colonial period.

Although the first non-official Europeans involved in the political and economic life of Burma during the nineteenth century were largely traders, during the twentieth century an increasingly large proportion came to be involved in the management of sizeable Western investments in banking, manufacturing, and especially mineral and timber extraction.[157] The total size of foreign investments in Burma tripled between the First and Second World Wars, chiefly because of interest that developed in the exploitation of petroleum, rubber and certain minerals, including wolfram (tungsten) and tin. These totalled nearly £40 million in value by the 1930s.[158] The three giants of Burma's oil industry were the Burmah Oil Company, the British Burma Petroleum Company, and Burma Shell, which between them controlled about 98 per cent of production. The biggest mining company was the Burma Corporation, Ltd., which was 'one of the largest silver and lead producers in the world' and which also mined zinc, iron ore, copper and nickel.[159] British firms dominated the export of teak and hardwoods,

---

156   Of the 30,851 Europeans, Anglo-Indians and Anglo-Burmese in Burma in 1931, only 7,819 had been born in Europe, the British Isles, Australasia and North America. Of that number, 6,426 had been born in the British Isles (*Indian Census, 1931, Burma*, pt. II, Imperial Table VI, Birth Place, pt. I). Of the British in Burma, almost 5,000 served in the army at non-commissioned officer rank or below, leaving less than 3,000 who could be considered members of the top group. Even if all the Anglo-Indians and Anglo-Burmese are included in the top group, along with the few Burmese in the élite civil service and other senior posts, the group cannot have numbered more than 31,000 to 32,000, less than 0.002 per cent of the total 1931 population of over 14.5 million.

157   Helmut G. Callis, *Foreign Capital in Southeast Asia* (New York: International Secretariat, Institute for Pacific Relations, 1942), p. 94.

158   Ibid., p. 89.

159   Letter, R.G. McDowell to D.T. Monteath, 16 Nov. 1933. BOF P&J(B) 1, pt. 1.

and the major timber companies also had sizeable interests in the rice trade, owning many of the largest rice mills; several also owned cement works, rubber estates, and oil refineries. These firms included the Bombay-Burma Trading Corporation, Steel Brothers, MacGregors, Foucar, and T.D. Finlay.[160] The total foreign investment in banking, trade and manufacturing in pre-war Burma was estimated at about £6,800,000, although if funds invested through Burma into neighbouring counties is excluded, the figure is probably nearer to £5,500,000. Of these investments, 75 per cent were considered to be in British hands.[161] The major banks operating in colonial Burma were British or Indian owned.[162] However, Indian investments, including loans to agriculturists, probably exceeded British and other Western investments before the Second World War.[163]

The new 'middle class'. Changes in the Burmese 'middle class' during the colonial period need to be analysed in order to highlight major aspects of social and political change during the period. From being essentially non-existent under the monarchical state, that class had emerged by the 1920s and 1930s into three analytically distinguishable groups: those involved in trade, commerce and industry; those involved in public administration,[164] the liberal professions and allied occupations; and those involved primarily in earning their living from land rents, money lending and the provision of

---

160   Callis, *Foreign Capital in Southeast Asia,* p. 91, provides an incomplete list.

161   Ibid., p. 92. It is not clear in Callis's estimate whether he has taken into consideration the level of Indian investment in British firms operating in Burma. It is safe to assume that 10 per cent of stock in most British firms in Burma was held by Indians. Chakravarti, *Indian Minority,* p. 92. Japanese assets in Burma immediately prior to the Second World War, including bank balances, did not exceed £150,000. They owned little real estate and most of their assets were trading capital. Telegram, Governor of Burma to Secretary of State for Burma, 12 Sept. 1941. BOF 286/40, p. 13.

162   *The Burma Gazette,* 26 March 1938, in BOF C67/46; Tun Wai, *Burma's Currency and Credit* (Bombay: Orient Longmans, rev. edn., 1962), p. 24.

163   Furnivall, *Colonial Policy and Practice,* p. 190. See also Harvey, *British Rule in Burma,* p. 68.

164   Cady, *History of Modern Burma,* p. 151, writes that 'the emerging Burmese bureaucracy constituted a new middle class (called *a-so-ya-min* or simply *min*) affiliated neither with the people generally nor with the British ruling group.' While it is quite correct to note that the indigenous government servants and, indeed, other members of the new middle class did live in a style separate from the bulk of the peasant population, it is misleading to conclude that their lives were divorced from the welfare and prosperity of the rest of society. The Burmese middle class was not a deracinated intelligentsia.

agricultural credit. As the middle class was a product of the colonial state and the economic forces it brought into being, its growth and strength was clearly a consequence of the new state structure. Unlike the evolution of the modern European state where the middle classes rose to challenge the authority of the absolute state, or India where the new middle class, although created by the colonial state, became powerful enough to take control of the state from the British, in Burma the middle class was the child of the state and remained ultimately dependent upon it.

While an in-depth study of the economic and class transformation of modern Burma has yet to be done, it seems apparent that the middle class evolved somewhat along the following lines. Former officials of the precolonial government often received appointments in the British administration or, because of their English education (usually at missionary schools), were taken into government employment. With their earnings, or perhaps with money borrowed from Indian moneylenders, they often went into business or invested in land. Through foreclosure on mortgages and further land speculation these families became wealthier and more powerful, and used their additional capital to send their sons to government schools and universities in India and England. After 1920 more of these students remained in Burma for their university education. It was from families with histories like this that the Burmese middle class emerged.

The 1931 census revealed that 557,248 individuals were involved in trade. Of that figure, 73.3 per cent were listed as indigenous, 17.3 per cent as Indian, and 9.4 per cent from other groups. Although the indigenous peoples made up over 85 per cent of the total population and 87 per cent of the total workforce, they held less than three-quarters of all positions in trade. Of the 10,914 persons engaged in larger businesses such as banking, insurance and import/export, Indians held 75.6 per cent of all positions.[165] In Rangoon in 1931, the indigenous population held only 13.2 per cent of all positions as traders and shop assistants.[166] As these figures indicate, what Burmese strength there was in the commercial sector of the economy was not in the more vigorous economy of the delta but in the more traditional economy further north.

---

165   Chakravarti, *Indian Minority*, p. 34; Taylor, 'Relationship between Burmese Social Classes and British-Indian Policy', table 8, p. 45.

166   In the remainder of the delta, excluding Rangoon, they held 52.6 per cent of all such positions. *Report on Indian Immigration*, p. 37.

The Indian middle class had the strongest hold on foreign trade of any group in Burma. Indian exporters '. . . handled the majority of commodities exported from Burma though mineral oil, minerals and rubber were important exceptions.'[167] Of an estimated total annual export trade before the Second World War of Rs. 4,800 lakhs, it is estimated that Rs. 2,500 lakhs were in Indian hands. By the early 1940s, Indian firms had increased their share of the import trade to an estimated 50 per cent.[168] Because Indian merchants as well as Europeans and Chinese traders had long secured control over Burma's foreign trade, the Burmese were unable to enter and compete to any large extent in this sector of the economy.[169]

Even though a majority of the traders in the internal market remained indigenous, their shops and holdings were smaller than those of many of their Indian competitors. As Chakravarti writes,

Indian participation in the local and domestic trade of Burma was ... very extensive. Indian shops, particularly grocery, departmental, food and drug stores, could be seen all over Burma in urban and rural areas. ... Most of the large shops in important centres of trade and in big cities such as Rangoon, Mandalay, Maymyo, Moulmein, Bassein, Pegu, and Akyab belonged to Indians and each and every district town, subdivisional town, and township centre contained several Indian shops. ... Indian hotels, restaurants, food centres, jewellery shops, and cinemas were fairly well distributed in all important cities and towns. Most of the traders also owned land and buildings at their places of business.[170]

In Rangoon, Indian merchants were the largest property owners. This was largely due to the fact that the money to pay for development of the city centres after 1852 was raised mainly from the sale of property, and Indians had been the principal buyers.[171] By the 1930s Indians paid over 55 per cent of all municipal taxes in Rangoon while the Burmese paid only 11 per cent, Europeans paid 15 per cent and all other groups paid

---

167   'India's Interests in Burma's Trade and Industry', by R. T. Stoneham, 24 Jan. 1944. BOF 60/44.

168   It was estimated that Burma's import trade amounted to Rs. 2,200 lakhs before the war; and of this figure 1,100 lakhs were controlled by Indian firms, ibid. Chakravarti conservatively estimates that Indian firms controlled 20 per cent of Burma's foreign trade before the war, *Indian Minority*, pp. 78-9.

169   Adas makes this point relative to the external rice trade, *Burma Delta*, p. 177, though it could be made for other commodities as well.

170   Chakravarti, *Indian Minority*, p. 79.

171   Ibid., p. 7.

18 per cent.[172] In the larger towns, including Rangoon, even much of the property owned by Burmese was under mortgage to Indian bankers and moneylenders.[173]

In the rural areas, Burmese ran most of the small shops but most of their imported goods had to come via Indian wholesalers. Besides these shops, there were commercial opportunities for Burmese as rice brokers and grain merchants. Their numbers greatly expanded with the rapid development of the delta rice economy from 1852 to the First World War, but later decreased because of the decline in the value of the rice trade and increased competition from Indians and other non-Burmese groups. Whereas there were 39,000 grain and pulse dealers in the delta in 1921, by 1931 there were fewer than 30,000 in all of Burma. While in 1921 82 per cent of these dealers were Burmese, by 1931, 77 per cent were Burmese.[174] As Adas notes, by the 1920s there was a struggle between Burmese and Indians for control of internal marketing and transport in the delta rice industry that was generally 'overshadowed by the rivalry ... in the rice processing industry and among dock laborers in Rangoon harbor'.[175] By the 1930s the same struggle had extended to a greater or less degree to the rest of central Burma.

The inability of the Burmese middle class to compete in the ownership and management of manufacturing and industrial concerns during the colonial period reveals a similar story. Of the 1,031 factories in Burma in 1939-40, Indians owned at least 303.[176] Indian firms owned mills and other factories in every major category of modern industry. Chakravarti estimates that the size of Indian investments in industry closely followed that of the British.[177] While Burmese owned a few more factories than did Indians, they were usually smaller, employed fewer workers, and were frequently capitalised by Indians. Similarly, Chinese industries were usually very small-scale operations. Two-thirds of the industrial concerns of prewar Burma were owned directly by non-Burmese. Of the 792 rice mills in Burma in 1940, 45 per cent were owned by Burmese, 24 per cent by Chi-

---

172   Riot Inquiry Committee, *Interim Report* (Rangoon: Government Printing and Stationery, 1938), p. 17; Chakravarti, *Indian Minority*, p. 91.

173   Especially Chettiars. N.C. Sen, *A Peep Into Burma Politics (1917-1941)* (Allahabad: Kitabistan, 1945), p. 71.

174   Adas, *Burma Delta*, pp. 176-7.

175   Ibid., p. 178.

176   Chakravarti, *Indian Minority*, p. 88.

177   Chakravarti contends that this is probably true for investment in mining, but this is doubtful.

2.4. Earners and Working Dependents by Ethnicity in Middle Class Positions, 1931

Occupation	Total	Burman	Other indigenous	Indigenous %	Indian	Indian %	Chinese	Indo-Burman	Europeans and Anglo-Burman	Others %
Trade	557,248	329,079	78,366	73.3	96,211	17.3	38,419	2,249	1,466	9.4
Public administration	44,867	17,003	11,003	63.4	12,822	30.8	572	869	1,441	5.8
Professional & liberal arts	198,890	133,890	49,386	91.9	10,418	5.2	1,490	1,594	2,268	2.9
Members of religious orders, etc.	128,280	89,257	36,945	97.9	156	1.5	128	156	156	0.6
Professional & liberal arts excluding members of religious orders	70,630	44,533	12,441	80.6	10,262	14.5	1,362	1,438	2,112	4.9
Private incomes	7,167	3,497	813	60.1	1,829	25.5	175	370	456	14.4

Source: Census of Burma, 1931

nese, 28 per cent by Indians, and only 4 per cent by Europeans. The few European-owned mills were by far the largest. Both internal and external transport were dominated by Indian and British firms or the state-owned railways. There were no Burmese-owned commercial banks and insurance companies in pre-war Burma. Most Burmese conducted such business with Indian banks and insurance companies that had branches in Burma [178] While Indians had substantial investment in British firms doing business in Burma—estimated, as noted above, at 10 per cent of total investment— there is no evidence of Burmese investment in British firms.

While the indigenous population clearly benefited less from the economic opportunities created by the colonial state than the Indian and European communities did, in public administration and the liberal professions they did somewhat better, and it was in this sector that the Burmese middle class had its greatest strength. Here Burmese predominated over Indians in total number but not in proportion to the country's total population. Table 2.4 shows the composition of this sector of the middle class. Of those in public administration, which in 1931 totalled about 45,000 persons, 63.4 per cent were indigenous, 30.8 were Indian and 5.8 per cent were members of other foreign groups. In the liberal arts and professional category, if the 128,280 members of religious orders or others primarily involved in religious activities are excluded, the indigenous peoples accounted for 80.6 per cent, Indians for 14.5 per cent and others for 4.9 per cent. [179]

Given the importance of the law in shaping the quality of the colonial state, the growth of the legal profession is an important indicator of social change. Of the 2,301 lawyers of all kinds in Burma in 1931, almost 77 per cent were indigenous, over 70 per cent being Burman. [180] Of the 20,658 persons employed in teaching (other than in religious institutions) about 56 per cent were Burman and 23 per cent were from other indigenous communities. Whereas the Burmans and other indigenous peoples held over 75

---

178   Chakravarti, *Indian Minority*, pp. 86-7.

179   If the Europeans and Anglo-Indians are excluded from the 'others' category, on the assumption that all of them were members of the top group, then the Chinese proportion of the public administration and professions category would be reduced to about half of the 'others' percentage noted here.

180   Over 2 per cent were Chinese, 14 per cent Indian (of whom almost 11 per cent were born outside Burma), 5 per cent Indo-Burman, slightly more than 1 per cent European, slightly less than 2 per cent Anglo-Burmese and 2 per cent from other groups. There were in addition to the lawyers, 2,148 lawyers' clerks, petition writers, etc., who presumably could have been distributed in much the same manner as the lawyers.

per cent of the posts in law and teaching, in medicine, a more financially secure profession, the Indian population held over half the positions in 1931. Almost 52 per cent of all doctors practising Western style medicine were Indians born outside Burma and almost 7 per cent were Indians born in Burma. Only about 20 per cent of doctors were Burman and another 5 per cent came from the other indigenous peoples.[181]

The third sector of the middle class was composed of those persons who owned agricultural land and provided credit for the cultivators. It had been the policy of the government of India from the time of the annexation to encourage cultivator ownership in Burma as the most desirable means of organising agriculture and creating a stable and peaceful society. Both utilitarian principles and the pre-British agricultural system convinced the government that it should protect and promote the interests of the small-holder.[182] The importance of continuing this policy was noted by the Land and Agriculture Committee in its reports in 1938-40, which held that the 'ownership of land by the small agriculturalists [was] the best suited to Burma and [the] one which [would] make for social and political stability since it [would] rest on the foundations of comfortable, contented and independent peasantry'.[183] The Land and Agriculture Committee further felt that land should be owned by permanent residents who had 'a direct interest in the maintenance of law and order and in the stability of national institutions'.[184]

By the 1930s these principles bore little relation to the reality of Burma's rural economy, especially in the delta, where there had gradually developed a class of landlords who invested in land for profit and rented their land to tenants. As early as 1880, settlement reports in Bassein and Henzada noted the passage of land into the hands of moneylenders and the trading class.[185] By the 1930s non-agriculturalists owned over half the agricultural land in the principal rice growing districts of deltic Burma.[186]

---

181   *Census of Burma, 1931,* p. 139.

182   Adas, *Burma Delta,* pp. 32-4.

183   *Land and Agriculture Committee Report* (Rangoon: Government Printing and Stationery, 1939), pt. I, p. 2.

184   Ibid., pt. II, p. 1.

185   Ibid., pt. I, p. 37; Mya Sein, *Administration in Burma: Sir Charles Crosthwaite and the Consolidation of Burma* (Rangoon: Zabu Meitswa Pitaka Press, 1938), p. 104, who adds pleaders to the list of new landlords.

186   *Land and Agriculture Committee Report,* pt. I, p. 39.

The pre-war decline of the cultivator owners as a class in Burma was precipitous. In 1931 there were 39,000 male landlords (non-cultivating owners in census terms), whereas in 1921 there had been only 33,000 male landlords. Female non-cultivating owners decreased in this same decade from 41,000 to 31,000, but as most of these women were probably widows of previous cultivator-owners, what this indicates is not so much a reduction in the number of landlords as a decline in the number of small, family-owned farms. The number of cultivating owners fell from 2,569,000 in 1921 to 1,248,000 in 1931, a decrease of more than 50 per cent. This is evidence of the decline of the more prosperous and independent segments of the agrarian population and the rise in wealth of a small number of land-lords. The amount of land owned by non-agriculturalists in the principal rice-growing districts of the delta almost doubled between 1930 and 1938, which suggests that the number of cultivator-owners continued to fall rap-idly after the 1931 census when the full impact of the depression on the rice economy began to be felt.[187] For all of Burma, similar generalisations can be made. In 1926, of the 18,271,818 acres of cultivated land, 14,799,950 acres were owned by agriculturalists, 1,012,505 were owned by non-agri-culturalists who were residents of Burma, and 2,459,363 by non-residents. By 1937, of the 19,304,164 acres occupied, 12,862,874 acres were owned by agriculturalists, 1,465,164 acres by non-agriculturalists, and 4,976,869 acres by non-resident non-agriculturalists. Whereas land held by landlords domiciled in Burma increased by about 150,000 acres in this eleven-year period, landlords not domiciled in Burma increased their holdings by al-most 2,500,000 acres.[188]

A further indication of the decline of cultivator-ownership is the decrease in the percentage of cultivator-owners in the male agricultural workforce between 1921 and 1931. From the time of the British conquest, when almost all land was effectively held by cultivators, to 1921, the proportion of cultivating owners had dropped to nearly half the total workforce. In the next ten years the proportion dropped to fewer than 37 per 100, while in the same period the number of landless agricultural labourers increased by 13 per cent.

The basic cause of the decline of the cultivator-owner in pre-war Bur-ma—the class that both the British administrators and the Burmese politi-cal elite had looked to as the foundation on which to build a stable political

187 Ibid., pp. 37-8.
188 Ibid.

order and a healthy economy—was the nature of the rice industry, especially the system of financing the rice crop. As Furnivall wrote,

In the capitalist system the weakest go to the wall and their share in the output tends to fall down or below the level of subsistence. Burmans were in the position of the weakest. Not only were they confined to agriculture but over large tracts where economic progress was most rapid, the peasantry was transformed into a landless proletariat.[189]

These conditions developed in the twentieth century; before then conditions had been different.

From 1852 to about 1907, the Burmese cultivator in the delta received a good price for his surplus produce and was able to spend his money on a variety of new imported goods.[190] Few made enough profit to invest, and the consumption opportunities the new state introduced were apparently enjoyed. Many Burmese moved from the dry zone to the delta to develop new areas of rice production.

In the last half of the nineteenth century, it was possible for an individual beginning as a landless labourer to work his way upward until he eventually attained the status of large landholder. The number of persons who began as laborers and rose to become landlords was small, but large numbers of agriculturalists moved one to two notches up or down the social scale.[191]

During this period there was little competition between the Indians and Burmese as each group had its own functions, the Indians providing seasonal labour and some finance, with the Burmese doing the bulk of the work. When almost all available land in the delta had been brought into cultivation, the 'problems inherent in the nature of economic development in Lower Burma grew more intense and an era of apparent prosperity and content gave way to decades of conflict and unrest'.[192] In fact, the crisis in agriculture which was so apparent in the 1930s had begun in the first years of the twentieth century in some parts of the delta and spread slowly.[193] The depression merely accelerated the decline of the Burmese cultivator-owner that had begun much earlier.[194] The doctrine of legal equality provided

---

189   J. S. Furnivall, *An Introduction to the Political Economy of Burma*, (Rangoon: People's Litearature Committee and House, 3rd. ed. 1957), p. 3.

190   Adas, *Burma Delta*, pp. 74-6.

191   Ibid., p. 70.

192   Ibid., pp. 128-9.

193   Grantham, *Studies in the History of Tharrawaddy*, pp. 31-2.

194   Adas, *Burma Delta*, p. 153.

equal opportunity but provided none of the personal security of the precolonial state's economic order.

Much attention has been given in previous studies of rural Burma to the role of the Chettiars, because they were the single largest agrarian creditor group. The Chettiars were the most obvious targets for critics of the rural credit system because by 1938 they owned at least 25 per cent of the occupied land in the most important rice growing areas.[195] Before discussing the Chettiars, however, it is important also to note the role of other Burmese and Indian moneylenders.

In the first few decades after 1852, most agricultural credit required by delta cultivators was provided by friends, relatives, shopkeepers and indigenous moneylenders. In the earliest years friends and relatives were probably the most important source of rural credit. Many entrepreneurs who prospered combined the functions of shopkeeper, moneylender and rice trader.[196] By the 1880s, when Chettiars had also started to operate in the delta, large landowners and established cultivators took the place of friends and relatives.[197] Others who had been sources of rural credit and who, through foreclosures, became landlords were traders, speculators, lawyers, government clerks, merchants, retired village headmen, school teachers and doctors.[198] All were individuals who had an opportunity to take advantage of the relatively sudden monetisation of the economy following the establishment of the colonial state. At the turn of the century many British officials felt that these Burmese moneylenders were greedier land grabbers than the Indians.[199] 'Agrarian debt tended to be highest in the tracts near large towns where moneylenders, paddy brokers and other credit sources were more accessible, and where holdings were generally larger.'[200] Adas has written,

throughout the last half of the nineteenth century land was the most secure, profitable and frequently chosen investment outlet for persons who had accumulated capital through trade, in the professions or in government service. The steady rise in the price of paddy was paralleled by a similar increase in the value of land. Wealth,

---

195   *Land and Agriculture Committee Report*, pt. I, p. 37.

196   Adas, *Burma Delta*, pp. 64-5.

197   Ibid., p. 67.

198   Ibid., pp. 71-4.

199   Ibid., p. 119.

200   Ibid., pp. 68-9.

status and local influence were rewards earned by those individuals who were able to acquire substantial holdings of rich paddy land.[201]

The only areas of Burma where indigenous moneylenders were able to meet the domestic demand for agricultural credit in the 1920s and 1930s were in Akyab district.[202] This situation was principally due to U Rai Gyaw Thoo and Company, the only large Burmese money-lending firm. It also owned sizeable amounts of land in Akyab and was involved in other commercial activities.[203] The only European institution directly involved in the provision of rural credit was Dawson's Bank, which primarily made loans to larger Burmese cultivators so that they would not have to borrow from Indian sources.[204] Efforts by the government to form a cooperative credit system as an alternative source of loans were a failure.

In addition to these sources of rural credit, Indians other than Chettiars participated in the money lending professions.[205] However, between 1907 and 1942, although the majority of moneylenders remained Burmese, the greatest amount of capital for rural credit came from the Chettiars.[206] The Chettiars were a caste of bankers and moneylenders from Madras. Their original homes were in Chettinad but their banking operations spread throughout India and much of the rest of Eastern Asia.[207] While many of the people who supplied rural credit to the Burmese cultivators from the 1880s to the 1930s were interested in land speculation and investment, and were thus eager to foreclose on mortgages, the Chettiars, being essentially bankers, did not wish to tie up their capital in land. The fact that by 1938 the Chettiars owned 25 per cent of the cultivable land in the great rice growing areas of Burma was undesirable not only from the perspective of

---

201   Ibid., p. 74.

202   Tun Wai, *Burma's Currency and Credit*, p. 58.

203   Ibid., pp. 55-7.

204   Adas, *Burma Delta*, pp. 138-9; Tun Wai, *Burma's Currency and Credit*, pp. 71-2; letter, Mr. Laurence Dawson to Under Secretary of State for Burma, 22 Sept. 1942. BOF E4173/46.

205   Chakravarti, *Indian Minority*, p. 93.

206   Adas, *Burma Delta*, pp. 136-7.

207   For a fuller description of the Chettiars, see Adas, *Burma Delta*, *passim*; Adas, 'Immigrant Asians and the Economic Impact of the European Imperialism: The Role of the South Asian Chettiars in British Burma', *Journal of Asian Studies*, XXXIII, 3 (May 1974), pp. 385-401; Chakravarti, *Indian Minority*, pp. 56-69 and *passim*; Tun Wai, *Burma's Currency and Credit*, pp. 40-52; Usha Mahajani, *The Rise of the Indian Minorities in Burma and Malaya* (Bombay: Vora, 1960), pp. 16-21.

the Burmese agriculturalists and the British administrators, but also from the Chettiars' own viewpoint.

This situation resulted from the great strength of the Chettiars' banking system relative to the indigenous middle class; the former were able to charge lower rates of interest than other moneylenders and were considered honest even by their creditors.[208] Naturally, they were able to develop a larger clientele than moneylenders with higher interest rates and poorer reputations for probity. The security of their finances was due to their 'connections with Western banks and joint-stock companies, such as the Imperial Bank of India and the Indian Overseas Bank, which provided them with sources of working capital which were not readily available to Burmese brokers, merchants and moneylenders.'[209]

Initially the Chettiars had not tendered loans directly to the cultivators but had remained in Rangoon and other towns where they provided loans to indigenous moneylenders. From the 1880s onwards, however, they expanded their operations into the delta and undercut the interest rates of the indigenous moneylenders.[210] Thus, 'while there were more Burmese moneylenders at the end of the 19th century than Chettiars, the Chettiars provided most of the capital and even some of that for indigenous moneylenders.'[211] Beginning with the depression in rice prices of 1907 the rivalry between Chettiars and Burmese moneylenders increased, so that by the late 1930s few indigenous moneylenders were able to borrow from the Chettiars to finance their operations.[212] Following the great slump in rice prices in 1930, many Burmese cultivator owners were unable to meet their payments, and the Chettiars, partly because of the pressure exerted on them by the great banks of India, were compelled to foreclose. From 1930 to the Second World War the Chettiars did not attempt to expand their businesses further, but hoped merely to regain their capital and protect their investments.[213]

The sector of the middle class which owned the other half of the land not held by agriculturists in the delta were 'mainly indigenous moneylenders, rice

---

208   Chakravarti, *Indian Minority*, p. 65, who cites the Report of the Government of Burma's Banking Inquiry Committee, 1929.

209   Adas, *Burma Delta*, pp. 114-15.

210   Ibid., pp. 66-7.

211   Ibid., pp. 112-13.

212   Ibid., p. 175.

213   Chakravarti, *Indian Minority*, p. 58.

merchants, successful Burmese cultivators, urban investors, and Indian merchants other than Chettiars, just as they had been in the preceding period'.[214] While the indigenous/alien proportions of this half of the delta landlords is not known, it is likely that Burmese owned less than 50 per cent.

Workers and peasants. As within the middle class, the much larger working class was divided both ethnically between Indians and Burmese and occupationally in terms of the nature of their work and places of employment or income. Because of the way the economy developed under British rule, the alien sector of the working class was concentrated in industry while the indigenous peoples were concentrated in agriculture. By the 1920s, however, this ethnic division of roles was breaking down as tenant cultivators and cultivator owners were pushed off the land. Simultaneously with the growth of a larger class of Indian landlords, Indians were moving into agricultural occupations, accelerating the flight of Burmese labourers from the countryside to the cities. The heightened competition for jobs and land resulted in greatly increased communal tensions between alien and indigenous workers throughout the 1920s and 1930s. In 1931, 96 per cent of the 4,321,356 persons working in agriculture and forestry were indigenous, compared with only 48.5 per cent of the 39,505 workers in mining and 80.8 per cent of the 664,376 in all types of industrial employment. In the largest and most important industries, the proportion of Indians and other aliens was much higher than that of the indigenous groups.[215]

Within major industrial establishments, the total number of workers fluctuated during the year as more workers were taken on after harvests to process crops prior to marketing. In the larger industrial concerns Indian labour held an absolute majority of positions in all seasons and at each of

---

214   Adas, *Burma Delta*, pp. 188-9.
215   Table 2.2 (p. 131) includes all workers and earning dependants in its calculations. If only wage earners are used to calculate the percentage of indigenous and alien workers in the labour force, the indigenous percentage decreases. Of the 2,704,427 male earners in the 1931 census involved in agriculture, 93.4 per cent were indigenous. Among the 435,293 unskilled and semi-skilled male earners in industry, 47.4 per cent were indigenous (*Report on Indian Immigration*, p. 36). In Rangoon, Indians accounted for 88.5 per cent of all unskilled and semi-skilled labour and 56.1 per cent of all craftsmen. Male members of the indigenous groups accounted for only 8.8 per cent of the unskilled and semi-skilled labourers and 26.2 per cent of the craftsmen. Excluding Rangoon, in the delta in 1931 Indians held 56.3 per cent of the semi-skilled and unskilled male labouring jobs and 20.8 per cent of the craftsmen positions. Ibid., p. 37.

two levels of skill.[216] With the growth in size of the labour force between 1933-4 and 1938-9, the percentage of Burmese employed increased in every category, indicating the increasing competition between Burmese and Indian workers for industrial jobs.[217]

As noted earlier, in the 1870s and 1880s the government of India adopted policies to encourage the immigration of Indian labour to Burma. With the termination of these programmes, 'the recruitment of Indian labour for work in Burma naturally fell into the hands of two of the most unscrupulous types of people, namely the shipping agents of companies plying steamships between India and Burma, and the Indian labour contractors popularly known as *maistry*.'[218] The *maistry* were middlemen between the European and Indian employers and the labourers. They hired out gangs of workers recruited in India, and served as gang paymasters, foremen, and housing and transport agents.[219] In India the labour gangs were normally organised on the basis of family or village of origin, and when vacancies in a gang occurred, others of the same group normally filled them, thus making it difficult for indigenous people to gain employment.[220]

The port of Rangoon was the busiest in terms of immigration in the world after 1924.[221] Most of the Indian labourers stayed in Burma for only two to four years, depending on how fast they could save enough to buy their return fare and have a little left over for their efforts. Most of them would then remain in India for several months before returning to Burma for another two- to four-year stay. Despite the low wages these men earned, they were in most cases sufficiently greater than what they could earn in their native provinces to justify their travel to Burma and long separation from their families.[222] It is estimated that between 200,000 and 350,000 of the over one million Indians in Burma entered or left the country every year in the 1930s.[223] The consequences of this migration were not only

---

216   Ibid., table I, p. 62.

217   Ibid.

218   Chakrarvati, *Indian Minority*, p. 43.

219   The *maistry* system and its attendant evils have been described in detail in Chakravarti, *Indian Minority*, pp. 43-55. See also A. Narayan Rao, *Indian Labour in Burma* (Madras: Keshari, 1933) and E.J.L. Andrews, *Indian Labour in Rangoon* (London: Oxford University Press, 1933).

220   *Report on Indian Immigration*, p. 55.

221   Harvey, *British Rule in Burma*, p. 70.

222   *Report on Indian Immigration*, p. 13.

223   Chakravarti, *Indian Minority*, p. 21.

the creation of the plural society, but also a growing level of tension and conflict between the indigenous population and the migrant labourers. The antagonism between these groups publicly expressed itself in the form of race riots and pogroms, and its political repercussions were still being felt in the 1980s.

This chapter has attempted to show the consequences of the nineteenth-century rationalisation of the state by the colonial authorities on other institutions of Burma's society. Removing the fetters on economic growth that had been part of the political strength of the precolonial order made an arena of fierce economic and social competition in the twentieth century. The resulting conflicts were the product of this structure, and it is to this that we now turn.

3

POLITICS UNDER THE RATIONALISED
STATE, 1886-1942

Introduction

The development of the rationalised state under British colonial auspices led to the emergence of a complex of factors in the political life of Burma which, though in some ways new, nonetheless shared important qualities and concepts found in the early modern state. Altering the forms and enhancing the secondary functions of the state was relatively easy, given the strength of the British-Indian empire. Developing indigenous ideas and organisations to respond to and to take control of the state was more difficult. But the process was remarkably rapid, and within fifty years Burma had created the private and public institutions normally associated with the modern state, including political parties, mass movements, and ideological constructs containing a justification for state intervention in social and economic affairs.

The formal organisation of the colonial state is easy to recognise as it stands out against the background of the precolonial state and society upon which it was imposed. Consequently, the new state structures were often seen as more important and powerful than the old. Their novel qualities impressed both indigenous leaders and foreign observers throughout the twentieth century. But the new aspects of political life that developed in nineteenth century and twentieth centuries, and the responses from the public that these elicited, should not obscure the strength and consequent importance of the background.

Among the political issues of the colonial period, the historical relationship of the central state with economically marginal but strategically

149

important peripheral zones was one of the most important. But the power of the colonial order kept this question from coming to the top of the political agenda until the very end of the period, when external forces threatened to dislodge the British. More important, especially in the years between 1920 and 1940, was the core population's relationship with the central state. Different segments of the new class structure had to concern themselves with different aspects of this relationship. For the peasantry there were the persistent demands by the state to pay taxes and rent in the face of declining levels of relative income and security. For the middle class, and the political élite that emerged from it, the major questions hung on the degree to which cooperation with the British order had to be balanced against the long-term goal of regaining the independence of the state. For the creators of the colonial state and their bureaucratic successors, the problem hinged on the maintenance of the state's authority and the interests which it served within a political context which denied their legitimacy and often spurned their values as the creators of wealth and order. For the British, Indian and other foreign commercial interests that had been created under the colonial state the perpetuation, as cheaply as possible, of the existing order was paramount.

One factor that obviously distinguished the colonial state from its predecessor was the way in which its controllers sought to manage these issues. The limited development of bureaucratic and rationalised means of rule in the face of persistent local and patrimonial opposition to central extraction in the early modern system made the amassing of wealth and power more difficult for the monarchical state than for the colonial state. However, the greater physical power of the colonial state and its methods of operation, in the end, could not halt the development of both passive and active opposition to it. In this we see the development of new political forms and the re-emergence of old political forces. The institutions of the rationalised state did not replace the precolonial order instantly, and then only following a good deal of trial and error, while anti-state and anti-British forces developed gradually and were much conditioned by the internal and external environment in which they had to operate.

What was the nature of politics under the colonial state and what was its basis? Previous analysts of Burma's politics have generally argued that colonial politics centred largely on opposition to British colonialism, and among a significant proportion of the population of Burma, or at least central and southern Burma, this opposition took the form of nationalism.

In tandem with this grew the idea that the Burmese people were one nation which had the moral right to self-determination and self-government, and that it was therefore illegitimate for Burma to be ruled by an alien people from another nation. This strongly held, emotive, and now almost unquestionable argument, upon which the politics of the globe have came to be structured in the twentieth century, provides in vast, if vague, terms an explanation for the development of anti-British forces in Burma during the twentieth century, if not the nineteenth. But such an argument assumes many things about human motivation and action in a large and heterogeneous population in which individuals faced different challenges and opportunities as a result of the existence not only of the state, but also of their personal, class, religious and ethno-linguistic identity.

The development of the concept of the Burmese nation stems from a variety of factors, some old but reinterpreted in twentieth century terms, others new and the consequence of modern developments. The existence since the Bagan period of a history of Myanmar and a simplified lineage of kings, in addition to the strength and continuity of the precolonial state, provided a semi-mythical but also historically grounded claim that a state called Myanmar had long existed and was not therefore a colonial creation incapable of self-rule. The rapid homogenisation of the population of the more important economic zones of the Toungoo and Konbaung polities had created a strong, if not yet complete, notion of an ethnic identity with the precolonial state. The importance of the Buddhist religion in terms of both the state-centred and ethnically grounded notions of identity of the precolonial Myanmar people provided an additional cultural tie for the majority with the notion of the Myanmar nation.[1] The colonial state further strengthened these sentiments in both negative and positive ways. The colonial authorities' insistence upon racial distinctiveness gave ethnicity a greater centrality in political thought than it had previously had. The development of more rapid and easier means of travel and communication throughout southern and central Burma by new roads, railways and river steamers enhanced people's understanding of their common ties within Burma's territory. The growth of printing and publishing in Myanmar, coupled with the development of nationalist newspapers and Myanmar novels and modern poetry, strengthened a notion of common identity, as did the archaeologists' explanations of the state's past glories. All of these

---

1   Donald Eugene Smith, *Religion and Politics in Burma* (Princeton University Press, 1965), pp. 81-6.

came to provide a bond between the individual and those movements that claimed to speak for the Myanmar nation. The growing assertiveness of Myanmar nationhood, however, also enhanced the fears and apprehensions of those people, foreign and indigenous, who did not share these terms of identity.

In order to understand what the force of nationalism meant in colonial Burma, one needs to analyse further the factors which went together at different times to form the basis of nationalist movements. Despite references to the historical glories of classical Myanmar, few nationalist leaders believed in the feasibility of re-establishing the monarchical state. The king's state had been no more a nation state than the colonial state, and its virtues were seen as too few and its vices, much emphasised by the colonial rulers and conceded implicitly by Western educated Myanmars, to be too great for it to be held up as a viable ideal. More important, the colonial state's rationalised features and its justification of production and efficiency had, by the twentieth century, been accepted by a significant proportion of the middle class political leadership who sought to capture the state in the name of the Myanmar people.

The growth of the rationalised state also led to the development of what came to be called nationalism but had its roots less in the desire to capture the state than in a wish to evade it. Among large segments of the peasant population, resistance to the greater demands of the modern state and the economic and social dislocation it created for them began to develop. Peasants' perceptions of the consequences of the modern state led to the growth of a movement which did not intend to glorify the achievements of the nation state in order to seize it. Rather, their movement had, as its major purpose, the denial of the legitimacy of the demands of the modern state and all that it had created by its policies on taxation, regulation, economic enterprise and labour and capital mobility. Rejection or boycott of the state was the key to political action among many peasants. They saw the removal of the British as essentially the same as the removal of the modern state; for to them, the two were inseparable. If the cause of the modern state, the British, were removed, the modern state and all it had created would go with them, it was believed.

The manner in which these two wellsprings of opposition to the colonial state coalesced as the nationalist movement from their radically different premises provided much of the internal political dynamic of most the twentieth century. This, paradoxically, made it easier for the British to maintain their position until they were ousted by an invading Japanese army in 1942, but more difficult for an indigenous government to control the society subsequently. The nation state ideal called for the acquisition of state power, either by evolutionary, cooperative means or revolutionary, violent means, while the boycott approach called for rejection of the modern state by either passive or active means in the name of the nation, but also in the interests of local and personal privilege and identity. But the leaders of these movements, and their successors, were able to use to their advantage similar sets of ideas, grievances and symbols in the internal and external political argument that raged during the colonial period and after. The major issues they used included the role and nature of the Buddhist faith and its institutions, the concept of equity and justice for the indigenous population, and the place of foreign or alien capital and labour in the economy, as well as the place of the British in the management and control of the state. But the fundamental division between those who accepted the legitimacy of the purpose of the modern state and those who did not still runs through these arguments, and in large measure explains the absence, during much of the colonial period and after, of clear and concerted cooperation between the political élite and much of the peasant population.

The crux of the problem was, and remains, legitimacy, the legitimacy of the rationalised state and of the power of the elite that controls it. To those who accepted its utility in terms of its progressive, efficiency-oriented nature and the power thus created, and who viewed the life of the nation in terms of its external relations as well as the internal problems of social control, economic provision and elite status, the existence of the modern state in a world of similar states was justification for its power. For those more concerned with their own personal and local security and immediate prosperity, who thought primarily in terms of local issues and historical privileges, the state, or an anti-state movement, if it was to be supported, had to provide some rationale other than mere efficiency, productivity and national independence. It had to provide an aura of emotion, sentiment and personal bonding, an 'imagined community',[2] which a merely utilitarian movement or institution could not create. It was through the skilful use of these sentiments, unconsciously reinterpreted to provide support for a power seeking movement, that political leaders eventually developed a following among people whose utilitarian interest was to boycott the state.

---

2   See Benedict Anderson, *Imagined Communities: Reflections on the Origin and Spread of Nationalism* (London: Verso, 1983).

By making the power seeking nationalist movement more legitimate than British rule, the political élite was able to combine with the peasantry to wrest control from the British in the name of ideals and interests contrary to those of the peasantry. The political upheavals in Burma after independence, and the eventual bankruptcy of the state in 1988, were the legacy of the nationalist movement and the class conflicts it temporarily submerged in the name of nation state autonomy.[3]

Early responses to the colonial state

During the first sixty years of British rule, when the colonial state was small and incomplete, it made few demands on the people, perhaps even fewer than the precolonial state had done in some areas. It was then relatively easy for people to comply with the new rulers and even, in some cases, cooperate with them. Those disenchanted with conditions under the kings in the north migrated to the south to take advantage of the economic opportunities developed there, as well as escaping from corvée and military service obligations. The unwillingness of the colonial state to recognise or sanction patron-client ties provided an incentive for those wishing to avoid their traditional obligations. Even so, the symbols of the old order, and the identity they provided through the continued existence of the monarchy and the permanency of the Buddhist faith, meant that there was little lost in terms of personal identity when taking advantage of these new opportunities. Especially in the period between the first and second Anglo-Burmese wars, the weakness of the colonial administration and its peripheral relationship to the core of the monarch's domains posed few problems for the people who remained under or migrated to British rule. For those people who found life under the new order unacceptable, removal to the north was always an open option.

The establishment of British rule in Arakan and Tenasserim evoked little violent opposition after the surrender of the king's forces. There are a variety of reasons for this. Neither Rakhine nor Taninthayi had been well integrated administratively or ethnically into the precolonial order. Rakhine had been conquered by the Innwa state only in 1784 and resistance to the central state had persisted, including a significant rebellion in 1797, which created the immediate cause of the first Anglo-Burmese war. Taninthayi, too, was a peripheral region with a small population. The land had been

---

3   See R.H. Taylor, "Disaster or Release? J.S. Furnivall and the Bankrupcy of Burma", *Modern Asian Studies,* Vol 29, Part I (February 1995), ppp. 45-63.

fought over repeatedly by the kings of Myanmar and Siam and the people there seemed to take some consolation from the fact that, with the advent of British rule, they would be exempt from these enter-state rivalries.[4] Being marginal territories, both contained a significant proportion of people who had fled from one authority or another, who did not share either a religious or an ethnic identity with the monarchical state, and who had indeed little sense of loyalty to any state in the region.

Equally important in easing the way for the peaceful establishment of colonial rule in these two regions was the rapid agricultural and commercial expansion that took place. Within the first year of British rule in Tenasserim, rice production increased 34 per cent. The security that the British created allowed the cultivators to spread throughout the province and redevelop their fields.[5] Conditions were similar in Arakan, where the price of agricultural goods rose dramatically and imports of inexpensive British cloth meant that more could be purchased with the new currency in circulation.[6] The individualism and legal equality fostered by British rule, coupled with abandonment of the sumptuary laws of the precolonial state and the growth of wage labour and a money economy, made first Arakan and Tenasserim, and later all of British Burma, attractive areas for entrepreneurs seeking release from the constraints on consumption and investment that had maintained the precolonial state.

The rapid growth of population in these regions is indicative of their attractiveness. The population of Tenasserim grew by 50 per cent between 1835 and 1845 and by another 50 per cent between 1845 and 1852.[7] Lower Burma's population doubled in the first decade of British rule.[8] In the earliest years much of the population growth was due less to the migration of people from independent Myanmar to British territory than to migration from other regions elsewhere in South and South East Asia, as well as China. The land connection between Chittagong and Arakan and the existence of the same government on both sides of the border encouraged the

---

4 *Selected Correspondence of Letters from and Received in the Office of the Commissioner Tenasserim Division from the Years 1825-26 to 1843-44* (Rangoon: Government Printing and Stationery, Burma, 1928), pp. 3-4; John F. Cady, *A History of Modern Burma* (Ithaca: Cornell University Press, 1958), p. 80.

5 *Selected Correspondence Tenasserim Division*, pp. 51-2.

6 *Report on Progress of Arakan Under British Rule from 1826 to 1875* (Rangoon: Government Press, 1876), p. 47.

7 Cady, *History of Modern Burma*, p. 84.

8 Ibid., p. 94.

migration of Bengalis into the region. Early efforts to encourage Myanmar people to migrate in large numbers to Tenasserim were unsuccessful,[9] but the government brought in labourers from south India, including convicts, and encouraged the migration of Chinese from the west coast of Malaya. Both Tenasserim and Arakan soon took on the character of international trading centres and settlements (which they still have).

Particular segments of the population of Arakan and Tenasserim were keener to cooperate with the British than others. This cooperation is normally explained in terms of the ethnic antagonism that was claimed by the British to exist between the Burmans of the north and the Arakanese, Mon and Karen populations. Great emphasis is given, for example, to the cooperation that Mons and Karens gave to the British forces during the first Anglo-Burmese war; these groups, it is claimed,viewed the British as liberators from 'Burman' rule.[10] Many members of the Mon and Karen communities had not yet been fully integrated into the state structure of the precolonial order and therefore felt little if any sense of identity with the old state. Moreover, many Karens were not Buddhists and had been denied opportunities for advancement under the crown.

The British interpreted their behaviour in terms of ethnic antagonism, and thus set the pattern for subsequent foreign and indigenous interpretation. Particularly among the Sgaw Karen population there was a significant minority of individuals who turned to British officials and American Baptist missionaries for the opportunities they provided for a distinctive identity, and thereby developed an attachment to the new order. A notion of Karen identity separate from the precolonial state was encouraged by the missionaries, who had had little success in converting Buddhists to their cause, and by the British, who were seeking a pool of reliable recruits for state service. Many of the animist Karens thus gained not only a distinctive identity but also a distinctive religion, connected ideologically and personally with the growing power of the Western world in southern Burma. 'Thus, especially among the Sgaw Karens, Christianity and pro-British Karen nationalism developed hand in hand'; the first Western-style voluntary political organisation in Burma's history, the Karen National Association, was formed in 1881 by Karen Christians and their American mentors as a pressure group

9   Ibid., p. 82.
10   Ibid., p. 73.

'to promote a broader sense of unity among all Karen peoples and to provide spokesmen for them in political matters.'[11]

The ease with which British rule was established in Arakan and Tenasserim should not, however, obscure the point that there were individuals and groups who did oppose the new order. Although the independent state in the north could provide them with little support, the gentry in particular attempted to defend the privileges and power they had enjoyed before the British arrived. After the second Anglo-Burmese war the extent of their opposition grew, for the British annexed not a peripheral region but a nuclear area of the precolonial state which had provided new opportunities to officials and others from the core during the previous century.

The majority of the resistance leaders during the nineteenth century were former princes and officials of the precolonial state and their supporters, as well as Buddhist monks. It was the officials who suffered first. In Tenasserim, 'none of the higher Burmese officials were retained by the British administration'.[12] While the Commissioner, Mr Maingy, was confident that 'the lower and middling classes appear ... mild, obedient, inoffensive people', and were 'attached' to the British, he was worried about 'some desperate gangs of thieves' who belonged 'to the party of the late Ye Woon or Second Governor' who had been despatched from office.[13] From the start, the British government tended to see any opposition to their rule as acts of thieves and dacoits, rather than in terms of economic, political or personal grievances against the colonial state and its masters, and thus denied such acts any justification.

In Arakan, there appears to have been no initial opposition to the imposition of British rule; however, within a few years resistance developed, and in 1836 there was a serious rebellion: 'Disaffection centred in men of property and social standing under the traditional order who were being denied influence under the new regime.'[14] But the strength of such opposition was not great and the improving economic conditions of Arakan, like Tenasserim, apparently undermined the support that the followers of

---

11   Ibid., p. 99; J.W. Baldwin, 'The Karens in Burma', *Journal of the Royal Central Asian Society*, XXXVI (1949), pp. 102-13.

12   *Correspondence for the Years 1825-26 to 1842-43 in the Office of the Commissioner Tenasserim Division* (Rangoon: Government Printing and Stationery, Burma, 1929), p. 1.

13   *Selected Correspondence Tenasserim Division*, p. 23.

14   Cady, *History of Modern Burma*, p. 85.

deposed officials had previously given them. Others drifted back over the border into independent Myanmar.

Following the second Anglo-Burmese war, there was a period of widespread disorder, although it could not be defined as a national uprising. It took more than three years for the British to feel confident that order had been restored. Here also the heart of the leadership of the rebellion was provided by officials and gentry of the precolonial state, especially *taik-thu-gyi*, many of whom had only recently received their appointments from the throne and had not yet established hereditary claims to office. Where an established *myo-thu-gyi* acknowledged the new rulers, presumably upon a promise of their continuing in office, turmoil rarely resulted.[15]

Still, as late as the final years of the 1850s, there existed organised bands of men opposed to British rule, though not all of these were led by officials who had served the monarchical state. The fact that people whom the colonial authorities called Mons and Karens were involved in anti-British activities and refused to comply with the new order caused officials concern. The statement of the Commissioner of Pegu in 1858 that some rebellious Mons 'would not acknowledge being Mons'[16] says more about the British construction of ethnic categories in Burma than about the nature of the resistance. By the beginning of the 1860s, however, the British-Indian forces had established a reasonable degree of tranquillity. Less widespread opposition to the state from then until 1885 was labelled banditry and dacoity, and although the number of these acts continued to grow, they were dealt with by armed military police units. The ease with which this was done was due in part to the fact that people who had been influential under the old order had mostly been captured and removed from their areas of influence, or had fled north to live under the patronage of the court. By 1882 a British administrator could lament that 'not a single Burman could be found with interest, position, or influence' in the whole of his district.[17]

Following the annexation of northern Myanmar and the deposition of King Thibaw, the British faced more intensive and extensive opposition. Unlike the first two annexations, the British now directly assaulted the personal identities of the majority of the population by removing the central

15   Ibid., pp. 89-90; J.A. Mills, 'Burmese Peasant Response to British Provincial Rule 1852-1885', in D. B. Miller (ed.), *Peasants and Politics* (Melbourne: Edward Arnold, Australia, 1978), pp. 83-5.

16   Mills, 'Burmese Peasants Response', p. 84.

17   Ibid., p. 96.

pillar of the old state, the monarch, and denying the backing of the state to the institutions he had supported, in particular the Buddhist faith.[18] Disturbances first occurred in the core areas of the precolonial state, but eventually spread south as well. Rebellious activity was not suppressed in some areas of central and southern Burma until 1890. In the hill areas, however, some of which had already fallen out of the grip of the central state before the British arrived,[19] or had had only a tributary relationship with the king, the *pax Britannica* was not established for another five years. The extent of the resistance to the British and the intensity of feeling behind it might have been reduced had the Viceroy of India not decided to abolish the monarchy. This action made clear to the royalty, the old nobility and the monkhood that there would be no role for them in the future of the state, and they therefore felt they had little option but to resist.

Much of the initial opposition was led by princes who were able to organise substantial followings, some of up to a thousand or more men.[20] Their appeal for support was put in terms of the defence of the old order. For example, the Myinzaing Prince, in his call to arms, after noting his descent from the royal lineage and the power of his personage, issued a statement encapsulating their fears. It said in part,

the heretics, savage and lawless *Kalas* [originally referring to Indians, but generalised to include Europeans] have now entered Burma, and are destroying religious edifices, such as pagodas, monasteries, etc., held sacred by the people, the Buddhist Scriptures and the Priesthood. They have destroyed the accounts and records of royal ceremonies which were generally referred to by the Kings of old. And these *Kalas* are using in the profane way the white umbrellas and other insignia which belong only to royalty.[21]

Others whose claim to princely status was doubtful, including one who previously had served as a vaccinator under the British, raised the standard of royalty to rally support against the invaders, perhaps hoping to emulate the founding of the Konbaung dynasty by Alaungpaya.[22] Though a few of the former officials of the court at Mandalay did join with some of the

---

18   Ni Ni Myint, *Burma's Struggle Against British Imperialism (1885-1895)* (Rangoon: The Universities Press, 1983), p. 156.

19   Ibid., p. 15.

20   Ibid., pp. 45-51. Profiles of some of these leaders are given in ibid., app. G, pp. 198-201.

21   Ibid., app. E, p. 194.

22   Ibid., pp. 53-4.

THE STATE IN MYANMAR

princes in rebellion, most stayed on to serve the state's new masters. As they were good bureaucrats (servants of the state, not the ruler) 'the replacement of King Thibaw by the British at Mandalay became for them only a change of master'.[23] One of the princes even cooperated with the British, perhaps in the hope of receiving the nominal throne for himself, and helped induce 'the bulk of the *Wuns* and *Myothugyis* in some areas not occupied directly by the British officers to carry on as officials of the new regime or to yield their places to successors appointed by Mandalay'.[24]

Although the British were able to enlist the cooperation of the head of the Buddhist order, the *thathanabaing*, who had served King Thibaw, to assist in maintaining order in both secular and religious affairs,[25] some of the resistance was led by monks. This happened mainly in southern Burma where monks had been outside the control of the central ecclesiastical organisation since 1852.[26] Many of the leaders of the smaller rebel bands were headmen and other local officials of the precolonial state. Dacoit leaders also joined the conflict with the new state, though whether this demonstrated 'a nobility of aspiration' rather than a desire to make a profit in the ensuing disorder is arguable.[27]

Though the extent of the opposition was great, requiring in the words of the Commissioner of British Burma 'the military occupation of a hostile country',[28] the lack of unity and cooperation among the rebel leaders eased the task of the British-Indian forces. 'Every village was a little republic', and without a single leader to rally these forces to a united purpose, 'Burma as a nation was broken up'.[29] This, at least, is the explanation given by twentieth century Burmese writers. But the possibility of routing the British from the country, given adequate organisation and leadership, did exist, because a little over a year after the annexation the British had to organise

---

23   Ibid., p. 58.
24   Cady, *History of Modern Burma*, p. 127; see also Ni Ni Myint, *Burma's Struggle*, p. 95.
25   Ni Ni Myint, *Burma's Struggle*, p. 97.
26   Ibid., pp. 75-7 and app. G, pp. 209-11.
27   Ibid., pp. 58-61, 77; app. G, pp. 205-8; app. H, pp. 218-21, lists a total of 71 prominent resistance leaders; see also Cady, *History of Modern Burma*, p. 134.
28   Quoted in Ni Ni Myint, *Burma's Struggle*, p. 66.
29   Lei Maung, *Myanmar Naingnanyei Thamaing* (History of Myanmar's Politics) (Rangoon: Sapei Biman, 1974), vol. 1, p. 1; Maung Maung, *Burma and General Ne Win* (New York: Asia Publishing House, 1960), p. 2.

a force of 40,500 men to restore order.[30] The advantages the British had over their opponents were not only in manpower, organisation and weapons. They also developed an effective strategy 'aimed at close occupation of the country', quelling unrest with military force, followed quickly by the imposition of civilian administration backed by the military police.[31] The commencement soon afterwards of major public works projects, especially the extension of the railways from southern to northern Burma, provided new opportunities for paid employment which further undermined the appeal of the disparate rebel leaders and helped end the uprisings.[32]

It took another five years for the British to 'pacify' the surrounding hill areas, for there it was more difficult to find figures willing to be placed in authority over the people, except in the Shan States.[33] Most of the resistance in the Chin and Kachin hills, except for that led by the Wuntho Sawbwa, was organised by local leaders who had had few if any relations with the former state other than through the payment of tribute. The British were able to get many of these leaders to accept their authority in exchange for a promise not to interfere with local customs and the chiefs' taxing powers over their subjects.[34] Where the chiefs were unwilling to obey the colonial authority, the British exacted retribution with punitive raids that met little resistance because of an inability 'to overcome local and sectional interests and mobilise wider loyalties'.[35] During much of the British period, the writ of the central state in the more remote areas amounted to little more than periodic 'flag marches' in which the symbol of state supremacy was displayed and the promise of punishment for unruly behaviour was made.

But the heart of the precolonial state's territories was now firmly under the control of the new rulers, and the local inhabitants increasingly turned their attention away from attempting to resist the foreign rulers and more towards taking advantage of the new opportunities being created. The migration of increasing numbers of people from the north to the expanding rice economy in the delta relieved political pressure on the new state as energies became concentrated on economic activities.[36] The massive human

30   Cady, *History of Modern Burma*, p. 134.
31   Ni Ni Myint, *Burma's Struggle*, p. 86.
32   Ibid., pp. 101-2.
33   Ibid., chs. 5, 6, and 7; app. G, pp. 211-17.
34   Ibid., p. 135.
35   Ibid., p. 137.
36   Michael Adas, *The Burma Delta: Economic Development and Social Change on*

endeavour that went into building of new railways, roads, irrigation canals and bunds, and clearing of the delta swamps for the rice industry, partially explains the air of political social quiet that settled over Burma for a generation after 1890.

The absence of effective and trusted leadership was another important factor. The British had removed the old elite from the central state and exiled the king and his immediate family while pensioning off other members of the nobility and court officialdom. Those *myo-thu-gyi* and other gentry who had not rebelled against the British were absorbed into the new administration and were busy learning their altered tasks. The destruction of the old township system weakened the social and political bonds of communities larger than the village. However, underneath this outward calm, forces were at work that would begin to erase the feelings of remorse, resentment and helplessness that the older generation of Burmese felt in the 1890s and the early twentieth century.[37] The economic transformation of the country was creating the new class and ethnic structures discussed in the previous chapter, and this would unleash massive peasant protests in the 1920s and 1930s, at first passive, later active. Yet, as there were still plenty of opportunities, the ethnic competition for jobs and land that was to become politically serious in the 1930s was not yet seen as a major problem.

Nonetheless, the growing prosperity of the people and their release from the constraints of the past were leading to new forms of social behaviour that threatened to remake Burmese culture and society. Established conservative interests, in particular the Buddhist monkhood, looked with displeasure upon these change. Moreover, that many of these consequences of these changes resulted in growing domination of the economy by foreign capital and labour came to be increasingly understood by much of the population, especially those in the towns and cities where the impact of colonialism was most immediate. But in the villages, too, the intrusion of the state's new institutions, laws and police was felt, and resistance to the violation of accepted norms of fairness and order was developing a political form. Except perhaps for those tied most closely to the state, for the majority of Burmese at the beginning of the twentieth century there were aspects of change that were felt to be immoral and unfair, and while differ-

---

an *Asian Rice Frontier, 1852-1941* (Madison: University of Wisconsin Press, 1974), pp. 41-3.

37   Maung Maung, *From Sangha to Laity, Nationalist Movements of Burma, 1920-1940* (New Delhi: Manohar, Australian National University Monographs on South Asia no. 4, 1980), p. xvi.

ent individuals and groups could not always agree on what these were, they could all agree that there was one cause: British imperial rule. But what was to be done about it?

In contrast to Vietnam, where in Confucianism the culture provided a state-centred and essentially secular philosophy which could be used—or so it was believed for a time—to find a solution to the colonial dilemma,[38] Burmese culture, and in particular Buddhism, provided no answer to the plight of the old élite nor the population at large. The challenge posed to Buddhist beliefs and institutions by the utilitarian ethic of the modern state and the international organisational power of Christian missionaries forced educated Burmese to rethink the basis of social and political action in terms appropriate to their transformed world. The institutions of the modern state and of modern Christianity, including elected leaders, committees, formal resolutions and voluntary membership, came to be seen as necessary instruments to be used to resist colonial rule. It was more than just the name that the founders of Burma's first large voluntary organisation, the Young Men's Buddhist Association (YMBA), adopted from the Young Men's Christian Association (YMCA). In fact, this was the least important, for the name of the organisation in Burmese, *Budda Batha Kalyana Yuwa Athin*—literally, the Association to Take Tender Care of the Wholesomeness of Buddhism—shared little with the YMCA. Rather, it was the Christian body's organisational form, use of printing and propaganda, and efforts at mass education that were crucial to the development of a Myanmar nationalism organisation.[39]

But first a new élite, aware of these models and lessons, had to rise from the ruins of the old order via the institutions created by the new state. The first outward evidence of the changes experienced and the lessons learned between 1885 and the first years of the twentieth century was the emergence of a new political élite that claimed to speak for Myanmar nationalism and was accepted as its voice by the British.

The emergence of the middle class political elite

The new urban-based political elite which emerged with the development of the colonial state was the product of and the spokesmen for the small

---

38   See David G. Marr, *Vietnamese Anti-Colonialism, 1885-1925* (Berkeley: University of California Press, 1971).

39   See the general comments of S.J. Tambiah, *World Conqueror and World Renouncer* (Cambridge University Press, 1976), p. 213 on this point.

and increasingly financially insecure Burmese middle class. Much of its behaviour can be explained in terms of an attempt to defend that class' position in society by taking advantage of the political opportunities provided by the British-Indian policy of increasing the role of liberal democratic institutions within the colonial state. The new political élite saw itself as having a responsibility for protecting and enhancing the middle class' political and economic power by creating conditions that would ensure that the state they would inherit from the British would guarantee the perpetuation of their class and its guarantees for liberal capitalism.

However, forces in society which predated the rationalised state and looked less favourably on its social and economic consequences were also emerging, and taking advantage of what opportunities they could to organise resistance not only to the British but to the modern state itself. Many of their grievances were, in fact, the result not so much of British rule but of the notion of the rationalised state, whoever managed it, which was taking on responsibilities and enforcing rules that ran contrary to their interests, historical privileges and status. Especially important among these groups were the peasantry, the largest sector of the population, and the Buddhist monkhood, whose role in society was being undermined by the educational, judicial, administrative and economic policies and general secular orientation of the state.

Towards the end of the colonial period another force, students and other youth, rose to challenge for the leadership of political life. These young men and women were disillusioned with what they regarded as the political elite's collaboration with the colonial power and were strengthened in their beliefs by new ideological constructs, especially the revolutionary rhetoric of Marxism-Leninism. But by then the middle class elite was near to taking control of the state, and was only stopped by foreign invasion in 1942. The politics of the end of the colonial period were thus dominated by rivalry between the youth, who attempted to champion some of the interests of the peasantry, and the established middle class political elite.

The membership of the political elite changed little throughout its rise to prominence. Many people who were founders of the first political organisations in the 1900s and 1910s were ministers and senior officials in the 1930s and 1940s. The first widespread organisation, the YMBA, formed the basis of many of the political parties of the 1920s, although its initial concerns were formally limited to cultural and religious questions. It was led by students and most of its membership was composed of young government officials and clerks,[40] all products of the new state. For example, the organisers of the YMBA's first nominally political act, the protest over the wearing of shoes by Europeans in the precincts of Buddhist pagodas, were all among the top leaders of a political party in 1942.[41] The YMBA's successor, the General Council of Burmese Associations (*Myanmar Athin Chohkyi* or *GCBA*), which was organised for more explicitly political and nationalist ends, was led by many of the same middle class lawyers, businessmen, landowners and journalists.[42]

The new legal profession developed by the needs of the colonial state provided a natural recruiting ground for the political élite. Indeed, in the early 1920s it seemed that politics in Burma was the 'monopoly of barristers'.[43] This situation changed very little during the succeeding twenty years. Lawyers, who by training possess the bureaucratic, verbal and drafting skills necessary for party leadership, lacked the financial security of doctors, large landowners, and contractors. Burmese lawyers even lacked the financial security of Indian lawyers,[44] but they mainly worked in Rangoon, the centre of political life, and this gave them time for political activities. Because of their financially insecure positions, however, the party leaders often had to rely on others for financial support, for personal as well as political reasons. This made them especially vulnerable to outside financial manipulation, particularly by Indian financiers.

There were wealthy Burmese involved in colonial politics, but for the most part they tended to keep their money for use at the local level. At least until the late 1930s, relatively little flowed to Rangoon for the use of politicians and parties at that level. One reason for this was that local leaders

40   Maung Maung, *Burma and General Ne Win*, p. 4.

41   Ibid., p. 6; for a fuller discussion, see Smith, *Religion and Politics*, pp. 86-92.

42   Maung Maung, *Burma and General Ne Win*, pp. 8-9.

43   Maung Maung, *Burma's Constitution* (The Hague: Martinus Nijhoff, 2nd edn., 1956), p. 11. Of the 75 Burmese and Indian members of the 1932 Legislative Council, 33 were lawyers. The next largest group were businessmen who held 18 seats, and landowners with 12. Seven members were teachers or former government officials, or employees of foreign firms, and of the remainder, one was an engineer, who was Chinese, one was a contractor, one a doctor, one a cultivator, and some for whom no occupational identification is known. Take from 'Brief Notes on the Status and Political Leanings of Member Elected to the Burma Legislative Council', G.B.C.P.O. no 387, Judl. Secy., 4 April 1933, BOF P&J(B) 1.

44   G. E. Harvey, *British Rule in Burma 1824-1942* (London: Faber and Faber, 1946), p. 36.

often felt those involved in Rangoon politics did not need or deserve their financial support since they were in the capital, the centre of government, and thus able to live off the state as officials had under the Burmese monarchy.[45] The necessity of financing parties that were not part of the government was generally recognised as an obligation of local leaders. There certainly was no tradition under the precolonial state of individuals giving financial support to aspiring officials, at least willingly.

Related to this was the fact that political parties were very new to Burma. National organisation was slow to develop, for although spontaneous support for a leader was easy to arouse, it was difficult to sustain a political body through the payment of membership fees and the like. The need for individuals to protect their local interests often appeared paramount, especially in the uncertain political and economic conditions of the late 1920s and 1930s. Besides, with the relatively limited powers of the few ministers under the dyarchy system until 1937, and the domination of local government bodies by civil servants, there were few concrete financial or political rewards that national leaders could give local supporters. Indeed, some members of the provincial middle class had achieved their wealth through the existing autocratic administrative system with its opportunities for corruption and the hoodwinking of uninformed and transient British and Indian administrators. Some did not wish to see the system change in favour of a new political elite, which they did not know and might not be able to control if it gained state power. A review of the nature of local leadership in the colonial period may shed more light on some of these points and give a better sense of the kind of political order the colonial state had created.

The elected and appointed membership of the town and city governing bodies, the municipal committees, provides one indication of the nature of local leaders in urban Burma. Of the 828 such persons for whom occupational data are available for April 1937, business people were the largest group among all the major ethnic communities. Among the Burmese, people in business or owners of real property held slightly over half the posts.[46] Another way to understand the nature of the colonial middle class

---

45   For example, Sir J.A. Maung Gyi, a leading politician of the 1920s and in the 1930s acting Governor, became know as the 'eater of 5,000 kyats' because of his position as a minister in the government, much as pre-British officials were known as *myosa*. Nyo Mya, 'Profile: Sir Joseph Augustus Maung Gyi', *The Guardian* (Rangoon) 2, 6 (April 1955), p. 11.

46   Robert H. Taylor, 'The Relationship Between Burmese Social Classes and British-Indian Policy on the Behaviour of the Burmese Political Elite, 1937-1942'

and its political leadership is to examine the pre-war political careers of people prominent in the 1950s. *Who's Who in Burma, 1961* includes 233 persons who had active careers in the 1930s. Their names are listed along with their fathers' occupations. Merchants and owners of real property account for 104 or 45 per cent of the fathers of these elite individuals. The elite's growing dependence upon the state, however, is indicated by the fact that individuals whose fathers were government employees accounted for the largest single group of these leaders.[47]

While such data suggest something of the nature of the middle class leaders who were elected to public posts or had active careers in the 1930s (and were still influential in the 1950s), it does not give an individualised picture of who the influential people in the colonial period were. The last pre-war Deputy Commissioner of Amherst District prepared a list of twelve important people in his jurisdiction for use by the reoccupying Intelligence section of the British army after the war. While Amherst was not a representative district, being in Tenasserim rather than the delta or central Burma, his list and description of these people gives an insight into the nature of local leadership under the late colonial state.[48]

The first on the list was the member of the House of Representatives from Moulmein North, U Ohn Pe. He was described as 'one of the wealthiest and most influential Burmans of the District. Landowner, millowner, and owner of the Moulmein Electric Supply.' His brother was the prominent Rangoon civic leader Sir U Thwin, a member of the Senate and former head of the Burmese Chamber of Commerce. U Ohn Pe was 'reasonably cooperative with Government, but kept in with both sides and had friendly contacts with some of the leading *Thakins*',[49] the most radical anti-British youths of the period. U Po Lun, the business manager of the Moulmein

---

(PhD, Cornell University, 1974), table 21, p. 155.

47   *Who's Who in Burma, 1961* (Rangoon: People's Literature Committee, 1962), tabulated in Taylor, 'Relationship Between Burmese Social Classes and British-Indian Policy', table 22, p. 157.

48   'List of Influential Persons in Amherst District' by W.I.J. Wallace, 19 October 1943. (Wallace Papers in the Indian Office Library and Archives, London).

49   *Thakin* was the title taken from the early 1930s by nationalists who wished to assert that they—rather than the British, who were normally addressed as '*Thakin*', like '*Sahib*' in India—were the 'master's of Burma, for this is what the word literally means. The term had been used to refer to officials of the king under the monarchy. The movement, and the implications of its name, will be discussed below.

Electric Supply Company, was the second person on the list, but he was not known to be interested in politics.

The third person was Thakin Maung Gyi, an engineer at the Moulmein Electric Supply Company. He had been to England and had an English wife. Although an active nationalist in the early 1930s, he later lost interest. U Toe Lon, the fourth person, was influential because of his wealth and standing as a timber merchant. He was very conservative, the Deputy Commissioner believed. Another influential older person was U Maung Nge, a Senator and wealthy landowner. Two persons of Sino-Mon descent were on the list; one was a large landowner and other ran the Modum Motor Bus Association. Also listed was the President of the Moulmein municipal government, a Muslim lawyer, who had been born in Moulmein. The next three men listed were headmen who were also substantial landowners. The last man was the Township Officer of Chaungzon who 'had the support of the influential and wealthy Burmans, including U Ohn Pe of Moulmein, who were interested in seeing law and order preserved under whatever Government'.

The type of local leader who expressed disdain for the Rangoon-based politicians and would have contributed nothing to support their political parties is described by C.J. Richards in *Burma Retrospect*.[50] In his account of U Kyan Aung, Richards, who was a former Deputy Commissioner, provides a description of one of the routes to local power and wealth in Burma in the 1920s and 1930s, if not earlier. Kyan Aung began by gaining the post of Revenue Surveyor, a 'badly paid and generally overworked' position which had ample opportunities for graft and corruption. A Revenue Surveyor was 'the first link in the administrative chain responsible for amassing something like one-third of the total Provincial Revenue of Burma'. Kyan Aung was responsible for assessing the tax that had to be paid on a cultivator's crop, obviously a position offering opportunities for corruption or the application of unofficial coercion. In time his corrupt activities were discovered by his British supervisor, but he 'easily escaped prosecution for bribery' as no one could be found to testify against him; 'but Government discharged him for bad work'.

With his bribe money, plus twenty acres of land he had inherited from his parents, Kyan Aung 'proceeded methodically to add various other hold-

---

50   C.J. Richards, *Burma Retrospect and Other Essays* (Winchester, England: Herbert Curnow, The Cathedral Press, 1951), pp. 62-6, from which all the following quotations are taken.

ings, partly by purchase, partly by foreclosure of mortgage, on money acquired through his exactions'. By the late 1930s, when land prices had risen again after the slump of the early 1930s, 'Kyan Aung was owner and mortgagee of something like a thousand acres, valued at something up to two hundred rupees an acre, most of which he had acquired at about one-tenth their worth' He then expanded his activities by securing the 'leases of two neighbouring fisheries for a good deal less than they were worth, by the process of buying out intending competitors, before the auctions took place'. He made further profits from paddy trading, something his neighbours with fewer liquid assets were unable to do. Kyan Aung also bought a bus and began a passenger and freight service to the township headquarters where he started a general store.

Having made his fortune through bribery and speculation, Kyan Aung decided it was time to make his mark in the political world, perhaps in order to protect his little empire and further diversify its activities. He stood for the District Council and ran against two other candidates, 'an obscure lower-grade pleader and a landowner of nearly U Kyan Aung's prominence, and it was thought that between these two there would be a close finish'. Several weeks before the election the other landowner candidate was shot through the head and his murderer was never apprehended. Safely elected as a member of the Council, 'Kyan Aung had ample opportunities of graft among contractors and the like'. He was even tried for organising robberies and dacoities while serving on the District Council, but was acquitted. Doubtless blind justice could feel a rupee in the hand.

Despite his prominence, wealth and active political career at the local level, Kyan Aung expressed 'outspoken mistrust of advanced nationalism' of the type advocated by the national party leaders. 'Thus at a meeting of local celebrities, when a discussion of politics arose, U Kyan Aung remarked –"Personally I do not want Independence. I do not like the Law of the Jungle." There were some rather dark glances when he said this, but U Kyan Aung did not seem to notice them.' It would, of course, be a mistake to assume that most, or even a great many, local political leaders behaved in a manner similar to Kyan Aung. But it would be equally a mistake to assume that all local political bosses viewed the colonial state and the system it had created as an unmitigated evil to be got rid of at the earliest opportunity. Furthermore, Kyan Aung's behaviour as an official and an entrepreneur goes some way towards explaining the negative response of the peasantry to the state which gave him his chances and which could do little to protect them from his illegal actions.

However, before turning to an analysis of the villagers' response to the colonial state, it is necessary to examine further the nature of the political elite and its institutions. The careers of several of the leading national political figures during the 1920s and 1930s indicate the consequences of the nationalist parties' inability to draw funds from the local middle class to support their organisational activities. The career of U Chit Hlaing expresses this dilemma, perhaps more than that of any other major figures of the 1920s and 1930s.

Chit Hlaing was born in October 1879, in Amherst district, an area that had known British rule for fifty-four years. His grandfather was said to have been a head constable who on retirement set up as a timber merchant. The teak industry prospered in the early years of British rule through exports to India and the shipbuilding industry in Moulmein. His father continued in the timber business and diversified into money lending. With such a prosperous family behind him, Chit Hlaing was able to study in England from 1898 until 1902, and became a barrister.[51] Chit Hlaing rapidly dissipated his financial legacy in support of the activities of the GCBA,[52] and by April 1932 was hiding in Moulmein to avoid arrest for debt.[53] There is no questioning Chit Hlaing's political courage and dedication to the nationalist movement. In addition to using his own funds to support the nationalist cause, he was arrested for his beliefs on several occasions.[54] As a key figure in the early GCBA, serving as its chairman for several years and nearly

---

51 Burma List no. 32, History Sheet of U Chit Hlaing, appended to letter, Government of Burma to Government of India, 4 April 1931, BOF P&J(B) 1. See also Sein Myint, *Hnit 200 Myanma Naingngan Thamaing Abidan* (Dictionary of 200 Years of Myanmar History) (Yangon: Sapei Yathana, 1969), pp. 74-6. This volume is useful for providing potted careers of political leaders and has been consulted in the preparation of this chapter. Also, details of the careers of political leaders have been taken from various files in the Burma Office as well as the standard publications noted in the bibliography, especially those of John F. Cady and the two Maung Maungs.

52 Cady, *History of Modern Burma*, fn. 37, p. 367.

53 Appreciation of the Political Situation, by Sir C. Innes and T. Lister, 12 April 1932, BOF P&J(B) 1.

54 Burma List no. 32, History Sheet of Chit Hlaing; N.R. Chakravarti, *The Indian Minority in Burma: The Rise and Decline of an Immigrant Community* (London: Oxford University Press for the Institute of Race Relations, 1971), p. 110; Maurice Collis, *Into Hidden Burma* (London: Faber & Faber, 1953) pp. 163-164.

made president-for-life, he was widely regarded in rural areas as one of the leading Burmese national leaders. He was known as the uncrowned king of Burma, and women were said to lay their hair down as a carpet for him.

This towering figure of the 1920s, touring the country in the style of a prince and possessing independent means and contacts with both the Indian and Burmese nationalist movements, was in the 1930s closely tied to the financial interests of the Chettiars and several Indian firms, in particular the Scindia Steam Navigation Company, one of the major transporters of Indian labourers to and from Burma. Scindia's Rangoon agent, S.N. Haji, was notorious in the 1920s and 1930s for the use of funds to 'buy' Burmese politicians. Chit Hlaing's personal financial plight came simultaneously with the political controversy over the separation of Burma from India and his decision to participate in the colonial political system. When he attended talks in London on the separation question he, like all the other Burmese politicians in the delegation, agreed on the desirability of Burma becoming a separate political entity. However, on his return to Rangoon, he changed his mind and advocated Burma remaining an integral province of the Indian empire. From 1932 until the Second World War, he almost invariably sided in any dispute with Indian financial interests.

Thus, from the early 1930s U Chit Hlaing was never to regain his national prominence, and his place was taken by two new politicians, Dr Ba Maw and U Saw. Ba Maw's career shows again the interplay between strategies of popular appeal and Indian financing which tugged at the major political figures of the period. To get elected by mobilising popular support, a politician had to reassure the Burmese peasant majority that he and any government he led would act to obviate the consequences of the rice economy, the indebtedness of the peasants to the Chettiars and other moneylenders, and the state's actions to protect existing contractual obligations. But to finance their political movements, they had to turn to the large financial interests, including the Chettiars, which could provide them with the funds they needed to finance elections, pay followers, and purchase votes in the legislature.

Born in 1893, the son of a former official in the court of King Thibaw, Ba Maw attended St Paul's English High School in Rangoon and took a BA with Honours from the Rangoon branch of Calcutta University in 1917, before travelling to England where he studied at Cambridge University from 1922 to 1924 while simultaneously preparing for the bar at Gray's Inn, London, to which he was called in 1923. Forced to withdraw from Cambridge when the authorities there discovered his London studies, he went to France and took a doctorate from the University of Bordeaux in 1924. Entering politics in the GCBA, while practising law in Rangoon, Ba Maw gained his early reputation by defending Hsaya San and other leaders of the 1930-32 peasants' rebellion at their trial. One of his British colleagues at the Rangoon bar subsequently described Dr Ba Maw at the Hsaya San trial as

an able advocate, and with a flamboyance and histrionic skill calculated to allure the gallery. ... He was within the law, but seemingly on the side of the rebels. It was an attractive combination, and the Doctor was hailed as the champion of the oppressed.[55]

In preparation for the 1932 elections on the separation of India question, he organised one of the two Anti-Separation Leagues. Unlike the leader of the rival league, Chit Hlaing, Ba Maw was not then beholden to Indian interests, and made clear that his anti-separation stance was intended for bargaining purposes with the British government. He always insisted that there would have to be a clause allowing for Burma's secession from India at whatever time the government of Burma chose. In 1934 Ba Maw accepted the post of Minister of Education in the dyarchy cabinet and in 1937 he became the country's first Premier under the new constitution. By 1939, however, he was seen as an ally of Indian interests and a collaborator with the British by Rangoon University students, and when he was unable to rectify their grievances they organised demonstrations with rival politicians, including U Saw, which led to the downfall of his government. Having been elected as the leader of the reformist Hsinyeitha (Poor Man's, or Proletarian) Party, championing peasant causes such as land reform and the abolition of indebtedness, he only remained in office with the assistance of Indian votes in the legislature and Indian financial backing until politicians less encumbered with these obligations were able to create such public disorder as to cause his downfall.[56]

The politician who succeeded Ba Maw as Premier was Shwegyin U Pu. He was an independent man who apparently had few contacts with Indian interests during his career, although he did have Chinese financial support. He was born in 1881, to parents who were timber merchants in Shwegyin. He received a BA at Rangoon College in 1903 and was called

---

55   E.C.V. Foucar, *I Lived in Burma* (London: Dennis Dobson, 1956), p. 75.
56   See Taylor, "The Relationship Between Burmese Social Classes and British-Indian Policy", chs. 4 and 5, for details.

to the English bar from the Middle Temple in 1908. While studying in London, Pu founded a Buddhist society, and on returning to Rangoon he became active in the YMBA and GCBA. His career was very similar to that of another leading figure, U Ba Pe. Ba Pe, born in 1883 in a small town in Tharrawaddy District, was the son of landowners. He received a BA from Rangoon College in 1906, but being unable to afford study in Britain, took a job as a teacher at St Paul's English High School. In 1906 he was one of the founders of the YMBA, and from 1907 to 1911 he continued in a leading role in the YMBA while working as a government clerk. He left government service to found the Sun Press Limited, and his newspaper *Thuriya* (The Sun) became the leading voice of Burmese middle class nationalism throughout the colonial period. Ba Pe's varied career included being an editor and publisher, party leader, businessman, Education Minister under dyarchy and Home Minister in the 1939 ministry of U Pu, and being jailed by Premier U Saw's government in 1941. He was for several years before the war the head of the Burmese Chamber of Commerce and as such served as one of the leading spokesmen for indigenous business interests.

Shwegyin U Pu and U Ba Pe, though both able to achieve high office briefly, were never able to capture the public's attention in the way that Chit Hlaing and Ba Maw did. This was partially due to differences in personality, neither having the histrionic skills of their opponents. Both were closely associated with the urban and business-oriented sector of the Burmese middle class that was increasingly dependent upon the colonial state. While probably more serious and orthodox Buddhists than Chit Hlaing (Ba Maw was a Plymouth Brother), they were less capable of using religious appeals to gain public support because of their belief that monks should not be involved in political activities. Furthermore, because of their reliance on funds for their parties from Burmese and Chinese sources, they were never able to compete financially with their Indian-backed opponents.

Dr Thein Maung and U Saw were politicians who gained greater freedom of action than some of their contemporaries by not becoming reliant on Indian funds. Both were able to gain financial assistance from the Japanese consul in Rangoon at different points in their careers, to maintain or enhance their independence of Indian supporters, and Saw developed a following among the largest Burmese landowners. Dr Thein Maung was born in Paungde in 1891 and entered politics with Ba Pe's People's Party in the 1920s after completing a medical degree at Calcutta University. A staunch separatist in 1932, and a firm supporter of Burma's industrialisation on a model similar to Japan's, he left Ba Pe in 1937 to join Dr Ba Maw's coalition government and stayed close to Ba Maw after his government fell in 1939. In 1940 he travelled to Japan where he received Japanese assurances of financial support for Ba Maw's new Freedom Bloc organisation that campaigned against Burmese cooperation with Britain in any future war.

The most successful politician of pre-war Burma was U Saw.[57] Although not averse to taking Indian money, Saw was more independent of Indian interests than other leading politicians and seemed the best hope of the Burmese middle class. Born in 1900, the son of a well-to-do landowner in Tharrawaddy district, Saw was educated only in Burma and, unlike almost every other member of the colonial political elite, did not have a degree. His formal occupation was that of a third grade pleader, one of the lowest ranks of the new legal profession. Saw's political career began in the early 1920s, and until the founding of his own Myochit or Patriot's Party in 1938, he was a member of Ba Pe's party. Because of his support for the Hsaya San rebels he was charged with sedition, although the charges were later dropped.

In 1935 Saw visited Japan, Korea and Manchuria, and was impressed with the efficiency and power of the Japanese. His account of his travels, *Gyapan Lan Nyunt* (Japan Points the Way),[58] describes the industrial and commercial prowess of the Japanese, their concern for cooperation with other Asians, and his belief that the Japanese model of economic development and cultural conservatism was appropriate for Burma. From the time of his visit to Japan, which was paid for by his hosts, until some time shortly before he became Premier in 1940, he maintained close contacts with Japanese diplomats and agents in Rangoon, and, in the words of the governor of Burma, 'there was good reason to think that he accepted money from them'.[59] After cultivating the favour of the Japanese consul in Rangoon, he had sufficient funds to become the sole owner of the *Thuriya* newspaper in February 1938, and the next month began to organise his Myochit Party by leading ten legislators out of Ba Pe's camp. His views and growing power also attracted support for his party from the wealthiest members of the middle class, who were increasingly aware of the consequences for private business of the growing class

---

57   A full account is given in ibid., chs. 8 and 9, and in Robert H. Taylor, 'Politics in Late Colonial Burma: The Case of U Saw', *Modern Asian Studies*, 10, 2 (April 1976), pp. 161-4.

58   Saw, *Gyapan Lan Nyunt* (Japan Points the Way) (Yangon: Thuriya Press, 1936).

59   'Report on the Burma Campaign, 1941-42', by Sir Reginald Dorman-Smith, p. 8, Dorman-Smith papers in the India Office Archives and Library, London.

tensions and socialist rhetoric in the country. Among these were U Ba Tin (a leading supplier of railway sleepers to the Burma Railways), Henzada U Mya and Pegu U Sein Win, members of the House of Representatives. The latter two were reputed to own in excess of 30,000 acres of land.[60]

The colonial elite was comprised of very different men from its precolonial predecessor. Unable to rely on the state and the appanage system to maintain themselves, they all developed careers in the new professions, using as a springboard the independent means of their parents. But their personal wealth was insufficient to pay the large costs of organising and maintaining the political machines needed to win votes and gain access to office. Except for Dr Thein Maung and U Saw, all who reached the pinnacle of domestic power did so on the backs of Indian financiers or by cooperation, even if it was grudging, with the colonial state. Consequently, only Thein Maung and Saw were not compromised in the eyes of the Burmese electorate.

It was the opportunities provided by the changing internal and external conditions that allowed Saw to break free from the dilemma that had trapped his political rivals. Japanese financing, the heightened class and national awareness of leading wealthy Burmese, and the political patronage provided to ministers who gained office under the 1935 constitution allowed the late colonial elite to become more independent both of the British and, more important, of Indian capital. How did this situation come about? The British-Indian policy of introducing liberal democratic political institutions and the subsequent fostering of political parties was one factor. A second factor was the increasing development of anti-state, peasant-based non-cooperation movements. A third was the growing radicalism of the younger generation of the educated middle class, the group which least perceived their financial stake in the existing economic order. Their rise to power in vastly altered circumstances after the Second World War created a very different Burma from that which was developing in the late 1930s.

The emergence of Burmese political parties

The idea of the political party as an institution for mobilising support for aspiring politicians and maintaining their power once in government, as

---

60   The author is indebted to Dr. Dorothy Guyot, who supplied this information from an interview she conducted on 26 September 1962, with U Ba Maung, a House member in the 1930s and Saw supporter. Conversations between the author and U Aye, a close associate of Saw in the Myochit Party, held in Rangoon in January 1975, further confirmed the details set out above.

well as implementing widely shared policy preferences with a justifying ideology, was totally outside the political experience of precolonial Myanmar.
However, once voluntary organisations began to be formed by the new
political elite, political parties developed rapidly. The formation of parties
is explained by a combination of factors. Members of the elite had become
aware of the party mode of popular organisation during their travels in
England and India. The creation of the 1923 dyarchy Legislative Council
and its attendant elections demanded the creation of some means of amassing votes for candidates and presenting a national political programme.
Meaningful opposition to cooperation in these elections required a means
of communicating with the populace as well. The growing politicisation
of the village population, led often by politically oriented young monks,
was another factor, for this new force provided the politicians with a ready
following if they found symbols and policies with which to elicit support.
Behind these obvious factors lay a growing belief among the new Burmese
middle class that it was necessary to form some means of defending their
interests and their perceptions of Burma's interests from the power and
wealth, and the social and cultural influence, of Britain, from Indian labour, and from both British and Indian capital. That the regaining of independence under middle class leadership was ultimately the only means to
protect their interests was obvious. But conditions were not yet deemed appropriate for that step. The first Burmese political leaders were constrained
to work within a new political universe under conditions imposed by the
colonial state and the consequences of the evolving class and ethnic structures of society.

Nonetheless, the nature of the political parties in Burma evolved rapidly
between the early 1900s and the late 1930s, reflecting both environmental
changes and the growing sophistication of the political elite. The parties
were never tightly knit organisations during these years, but over time they
became increasingly 'national'[61] in scope and hierarchical in structure. For
analytical purposes, there were three phases of party development. The first
phase lasted from the mid-1900s to around 1920, the second from the
early 1920s to around 1936, and the third from 1935 to 1942. The first
phase was essentially one of urban, elite organisations that were marked by
greater unity among the leadership than at any later period. The second was
noted for great divisiveness at the top but also for mass support at the village level for those parties that espoused rejection of the colonial state. The

---

61   They were constrained to operate almost entirely within 'Burma proper'.

third phase saw the beginning of both mass support at the base and more unified leadership at the top, but owing to the brevity of the period the full implications of these trends were never realised.

The unity at the top in the first phase was a result not only of the small number of leaders in the initial years, but also of the lack of opportunities in this period of administrative rule. The repeated bifurcation of parties in the second phase was a result of both the opportunities for a limited number of leaders to gain political office under dyarchy and the absence of sufficient indigenous funding for all the party organisations. Contention over the proper role of political monks and of radical and often illegal peasant organisations was also a highly divisive influence. The third phase was conditioned by the existence of a great many more opportunities for patronage for party members from the controlling party in the legislature and cabinet, coupled with other sources of party finance not tied to Indian interests. The unity and strength of the parties from about 1936 onwards was also aided by a growing sense of class and communal consciousness on the part of the Burmese middle class. This consciousness increased as their position in society was increasingly challenged by Indian capital on the one hand and the Burmese peasantry on the other.

During these years the intellectual and ideological underpinnings of party life also evolved through successive short phases. The first nationalist leaders sought to save Burmese society from the corrosive effects of colonial rule and the new state. Later leaders sought to change and redefine society to regain national independence while preserving those traditional elements that were compatible with a rationalised economy and state. The eventual result was that nationalists began to reorient Burmese political thinking away from notions appropriate for a patrimonial society and monarchical state towards ideas of nationhood with economic and class interests and a world perspective relevant to modern party politics and mass movements.

As a consequence, Burmese political thought shifted from concern for religious honour, social respect and proper behaviour in the 1910s to demands for explicitly political and economic reforms in the 1920s and anti-imperialist, anti-capitalist sentiments and calls for action in the 1930s. However, the incorporation of new political ideas into Burmese political life was not a rectilinear process. Until the 1930s, and especially in the 1920s, there was incongruity between the content of political demands and resolutions and the format through which the leadership of the major nationalist organisations presented these ideas in conferences and meetings of their supporters. While the nationalist movement was essentially restricted to a few Rangoon-centred university graduates, teachers and government servants, the national organisation was modern and secular in form: its programme was cautious, being both culturally and socially conservative. When the nationalist movement sought to widen its support in the 1920s, the leadership, increasingly under the sway of Buddhist monks, felt it had to present its still essentially conservative goals through religious and culturally recognised mediums and symbols. Only in the later 1930s did the content and form of Burmese nationalism began to coalesce. Nonetheless, the ideas of the 1930s were interpreted in the context of Burmese culture, which was the product of a thousand years of patrimonial rule justified by Buddhist philosophy.

It is perhaps a misnomer to refer to the predominant institution of the first phase of party development, the Young Men's Buddhist Association, as a political party. It was founded in 1906 as a religious, cultural and welfare oriented group by a small number of Western educated men. They 'basically accepted British rule as an unavoidable part of life in Burma, and began using western organisational and institutional forms in setting up various Buddhist associations, missions and schools.'[62] Having brought together under one umbrella disparate organisations of Buddhist laymen in various towns, the YMBA held conferences and debates on social and religious questions, but until 1916 the nearest it came to political activity was voting resolutions urging Burmese to use indigenous products and proposing a unified educational code.[63] In that year the annual conference passed a resolution demanding government action to ban the wearing of shoes inside pagodas by Westerners, and the YMBA joined monks in the organisation of public protests against such acts of disdain for Burmese culture by non-Buddhists. Eventually, in 1918, the government ruled that it was in the power of the head of a monastery to determine the standards of dress required for admission to their premises, the first instance in Burma's colonial history when the government made a concession to public demands.

The outwardly cautious and conservative action preceded a split in the organisation in 1917 between the so-called radicals, led by the YMBA

---

62   Maung Maung, *From Sangha to Laity*, p. xvi.

63   Ibid., pp. 3-4; Maung Maung, *Burma and General Ne Win*, p. 5; partial translations of the YMBA conference resolutions are found in Maung Maung, 'Nationalist Movements in Burma, 1920-1940: Changing Patterns of Leadership: From Sangha to Laity' (MA, Australian National University, 1976), app. A., pp. 552-77.

founder U Ba Pe and other younger leaders, and an elder faction which had taken the organisation over in the late 1900s, over the question of sending a delegation to Calcutta to discuss the future of Burma with Montagu and Chelmsford (who were then considering the outline of the dyarchy system for India). The organisation, and the majority of its forty-five branches, remained with the younger group and prepared the way for the formation of the more explicitly political GCBA. The growing political awareness of the YMBA leaders was also reflected at the fifth conference when a resolution was passed objecting to the Governor's schemes to use the schools for the inculcation of the 'imperial idea' in Burmese youth.[64] At the next conference proposals for repeal of the capitation and *thathameda* taxes, reflecting the organisation's concern with ameliorating the conditions of the peasantry, and for the formation of a women's section or a YWBA were also made.[65] The second phase of party development began with the shattering of the remaining unity of the YMBA. This resulted from its efforts to persuade the British government to apply the Indian dyarchy reforms to Burma.[66] In 1919 the leadership divided over whether to accept the Craddock reforms or to continue to lobby in London for equal treatment with India, as well as over differences among the members over finances and pongyi involvement in politics. The elder faction was willing to accept Craddock's proposals but the younger group insisted on mounting a protest to the British government over the exclusion of Burma from the dyarchy reforms.

The leadership of the younger faction formed the nucleus of the major parties of the second phase of party development. In addition to U Ba Pe and U Thein Maung, these included the leading political monk U Ottama and others such as U Chit Hlaing, Tharrawaddy U Pu and U Tun Aung Kyaw. In March 1920, at its fifth conference held in Prome, the YMBA changed its English name to the General Council of Burmese Associations and its Burmese name to the *Myanma Athin Chokkyi*, meaning 'Myanmar's great controlling group'. The policies and membership of the newly named organisation were much the same as the younger faction of the YMBA. The

---

64   See pp. 119-120 above.

65   Maung Maung, *From Sangha to Laity*, p. 13.

66   The following discussion of the development of the parties up to 1932 relies upon the standard historical sources noted in the bibliography as well as *Special Confidential Supplement to the Police Abstract of Intelligence*, no. 1, XXXVI, 17 Sept. 1932, no. 37, 'The Burmese Political Tree', BOF P&J(B) 1; Maung Maung, 'Nationalist Movements in Burma', app. B, pp. 604-13; and Maung Maung, *From Sangha to Laity*, chs. 3 and 4.

more activist group extended party activities to the districts and outlying towns and villages by bringing the 200 or so branches of the old YMBA into closer contact with the Rangoon leadership.[67]

With the change in style of party organisation and the withdrawal of the most conservative leaders in 1920, the GCBA began to involve itself directly in popular political protests and demonstrations. In doing so, it adopted the techniques of the Indian National Congress under Gandhi, the boycott or *hartal*, as for example in the successful boycott organised in protest against the election of members from Burma to the Indian Legislative Assembly and the Council of State at Delhi in October 1920. Such an action appeared to British observers at the time as mere imitation of, if not infiltration by, Indian nationalists in Burma's previously tranquil political life.[68] This conclusion might be easily drawn on one level, for the Burmese political elite were certainly aware of the Indian nationalists' techniques and intentions and shared the same colonial opponents. Yet even though several of the most important early Burmese nationalist leaders, particularly Chit Hlaing and Ottama, had close relations with the Indian National Congress and other groups, Indian organisational techniques, much less political agents, had little to do with the development of Burma's popular political organisations throughout the colonial period.[69]

The boycott of the central Indian elections of 1920 was a minor affair. Because the franchise was tightly restricted and the issue of no intrinsic importance, very few people were involved. However, less than two months later the development of a countrywide student boycott added impetus to the development of the nationalist parties and demonstrated to the political leaders the depth of feeling and potential support for anti-British actions which existed in the country away from the artificial atmosphere of colonial Rangoon. On 4 December 1920, the day now celebrated as 'National Day' in Myanmar, a few students from Rangoon College organised a protest against the government's plan to set up and develop Rangoon University as an elite institution designed to produce only a few qualified Burmese men and women who could take over the jobs then done by foreigners.

---

67   Maung Maung, *From Sangha to Laity*, p. 19.

68   Cady, *History of Modern Burma*, pp. 215-17; Albert D. Moscotti, *British Policy and the Nationalist Movement in Burma, 1917-1937* (Honolulu: Asian Studies at Hawaii, no. 11, Hawaii University Press, 1974), p. 20.

69   Cady, *History of Modern Burma*, p. 193.

This small group had little idea of the effect its action would have.[70] Within days most of the indigenous students at both Rangoon College and Judson College (run by American missionaries)[71] were boycotting classes, and by early 1921 the strike had spread to all government schools and some missionary schools throughout Burma proper.[72] The organisers of the strike were not 'radicals' set to oust the British from power,[73] but the support they received from their parents, older sections of society and the leadership of the GCBA demonstrated the potential for political pressure on the colonial government to modify its policies.

For the long-term development of nationalist politics, the 1920 university boycott spawned another movement that provided an important outlet for nationalist energies. This was the national schools movement. GCBA branches and individuals in most towns and cities organised alternative, non-government schools during 1921 in order to maintain the strike and also to ensure their children's education for advancement in the new professions. Though lacking the resources of the state schools, they increased popular awareness of the potential of local organisation in the face of state opposition. The national schools persisted into the 1930s, though on a much reduced scale, as the movement split over the issue of acceptance of government funds.[74]

Thus began the mobilisation of increasing numbers of people from various sectors of Burmese society into political and social action. Different groups responded for different reasons, but all did so under the cloak of nationalism. For the leaders of the GCBA, national independence meant taking control of the state and protecting the economic status and preroga-

---

70   Moscotti, *British Policy and the Nationalist Movement*, p. 29.

71   Karen and Anglo-Indian students did not join the strike, although at first Karen students at Judson College were encouraged to do so, as the government's initial plan for the new university had no provision for the missionary college. Lu Pe Win, *History of the 1920 University Boycott* (n. p. [Rangoon?], the author, for the Organisation for the Celebration of the Golden Anniversary of the National Day, November, 1970), p. 17.

72   Cady, *History of Modern Burma*, pp. 213-21.

73   Many of the leaders of the 1920 student boycott returned to the new university and later became prominent officials. Eleven entered the elite ICS, while seven joined the Indian Police Service and another seven the Indian Forest Service. Many others became teachers and government officials of lesser rank. Lu Pe Win, *History of the Strike*, p. 33.

74   Maung Maung, *From Sangha to Laity*, p. 21-3; Cady, *History of Modern Burma*, p. 220.

tives of the new middle class. For the students, most of whom were also from the middle class, expanding educational opportunities meant more jobs for teachers and lower standards of admission and graduation.

A third group, the monkhood, which had not involved itself in political activities since the rebellions of the 1880s and 1890s, now became politically organised. As discussed in Chapter I, the monkhood had fulfilled important and sometimes political roles under the precolonial monarchical order. These functions were now being absorbed in new institutions shaped by the needs of the colonial state. Education, a monopoly of the monks under the old order, was now either a state, missionary or state-supervised private secular activity, and this meant the monkhood losing one of its major claims to respect and authority in town and village life. The growth of British law and the development of the legal profession meant also that the monk's function as the interpreter of the meaning of Buddhism as the basis of the settlement of disputes was now receding.[75] The state also no longer provided the *sangha* with patronage or protection, and while it continued to maintain and support Pali scholarship[76] it jeopardised the monkhood's financial position by creating areas of investment for private capital belonging to the new, secular middle class which the monarchs would have confiscated and in part donated to the monkhood. The monkhood did receive substantial gifts from middle class people who were more affluent than private individuals had ever been before in Burma, but this support had about it an air of conspicuous social display and private reward that the patronage of the royal court had never had.[77]

At the time of the formation of the GCBA a minority of the approximately 120,000 monks in the country began, wrote U Tin Tut, 'to take an interest in politics seeing ahead a result by which the Government of Burma would again become Burmese and the Order would again become associated with government power for the advancement of the religion

---

75   Smith, *Religion and Politics in Burma*, p. 31.

76   Ibid., pp. 66-71.

77   One was struck in visiting important and less important pagodas and monasteries in Burma in the 1980s by the large number of donation plaques erected in the 1920s and 1930s, as well as the 1950s, by individuals and families. These often include, in addition to the donors' names, their social status, such as landowner or owner of a shop or small commercial concern. However, throughout the colonial period there were no major new pagodas constructed. Buddhist monumental architecture had to wait until the return of independence for the government to undertake the construction of new, large complexes such as the Kaba Aye (World Peace) pagoda and its precincts in the 1950s.

and the people of Burma'.[78] In 1920, monks came together to form the General Council of Sangha Sammeggi (GCSS), parallel to the GCBA. As with so many organisations in Burma's colonial history, religious or secular, its founders were intent upon essentially moral goals. The uplifting of lay standards of Buddhist practice and the imposition of discipline on the monkhood itself were pre-eminent among these, as the absence of effective government control to maintain discipline meant that the *sangha* was becoming increasingly factionalised and lax in application of the rules of the *Vinaya*.[79] However, thanks primarily to the leadership of one monk, U Ottama, the GCSS soon became a major political force and turned itself and the GCBA in different directions from those its founders had intended.

U Ottama, who had travelled in India and Japan and spent most of the first two decades of the twentieth century outside Burma, returned advocating an interpretation of Buddhism that quickly found favour with younger monks, though the established *sayadaw*s who provided the *sangha*'s hierarchy looked with much distrust upon his message and tactics. Ottama's simple argument had clear appeal, particularly to monks in the villages who shared the peasants' relative declining standards of living, security and status. He argued that since the wellbeing of the religion was dependent upon the wellbeing of the people who supported it, the monkhood, like the king who claimed to be a *Bodhisatta*, had to involve itself in secular affairs until such time as conditions were appropriate to resume purely religious obligations.[80] The symbiotic relationship between the state and religion was now recast in terms of a symbiotic relationship between the people and the religion, with the state the cause of distress to both.

At first U Ottama's message was largely ignored and criticised by senior monks, but after his arrest and conviction for sedition in June 1921, the GCBA took up his cause[81] and the GCSS pledged to continue his agitational tours of the countryside, multiplying the number of monks preaching his message of non-cooperation with government. The GCSS founded a group of political monks known as *dhammakatika* who served as political leaders and tutors to the newly formed *wunthanu athin* (village nationalist and self-defence organisations which were affiliated with the GCBA). There were an estimated 200 of these monks touring the country in the

---

78   'The Problem of the Pongyi', by U Tin Tut, 6 Nov. 1943, BOF 4811/38.

79   Maung Maung, *From Sangha to Laity*, p. 24.

80   Ibid., p. 14-16; see also Smith, *Religion and Politics*, pp. 91-107.

81   Moscotti, *British Policy and Nationalist Movement*, p. 32.

1920s,[82] spreading the nationalist messages of Buddhist protection and personal benefit to the population. The 12,000 branches of the GCBA assisted them in their work.[83] But the government's arrest of Ottama was only the beginning of the suppression of political monks. Even among the most conservative Buddhists, who disapproved of monks becoming involved in politics, it created hatred of British treatment of the religion. Throughout the 1920s monks were arrested and imprisoned with little regard as to their religious status. One monk was killed in a demonstration in Mandalay in 1924. The extent of their involvement in what the government regarded as seditious activities was so great by 1928 and 1929 that over 120 monks were arrested, and one, U Wisara, fasted to death in a government gaol.[84]

The influence of the political monks soon gave them a controlling say in many of the activities of the GCBA and was one of the causes of the organisation's eventual decline. The GCSS became subject, as it involved itself in secular activities, to the same factional tendencies found in the YMBA and GCBA, but the most militant faction of monks also stood with that group of lay leaders who refused to cooperate with the government by voting or by standing in elections to state bodies. By the early 1930s there were GCSS factions supporting at least four political offshoots of the original GCBA, although the largest remained with the staunchly pro-boycott leader, U Soe Thein, and was the only body never to enter into the colonial political system. Nonetheless, as late as 1937 most of the major political parties had some connection with pongyi groups. Dr Ba Maw's party, as well as U Chit Hlaing's and U Ba Pe's, had advisory boards of sayadaws. Critics of the monks' role in politics claimed that the party leaders had to clear appointments and party decisions with these boards, although once in office, politicians felt able to ignore their monk supporters. Before then, though, the support of the political monks was crucial.[85]

As part of the package of political reforms intended to prepare the population for what the British saw as responsible self-government, the govern-

82   Maung Maung, 'Nationalist Movements in Burma', app. C, pp. 614-8, provides a partial listing.

83   Moscotti, *British Policy and Nationalist Movement*, p. 32.

84   Ibid., pp. 51-4.

85   For example, see *The All Burma Sangha Samaggi Orders of the Thetpan Sayadaw on the Question of the Policy of the G. C. B. A. in Respect of Separation and Federation Issue* (short pamphlet) (Rangoon, 26 Aug. 1933), which expelled Dr Ba Maw from the GCBA; Taylor, 'Relationship Between Burmese Social Classes and British-Indian Policy', pp. 220, 222.

ment introduced in the early 1920s a system of circle boards to be elected at the district and township levels. These were to take control of the administration of education, roads and sanitation in 28 of Burma's 37 districts, although full powers were granted to only 17 of the boards.[86] Urged on by the GCSS and perhaps not wishing to be seen to lag behind popular sentiment, as happened at the time of the university boycott the previous year, the GCBA leadership organised an election boycott. This proved distinctly successful. Only 6 per cent of the eligible voters participated in the election and, for nearly 600 of the 2,700 boards to be to be elected, no candidate was put forward, while in another 800 or so only one candidate stood. The level of participation in these government-sponsored bodies was even lower in the 1925 elections and the experiment was considered a failure by the government.[87] It would seem that the only individuals who could see the advantages of such 'democratic institutions' were political rogues like U Kyan Aung. The GCBA was equally successful in organising boycotts of the elections for the Legislative Council held in 1922. Less than 7 per cent of the electorate voted in that year, but after a split in the movement in 1925, over 16 per cent voted. In 1928 still only 18 per cent were willing to vote.[88]

The development of the GCBA and the GCSS, coupled with the growing advocacy of the boycott by part of the political elite, indicates the radicalisation of party politics during the 1920s.[89] The growing involvement of monks and villagers in political organisations enhanced the power of the nationalist movement by mobilising increased support for the central leaders. There was, however, a serious dilemma, for on the one hand the British were holding forth to those members of the elite willing to cooperate with their constitutional policies the possibility of power, while on the other hand their ability to pressure the British to speed the transfer of more power to them was dependent on the support they received from the mass of the population. The latter, encouraged by the political monks, viewed cooperation with the colonial state as a form of collaboration with

---

86   Cady, *History of Modern Burma*, p. 263.

87   Ibid., p. 265.

88   Ibid., pp. 241, 260. Cady (p. 245) notes that Karen Christians participated actively in the election of 1922; Maung Maung, *From Sangha to Laity*, p. 44.

89   At the 1921 GCBA conference 'within the empire' were deleted from the resolution demanding home rule. Translations and summaries of all major GCBA conference resolutions are provided in Maung Maung, 'Nationalist Movements in Burma', app. A, pp. 577-601.

the source of their economic and cultural complaints. The consequences of this dilemma were seen in the splits within the GCBA throughout the 1920s and to the end of its political effectiveness in the early 1930s.

In 1922 the GCBA suffered the first of these splits when it was announced that dyarchy would be extended to Burma. Although personal clashes and financial chicanery also lay under the surface of elite conflicts,[90] the political issue was whether or not to cooperate with and participate in the elections for the Legislative Council. The faction willing to cooperate was known as the Twenty-One Party, after the 21 GCBA members who resigned to form the National Party to participate in the elections. Its central figure was U Ba Pe, who led it as well as its successor parties, the People's Party and the United GCBA. The party was considered to have more support from the educated middle class than its rival, the Hlaing-Pu-Gyaw GCBA—or perhaps, more accurately, the boycott advocating GCBA had the support of the peasantry.

Taking its name from its three leaders, the Hlaing-Pu-Gyaw GCBA not only advocated non-cooperation in elections, but also demanded home rule outside the empire. Under the auspices of this group, the village and township movements created by the political monks (the *wunthanu athin*) became its local branches. Each was affiliated with the new higher party level through the payment of dues. Supported and in time dominated by the GCSS, the conferences of the Hlaing-Pu-Gyaw GCBA were attended by thousands of delegates, and these increasingly forced the urban, educated leadership to bow to the demands of the local activists. The force of their demands led to another GCBA split at the time of the eleventh national conference in 1924, when the political pongyi forced through a resolution advocating a campaign for non-payment of taxes as well as an election boycott. As will be discussed below, the strength of peasant feeling against the *thathameda* and capitation taxes was so strong at this time that even politicians who were cooperating with the British state attempted to get them repealed in the Legislative Council.[91]

The question of Pongyi involvement in party activities, as well as the mismanagement of party finances, resulted in another split of the Hlaing-Pu-Gyaw party in 1925. One of the new groups, the Pongyi's GCBA, was

90 Maung Maung, *From Sangha to Laity*, pp. 27-8. Chapter 3 of this work, entitled 'The Sangha Takes over the GCBA', is an account that follows closely the major histories of the period published in Burmese.

91 Moscotti, *British Policy and Burmese Nationalism*, pp. 50-1.

headed by U Soe Thein, a chemist educated in Germany and the United States, whose family had controlled oil wells before the development of the modern industry in Burma. The Pongyi's GCBA maintained the non-cooperation policy of the old Hlaing-Pu-Gyaw party, and was dominated by the monks who had control not only of the policy but also of party funds. The other party remained under the control of Chit Hlaing and Tharrawaddy U Pu. Pu soon withdrew and formed the Home Rule Party, still advocating non-cooperation, while Chit Hlaing and his dwindling band of followers contested the 1925 Legislative Council elections. From then on the GCBA as a national force diminished in influence and even the Pongyi's GCBA split in 1929.[92] Having cut themselves off from the political monks and peasant base of the original GCBA, the cooperating parties did not regain their national prominence until the late 1930s when they adopted a new middle class base and a cooperative relationship with the colonial state.

The lack of secure organisational bases for the parties was shown by the way they organised and reorganised frantically in the run up to elections. When the British announced that the 1932 Legislative Council elections would determine whether or not Burma would separate from India, there was more than the usual flurry of party activity. In addition to the Separation League, which was a direct outgrowth of Ba Pe's United GCBA, two Anti-Separation Leagues were founded in July 1932. Both were products of the Free State League that had been formed in March of that year. In the 1932 elections the success of the Anti-Separation Leagues, which received 529,127 votes to the separationists' 293,942 votes, with a turnout of 40 per cent of the electorate,[93] indicated both the power that Indian financial support gave to political leaders (for the majority of them, as well as the electorate, probably favoured separation) and the crumbling of the boycott tradition among the party leadership.

The ineffectiveness of the Burmese political elite during the second phase of party development led to a large degree of cynicism and mistrust of the

---

92   In addition to the parties which developed of the original GCBA, there were several other parties or factions. The most important in the 1920s was the Golden Valley or Independent Party. It took its name from the wealthy district of Rangoon in which most of its members lived. It provided most of the ministers of the governor's council until 1932. The party was led an Irish barrister and a Burmese barrister.

93   Telegram, Governor of Burma to Secretary of State for India, 29 Nov. 1932, BOF P&J(B) 1.

middle class leadership among both the peasantry and the younger middle class. The champions of the nationalist cause of 1920 had, by the mid-1930s, become collaborators with the state and those foreign groups who most benefited from it. The majority of people in the districts did not look to the elected legislators as their leaders, spokesmen or protectors. When the Burmese ministers took office in 1937 under the new constitution, there was no expression of popular support for them despite the greater power that they now yielded. Apparently the ministers also did not believe that the people supported their government. British and Burmese officials and politicians were aware of this situation and for that reason sometimes despaired of the possibility of making the democratic features of the 1935 constitution work. As one high official wrote, as long as it was known that the Burmese ministers were kept in office with the aid of Europeans and Indians, 'the fight will be taken outside the Legislature on to the streets of Rangoon, Mandalay and elsewhere'.[94] Nonetheless the political importance of elections as a means of taking control of the state from the British was changing, and the political elite was intensely keen to gain access to office and to the privileges and protections that the mantle of state authority would provide them with, both in their intra-elite conflicts and in their contest with British officialdom. The strategy of boycotting elections had crumbed away further by the 1936 election, the only one held under the 1935 constitution, for approximately 52 per cent of the electorate voted on this occasion.[95]

The third phase of party development saw a struggle between two parties that had both rejected the earlier basis of party life. Myochit, led by U Saw, seized the opportunities provided by the 1935 constitution and the evolving international situation to develop a mass-based party which would defend and enhance the position of the middle class and regain Burma's independence by making its cooperation indispensable to the British. The other, the Thakin movement, sought similar goals but hoped to achieve them through the subversion of the constitution and, perhaps, through a revolutionary struggle. The full flowering of this rivalry between the sec-

---

94   Personal letter, James Baxter to D.T. Monteath, 4 April 1939, BOF P106, part 1.

95   Based on calculations from Ganga Singh, *Burma Parliamentary Companion* (Rangoon: British Burma Press, 1940), election results statement on pp. 341-61. Dorothy Hess Guyot, 'The Political Impact of the Japanese Occupation of Burma' (PhD, Yale University, 1966), table 2, p. 21, gives a turnout figure of 31 per cent.

tion of the middle class with a stake in the colonial system and that section, increasingly socialist in its ideological orientation, without such a stake emerged just before the Japanese invasion in 1942.[96] This rivalry was submerged during the war years, but re-emerged in the internal politics of the post-war independence struggle, and culminated in the post-independence civil war.

Peasants and politics under the colonial state

One of the established myths about politics in Burma in both the colonial and the postcolonial periods is the so-called 'elite mass gap'.[97] The myth grew up through taking insufficient account of the nature of politics under the precolonial state in terms of the people's relationship with the state. It is also based on unquestioning acceptance of certain folk statements, usually passed on by members of the elite, such as 'government is one of the five great evils to be avoided'. According to the myth of the elite-mass gap, the imposition of the modern state and the political elite who managed it meant that, over the past hundred years, a vast gulf of misunderstanding and mistrust developed between the peasant population and the controllers of the state or the indigenous political leadership. This shaped the nature of both elite and mass responses to different political situations, making the Burmese polity less stable than it might otherwise have been. There certainly was, and remains, a gap in the perceived interests of the peasantry and the political elite, but it exists because these two groups *do* understand each other and their contradictory interests.

An important corollary of the standard elite-mass gap theory is the assumption that the political attitudes and views of the mass of the peasant population have remained essentially unchanged from the time of the classical state, and that these are attitudes and views inappropriate for modern conditions. At the same time, it is suggested, the political elite,

---

96 See Taylor, 'Politics in Late Colonial Burma'; also James F. Guyot, 'Bureaucratic Transformation in Burma', in Ralph Braibanti (ed.), *Asian Bureaucratic Systems Emergent from the British Imperial Tradition* (Durham, NC: Duke University Press, 1966), p. 365. The growing power of politicians to interfere in administration during this period tended to undermine the authority of district officers and other civil servants as well as to add to their work load. F.S.V. Donnison, *Public Administration in Burma: A Study of Development During the British Connexion* (London: Royal Institute for International Affairs, 1953), p. 57.

97 Guyot, 'Political Impact of the Japanese Occupation', pp. 16-21; Josef Silverstein, *Burma, Military Rule and the Politics of Stagnation* (Ithaca: Cornell University Press, 1977), pp. 198-200.

and the new urban or middle class generally, have lost any understanding they may have once had of their own social origins. The credence given to this theory has done much to obscure the lively political life of the rural population and its impact upon the political behaviour of the political elite and the modern state.

It is perhaps true that the colonial state of the nineteenth and early twentieth century, with its foreign rulers governing through a new bureaucratic structure and with the force of an empire behind it, had little need to relate to and understand the political and economic perspectives of the mass of the population. The same is not true of the indigenous elite that led the political organisations of the twentieth century. The new state was making demands on the peasantry in particular to which the elite was forced to respond. The replacement of patron-client ties by bureaucratic officials at the local level altered the peasants' legal and fiscal relationship with state authority. The rapid development of the Irrawaddy delta rice fields demonstrates the Burmese peasant's clear and ready grasp of the profit motive and the advantages of trade for the social advancement of himself and his family. The speed with which peasant political organisations developed in the 1920s, in league with, or in opposition to, the plans and programmes of the political elite, demonstrates awareness of the opportunities available in altered circumstances. The apparent 'fact' that the political behaviour of the peasantry during the 1920s and 1930s had aspects of precolonial practices and beliefs does not invalidate the relevance of their response to the conditions in which they took place. All indigenous political movements are shaped by the culture in which they develop, and many of the political practices of the peasantry under the precolonial state were modified to meet the circumstances created by the colonial state.

Several factors motivated peasants to involve themselves in political action. The administrative, economic, geographical and demographic changes that British policies imposed ended the precolonial stability of the settled village, providing a population base that could be easily mobilised for political action. The colonial state's lack of legitimacy in the eyes of the population was a key psychological factor in encouraging individuals to strike against the state: the relative deterioration in most peasants' economic position in the 1920s and 1930s merely compounded their sense of grievance. This growing sense of discontent, perhaps linked with the anomic conditions of the plural society, provided the political elite with an army of rank and file followers when the leaders could produce a programme and organisation that addressed their perceived needs. The fact that the political elite's interests often ran counter to those of the peasantry provided much of the internal tension within Burma's domestic politics in the late colonial period.

As discussed in Chapter II, the closing of the rice frontier was one of the underlying factors contributing to the crisis of the Burmese peasant class during the 1920s and 1930s. The growing surplus of potential tenants and their weakened bargaining position led to widespread rural insecurity. Declining rice prices and rapid price inflation contributed to the peasants' plight. The rise in the number of indigenous landless cultivators and increasing competition by Indian labourers to gain land combined to heighten the insecurity of tenure of those who were able to remain cultivators. The rootlessness of the tenant class is indicated by the small percentage of cultivating tenants who lived on the same land for more than four years. Short tenancy (a consequence of the growing competition among cultivators for land to till, leading inexorably under the prevailing economic situation to higher and higher rents) became a major feature in districts such as Tharrawaddy before the First World War.[98] After the collapse of the international rice market in 1930 the problem reached crisis proportions, leading to even greater communal tensions,[99] and reflected the complications of class and ethnicity in colonial Burma's politics. The size of the crisis in the 1930s should not, however, overshadow the fact that for some cultivators personal dislocation predated the First World War and led to expressions of peasant discontent and political action at least fifteen years before the Hsaya San peasant rebellion of 1930-32. Serious falls in the price of rice early in the First World War, coupled with general inflation as imported

---

98   S.G. Grantham, *Studies in the History of Tharrawaddy* (Cambridge: Printed at the University Press for private circulation, 1920), pp. 31-2.

99   In Insein District, for example, in 1933-35, over 22 per cent of all tenants had had the same land for four or more years, 10 per cent for three years, 21 per cent for two years, and 47 per cent for one year. Conditions were similar in Amherst, Pegu and Myaungmya. In districts further from Rangoon, security of tenure seemed to be greater. For example, in one Henzada tract in 1936-37, 63 per cent of tenants had had their land for four or more years, 22 per cent for two or three years, and 15 per cent for only one year. *Land and Agriculture Committee Report*, part I, p. 15. Conditions were different in the delta compared to the dry zone. Whereas 47 per cent of all land was rented in 1938 in all of Burma, 58 per cent was rented in lower Burma compared to 33 per cent in upper Burma. Ibid., p. 8.

consumer goods became scarce, began an absolute decline in the financial security of an ever growing segment of the peasant class.[100]

The capitation tax in the south and the *thathameda* tax elsewhere contributed to peasant grievances against the state.[101] While high rents and insecurity of tenure could be explained away as the consequence of the economic system, these taxes could not. Both were essentially head taxes, especially aggravating to the peasants, for as a fixed tax payable in cash they fell equally on the poor and the prosperous. Although the *thathameda* was a precolonial tax carried over by the British, as a result of the efficiency of the modern state's collection system it became a greater source of grievance because the headmen were no longer able to adjust it on an informal basis to fit changing economic conditions. The end of the sumptuary laws and the growth of obvious distinctions in wealth within the village made the tax even more galling, for the gap in different individuals' ability to pay had become common knowledge. While other taxes, direct and indirect, may have actually taken more of the peasant's income, these taxes were annual reminders of the state's limitations on his freedom as well as a threat to his pride.

In the early years of the development of the rice industry, growing prosperity and the absence or low rate of land taxes made the head taxes seem less onerous. Tenancy, too, was then seen by Burmese migrating to the delta as a step in the process of social advancement to cultivator-ownership. However, in the period after the First World War, tenancy became 'a dead-end for most agriculturalists or a temporary respite in their fall from cultivator-owners to landless labourers, rather than the avenue of upward mobility it had been in the nineteenth century'.[102] Political conditions, including the growing power of local administrators and bosses like U Kyan Aung, and the rise of land prices and the decline of paddy prices combined to benefit the landlord class, so that class distinctions within the agricultural communities became more distinct. The corruption of subordinate employees of the Land Records Department by land-grabbing landlords,[103] and the efforts of headmen to take more land for themselves, meant that the peasants

---

100   Cady, *History of Modern Burma*, pp. 187-8.

101   Ibid., p. 91; Maung Maung, *From Sangha to Laity*, p. 47; James C. Scott, *The Moral Economy of the Peasant, Rebellion and Subsistence in Southeast Asia* (New Haven: Yale University Press, 1976), pp. 99-102. The definitive study is Ian Brown, *A Colonial Economy in Crisis: Burma's Rice Cultivators and the World Depression of the 1930s* (London: Routledge Curzon, 2005).

102   Adas, *Burma Delta*, p. 147.

103   Ibid., pp. 142-43.

had less and less legal protection and came increasingly to see the agents of the state as the agents of their misery. The rapidity with which the pioneer peasants fell to the lowest categories of rural population can be seen by the fact that by the 1930s 'landless laborers became the dominant element in the population of many villages in lower Burma'.[104]

After the *thathameda* or capitation tax, the most irritating tax for the peasants was the land tax. Land tax was set at about 10 per cent of the cultivators' gross return, but this could amount to as much as 25 to 50 per cent of their net produce. In bad years, although it was intended that the tax would be reduced or remitted by the Deputy Commissioner, this often did not happen, and the burden on the farmer could be even greater. In some instances, he had almost nothing to show for his year's labour. Though less regressive in form than the head taxes, the land tax was a greater burden on small cultivators than on larger ones, thus increasing rural economic inequalities.[105] Revenue from land tax formed the largest proportion of the colonial state's receipts.

The second most important source of government revenue was an indirect tax on rice production. This was initially less of a burden on the cultivator. It took the form of an export duty on the country's rice and was justified by the government in terms of keeping down the rates of land tax.[106] Its implications for peasants' incomes became apparent in 1918-19, when the government established the Rice Control Board to keep the domestic price of rice low for urban consumers in the wake of the rapid increase in the international price after the war. The government also hoped to limit the huge profits that would be made by the large rice exporting firms. However, the action drew clearly to the cultivators' attention the direct involvement of the state in the regulation of the price they could receive for their crop, and thus added to the head taxes and land tax as a source of peasant grievance against the government.[107]

The peasants' political response was to form the *wunthanu athin*. These were intended to protect local interests, but became linked through the activities of the GCBA and GCSS that helped set them up to the nationalist movement of the urban political élite. The term *wunthanu* came into common use as early as 1915. It was derived from Pali and means 'supporting

---

104   Ibid., p. 152.

105   Scott, *Moral Economy of the Peasant*, pp. 102-5.

106   Shein, *Burma's Transport and Foreign Trade*, pp. 129-30.

107   Cady, *History of Modern Burma*, pp. 221-3.

own race', and was used in the sense of 'nationalist' or 'patriotic'[108] (*athin* means organisation). The rapid growth of the *wunthanu* movement was a consequence both of the organising activities of the political monks sent out by the GCSS and of the peasants' perceived need to have a voice in the growing nationalist movement.[109] Delegates from the village *athin* attended the major GCBA conferences and pressed for the increasingly radical resolutions passed there.[110] By 1924 there were *wunthanu athin* organised in almost every village in Burma.[111]

The effect of these organisations was to give the villagers a greater sense of their own power in their conflicts with the state and its officials. As U Maung Maung has written,

with an organized body holding them together, the people in the villages and towns became bold enough to refuse to comply with, or to complain against, unjust orders and ill-treatment by administrative officers, the police or the village headmen. The signboard '*wunthanu*' on a placard (in Burmese) would be hung in every home and shop like a good luck charm. People purchased from shops with such signs.[112]

The initial importance of the *wunthanu athin* for the leaders of the GCBA was that through them they were able to organise the election and other boycott campaigns which were successful in protesting against the British government's unwillingness to give Burma home rule.[113] In this way they were able to link the national political goals of the urban elite with the interests of the villagers, who extended the idea to the organised general boycott of the local state apparatus and its agents. The *wunthanu* organisations involved not only laymen but also women and monks, often as leaders, in their activities.[114]

The link between the village *athin* and the central executive committee of the GCBA paralleled that of the government established under the Rural Self-Government Act of 1921. Ignoring the state's plans for self-

---

108   Patricia Herbert, *The Hsaya San Rebellion (1930-32) Reappraised* (Melbourne: Monash University Centre of Southeast Asian Studies Working Paper no. 27, 1982), fn. 28, p. 15.

109   Moscotti, *British Policy and Nationalist Movement*, pp. 40-1; Maung Maung, *From Sangha to Laity*, pp. 28-32.

110   Cady, *History of Modern Burma*, p. 231.

111   Moscotti, *British Policy and Nationalist Movement*, p. 33.

112   Maung Maung, *From Sangha to Laity*, p. 20.

113   Moscotti, *British Policy and Nationalist Movement*, p. 41.

114   Cady, *History of Modern Burma*, fn. 66, p. 235.

government, they set up their own with a hierarchy of village, circle and district boards.[115] Through these the *wunthanu athin* organised a variety of activities in defiance of the state. They encouraged the people and monks to refuse services, including food and religious ceremonies, to non-European officials. These people were the most vulnerable to such pressures, as they were dependent on the communities in which they lived for their sustenance and authority. Headmen were especially singled out for this treatment and some were even killed.[116]

As part of their shadow administrative structures, the *wunthanu athin* organised their own courts, boycotting the state's legal system and reinstating Burmese arbitration techniques to settle disputes, often with the involvement of village monks.[117] They organised protests against specific legislation they found objectionable, especially the collective defence and punishment provisions of the Village Act.[118] After 1923 *bu* or 'No' *athin* were organised, often within the *wunthanu athin*, as the campaign grew more radical. These bodies organised boycotts of the state's auctions of fisheries and fallow lands and refused to acknowledge the state's right to control these resources. They encouraged villagers not to pay taxes and to defy the orders of the headmen, and they attempted to thwart the legal sale of alcohol and opium.[119] Similar *sibwayei* (economy *athin*) were also organised, sometimes using violence, in order to persuade Chettiars to lower debt obligations.[120] The height of the anti-tax campaign was reached in 1923-5, when the GCBA was most under the control of the radical delegates of the village *athin*.[121] They even succeeded in getting the 1924 GCBA conference to pass an illegal resolution authorising the non-payment of taxes.[122]

115   Herbert, *Hsaya San Rebellion*, p. 8; Moscotti, *British Policy and Nationalist Movement*, pp. 34, 42.

116   Moscotti, *British Policy and Nationalist Movement*, p. 33; Cady, *History of Modern Burma*, pp. 234-5, 253.

117   Moscotti, *British Policy and Nationalist Movement*, p. 42; Cady, *History of Modern Burma*, pp. 234-5.

118   Herbert, *Hsaya San Rebellion*, p. 11.

119   Maung Maung, *From Sangha to Laity.*

120   Cady, *History of Modern Burma*, p. 252; Moscotti, *British Policy and Nationalist Movement*, p. 43.

121   Cady, *History of Modern Burma*, p. 253; Moscotti, *British Policy and Nationalist Movement*, pp. 42-43, 44.

122   Moscotti, *British Policy and Nationalist Movement*, p. 45.

Though relatively quiet during 1926, the movement was revived after the release of U Ottama from prison in 1927.[123]

The formation of the *wunthanu athin* was part of the general process of mobilisation of the peasant population into the modern national political arena. Led by both the secular political elite and more traditionalist political monks, they provided the substitute for local leadership that the *myo* and village headmen had provided under the monarchical state. New forms of collective action, based on traditional patterns of avoidance of unjust or exorbitant demands by the state and its officials, precolonial and colonial, were used as methods not only of self-defence but also of political expression. A tradition of resistance through avoidance was added to forms of direct political action in the face of the greater power of the colonial state that the indigenous political elite initially encouraged and the colonial officials could not ignore. The range and intensity of these non-cooperative forms of behaviour are difficult to assess and have been little discussed in the literature, but they provide the background to the political behaviour of other elements in the state and society throughout the colonial period.[124] Although the *wunthanu athin* movement as an organised force was suppressed after the Hsaya San rebellion, the tradition of boycott and avoidance of the state had been re-established under modern conditions.

The *wunthanu* movement itself lived on in popular memory as a reminder of the political potential of the peasantry and the linkage between local political interests and the national political elite. If that elite was to increase its power through the support of the mass of the people, it would have to attune its policies and ideas to their interests and views. As Maung Maung makes clear in *From Sangha to Laity*, when the leaders of the GCBA abandoned the boycott movement in order to participate in the dyarchy elections of the colonial order, they lost the support of the peasants. The latter then drifted under the control of Soe Thein's Pongyi's GCBA and eventually into Hsaya San rebellion.[125] When neither proved effective in rectifying their grievances, the peasantry was briefly cut off from the national elite until the organisation of new movements in the 1930s that gave them an opportunity to express themselves in organised political action.

<hr>

123   Ibid., pp. 46, 51; Cady, *History of Modern Burma*, pp. 232, 260.

124   Andrew Turton, 'Limits of Ideological Domination and the Formation of Social Consciousness in South East Asia', in Andrew Turton and Shigeharu Tanabe (eds), *History and Peasant Consciousness in South East Asia* (Osaka: National Museum of Ethnology, Senri Ethnological Studies no. 13, 1984), p. 65.

125   Maung Maung, *From Sangha to Laity*, pp. 62-4.

The ideas of the *wunthanu* movement organisers were consonant with the views of the peasants themselves. *Wunthanu Rethkita*, which was written in 1924 for the use of the political *dhammakatika* monks as they toured the villages organising the *wunthanu athin*, expressed these ideas well. Its author, C.P. Khin Maung, an ardent boycottist in the Hlaing-Pu-Gyaw GCBA, demonstrated in his *Wunthanu Rethkita* (National Principles) that the ideas of the *wunthanu* movement were moral and just, as they were 'in accordance with the Buddha's wishes'. He further pointed out the differences between a good state and the then existing state that they were to boycott. The good state of the Myanmar kings and their officials, he argued, 'had to observe certain principles and duties and swore to act for the people's good'. The king's ministers, the *wun-gyi*, bore 'the king's burden and the people's burden and these are that the king should make no errors, that there should be no conflict and opposition with the people, and that the country should be populous and pleasant and the people tranquil and contented'.[126] These are ideas which reappear in the ideological justification of every successful political organisation in modern Burma's history, and have their roots in the precolonial state's ideology.

Despite the widespread support and deep commitment to the *wunthanu* movement in the villages and its link with national politicians, the colonial state was able to amass sufficient force and law to keep the movement under control. Existing legislation such as the 1887 Village Act, the Anarchical Revolutionary Crimes Act or Rowlatt Act of 1919, the Habitual Offenders Restriction Act (1919) and Section 144 of the Criminal Procedure Code, and new laws specifically drafted to deal with the boycott movement, the Criminal Law Amendment Act (1922), the Criminal Tribes Act (1924) and the Anti-Boycott Act were used by the state throughout the 1920s.[127] Military police units were sent to punish recalcitrant villages, and they even, on occasion, razed buildings.[128] The *bu athin* were declared illegal and banned in 1923.[129] Coercive measures were used to collect taxes in the face of peasant opposition. In 1923-4, 2,802,000 rupees were collected in this way.[130]

---

126   Herbert, *Hsaya San*, pp. 8-9.

127   Moscotti, *British Policy and Nationalist Movement*, p. 34; Maung Maung, *From Sangha to Laity*, pp. 42-3; Cady, *History of Modern Burma*, pp. 233-4.

128   Moscotti, *British Policy and Nationalist Movement*, p. 42.

129   Maung Maung, *From Sangha to Laity*, p. 46.

130   Moscotti, *British Policy and Nationalist Movement*, p. 45.

The form of these coercive tax collections only served to reinforce the peasants' dislike of the state and those who benefited from its method:

The *myooks* came with the military police, an armed Indian sepoy force, and a few Indians in business or a butcher in the neighbouring town. The *myook* held court and upon failure of residents to pay taxes due, the properties of the delinquents were auctioned off. . . the villagers would not buy each other's property; but the Indian business man was thereto pick it up at the cost of the dismantled material alone. The villager's animals, his means of earning a living, his bullock carts, and other movable property was also disposed of in the same manner.[131]

The *myo-ok* himself often profited from these auctions, which sometimes went as far as selling the food in the villager's home.[132]

Far from ignoring the consequences of the state's actions in putting down the boycott movement of the *wunthanu athin*, the indigenous political elite, including those who cooperated with the Legislative Council, attempted to halt or ameliorate the actions of the officials and thus regain the support of the peasantry. The National Party under U Ba Pe attempted in the Council to halt the imposition of communal fines on villages and opposed the outlawing of the *bu athin*. In a creative political act, the politicians 'almost succeeded in passing a resolution (37 to 39) to lift the emergency ban against allegedly subversive *athins*', providing that only 'legislative councillors acquainted with the problem certify that the assumed emergency no longer existed.'[133] This resolution, had it been passed, would have removed from the officials and placed in the hands of the elected representatives a significant degree of political power within their constituencies. Thus the politicians who worked within the state's structures would have been provided with evidence to demonstrate that cooperation was actually beneficial to the indigenous population. Their failure lent credence to the arguments that no genuine Myanmar nationalist cause could gain from cooperation with the British and their electoral institutions.

The suppression of the *wunthanu* movement, coupled with the growing agrarian crisis after the 1930 depression in rice prices and the increasing competition for jobs and land, led to a significant rise in communal and class tensions in the towns and cities of Burma, as well as the most widespread peasant uprising of the colonial period. The first major demonstration of these growing tensions was two weeks of rioting in May 1930 in

131   Maung Maung, *From Sangha to Laity*, p. 48.
132   Herbert, *Hsaya San Rebellion*, p. 10.
133   Cady, *History of Modern Burma*, p. 249.

Rangoon, between Indian dock workers and Burmese labourers who had been used as strike-breakers. After the strike by the Indian workers was settled the Burmese were fired; they took their anger out on the returning Indians. There were several hundred reported deaths and many more injuries. The rioting spread from Rangoon to surrounding towns, 'and especially to the Hanthawaddy district towns of Kayan, Thongwa, and Kyauktan, where a concentration of Indian landowners and tenants had gained footholds among the predominantly Burmese lands'.[134]

In December the Hsaya San peasants' rebellion broke out. Hsaya San, a district leader of the GCBA who had grown frustrated at the inability of the élite politicians to alleviate the peasants' conditions, had in 1928 secretly begun to organise associations to resist the collection of the capitation tax following the governments' suppression of the anti-tax campaign of 1927.[135] In addition to the anti-tax issue, he also developed peasant support for opposing the state's restrictions on the use of timber and bamboo by the villagers, a traditional privilege that the colonial state had appropriated as a monopoly. When the acting Burmese Governor, Sir J.A. Maung Gyi, refused to remit or reduce taxes following the dramatic decline in paddy prices of 1930, an apparently spontaneous peasant revolt broke out at the end of December in Tharrawaddy district. By early January it had spread to surrounding areas, especially the delta. The initial anger of the peasants was directed at the village headmen, and within two days four had been killed. In the 18 months of the rebellion, a total of 38 headmen were killed and 150 others attacked and wounded. The government, initially unprepared for the rebellion, brought in additional troops from India, and before the rebellion was suppressed killed over 1,300 rebels and arrested, captured or received the surrender of another 9,000.[136]

While at the time the government explained the Hsaya San peasants' rebellion as the last gasp of the dying traditionalism of the Burmese peasantry (a view shared by many commentators subsequently), it can be more appropriately seen as a consequence of the inability of the *wunthanu* movement and its national level GCBA leaders to ameliorate peasant grievances

---

134 Maung Maung, *From Sangha to Laity*, p. 73; see also Moscotti, *British Policy and Nationalist Movement*, pp. 55-6.

135 Moscotti, *British Policy and Nationalist Movement*, p. 57.

136 The fullest account is Maung Maung, *From Sangha to Laity*, ch. 7, 'The Peasant Revolt', pp. 83-107.

to any significant extent.[137] The government's suppression of the *wunthanu athin* had demonstrated to the peasants the failure of nonviolent political action and suggested that force was the only resort. The rationalised state, and the effective closure of the rice frontier, had also effectively abolished the option of avoidance that the peasantry had under monarchical rule. The rebellion, which was eventually put down by the massive armed forces of the state, taught them two further lessons: first, that for the time being there was little they or the national leaders could do to protect them, and second, that independence was the only way of gaining a state that might listen to them.

The extent of communal discord that existed in Burma in the early 1930s was further displayed by an outbreak of anti-Chinese rioting in Rangoon in January 1931, at the start of the peasants' rebellion. Fourteen deaths occurred in Rangoon and many Chinese fled the city.[138] The rioting spread to parts of Toungoo, Pegu and Hanthawaddy districts.[139] Although the Chinese population of Burma was then relatively small, and relations between Chinese and Burmese had never suffered from the cultural and economic strains that affected Burmese-Indian relations,[140] the indigenous population felt mounting hostility towards any group that seemed to be prospering under the prevailing conditions. In areas not directly involved in the Hsaya San rebellion, Burmese and Indians took the opportunity of the state's preoccupation with the urban riots and peasant rebellion to attack each other. Race riots occurred in Syriam, Thongwa, and Kyauktan townships around Rangoon in April, May and June 1931.[141]

The last major outbreak of communal conflict before the Second World War started on 26 July 1938, when five days of anti-Indian rioting began which extended to almost all of southern and central Burma. The rioting began in Rangoon and spread throughout the districts, reaching Mandalay

---

137   Herbert, *Hsaya San Rebellion*, p. 7.

138   Moscotti, *British Policy and Nationalist Movement*, p. 120.

139   Maung Maung, *From Sangha to Laity*, p. 74.

140   In contract to other South East Asian countries, there has been very little written on the place of the Chinese in Burma's political and society. This is primarily due to the small size of the community and its reasonably easy and rapid integration into Burmese society, and their being dwarfed by the importance of the Indian community. The best short summary is found in Victor Purcell, *The Chinese in Southeast Asia* (London: Oxford University Press, 2nd edn., 1966), pp. 41-80.

141   Maung Maung, *From Sangha to Laity*, p. 74.

on the 30th. In the words of the government appointed committee which investigated the causes, the riots 'spread ... almost in concentric circles radiating from Rangoon as fast as news of what had happened there could travel by means of Burmese newspapers, passengers, and other carriers of information and rumour'.[142] The ostensible cause of the riots was the publication of an anti-Buddhist tract by a Burmese Muslim. The book had been originally published in 1931 but its existence was publicised in the anti-Ba Maw press only in July 1938, as part of the campaign to bring down his government by demonstrating that it could not maintain order. Monks took a leading part in organising the agitation against the book.[143] On 2 September another outbreak of anti-Indian rioting occurred in Rangoon. Although it was less severe and restricted primarily to the capital, the disturbances last six days.[144]

These disturbances were orchestrated by political opponents of Dr Ba Maw, both from the established parties, particularly U Saw's Myochit, and from the younger nationalists of the Do Bama Asiayon. Burmese entrepreneurs were encouraged by the belief that Indians might be forced to leave Burma as a result of the widespread anti-Indian sentiment then so forcefully apparent in the country. Plans were made to establish Burmese cooperative stores and a Japanese-owned trading firm was asked to advise.[145] The government's official inquiry into the riots concluded that they were caused by discontent among peasants over land tenure and related matters, anti-Indian feelings, the problems over the rights of Buddhist women who married Muslim men, and the political campaign against the Ba Maw government.[146] Under the relatively open political system of the late colonial state, opposition forces could always champion one or another of these problems in order to create political instability and personal insecurity, and perhaps bring down a government.

142   Riot Inquiry Committee, *Interim Report* (Rangoon: Government Printing and Stationery, 1938), p. 9. See also Smith, *Religion and Politics*, pp. 109-14.

143   Riot Inquiry Committee, *Interim Report*, p. 8; Cady, *History of Modern Burma*, pp. 393-4; Burma Monthly Intelligence Summary, vol. II, no. 7, for July 1938, 1 Aug. 1938, BOF I 37, part II.

144   Cady, *History of Modern Burma*, p. 394.

145   Burma Defence Bureau Intelligence Summary no. 9, 26 Sept. 1938, BOF I 358.

146   Riot Inquiry Committee, *Interim Report*, pp. 11-12, 22, 28-29, 33-37, and *passim*.

Even in what would be called normal periods of political and communal peace during the colonial political period, class and communal tensions were always apparent. A review of just a few months in 1939 will suggest the nature and extent. In March 1939, for example, there were communal and agrarian troubles in Shwebo and Myaungmya, of sufficient importance to be brought to the attention of the Governor.[147] Later in the same month additional Military Police units had to be sent to Myaungmya because of Burmese attacks on Indians. Military police were also patrolling Shwebo and parts of Katha in the north because of attacks by Burmese on Muslim and Zerbadi (Indo-Burmese Muslim) villages. Some of the Zerbadi villagers were being armed by the state for self-defence.[148] The troubles were spreading to Tharrawaddy district as well. From there one official report stated that

in Minhla and Okpo ... payment of rents has left many persons with hardly any food to live on. In fact, my firm conviction is that the basis of half of the Tharrawaddy trouble consists in the exorbitant rents charged by the Chettyars and moneylenders. This rent will to have come down if we are going to expect even comparative peace here. In fact these Chettyars who live safely in Rangoon and come to the districts only to screw the last basket of paddy out of the tenants are the direct cause of crime and should be made to pay for the results.[149]

By April the troubles had spread to Pyapon, Bassein, Pegu and Lower Chindwin, as well as Shwebo and Myaungmya. In Myaungmya, because of the large number of Indian tenants, more military police were sent in an effort to stop a rick and hut burning campaign that was being conducted in an effort to drive off Indian tenants.[150]

Not all the conflicts were communal in nature, and some clearly indicated the class basis of much of the unrest. In one instance, 'where the culprits in an attack on a field hut of an Indian tenant were caught red-handed, they proved to be all Indians who resented the fact that the victim had accepted a tenancy on the landlord's terms.'[151] By mid-May the level of attacks had lessened, but the tenants stepped up their programme of

---

147 Governor's Confidential Report no. 6, 16 March 1939, BOF P 39, part II.
148 Burma Defence Bureau Intelligence Summary no. 3, 27 March 1939, BOF I 358.
149 Ibid.
150 Ibid., no. 4, 25 April 1939. Home Secretary's Fortnightly Report, first half April 1939, 26 April 1939, BOF P 39, part II.
151 Governor's Confidential Report no. 9, 2 May 1939, BOF P 39, part II.

organising cultivators' associations so as to present a united front before the landlords when the time came to prepare new leases.[152] The burning of hayricks and field huts continued mostly in Pegu and Irrawaddy divisions. The Home Secretary wrote,

The crimes are not communal but are committed to intimidate tenants who have renewed their leases at the old rates. Armed patrols are now operating in the effected areas and where no evidence is obtainable against the culprits, the villagers are being called to show cause why fines should not be imposed under the Village Act; prosecutions are being instigated where possible.[153]

Communal conflicts abetted by class tensions, often called 'agrarian outrages', continued throughout June and July.[154] As the conflicts continued into August, especially in Irrawaddy division,[155] the Commissioner of Police drew official attention to 'unusually large demands for revolver licenses, particularly on the part of landowners'. It was also noted that rent collectors were becoming more common in the delta as Chettiars' fears of collecting their rents in person increased.[156]

With the resumption of cultivation, the tensions diminished as the farmers returned to their work. In the next year, apparently, the landowners gained the initiative in the struggle. It was reported that because of the intensified competition among would-be tenants, landlords were having an easier time getting contracts, and that in Akyab and Tharrawaddy the Landlords' Association was causing more trouble than the cultivators' associations.[157]

Youth and students in late colonial politics

From the 1920s students strike over the formation of Rangoon University until the Japanese invasion in 1942 the importance of secular youth in

---

152   Ibid., no. 11, 17 May 1939. Home Secretary's Fortnightly Report, first half May 1939, 26 May 1939, BOF P 39, part II.

153   Ibid.; reports of these events were published in British newspapers. See, for example, *The Daily Telegraph*, 22 May 1939.

154   Burma Defence Bureau Intelligence Summary no. 7, 27 July 1939, BOF I 358.

155   Home Secretary's Fortnightly Report for second half July, 1939, 9 August 1939, BOF P 9, Part II.

156   Burma Defence Bureau Intelligence Summary no. 8, 26 Aug. 1939, BOF I 358.

157   Extract from the Home Secretary's Fortnightly Report, send half March 1940, 9 April 1940. BOF E 1241/46, Home Secretary's Fortnightly Report for the first half May 1940, 27 May 1940, BOF P 39, Part III.

colonial politics increased. In the latter half of the 1930s, every political leader had to take account of student politics. Politicians in power were generally keen on restricting student activities, but those out of power were interested in aiding and abetting student anti-government and nationalist campaigns. The contacts the student leaders had with the colonial political elite increased their own sense of power and importance and led to a growing belief on their part that they would, in a few years, succeed the current leadership with a purer and more principled anti-colonial movement.

Although student and youth politics was a national phenomenon by the 1930s, Rangoon remained the centre of student politics. Here was the capital of the state and the site of Rangoon University, the largest and most prestigious centre of higher education in the country. The emotional and intellectual impact of Rangoon, with its large foreign communities and businesses, on youth coming from the districts, as most Burmese students did, was very great. Before they went to Rangoon the students of the 1930s may have intellectually apprehended the meaning of their country's dependent status and have experienced national or racial slights at the hands of Indian merchants or British officials, but the visual impact of Rangoon could only underscore boldly the structure of power in the country.[158] In addition, in Rangoon students had access to various forms of leftist literature, especially tracts on imperialism, much of which was imported from Britain. This literature, more than the students' formal study of European history and law in the University, provided them with a theory to explain their country's and their class's historical dilemma.

If these factors stimulated youthful nationalist feeling, the political, economic and constitutional ferment of the decade suggested to the students that concrete political action might be of use in freeing Burma from British rule and Indian money. The Hsaya San rebellion showed young people that the national spirit was strong among the peasants, and the general interpretation of the meaning of the rebellion provided a romantic link back to the military and political achievements of Burmese kings and generals. Moreover the constitutional reforms of the 1930s led to heightened interest and opportunities for participation in electoral politics. The party leaders, especially Dr Ba Maw in the 1936 election and U Saw in his 1939 campaign to bring down Ba Maw's government, sought and encouraged

---

158   The flavour of the period is delightfully portrayed in Thein Hpei Myint, *Asheika Neiwunthwetthe Bama* (As Sure as the Sun Rises in the East) (Rangoon: Hpyanchieyi Dana, Myat Sa Pei, 1974 and other editions). The title is taken from a line in Burma's national anthem, the old *Do Bama Asiayon* song.

student assistance. After Ba Maw's fall from power, he once more allied with the major youth leaders to form the anti-war Freedom Bloc. Perhaps even more than these specific political events, the economic crisis of the 1930s made students see the direct importance of political and nationalist action for their generation.

Up to the 1930s, young Burmese with education and ambition had been able to secure adequate if not always lucrative positions with the government or with foreign firms. New positions for clerks, pleaders, barristers, civil servants, teachers and the like generally became available as the economy of the cities developed. In the 1930s, however, two events limited such opportunities. First, the effects of the worldwide depression put an end to the expansion of government and private employment, and retrenchment caused some already in employment to lose their jobs. Secondly, the number of university graduates multiplied rapidly. Young people coming from rural areas saw their families' fortunes sink as the financial impact of the depression on Burmese agriculture took its toll even of the better off Burmese peasants, landlords and shopkeepers. In contrast to the generations of the 1910s and 1920s, that of the 1930s saw their parents' and their own opportunities for prosperity and advancement receding.

Such factors help explain the increased political involvement of middle class youth who came to lead some of the new political movements, but they were supported in their endeavours by the increasing politicisation of younger and less privileged students in towns and villagers. As many of the university students were themselves from these districts, making contact with those who remained behind was easy. The increased interest of youth and students outside Rangoon in politics was manifested in the proliferation of youth movements, volunteer corps, students unions and local level Thakin organisations in the late 1930s.[159]

Some data indicate not only the extensive nature of such movements, but also their organisational instability, as youth sought effective outlets for their political energies. In April 1937 British military intelligence reported

---

159   The Burmese Defence Bureau Monthly Intelligence Summaries under the heading 'Youth Movements' listed large numbers of new organisations. They also made a distinction between political and non-political youth organisations. Although it was not made explicit what criteria were used for making such distinctions, in all probability, groups which formally acknowledged affiliation with a political party or anti-government movement were labelled political, and those which either supported the official government or appeared to be neutral, were considered non-political.

that twenty-two new clubs, corps, etc., had been formed, of which three were considered political: one students' union and two Thakin branches.[160] In May of that year there were thirty-two new clubs, corps, etc., of which fifteen were political: three students' unions and eight Thakin branches.[161] In January 1938, there were fifty-three new organisations, forty of which were political. During the next month another twenty-eight new clubs, twenty-three of which were political, were formed.[162] In January 1938 there were fifty-three new organisations, forty of which were political. During the next month another twenty-eight new clubs, twenty-three of which were political, were formed.[163] Reports for subsequent months contain similar numbers.

In the first six months of 1938 there were over 230 such organisations formed, of which over 160 were considered to be explicitly political. Such a large number of new groups would indicate that while they were relatively easy to form, as there was a great deal of youthful energy seeking organisational outlets, the groups did not last long. This was for the simple reason that there were few activities for such groups to engage in after the initial details of organisation had been completed. The members would slowly drift away and perhaps join other, new groups. Another indication of the amount of youthful energy in Burma in the late 1930s was the large numbers of meetings and parades conducted each month.[164] These youth meetings, parades and the like were certainly not all anti-government in inspiration or character. Many were not concerned with the struggle against

160   Extract from Intelligence Summary no. 4, 24 April 1937, BOF I 20.

161   Ibid., no. 5, 26 May 1937.

162   Burma Defence Bureau Intelligence Summary no. 1, 26 Jan. 1938, BOF I 358.

163   Ibid., no. 2, 1938.

164   These, like youth organisations (see fn. 157 above), were tabulated in the monthly intelligence summaries. For example, in January 1938, there were 170 parades and 122 meetings, 74 of the meetings held by Thakins (ibid., no. 1, 26 Jan 1938). In February 1938 there were 166 parades, 105 conducted by volunteer corps affiliated with political parties and 61 by volunteer fire brigades. In the same month there were 164 meetings, 140 promoted by Thakins (ibid., no. 2, 23 Feb 1938). In March 1938, there were 365 parades but nearly 300 of these were conducted by fire brigades. Of the 161 meetings that were held, 121 were held by Thakins (ibid., no. 3, 26 March 1938). In May 1938, there were 302 parades, 201 conducted by members of the Green Army, the *Dahma Tat* of Dr Ba Maw's party, and the *Bama Letyon Tat* of the Students Union. Of the 275 meetings held, 202 were organised by Thakins (ibid., no. 5, 27 May 1938).

imperialism but instead expressed a general but unspecific sense of national pride.[165]

The various volunteer corps organised to conduct these parades and rallies in the 1930s, often referred to somewhat grandly as private armies, were the most organised mass groups in pre-war Burma. Every major political party had its own volunteer corps, as did the All Burma Students' Union and the Hindu, Muslim and Chinese communities. The oldest of the volunteer corps, the *Ye Tat,* usually referred to in English as the Green Army, was founded by conservative politicians in the 1930s but did not become politically involved until after the introduction of the 1935 constitution. The success of Fascism in Europe in the 1930s provided part of their inspiration. While they could be used to terrorise political opponents, the volunteer corps were rarely used to break up meetings and public speeches. They were not armed but did have uniforms, usually khaki shorts and shirts of distinguishing colours from which they took they popular name. Their most important function was usually the extortion of money from wealthy individuals through the threat of a beating or the destruction of property.[166] There were occasional clashes between the different 'armies' but they were never a serious threat to domestic order.[167]

Linking the relatively sophisticated, politically active students of the university and the students and other youth of the towns and districts by the end of the 1930s were the All Burma Students' Union (ABSU) and the organisation of the Thakins, the Do Bama Asiayon. These two groups, often working together so closely as to be indistinguishable, were the primary focus of the energies of nationalist youth. Their leadership, often overlapping and almost identical in perspective on many issues, came from the youth of the Burmese middle class. Their behaviour, however, often in violation of traditional codes of conduct for young people in Burmese cul-

---

165   Maung Maung, *From Sangha to Laity,* pp. 76-8.

166   Interview with F.S.V. Donnison, I.C.S. (retired), London, 14 Dec. 1971.

167   For example, 'A party of Dobama Red-shirt Volunteer Corps, while patrolling Kyaukpadaung [Myingyan] by night came into collision with the local Green Army. Blows were exchanged with the result that a number of Red Shirts are now "off parade". It was the "Red Shirts", however, who laid complaint at the Police Station.' Extract from Intelligence Summary no. 4, 24 April 1937, BOF I 20. In mid-1938 there were clashes between Galon U Saw's Galon Tat and parties of Thakin in central Burma. Burma Defence Bureau Intelligence Summary no. 6, 26 June 1939. BOF I 358. For a fuller discussion of the development and use of the private armies, see Taylor, 'Burmese Social Classes and British-Indian Policy', pp. 184-91.

ture, led them into conflict not only with the political authorities but also with the older generation. In the first years of the 1930s some young people who felt a great deal of frustration with the inability of the older politicians to dislodge the British from Burma established study groups and other bodies to develop discipline and principle among themselves. They sought to avoid the temptations of office and apparent apeing of British ways by many youths in Rangoon at that time. A Youth Improvement Society of this type was formed in 1930,[168] followed a few years later by an All Burma Youth League. This small group contained several of the most important political leaders of the 1950s, including U Nu, U Ohn and U Thi Han.[169]

Emerging out of the first efforts of the 1930s generation to organise politically, the Do Bama Asiayon was the political grouping that provided many of Burma's government leaders of the 1940s and 1950s with their first political experience at national level. The name 'Do Bama Asiayon' means 'We Burmans', or, more literally, 'Our Burma Association', and has its parallel in the Sinn Fein of Irish nationalism. 'Do Bama' was also the slogan called forth by many of the Burmese involved in the anti-Indian riots of the early 1930s. The organisation was criticised by Marxist nationalists in the late 1930s for being racist and sectarian because of its original narrow appeals to Burman (Bamar) Buddhists. As noted earlier, the name *Thakin* that the members of the Do Bama Asiayon adopted is an old Burmese word meaning 'master', and, like *Sahib* in India, was the title by which Europeans were addressed by subordinates during the colonial period. By taking the title for themselves, Burmese nationalists were demonstrating that they were the masters of Burma; but also, perhaps unconsciously, the elite youth who appended the title to their names were telling other Burmese that they were the emerging governing elite.

The Do Bama Asiayon was formally organised on 4 July 1933, but it did not rise to prominence until it was taken over the former leadership of the ABSU, including Thakin Aung San, in 1938. The ABSU, with its affiliated student unions at secondary schools and centres of higher education in Mandalay, Pyinmana and Rangoon, was one of the groups seeking to organise politically interested youth. Initially it concentrated on matters directly affecting students. It had grown from efforts of the Rangoon University Students' Union to enlist the support of other students for the 1936 student strike against the University Act, the cause of the first student

168   Maung Maung, *From Sangha to Laity*, p. 75.
169   Ibid., pp. 78-79.

strike in 1920. By the late 1930s, it had become involved in political action touching all aspects of the life of the peasants and workers.[170]

Because of the earlier importance of students in Burmese politics before they were organised on a national basis, the formation of the ABSU was the cause of much concern to British officials responsible for internal security. One of them wrote in September 1937, 'this new tendency to combine unions and to accept orders from extremist organisations in Rangoon is pregnant with danger and the next school or university strike will probably be much more troublesome than any in the past.'[171]

The concerns of the annual conferences and other meetings of the ABSU reveal its interests and the nature of its political activities. At the third annual conference held in 1938 there were 53 delegates from schools in southern and central Burma as well as 250 other persons, including two of the four members of the House of Representatives from Bassein town district where the meeting was held. 'The background of the dais on which the President's chair [occupied by Aung San] was placed was decorated with a large picture of the famous Burmese General Maha Bandoola on horseback receiving the salute of a British army officer.' The meeting passed resolutions calling for free compulsory elementary education, technical and vocational education for those who passed the primary level, the sending of state scholars abroad for technical and vocational education, and a pledge not to assist the British in the event of war.[172] At the annual conference held in December 1940, over 4,000 students attended an illegal ceremony honouring the 89 students who had been injured in the anti-Ba Maw and anti-British demonstrations held in Rangoon during 1938-9, and a bust was unveiled of Maung Aung Gyaw, a student who had been killed by the police in these demonstrations.[173]

At its ideological and political training classes, the ABSU leaders encouraged students to read and discuss the implications for Burma of the various Marxist and Marxist-derived books and articles then in common

---

170   See ibid., pp. 122-40; also Cady, *History of Modern Burma*, pp. 378-83, for an account of the 1936 students' strike.

171   Burma Defence Bureau Intelligence Summary no. 9, 25 Sept. 1937, BOF I 20.

172   Maha Bandoola was a Burmese officer who led several successful battles against the British Indian army in the first Anglo-Burmese war. He was known for his headstrong bravery and died during the ill fated defence of Rangoon toward the end of the war. Ibid., no. 5, 27 May 1938, BOF I 358.

173   And after who Aung Gyaw Street in downtown Yangon is today named.

circulation. Many of these volumes were written by leaders of the Do Bama Asiayon and were easily available through the Nagani (Red Dragon) Book Club run by Thakin Nu and others. Thakin Soe's *Socialism* and Thakin Ba Hein's *The Capitalist World* were among the most widely read volumes in Burmese, and Lenin's works were also much sought after.[174] The Marxist-oriented leaders of the ABSU, having graduated from student politics, if not always from the university, took over the Do Bama Asiayon from its more conservative and older leaders in 1938 and elected Thakin Thein Maung President and Thakin Aung San Secretary-General. Before then the organisation had been led by men whose ideological views tended to be somewhat closer to the moralistic principles of the founders of the All Burma Youth League and the other student self-strengthening movements of the early 1930s from which it had developed. The man who was the inspiration behind the Do Bama Asiayon and who gave it its name, Thakin Ba Thaung, was the author of several tracts urging Burmese to have greater self respect and to avoid involvement with foreigners and the purchase of foreign made goods.[175] The political leader of the 1930s who bridged the gap between the Do Bama leaders of the early 1930s and the Marxist leaders of the late 1930s better than any other was Thakin Nu, the man who became Prime Minister at independence.

The dominance of Marxist-oriented students in the leadership of the Do Bama Asiayon led to a split within the organisation after the 1938 conference; the majority remained with Aung San and the old ABSU leadership which had the patronage of one of the oldest Thakins, the essayist and poet Kodaw Hmaing. This outward split was only one manifestation of the divisions that existed within the organisation and the youthful political group more generally. Although they were able to arouse widespread popular support from peasants and workers for anti-government campaigns in the late 1930s, the leaders were constantly torn, as the previous generation had been, between those who wished to work with the British state structures in

174   This is discussed further in Robert H. Taylor, 'Introduction: Marxism and Resistance in Wartime Burma', in the author's *Marxism and Resistance in Burma 1942-1945: Thein Pe Myint's 'Wartime Traveller'* (Athens, Ohio: Ohio University Press, 1984), pp. 2-3.

175   Tin Htun Aung, *Myanma Naingngnanyei hnit Thakhin Ba Thaung* (Burma's Politics and Thakin Ba Thaung) (Rangoon: Sapu U Sa Pe Hpyanchiyei, 1980). App. D(1) of Maung Maung, 'Nationalist Movements in Burma', pp. 619-28, contains translations of Ba Thaung's first two *'naingnganpyu sasu'* or 'national building' articles.

order to regain independence and those who sought to subvert the state, or at least boycott its institutions, on the assumption that without collaborators, the colonial order would collapse. By this time, however, the situation was more complicated, as the changing international order, particularly the development of Japanese militarism and the Chinese Communist Party, as well as the growing strength of the Indian National Congress, suggested to some leaders of the Do Bama Asiayon that outside support, perhaps even arms, would be made available to assist them.[176]

In the four years prior to the Japanese invasion, the Do Bama Asiayon's young leaders were searching for ways to solve their political dilemma. While it was clear to many of them that the existing political system did provide opportunities for personal advancement and even power, it did not allow for the kind of revolution that they felt was necessary in order to establish a more just distribution of economic and political power. Examination of the records of the period suggests that in searching for a solution the leaders were unable, under the existing order, to act upon their often creative and potentially effective ideas. Like the first generation of national leaders they were caught in the web of the state, and only its destabilisation as a result of external change could create a situation where they might seize power and alter the nature of the state.

The stresses of the period laid bare the disorder among the younger political leaders. Within the Do Bama Asiayon there were socialists, militarists and reformers, and those who looked to Japan or the Soviet Union or the British Labour Party for inspiration. Various committees and divisions of the organisation became enclaves of these differing perspectives and a great deal of time was spent in fairly academic debate. The first conference of the Do Bama Asiayon, held in Yenangyaung in 1934, had about it the flavour of the old GCBA conferences of the 1920s.[177] Following the second conference in 1936, a parliamentary branch, the Ko Min Ko Chin (One's Own King, One's Own Kind) party, was established. With its formation, the Do Bama Asiayon entered into electoral politics and competed in the 1936 general election. This action, which placed the Asiayon on the same footing as the political parties which cooperated in the state's structures, was followed soon after the inauguration of the new constitutions by an

---

176   Taylor, 'Marxism and Resistance', pp. 8-11.

177   App. D(2) of Maung Maung, 'Nationalist Movements of Burma', pp. 629-43, contains translations of the resolutions of the five Do Bama Asiayon conferences.

announcement that echoed the boycott and non-cooperation movement of the *wunthanu athin* and the original GCBA. In July 1937, the Do Bama Asiayon leader Thakin Tun Ok was reported to have indicated

that the ultimate aim of the Thakin Party is to establish a system of administration parallel to the existing Government system, and that the first step toward this end will apparently be to undermine the present system of village administration and the authority of the village headman. The apparent idea is that the ... system of government from the village headman upwards would have its counterpart in the appointment of Presidents of village, township and district Asi-ayons, with the Central Baho Dobama Asia-yon at the head of the organisation.[178]

The following January it was reported in Bassein that the idea of a parallel administration was to be put into effect.[179] While occasional references to this scheme appeared from time to time subsequently, it seems it was never attempted on any broad scale.

The new generation of political leaders recognised that the modern state could not be ignored and that the gaining of independence would not mean restoration of the economic and political practices of the precolonial era. The postcolonial state would have to be used to transform Burma, and from the time the young Marxists took control of the Do Bama Asiayon, its rhetoric and policies were cast in the mould of the modern state. The clearest statement of this new view is found in 'The Manifesto of the *Dobama Asiayone* ... Its Policy, Its Explanation, Its Future Work' prepared by the Fourth Working Committee of the organisation under the leadership of Aung San.[180] The novelty of the organisation's ideas and behaviour had created a good deal of opposition to it from established sectors of Burmese society; this was acknowledged at the beginning of the Manifesto. Stating that 'it has met with imperialist and bureaucratic repression', it went on to say,

for a time and still among sections of the public, it is regarded as a socially evil phenomenon. Its members are virtually ostracised. With political persecution on the one hand and social tyranny on the other, it has undergone innumerable trials and tribulations which are but the signs of its birth pangs.

---

178 Burma Monthly Intelligence Summary no. 4, for month ending 31 July 1937, BOF I 37, part I.

179 Burma Defence Bureau Intelligence Summary No. 1, 26 January 1938, BOF I 358.

180 Translated in CID Burma, Intelligence Branch Department no. 694/C, 11 July 1939, BOF P 39, part II. The manifesto was reprinted in *The Guardian* (Rangoon) in 1959 during the time of the first military government.

Turning to explicitly political matters, the Manifesto described the organisation as 'anti-imperialist and democratic'. The Do Bama Asiayon stood for 'full "*Ko Min Ko Chin*" a free democratic republic'. The details of the policy included the abolition of the Government of Burma Act of 1935, and the drafting of a new constitution by a constituent assembly exercising full self-determination. 'Mass struggle' was the strategy with which to accomplish this. Among the available tactics was parliamentary action. On the question of accepting political office the Manifesto noted that this was merely a question of tactics, but doubted whether accepting office would be of any use under the existing constitution, which did not allow for effective means of solving Burma's problems. Neither India's experience nor Burma's under the 1935 constitution offered convincing evidence to the contrary. The strategy of mass action entailed four main tasks:

To raise the social and economic consciousness of all toilers of the land on their day to day needs, local, municipal, economic, cultural, etc.

To resist an encroachment upon our civil liberties and democratic rights.

To introduce effective measures which will ultimately turn the Dobama Asiayon into a full-fledged organ of the people's will -- a united democratic national front against Imperialism, for freedom and democracy.

To hold a Plebiscite in regard to the constitution on every Anti-Constitution Day [April 1].

To achieve this strategy, organisation was needed 'to purify, regulate, extend and strengthen' the Asiayon. Also needed were a 'properly equipped and well-regulated headquarters and its staff.' The Working Committee felt that half of that goal had already been achieved.

The Do Bama Asiayon was often accused by British officials and more conservative Burmese of being a Communist organisation as well as being corrupt. It sought to defend itself against such charges as it did in the Manifesto.

To many the ideology and character of our Asiayone has not been clear. The ... vested interests call our Asiayone communistic in origin. But everyone who knows something of a Communist Party would laugh at the suggestion. No, the Dobama Asiayone is not a communist organisation. What is it then? Of course, unlike reactionaries and vested interests, we are not alarmed by 'the Spectre of Communism'. Within our organisation, communists, socialists, nationalists, others, all can exist, provided they will sincerely fight and live and die for freedom.

213

Now there is another criticism that our organisation is corrupt. But this is such a big bluff for any sensible man to swallow. Whether it is corrupt or not will be more and more clearly seen. After all, some members of it may be corrupt. This is not peculiar to the Dobama Asiayone alone. But this is no reason why the whole organisation should be condemned. This is however a good propaganda of our political opponents.

In addition to its broad policy goals of independence, self-determination and anti-imperialism, the Do Bama Asiayon adopted a variety of other specific goals that it attempted to get the existing government and parties to implement. These policies were directed towards improving the conditions of the masses, which, according to the Asiayon constitution, were composed of 'labourers, cultivators, students, shopkeepers, hawkers, traders, brokers, clerks and working people'. The purpose of these other policy goals was not to promise the masses 'heaven and earth all of a sudden', but to indicate what an independent state led by them would achieve in governing Burma.

Though the groups defined by the Asiayon as the masses accounted for the overwhelming majority of the population, the peasants were the most important sector to which all the parties had to appeal. On the questions of peasant indebtedness and landlessness, the moderate policy of the Do Bama Asiayon suggests a certain ambiguity in its position. While at times advocating a militant pro-landless cultivator and even pro-revolutionary line at the rhetorical level, at the practical level the national leadership followed a reformist line suggesting an internal conflict of interest between the organisation's need for political support and its leaders understanding of their own interests within the political economy.

Indeed, the Do Bama Asiayon's policy was much in keeping with the policies of the major parties in the government. In the July 1939 Manifesto, the goals of the Asiayon were not greatly different from those of the Legislature's Agrarian Inquiry Committee or the British policy makers who had been advocating small scale peasant proprietorship since the 1880s. 'The agrarian problem will, we are afraid, for some time come to absorb most of our attention, because [the peasants] form the core of our national economy for the time being. Our policy in this connection is to create a prosperous peasant population.' While the Do Bama Asiayon expressed dissatisfaction with the terms of the government's agrarian policies, it also said it would 'give them full trial'.

The central Do Bama Asiayon's reformist policies in agriculture were demonstrated in 1939 when, during a spate of rick and hut burnings accompanied by Burmese-Indian communal tensions and clashes, the Thakins' central leadership urged the cultivators to abide by the law and cease such activities.[181] However, local Thakin working with the peasants apparently paid little heed to this advice and encouraged them to begin ploughing in areas where no contracts had been signed with the landlords, as happened in Myaungmya district in June of that year.[182] Local actions of this kind, in keeping with the old *wunthanu* methods, were opposed by the President of the Do Bama Asiayon, who called upon the peasants to abandon their non-payment of tax campaigns and urged them to work through legal procedures for a lowering of taxes and rents. He further suggested that the peasants were acting precipitately in their efforts to throw out the British.[183] The central leadership 'brought to the notice of its rural branches the provisions of the Tenancy Act and ... urged them to impress on their members the necessity for complying with the provisions of the Act and behaving in a law abiding manner.'[184]

The Thakins' central leadership, perhaps in the belief that only industrial workers could lead a progressive movement, spent a great deal of effort in trying to organise factory workers and labourers in the oil fields at Yenangyaung and Chauk.[185] Here one of the major problems they faced was the fact the most of the industrial workers were Indians who were aware of the implicit pro-Burman attitude and leadership of the Asiayon. Its labour programme included the abolition of the *maistry* system and the establishment of a Labour Exchange Department run by the state to replace it. The most complete statement of the Do Bama Asiayon's labour policy was made in a May Day manifesto signed by Thakin Soe, Burma's premier Marxist theoretician, and Thakin Kyaw Sein. Its distribution was banned by government order. Among other things, it called for a 35 per cent increase in wages, a forty-hour week, and the improvement of working and living conditions through government action.[186] Its organisational activities, along with the ABSU leadership, enabled the Asiayon to gain the

181   Governor's Confidential Report no. 11, 17 May 1939, BOF P 39, Part II.

182   Home Secretary's Fortnightly Report for the 2nd Half May, 1939, 10 June 1939; Governor's Confidential Report no. 13, 16 June 1939. BOF P 39, part II.

183   Burma Defence Bureau Intelligence Summary no. 4, 25 April 1939, BOF I 358.

184   Governor's Confidential Report no. 12, 5 June 1939, BOF P 39, part II.

185   Report of an Officer of this Department (CID), 15 Aug. 1939, BOF P 233.

186   Extract from the May Day Manifesto to be issued by the DAA, 1940, BOF P 39, Part III.

support of many oil workers during the 1938 strike.[187] The Thakins also made appeals for support from members of the police, army and civil service, and their successes was sufficient to cause the government concern.[188]

The Thakins' claim that the organisation was not Communist was clearly correct. Their policies were too eclectic and their hope of working through existing institutions of the state indicate their ambivalent attitude towards revolution There were several reasons for this, one of which was the origins of their socialist ideas. There were a variety of sources, none coming directly from the any of the internationally recognised centres of revolution. Rather, the Thakins learned their socialism from popular British and Indian tracts, particularly the publications of Gollancz's Left Book Club and the writings of people such as Palme Dutt and John Strachey. As the leading Eastern European student of Burmese ideological practices has written, the Thakins 'tended to accept some Marxist principles in a dogmatic and simplifying manner', and this 'produced a contradictory response among the Thakins.' The ideology was appealing to some because of its connection with the rapid development and power of the state in the Soviet Union, but for others its value was found in its 'explanation of the nature of colonialism and imperialism'. Most of the Thakins saw Marxism as 'a mere instrument in their anti-colonial struggle'.[189]

The ideological inconsistencies of the Thakins can also be explained by examining their social backgrounds, most of which were to be found among the landowning, commercial and government service sector of the state-dependent middle class. While full information on the class positions of the Thakins is not available, it seems that most of the leaders and perhaps many of the district leaders, like the student political leaders of the period, came from the declining landowning and trading class of the rural areas. Of the nineteen persons listed in *Who's Who in Burma, 1961* who were active Thakins in the 1930s, and whose father's occupation is given, only one was an agriculturist. Most of their fathers were traders and merchants, four

---

187   For a discussion of the 1938-39 oilfield workers strike, see Taylor, 'Relationship Between Burmese Social Classes and British-Indian Policy', ch. 5. The Burmese language literature, in which it is often known as the 1300 Revolution, is extensive.

188   Burma Defence Bureau Intelligence Summary no. 12, 31 Dec. 1941, BOF I 358.

189   Jan Becka, *The National Liberation Movement in Burma during the Japanese Occupation Period (1941-1945)* (Prague: Oriental Institution, Dissertationes Orientales, vol. 42, 1983), p. 38.

were landowners, two were timber and rice mill owners, and two were government employees. Thakin Aung San's father was a pleader, Thakin Tun Ok's father was a landowner and Thakin Hla Pe's was both a landowner and a miller. Thakin Tun Shein was the son of a trader and Thakin Nu's parents were landowners and shopkeepers. Other prominent Thakins were the sons of contractors, merchants and landowners.[190]

Thus, the Do Bama Asiayon was a new force in Burmese society and politics, and it was based upon the youngest generation of the middle class. Generational differences determined their complaints against the older parties and leaders more than did ideological goals. While they used the language of Marxism, they were no more, and no less, anti-imperialist than the older party leaders. They may have seen the strategic possibilities of the anti-imperialist campaign in Burma in the late 1930s differently, but not necessarily more correctly. Their generation had not witnessed the defeat of the Hsaya San rebellion; it just remembered it as a glorious attempt to throw off foreign rule. The Indian population, as far as they had experienced, had always been in Burma, and while they may not have liked to compete with Indians for employment, they had a different perception from their seniors of India's relationship with Burma. Moreover, the Thakins did not look upon King Thibaw as the king who could not fend off the British, but rather as the Myanmar king that the British had arrogantly deposed.

These differences altered the world views of the two rival generations of political leaders in pre-war Burma. They affected their perceptions of what could and should be done to regain the state's independence and remove policy making from control by the interests of foreign capital and labour. They did not, however, change to any significant degree what the political leaders wanted Burma to become once it was again free of foreign rule and economic domination. Conflicts over the goal of the independent state were to occur in another decade, when independence was imminent and the consequences of internal class conflict made themselves felt. The ideas of the student political activists of the 1930s persisted after the fall of the colonial state, to shape the first 40 years of Burma's post-colonial independence. So also did the their legacy of political mobilisation, which achieved success as the state was dislodged from its dominant relationship with civil society.

---

190   Guyot, 'Political Impact of the Japanese Occupation', app. I, pp. 419-21; Nu, *U Nu – Saturday's Son* (edited by U Kyaw Yin and translated by U Law Yone) (New Haven: Yale University Press, 1975), p. 10.

4

THE DISPLACEMENT OF
THE STATE, 1942-1962

War, revolution and the state

The relationship between the state and civil society in Burma was radically altered in the period between 1942 and 1962. As a result of the Second World War and the civil war that followed independence, the state was displaced as the creator of political order and economic direction and lost its hegemonic position. No longer able to determine many of the conditions of social and economic life, the state became a rival object for control by groups possessing different perceptions of what kind of society Burma should be. After independence from Britain was formally granted on 4 January 1948, these groups sought to dislodge those who had been bequeathed the shell of the state in order to reconstruct society in accordance with their own concepts of politics and morality. For twenty years, capture of the carapace of the state became the purpose of almost all political action, and as no group was willing to grant the state and its personnel pre-eminence, a stalemate ensued. The state remained enfeebled, and a generation came of age in a society where non-state institutions were often perceived as more powerful than the state itself.

It has usually seemed logical to divide analyses of the 1940s and the 1950s into six or eight reasonably distinct periods of two to five years. This implied that the primary objectives, the leading personalities and perhaps even the purpose of politics during these years changed from one reasonably discrete unit of time to the next. These periods are the Second World War, 1942-45; the regaining of independence, 1945-48; the post-independence civil war, 1948-52; the government of the Anti-Fascist

People's Freedom League (AFPFL), 1951-58; the military 'caretaker government', 1958-60; the return to civilian rule under U Nu, 1960-62; and the military coup of 1962. Viewed from the perspective of the evolution of the state *qua* state, these twenty years can also be seen as a whole, during which the state, denied the support of the British-Indian empire and briefly and ineffectually backed by the Japanese empire, disintegrated and was displaced. The two decades after 1942 can be conceived as years of contest between competing groups over which one would resurrect the state, in what form, and in whose interest. Because of its complexity, it is difficult to deal with the period chronologically and still grasp meaning from the passing events. The only significant change in the nature of the contest came in the months between October 1946 and January 1947, when, after the British had made it clear that independence would be granted within one year, the basic issues became fundamentally domestic and internal rather than imperial or international.

Many of the interweaving strands of political and economic developments during these twenty years have pre-war roots. As argued in Chapter 2, the rationalisation of the state under colonial auspices altered the nature of the society in many ways. But in the realm of popular ideas and symbols, many political and moral ideals of the precolonial order persisted in people's minds. When the Japanese invaded, only fifty-six years had elapsed since a Myanmar monarch had reigned in Mandalay. While very few people in 1942 expected that it would be possible to return to political structures and state relations comparable to those of the late Konbaung dynasty, many looked forward, more in nostalgia than in clear memory, to a new version of the alleged order and justice of the precolonial state. Some felt there should be no return to the 'feudal' past and that Burma would have to 'skip historical stages' in order to 'catch up' with the modern world. Others, making less sweeping assumptions about the plasticity of the state and society, sought merely to guide the state along recent familiar paths. The struggle of the political groups holding these conflicting views and the interests they represented, together with efforts by local leaders to fend off the demands of the centre, form the essence of Burma's politics from 1942 to 1962.

The more attempts are made to reorganise the state in a particular period, the more obvious does it become that its controllers are trying to reassert its position. Whereas the Myanmar kings only recognised their state system on the founding of a new dynasty and the British merely elaborated the institutions of the colonial state, in the twenty years after 1942 incumbents attempted to restructure the state nine different times. Not all of these attempts were fundamental in intent, but all forced the ruling elite to rethink the nature and purpose of the state in order to construct institutions that would last. The range of options for state reorganisation was limited by the experiences and knowledge of the dominant political group, and by what its members thought would be acceptable to their followers. Ideas of reorganisation ranged from 'traditional' kingship to 'modern' ideas of socialism, and from Western notions of liberalism to varieties of militarism and statism as found in Japan or the socialist world. Crucial in shaping ideas for reorganisation was the belief that some 'new' form of state was necessary to demonstrate that the ruling élite was not captive to the old order, but was creating a new order that would be able to deal with social and economic issues more effectively than their predecessors or rivals.

The question of the nature of the state had been a factor in the ideological debates of the nationalist movement throughout the 1930s. Politicians nearest to the state power realised that even if the British were not defeated by the Axis powers in a major war, it was unlikely that Britain would remain the master of Burma for much more than another decade or two. The political evolution of India, the relative decline in the economic power of Britain and the successful operation of the 1935 constitution by politicians such as U Saw were factors favouring the attainment of full and genuine internal self-government by leaders from the new middle class. The apparent rise of anti-capitalist left-wing movements as well as the continuing threat of peasant unrest demonstrated to the more far-sighted British officials and politicians the desirability of placing the social control functions of the state in the hands of Burmese officials and politicians whose interests were linked with the British Empire/Commonwealth. If nothing else, the maintenance of the internal order upon which Britain's economic interests depended necessitated a steadily growing identification of the state with the interests of the most conservative state centred classes and groups in Burmese society.

The efforts of groups that opposed the policies and institutions of the colonial state and refused to identify with it had grown during the inter-war decades. It was their strength, especially when they were able to mobilise support from the peasantry and from the youth, that most seriously challenged the attempts of the indigenous political élite after 1947 to assert the dominance of the state. The economic and ideological issues that motivated

221

peasant and worker discontent were little touched by the transitions after 1942. While day to day rivalries monopolised political attention, the underlying issue of the state's ability to provide the focus of individual identity and social order (and thus dominate anti-state forces) was not resolved. Order remained uncertain, and extra-state agents of coercion and control continued to play a large role in the lives of the population.

The continuing grievances of the peasantry provided a motivation for political mobilisation on the part of the majority of the population. The last pre-war government had attempted to improve the conditions of the peasantry by introducing moderate tenancy and land reform legislation, but no solution was possible which both dealt with the massive level of peasant indebtedness and preserved the capital of politically powerful foreign and indigenous moneylenders and landlords, the *sine qua non* for political success under the late colonial order. Land tax also remained a complaint of the peasants, though the first government under the 1937 constitution had abolished the capitation and *thathameda* taxes. But with a large proportion of the peasant population still landless, anti-state groups had a ready supply of the discontented to mobilise against the state.

As the political dilemma of peasant indebtedness indicates, the promise of internal political power and greater control over external affairs held out by the British to the indigenous political elite did not provide a solution to the middle class' major economic problems, including competition with Indian and, to a lesser extent, Chinese businessmen. As long as the credit system and the internal economy remained largely in foreign hands, it was impossible for the indigenous middle class to feel assured that the political power that its leaders held was secure and would be used in the interest of political stability and indigenous economic advantage. The problem of Burmese professionals was easier to resolve through the passage of legislation requiring that individuals must be citizens in order to pursue particular occupations such as teaching or the civil service. But comparable legislation concerning trading, money lending and other commercial activities could be easily circumvented.

A fundamental issue that remained unresolved between 1942 and 1962 was the legitimacy of the state. In the eyes of most of the urban middle class, political parties, elections and the rhetoric of nationalism and populism were sufficient to legitimise the state in the modern world. But as the heirs of the colonial state and the victors over their Communist colleagues in the independence movement, the wielders of state power in the 1950s, led by U Nu and the Socialist group, were uncertain of their own legitimacy[1] and perhaps that of the postcolonial state itself for the larger society. To many others, including the culturally more conservative members of the middle class and the Buddhist *sangha*, the state ought to have been rooted in older Myanmar idioms and symbols. Despite acceptance of the colonial-style state with its advantages for political control by the middle class, the majority of the population received few of the permanent advantages that were commonly expected to follow from independence and the end of foreign exploitation. The departure of the British did not mean an end to the modern state and its concomitant economic and social institutions.[2] Nor did the achievement of independence make it possible for peasants and others to gain redress for their grievances (as allegedly occurred under a righteous king whose moral order limited the excesses of his state and its officials). The development of a legitimising myth which combined a justification for the activities of the modern state with Burmese rather than British notions of justice had not occurred, and the state provided little focus of identity for much of the population.

These fundamental issues in the life of the state were largely irrelevant prior to 1942 because the external power of the British-Indian empire was sufficient to maintain the dominance of the state despite its perceived illegitimacy. The initial consequence of the Japanese invasion, of course, was to remove the British-Indian armed forces. The British and Indian civil servants and many of the Burmese politicians who had managed the late colonial state were immediately replaced by Japanese army officers and civilians and by Burmese politicians and officials who, for reasons of idealism, opportunism, or a degree of compulsion, cooperated with the new regime. Many, like Thibaw Min's officials at the time of the British conquest, felt obligated to continue to serve the state regardless of its master.

The Japanese invasion set in train other economic, social and political processes which undermined the state. Two major factors were at work.

---

1   Khin Maung Kyi, 'Patterns of Accommodation to Bureaucratic Authority in a Transitional Culture: A Sociological Analysis of Burmese Bureaucrats with Respect to Their Orientations Towards Authority' (PhD, Cornell University, 1966), pp. 106-7.

2   These feelings of loss and betrayal are portrayed fictionally in Thiha, *The Chindits and the Stars* (London: Regency, 1971) and in the post-independence stories in *Selected Short Stories of Thein Pe Myint*, trans. And edited by Patricia M. Milne (Ithaca: Cornell University Southeast Asian Program Data Paper no. 91, June 1973), pp. 47-105.

First, the removal of British power meant that many of those individuals and interests associated with the colonial order and ultimately dependent on it either left the country or sought protection from indigenous or other foreign forces. Secondly, mass political groups were organised and mobilised in support of Burma's independence. With the encouragement of the Japanese military there arose a new, indigenous power in the form of the Burma Independence Army (BIA), which briefly assumed power as the British withdrew. There subsequently developed other groups opposed to the Japanese fascists, often calling themselves Communists or Socialists, or acting in the name of the Karen community, willing to cooperate with the British to remove the Japanese. While the Karen leaders sought to bring about a return of the British, the Marxist-oriented groups wished to ensure that imperialists would play no role in the future of Burma. Both the BIA and the underground leftists, who formed a Communist Party in 1943, received the support of students and peasants who believed that they would benefit from the creation of a new and indigenously managed state. For the Karen Christian leaders, and for the 'traditional' authorities recognised by the colonial state as its agents in the hill areas, the threat of a new state formed upon egalitarian principles and indigenous rule meant an end to their protected positions.

The reorganisation of the state

The terminology used in a discussion of the displacement of the state tends to make the subject seem abstract and remote from the lives of individuals. In fact, the resulting turbulent conditions directly affected the lives and property of most of the population. For many, the upheavals that resulted from war and revolution brought opportunities as well as difficulties. The uncertainty of these years can be gathered from talking with people who lived through them and from studying various written accounts. For example, one left-wing nationalist wrote of a group of villagers who at the time of the British withdrawal were primarily worried about the unchecked activities of dacoits in their area and who lamented that 'the government is no more'.[3] The echoes of the collapse of the monarchical state 63 years earlier, which resulted in the establishment of a British military administration, were heard in these remarks.

---

3   Thein Pe Myint, *Wartime Traveller*, in Robert H. Taylor, *Marxism and Resistance in Burma, 1942-1945: Thein Pe Myint's 'Wartime Traveller* (Athens, Ohio: Ohio University Press, 1984), p. 122.

In another parallel with the fall of Thibaw, the sudden dislocation of the state in 1942 provided opportunities for individuals on the periphery of colonial society to acquire positions and wealth or to settle old scores unhindered by established and recognised authorities. Property abandoned by fleeing British, Indian and Chinese businessmen fell, at least temporarily, into indigenous hands. For those seeking local administrative control the departure of the personnel of the colonial state provided opportunities for office, and individuals acted alone or in groups to assume the mantle of authority. Governing roles were quickly taken up by audacious or more authoritative individuals. In particular, Thakins and members of the BIA took it upon themselves to administer local areas and to establish new township and urban governing committees, often in conflict with each other, as well as with older politicians or the Japanese army. The committees dominated by youths saw the departure of the British as 'the dawn of a new Burmese era', in which traditional values could be resurrected and Western cultural influence eradicated. Many of their actions, however, were merely symbolic, such as the renaming of streets and public buildings.[4] They had too little time and too little authority to do more.

The chaos of local government was mirrored in the confusion and disorder of the central state. The political leaders in the capital often believed that if they could correctly organise their central institutions, the disorder below them would be eliminated by new laws and edicts and by the examples they set. The first wartime attempts at reorganisation came immediately in the wake of the Japanese invasion. A *Baho* or Central Administration was established by the Japanese and nominally headed by Thakin Tun Ok. Pleading the exigencies of war, its leaders merely attempted to maintain functions equivalent to the British administration. From its beginning in early April the *Baho* administration, recognising its relative powerlessness, made little attempt to guide local administrative bodies, seeking 'only to review local policies after they had been made'.[5] Indeed, for a brief period, Burma again became a series of little republics, as the authority of the central state extended to little more than the capital. Given the uncertain authority of Burmese officials in their relations with both the Japanese and

4   Jan Becka, *The National Liberation Movement in Burma during the Japanese Occupation Period (1941-1945)* (Prague: Oriental Institute, Dissertationes Orientales Volume 42, 1983), p. 90.

5   Dorothy Hess Guyot, 'The Political Impact of the Japanese Occupation of Burma' (PhD, Yale University, 1966), p. 143.

the initially autonomous township and town committees, the central administrators fell back on the forms of the old order.[6]

Faced with an inept and nearly powerless indigenous administration, in August 1942 the Japanese created a new order which would relieve the occupying army of administrative tasks. The *Baho* administration was replaced by a government led by Dr Ba Maw which invited civil servants and politicians who had worked with the British to join it; the autonomous committees of the BIA and other local bodies were suppressed and replaced with centrally sanctioned authorities. The Ba Maw administration was greatly hampered, however, by poor communications and by the existence of rival centres of authority, especially the Japanese army.[7] The indigenous authorities were left only the functions of law and order, plus justice and revenue collection, while the Japanese managed major economic enterprises and the means of transport and communications necessary for prosecution of the war. Local government officials, especially district officers, using the same organisational methods as their pre-war predecessors, were forced to make administrative decisions without central supervision. More than two-thirds of the district officers had no experience of such autonomy. At the centre most of the administrators were also former British employees, except in the newly created departments such as labour, war cooperation and religion, which were filled with political appointees. Perhaps the major innovation in the procedures of the state during war was to change the official language to Burmese, though English-language manuals and forms were still the norm.[8]

Despite their reliance upon British procedures, the administrators under Ba Maw made great efforts to show that the state they were creating was radically different from the one it had displaced. Although the state's goals of security, order and economic wellbeing remained the same, the terminology used to explain these goals was altered to make the purpose of the state seem new and laudable. 'National unity' and 'strength' became the avowed purposes of the state, and these were to be achieved in the first instance by reorganisation of the administrative machinery 'to make a fit and proper instrument for the service of the new State'. The initial problem

---

6   Ibid., pp. 144-5.

7   Ibid., pp. 145-6.

8   James F. Guyot, 'Bureaucratic Transformation in Burma', in Ralph Braibanti (ed.), *Asian Bureaucratic Systems Emergent from the British Imperial Tradition* (Durham, NC: Duke University Press, 1966), pp. 386-7.

to be dealt with was the composition of the personnel of the state. This was vital, Ba Maw argued,

especially when a State is defending its very existence. At such a time a State must be completely assured of the loyalty, integrity, competence and discipline of its servants or else it cannot survive. A house divided against itself must fall sooner or later. This is proved by what happened in the last days of British rule in Burma ... when one of the contributory causes of the British defeat was a sudden breakdown of the administration. Such a contingency must be avoided at all costs in the new State by the means of timely action. Furthermore, there cannot be a sound and stable State if its administrative services are unsound or unstable.[9]

Every attempt to resurrect the state since that time has placed equal emphasis upon the need to ensure the loyalty of the officials and agents of the state. While the British sought to ensure that there was a pool of trained manpower to staff the administrative services, the loyalty of officials was ensured by the unique foreign origins of those at the top and by the relatively munificent salaries they and their subordinates were paid. An indigenously based, impecunious state could afford neither of these options, and was forced to rely on staff training that emphasised unity and loyalty. But without the centrality of the Buddhist king to provided a focus of loyalty, and with the existence of many powerful alternative symbols appealing for the allegiance of individuals, it was intended that the state and the nation it claimed to represent would become the focus of loyalty. Ba Maw's call for 'One Blood, One Voice, One Command' was not so much the order of a dictator as an appeal for a nation-state centred sense of loyalty of a kind that the state in Burma had not encouraged before. Nationalism had now become official.

The constitution installed with the Japanese grant of independence in August 1943, like the British-drafted constitution of 1937, reflected more the ideas of its foreign sponsors than those of the leading personnel of the state. Intended to provide a means to carry out the government's New Order Plan, the constitution was similar to the 1889 Meiji constitution of Japan, placing ultimate authority, including control of the armed forces, in the hands of the head of state. The Minister of War, however, was always to be a serving military officer.[10] This was the constitutional basis of the

9   Ba Maw, 'A Review of the First Stage of the New Order Plan', *Burma*, I, 1 (Rangoon: Foreign Affairs Association, Burma, Sept. 1944), pp. 110-11.

10   Abu Talib bin Ahmad, 'Collaboration, 1941-1945: An Aspect of the Japanese Occupation of Burma', PhD, Monash University, pp. 240-2.

position in the cabinet of General Aung San as head of the Burma National Army (BNA), and was the beginning of a pattern of political equality between the head of state and head of the army in the state which lasted till 1962 and is reasserted in the 2008 draft constitution. Below the head of state there was a Planning Board as well as an embassy in Tokyo, a supreme court, and the cabinet. There was no role for bodies such as a legislature, or for local self-government as attempted under the British. However, in the most important aspects of state administration, the constitution followed the pattern of the colonial state. For example, 'local administration was put under the Home Ministry with the exception of the Shan States which were administered by the Prime Minister's Department'.[11]

The divergent treatment provided for the Shan States within the organisation of the wartime state was a continuation of colonial state practices. Little distinction was made, however, between the administration of central Burma and the western and northern frontier areas known subsequently as the Chin and Kachin States. Although these were nominally under the control of the central administration, as they were zones into which British and American military units made forays they remained under Japanese military control.[12] In the eastern areas the Japanese initially maintained a system of 'indirect' rule similar to that of the British. The Shan sawbwas individually came to terms with the Japanese and in the process succeeded in ensuring that troops of the central state did not enter their domains.[13] The most eastern Shan State, Kengtung, was ceded by the Japanese to Thailand, but the other Shan States, as well as the Wa and Karenni States, were under central control after December 1943.[14]

Upon their return in 1945, one of the conditions the British insisted upon before granting independence was that the leaders of the Shan States and of the hill tribes had to agree to cede their territories to an independent government in Rangoon. Barring such an agreement, Burma would be truncated between an independent central Burma and a surrounding horseshoe of sparsely populated mountains remaining under British sovereignty.

---

11   Ibid., pp. 248-9.

12   With the exception of the Chin Hills around Tiddim. See Desmond Kelly, *Kelly's Burma Campaign*, London: Tiddim Press, 2003.

13   Ba Maw, *Breakthrough in Burma: Memoirs of a Revolution* (New Haven: Yale University Press, 1968), p. 200.

14   'The Address of His Excellency Thakin Mya, the Deputy Prime Minister, at the Third Session of the Privy Council on Monday, the 20th March 1944', *Burma*, I, 1, p. 129.

Such a scheme had little rationale other than as a bargaining point in 1946 and 1947 between the British government and the leaders of the nationalist united front, the Anti-Fascist People's Freedom League (AFPFL).

Once the British had decided that they had to leave Burma as expeditiously as possible, means were found for doing so with the 'consent' of the hill tribes' leaders. As called for in the 1947 Aung San-Attlee agreement, the Shan sawbwas and 'leaders of the Chins and Kachins' with delegates from the Supreme Council of the United Hill Peoples (the traditional leaders' organisation) agreed to join Burma in a 'federation'. This agreement was ratified by a British House of Commons special committee in April and the way was paved for Burma's independence as a federal union.[15] The constitution of independent Burma, later ratified by a constituent assembly in 1947, delineated the federal state but in reality provided for a centralised governmental system. The states, eventually numbering five, had no substantial legislative powers and little say in taxation or state finance. The Shan, Karenni, and Kachin States, together with the Chin Special Division which had less formal internal arrangements, were created in the initial constitution and a Karen state was created later by constitutional amendment. The drafters of the constitution had no intention of establishing a federal system similar to that of the United States or Switzerland. Something more like the relationship between Scotland and the British government in London prior to 1999 was intended.

Although in theory Burma in 1948 came under one legal authority, in fact this was not the case. In certain respects, such as the criminal law, the Shan States and other former reserved areas remained outside the central state system until 1962. It could be argued that independence, rather than establishing the principle of nationalism as the basis of the state (as formally enunciated in the preamble of the 1947 constitution), actually reversed the egalitarian trend of the British period by increasing the powers and privileges of the Shan and Karenni sawbwas.

The amalgamation of the federated Shan States in 1948 occurred when there was a shortage of personnel and of political will at the centre to impose a single government on the region. The sawbwas had, by their cooperation with the non-Communist AFPPFL leadership in accepting inclusion

---

15   Maung Maung, *Burma's Constitution* (The Hague: Martinus Nijhoff, 2nd edn., 1961), pp. 79-80. Kyaw Win, Mya Han and Thein Hlaing, translated by Ohn Gaing and Khin Su, *The 1947 Constitution and the Nationalities*, Volumes I and II (Yangon: Universities Historical Research Centre and Innwa Publishing House, 1999).

within the new order, gained a degree of recognition for their continuing political utility. After 1948 the sawbwas were able to maintain their own budgets, police forces and local tax regimes, as well as appointing their own officials, but without the supervision of central civil servants as the British had insisted upon.

The democratic principles of the 1947 constitution logically required the abolition of the hereditary 'traditional' leaders of the frontier areas. While the constitution called for the establishment of a socialist and egalitarian society, it provided the state with few means of carrying out social reform, for it was based upon a political compromise between the central AFPFL leadership and the frontier area leaders. To have abolished their positions would have been a genuinely revolutionary act, but that was not to occur for another ten years.

This review of the constitutional evolution of the Shan States and other peripheral territories during the 1940s highlights an aspect of the displacement of the state. The post-independence constitution was framed upon the same liberal principles of government that had been the basis of the 1935 Government of Burma Act. The bureaucratic structures of the colonial state which had not been destroyed by the war, or had been rebuilt by the postwar British Military Administration, were retained. Legislative powers were lodged in a bicameral legislature in which the Upper House, the Chamber of Nationalities, served as a brake on the radical democratic possibilities of the lower house which was organised on the basis of one-person-one-vote and therefore held out the prospect of influence for the peasantry. The Chamber of Nationalities was created in order to serve the interests of the 'traditional' leaders in the frontier areas rather than those of urban wealth and status, as did the colonial upper house. The governor was replaced by a nominal president possessing few effective veto powers. State power now became constitutionally lodged in the cabinet led by a prime minister, but because of the maintenance of the Secretariat structure between the ministers and the operative departments, ministers were still dependent upon the willingness of the permanent officials to carry out their orders.

The establishment of this political order within the independent state was not an inevitable process. The constitution was written by the conservative interests which had won an internal power struggle within the AFPFL during the period between the autumn of 1946, when the British government decided to grant independence, and mid-1947, when power was handed to the non-Communist groups. The losing elements in that struggle were excluded from state power and formed the core of the groups in rebellion during and after the four-year civil war. What differentiates the state before 1942 from that after 1948 was that after independence the incumbent political elite tried to control the country through the institutions of a liberal constitution while lacking the coercive force of the their British predecessors. The consequence was perhaps inevitable. Forces unwilling to accept their exclusion from state power in 1948 launched the civil war in an attempt to achieve political power. The following section briefly describes the nature of the contestants for state power during the 1940s and 1950s.

The contestants for state power

During the six years between the Japanese invasion and the formal departure of the British there arose a variety of political organisations and groups which sought to seize control of the authority of the state either in all or in part of the territory internationally recognised as Burma. The most important of these groups, the Anti-Fascist People's Freedom League (AFP-FL), the Burma army, the Communist Party of Burma (CP[B] or BCP), the Karen National Union (KNU), and many less well known groups, all worked assiduously to organise and maintain popular support for their leaders and their policies. The most effective period of mass mobilisation was during the war,[16] but the most dramatic and lasting consequences are seen in the politics of the post-war independence contest and the resulting civil war. The leaders of the various groups formed during the war years, secular and religious, Communist and non-Communist, each vigorously disputed the legitimacy of those who received the carapace of state sovereignty from the British.

The leaders of the most vehemently anti-British groups, most of whom had worked together in the nationalist and students' movements of the 1930s, believed that success in driving out the foreigners would mean that state power would accrue to them. In contrast, the leaders of various minority communities, especially the Christian Karen and the Shan sawbwas, were aware that their influence would be diminished if independence were won in the name of the Burmese nation-state, and thus they sought to mobilise support as a countervailing power to that of the state-centred

---

16   See the discussion of the mobilisation of groups during the war in Guyot, 'Political Impact of the Japanese Occupation'. A summary is provided in Table 13, Wartime Mass Organisations, p. 275.

nationalists. Many of these leaders were able to find allies and friends in foreign communities resident in Burma or in governments and political movements outside. For this reason, indigenous minority leaders often had a greater feeling of power and support that they actually possessed. For many of them, their experiences during the war when they led a variety of seemingly invincible foreign-armed irregular guerrilla forces underscored their belief in their own power.[17]

Representing so many conflicting interests and ideologies, and backed by followers intent on achieving or maintaining their goals, the leaders of the different groups found it impossible to reach compromises with each other and still retain their supporters. To defend themselves against rival leaders within their own organisation, incumbents often escalated demands to prove their militancy and dedication. The multiplicity of political movements in the 1940s and 1950s and the cumulative sacrifices that their followers made prevented leaders from accepting compromises which could have lead to their incorporation into the state. The resultant political confusion was made worse by the existence of multiple offers of political alliance or collaboration, resulting in temporary cooperation between ideologically incompatible groups. The emotional atmosphere often bred unrealistic expectations, making leaders prisoners of their own rhetoric. Failing to win a place in the formal distribution of state power after 1948, opposition leaders felt they had no alternative but to resort to arms, either to carve out a separate state, or to seize state power.

The major conflicts that underlay the civil war did not erupt until independence was assured. As long as the possibility of external control remained, the majority of internal groups were willing to submerge their differences. The defeat of the Japanese in Burma between February and late May 1945, three months before the surrender of the imperial Japanese government, created an illusion for individuals and groups attached to the colonial state that the return of the British would lead to a restoration of the political *status quo ante bellum*. This was the intention of the government in London and the governor-in-exile in India, and of those within Burma who had prospered under the colonial state. The returning British-Indian army was instructed to prepare the way for a return to civilian government under the pre-war governor, with temporarily enhanced administrative

---

17   See Richard B. Laidlaw, 'The OSS and the Burma Road 1942-45', in Rhodri Jeffreys-Jones and Andrew Lownie, eds, *North American Spies: New Revisionist Essays* (Lawrence, Kansas: University of Kansas Press, 1991), pp. 102-22.

powers until pre-war economic and political 'normality' could be restored. That was not to be, however, for between May 1945 and October 1946 the major internal political groups gathered together under the umbrella of the AFPFL maintained sufficient cohesion to apply pressure on the British to depart. The AFPFL persisted with its threat of rebellion, and once it had been made clear to London by the Indian National Congress that the British-Indian army was no longer at the disposal of the colonial authorities to suppress 'freedom movements', there was no viable alternative to granting independence.[18] The British Labour government recognised that to attempt to hold on to power in the face of widespread nationalist armed resistance, even if Britain could muster a military force for an unpopular and expensive colonial war, might result in victory for the Burma Communist Party. Such a result would have undermined Britain's remaining strategic and economic interests in other parts of South and South East Asia, as well as in Burma.[19]

Once independence was assured following the Aung San-Attlee agreement of January 1947, the energies of all the political groups in Burma turned to internecine struggle for a place in the new order. Nationalist unity now took second place to political advantage. While all the major contending groups had their origins in Burma's pre-war political history, the forms they took in the late 1940s were new. Some of the parliamentary style parties of the 1920s and 1930s had had their own 'pocket armies' but had been forced for the most part to accept the conditions of electoral politics within the order upheld by the colonial state. Under that order, groups who cooperated were guaranteed rights and privileges denied to those who voiced revolutionary opposition. But unlike in India, where the same laws had applied, none of the political parties of the colonial era survived, other than in name, into the postcolonial political world, and extra-state coercive capacities became necessary for political survival after 1948.

During the war years, although the government of Dr Ba Maw attempted to develop a monopolistic political organisation, Maha Bama (Greater Burma), out of the pre-war Thakin movement and the Hsinyeitha party, this grouping had little effect on the political life of the country other than

---

18   See Chapter 10 of the 'Memoirs of Lord Listowel', 'Burma Independence: 1947-1948', www.redrice.com/listowel/CHAP10.html, accessed on 28/902/06.

19   See Robert H. Taylor, 'Burma in the Anti-Fascist War', in Alfred W. McCoy, ed., *Southeast Asian Under Japanese Occupation* (New Haven: Yale University Southeast Asia Studies Series no. 22, 1980), pp. 162-3.

to provide a cover for activists in underground resistance cells. The absence of electoral politics and the creation of a one-party pseudo-fascist state by Ba Maw and his associates, coupled with the economic and social disloca-. tion caused by the war, provided no focus for political loyalty and little opportunity for individuals with organisational skills who sought to operate under state auspices. But below the surface of Maha Bama and officially sanctioned subordinate organisations there developed a politicised officer corps in the Burma army, the sizeable Marxist-oriented movements calling themselves Communist or Socialist, and the religious/ethnic minority political and paramilitary organisations exemplified by Christian Karens who worked closely with British wartime intelligence bodies. All of these groups emerged at the end of the war to cooperate briefly but uneasily in the AFPFL. But the people they mobilised to oppose first the British, then the Japanese, and then again the British were turned against each other in civil war, which lasted longer and was far more destructive than the struggle between British and Japanese imperialism.

The army. The core of the Burma army, though it was the longest established armed group at the start of the civil war, was formed only in July 1942 when the Burma Defence Army (BDA) was established under Japanese supervision from the 23,000 or so youths who had made up the Burma Independence Army (BIA). The BIA had swollen in number during the previous four months as young nationalists rallied to the call of the 'Thirty Comrades' whom the Japanese had trained to lead an anti-British force. Only 5,000 were selected to form the 'professional' BDA. Renamed the Burma National Army (BNA) in August 1943 at the time of the grant of nominal independence by the Japanese, the army was then a small infantry force used primarily for garrison and ceremonial duties. Its first officer training school, founded in 1942 at Mingaladon north of Rangoon, provided a large proportion of the politicised officer corps which split between supporters of the AFPFL government and the Communist party soon after the beginning of the civil war.[20]

The BIA had provided a model of youthful adventure and independent political action, especially as its leader, General Aung San, already well known among the student population for his leadership of the student

---

20   This section is based upon a fuller discussion of the development and political role of the army in Robert H. Taylor, 'Burma', in Zakaria Ahmad and Harold Crouch, eds, *Military-Civilian Relations in South-East Asia* (Singapore: Oxford University Press), pp. 13-49.

union and the Thakin movements in the late 1930s, had spurned the prevailing wisdom about what was politically possible under the colonial state, creating a style of political daring that many others were to emulate during the succeeding years. The BIA grew out of the desire of leading Thakins and students to find a source of foreign assistance that would provide arms and training for the raising of a force to drive out the British. The approach of the Second World War, together with the progress of the Chinese Communist revolution, led nationalists to look to Japan or China as possible sources of such aid. On 8 August 1940 Aung San and another Thakin sailed from Rangoon in search of Chinese Communist assistance, but in the meantime Ba Maw and his party made contact with Colonel Suzuki of the Japanese Imperial Army. In their discussions it was arranged that the Japanese should find Aung San in Amoy and take him to Japan. This was done and he returned to Burma in February 1941 to recruit a band of colleagues for training as the officer corps for a new Burmese military force. By July 1941 thirty men had been assembled on Hainan Island under the Japanese, and these formed the core of the BIA which was raised in Bangkok and south-eastern Burma in December 1941 and January 1942.

The BIA was different in character as well as in purpose from the army of the colonial state. The bulk of the indigenous forces of the colonial state were recruited from various hill peoples living along the borders with China and India or from the Karen community. Lowland troops other than those designated as Karens were not recruited except for a brief period during the First World War and immediately before the Japanese invasion. The British force disintegrated as the Japanese advanced and the much larger regular British Indian army retreated to India. However, some of the troops, especially Karens from eastern border regions, remained in the country and towards the end of the war played leading roles in the formation of an anti-Japanese Karen resistance force while working with the BIA to lessen communal tensions in the delta.

The BIA was nationalist in the narrowest sense. It did not pass through the major frontier zones as it advanced into the country with the Japanese, and therefore its recruits were mainly from the most highly commercialised regions of southern Burma. Excluded from its ranks were members of the major immigrant communities as well as the hill peoples. Most of the officers of the BIA as well as their successors were from urban communities and many had secondary and, in some cases, university education. The ordinary soldiers were youths, disproportionately drawn from groups other than the peasant class until the final mobilisation against the Japanese in 1945.[21] Given its narrowly nationalist basis and social origins, it is not surprising that the BIA officer corps tended to perceive Burma's political problems primarily in cultural and ethnic terms, rather than in terms of class or ideology.

The post-BIA officer corps which became the core of the Burma army after July 1942 developed careers within the confines of a small and corporately self-conscious organisation. For those on the fringes of wealth and power in colonial society the army served as an important route of social mobility. Its popularity as a liberating force was, however, short-lived, and within a year of its formation officers had to seek means of regaining popular support. As the army became identified with Japanese brutalities and the economic hardships of war, officers, including the Minister of War Aung San, sought to alter the attitude of their troops towards the civilian population while seeking a political alternative to the Japanese alliance. The army's unpopularity had become so great by the middle of the war that it was difficult to recruit additional men to expand the force to its authorised size of 10,000.

During the war the BNA developed two characteristics. One was its officers' and men's loyalty to the notion of Burmese independence and the necessity of having the support of the people. The other was that the army felt it necessary to involve itself in politics in order to compete with other political groups and to achieve the officer corps' notion of a correct social and political order. The wartime officer training school graduated five classes, passing out 791 officers. These men received a thorough Japanese-style military education, but many secretly studied Chinese and other Communist writings on the nature of a 'people's army' made available to them by cadres from the underground Communist Party. Professionalisation was thus combined with a political and populist purpose encouraged by leading officers.

The BNA faced a serious external threat to its existence in 1944-45 as Japanese power began to wane relative to the force of the Allies in India and China. In the eyes of the British, the BNA in 1944 was a 'quisling' organisation that could on moral and legal grounds be denied any role in postwar Burma; the BNA was guilty of treason against the King/Emperor and would be punished accordingly. The BNA leadership had thus to search for a way not only to redeem its political popularity in Burma but also to make

---

21   Guyot, 'Political Impact of the Japanese Occupation', p. 334.

itself acceptable to the Allies, if it was to have a role in the post-war campaign for Burma's independence. Such a way appeared in the form of a coalition with the Burma Communist Party. The BCP had made contact with the Allies in 1942 and since that time had been organising the peasantry in Burma to oppose fascism and take power in an anti-imperialist revolution. The Anti Fascist Organisation (AFO), formed under the leadership of General Aung San and the Communist leader Thakin Soe in August 1944, was the answer to the BNA's dilemma.[22]

When the army, secretly renamed the People's Army, marched out of Rangoon on 27 March 1945 to fight the Japanese as the armed force of the AFO united front (renamed AFPFL), it helped to guarantee that the officer corps a role in the future of Burma. In so doing it demonstrated its patriotism and its power to the British. The army also managed to make itself seem indispensable as an armed force to the civilian political leadership, including the Communists. 27 March, now celebrated annually as Army Day or Resistance/Revolution (*Towhlanyei*) Day, marks the army's position as a major force in Burma's politics.

The success of the army in ensuring a political future for itself was the result of the astute political leadership of Aung San, who until his assassination at the age of 32 in July 1947 was able to lead the Communist-inspired AFPFL national front in negotiations with the British, while reassuring the growing conservative elements within the League that the Communists would not control the post-independence state. After the return of the British, Aung San concerned himself with ensuring the integrity and political loyalty of the army to the AFPFL, of which he became President in May 1945 in place of Thakin Soe. Abandoning an initial demand that the British recognise the AFPFL as a provisional government and the BNA as an allied army, Aung San, in collaboration with Thakin Than Tun who replaced Soe as leader of the Communists at this time, settled for a compromise with the newly established British Military Administration. The essence of the agreement allowed for a continued role for the army by placing it legally under the control of British military law while maintaining a popular and anti-British force in the form of the People's Volunteer Organisation (PVO), a veterans' body primarily loyal to Aung San but with ties to various other officers serving in, or demobilised from, the BNA.

---

22   See Robert H. Taylor, 'Introduction: Marxism and Resistance in Wartime Burma', in Robert H. Taylor, *Marxism and Resistance in Burma 1942-1945: Thein Pe Myint's 'Wartime Traveller'*, pp. 51-69.

The Kandy agreement—as the deal struck between Aung San and the British South East Asia Commander, Admiral Lord Louis Mountbatten, became known—was viewed by many in the officer corps, who feared that the disarmament of most of their troops and the command of the remainder by British officers, as a means to allow the Communists to take control of the independence movement. It had been the policy of most leading Communists since 1944 to cooperate with the returning British, and anti-Communist officers interpreted this strategy as directed as much against them as against the Japanese fascists with whom followers of Thakin Soe said they were aligned. Nonetheless, Aung San conceded in September that the army was not the legal force of an independent state as he had claimed in May. But in the long term the Kandy agreement was distinctly to the advantage of those officers and men who sided with the British.

The Kandy agreement provided the AFPFL with a body of men loyal to it and yet within the British colonial army, thus allowing the independence movement to penetrate a principal pillar of state power. But the army was then placed in a position to side with the British against the rivals of the state, especially the Communists. In the meantime, the British became increasing dependent on the former BIA troops as regular British and Indian troops were withdrawn. The former People's Army was engaged in pursuing Communist guerrillas and dacoits in the area around the oil fields at Yenangyaung during 1947. Called 'Operation Flush', it was the first major campaign conducted by a wholly indigenous state force since 1885. The unit which carried out the operation was the 4th Burma Rifles, under the command of Lt.-Colonel Ne Win.[23]

The civil war of 1948-52 provided the army with important corporate experience. In 1942, and again in 1945-6, it had been forced to shed some politicised officers and men in the interest of discipline and order, as required by the Japanese and the British. In 1948-9 the army experienced a third major shedding of personnel, but this time many officers and men went voluntarily, deserting to join one or another of the paramilitary organisations which took up arms against the state. By mid-1948 three battalions of the army, along with more than half of the PVOs known as the White Band, had joined the Communist side. The only units to remain loyal to the AFPFL government were Ne Win's 4th Burma Rifles and Karen, Kachin and Chin units which the independent state had inherited

---

23   Maung Maung, *Burma and General Ne Win* (New York: Asia Publishing House, 1969), pp. 180-4.

from the British. In December 1948 the 3rd Battalion Karen Rifles along with many Karen military and civilian police joined the rebellion of the Karen National Union, and the following month they were joined by the 1st Kachin Rifles.

The remaining officer corps drew two lessons from these experiences. The first lesson was the need to keep party factionalism out of the army by maintaining corporate loyalty over ideological or party loyalties; the second was the need to ensure that extra-military ethnic loyalties were not encouraged by organisational structures. The British practice of organising troops on the basis of ethnicity had been perpetuated after 1945 at the insistence of the AFPFL leadership in order to ensure the loyalty of former BNA troops to them. During the civil war, this policy greatly weakened the solidarity of the armed forces of the state.

The army's military and political experiences, both domestic and international, were crucial in shaping the officer corps' attitudes and policies in subsequent years. Faced by a plethora of enemies, Communist and ethnic separatist, and supported by a weak and uncertain civilian government backed in many cases by local thugs and racketeers,[24] the army leadership developed the ability to function independently of civilian control. The fact that the civilian government was unable to gain any significant external aid or equipment for the army during the most perilous years of the civil war, coupled with the backing that the Chinese Nationalist KMT troops in the Shan State received from Taiwan, Thailand and the United States, convinced the army leadership of the necessity of self-reliance.[25]

The inclusion of the army Supreme Commander General Ne Win in the cabinet in April 1949, as Deputy Prime Minister and Minister for Home Affairs as well as for Defence,[26] made official for a brief period what was the practical reality throughout the first fourteen years of Burma's independence. All civilian governments were dependent on the army for office, for it was only the army's loyalty to the civilian leadership and the norms of the constitution that kept one or another of the rival insurgent groups from

---

24   See Mary P. Callahan, 'The Sinking Schooner: Murder and the State in Independent Burma, 1948-1958', in Carl A. Trocki, ed., *Gangsters, Democracy, and the State in Southeast Asia* (Ithaca, New York: Cornell University Southeast Asia Program, 1998), pp. 17-38.

25   For details of the KMT affair and its effects on the politics of Burma, see Robert H. Taylor, *Foreign and Domestic Consequences of the KMT Intervention in Burma* (Ithaca: Cornell University Southeast Asia Program Data Paper no. 93, 1973).

26   Maung Maung, *Burma and General Ne Win*, pp. 214-16, 222.

seizing state power. Despite its formal adherence to principles of the constitution between 1948 and 1962, the army remained a politically involved
group even after Ne Win left the cabinet in September 1950. Several officers maintained close personal and political ties with the leading Socialist
group in the cabinet. And political ambition, the motivation for joining the
army in 1942, had not evaporated with the development of a regular state
army. Many of the non-commissioned and commissioned officers recruited in the civil war and afterwards joined for political reasons, and many
NCOs who had joined in the anti-Communist and anti-KNU struggles
were given commissions as the army rebuilt after the civil war.[27]

The Communists. The Communist movement in Burma was never a well
organised political force like the Communist Party of Vietnam. Its roots lie
very late in the colonial period. The first 'party cell' was formed by Aung
San, Soe and other Thakins in 1939, and the first underground 'party congress' was held in 1943 by Soe and six others. It had few articulated institutional structures and its pretentiously named central committee was little
more than a rallying point for local enthusiasts. Nonetheless, the Communist movement soon assumed a major role in the political life of the country
through the 1940s and 1950s, and its leaders thought themselves to be near
to taking state power in the period between 1945 and 1948. The strength
of the Communist movement stemmed from the importance of its leaders
in providing the ideas and formal organisational structure of the national
united front after 1944, and from the power they appeared to demonstrate
through the support of workers and peasants in opposing the policies and
programmes of the Japanese, the British and the AFPFL controlled government. Internal party feuding, including a split in 1956, contributed to the
decline of the Communist movement in the 1960s, but by then much of its
programme had become less relevant and its ineffectual leadership had led
to a decline in the respect which it had previously enjoyed.

The leadership of the Communist movement centred upon a few intellectuals and activists from the pre-war Do Bama Asiayon. Though assisted
by others the key figure, Thakin Soe, and Thakin Than Tun were the focus
of the movement. Soe, the most important left-wing polemicist in colonial

---

27   Moshe Lissak, 'Social Change, Mobilisation, and Exchange of Services between
      the Military Establishment and the Civil Society: The Burmese Case', *Econom-
      ic Development and Cultural Change,* XIII, 1, pp. 5-6. See also Mary Patricia
      Callahan, 'The Origins of Military Rule in Burma', PhD, Cornell University,
      1996, published as Mary P. Callahan, *Making Enemies: War and State Building
      in Burma* (Ithaca and London: Cornell University Press, 2003).

Burma, was largely responsible for introducing Marxist-Leninist political concepts through the idiom of Burmese Buddhist thought to politically active students and others before the war. Convinced of the political and moral correctness of current international Communist strategy, he did not believe in 1940-1, as did the leaders of the future army, that it was possible to enter into an alliance with the Japanese fascists in order to gain Burma's independence from the British imperialists. Taking a longer view of the political situation inside and outside Burma, and sharing the beliefs of left-wing political forces in much of the world at that time that fascism and militarism were the primary enemy of colonial liberation movements, he argued that it was necessary first to attack the Japanese in collaboration with the British and other capitalist allies then in alliance with the Soviet Union. Despite its initial unpopularity at the start of the war, the Communist Party's ideological and strategic views of 1941-2 were interpreted as having been correct in 1944-5 (in contrast to those of the army and civilian leaders who had worked with the Japanese), and their advice on political strategy and tactics at the end of the war was thought to be grounded in a historically valid theoretical perspective.

Furthermore, untainted by collaboration with the Japanese, Soe and other Communists spent the war years travelling to rural villages, setting up anti-fascist units and teaching the peasants Soe's particular understanding of Communism and the importance of organisation in ending foreign rule and achieving revolution. The fact that the Communists were able to maintain contacts with the outside world through India via their association with the British intelligence organisation Force 136 (the Asian section of the intelligence and sabotage agency established by the British war cabinet, Special Operations Executive) also gave them a superior knowledge of international affairs; this proved an advantage in political debates. At the end of the war, accepting the advice of the Indian Communist Party and its interpretation of the wartime 'Browderist line' (which advanced the view that an anti-imperialist revolution would not be necessary after the war in order to achieve independence and socialism because the United States and other capitalist states would be forced to come to terms with new, radical world-wide class forces), the Communists were able to join with the army and cooperate in the speedy defeat of fascism. This would lead, inevitably they thought, to independence under the guidance of left-wing forces.

The other major Communist figure was Thakin Than Tun. Although less of an intellectual than Soe, he was a superior organiser. During the war he served as Minister of Agriculture in Ba Maw's cabinet and achieved a reputation as an effective administrator with a good understanding of agrarian problems. In that capacity he toured the countryside, meeting peasants and making himself known as their champion. Towards the end of the war he joined with Soe and the Communist Party (Burma) (CP[B]) in circulating the underground propaganda of the anti-fascist national front. In mid-1945 he succeeded in ousting Thakin Soe from the leadership of the party over issues of strategy as well as of personal behaviour. From then on Than Tun was considered to be, along with General Aung San, his brother-in-law, one of the two most important political figures of the country. Than Tun's removal of Soe from the leadership of the CP(B) set in motion a split between them and their followers which eventually made it easier for the anti-Communist forces to halt their drive for power.[28]

Both before and after the defeat of the Japanese, the Communists gained a great deal of influence among the peasantry because of their advocacy of popular agrarian policies, especially the non-payment of rent and taxes and the abolition of peasant debt. Many of their local leaders were first mobilised as cadres of the Japanese-sponsored East Asia Youth League,[29] but at the end of the war they continued to agitate for the redress of peasant grievances. Other groups, all of whom adopted leftist slogans and symbols, emulated their efforts. As an American diplomat made clear in a report written in March 1946, the Communist programme was the most appealing to the peasantry, and even politicians such as General Aung San, who did not consider it to be practical, felt they had to accept it. Echoing the programme of the *wunthanu athin* and *bu athin* of the 1920s, the Communists after the war

advocated cancelling agricultural debt (owing mainly to Indian Chettyars), establishing the cultivators as owners of their land, and reserving the country's oil, timber and mineral resources for the benefit of the Burman. Not all of the Peasants' Unions were Communist led, but the most effective appeal everywhere was to denounce landlords, moneylenders, and rice exporters, mostly Indian, who under protection of British rule had despoiled the Burman people. ... Cultivators must unite to forestall the repayment of Government loans and to obtain cancellation of

---

28   A detailed discussion of this period is found in Taylor, *Marxism and Resistance in Burma*, 'Introduction: Marxism and Resistance in Wartime Burma', pp. 51-69.

29   Guyot, 'Political Impact of the Japanese Occupation', pp. 296-8.

land rent and taxes for the current year. Aung San acquiesced in the program for political reasons. ... [30]

The popularity of the appeal was obvious, and no political leader wishing to demonstrate his ability to maintain mass opposition to the British could afford to stand against it until he was assured of state power.

In the organisation of peasant support for the nationalist movement, and the maintenance of an air of political uncertainty and revolutionary fervour, the Communists were the most visible political force in the three years between the end of the war and the formal grant of independence. Their leaders, however, were gradually squeezed out of the leadership of the anti-imperialist national front after the AFPFL's non-Communist leaders amended its constitution in May 1946 to exclude political parties.[31] When the British offered control of the Governor's Executive Council (effectively the cabinet) to Aung San and the AFPFL in October 1946, the BCP refused to cooperate because the Labour government in London had yet to promise independence—a prerequisite for cooperation with the imperialists stipulated in AFPFL resolutions for over a year.[32] According to Than Tun's version of events during 1947, before and after the assassination of Aung San the BCP continued to seek to cooperate with the League in order to ensure independence, and to limit the degree of control that right-wing and imperialist forces could gain over the soon-to-be-independent state. They were, however, rebuffed in these efforts.[33]

Thus, when independence came, the Communists were denied any role in the state other than that of a loyal but powerless opposition. The CP(B) split in January 1946 between the smaller Soe faction, the Red Flags, and Than Tun's newly named White Flag Communist Party (BCP) over collaboration with non-Communist groups and the passive revolutionary

---

30   John F. Cady, 'The Character and Program of the Communist Party in Burma' (Rangoon: American Consulate General, 16 March 1946), p. 2.

31   Walter D. Sutton, 'Aung San of Burma', *The South Atlantic Quarterly*, vol. XLVII, 1 (Jan., 1948), pp. 1-16.

32   San San Myint, 'Hpa Hsa Pa La Hkit Myanmar Naingnganyei Thamaing' (Political History of Myanmar in the AFPFL Era) (MA, Rangoon Arts and Sciences University, pp. 73-4, citing *Pyithu Ana Gyone* (*People's Power Journal*), Vol. 3, no. 1 (2-10-46), p. 4. See also Sein Win, *The Split Story* (Rangoon: Guardian Press, 1959).

33   *Hpa Hsa Pa La -- Konmyunit Apyanahlan Peisa (AFPFL-Communist Correspondence)* (Yangon: Pyithu Ana Punhnat Taik, 1947), pp. a-b, Introduction written by Thakin Than Tun.

strategy of Than Tun. Subsequently, the major civilian group within the AFPFL stood by and watched politicians who had worked with the British before the war or with the Japanese during it form the first independent government of Burma since 1885.

After the expulsion of the Communists from the League, the CP(B) and BCP agitated to undermine the legitimacy of the AFPFL-led state, alleging that its leaders had abandoned the goals of the anti-fascist revolution. The Communists opposed the government both for its agrarian policies and for its post-independence agreements with the British, including (a) the acceptance of a debt obligation, (b) the maintenance of a military advisory mission, and (c) British rights to use staging bases in Burma for military action elsewhere in Asia.[34] Believing that their popular support was wider than it apparently was, the two Communist factions claimed that they would bring down the government—Soe's faction by armed revolution and Than Tun's by mass organisation. Soe's group had been declared illegal by the British in 1946 but Than Tun's party remained a legal organisation into the early 1950s. However, on the night of 27 March 1948 the government ordered the arrest of the BCP leaders. Having been notified of this by Party sympathisers in the bureaucracy (the state apparatus was riddled with supporters of various political groups), the Communists went underground.

Despite their organisational weaknesses, at the beginning of the civil war the Communists were probably the most popular political party in large sections of the country, especially the rice growing areas. Loyal to them were between 15,000 to 20,000 armed troops, mostly veterans of the anti-Japanese resistance movement. In addition, they were joined by about 9,000 former BNA troops in the White Band PVO and several hundred troops from the government army in mid-year.[35] The Communists had their greatest success in areas where they had been active during and after the war, such as the delta and around Pyinmana. As early as 1946 the Communist-led Peasants' Union in Yamethin District claimed to have enrolled 33,000 members; its activities greatly overshadowed the organisation efforts of the peasants groups which supported the AFPFL and its Socialist Party leaders. The Socialists had lost what support they had among the

---

34   Ibid., pp. c-d; San San Myint, 'Hpa Hsa Pa La Hkit', p. 206, p. 211. See also John F. Cady, *Post-War Southeast Asia: Independence Problems* (Athens, Ohio: Ohio University Press, 1974), pp. 63-4.

35   San San Myint, 'Hpa Hsa Pa La Khit', p. 211.

peasants by their advocacy of cooperation with landlords and the payment of rents and taxes.[36]

But the Communists were unable to sustain their drive against the government's forces, especially as they were short of equipment and ammunition. Some Communist forces rallied to the government in early 1949 when the Karen National Defence Organisation (KNDO) also went into rebellion. The Communists' lack of organisation and their inability to provide protection for peasant families, or to implement policies in the face of the refusal of the government to recognise their actions, removed much of their initial support. Even though a good proportion of the public thought the Communist leaders had been denied state power by the scheming of the Socialists,[37] support drifted away from them in the early 1950s because they lacked the organisational structures and military power to sustain their campaigns. Nonetheless, a great deal of sympathy for the Communist agrarian programme and the Party's leaders persisted into the 1950s. The fact that they had come close to taking power twice in Burma's post-war history, once peacefully in 1947-8 and once by arms in 1948-50, gave the Communists a degree of prestige that they would not otherwise have had. Much of the electoral support given to anti-AFPFL left-wing legal political parties in the 1950s reflected the continuing popularity of the Communists long after they had been declared an illegal organisation.

Non-communist movements and political parties. Throughout the two decades of the contest for control of the state prior to 1962, there emerged a variety of other political parties and movements besides the army and the Communists. These alternative organisations represented various ideological perspectives, class or sectional interests, and religious and ethno-linguistic groups. A few of these movements were developed by the controllers of the government of the day, such as the Maha Bama movement of the Second World War or the National Solidarity Association founded by the army during the 1958-60 'caretaker' period. These were not of lasting significance, but the model of political organisation they provided was often emulated by more autonomous movements.

Some of the more important political parties and movements had their roots in the colonial period. The oldest was the Karen Central Organisation (KCO), which, though formed only in 1945, was a lineal descendant

---

36   Cady, 'Character and Program of the Communist Party in Burma', p. 3.

37   Khin Maung Kyi, 'Patterns of Accommodation to Bureaucratic Authority', p. 107.

of the Karen National Association that had been established in 1881 and was Burma's first modern political organisation.[38] The KCO divided in 1947 when the Karen National Union (KNU) was founded. Others had much shorter lineage. The AFPL can perhaps be traced back to the pre-war Thakin movement, but its organisational form emerged in August 1944, and between then and 1947 it lost its two formative members, the Communists and the army. Subsequently it was a rump organisation.

Many minor parties sprang up at the time of elections. The Patriotic Alliance, for example, formed in the early 1950s and composed of a motley collection of older politicians and a few new ones, made little impact on the public scene. Other parties were founded by leaders of minority communities in the border areas which were drawn into state-centred politics for the first time. These served as the vehicles for the political support of various traditional leaders and groups, such as Kachin Duwas and Shan and Karenni Sawbwas. The People's Economic and Cultural Development Organisation, for example, was founded in 1953 by the Buddhist Sima Duwa to rival the power of the Christian-oriented Kachin National Congress head by Duwa Zau Lawn. The United Hill People's Congress was founded in 1947 by Shan Sawbwas to counter the growing influence among their subjects of the egalitarian and Rangoon-focused Shan State People's Freedom League.[39]

When it became the basis of the first government of independent Burma under the leadership of Thakin Nu in 1948, the AFPFL was a very different organisation from the one which had led the fight against the Japanese and the British in 1945. The AFO had expanded under the name of the AFPFL in March 1945 by including in its nine-member executive committee three representatives of the People's Revolution group, the forerunners of the postwar Socialist Party. Following the example of the BIA in 1942, in 1945 local AFPFL leaders assumed administrative powers in areas abandoned by the Japanese before the returning British Military Administration could take control. The League's cooperative policy towards the British, despite opposition from some regional leaders and army commanders who argued that they were abandoning a chance for genuine independence, was carried out on orders from the central army and Communist leadership in Rangoon.

38   J.W. Baldwin, 'The Karens in Burma', *Journal of the Royal Central Asian Society*, XXXVI (1949), p. 108.

39   A fuller discussion of political parties during this period is found in Robert H. Taylor, 'Burma', in Haruhiro Fukui (ed.), *Political Parties of Asia and the Pacific* (Westport, Conn.: Greenwood Press, 1985), vol. I, pp. 99-154.

The policy of cooperation with the British and the consequent opening of membership in the League to conservative nationalist leaders and groups led to the first major fracture in the Communist Party and hence in the AFPFL. Subsequently, the League became increasingly heterogeneous in membership, with smaller groups joining, such as some of the pre-war organisations for women and youth. Although they had little impact on its level of support among the publicly generally, their leaders demanded a say in policy, lessening the AFPFL's revolutionary potential as it adapted to less radical urban and middle-class interests. The Socialist leaders were keen to use the support of the older conservative elements in order to lessen the power of the Communists, and this was one of the reasons for their opposition to the no-rent/no-taxes appeal of the Communist-led peasant unions.

However, until the removal of Thakin Than Tun as League General Secretary, the AFPFL remained under strong but politically moderate Communist and left-wing influence. The Communist candidate for succession to Than Tun, Thein Pe (Myint), lost the leadership struggle in June 1946 by one vote to the Socialist leader and future Deputy Prime Minister Kyaw Nyein. After the Communists were expelled from the League five months later, the best organised leftist groups remaining within it were the PVO, the Trade Unions Congress (Burma) (TUC[B]) and the All Burma Peasants' Organisation (ABPO). The PVO was badly factionalised and the majority joined the Communists in the civil war. The TUC(B) and ABPO both lost many members when the Communists were expelled from the League and rival Communist-led organisations were established.

As the civil war raged in the months immediately after independence, the AFPFL government of Prime Minister Nu exercised little influence outside of Yangon. The government relied increasingly on non-AFPFL support from various groups in addition to the army and the bureaucracy, and on foreign aid, to remain in power. The last ardently radical members of the League were expelled in December 1950, when left-wing Socialists quit the Socialist Party to form the Burma Workers' and Peasants' Party (BWPP). In their view, the AFPFL government and its right-wing Socialist ministers had abandoned the goals of Burma's revolution by shifting away from Marxism-Leninism, by accepting United States aid and the American position on the Korean War in the United Nations, and 'by the enactment of legislation dealing with religion', specifically the Buddha Sasana Council Act. This act 'created a state-financed agency for the promotion and propagation of Buddhism', whose purpose, according to the Prime Minister, was to 'challenge openly other ideological forces [but not other religions] at work in the country'.[40] The loss of popular support by the League following independence made it increasingly reliant on the instruments of the state to remain in power, as well as the support of local bosses.[41] As the power of the state was weak and fractured, the ability of the League to control affairs remained tenuous. Nonetheless, the League remained the country's major legal political party until it split in 1958, for no other group was able to tap directly the patronage and fiscal powers of the state during that time.

As it abandoned its founders and their Marxist ideology, the AFPFL lost its initial unifying set of beliefs. The heroism and martyrdom of General Aung San and the story of the independence movement provided the symbols and ideals which were its main assets, along with the charisma of U Nu. The leaders of the League, with the exception of Nu, were mainly members of the Socialist Party and espoused a variety of welfare socialism similar to that of the British Labour Party in the 1940s and 1950s. The League increasingly based its strength on its control of the state bureaucracy. AFPFL ministers and cadres closely involved themselves in administrative decisions to ensure that their supporters were rewarded and their opponents denied preference. League organisers directed vital programmes such as land reform by supervising the work of the village land committees and the granting of annual government crop loans. Import/export license awards were a mainstay of support for the League amongst the business community, where, despite attempts at creating government monopolies and encouraging Burmese entrepreneurs, Indian businessmen still played a major role. The executive committee of the League was the real centre of decision-making, not the government cabinet room.[42]

Ministers' power came from the personal influence they had over key subordinate organisations of the League and the government. Ba Swe, a Deputy Prime Minister through much of the 1950s and briefly Prime Minister, was vice-president of the AFPFL and head of both the Socialist

---

40 Donald Eugene Smith, *Religion and Politics in Burma* (Princeton University Press, 1965), pp. 126-27.

41 For more information on local bosses and politics during the 1950s, see Mary P. Callahan, 'Sinking Schooner' and Mary P. Callahan, 'On Time Warps and Warped Time: Lessons from Burma's 'Democratic Era'', in Robert I. Rotberg, ed., *Burma: Prospects for a Democratic Future* (Washington, DC: Brookings Institution Press, 1998), pp. 49-68.

42 See Maung Maung, "The Search for Constitutionalism in Burma", in R.N. Spann, ed., *Constitutionalism in Asia* (London: Asia Publishing House, 1963), pp. 114-29.

Party and of the TUC(B). Thakin Tin, holder of the Agriculture ministry, was head of the ABPO. Kyaw Nyein, a Deputy Prime Minister and secretary of the League, forged a power base from the great influence he wielded through the Home Ministry, with its control over the police, especially the Union Military Police, and the judicial system.

Local units of the League had little influence upon the centre. They were largely moribund between elections. The active units were often rife with factionalism between supporters and opponents of the Socialists. Most local leaders worked for the organisation in order to gain access to the patronage and favours that their patrons at the centre could provide. Although the leaders claimed that there were 1,287,290 members of the League in 1957, many of these were nominal, for membership came automatically with enrolment in one of the subordinate organisations such as a trade union. So uncertain were the leaders of their support in the League that they failed to hold a national congress between 1947 and 1958. The 1958 congress was held only because by then the leadership had become so factionalised that it needed to determine which group had support amongst the rank-and-file.

In its thirteen years of existence, the AFPFL faced three nation-wide elections.[43] The first, held in April 1947, was for the constituent assembly to draft an independent constitution. Two hundred and fifty five members were elected, 210 in 'Burma proper' and the other 45 in the former 'frontier areas'. The AFPFL or affiliated organisations won all but seven of the seats. The victory was less impressive that it seems, for the two principal opposition parties, the BCP and the KNU, urged voters to boycott the polls as the *wunthanu athin* had done in the 1920s. Nevertheless, seven independent Communists were elected against AFPFL candidates. The League and its associates in the PVO controlled the machinery of the election because many of their members were by then employed in government service and staffed large sections of local government. In some areas of central Burma, Indian, British and Burmese troops were used to maintain sufficient government control to allow campaigning and polling to proceed. The AFPFL dominated assembly elected at that time served as the parliament until 1951.

The national elections held in 1951 were conducted in three stages because of the continuing civil war. Out of 8 million eligible voters, only 1.5

---

43   For a history of elections in Burma, see R.H. Taylor, 'Elections in Burma/ Myanmar: For Whom and Why?', in R.H. Taylor, *The Politics of Elections in Southeast Asia* (Cambridge and New York: Cambridge University Press, 1996), pp. 164-83.

million cast their ballots, a turnout of less than 20 per cent, little more than during the boycotts of the 1920s and less than in 1936. The AFPFL was the victor in this election also, winning 147 seats out of the total of 250 in its own name and gaining the support of another 50 or so candidate from affiliated organisations. The remaining seats were won by independents and left- and right-wing parties. But despite its sweep of the legislature, the League actually won only about 60 per cent of the votes cast.

The League last faced the voters in 1956. At that time the major legal opposition party banded together in a coalition, the National United Front (NUF), in an effort to break the AFPFL's domination of the government. Issues such as inflation, social stability and corruption were prominent in the campaign. More than twice as many voters cast their ballots in 1956 as in 1951. Again, the AFPFL won control of the legislature, with the NUF winning only 48 seats. The AFPFL's share of the popular vote, however, fell to about 48 per cent.[44] The decline of popular support for the League accelerated through the 1950s as its leaders became increasingly distrustful of each other as they fought over the spoils of power for distribution to their factional supporters. The result was not only a split in the AFPFL but also the collapse of the government in 1958, threatening a 'Civil War among the anti-Communists'.[45]

Following the bifurcation of the League earlier in the year, Prime Minister Nu's ally Bo Min Gaung succeeded Kyaw Nyein as Home Minister and thus gained control of the Union Military Police. The Socialist leaders, Ba Swe and Kyaw Nyein, both close allies of senior army officers, including Brigadier Maung Maung and Colonel Aung Gyi, sought the support of the army to return to power. Ba Swe had claimed publicly that their faction, referred to as the 'Stable AFPFL', had army backing, and Nu's so-called 'Clean AFPFL' faction claimed that a coup was imminent.[46] By September 1958 the capital was surrounded both by troops of the regular army and by the Union Military Police. In order to forestall armed conflict between them and thus a new possibility of the Communists taking power, Maung

---

44 Maung Maung, *Burma and General Ne Win*, pp. 226-7; Josef Silverstein, *Burma, Military Rule and the Politics of Stagnation* (Ithaca: Cornell University Press, 1977), p. 69.

45 Richard Butwell, *U Nu of Burma* (Stanford, CA: Stanford University Press, repr., 1969), p. 205.

46 Louis J. Walinsky, *Economic Development in Burma, 1951-60* (New York: Twentieth Century Fund, 1962), pp. 247-8.

Maung and Aung Gyi convinced Nu to 'invite' General Ne Win to head a six-month 'caretaker' army government.[47]

The military caretaker government attempted to 'clean up' the country and its politics. After remaining in power for eighteen months, it conducted a national election. In the campaign the radical Marxist and socialist rhetoric of the 1940s and early 1950s was largely forgotten, except by minor party or non-party independent candidates such as former Brigadier Kyaw Zaw, who attacked the continued role of the United States in backing the KMT in the Shan State, or by the candidates of small leftist parties which did not possess the financial backing of the two major parties. The major parties' campaign slogans centred on the relations between religion, especially Buddhism, and the state, and on the issue of whether the nominally ethno-linguistic states created in the 1947 constitution should be increased in number and granted greater autonomy. The continuing role of foreigners in the economy was also raised, but this was played down by U Nu and his followers because of their continuing contacts with foreign businessmen.[48] The election was won by Nu's 'Clean' faction, soon renamed the Union Party, despite or perhaps because of the support that the army had given to the 'Stable' faction.

The political discord in Rangoon was not resolved by the election, however. While the split in the AFPFL in 1958 might have been seen, at least by the League's sincere supporters, as a tragedy, the factionalisation of Nu's Union Party had, by 1961, assumed the proportions of a farce. His party and government were held together by little more than the name of one man, and when Nu threatened to resign after the next election a scramble for succession commenced. By early 1962 the ruling party had lost what little popular support it had still retained.[49] But the increasingly chaotic politics of the political élite during the late 1950s and early 1960s was not merely a function of rivalries over the leadership and the spoils of office.

The politics of this period was symptomatic of the condition of the state. Rather than guiding the political agenda, the state largely responded to demands made upon it by often contrary political interests enunciating first principles as non-negotiable and axiomatic. Calls for ethnic autonomy

---

47   Butwell, *U Nu of Burma*, pp. 204-5; 'Parliament Meets', *Burma Weekly Bulletin*, vol. 7, no. 30 (6 Nov. 1958), pp. 258-9; Maung Maung, *Burma's Constitution*, p. 48; Nu, *U Nu -- Saturday's Son* (New Haven: Yale University Press, 1975), pp. 326-7.

48   Silverstein, *Burma, Military Rule*, p. 70.

49   Ibid., p. 66.

and religious freedom were countered by demands for a unitary state and for the support of the faith of the majority. Demands for socialism and a workers' state were countered by demands for the opening of the economy to foreign capital and an end to state regulation and economic planning. With no clear ideals or institutions to guide them, state managers in the 1950s operated as best they could. The charismatic appeal of Prime Minister Nu was crucial for the perpetuation of the state, but his behaviour was too erratic to allow respect and loyalty to the state to become routine. Further complicating the political picture, the alternatives posed by the underground Burma Communist Party and ethnic insurgents in minority areas were always before the public, denying the claim that there was no option but Nu's brand of politics.

Old and new functions of the state

Evidence of the displacement of the state between 1942 and 1962 is most clearly seen in the fact that it was much less capable of carrying out the minimal functions of maintaining order and regulating non-state institutions than the state had been under either the kings or the British. In addition, many of the functions the state had assumed during the colonial period in the spheres of health, education and human welfare were carried out neither universally nor with great efficiency. Despite the widely-held belief that the functions of the state would change with independence and the placing of power in the hands of indigenous leaders, one major consequence of the displacement of the state was that state managers paid increased attention to the functions of law and order and social control. In the meantime, repeated claims were made on the state by political leaders and by others to assume even greater responsibilities in regard to the management of the economy in the name first of wartime exigencies, then of nationalism, and finally of socialism. Ironically, the abandonment of the professed *laissez-faire* of the colonial state for the planned economy of the socialist state coincided with the undermining of the power of the state necessary for economic management.

Law and order. The displacement of the state from 1942 onwards was first experienced when the police and the military were unable to maintain social control during the Japanese invasion. The departure of nearly half a million people with the British was not the consequence solely of the change in administration and related personnel. Many, if not most, of the Indian and other non-European population who fled to India did so because of the breakdown of the control mechanisms of the state. The chaos of invasion led to a near collapse of the police and other instruments of order which had made life possible for the immigrant populations of colonial society. It has been estimated that about 1.5 million persons 'had their lives disjointed by military action'. From one half to four-fifths of the remainder of the population 'were adversely affected by the breakdown of administration'.[50] The most telling figures on the breakdown of social control at this time are provided by the estimates for the rates of murder and dacoity. It is thought that more than 500 acts of murder per million inhabitants occurred between February and June 1942, compared with 73 per million in 1940. Dacoities during the same period probably reached more than 2,000 per million, compared to 41 per million two years previously.[51]

Although Dr Ba Maw's government did little to change the organisation and functions of the police from those which had been created by the British, one of its first acts was to increase their number. By 1943 the force had been 'increased by 20 per cent over its pre-war strength or to 15,900 officers and men'. Men who had served the British and new personnel were recruited 'in equal proportions'.[52] Nonetheless, the police remained ineffectual, and the most important coercive force in the country during the war was the Japanese army, especially the Kempetai (military police), which replaced the 'punitive police' of the colonial period as the most feared organisation in the country. Even so, the costs of the indigenous police tripled during the war years while the total government funds devoted to law and order increased about one-third to about one-half of the total budget of the state.[53]

During the British interlude between 1945 and 1948, efforts were made under both the British Military Administration (CAS[B]) and the civilian governors to restore the effectiveness of the police. Elaborate plans to ensure a better policed society had been drawn up by British officials in exile in India. Their efforts were, however, largely in vain. After the war, the police became highly politicised and strikes by the Rangoon police force in 1946 were among the events that prompted the handover of power from the Governor to the AFPFL. In the first three months of 1947 the crime

---

50   Guyot, 'Political Impact of the Japanese Occupation', p. 86.
51   Ibid., Table 3, p. 152.
52   Abu, 'Collaboration, 1941-1945', p. 203.
53   Guyot, 'Political Impact of the Japanese Occupation', Table 9, p. 212.

rate was higher than at any time for which records were available, except for the actual months of the Japanese invasion in 1942. The murder rate was more than double that of 1940 (180 per million population) while the dacoity rate was up from 41 per million to 1,260 per million.[54]

Such statistics become increasingly rare after independence, another indication of the decline of state control over society. The civil war resulted in widespread disorder, with violent death rates probably higher than at any time in history of modern Burma. Then, after the civil war subsided, the police were in many areas the least important of the agencies of social control. The army had responsibility for order, often assumed by local officers rather than authorised by the civilian ministers, and in some areas, as will be discussed below, local political bosses of the ruling AFPFL became the effective enforcers of whichever laws they found useful for maintaining their political base. The state continued to apportion a large percentage of its budget to law and order. In 1956, for example, 23 per cent of capital expenditure, the largest single capital heading, was devoted to law and order and defence.[55] In the first six years of independence, military expenditure grew at an average rate (in constant price terms) of 35 per cent[56] and reached a peak equalling 6.7 per cent of gross domestic product in 1954.[57]

Those responsible for the maintenance of law and order in the 1950s often looked back with some nostalgia to the colonial days when the state was able to maintain public order and thus allow a greater degree of public political activity. After the army caretaker government had worked for nearly eighteen months to suppress the private armies of the local political bosses, General Ne Win, as commander of the armed forces, noted that under the British, even though there had been a great deal of internal political conflict, 'the factional struggles did not end up in violence and bloodshed. The British Government could afford to stay neutral, the entire administration

54   Ibid., Table 3, p. 152.

55   *Economic Survey of Burma 1958* (Rangoon: Government Printing and Stationery, 1958), p. 120.

56   Stockholm International Peace Research Institute, *SIPRI Yearbook of World Armaments and Disarmament, 1968/69* (Stockholm: Almqvist and Wiksell, 1969), Table 1A.12. Far East: Constant price figures, pp. 208-9.

57   Stockholm International Peace Research Institute, *World Armaments and Disarmament SIPRI Yearbook 1976* (Stockholm: Almqvist and Wiksell, 1976), Table 6A.19. Far East: military expenditure as a percentage of gross domestic product, pp. 160-1; ibid., 1977, Table 3A.4, p. 234; ibid., 1984 (London: Taylor and Francis, 1985), Table 3A.4, pp. 280-4.

kept aloof. Hence the fight was contained in a narrow arena.'[58] The postcolonial state was never removed to the same degree from political struggles because it did not possess the power of the colonial state to contain 'in a narrow area' what had become stronger and ultimately more important political antagonisms.

As discussed earlier, one of the major changes in the state during the colonial period was in the nature of law and the courts. Arbitration was replaced by codified law with an emphasis on written documentation, established precedent and a search for justice based on 'facts' in order to determine legal rights. The peasantry in particular felt that the colonial legal system provided inadequate protection of their interests and rights in society. The colonial state's emphasis on the rights of property against those of the person was felt not only to be morally wrong, but designed intentionally to ensure that the poorest had no chance of achieving justice. Since the poorest were the peasants, there was a clear wish on their part to see the system changed. However, little was done between 1942 and 1962 to alter the nature of the colonial legal system. The independent state after 1948 continued to enforce the same codes of law as had been imposed by the British in the nineteenth and twentieth centuries, and court procedures, rules of evidence and other aspects of the British-Indian legal system remained in place. The only major change was that appeals at the highest level to the Privy Council in London were abolished at independence and a new Supreme Court was installed to interpret the meaning of the constitution.[59] To most Burmese the continuation of the British-style legal system after independence was a clear sign that the nature of the state had not changed despite the departure of the colonial masters.

Economic and financial. The displacement of the state in the economic sphere was camouflaged by the greater attention state institutions devoted to economic planning and regulation in the name of nationalism and socialism. While control by the state of some economic functions did increase during these two decades, this came about primarily because the state assumed responsibilities for many economic operations previously owned by foreign capitalist enterprises, rather than through the development of new economic functions. Even at the end of the fiscal year 1961-2 the bulk of

---

58   Quoted in Maung Maung, *Burma and General Ne Win*, p. 25.

59   Alan Gledhill, 'Burma', in John Gilissen (ed.), *Bibliographical Introduction to Legal History and Ethnology*, vol. E, no. 7 (Brussels: Editions de l'Institut de Sociologie, Université Libre de Bruxelles, 1970), p. 11.

agriculture, accounting for 26 per cent of gross domestic product (GDP), and more than half of trade, accounting for 29.3 per cent of GDP, were in private hands, though the state had assumed greater regulatory control over these activities. Only in the major capital intensive areas of the economy which had been controlled by the state before independence (power generation, construction, communications, and social and administrative services) did the state have a major share of GDP in 1961-62.[60]

Between 1942 and 1962, planning became a substitute for the economic management which was beyond the capability of the state to develop. During the war planning was intended to increase production for the war effort; throughout the period of the British Military Administration and up to independence planning was intended to restore the economy to the conditions that existed before the war; with independence planning was to create a more prosperous and equitable socialist society. In each period planning was seen as a short cut to economic management, but given that the state had little control over the institutions of the economy it failed to meet the goals set. The first attempt was made in 1942-3 with the issuance of the 'New Order Plan', which was intended to provide a means of 'concentration, of power and control of action, of means and ends.' With the proper administrative structures Dr Ba Maw and his associates thought it would be possible to use the civilian and military manpower of the state to meet the demands upon it and thus create a new order justifying independence.[61]

Although the managers of the state in 1942 had ideas about economic planning, these remained rather vague, as did all subsequent plans. Their rhetoric and style were belied by the inability of the state to implement its plans for lack of both economic resources and persuasive capacity. Planning became a talisman. Ba Maw argued in 1943 that the plan itself would create power for the state:

All planning is concentration, of power and control, of action, of means and ends. Looking at it as a structure, a plan just follows this theory logically to the end and by doing so generates its own power. The ground-elements in planning are really concentration in one form or another, mass organisations, national unity, mobilisation of wealth and labour, collective action, leadership, and so on.

---

60   *Report to the Pyithu Hluttaw on the Financial, Economic and Social Conditions of the Socialist Republic of the Union of Myanmar for 1977-78* (Rangoon: Ministry of Planning and Finance, 1977), Tables 9 and 10, pp. 21-22.

61   Tin, 'Commentary of the New Order Plan', *Burma*, 1, 1, pp. 17-18.

The basic unit is human energy, human labour and its values. It is radically different from the old democratic plan [sic] which was based upon vote-value instead of labour-value. A real plan, that is a revolutionary plan now-a-days, must be built upon labour-value whether it gets the votes or not. ... [62]

After independence, however, 'vote-value' was resurrected, and while the economic planners and the politicians were aware of the contradiction between the rhetoric of their planned economy and the realities of the political system, they did not want to jeopardise their chances for re-election by demanding sacrifices in immediate consumption for long-term investment plans.[63]

The objective of state planning during the war was 'to create a personal stake in the State as well as in the war among the masses'. The managers of the state argued that the threat of losing independence to the British once again was the initial issue in the war effort shared by the masses. But Ba Maw argued that it was necessary to 'create a more material stake than that'. One way of doing this was land redistribution, giving priority to those who served the state. The other was to give 'preferential consideration' in the granting of employment, leases, licenses, contracts and the like to those who had served the state.[64] Planning was replaced in practice with the power of patronage and with the construction of a political machine. By the 1950s, the most politically articulate sectors of society under the AFPFL—small shopkeepers, small businessmen, and farmers other than rice cultivators—were protected from taxation and enforced economic direction to ensure their continued support for the managers of the state.[65]

The decline in the economic capacity of the state after 1942 is revealed by examining the decreasing rates of government expenditure. The average level of government expenditure in the period 1937-41 was 158 million rupees per year. Despite massive inflation during the war years, actual government expenditure in 1943-4 was only 30 million rupees. Calculated in rupees at their 1937-41 value, actual expenditure in 1943-4 was only 5

62   Ba Maw, 'Burma's New Order Plan', ibid., p. 105.

63   Khin Maung Kyi, 'Patterns of Accommodation to Bureaucratic Authority', p. 101.

64   Ba Maw, 'Review of the New Order Plan States', *Burma*, 1, 1, pp. 118-19.

65   Khin Maung Kyi, 'Patterns of Accommodation to Bureaucratic Authority', p. 101.

per cent of the pre-war level. Budget estimates for 1944-5 put government expenditure at 3 per cent of the pre-war level.[66]

The cause of this precipitate decline in state expenditure during the war was the dramatic fall in revenue as the state lost the ability to tax. The Japanese military pre-empted revenues from customs, business income tax and forests which had together amounted to 42 per cent of government income under the British. Land tax, which had accounted for 30 per cent of tax revenue before the war and had been a major cause of peasant discontent, became the major financial base of the wartime state, but the collapse of the administrative system meant that only 12 per cent of pre-war land taxes were collected. This decline was partially due to the collapse of the domestic agricultural economy because of a lack of export opportunities as the Japanese lost control of the Asian shipping lanes.[67]

The ability of the state to tax the peasantry directly through land revenue was never subsequently revived and indirect taxation of imports became the major source of state income after independence. By 1956-7, land tax revenue amount to only 4 per cent of tax revenue and 2 per cent of all state income. By that time non-tax revenue in the form of earnings by ministries and departments, state trading boards and Japanese war reparations amounted to 38 per cent of all state revenues, with customs making up another 25 per cent of income. Only income tax, paid largely by state employees as most individuals in the private sector did not pay taxes,[68] provided another significant revenue source (22 per cent).[69]

The underlying cause of the weakness of the state vis-à-vis the economy was the destruction of productive capacity caused by the Second World War and by the civil war after independence. Real GDP, in 1970-71 prices, stood at Kyat (Kt) 5,483 million in 1938/39 but fell to Kt 4,663 million in 1947/48 and to a post-war low of Kt 3,983 million in 1948/49, the first year of the civil war. Production then steadily rose to Kt 7,758 million by 1962/62.[70] This increase was primarily due to an average GDP growth be-

---

66   Guyot, 'Political Impact of the Japanese Occupation', Table 8, p. 208.

67   Ibid., pp. 209-10.

68   Khin Maung Gyi, 'Patterns of Accommodation to Bureaucratic Authority', p. 101.

69   These percentages are calculated from Table 37: 'Union Government Budget Receipts, 1956-57 actuals', *Economic Survey of Burma 1958*, p. 54.

70   David I. Steinberg, *Burma's Road Toward Development: Growth and Ideology Under Military Rule* (Boulder, CO: Westview Press, 1981), Table 5.1, per Capita GDP, p. 78.

tween 1952 and 1960 of about 5 per cent per annum.[71] Growth rates fluctuated markedly during the period, as the economy was highly dependent
upon trade, especially rice, timber and other primary products. In the early
1950s, thanks to the boom in primary products caused by the Korean war,
export earnings grew rapidly, though mainly to the benefit of the state, as
the price which farmers received for their crops remained under its control.
But a subsequent downturn in trade caused GDP at constant prices to decline an estimated 3 per cent in 1958, the year of the political crisis which
led to installation of the military caretaker government.[72]

Despite the expressed goal of the government to improve the economic
wellbeing of the population through planning and reinvestment of profits in
the country (instead of losing these to foreign owners), the incomes of most
individuals remained through the 1940s and 1950s well below what they
had been at the end of the depression in the 1930s. Real per capita GDP
in constant 1970/71 prices stood at Kt 395.3 in 1938 but fell 45 per cent
because of war destruction to Kt 218.1 in 1947/48. But despite the growth
of the 1950s, this figure had still only reached Kt 335.4 in 1961/62.[73] Per
capita consumption also declined in 1947/48 to 84 per cent of its 1938/39
level and fell to 72 per cent of the pre-war level in 1953/54. By 1960/61
per capita consumption had risen to 94 per cent of the pre-war level.[74] The
failure of the state to keep promises was one cause of its inability to counter
the political cynicism that greeted the authorities' platitudes.

The most obvious aspect of the enlarged economic role of the state after
the Second World War was its management of enterprises formerly run by
private British firms. Many of these were taken over by the British Military Administration in 1945 and were already operating under partial state
management when nationalised after independence. The Irrawaddy Flotilla Company became the State Inland Water Transport Board, and the
various timber extracting and exporting firms were nationalised under the
State Timber Board. Rice purchasing and export became a monopoly of
the State Agricultural Marketing Board (SAMB). More technically complex
foreign owned endeavours, such as the oil industry, became the subject of

---

71   Mya Maung, 'Socialism and Economic Development of Burma', *Asian Survey*,
      IV, 12 (Dec. 1964), p. 1119.

72   *Economic Survey of Burma 1958*, p. 1.

73   Steinberg, *Burma's Road Toward Development*, Table 5.1, p. 78.

74   Frank N. Trager, *Burma: From Kingdom to Independence* (New York: Praeger,
      1966), Table 3, Gross Domestic Product, Per Capita Gross Output and Con-
      sumption in 1947-48 Prices, p. 160.

joint venture agreements between the state and their mainly British owners. Many other enterprises were also nationalised and placed under government appointed boards which were intended to manage them as businesses, returning a profit which would accrue to the state rather than to British or Indian shareholders. However, the majority of state enterprises ran at a loss and depended on state subsidies in the 1950s.[75] Furthermore, the government organisations—except for several of the larger export oriented boards, particularly the SAMB—were run in a way politically beneficial to the ministers to whom they were responsible, and many managerial appointments were made on the basis of political patronage rather than merit.[76]

The major exceptions to this pattern were the economic enterprises managed by the Defence Services' Institute (DSI), which had been established by the army in the early 1950s to provide inexpensive consumer goods to members of the forces, but which expanded later to incorporate a wide range of economic activities. By the time of the 1958 caretaker government it had become the country's largest economic enterprise.[77] With the return to civilian rule in 1960, the DSI was renamed the Burma Economic Development Corporation and, despite its nominal position under the prime minister, remained in effect under army control.[78]

One of the main problems the state faced in attempting to develop the economy was capital formation for investment. The initial nationalisation programme resulted in an annual average net private capital outflow of Kt 14.3 million per year between 1951 and 1954, but this trend was reversed from 1955 to 1959 when there was an annual net private capital inflow of 11.3 million. In the following year, 1960, there was however a new private capital outflow of Kt 50 million and an additional Kt 13 million outflow in 1961.[79] Domestic capital formation was more successful after the civil war in both the private and state sectors, but it never achieved the targets

75   Aye Hlaing, 'Observations on Some Patterns of Economic Development', *Burma Research Society Fiftieth Anniversary Publications No. 1* (Rangoon: Burma Research Society, 1961), p. 10.

76   H.V. Richter, 'The Impact of Socialism on Economic Activity in Burma', in T. Scarlett Epstein and David H. Penny, eds, *Opportunity and Response, Case Studies in Economic Development*, (London: C. Hurst, & Co. 1972), p. 225.

77   Walinsky, *Economic Development in Burma*, p. 261.

78   Lissak, 'Social Change, Mobilization', pp. 15-16.

79   Frank H. Golay, Ralph Anspach, M. Ruth Pfanner, and Eliezer B. Ayal, *Underdevelopment and Economic Nationalism in Southeast Asia* (Ithaca: Cornell University Press, 1969), p. 162.

drawn up by the economic planners. State gross capital formation exceeded private gross capital formation in the years from 1953/54 to 1956/57 when they reached parity, but after that year until 1959/60 private capital accumulation exceeded that of the state.[80] This reflected the more settled economic conditions of the later period as well as declining government export revenue and reduced adherence to socialist policies.

The emphasis placed on development of a domestic manufacturing base indicated the desire of the independent state to make itself less dependent upon the outside world. In addition to investment in import substitution industries, a large amount of capital was directed towards power and transport development.[81] Between 1952/53 and 1959/60, 9.4 per cent of all capital expenditure was devoted to the industrial sector and another 12.8 per cent to power generation. The only sectors to receive a larger proportion of capital expenditure were construction and law and order.[82] This emphasis upon import substitution and the development of the industrial sector was reflected in a reorientation of imports. Whereas in 1938/39 only 22 per cent of all imports were for capital goods, in 1955/56, 33 per cent of imports were for capital goods.[83] However, the state could not further reduce imports of consumer goods so as to allow for more capital goods imports, because of the political protests this would have caused among influential shopkeepers and businessmen. Indeed, before the 1956 general election the government, with its limited foreign credits, purchased Kt 1.5 million worth of consumer goods from India with Indian credits in order to replenish shops with consumer goods then in short supply.[84]

---

80   Trager, *Burma: From Kingdom to Independence*, Table 4, Capital formation, Planned and actual, p. 162.

81   Khin Maung Kyi, 'Modernisation of Burmese Agriculture: Problems and Prospects', in Institute of Southeast Asian Studies, *Southeast Asian Affairs 1982* (Singapore: Heinemann, 1982), p. 116.

82   Trager, *Burma: From Kingdom to Independence*, Table 2, Allocation of Capital Expenditure Spent, p. 159; Walinsky, *Economic Development in Burma*, Table 56: Percentage Distribution of Public Capital Expenditure by Economic Sector, 1952-53 to 1959-60, p. 354.

83   Frank N. Trager, *Building a Welfare State in Burma* (New York: Institute of Pacific Relations, 1958), Table 2: Imports by Value, pp. 28-9.

84   R.J. Kozicki, 'India and Burma, 1937-1957: A Study in International Relations' (PhD, University of Pennsylvania, 1959), pp. 403-4; Nu, *U Nu -- Saturday's Son*, p. 228. Nu records that the goods were provided as a loan; Kozicki states that the loan funds were not used. See also Guyot, 'Bureaucratic Transformation in Burma', p. 393.

The events of the two decades between 1942 and 1962 resulted in relatively little restructuring of the economy despite the intentions of political leaders of the state. According to their plan, the size of the government's share in economic activities should have increased dramatically in all spheres in the 1950s compared to the 1930s. As table 4.1 shows, only in the sphere of government expenditure itself was there a significant change in the state's share of the economy from before the war to the end of the 1950s. Even in the state marketing and transport sectors the independent nationalist state had control over a smaller proportion of all activity than had the colonial *laissez-faire* state.

4.1.   Distribution of Gross Domestic Product

	1938–9	1959–60
Agriculture and fisheries	38.6	34.5
Forestry	7.3	7.1
Mining and quarrying	5.5	2.3
Rice processing	3.7	2.9
State marketing	12.8	9.2
State transport	2.4	1.6
State banking	0.0	0.3
Other public utilities	0.6	1.0
General government	3.1	11.3
Rental value of housing	3.3	4.1
Other industries and services	22.7	24.7
GDP	100.0	100.0

Source: Calculated from Louis J. Walinsky, *Economic Development of Burma* (New York: Twentieth Century Fund, 1962), Table 57, Gross Domestic Product in 1947–48 Prices, 1938–39 to 1959–60, p. 355.

External relations. With the end of colonial rule, the managers of the state in Burma had to develop new external relations. As with all states, their primary goal was to establish and maintain the security of the state, but that security had reciprocal internal and external aspects. Inasmuch as state managers often saw their personal or institutional longevity as identical with the security of the state, external security decisions were often made for internal reasons, and economic aspects were often as important as political ones in the making of foreign policy.

Burma's external relations may have begun formally on 4 January 1948, but state managers and would-be state managers had been conducting external political relations for centuries under the kings and, in the context of the European state system, since the 1920s. The negotiations that British officials in Rangoon conducted through the Governor with Calcutta, Delhi or London over immigration, defence and financial relations in the

1930s were the beginning of more formal relations after independence. These 'imperial' external relations came together when Premier U Saw, in order to secure his political position at home, journeyed to London in 1941 to try to gain a pledge of post-war formal independence. When the Churchill government refused to cooperate, Saw broke out of the imperial framework that had determined external relations from 1886 to 1941 and went as a head of government to lobby Washington for support against the British. Failing to get support from the Roosevelt administration, Saw then turned to the Japanese. State managers seek their friends where they can find them, and by the end of the British colonial state the Premier of Burma was attempting to conduct external relations like any other head of government.[85]

As the rising power in East and Southeast Asia in the late 1930s, Japan was an important focus of attention for Burmese political leaders. Several Burmese travelled to the country, and while Japanese assets in Burma were small, Japanese military and trading interests were considerable. But Japan's primary interest was strategic. The imperial Japanese army's 1942 invasion of Burma was intended to close the Burma Road which was the major supply link to Japan's enemy, the government of China under Chiang Kai-shek. But having occupied Burma and promised Burmese nationalists an independent state, Japan had to attempt to buttress the power of the state vis-à-vis domestic society in order to gain the cooperation of Ba Maw and other leaders in the war effort.

Thus the Japanese recognised the autonomy of the state in Burma, which, weak as it was, was the only institution through which they could work to achieve Japanese economic, political or strategic gaols. Similarly, after 1948, the fact that the state did not have effective control over society meant that other states' demands had to be tempered by a recognition of the state's limited ability to implement its policies. Occasionally, foreign assistance was needed to shore up the state and support it financially.

The ambivalent relationship between Japan and Burma in the 1940s is indicated by the ways in which heads of state or leading political figures were elevated to office in that decade. Ba Maw was made head of state in 1942, like Thakin Tun Ok before him, because he was thought the best man for the job by the Japanese army commander. The elevation of Aung San to the position of Burma's leading nationalist figure over Than Tun or

---

85 Robert H. Taylor, 'Politics in Late Colonial Burma: The Case of U Saw', *Modern Asian Studies*, 10, 2 (April, 1976), pp. 161-194.

Saw was a consequence of his being accepted by the Japanese as the creator of an anti-British armed force. Similarly, Aung San was viewed by the Supreme Allied Commander South East Asia, Mountbatten, as the man to cultivate in order to maintain peace in Burma. When Aung San was assassinated, it was the British Governor who chose Thakin Nu to succeed him. This is not to argue that these men lacked support in the country; it is merely to suggest that in the balance of political power within the state during the 1940s, external relations were crucial in determining the allocation of leading positions.

Formal independence modified but did not end the ability of external states to effect the functioning of the state and its leading personnel. However, the instruments through which such efforts were made had to be altered. The rhetoric of the AFPFL leaders called for external relations to be conducted in such a way as to avoid entering into alliances that would compromise Burma's independence. On the other hand sentiments of loyalty and existing economic and political ties, as well as treaty commitments made before independence, linked Burma to Britain and India. The Aung San-Attlee and Let Ya-Freeman agreements reached in 1947 placed obligations on Burma in exchange for the receipt of British military aid and training facilities.

Thus the military and economic position of the state in 1948-9 pointed towards forming external links with the West. It was also from the West that military and economic assistance could have been expected to come to shore up the state's position against its multiple internal opponents. By mid-1949, when conservative ministers from the pre-war political and administrative elites as well as from the army dominated the government, thought was apparently given to relationships for defence and economic cooperation with the West. However, the idea of a formal treaty commitment, which would have raised a great deal of opposition within the country, was subsequently dropped. Instead, established but technically informal relationships with the old imperial connections were allowed to provide the beleaguered state with a modicum of military and economic aid at the height of the civil war. Both India and Britain provided Burma with 10,000 small weapons each and arranged with other Commonwealth countries, including Australia, Ceylon and Pakistan, to provide a loan of £6 million in the 1950s to tide the state's treasury over until the insurgency was suppressed.[86] At the same time the United States, the rising hegemonic state in the region, was asked by Prime Minister Nu to provide $50 million in aid. This resulted in an aid agreement worth from $8 to $10 million.[87]

The outbreak of the Korean War provided an object lesson in the state's external relations and served to reinforce neutralist attitudes about security and foreign affairs. The initial United Nations response to the North Korean aggression was viewed by the non-communist state managers in Burma as a guarantee that if they were attacked by another states—China being the state they thought most likely to do this—the world organisation would come to their assistance. Subsequently, as it became increasingly apparent that the actions of the United Nations were being determined primarily to further United States' Cold War policies toward the Soviet Union and China, Burma's leaders began to question the extent to which they could rely on the UN for support.[88] The subsequent recognition of United States support for the activities of Chinese Nationalist (KMT) troops in northern Burma, raising the prospect of a Chinese People's Liberation Army incursion into Burma's territory, re–emphasised that Burma's government would have to develop its own independent foreign policy if it was to avoid entanglement in the Asian Cold War.[89]

Burma's leaders recognised that siding with either the United States or the Soviet Union and China would raise greater threats to state security than abstaining from involvement in the major Asian international conflicts of the early 1950s. This recognition, aided by the Korean War, was to evolve later into state policy. The increase in Burma's export earnings in the Korean war years gave the government financial latitude to pursue an independent foreign policy and even to order a curtailment of United States aid because of American assistance to the KMT troops in Burma. By the end of the war, when commodity prices declined, Burma's external financial position became much more perilous and it sought external assistance where it could without publicly compromising the country's independence. Thus the practice of seeking aid from a multiplicity of sources was established.

---

86   Kozicki, 'India and Burma, 1937-1942', pp. 310-14; Evelyn Colbert, *Southeast Asia in International Relations 1941-1956* (Ithaca: Cornell University Press, 1977), pp. 107-108.

87   Moses Than Aung, 'A General Study in the Economic Development of Burma with Special Reference to Economic Planning (1948-1958)', MA, Rangoon Arts and Sciences University, 1973, p. 13.

88   Colbert, *Southeast Asia in International Politics*, pp. 154-5, 157, 159.

89   Taylor, *Foreign and Domestic Consequences of the KMT Intervention*.

Burma's acceptance of aid in the latter half of the 1950s reveals the dilemmas the state's managers faced. Capital accumulation was difficult and the country's economic prospects were in gradual decline in the mid-1950s. The state's ability to import consumer goods was especially at risk immediately prior to the holding of national elections in 1956, and the government of India came to the AFPFL government's assistance with a loan of $42 million. As hard currency earnings become more difficult the state entered into barter agreements with the Soviet Union, China and Eastern European socialist states for development resources while once more accepting United States and British Commonwealth aid. Soon, Japan's war reparations became a major source of aid, enabling it to establish pre-eminence among those countries active in the economy.[90]

In the 1950s Burma's efforts to establish a neutral foreign policy made necessary the development of an independent defence policy. By declaring neutrality Burma was tacitly siding with one of its two largest neighbours, India, without at the same time antagonising Communist China in the way in which an alliance with the United States would have done. But the state did enmesh itself into a web of informal economic relations with the outside world. Unable to raise adequate revenue internally, by 1957-8 the state had come to rely 'upon foreign grants and loans for 46 per cent of its capital expenditures, and this dependence rapidly increased to 74 per cent in 1958-59 and then to an estimated 82 per cent in 1959-60'. It has been suggested that by 1959, 70 per cent of the state budget was financed by external loans and aid.[91] The financial weakness of the state was threatening to make it dependent on the outside world by the end of the 1950s.

The rise of alternative authorities

The collapse of state power after 1942 is demonstrated by the way many individuals could, with relative ease, circumvent the institutions of the state and ignore the orders of its officials. The most ambitious individuals could find means of achieving power and wealth outside the structures of the state as society regrouped itself on the basis of local centres and paid little heed to the capital. Unlike under the precolonial or the colonial order, there

---

90 See the discussion in Walinsky, *Economic Development in Burma*, pp. 507-45; Trager, *Burma*, pp. 305-43; John D. Montgomery, *The Politics of Foreign Aid: American Experience in Southeast Asia* (New York: Praeger, 1962), *passim*.

91 Montgomery, *Politics of Foreign Aid*, p. 31, though published government sources do not reveal such a large figure.

were for twenty years frequently used routes to power and wealth outside the structures sanctioned by the state. The expansion of dacoit gangs and insurgent bands is the most obvious example. Influence and loot accrued to their leaders through the coercive power they possessed.

For others, however, there were more lasting ways of gaining power and wealth. Politics was the most promising of these and replicas of the U Kyan Aungs of the colonial period (described in Chapter 3) came into their own in the 1950s. Then, in exchange for the authority that acting in the name of the state provided, local bosses offered the centre the promise of keeping their areas under control. The central state in turn sought such alliances in order to re-establish some partial control over society at the least cost to itself. In effect, the displacement of the state resulted in local leaders being able to dictate conditions to the central authorities, and thus inverted the relationship of state and society which had been the norm since the nineteenth century.

Although the colonial state's authority collapsed with the departure of the British, many subordinate officials remained in post as servants of the new regime. During the war, because they were no longer the agents of a power state able to protect or coerce the population, these officials lost much of their influence.[92] At the same time, the phenomenon arose of private individuals assuming for themselves responsibilities of administrative and political control. Sometimes this was done by local 'elders', but often by upstarts or individuals with personal connections with the local BIA commanders.

After the war, the British Military Administration and the returning colonial civil service, staffed largely by the same personnel, attempted to resurrect the pre-war system. However, the political and social mobilisation of the war years and the resulting upheaval, coupled with widespread political opposition to the British, made this extremely difficult. One obvious problem was a shortage of personnel familiar with the old state system and still willing to work within it. Only 70 per cent of Burmese and 60 per cent of British and Eurasian officials returned to duty in 1945. As more of these officers were required to take on new administrative responsibilities relating to reconstruction and the distribution of consumer goods, their places were taken by subordinate officials. The result was a rapid turnover

---

92   Guyot, 'Political Impact of the Japanese Occupation', pp. 204-5.

of personnel that made it nearly impossible to revive the more ordinary administrative routines of the pre-war period.[93]

The loyalty of its personnel that the state had developed in the colonial period was now destroyed and opponents of the British permeated the administration. For example, the typist in the Governor's office made copies of his papers for the leadership of the AFPFL.[94]

The top layers of the bureaucratic order which had held the colonial state together were further eroded in the months immediately before and after formal independence. Between October 1947 and April 1948, nearly 58 per cent of the top grade civil servants resigned along with 84 per cent of the senior police service officers, 50 per cent of civil medical officers and 78 per cent of the senior public works officers.[95] The result was rapid promotion for officers from the subordinate services and the recruitment of many new, junior civil servants.[96]

By the 1950s, district officers were by and large unable to command respect in their regions. Power had passed to the politicians and army commanders on the spot who held the real authority over the local populations. The plan of the newly independent state to use the colonial administrative system for economic development and the advance of social welfare proved impossible. The district officers and their staffs had their authority limited not only by the interposition of new, local extra-legal agents, but also by the intention of the politicians to introduce a more participatory form of local government. The prevailing notion in the 1950s was that it was necessary to turn the centrally appointed state officials into servants of locally elected councils capable of representing local demands. However, the councils rarely operated as intended. Rather than representing the people, they became the fiefs of political bosses and just another arena for factionalism to be manifested. The bureaucratic procedures required by local officials in order to satisfy both their central employers and their local bosses multiplied by a factor of six or seven. They soon became overwhelmed with office work and the authority which the colonial administrators had shifted

---

93   Guyot, 'Bureaucratic Transformation of Burma', p. 383.

94   Leslie Glass, *The Changing of the Kings: Memories of Burma, 1934-1949* (London: Peter Owen, 1985), p. 201.

95   Guyot, "Bureaucratic Transformation in Burma"' Table 4, p. 420.

96   Ibid., p. 421.

to members of the central legislature, to the nearest military commanders, or even, in some cases, to local insurgent leaders.[97]

The situation in Arakan in the early 1950s illustrates the loss of central state dominance. After independence, the Arakan branch of the AFPFL took control of the region. The expanded police force was filled with recruits from the demobilised forces of the PVO, but when the civil war broke out and the government declared the pro-Communist White Band PVO an illegal organisation, many members of the police joined the insurgents. A local AFPFL leader was then appointed as Special Deputy Commissioner to oversee the police and administrative system, but his authority disintegrated after his main political opponent, a conservative Arakanese and former élite colonial civil servant, U Kyaw Min, won a by-election in 1950. Kyaw Min then became the boss of the region[98] and, being unable to accept the socialist pretensions of the AFPFL leadership, formed his own political party, so named as to imply it represented the people of Arakan.

One Burmese analyst has noted how the collapse of the administrative power of the state in the districts allowed the rise of local *Bo*.[99] These men rose to leadership in their districts during the civil war by 'defending their own towns' when the armed forces of the state proved unable to do so. They were subsequently recruited by the AFPFL leadership as parliamentary representatives and they 'controlled the districts with the own para-military bands. They enjoyed their power independent of the legal authority' of the state.[100] Managing local affairs on their own, or running 'a government parallel to the bureaucracy' and arbitrating disputes and enforcing 'their decrees with their own power',[101] the local *Bo* became states with the state. Their authority was further enhanced by the wealth they accumulated and used in the construction of pagodas and other acts of Buddhist merit, and they developed their own networks of patron-client ties which made them increasingly independent of the state.[102]

---

97   Ibid., pp. 415-418.
98   ASMI, 'The State of Arakan', *The Guardian*, 1/10 (Aug., 1954), pp. 28-9; 1/11 (Sept., 1954), pp. 22-3; 1/12 (Oct., 1954), pp. 17-20.
99   *Bo* is a term used to refer to military officers and also to Europeans. In time it has come to mean any strong figure in an area.
100   Khin Maung Kyi, 'Patterns of Accommodation to Bureaucratic Authority', pp. 110-11.
101   Ibid., pp. 123-4.
102   Silverstein, *Burma: Military Rule*, p. 65.

During its attempts to re-establish order in the districts between 1958 and 1960 the military caretaker government worked to eliminate the power of the *Bo*. It was the intention of the army to reinstate the authority of the village headmen and district officers. The effect was to increase the opposition of civilian politicians within the AFPFL toward the military,[103] because the attempt to resurrect the dominance of central state agents in the district undercut the power bases of the party machine. During the caretaker period the army also organised National Solidarity Associations as part of its psychological warfare programme. These were under the leadership of headmen and local officials and were intended to develop within the public a willingness to resist the power of the local *Bo*.[104] At the end of the caretaker period the military felt they had successfully disbanded the *Bo*'s pocket armies.[105] Much of the military's success in restricting the power of these extra-state bodies came from the centralisation of district responsibilities in the hands of security and administration committees, which had the effect of placing the power of the army and the police behind the local administrative officers.[106]

The army caretaker government attempted to resurrect the power of the central state not only in the district administrations of central Burma where the AFPFL *Bo* had their power bases, but also in the surrounding hill areas where the 'feudal' powers of the traditional leaders had been perpetuated despite the egalitarian principles of the independence constitution. As Josef Silverstein has written,

in the states located on the nation's frontiers, the [army] government recreated a form of administration used originally under the British [sic]. The Frontier Areas Administration assumed direct jurisdiction over remote border areas and took responsibility for security and improvement in services to the peoples in those areas. As a result of these changes a more centralised administration was developed throughout the nation, and internal security improved. At the same time, control by the states over their own territories was weakened, and their peoples were tied more closely to Rangoon.[107]

103   Lissak, 'Social Change, Mobilization', p. 13.
104   Butwell, *U Nu of Burma*, p. 211; Lissak, 'Social Change, Mobilization', fn. 51, p. 16.
105   Maung Maung, *Burma and General Ne Win*, p. 24.
106   Silverstein, *Burma: Military Rule*, p. 78.
107   Ibid.

The authority of several of the sawbwas had first been undermined and partially superseded during the civil war and the subsequent occupation of parts of the Shan States by the Chinese Nationalist troops which had crossed the border from Yunnan Province in 1949 and 1950. Earlier, Karen National Defence Organisation troops had passed through the territories of some of the sawbwas, and the rulers' forces were unable to maintain control in the face of the insurgents. Martial law was then declared so the central army could reimpose order. According to a Burmese historian who had access to government records, the authorities felt that the consequence of unrest in the Shan States in the early 1950s would be the creation of a Communist government in collaboration with forces of the Kachin insurgent Naw Seng (the former commander of the colonial army's 1st Kachin Rifles), who had fled across the Chinese border. Government officials alleged that if the army had not taken over, the inefficient governments of the sawbwas would have fallen to the Communists.[108] (Former sawbwas have privately suggested that the army overstated the level of insurgent activities as a pretext for intervention.)

The primary consequence of the civil war for the Shan States was the undermining of the position of the sawbwas. On 13 September 1952, a state of emergency was declared in the state. At the end of November 1952, military administration under the control of General Ne Win was imposed in all areas. The state's and the sawbwas' police forces were amalgamated during the same period. The minister responsible in the central cabinet in Rangoon announced at a meeting in Taunggyi on 28 October 1952 that upon the termination of the military government, the sawbwas would be replaced with a form of democratic government. The sawbwas had agreed to the abandonment of their traditional powers at a meeting two days previously.[109]

Nonetheless, the politics of the situation were so complex that little was actually done to replace the sawbwas with an elected government before central military rule was withdrawn on 10 September 1954. The Shan State Military Co-ordination Committee did not meet for six months after the establishment of army rule. In fact, it appeared that the administration was merely imposed on top of the state and sawbwa administrative systems.[110] However, the military government did manage to implement

---

108   Ba Thann Win, 'Administration of the Shan States', pp. 109-110'; interview with Jimmy Yang, Rangoon, August, 1984.

109   Ba Thann Win, 'Administration of the Shan States', pp. 119-27.

110   Ibid., pp. 128-33.

some reforms, strengthening the power of the centre and weakening the position of the sawbwas. Police powers had been concentrated in the Shan States' government, as had all revenue collection. Principles of democratic local administration were enunciated with the removal of the power of the sawbwas to appoint village headmen. They were now to be elected. Also, a uniform code of law was introduced in the state, removing the individual judicial powers of the sawbwas. But theory was one thing, fact another. As no administrative mechanisms had been created to implement these reforms, the central government had to ask the sawbwas to continue to function in its place.[111]

Nonetheless, the sawbwas realised they could soon lose their positions, and in order to defend themselves established a political party, the Social Democratic Party, in May 1955.[112] They remained in control of all the seats in the two houses of the central legislature in the election that year, thus demonstrating their power to the central authorities. The contradiction between their powers and the egalitarian principles of the constitution provided a continuing ideological problem for the central state. In June 1957 it was rumoured that the Shan States would choose to secede from the Union under a clause in the 1947 constitution providing for such an option after ten years, and furthermore, would allow the establish of a United States air base in north-east Burma opposite China.[113] The central state thus felt obliged to act in order to preserve its sovereignty, territorial integrity and neutralist foreign policy.

The military caretaker government completed the formal process of ending the powers of the Shan and Kayah sawbwas with a handover of power to the state on 24 April 1959, in exchange for sizeable pensions and payments.[114] However, the sawbwas continued to exercise a great deal of authority, as demonstrated by their dominance of the electoral process, in their former states, thus guaranteeing continued political influence and safeguarding their 'traditional' positions.

Upon the return of civilian government in 1960, conditions in the countryside began to return to their pre-1958 condition. The government of U Nu attempted to rely once more upon local politicians and parliamen-

---

111   Ibid., pp. 152-6.
112   Ibid., p. 157.
113   Ibid., p. 193.
114   'Dawn of a New Ear in the Shan State', *Burma Weekly Bulletin*, 8, 4, (21 May 1959), pp. 25-40.

tary representatives but, as many of these had sided with his opponents or had their power undermined by the reforms of the caretaker government, the power of the state in relation to society was further undermined. In the Shan and Kayah areas where the power of the central state was no longer mediated through traditional authority, the growth of anti-state insurgency under the leadership of the families and officials of the former sawbwas was also weakening the power of the centre.[115]

Economic and social change

Although there was no fundamental change in the economy, the displacement of the state led to changes in Burma's social structure and domestic economic relations during the 1940s and 1950s. These changes reversed some of the trends begun by the colonial state and eventually facilitated reassertion of the state's dominance over other institutions. But the process was uncertain, especially in the 1940s, when change was almost entirely the consequence of forces and pressures outside the control of the state. The political leaders of the 1950s had specific ideas about the restructuring of Burma's ethnic and class composition, but these were only partially implemented as countervailing pressures in the political process protected powerful elements in the existing order.

Rapid social restructuring had commenced with the Japanese invasion and the immediate departure of the British and other communities most closely dependent upon the colonial state. In little more than a few months, the British withdrew in a manner quite unexpected only a few months before. Between January and June 1942, 600 government employees, 3,600 businessmen, 170 missionaries, and 500 professionals, together with their families, totalling 12,000 people, left for India. They were accompanied by more than 400,000 less exalted individuals, including nearly half of the Indian and Anglo-Indian or Anglo-Burmese population; 9,000 Burmese also joined the exodus.[116] The cities were most dramatically affected. The popu-

---

115   See Jon A. Wiant, 'Insurgency in the Shan State', in Lim Joo-Jock and S. Vani, *Armed Separatism in Southeast Asia* (Singapore: Regional Strategic Studies Programme, Institute of Southeast Asian Studies, 1984), pp. 81-110; Bertil Lintner, 'The Shans and the Shan State of Burma', *Contemporary Southeast Asia*, 5, 4 (March 1984), pp. 401-50.

116   Guyot, 'Political Impact of the Japanese Occupation of Burma', p. 103; Golay et al., *Underdevelopment and Economic Nationalism*, p. 213.

lation of Rangoon fell from half a million to only 150,000 between the first Japanese bombing in December 1941 and the end of February 1942.[117]

The loss of such a sizeable proportion of the Indian population had a dramatic impact on the structure of society, especially in terms of employment and the distribution of economic functions. Many professional, transport, industrial and trading roles became vacant and were either left unfilled or taken up by Burmese. Apparently, only a small proportion of those who fled in 1942 returned after the war, though other Indians came to Burma from 1945 to 1947. Consequently the Indian population, which stood at over one million in 1931, was reduced to about 700,000 in 1947-8.[118] After 1947 it was no longer possible to re-establish the colonial immigration pattern between South Asia and Burma.

Strict limitations on large-scale Indian immigration, long sought by Burmese politicians, were made law in June 1947, when the British Governor promulgated the Burma Immigration (Emergency Provisions) Act requiring visas for entry into Burma.[119] Furthermore, the unleashing of previously controlled antagonisms during the civil war made the country an uncertain place for South Asian migrants, and at the height of the conflict the rate of departures increased, so that in 1949, 80,995 Indians left Burma but only 32,676 arrived by sea.[120] Together with those travelling by land routes, there was a total of 118,382 departures and 65,414 arrivals, giving a net population decrease by immigration of 52,968 in 1949. Net movements resulted in a loss of 3,538 in 1950, but with the restoration of control over the cities and central sections of the country, conditions once more encouraged Indian immigration. From 1950 until 1955 there was a net increase in population caused by immigration each year, with the exception of 1954. After 1955 recorded departures surpassed recorded entries for every years, with particularly large upswings in net departures in the politically uncertain years of 1958, 1959 and 1960.[121]

Despite the many family and business connections between Burma and India, immigration had become more and more difficult. Greater restrictions were placed on the activities of Indian businessmen in the name

117   Guyot, 'Political Impact of the Japanese Occupation of Burma', pp. 94-6.
118   Kozicki, 'India and Burma', p. 225.
119   Ibid., p. 222.
120   Ibid., pp. 316-17.
121   Golay et al., *Underdevelopment and Economic Nationalism*, Table 13: 'Recorded Movement of Population (Sea, Air and Land)', p. 214.

of socialism and nationalism, and their lives and property became increasingly uncertain. Nationalised property was often 'compensated for' with government non-negotiable bonds redeemable only in Burma. As the President of the Indian National Congress stated in 1950 when discussing the problems of Indians were having in repatriating money from Burma to India, 'sometimes we are told that we can enjoy [our pre-war] money in Burma itself, but one does not know how long … by people who cannot feel a sense of peace and security in living there as they used to once during the British regime.'[122]

The peasantry. For the peasantry, the political cataclysms of the 1940s and 1950s provided unplanned and uncertain relief from the problems of landlessness, tenancy and indebtedness that had developed during the colonial period. The uncertainty and confusion caused by war, revolution and partially implemented government land reform and credit schemes made their positions no more secure than under the colonial state. The high expectations of relief from economic insecurity and predatory landlords, moneylenders, and state officials that peasants had shared in the 1920s and 1930s were not fulfilled after independence, but the weakness of the state in the 1940s and 1950s did provide opportunities for revolt or withdrawal which some peasants were able to exploit. The state's leaders were very uncertain of their ability to control the peasantry and could not ensure that the majority of the population, often under local leaders, did not, by non-compliance or violence, destroy their plans for social and economic change.

The partial exodus of Indians in 1942 included most of the alien landlords and moneylenders to whom the peasantry were beholden. The collapse of the state's judicial system during the war years also meant that land rent and debt repayments owed to indigenous landlords were ignored, as these obligations could not be enforced. Consequently, very few indigenous landlords were able to collect rents from their tenants during the war.[123]

For most peasants, however, the war period provided little of benefit and the advantages of being free of landlords, indebtedness, rent payments, and often land tax, were outweighed by the disadvantages of the collapse of the economy and of social order. Disease spread among the peasants and the standard of life declined generally. The availability of imported consumer goods was greatly reduced and items such as textiles and soap became scarce

122   Quoted in Kozicki, 'India and Burma', p. 354.
123   Becka, *National Liberation in Burma*, pp. 110-12; Golay et al., *Underdevelopment and Economic Nationalism*, p. 223.

and expensive. Prospects for achieving even depression level returns from the cultivation of export crops collapsed because of the curtailment of the international rice trade and a severe shortage of shipping to Japan and the rest of the East Asia Co-Prosperity Sphere. More than half of the draught cattle in the country were lost during the war through disease and Japanese requisitioning. Peasants were also obliged to provide transport, construction and other labour services, often for little or no payment, for the Japanese army. The 'Sweat Army' of the Japanese era was only the most notorious of the forced labour gangs organised from among the peasantry.[124]

Many peasants adjusted to the precipitous decline in their conditions by undertaking only subsistence agriculture. As a result, half of all the pre-war paddy acreage was left uncultivated. Yields per acre fell by a third or more. In the face of this decline in production, the state attempted to alleviate the peasants' conditions and to increase output, but its actions had little effect. In 1943, a 50 per reduction in rent was ordered in a largely meaningless effort to improve rural incomes and to increase cultivation. The state also became a major purchaser of paddy in 1942 and 1943 in an attempt to keep prices and production up.[125]

The peasantry in the export-oriented delta suffered more during the war years than did those in the central dry zone. Many peasants in central Burma, because of their diversified agriculture, were actually able to improve their economic positions, in particular by paying off their debts with increasingly worthless Japanese money.[126] The government encouraged farmers to diversity away from paddy to cotton and jute in order to provide supplies of raw materials for the manufacture of goods no longer imported from abroad, such as gunny sacks and cloth, though without much success.[127] The reason for this failure was probably the collapse of the credit systems of the colonial period which had provided peasants with the means of planting. Without state assistance or private credit, the cost of diversification was prohibitive.

At the end of the war the returning British Military Administration and its civilian successors made revitalisation of the rice industry a top priority. There was then a worldwide shortage of food and not only the colonial au-

---

124   Becka, *National Liberation in Burma*, p. 111.
125   Abu, 'Collaboration, 1941-1945', p. 209.
126   Becka, *National Liberation Movement in Burma*, p. 110.
127   Abu, 'Collaboration, 1941-1945', pp. 210-211; Golay et al., *Underdevelopment and Economic Nationalism*, p. 223.

276

thorities but also the leaders of the AFPFL set a high premium on Burma's ability to help feed the world. But for the peasantry the return of the British meant a return not only to the international market but also to increasing attempts by the state to control the production and marketing of the agricultural surplus. The programmes introduced by the British in 1945-6 to strengthen state control of agriculture in order to increase harvests and regulate prices were the basis of subsequent state attempts to control the production and profits of farmers. *Laissez-faire* in relation to the mainstay of Burma's economy ended in 1942, not at independence six years later.

The initial policies of the post-war British administration were successful inasmuch as rice production, and the system that supported it, returned to a relatively high level of efficiency in a very short period. Soon, planted acreage rose to a level more than two-thirds that of the pre-war period and yields per acre increased. By 1949-50 total paddy production was about five-sevenths of the pre-war level.[128] The government regulated the price of paddy through a state agricultural purchasing organisation and in the immediate post-war years set the official price below the cost of production. At the same time the colonial state apparatus which enforced payment of rent and taxes was resurrected, though apparently the peasants were led to believe this would not occur until economic conditions had improved. Even in areas where the economic well-being of the peasantry was not acute, the Communist-led peasants' unions received widespread support for their campaigns attacking the state's rice policy.[129]

Recognising the support the Communists received for their 'no rent' and 'no tax' campaigns, but also faced with the problems of raising revenue and capital and protecting property rights, the AFPFL was able to persuade the colonial authorities to introduce ameliorating legislation. Improvement in the security of tenure was one of the objects of the AFPFL's programme. The 1947 Tenancy Standard Rent Act limited paddy land gross rents to twice the level of land tax and placed the burden of land tax payment on the landowner rather than the tenant.[130] This allowed the state to determine

---

128   John S. Ambler, 'Burma's Rice Economy under Military Rule: The Evolution of Socialist Agricultural Programs and Their Impact on Paddy Farmers' (unpubl. Paper, Cornell University, 1983), Table 1: 'Paddy Acreage, Production, Yield and Population Estimates -- Burma, 1940-41 to 1961/62'.

129   Cady, 'Character and Progress of the Communist Party in Burma', p. 4.

130   Golay, et al., *Underdevelopment and Economic Nationalism*, p. 223. The amount of rent payable was reduced to the same as the rate of tax by an amendment to this legislation in 1954, ibid., fn. 47, p. 223.

the value of land, but placed the burden for the extraction of funds for the payment of tax onto the landlord. The government thought, mistakenly, that this arrangement would provide an alternative to the need for rural credit, as the lower rents would allow sufficient savings for tenants to finance their own annual crop.[131]

Some legislation introduced to further peasants' rights and undercut the appeal of the Communists' agrarian policies had the effect of putting the cultivators more under the control of both the state and the landlord. For example, the 1948 Disposal of Tenancies Act made security of tenure dependent upon payment of rent, cultivation of the land and repayment of agricultural loans. Other legislation was more helpful to the peasants and alleviated some of their prior obligations. The 1947 Agriculturalists' Debt Relief Act cancelled all pre-war debts and imposed an obligation only to repay the principal under loan agreements entered into between October 1946 and the date the legislation was passed. While in theory these acts provided peasants with 'security of tenure, nominal rents, and reinstated the titles of many cultivators',[132] given the breakdown in the administrative system it is doubtful whether many peasants were in a position to extract support from the state in exercising their newly acquired rights.

After independence more radical legislation was enacted in the form of the 1948 Land Nationalisation Act. According to the government, in 1948 there was a total of 11,120,343 acres of land in cultivation in the delta. Of this land, slightly less than 52 per cent was held by peasant proprietors, about 9 per cent by resident landlords, and the remaining 42 per cent by non-resident landlords. In central Burma the situation was different. There, nearly 87 per cent of the 8,203,498 acres in possession was held by peasant farmers and only 7.5 per cent was held by alien landlords.[133] The purpose of the Land Nationalisation Act was to return the land held by foreign and indigenous landlords to the tenants who worked it. The act was implemented in only one township and then abandoned. The reason advanced by some for the failure of land reform in 1948 was the distractions of the civil war; others have blamed the absent of sufficiently well trained administrative personnel to implement the measure.[134]

---

131   *Two Year Plan of Economic Development for Burma* (Rangoon: Supt., Govt. Printing and Stationery, Burma, 1948), p. 10.

132   Golay, et al., *Underdevelopment and Economic Nationalism*, p. 224.

133   Than Aung, 'General Study of Economic Development', pp. 79-80.

134   Golay, et al., *Underdevelopment and Economic Nationalism*, p. 224.

However, given that one of the rallying points of the Communists against the AFPFL government was that the state under its management favoured landlords over the peasants, it would appear to have been in the interest of the government to implement the act expeditiously in order to regain the support of the majority of the population which was supporting or sympathising with the Communist insurgents. The reasons given by J. S. Furnivall, at that time an economic adviser to the government , for the failure to implement the act were 'favouritism, mistakes and bribery. The whole plan was ruined by the incompetence and corruption of the politicians and officials who used it for their own benefit.'[135] Another obstacle to implementation of the 1948 Land Nationalisation Act was the interference of the Indian Ambassador to Burma, who was demanding full compensation for the nearly 5 million acres of land held by Indian and other foreign landlords. The Ambassador, Dr M. A. Rauf, was the brother of the AFP-FL's Housing Minister and a leader of the Muslim community in Burma, M.A. Raschid.[136] Thus it appears that the weak political structures of the independent state and the interests of its managers combined to make implementation of the measure impossible.

A second Land Nationalisation Act was introduced in 1954. Like its predecessor, it was not intended establish socialist forms of ownership and production similar to land reform then being implemented in China, but rather to redistribute land ownership from foreign and indigenous landlords to sitting tenants. The revised legislation provided for the compensation of the Chettiars and other landlords, but at only a fraction of the value they set on the land and largely in the form of fifteen-year, three per cent, non-negotiable, non-transferable government bonds of little genuine value unless used for investment in Burma.[137] The act was implemented very slowly. Between 1954/55 and 1957/58, when the caretaker government halted the administration of the act, only 17 per cent of all cultivated land had been redistributed.[138] By late 1955 just six per cent of the target of 10 million acres had been reached,[139] and only about 59,627 peasants households had been affected.[140] Assuming that most of the 3,357,000 acres

---

135   Quoted in Than Aung, 'General Study of Economic Development', p. 80.

136   Ibid., p. 81; Golay et al., *Underdevelopment and Nationalism*, p. 224.

137   Kozicki, 'Indian and Burma', pp. 347, 350.

138   Golay et al., *Underdevelopment and Economic Nationalism*, p. 224.

139   Than Aung, 'General Study in the Economic Development', pp. 82-3.

140   Kozicki, 'India and Burma', p. 349.

THE STATE IN MYANMAR

eventually redistributed was paddy land, this represented about 25 per cent of this land category. Of these 3,357,000 acres, only 1,480,000 was actually redistributed to 178,540 previous tenant cultivators, while more than half of the resurveyed land was confirmed to be in the control of 305,490 households.[141] The implementation of the act, which included surveying work of a kind which had been largely neglected since before the war, did provide the state with an opportunity to improve its control of land use and taxation. The ultimate failure of the land nationalisation programme is indicated by the statement that as late as 1963, tenants were still paying rent to 350,000 landlords, one third of whom were alien.[142]

A study of the consequences of land redistribution in one area has shown that the programme was more beneficial to the better off members of the peasantry than to the poorer sections. Tenants who had been landowners were more likely to be granted land than were previously landless labourers, because to be eligible for a land grant, a farmer had to possess the means to cultivate the land. Many landless labourers were too poor to own either draught cattle or ploughs.[143]

In the 1950s government schemes to assist the peasants also tended to help the better off in other ways. One of the government's major organisations which helped cultivators was the State Agricultural Bank (SAB). The SAB was developed as a means of providing credit to farmers in order to avoid the necessity of becoming once again indebted to Chettiars and other moneylenders. Research conducted by an American anthropologist in the 1950s revealed that in the delta better off cultivators who did not need cheap credit borrowed from the SAB and then reloaned at higher rates to poorer peasants who could not meet the SAB's conditions for the granting of credit.[144]

Tampering with the margins of the land distribution and credit systems probably had less effect on how peasants saw their relationship with the state and the economy than the government's monopolistic practices in the purchase and export of paddy. Following the practices of the British Military Administration, the independent state assumed direct responsibility

---

141   Silverstein, *Burma, Military Rule*, p. 75.
142   Golay et al., *Underdevelopment and Economic Nationalism*, p. 225.
143   Ambler, 'Burma's Rice Economy', p. 15, citing David E. Pfanner, 'Rice and Religion in a Burmese Village' (PhD, Cornell University, 1962), p. 241.
144   David E. Pfanner, 'A Semisubsistence Village Economy in Lower Burma', in Clifton R. Wharton, Jr., ed., *Subsistence Agriculture and Economic Development* (Chicago: Aldine, 1969), p. 58; Ambler, 'Burma's Rice Economy', p. 18.

for the management of the rice trade. The Socialists in the AFPFL changed the scheme's public justification from increasing production to increasing peasant welfare, but the effect was to benefit the state.

Rice purchasing and resale were the source of a large proportion of the state's revenue and foreign exchange and served, effectively, as a form of indirect taxation on cultivators. In the years of high international rice prices during the Korean war, as much as 40 per cent of all state revenue was provided by the state rice trade.[145] All the profits of the State Agricultural Marketing Board (SAMB), first a monopsonistic buyer and then a monopolistic supplier of rice, accrued to state revenues. The purchase price set by the SAMB was the minimum price in the domestic market regardless of other economic factors. Throughout the 1950s, the SAMB purchase price never varied though the average annual export price of rice and rice products varied from Kt 446 to Kt 838 per ton (f.o.b.). 'The SAMB buying price for paddy, as compared with pre-war, remained below parity prices of other goods.' In the face of criticism concerning the unfairness of this arrangement, as well as its denial of 'market forces', the government maintained that the cultivators were actually better off than before the war because of its land reform programme and because of reductions in rent, taxes and interest rates.[146]

After independence, the failure of the State Agricultural Bank to provide adequate credit for the bulk of the peasantry led to the re-emergence of the class of indigenous moneylenders. Wealthier members of villages who under the state's tenancy legislation were unable to invest in land turned their surplus cash to money lending. There appeared in the 1950s a form of local credit not unlike that of the precolonial period, unsanctioned by law and parallel to the official controls on the economy.[147] As early as 1949-51 the absence of state legal protection for mortgages had led to a rapid drop in the registration of mortgages,[148] but it is not possible to assess the effect of these changes on the broad mass of the peasantry.

---

145   Richter, 'Impact of Socialism', p. 229.

146   Golay, et al., *Underdevelopment and Economic Nationalism*, p. 242.

147   There are no complete studies, but see Pfanner, 'Semisubsistence Village Economy', p. 58.

148   Kozicki, 'India and Burma', fn. 49, p. 342, citing *Report on the Administration of the Registration Department in Burma during the Three Years 1949 to 1951* (Rangoon: Government Printing and Stationery, 1954), p. 4.

Urban classes. For the relatively small indigenous working class, social change and state policies during the two decades between 1942 and 1962 provided a new level of security. One reason was the return to India of many urban labourers and a consequent lessening of job competition in the cities, especially in the transport and processing sectors. Another reason was the greater power that unions developed under the AFPFL government because of the influence of the TUC(B) as a major constituent of the ruling front. However, during the war years the situation was initially less positive. Unemployment grew rapidly, especially in manufacturing and the extractive industries including mining, oil production and the timber business. Many previously organised labourers migrated back to the villages in search of subsistence. The urban proletariat which had begun to develop under the British was thus dispersed during the war years.[149]

Nevertheless, organised urban labour was of critical importance after the war in maintaining immediate political pressure on the British to grant independence. Strikes, especially by government employees, were very effective in 1945, 1946 and 1947. As inflation increased, the power of the strike was used after independence by government employees to defend their incomes from government fiscal stringency. The state's employees developed a great capacity for bargaining with the government because of their strategic positions in the administrative system of the capital and elsewhere. The need to ensure the support and loyalty of the lower ranks of the administrative services weakened the government's ability to impose labour discipline on the economy, especially before elections. The political power of the state sector of the workforce had also increased as nationalisation provided workers with higher rates of pay and greater job security than they had received in the private sector. The result was low productivity and high labour turnover as workers moved from job to job in search of the best conditions.[150]

The middle class, which should have benefited most from independence, was placed in a highly ambivalent position after 1942. During the previous twenty years it had developed uneasy relations with groups striving for state power. The political elite was dependent upon the administrative and economic skills of the members of the middle class and it enunciated ideas of liberal democratic rule which would eventually have given the middle class a dominant position in relation to the state and to other classes. But

---

149   Becka, *National Liberation Movement in Burma*, p. 110.

150   Aye Hlaing, 'Observations on Some Patterns of Economic Development', p. 11.

the military requirements and socialist or statist ideological beliefs of most of the major political leaders after 1942 meant that policies that would have encouraged the growth of a large indigenous bourgeoisie were rarely enunciated, much less implemented. Rather, the middle class remained dependent upon the state, regardless of who controlled it, just as it had been before the war.

During the Japanese occupation, although indigenous businessmen no longer suffered from competition from Indian and British shops and companies, they were greatly restricted by the monopolistic activities of the Japanese trading firms.[151] The state attempted to come to their assistance in 1944 by making regulations limiting the ownership of property in Burma to citizens and by requiring 60 per cent indigenous equity in all companies. These rules, however, did not become law until almost the end of the war and the Ba Maw government in 1945.[152]

An indication of the ambivalent relationship of the middle class with the post-independence state was the policy of maintaining the government monopoly over rice trading. While the colonial state's managers had perceived no objections to using state economic and social policy to assist the development of an independent, entrepreneurial middle class, the socialist ideology of the post-independence state managers viewed such a development with misgivings. The State Agricultural Marketing Board, in the process of replacing the Indian and British middlemen, placed this large sector of external trade not in the hands of indigenous businessmen but under the management of state employees. For those entrepreneurs who were permitted to work in the interstices of the state monopoly as millers and brokers, the many restrictions placed on their operations by the state meant that profits were small.[153] As a result, wealth that might have gone towards the middle class and strengthened its independence was drained off by the state.

In smaller trading activities, indigenous businessmen benefited more. However, even after independence less than 40 per cent of all commercial dealers were Burmese. The predominant position of Indians and Chinese in trading concerns of all sizes, including the smallest, was not seriously disturbed by the social change that followed the war and independence.[154]

---

151   Beck, *National Liberation Movement in Burma,* p. 112.

152   Ibid., pp. 131-2.

153   Golay et al., *Underdevelopment and Economic Nationalism,* p. 243.

154   Ibid., Table 23, Dealers [any seller after the importer] Registered by the Commercial Taxes Service, November 1949 through May 1951, p. 252.

In private industry, the indigenous middle class did rather better and by the end of the 1950s Burmese owned over 90 per cent of all firms while foreigners owned only 3.5 per cent.[155] However, the largest industrial and processing concerns were jointly owned by the state and foreign, mainly British, companies, which controlled top managerial posts. When the government lost enthusiasm for state ownership in the mid- to late 1950s because of their inefficiency and high costs, attention was given to turning the nationalised industries over to private hands. The army caretaker government of 1958-60 opened rice exporting to private enterprise with preferential treatment given to Burmese firms, but its concern for economic rationality and the expansion of domestic and indigenous trade did not stop it placing an increasingly large part of the import trade in the hands of quasi-government corporations.[156] In those areas where the government wished to encourage the growth of private indigenous enterprises (banking, pawnshops, money lending and insurance) it was unsuccessful, for foreign competition remained strong and Burmese entrepreneurs were unable to raise the capital required for such operations.[157] The result was often further nationalisation, the threat of which made it difficult for large commercial and manufacturing investments to be made.

Paradoxically, the displacement of the state meant that the state became increasingly important as a source of middle class employment. Many factors were at work in increasing the public sector workforce. One was the increasing use of the state bureaucracy as a source of reward for political followers. This was a trend which predated the Japanese occupation, but in the less restrained administrative atmosphere of the 1950s it grew apace.[158] Another reason was the increasing range of activities the state attempted to undertake in the name of either socialism or economic planning.

The state had been the largest single employer under the British, and this situation was enhanced in the 1950s. Between 1930 and 1953/54, the total number of public service employees increased by 75 per cent, from 88,100 to 154,432.[159] By the end of the 1950s, nearly 250,000 people

---

155   Ibid., p. 232.
156   Ibid., p. 263.
157   Ibid., pp. 212, 258.
158   Richter, 'Impact of Socialism', pp. 212, 258.
159   Khin Maung Gyi, 'Patterns of Accommodation to Bureaucratic Authority', Table IV-1, Increase in Public Service Employees in Burma, p. 92.

worked for government departments, boards and corporations, compared with 56,400 in 1940.[160] Growth was less rapid, 55 per cent in the period between 1930 and 1953/54,[161] in the professional and technical services to which individuals from the old middle class were especially drawn. The most rapid growth was in positions for top-level managers and directors of various governmental organisations. These increased nearly threefold from 35 in 1940 to 96 in 1957, of which 35 were government boards and corporations.[162] Highly prized and well paid posts in the central secretariat increased 233 per cent between 1940 and 1957, with senior positions numbering 130 in 1957, compared with 39 in 1940.[163] The size of the civil service and its leading figures' influence in the state at the height of the civil war were such that they even attempted to install a government without politicians.[164] However, their dependent position and lack of any independent power limited their political effectiveness. The middle class and its leading bureaucratic elements were in fact no more powerful than the weak state they served.

The greatest source of influence the urban middle class had with the state was its proximity to the political elite and its hold over policy as a result of the ballot. Because small shopkeepers and businessmen were more politically vocal and articulate than the majority peasant population, they were better able to be heard within the leadership of the AFPFL and the bureaucracy. The urban middle class during the 1950s also increased its buying power as a result of public expenditure on development projects, and the government was forced to spend scarce foreign exchange on imports of luxury goods to offset inflationary pressures. The wives of many political leaders were themselves involved in 'trade' and were keen to see their interests protected. 'Very few taxable persons in urban areas paid income tax' because of the influence they had and because the government was unwilling to attempt to tax them for fear of the political backlash it would cause.[165] The weak state could only tax the least influential group in society, the peasantry, and then only indirectly.

---

160   Ibid., p. 398.
161   Ibid., p. 92.
162   Ibid., Table IV-2, Growth of Government Organizations, p. 93.
163   Ibid., Table IV-3, Growth of the Secretariat, p. 94.
164   Ibid., p. 120.
165   Ibid., p. 101.

The search for legitimacy

The search for a set of ideas and symbols to provide the state with the seal of legitimacy and thus help its perpetuation was a constant concern for political leaders after 1942. Nationalism alone proved insufficient to justify the continued exactions of the modern state, and so the state stood exposed as an immoral and perhaps even exploitative instrument of a narrow ruling group. The constant experimentation with alternative legitimising symbols and political slogans during the 1940s and 1950s stands in stark contrast to the consistency of the legitimising myths of the monarchical state and even of the colonial state. The legitimacy claims of the state under Dr Ba Maw between 1942 and 1945 were based on the contention that by siding with the Japanese in their battle against European imperialism in Asia, Burma was on the side of an obviously just historical trend. 'Asia for the Asiatics' and the 'Greater East Asia Co-Prosperity Sphere' had about them an aura of righteousness which wartime experience under the Japanese military eventually exposed to be hollow. After the August 1943 declaration of independence, Ba Maw chose for himself the title of *Adipati Ashin Mingyi*, a title with an historical resonance going back to the Burmese kings. He then claimed that the state he led, based on the contemporary dictatorial and nationalist slogan, 'one voice, one blood, one nation', was in keeping not only with authoritarian trends in German, Italian and Japanese politics throughout the 1930s and 1940s, but also with expectations in Burma. Popular Burmese newspapers and magazines in the 1930s frequently posed the question of who would be Burma's Mussolini or Hitler. The reality of the war years, however, made these claims increasingly derisory and there were few who felt that a legitimate government had been overthrown when Ba Maw fled the capital in April 1945.

The opposition to the Japanese-backed state was based on claims put forward by the Anti-Fascist Organisation at the time of its formation in August 1944. The AFO began its appeals with round condemnation of the evils of Japanese fascism and militarism, before proposing to create a free and fair society. Subsequent statements called for economic reforms and for improvement of the conditions of the workers and peasants after independence was gained. The language of these claims had a Marxist ring to them. Following the gradualist line that they were pursuing at the time, the central Communist leaders of the AFO and then the AFPFL, with the exception of Thakin Soe, were careful not to set forth radical economic plans until after independence. After the AFPFL fell under more conservative leadership, the ideological claims of the League were expressed essentially in nationalist terms. The first AFPFL congress in 1947 stated that its economic and social policy would encourage private enterprise and that foreign, including British, economic interests would be able to continue to function—though in the interests of the nation. The ideological statements of the AFPFL before and after 1948 were based on the equality of all peoples within the country and on economic reforms for the benefit of all nationals. The AFPFL did not publicly appeal in the name of any specific ethnic or religious community, though much of the organised opposition to the League was couched in terms of the protection of the special rights or privileges of Muslims, Christians, Buddhists or the Karens and other minority groups.

The preamble to the 1947 constitution set forth the liberal basis of the claims to legitimacy by the postcolonial state, and represented the thinking of the conservative leadership of the League after the ouster of the Communists. It began thus:

WE THE PEOPLE OF BURMA including the Frontier Areas and the Karenni States, determined to establish in strength and unity a SOVEREIGN INDEPENDENT STATE, to maintain social order on the basis of eternal principles of JUSTICE, LIBERTY AND EQUALITY and to guarantee and secure to all citizens JUSTICE social, economic and political; LIBERTY of thought, expression, belief, faith, worship, vocation, association and action; EQUALITY of status, of opportunity and before the law ... ADOPT, ENACT AND GIVE TO OURSELVES THIS CONSTITUTION.[166]

Echoing later clauses in the constitution, the independent government's first major economic statement indicated that the state's management also believed that the state had important economic functions, and that these, too, were the basis of its legitimacy. As stated in the initial Two Year Plan, the government was seeking to lay 'the foundations of a planned economy and to transform Burma into a country where the Welfare of the common man constitutes the main motive of State activity'.[167] The civil war, however, revealed how meaningless these doctrines were considered by much of the population, except the most Westernised individuals such as the authors of the constitution and the governments' first economic planners. To many

166   The 1947 constitution and its amendments are reprinted as Appendices VII, VIII, and IX of Maung Maung, *Burma's Constitution*, pp. 258-313.

167   *Two Year Plan of the Economic Development of Burma*, p. 2.

others, ethnicity, religion, or Communism inspired more loyalty than did the state.

Claims to protect the rights of ethnic minorities had been one of the bases of the legitimacy of the colonial state. As discussed in Chapter 2, individuals who referred to themselves as Karens were given special rights of employment and representation under the British, and the leaders of the communities in the hill areas and the Shan States were guaranteed a role in the state. The intellectual justification of this policy survived into the politics of twentieth century Burma. By use of ascriptive notions of ethnicity common in nineteenth-century Europe, and claims that the Karens, Shans or other groups were ethnic categories embodying living social formations with unique and independent histories, ethnic labels became reified into claims for the existence of political nations within Burma other than that recognised as the 'Burmese state'. Of course, the state *qua* state has no ethnicity other than that which may be given to it by its subjects. In the modern age of nationalism, almost all states have ethnic labels that may incorporate within them one or more non-political ethnic groups.

The prevailing mood of nationalism in the 1930s and 1940s gave emotional and intellectual credence to claims for unique national status for the 'Karen', 'Karenni', 'Chin', 'Kachin' and 'Shan' groups which the British had nominated as ethnically (or in those days 'racially') distinct from the 'Burman' who lived in the plains. Even Burma's Communists, borrowing from Stalinist doctrines about nationalities, accepted the legitimacy of these labels and it was their ideas, along with notions about nationality common in liberal thought at the time, that shaped the 'federal' nature of the Union of Burma as set forth in the 1947 constitution.

The experiences of the colonial period, compounded by stories about the oppression by the 'Burman kings' of minorities before the British came to rescue them in the nineteenth century, and by conflicts between communities in the delta during the Second World War and the civil war, heightened perceptions of ethnic distinctiveness in the post-war period. The British requirement that leaders of the 'hill tribes' and the Shan States indicate their willingness to join with the government in Rangoon in an independent Burma, culminating in the 1947 Panglong Agreement,[168] meant that ethnicity became part of the independence process itself. In several ways, individuals sought to put themselves forward as ethnic leaders in order to increase their influence in the government. The growing perception that the state could

---

168   Kyaw Win, *et al.*, *The 1947 Constitution and the Nationalities.*

not protect the Karen Christian community, and that the Karens thus owed a higher loyalty to their ethnic label than to the state, was the basis of one prong of the post-independence civil war.

The establishment of egalitarianism as a principle of the state, 'the eternal principle of equality' as stated in the constitution's preamble, and the implementation of universal suffrage meant that the unique privileges created by the colonial state were denied to some groups after independence. Especially for the leaders of the Karen Christian community, the denial of ethnicity as a political principle in an all-Burmese order meant an end to their unique power not only within the state but within their own communities, for they had no 'traditional' claim to authority (their influence having come from their ability to gain special treatment for their followers from the state). Similarly, the principle of equality meant that in the frontier areas, the 'feudal' powers of the sawbwas and other rulers were now in contradiction to state principles. The constitution in its detail, however, skirted this issue by allowing the Shan and Karenni state rulers to remain in office. The constitution's authors had no choice but to obfuscate the issue of ethnicity, for there is no logical limit to nationalist claims.[169]

The perception of an illegitimate grab for power by the non-Communist leaders of the AFPFL provided the basis for the other, Communist prong of the civil war. The popularity of the Communist leadership and its organisational activities after 1943 was only part of the basis of the support it received. The failure of the government to implement many of the egalitarian promises made by the AFPFL before independence was another factor. The state's search for legitimacy in the face of rival claims of politicised ethnicity and Communist ideology initially centred on several options: these included an extension of the federalist front to the unitary constitution with the creation of a Karen state and the placement of leading Karens in important positions in the state's structures. The initial promise of a socialist programme, including land reform, was intended to remove support from the Communists. However, during the 1950s religion, especially Buddhism, became the most important element in the state's search for legitimacy.

Although Aung San and the Communist founders of the AFO were ardent believers in the separation of politics from religion,[170] their successors

169　A fuller elaboration of this argument can be found in Taylor, 'Perceptions of Ethnicity in the Politics of Burma', *Southeast Asian Journal of Social Science*, vol. 10, no. 1 (1982), pp. 7-22.

170　Aung San, *Burma's Challenge* (South Okkalapa: Tathetta, 1974), pp. 61-5.

in the leadership of the AFPFL, particularly Prime Minister Nu and many of the older, more conservative figures in the government, believed that the state had an obligation to support the Buddhist religion just as the precolonial state had done. Others, such as the Socialist leader Ba Swe, argued that Marxism and Buddhism were actually comparable doctrines and that good Buddhists could equally support both. What distinguished the Socialists from the Communists, they argued, was that the Communists were opposed to religion.[171]

How much the state's leaders in the 1950s consciously used Buddhism as a religious weapon against the state's rivals, and how far they genuinely believed that the faith should be upheld by the state, cannot be known. Nu and others certainly believed, however, that strengthening Buddhist beliefs among the population would prevent Communists from coming to power.[172] Devout Buddhists had long been opposed to Communism and in the 1930s the colonial authorities had considered how they could use the monkhood to stop the spread of radical ideas. By the end of 1945, the Buddhist hierarchy had begun a programme of its own, criticising the Communist Party for being anti-religious; Burmese language newspapers also attacked the BCP for being opposed not only to private property but also to racial distinctions, thus allegedly making it impossible to oust Indians from Burma's economic life.[173]

Formal action was taken as early as 1949 with the passage of the Ecclesiastical Courts Act to use the state to support Buddhism. In 1950 Nu introduced into parliament legislation to establish a lay Buddhist Sasana Council, and a Ministry of Religious Affairs was established to implement legislation dealing with religion.[174] Not only did the Council support Buddhism among existing members of the faith; it also undertook missionary work to encourage the development of Buddhism among animists and others living in the hill areas, under the auspices of agencies such as the Society for the Propagation of Buddhism.[175] Other legislation passed in the early 1950s established a Pali University and continued the colonial state's practice of supervising examina-

---

171   Smith, *Religion and Politics in Burma*, pp. 128-9.

172   John Everton, 'The Ne Win Regime in Burma', *Asia*, 2 (Autumn, 1964), p. 3.

173   Cady, 'Program and Character of the Communist Party', pp. 4-5; Than Htun, *Pyithu Sit Pyithu Ana* (People's War, People's Power) (Rangoon: publisher unknown, 1946), pp. 28-9.

174   Smith, *Religion and Politics in Burma*, pp. 117, 148.

175   Ibid., p. 154.

tions for Buddhist scholars. In October 1951 Nu announced the holding of the Sixth Great Buddhist Council to correct and maintain Buddhist texts. Government funds were used not only to construct the great artificial cave in which the proceedings of the council were conducted over two years but also to build adjacent to it the Kaba Aye (World Peace) pagoda. This council, like the last one held under the auspices of King Mindon, served to link the state clearly with the support and propagation of the faith.[176] The socialisation of youth into Buddhist beliefs was also sought through the introduction of Buddhist instruction in schools, but this, like other state actions to support Burma's majority religion, provoked strong opposition from the leaders of other religious communities.[177]

The attempt to use Buddhism as the basis of the state's legitimacy was opposed not only by Christian, Islamic, Communist and animist leaders, but also by Socialists within the government. During the colonial period the previous consensus on the state's role as a supporter of Buddhism had been shattered, and although leaders like Ba Swe and Nu argued that socialism and Buddhism were compatible politico-religious doctrines, when they came to discuss the epistemological and moral bases of the two doctrines they were forced to differ.[178] After the split in the AFPFL in 1958, Nu was no longer constrained in his use of Buddhism as a source of political legitimacy. Given a completely free hand, he went even further and revived *nat* worship (a popular but non-Buddhist-derived practice), which he had conducted privately since 1948.[179] After 1960 Nu made *nat* worship almost an official state ceremony, once ordering the construction of 60,000 sand pagodas as a means of establishing peace in the country.[180] He also instituted the use of the Buddhist lunar calendar, abolished cattle slaughter, and reinstituted many Buddhist support programmes which the military had dropped after 1958.[181]

---

176   Ibid., pp. 117, 165. See also E. Michael Mendelson, *Sangha and State in Burma, A Study of Monastic Sectarianism and Leadership*, edited by John P. Ferguson (Ithaca: Cornell University Press, 1975), pp. 270-6.

177   Mendelson, *Sangha and State in Burma*, pp. 178-80.

178   Ibid., pp. 128-33.

179   Butwell, *U Nu of Burma*, p. 71.

180   Smith, *Religion and Politics in Burma*, p. 171.

181   Winston L. King, 'Contemporary Burmese Buddhism' in Heinrich Dumoulin (ed.), *Buddhism in the Modern World* (London: Macmillan, 1976), p. 92. Of course, during 1958-60, in an attempt to halt the spread of Communism, the army itself used the cry that Buddhism was in danger as a major part of its psychological warfare programme. The resultant public response is said to have been one of the main reasons for the pious Nu's election triumph in 1960 (against the

Nu's attempt to create state legitimacy on the basis of the symbols and beliefs of the Burmese monarchs failed partly because the society upon which he attempted to impose those ideas was much more religiously and educationally diverse and sceptical than that of the nineteenth century and before. It failed also because the state lacked the power to impose its control upon the Buddhist monkhood and because, unlike the strong kings of the past who were able to use the *sangha* and its institutions to prop up the state, in the 1950s mobilised factions within the monkhood used the state for their own political purposes. The continuing sectarianism of the monkhood reflected the fact that the state could not enforce 'purification' upon them by championing one sect and its interpretation of the *Vinaya* over the others. The AFPFL thus became riven with the same sectarian feuds as the monkhood,[182] and factions within the monkhood supported different leaders of the League. The holding of parliamentary elections during the 1950s in particular increased the power of the monkhood over the state, for influential sect leaders could often sway votes towards one party or another.[183]

The controversies that surrounded the state's legitimacy were not lessened but rather exacerbated by the policies that Nu implemented. Nu's final desperate acts, seen by his critics to be politically expedient rather than serious efforts at national consensus, reveal how the state's legitimacy had largely dissipated by the early 1960s. In keeping with his campaign promises, Nu introduced legislation amending the constitution to make Buddhism the official state religion. In the face of protests from other religious communities, he then introduced a second constitutional amendment guaranteeing freedom of religion. Neither measure achieved anything in terms of creating a legitimising doctrine for the state; both rather kept the issue of the state's legitimacy at the centre of public attention. Furthermore, in order to attempt to end ethnic separatist insurgency, in the 1960 election Nu promised to create more ethnically designated regional governments, a Mon State and an Arakan State. As with the creation of the first five ethnic states, this proposal created no autonomy for the ethnic leaders, for their states were fiscally and military tied to the centre. But the promise, as well as its non-fulfilment, also kept the question of ethnicity and the basis of the legitimacy of the state at the centre of public attention. Twenty years after the collapse of the colonial state, no new basis for the state had been developed.

---

wishes of many in the army). Smith, *Religion and Politics in Burma*, p. 135.
182   Mendelson, *Sangha and State in Burma*, pp. 25-26.
183   Smith, *Religion and Politics in Burma*, p. 138.

5

REASSERTING THE STATE, 1962-1987

The consequences of the March 2ⁿᵈ Coup

The overthrow of the civilian government of Prime Minister Nu and his Union Party by a military Revolutionary Council headed by General Ne Win on 2 March 1962 was not seen at the time as a particularly momentous event. Foreign observers saw the coup as a reassertion of the disciplined government of 1958-60 caretaker period, and therefore primarily as an attempt to restore order in an increasingly chaotic political scene.[1] It evoked no outward manifestations of public opposition either in Rangoon or in the central or peripheral regions of the country. The coup, conducted with the loss of one life, began with the arrest of the President, the Prime Minister, five other cabinet ministers, the Chief Justice and some thirty politicians and former sawbwas from the Shan and Kayah States. Although it took place during a strike by Rangoon's importers and retail traders against government plans to turn more trade over to citizens,[2] this apparently had no bearing on the decision by the army to replace the civilian government.

Rather, the army justified its action in the name of ensuring the continued unity of the nation. Nu's policies since 1960, especially the establishment of Buddhism as the state religion, the organisation of the Mon and Arakan States, and the continuing negotiations with politicians from the Shan and Kayah States over increasing regional autonomy, raised the prospect to the army leadership and many others of increasing disunity of

---

1   John Everton, 'The Ne Win Regime in Burma', *Asia* (Autumn 1964), p. 6.

2   Frank N. Golay et al., *Underdevelopment and Economic Nationalism in Southeast Asia* (Ithaca: Cornell University Press, 1969), pp. 249-50.

the state and the possible loss of central control over peripheral regions. The examples of Laos and South Vietnam were then very much alive in the minds of many people, including the coup leaders.[3]

The issue of federalism and the possibility of trying to apportion state sovereignty were intimately related to other central questions. The granting of greater autonomy to the states would have allowed them to pursue different patterns of economic development and further undermined socialism, which was of decreasing importance to Nu in any event.[4] The possibility of secession of the Shan and Kayah States raised the prospect of independent foreign policies for these regions and, if they opted for this, of their alliance with an outside power such as the United States. This would have posed a major threat to the security of the remainder of the country, with the possibility of direct conflict between China and the United States extending beyond Laos and Vietnam to the heart of Burma. Such possibilities were not considered fanciful in 1962.

The federal issue was part of a general critique, widely shared within the army, of the nature of parliamentary democracy as it had been practised in Burma. Federalism and multi-party democracy were considered open to abuse by politicians representing landlords, capitalists and others seeking power and wealth for personal rather than public ends. This critique subsequently became the justification not only for the coup but also for the changes in the nature of the state that followed from military rule.[5] It soon became clear, as a result of this critique, that the consequences of the coup for the state and society were far more significant than just the temporary replacement of one set of rulers by another. The weakness of the postcolonial state was attributed to parliamentary democracy and federalism, and therefore it seemed obvious that their abolition was necessary for the state to reassert itself over other institutions in civil society. While the ambition to strengthen the state vis-à-vis civil society failed, the next

---

3   Richard Butwell, *U Nu of Burma* (Stanford, CA: Stanford University Press, 2nd printing, 1969), quoting Brigadier Aung Gyi at a press conference on 7 March 1962.

4   See Nu's assessment of nationalisation and the economy in his memoirs, *U Nu – Saturday's Son* (transl. by Law Yone, edited by Kyaw Win, New Haven: Yale University Press, 1975), pp. 215-20.

5   'Political Report of the General Secretary', in Burma Socialist Programme Party Central Organising Committee, *Party Seminar 1965* (Rangoon: Sarpay Beikman, 1966), pp. 28-33. See also Hpo Kyaw Hsan, *Paliman Dimokayeisi Sannit hnit Myanmar Naingngan* (Parliamentary Democracy System and Myanmar) (Rangoon: San Pya, nd).

26 years were to see a significant weakening of independent civil society and economic institutions.

Although the Revolutionary Council did not initially phrase its seizure of power in the name of reassertion of the state, it did so twelve years later when formally passing power to the new legislative body, the Pyithu Hluttaw or People's Assembly, formed under the constitution inaugurated on 2 March 1974. In a detailed but unpublished report of its stewardship of the state, the Revolutionary Council wrote that after it 'took responsibility for the condition of the state (*naingngantaw*), it began a transitional revolution with the intention of establishing a socialist society of affluence and without human exploitation, with a strong governing power, and the long term independence for the state.'[6]

The achievement of state dominance after 1962 was prolonged and dangerous, and ultimately put to the test, given the history of the previous twenty years. Institutional rivals were forced to accept the Revolutionary Council's terms for participation in a new political order or were eliminated by law. Those institutions allowed to continue were made dependent on the state, either through their personnel or through their finances, and were therefore unable to organise opposition. The process of state reassertion was gradual, and in the end many compromises had to be made between the ideal of state autonomy and dominance and the reality of the political, economic and social conditions within which the state and its leading personnel functioned. Given the corporate experiences of the coup group prior to independence, a strategy of action avoiding foreign military or financial involvement seemed possible. A necessary measure was to ensure that no outside power had reason to intervene and capture the state immediately after the coup. Thus it is not surprising that the Revolutionary Council's first policy statement was to pledge to maintain the neutralist foreign policy of its predecessors.

In the two years between the coup and March 1964, by which time the bulk of the economy had been nationalised, the Revolutionary Council declared all political opposition illegal, took over the direct management of most educational and cultural organisations, and established the nucleus of a political party with ancillary mass organisations and its own ideology, through which it was intended to mobilise support for the state. The proc-

---

6   *Tawhlanyei Kaungsi ei Hluthsaungchet Thamaing Akyinchut* (Concise History of the Actions of the Revolutionary Council) (Rangoon: Printing and Publishing Corporation, 2 March 1974).

THE STATE IN MYANMAR

ess required the demobilisation of institutions which had rivalled the state
for allegiance during the previous two decades, and the creation of institutional substitutes tied directly to the state. Initially there was a good deal
of enthusiasm for these organisations but in time their ability to engender
popular support waned.

After organising itself as a government of eight members and issuing its
announcement on foreign policy, on its second day in power the Revolutionary Council eliminated the major organs established by the 1947
constitution, including the central legislature and the councils set up as
the putative governments of the Kachin, Shan, Karen and Kayah States
and the Chin Special Division. Administrative staff were drafted in to replace the latter.[7] Two days later, on 5 March, all legislative, judicial, and
executive powers were placed in the hands of the Chairman of the Revolutionary Council. As head of both state and government, Chairman Ne
Win in theory possessed all state power and thus achieved a position of
formal dominance within the state unprecedented since 1885. However,
an attempt was made to suggest the collective nature of the Revolutionary
Council government by substituting the designation 'Chairman' for 'Prime
Minister' or 'President'.

Revealing the Revolutionary Council's initial desire to gain the cooperation of other political groups in its attempts to recast the structures of the
state, Council Chairman Ne Win met the leaders of the civilian political
parties on a number of occasions. Not surprisingly, the leadership of the
political groups which had been consistently denied state power during the
previous fourteen years pledged their support for the Revolutionary Council, whereas the groups which had held power previously refused to cooperate, for fear of losing their independence or because they believed that the
military government would not last long. In meetings in April and May,
the civilian party leaders refused to join with the Revolutionary Council in
forming a single political party under its auspices.

The Revolutionary Council's state-centred and comparatively radical
socialist economic policies were little in evidence in the first months of
its rule. Although the Revolutionary Council made it clear that one of

7   This discussion of the development of the Revolutionary Council government
     is based on *Tawhlanyei Kaungsi ei Hluthsaungchet Thamaing Akyinchut*, David
     I. Steinberg, 'Burma Under the Military: Towards a Chronology', *Contemporary
     Southeast Asia*, 4, 2 (Dec. 1981), pp. 244-85; 'Political Report of the General
     Secretary' in BSPP, *Party Seminar 1965*, and other publications listed in the
     bibliography.

296

the purposes of the coup was to put the economy back on the road to the socialist goals of the original AFPFL, within six day of the coup the Minister for Trade, the 'pragmatic' Brigadier Aung Gyi (then considered the second most influential member of the coup group), stated that any plans for nationalisation of import trade would be postponed for at least two years, thus reversing the policy of the previous government.[8] Not until 1 August, when Imperial Chemical Industries was nationalised, was a major economic measure taken. Evidence of what was to come became clear in November when the government abolished the ten-year guarantee against the expropriation of foreign investments. More radical economic policies were not, however, introduced until after the resignation of Aung Gyi from the Revolutionary Council of 8 February 1963. The departure of Aung Gyi was probably necessary to facilitate the abrupt change in economic and political policy which followed. It also made clear General Ne Win's domination of the new government.

But the change in economic policy in early 1962 lay in more than just a clash of wills between Aung Gyi's supporters and those of the Chairman of the Revolutionary Council. During the preceding ten months the Revolutionary Council had sought—but from the perspective of its more ardently socialist members, had not received—the cooperation of party leaders and national businessmen. Thus a majority of the government thought they would have to pursue their goals without the cooperation of other institutions and groups. A week after Aung Gyi's resignation, the chairman announced thoroughgoing policies to nationalise both foreign and domestic trade as well as banking and manufacturing.

Earlier, however, the Revolutionary Council's intention to intervene in aspects of society previously considered private was apparent. In a serious of orders issued in March 1962 it was announced that horse racing would be banned in one year's time, that beauty contests and all government sponsored music, song and dance competitions would be prohibited, and that gambling was banned in the Shan State.[9] The state assumed direct control of the universities on 14 May and divorced itself formally from the Buddhist faith on 17 May by dissolving the Buddha Sasana Council. In the next month the American Ford and Asia Foundations and the Fulbright programme, as well as British and American language training schemes, were closed, and from then on only governments or international agen-

---

8   *The Guardian*, IX, 4 (April 1962), p. 10.

9   Ibid., IX (April 1962), p. 11; IX, 5 (May 1962), p. 8.

cies (having been granted state approval) were permitted to train Burmese nationals.[10] In August the state assumed control over all publishing by establishing a system of registered printers. By these moves, and others such as an officially sponsored National Literary Conference in November, the state began to seal Burmese culture from outside influences and to focus public attention on state-sanctioned cultural activities. At the same time, the state was distancing itself from social and religious issues which in its frame of reference were too politically threatening for the state to attempt to control, and which had, in the past, led to dissatisfaction among followers of different religious faiths.

The Revolutionary Council was aware of the usefulness of a state ideology around which the populace could focus its beliefs and loyalties, and which could be used as a means of mobilising popular support for the state. The experiences of the military leadership during the anti-fascist resistance of the 1940s had convinced them of the need for a form of 'united front'-style organisation to direct popular energies. A first step in the direction of shaping public opinion was taken on 30 April with the publication of the Revolutionary Council's policy statement, 'The Burmese Way to Socialism'.[11] To be useful to the state as a long-term doctrine, this statement had to be sufficiently vague not to tie the government to an explicit set of policies, but sufficiently emotive to appeal to public sentiment. Following the failure of the major civilian political party leaders to join them in forming a new national front, the Revolutionary Council launched its own party, the Burma Socialist Programme Party (BSSP, Myanma Hsoshelit Lansin Pat, MaHsoLat) on 4 July. Many of the Revolutionary Council's ideas and much of its style echoed the Do Bama Asiayon's pre-war manifesto and evoked much the same response from established interests. At first the Party was composed only of members of the Revolutionary Council, although other politicians, especially of the left, became involved in its

10   John F. Cady, *Post-War Southeast Asia* (Athens: Ohio University Press, 1974), p. 471; John H. Badgley, 'Burma: The Nexus of Socialism and Two Political Traditions', *Asian Survey*, III, 2 (Feb. 1963), p. 93.

11   'Myanmar Hsoshelit Lansin' (Myanmar's Socialist Way), repr. as an app. to Myanmar Hsoshelit Lansin Pati (Myanmar Socialist Programme Party), *Lu hnit Patwunkyindo ei Anya Manya Thabawtaya* (Law of the Interaction of Man and the Environment) (Rangoon: Printing and Publishing Corporation, 9th ed., 1973), pp. 81-96. An official translation entitled 'The Burmese Way to Socialism' is printed as an appendix to Burma Socialist Programme Party, *The System of Correlation of Man and His Environment* (Rangoon: BSPP, 1964), pp. 43-52.

early organisation.[12] A philosophical underpinning of the Party's ideology was issued the following January as the *System of the Correlation of Man and His Environment*.[13]

The behaviour of the state after the coup baffled many observers both inside and outside Burma. It was not the business-like military regime expected by many, and the actions and words of the state's leading personnel soon seemed bewildering. The regime's rhetoric owed much to leftist anti-imperialist thought current in Burma during the 1930s and 1940s, which had persisted in critiques of the government of the 1950s as expressed by the legal left in the National United Front and by students and other left wing intellectuals in Rangoon. But this rhetoric was now used to attack the cautious Socialists and the radical Communists of the 1950s. The analysis of the past provided by the state's ideologies was remarkably consistent between 1962 and 1988, thus indicating the lack of organic growth in the thinking of the Party and the absence of a connection between theory and practice once the basic ideology had been outlined.[14]

The following extract from the 1965 report of the BSPP General Secretary conveys the flavour of the ideology:

The national bourgeoisie, the class which had supplied in varying measures the political leadership in the nationalist movement for freedom from foreign rule, and political parties of the rightist or the leftist inclinations which operated under the influence of the bourgeoisie, made some efforts to reform the social life of the Union of Burma. Yet, those parties, rightist and leftist, born in the shadow of the feudal social system, nourished on the educational and spiritual values of the imperialists, wore the badge of their origins in all their activities. Their ideas, attitudes and policies were unwholesome with petit bourgeois sectarianism, narrow-minded pragmatism, dogmatism, opportunism, fellow-travellerism, charlatanism, superficialism, bourgeois reformism, bureaucratic stylism, anarchistic stylism, 'leftist' infantile disorder, bourgeois militaristic style, and such evils and 'isms'.[15]

Difficult as it may seem, the Revolutionary Council intended to avoid this near universal list of political errors through the ideology of the BSPP, which was described as a middle path between the social democracy of the

12   Badgley, 'Burma: The Nexus', p. 94.

13   See fn. 11.

14   U Chit Hlaing, a civilian who had studied in the early 1950s in Europe, primary in Paris, and had worked in the army psychological warfare department subsequently, was the major author to the Party's ideological statements. He resigned from the Party in 1971. See *Soe: Socialism and Chit Hlaing: Memories*. Passau, Germany: Myanmar Literature Project Working Paper No. 10, 2008.

15   BSPP, *Party Seminar 1965*, p. 29.

bourgeois right and the Communism of the bourgeois left. The BSPP was to be the party of all the working people and therefore the Revolutionary Council and the post-coup state claimed a different class bias from its left- and right-wing predecessors. As made explicit in a document called 'Specific Characteristics of the Burmese Way to Socialism', published on 4 September 1964,[16] the Revolutionary Council, in an attempt to defend itself from charges of being Communist and anti-religious in orientation, argued that the state had now come to be based not on the narrow capitalist and landlord class which had primarily benefited from independence, nor on that class's enemy, the Communist Party, but rather on all the people.

The development of these ideological expressions stemmed from two characteristics of the coup group. First, the major figures had been raised on the anti-imperialist and anti-capitalist rhetoric of the Do Bama Asiayon and the Anti-Fascist Organisation. During the war organisers from the Communist movement had worked among the Japanese-trained officer corps, instilling the rhetoric of Marxist-Leninist politics. Secondly, some former Communists and others of the left were among the first civilians to express support for the Revolutionary Council, and their skills with language and propaganda were thus used by the state. But unlike previous political movements in recent Burmese history, the Revolutionary Council did not want to use the rhetoric of its ideology to mobilise one class against another in revolution or elections. It rather wanted to unite the entire nation by demonstrating that all classes had made their contribution to the national effort, but that, because of improper leadership, the revolution had gone astray.

The rhetoric of the Revolutionary Council belied its early appearance and behaviour. While it said it was conducting a revolution, efforts were made to gain the cooperation of both previously legal and illegal political groups, and initially few political opponents were arrested.[17] In the first months after the coup, life went on much as before for most Burmese, and even when sweeping economic changes were introduced, they tended to be implemented piecemeal. For example, although the press came under effective government control as early as August 1962, the Burmese-language

16   Pyihtaungsu Myanma Naingngan Towhlanyei Kaungi (Union of Myanmar Revolutionary Council), *Myanmar Hsoshelit Lansin Pati ei Witheitha Latkangmya* (Specific Characteristics of the Myanmar Socialist Programme Party) (Yangon: Myanmar Socialist Programme Party, Party Affairs Central Committee, 4 Sept. 1964).

17   Badgley, 'Burma: The Nexus', p. 94.

newspapers *Hanthawaddy* and *Myanmar Alin* were not nationalised until January 1969.

What most determined the style of the Revolutionary Council, and was consequently characteristic of its style of state management, was the fact that the majority of its leading personnel had their formative administrative and political experience within the army. Thus the army style of command and planning tended to become that of the state. Military analogies and examples most readily came to the minds of senior leaders. Three years after the coup, for example, General Ne Win described his position as the leader of the Revolutionary Council in military terms: 'Like the commander of a military unit in disarray, I am faced with the problem of how to mobilise and regroup the people in order to set up an organisation that will serve the interests of the country in a spirit of unity.'[18] The leadership's working concept of a socialist economy was more like a system of military post exchanges than a complex organisation of production and trade. Again, a phrase from General Ne Win is suggestive: 'Internal trade is our real problem. I said trade only by convention. Internal distribution may be more appropriate for socialism.'[19] Military metaphors were common in state and party documents also. For example, in describing the first year of nationwide monopoly paddy purchasing by the state, the Revolutionary Council's unpublished report to the first Pyithu Hluttaw noted that the local administrative committees 'supervised the whole process effectively in the form of a military operation.'[20]

After 1962, until 1988, the state in Burma appeared to much of the rest of the world as isolated and *sui generis*. By the mid-1960s the economy was becoming less and less involved in world trade. Whereas in the 1950s the ratio of Burma's foreign trade (imports plus exports) to gross domestic product, a common indicator of an economy's external involvement, was 40 per cent, it fell to 26 per cent between 1960 and 1970, and to 13 per cent between 1970 and 1977, one of the lowest among developing economies.[21] The state's radical economic autarky and general disengagement from the world, including leaving the Non-Aligned Movement in 1979,

---

18   'Address of General Ne Win … at the Opening Session', BSPP, *Party Seminar 1965*, pp. 9-10.

19   *Address Delivered by General Ne Win at the Closing Session of the Fourth Party Seminar on 11ᵗʰ November 1969* (Rangoon: Sarpay Beikman, 1969), p. 6.

20   *Tawhlanyei Kaungsi ei Hluthaungchet Thamaing Akyinchut*, p. 289.

21   Stephen D. Krasner, *Structural Conflict: The Third World Against Global Liberalism* (Berkeley: University of California Press, 1985), p. 295.

was exceptional. Its domestic economic policies—which appeared to be intended to reduce the level of the cites to that of the countryside rather than the reverse, which was the normal pattern for the remainder of non-Communist Asia—seemed perverse to observers who judge 'development' and well-being in terms of international hotels and 'GNP per capita' in US dollar terms. Indeed some of their policies, such as the 1964 edict which 'unified retail prices throughout Union at the prices ruling in the Delta',[22] had to be abandoned because of their economic impracticality. Why, then, did the Revolutionary Council propose policies that seemed to fly in the face of 'common sense'?

Faced with what they perceived to be an obligation to strengthen and perpetuate the state, and having abandoned the option of turning to the outside world for material support, the Revolutionary Council had no option but to turn inwards and restructure the relationship of the state with the institutions of civil society. The postcolonial state stood, as it were, weak and suspended between the world economy—dominated by Western financial institutions, markets, and states—and its own population. Rejecting the threats to security and independence that an outside alliance would have entailed, they turned to find means of gaining the cooperation and support of the largest sector of the population, the peasantry. Unlike the state-builders of Western Europe or North America, they did not seek to please an entrepreneurial class of manufacturers or traders. No significant bourgeoisie existed in Burma. Rather, the only internal group powerful enough to bring down the state was the peasantry, and so this class's inherent and historical antipathy toward the state and its exactions had to be overcome.[23] The resulting lack of economic and institutional growth in Burma led to the urban uprising which once more challenged the state's dominance, and the military's dominance of the state, in 1988.

Territorial reorganisation

The trend since the Restored Toungoo dynasty towards greater uniformity and simplicity in the territorial organisation of the state was resumed after

22   H.V. Richter, 'Development and Equality in Burma' (unpubl. Paper, Department of Economics, Research School of Pacific Studies, Australian National University, 1974), p. 32; Richter, 'The Union of Burma' in R. T. Shand (ed.), *Agricultural Development in Asia* (Canberra: Australian National University Press, 1969), p. 164.

23   See the stimulating remarks of Hans O. Schmitt, 'Decolonisation and Development in Burma', *Journal of Development Studies*, IV, 1 (Oct. 1967), pp. 103-5.

1962 following the partial reversal during the previous twenty years. The reification of 'race' or ethnicity, which had become part of the state's structure after 1948 with the creation of the Shan, Kachin, Kayah, and Karen States and the Chin Special Division, with additional Mon and Arakanese States promised after 1960, was modified so that while the cultural plurality of Burma was recognised, this was to have no bearing on the political structure of the state.

As the possible dissolution of the Union was perceived as justification for the 1962 coup, it is not surprising that the Revolutionary Council's first act after the dissolution of the legislature was the abolition of the councils of the four states and one special division and their replacement with administrative staffs under central control. On 30 April the separate Mon and Arakan ministries were dissolved, thus ending the prospect of semi-autonomous states for those regions. An additional complication in the structure of the state was terminated on 1 February 1964, when the special border districts which had been established during the civil war were abolished.[24] These had allowed the prime minister to directly govern areas along the border with East Pakistan (now Bangladesh) and China where insurgent activities were especially strong.

In its published accounts of its activities in the months following the coup, the Revolutionary Council did not discuss these actions or provide a full explanation for them. Rather, the reorganisation of the territorial structure was largely ignored while political means were used to try and persuade the population of the border areas that their cultural diversity and rights would be protected without the existence of nominally ethnic subordinate political organs. Even though the ethnic states, special divisions and ministries before 1962 had not provided fundamental protection for any alleged unique political position, the ethnic claims they represented had become highly emotive. After 1962 the state's leading personnel sought means to de-politicise ethnicity. Ethnic identities, when politicised into non-negotiable demands for administrative and policy autonomy, are normally irresolvable by short-term political means, and every state attempts to translate such demands into lesser ones of a negotiable and non-personal nature. The effect of the Revolutionary Council's policies was to eliminate ethnicity as a constitutional issue and replace it with more tractable ones such as regional development and cultural diversity. While initially this

---

24   *Tawhlanyei Kaungsi ei Hluthsaungchet Thamaing Akyinchut*, pp. 8, 143, 159-60, 180.

strategy may have been counter-productive, by the 1990s it apparently began to pay dividends.

During 1963, two further attempts were made to terminate ethnic politics and the federal question by replacing them with other issues. At the annual Union Day celebrations held on 12 February, General Ne Win outlined the Revolutionary Council's policies; these were quite simple and avoided any discussion of separate political institutions for ethnically defined categories. Rather, the basis of the policy was equal rights and equal status for all minority group members within the state. In striving to make this principle a reality, economic equality would be given first priority. This, of course, was one aspect of the decision to equalise rice prices throughout the country in 1964, and there is significant evidence that the Revolutionary Council made efforts to carry out its promise in subsequent years.[25] Equal access to health and educational facilities was also pledged. In order to ensure better medical treatment in remote areas, one of the first pieces of legislation promulgated by the Revolutionary Council was an amendment to the People's Military Service Law conscripting doctors into the armed forces in order to deploy them where most needed.[26] While promising equal treatment, the state reiterated its pledge to protect minority cultural practices as long as these did not run contrary to accepted health standards and other norms.[27]

In subsequent years, the state carried out other steps to unify the population around symbols and institutions of a non-divisible nature. In 1965 an Academy for the Development of National Groups was opened to train individuals from border areas to appreciate the diverse culture of the country while recognising the need for the unity of the state. Graduates returned to their home areas where they taught and often assumed leadership positions in state and party organisations. Also, in keeping with the imposition of a uniform administrative pattern throughout the state's territories, legal codes previously applicable only to certain ethnic groups or areas were

25   John W. Henderson, et al., *Area Handbook for Burma* (Washington, DC: United States Government Printing Office, 1971), p. 76.

26   *Tawhlanyei Kaungsi Hluthsaungchet Thamaing Akyinchut*, p. 133.

27   See Myanmar Hsoshelit Lansin Pati Baho Komiti Dana Chok (Myanmar Socialist Programme Party Central Committee Headquarters)), *Taingyintha Lumyomya Ayei hnit Patthet ywei Towhlanyei Kaungsi ei Amyin hnit Khanyuchet* (Views and Considerations of the Revolutionary Council in Regard to National Groups) (Rangoon: Sapei Biman, 1963, 5th edn, 1982), such as, for example, the crushing of Palaung women's chests by placing brass rings around their necks.

standardised. By the end of the 1960s, for the first time a basically common administrative and legal system for the entire state had been achieved.

Another step the Revolutionary Council took, in 1963, was to invite the leaders of the insurgent groups to meet it and attempt to negotiate a solution to their grievances. On 11 July, not only ethnic insurgent leaders but leaders of the illegal Communist groups were invited to come to Rangoon for unconditional negotiations. This offer issued on 1 April was made only after a general amnesty for all prisoners other than rapists, murderers, and certain politicians arrested at the time of the coup. Little success came from the negotiations, apart from an agreement reached with one small Karen group in March 1964; otherwise all the insurgent groups returned to insurrection within a few months.[28]

Given the historical memory of the state and the desire of the state's leading personnel to use known symbols to enhance its legitimacy, it was decided to maintain the existence of states named after ethnic groups, though in reality there was nothing linked to ethnic distinction in their organisation and they were identical in structure and authority with the 'divisions'. Seven states were established named Kachin, Kayah, Karen, Chin, Mon, Rakhine (Arakan), and Shan, along with seven divisions called Sagaing, Tenasserim, Pegu, Magwe, Mandalay, Irrawaddy and Rangoon. The administrative equality of the 'ethnic' states and of the divisions obscures the fact that in the 1980s, when the last census was taken, 72 per cent of Burma's population lived in the seven divisions; only the largest territorial state, Shan, had a higher population than the smallest division, Magwe. Both the importance of the border states to the security of the state and their 'feudal' historical legacies were recognised in the official Union Day celebrations. Every year the 1947 Panglong Agreement—whereby the British-recognised leaders of the frontier areas and the Shan States pledged their loyalty to the state by agreeing to join the Union—was commemorated along with the pledges of equality made by the Chairman of the Revolutionary Council on Union Day in 1963.[29]

---

28   *Tawhlanyei Kaungsi ei Hluthaungchet Thamaing Akyinchut*, pp. 12-13, 144; BSPP, *Party Seminar 1965*, pp. 44-8; Pyithaungsu Myanmar Naingngan Towhlanyei Kaungsi (Union of Myanmar Revolutionary Council), *Pyitwin Nyeingchaneyei Hswenwei Pwe* (Internal Peace Discussions) (Rangoon: 1964).

29   See, for example, the speech of BSPP General Secretary Aye Ko to the 1984 Union Day rally in *The Working People's Daily*, 13 Feb. 1984, as well as the annual proclamations of the President on this occasion.

The wording of the 1974 constitution made it absolutely clear that the sub-states of the Union possess no political or administrative sovereignty or autonomy. Reiterating at many points that Burma is a country composed of many national groups (*taingyintha lumyo*), article 4 state explicitly that 'state (*naingngantaw*) sovereignty must reside in the entire nation (*naingngan*)'.[30] The constitution is also explicit on the equality of all native born individuals, regardless of ethnicity. The only deviation from the principle of the irrelevance of ethnicity is made in reference to cultural practices. The constitution states in article 46 that the Pyithu Hluttaw 'will have the right to enact law if said laws concern the cultural (*wunkyeihmu*) of a national group only if more than half of the *Pyithu Hluttaw* members from the relevant state or division concur.' In the explanatory notes on the meaning of the constitution distributed before the constitutional referendum, the protection given to the states was made to appear somewhat broader; it was explained that decisions could only be made by representatives of the affected states and divisions in the national legislature.[31]

The structure of the state was elaborated in Chapter III of the constitution, where it was noted that 'in organising the state, the system used is central leadership and local management' (clause 28) or, as stated elsewhere in the constitution and numerous BSPP publications, the state is organised on the basis of 'socialist democracy', which means democratic centralism. The basic unit of rural society is the village; in urban areas the basic unit is the ward. Villages are grouped to form village tracts and these, like the urban wards, are the primary unit of government and administration, maintaining the pattern established by the 1920s. Wards are organised into towns, and towns and village tracts form townships. Townships are in turn grouped into the fourteen states and divisions which form the state's territorial organisation. Missing from this structure was the district level of administration between the state or division and the township. (See table 5.1)

---

30   Translations are unofficial.

31   *Pyi Htaungsu HsoshelitThammata Myanma Naingngan Phwetsinpun Akheyikan Upadei hnit Pattaem thaw Asiyinhkansa* (Report Concerning the Constitution of the Socialist Republic of the Union of Myanmar) (Rangoon: Printing and Publishing Corporation, 1973), pp. 55-6.

5.1.   Data on the Territorial Organisation and Population of States and Divisions, 1974, 1983, 2005

State/Division	Townships (1974)	Towns (1974)	Wards	Villages tracts	Villages
Kachin	18	17	83	614	2,635
Kayah	6	6	27	79	625
Karen	7	7	33	377	2,096
Chin	9	9	29	376	1,358
Sagaing	38	38	165	1,816	6,281
Tenasserim	10	09	54	263	1,255
Pegu	28	32	233	1,391	6,504
Magwe	25	26	153	1,542	4,814
Mandalay	29	28	216	1,980	5,362
Mon	10	10	62	381	1,207
Rakhine	17	17	119	1,041	3,871
Rangoon	39	13	503	641	2,113
Shan	52	48	303	1,628	15,393
Irrawaddy	26	28	207	1,922	11,705
Total	314	288	2,189	13,751	65,319

State/Division	Area in sq. miles	Population (x1,000) (1983)	% of Total	% Urban
Kachin	34,379	904	2.56	20.13
Kayah	4,529	168	0.48	24.67
Karen	11,730	1,058	3.00	10.44
Chin	13,906	369	1.05	14.72
Sagaing	36,534	3,856	10.92	13.72
Tenasserim	16.735	918	2.60	24.12
Pegu	15,214	3,800	10.76	19.46
Magwe	17,305	3,241	9.18	15.22
Mandalay	14,294	4,581	12.97	26.49
Mon	4,747	1,682	4.76	28.15
Rakhine	14,200	2,046	5.79	14.85
Rangoon	3,927	3,974	11.26	67.78
Shan	60,155	3,719	10.53	17.66
Irrawaddy	13,566	4,991	14.14	14.89
Total	261,228	35,314	100.0	23.95

State/Division	Estimated Population (2005) ('000s)	Density Per Square Mile	Density Per Square Mile	Estimate Density Per Square Mile
		(1973)	(1983)	(2005)
Kachin	1,423	21	26	41
Kayah	310	28	37	68
Karen/Kayin	1,641	74	90	140
Chin	510	23	27	37
Sagaing	5,901	85	106	162
Tenasserim/Tanintharyi	1,525	43	55	91
Pegu/Bago	5,514	209	250	362
Magwe/Magway	5,080	152	187	294
Mandalay	7,571	296	320	530
Mon	2,801	277	354	590
Rakhine	3,023	121	144	213
Rangoon/Yangon	6,322	812	1,012	1,612
Shan	5,223	53	62	87
Irrawaddy	7,455	306	368	550
Total	54,299		135	208

Sources: Nyi Nyi, *Myanma Naingngan Amyotha Mawkun (1975)* (Burma's National Record, 1975) (Yangon: Pugan, 1978), pp. 125 and 139; *The Working People's Daily*, 18 November 1983; Central Statistical Organisation, *Statistical Yearbook 2005* (Naypyitaw, 2007), pp. 20-21.

Changing relations with state authority

Unlike the representative principles that underlay the 1947 liberal democratic constitution, the Revolutionary Council attempted to develop forms of democratic socialism whereby the leadership of the state would establish direct relations with the population, especially the workers and peasants. In order to achieve these goals, the Revolutionary Council pledged to organise the working and peasant classes into a coalition to defend their rights and privileges.[32] Among the activities set up to achieve this was the holding of five peasants' 'seminars' between the end of 1962 and 1966 and several mass workers' 'seminars' in 1963 and 1966. These mass meetings provided a means by which the ideas of the administration of mass organisations for

---

32   *Tawhlanyei Kaungsi ei Hluthsaungchet Thamaing Akyinchut*, pp. 20-3.

the workers and peasants could be presented.[33] While these mass and class bodies primarily served the state as means of directing the political and economic activities of much of the population, the initial direct approach of the Chairman of the Revolutionary Council to the mass peasant and worker meetings in the first years after the coup proved to be very popular. Several hundred thousand individuals attended, and they created a sensation of participation by people who had rarely before been involved in matters of state.

An indication of later, more formalised attempts by the leadership to change the people's image of the state was the laborious means by which the 1974 constitution was inaugurated. Using the argument that the 1947 constitution had been drafted by lawyers and conservative politicians without the participation of the people, and therefore had been incapable of achieving socialism and national unity, the leaders of the state developed a four-year process designed to give the perception of popular participation in the drafting, amending, and implementation of the new constitution. At the 1966 peasants' seminar in Rangoon, the Revolutionary Council reiterated its 1962 pledge that it was merely holding state power temporarily, and that power would be returned to its rightful possessors, the people, who would then govern through their own political party.[34] At the 1969 BSPP seminar the Revolutionary Council Chairman and Chairman of the BSPP, Ne Win, announced that a new constitution would be drafted to implement this pledge.

At the First Congress of the BSPP, held in mid-1971, guidelines for the drafting of the constitution were laid down, and the constitution in its various drafts never deviated from these. Nonetheless, the State Constitution Drafting Commission appointed by the BSPP made various attempts to involve the public. The day after its formation, the Commission requested groups and individuals to submit suggestions. A month later a list of subjects was distributed to help elicit ideas from the public, and fifteen teams of Commission members toured the country soliciting ideas. During the final two and a half months of 1971 these teams met over 100,000 people and received suggestions from 3,458 individuals as well as 1,883 letters sent

---

33   Initially as the Worker's Council and the Peasants' Council, subsequently as the Workers' *Asiayon* and the Peasants' *Asiayon* under the auspices of the BSPP.

34   Ibid., pp. 31-4; *The Guardian* (Rangoon), Jan., 1974, pp. 10-20, and Feb., 1974, pp. 14-15, repr. in Albert D. Moscotti, *Burma's Constitution and Elections of 1974* (Singapore: Institute of Southeast Asian Studies Research Notes and Discussions, no. 5, Sept., 1977), pp. 3-26.

directly to the Commission. A draft of the constitution was then discussed at a Commission meeting in February and the Commission used the advice it had received from the people to justify the establishment of a unitary state. After being discussed within the Central Committee of the Party, the draft constitution was published on 30 April. Afterwards, the fifteen Drafting Commission teams toured the country for two months, visiting every township. In their wake, 16,969 task groups were established at the local level to discuss the constitution and the Commission claimed that this process involved over 7 million people, or perhaps as much as 40 per cent of the population over fifteen years of age. These local discussions were followed by two more months of touring by Commission teams in October and November. A further 2,000 letters were also sent to the Commission by individuals and groups.

A second draft of the constitution was then prepared and approved by the Party Central Committee in March 1973, and during May the fifteen teams toured the country once again, meeting large numbers of people. After the Commission agreed on various laws and bye-laws necessary for the implementation of the constitution, as well as the modalities of a national referendum to approve it, the fifteen teams made one final tour, again holding public meetings. At the Second Congress of the BSPP in October it was announced that the draft constitution would be passed on to the Revolutionary Council which would then implement it when approved by a national referendum. After a national census was conducted which gave the state its first complete count of the national population since 1931, referendum and election commissions were established at various levels to compile voting lists.

The BSPP's local units and mass organisations were all involved in the referendum campaign and, according to the government, over 95 per cent of the 14,760,036 eligible voters cast ballots. Of these, 90.19 per cent voted in favour of the new constitution, but the populations in the border regions were less enthusiastic than those more closely tied to the central state. The percentages in the states ranged from 66.30 per cent in the Shan State to 77.69 in the Karen State, while the redesignated Arakan State reported 86.09 per cent and the Mon State, carved out of Tenasserim Division, 90.62 per cent for the new constitution.[35]

The state's managers after 1962 also tried to bring the state closer to the people and to make it seem a less awesome and distant institution by chang-

---

35   *The Guardian*, 4 Jan., 1974, repr. in ibid., p. 72.

ing its nomenclature. Terms under the civilian government were replaced with those considered more in keeping with a revolutionary government. Thus the word for ministers used since the time of the monarchical state, *wun-gyi*, was replaced with *ta-wun-gan*, a rather perfunctory and matter of fact term. Even the royal suffix *taw* was deleted from *naingngan* in the state's formal title.[36] With the passage of time and the slackening of the revolutionary spirit, such adjustments to nomenclature were abandoned, and the state and its officials once more took titles linking them to linguistic usages of two centuries or more before.

'Bureaucracy', the word issued in Burmese as in English to describe the corpus of state officials, had become anathema in nationalist thought in the 1930s. Just as it was only used pejoratively in the Soviet Union,[37] so too has it been used in Burma since independence. One of the Revolutionary Council's allegations against its predecessors was that the politicians had been unable to take control of the state from the bureaucrats who had worked for the British. But Burma, like all modern states, functions at its core through bureaucrats. The Revolutionary Council at the beginning of its tenure was quite aware of this, and strove to ensure that the civil servants who staffed the state were well treated and loyal. In keeping with its egalitarian sentiments, some distinctions previously made between higher and lower grades of employees were abolished; lower grade employees such as drivers and cooks received enlarged benefits and many temporary employees were made permanent.[38] With the passage of time and the increasing poverty of the state, however, employees' salaries failed to keep pace with inflation, and this encouraged widespread continuance of the petty corruption which had afflicted the administration under the AFPFL regime.

Despite the Revolutionary Council's theoretical aversion to bureaucracy, though consistently with its efforts to reassert the state, the civil service grew between 1962 and 1974 disproportionately to the increase in population. This is not surprising given the increasing number of functions the state assumed. However, despite the egalitarian impulse of the Council, increasing administrative costs prompted the state to resort once more to part-time

---

36   Hla Pe, *Burma: Literature, Historiography, Scholarship, Language, Life and Buddhism* (Singapore: Institute of Southeast Asian Studies, 1985), p. 126.

37   Theodore H. Friedgut, *Political Participation in the USSR* (Princeton University Press, 1979), p. 38.

38   James F. Guyot, 'Bureaucratic Transformation in Burma', in Ralph Braibanti (ed.), *Asian Bureaucratic Systems Emergent from the British Imperial Tradition* (Durham, NC: Duke University Press, 1966), pp. 426-7.

5.2. Growth in Full-Time Central State Employment, 1962-1975

	1962	1973	% change
POLITICAL FUNCTIONS			
Revolutionary Council Chairman	0 ⎫	130 ⎫	
Prime Minister	175 ⎬	55 ⎬	7.4
Central SAC	151 ⎭	286 ⎭	89.4
Foreign Affairs	339	430	26.8
Sub-Total	665	901	35.5
SOCIAL CONTROL FUNCTIONS			
Judicial Affairs	6,266	8,212	31.1
Home and Religious Affairs	91,542	84,006	– 8.2
Information	2,553	11,554	352.6
Sub-Total	100,361	103,772	3.4
ADMINISTRATIVE AND SERVICE FUNCTIONS			
Planning and Finance	12,277	16,399	33.6
Labour	1,311	1,779	35.7
Health	15,411	29,485	29.3
Education	69,265	105,649	52.5
Culture	498	779	56.4
Social Services	445	1,004	125.6
Sub-Total	99,208	155,095	56.3
ECONOMIC FUNCTIONS			
Agriculture and Forests	33,592	67,630	101.3
Mining	27,599	41,595	50.7
Industry	31,120	78,765	153.1
Construction	6,471	8,068	22.8
Transportation	49,827	76,978	54.5
Trade	17,726	77,957	339.8
Cooperatives	1,732	12,768	637.2
Sub-Total	168,067	363,761	116.1
Total	368,301	623,529	69.3

Source: Author's calculations based on data in Towhlanyei Kaungsi ei Hluthsaunchet Thamaing Akyinchut.

employees. While the total population of Burma grew by about 32 per cent between 1962 and 1974, the total number of employees increased by 89.6 per cent and the number of part-time employees by 324.3 per cent. Table

5.2 shows the growth in departmental employment between the time of the military coup and the establishment of the new constitutional order.

Not unexpectedly, following nationalisation, those ministries whose primary responsibilities centred upon the economy experienced the greatest growth in full-time personnel. What is more surprising is the decline in the numbers of full-time employees in the Ministry of Home and Religious Affairs. The reduction of over 8 per cent was probably the consequence of transferring many of this ministry's former duties to other and often lower level state and party organisations. Changes in ministerial expenditure during the period of the Revolutionary Council reveal parallel trends.

Total expenditure growth (see table 5.3) in current terms was 172.8 per cent during the period of the Revolutionary Council. The only areas of government expenditure to exceed that figure were those related to economic activities and information. Overall, the proportion of state expenditure devoted to political, 'social control', and other non-economic functions actually decreased. Unfortunately, comparable government data do not exist for changes in military expenditure, but estimates made by the Stockholm International Peace Research Institute (SIPRI) show defence expenditure increasing by only 42.2 per cent, from 409 million Kt to 581 million Kt.[39] These patterns of employment and expenditure suggest that in terms of its relations with the populace, the central state played an increasingly significant role between 1962 and 1974 as a larger proportion of the adult population came to depend directly upon it for their livelihood. Also, because of its increasingly involvement in public information campaigns, coupled with the general suppression of non-state publications, the message that the state wished to convey got access to a larger proportion of the population. Although the range of media available was very limited, the state view of reality became the dominant one through almost all outlets.

In terms of the internal management of the state, little at the central level changed formally between the time of the coup and 15 March 1972, when the colonial-style Secretariat was abolished and ministers were formally able to communicate directly with their subordinate government departments rather than through permanent secretaries. However, this change was largely cosmetic, since from 1962 most of the secretaries were military officers who worked under the direction of senior officers serving

---

39   *SIPRI Yearbook of World Armaments and Disarmament 1968/69* (Stockholm: Almqvist and Wiksell, 1969), Table 1A.13, p. 209, and ibid., 1977, Table 7A.18, p. 232.

THE STATE IN MYANMAR

5.3. Growth in Total Expenditure of Central Ministries, 1961-1973

	1961–2	1972–3	% change
POLITICAL FUNCTIONS			
Revolutionary Council Chairman	0	5,161	
Prime Minister	3,531	2,305	111.4
Central SAC	0	20,905	
Foreign Affairs	13,757	20,288	47.5
Sub-Total	21,983	48,719	121.6
SOCIAL CONTROL FUNCTIONS			
Judicial Affairs	19,927	30,747	54.3
Home and Religious Affairs	221,068	278,258	25.9
Information	19,898	116,238	484.2
Sub-Total	260,893	425,243	63.0
ADMINISTRATIVE AND SERVICE FUNCTIONS			
Planning and Finance	71,045	144,480	103.4
Labour	9,036	10,711	18.5
Health	59,564	146,779	146.4
Education	141,504	353,804	150.0
Culture	2,104	6,053	187.7
Social Services	4,789	7,101	48.3
Sub-Total	277,291	538,927	94.4
ECONOMIC FUNCTIONS			
Agriculture and Forests	212,498	948,241	346.2
Mining	242,761	745,106	206.9
Industry	255,678	1,397,500	446.8
Construction	132,193	395,546	199.2
Transportation	304,602	617,842	102.8
Trade	1,171,989	2,713,226	131.5
Cooperatives	4,135	37,587	809.0
Sub-Total	2,323,848	6,855,048	195.0
Total	2,884,015	7,867,937	172.8

Source: Based on data in *Towhlanyei Kaungsi ei Hluthsaunchet Thamaing Akyinchut.*

as ministers, and thus never had much possibility of frustrating the intentions of the cabinet. But at the same time as this reform was implemented,

314

there was a significant change when the district level of administration introduced by the British, which had been the linchpin of the initial rationalisation of the state, was abolished. Administrative guidelines and policy
henceforth had only to pass from the centre to the townships through the
states and divisions.[40]

Security and Administration Committees (SACs). The administrative changes
which allowed the abolition of the districts were only hinted at in May
1962, when the Home Ministry held a two-day conference to discuss the
creation of a system of Security and Administration Committees (SACs)
which came to serve as the main structure of the Revolutionary Council's
control of subordinate administrative organisations.[41] A similar system had
been used during the 1958-60 caretaker period and reinstalled in modified
form by the civilian government in 1961 when it proved effective in helping 'arrest the growing insecurity in the countryside'.[42]

The SAC system was organised from the centre downward through all
levels of administration to village tract or ward. The Central SAC in Rangoon was directly responsible to the Revolutionary Council and was chaired
by the Home Minister. The Committees, composed of local military commanders with police and civilian administrative officers from the relevant
level of administration, were chaired by soldiers at the divisional and state
levels, and also commonly at lower levels. The intention was to strengthen
the state's administrative authority by increasing the power of the centre
relative to the increasingly powerless district and other lower level executive officers. This was to be accomplished by improving the administrative
coordination with a given region. In actual administrative routine, 'the role
of the regional military commander as Chairman of the District SAC [was]
probably less important in non-military activities' but had a crucial role
in security matters.[43] The main functions of the SACs seem to have been
to check on local initiatives and to ensure that central directives were fol-

---

40   *Tawhlanyei Kaungsi ei Hluthaungchet Thamaing Akyinchut*, pp. 8-9, 158; Jon A.
      Wiant, 'Loosening Up on the Tiger's Tail', *Asian Survey*, XIII, 2 (Feb., 1973), p.
      181.

41   *Party Seminar 1965*, p. 35; *Towhlanyei Kaungsi ei Hluthaungsuchet Thamaing
      Akyinchut*, p. 8.

42   Josef Silverstein, *Burma: Military Rule and the Politics of Stagnation* (Ithaca:
      Cornell University Press, 1977), fn. 19, p. 93.

43   Jon A. Wiant, 'The Burmese Revolutionary Council: Military Government and
      Political Change' (seminar paper, Dept. of Government, Cornell University,
      1971), p. 18.

lowed. Having army personnel in coordinating positions at all levels gave the Revolutionary Council direct access to all subordinate administrative organs through two networks, the civil administrative hierarchy and the military chain of command.

During the first ten years of their existence, the SACs had no non-official personnel among their members. However, in July and August 1972, at the time when the district level of administration was abolished, the SACs were instructed to add to their membership representatives from the relevant Party units and Peasants' and Workers' Councils, with others appointed by the government.[44] In preparation for turning the SACs into elected People's Councils as the core of the new socialist democratic state under the 1974 constitution, the SACS were given executive and judicial powers.

Organising the state/party and mass/class organisations. After its formation in mid-1962, the Burma Socialist Programme Party was developed as the main means for mobilisation of support for the state. The Party and its subsidiary organisations—initially the Peasants' and Workers' Councils, subsequently the Peasants' and Workers' Asiayon, followed by the Lansin Youth, the War Veterans' Organisations and groups for writers and artists—have all served the state as means of organising the population into groups. This also obviated the possibility of independent mobilisation organisations being formed which would create or express unacceptable or unattainable demands. In so doing, the BSPP system also served to create participatory institutions of the type normally associated with the modern state but having no independent power separate from the regime. Members of such organisations tended to development an attachment to the state, and this encouraged the individual to feel that along with his organisation, he was playing a role in state management. Membership also brought ancillary benefits such as access to officials and rewards. However, in time the ineffectiveness of the organisations led to growing cynicism about their efficacy, and membership activities became increasingly ritualistic.

For the first decade of the BSPP's existence, the Revolutionary Council was, in the words of the party constitution, 'the supreme authority of the Party during the transitional period of its construction.'[45] At the First

---

44   *Tawhlanyei Kaungsi ei Hluthaungchet Thamaing Akyinchut,* p. 9; Wiant, 'Burmese Revolutionary Council', pp. 181-2; Silverstein, *Burmese Military Rule,* pp. 93-4.

45   'The Constitution of the Burma Socialist Programme Party', section 2, printed as an app. to *System of Correlation of Man and His Environment,* p. 61.

Conference of the Party, in 1971, its status was changed from that of a nucleus party to that of a mass party. Subsequently the Party was to lead the state, rather than the Revolutionary Council leading the Party. Between July 1962 and March 1964, it was not entirely clear what role the BSPP would play in the future. During the 1958-60 caretaker period, the army had organised a National Solidarity Association with subordinate local councils as part of its psychological warfare campaign against both legal and illegal political parties, and in some ways the Party was a descendant of that organisation. While the Party was described as part of the machinery needed to teach the people the ways of a socialist democratic state and to organise the 'vanguard' of such a state to avoid the workers and peasants being 'misled' by parties of the left or the right, it was not until the March 1964 Law to Protect National Solidarity was promulgated that all other political parties were declared illegal.[46] Under the terms of this law, all organisations, including religious bodies, were required to register and all political parties except for the BSPP were to disband and turn their assets over to the state.

The pace of change in the state's relationship with society accelerated at this time. Politically, BSPP units began to be organised in district centres as the Party began the process of its conversion into a mass party. At the same time, the first steps in the nationalisation of internal trade were undertaken. With the March promulgation of the Law to Protect the Construction of the Socialist Economy, the state adopted wide powers of arrest and seizure against crimes such as smuggling and blackmarketeering that were disrupting the its economic policies and financing its political and military opponents. Then, on 19 March, all trading and general merchants in Rangoon were nationalised, and on 9 April, trade in the remainder of the country was also nationalised. From then on, through a series of shops known as People's Stores, internal trade became the legal monopoly of the Ministry of Trade's Trade Corporation No. 1.[47] For a variety of reasons, of course, the government proved to be incapable of supplying sufficient goods to meet demands, and the black market continued to expand throughout the period of Revolutionary Council and BSPP rule.

---

46   *Tawhlanyei Kaungsi ei Hluthaungchet Thamaing Akyinchut*, p. 15; *Party Seminar 1965*, pp. 55-57.

47   *Tawhlanyei Kaungsi ei Hluthaungchet Thamaing Akyinchut*, pp. 40-1, 45; *Party Seminar 1965*, pp. 67.

5.4. BSPP Membership Figures

Occupation	Full members	Candidate members	Total members	Party friends
1965				
Total	20	99,638	99,658	167,447
1966				
Armed forces	20	54,028	54,048	
Workers	0	91,999	91,999	
Peasants	0	15,383	15,383	
Police	0	2,975	2,975	
Others	0	21,662	21,662	
Total	20	185,947	185,947	185,967
1970		257,463		728,056
1971				
Armed forces			65,555	
Total			239,019	
1972				
Armed forces	42,359	63,537	107,896	
Workers	20,316	123,098	143,414	
Peasants	8,207	43,553	51,760	
Police	309	4,644	4,953	
Others	2,179	26,025	28,204	
Total	73,369	260,857	334,226	
31 March 1973				
Peasants	12,941	104,283	117,224	
Workers	76,883	185,448	262,331	
Others	6,877	80,994	87,871	
Total	96,701	445,449	542,150	
1 March 1977				
Total	171,153	517,426	688,579	819,511
31 Jan. 1981				
Armed forces	70,563	73,184	143,747	
Peasants			408,601	
Workers			242,532	
Total	425,789	1,075,113	1,500,902	981,859
31 Jan. 1985				
Armed forces	113,540	56,114		
Peasants			842,308	
Workers			478,616	
Total			2,230,000 +	1,200,000 +

Source: 1965: Burma Socialist Programme Party Central Organizing Committee, Party Seminar, 1965 (Rangoon: Sarpay Beikman, 1966), p. 130; 1966 and 1972: Josef Silverstein, Burma: Military Rule and the Politics of Stagnation (Ithaca: Cornell University Press, 1977), Table 5, p. 103; 1970: The Guardian, Feb. 1971, p. 12; 1971: Working People's Daily, 1 July 1971, 31 March, 1973: Myanma Hsoshelit Lanin Pati Ayeipaw Patia Nyilakhan 1973 (Special Conference of the Burma Socialist Programme Party, 1973 (Rangoon: Printing and Publishing Corporation, May 1973), p. 106; 1 March 1977 and 31 Jan. 1981: Burma Socialist Programme Party Central Committee Headquarters, The Fourth Party Congress 1981 (Rangoon: Printing and Publishing Corporation, 1985), pp. 83–5; 31 Jan. 1985: Working People's Daily, 3 Aug. 1985.

The expansion of the Party was at first largely confined to individuals from organisations most trusted by the Revolutionary Council: the scrutiny of applications served to create an aura of an elite and select organisation. Until 1971, full membership was restricted to the members of the Revolutionary Council. On the first anniversary of the coup, the Party invited applications from 'candidate members'.[48] Nineteenth months later the Party received 681,906 applications for candidate membership,[49] many from individuals who had been excluded from positions in the old legal political parties. Members of previously powerful organisations usually refused to apply, believing that the BSPP would not last or would not be an avenue to influence. As shown in table 5.4, most of the early applicants were from the armed forces and from nationalised industrial organisations in towns and cities which were the easiest to organise. Peasants and others living in rural or remote areas, especially in the hill areas, found enrolment difficult, if they knew of the possibility at all. Despite the Party's intention of representing all of the population, peasants did not become the majority of members until the Fourth Party Conference in 1981.

Upon admission to the Party, individuals were given a membership card and number. These indicated the length of service, and the lower the number, the greater the probability that an individual possessed influence in the early years of the Party's formation. Of the 260 individuals who were elected in 1981 to the Party Central Committee, the body which guided the Party between quadrennial Party Conferences, 121 possessed party numbers below 1001000, and 44 below 1000200.[50] Over 75 per cent

48   Ibid, p. 19.
49   Ibid., p. 128.
50   Party numbers and other data concerning the membership of the 1981 Party Central Committee comes from short biographies of the members printed and distributed at the Party Conference. A photocopy has been made available to the author by a non-official source. Statements of a comparative nature about changing memberships in the leading committees of the Party must not be accepted as wholly accurate. They have been made on the basis of analysis of lists of the names of the members in Burmese and English, and as Burmese do not have family names and several individuals can have the same name, perfection in analysis was impossible with the resources available. The following table gives the length of party membership of BSPP CC members in 1981:

Years	Number	%
19	3	1.15
18	198	76.15
17	38	14.65
16	9	3.56
15	3	1.54
13	1	0.39

of Central Committee members had been either full or candidate members for eighteen or more years, and the longer the membership, the greater the probability that an individual would have held high office in the state or Party.[51]

As the Party expanded, efforts were apparently made to make it more representative by recruiting more vigorously in the peripheral states and from groups not attached formally to the state. An ethnic breakdown of the total membership of the Party is not available, but of the 260 members of the Central Committee in 1981, 72 per cent identified themselves as Burman (*Myanma*) and the remaining 28 per cent said they came from minority ethnic communities. Of the Burman members, 83 per cent joined within the first thirteen months of the Party's existence, while only 64 per cent of the minority group members joined during the same period. In subsequent years, however, ethnic minority recruitment into the ranks of the Party elite increased faster than the Burman rate. Civilian recruits into

12	0	0.0
11	3	1.15
10	1	0.39

51   Serving in leading positions in the state in 1981 from among the lowest 200 numbers were:
U Ne Win President (10000001)
U San Yu, Secretary of the Council of State (10000003)
U Thaung Kye, member of the Council of State (10000005)
U Myint Maung, Chairman of the Council of People's Attorneys (10000025)
U Ye Gaung, Minister for Agriculture and Forests (10000037)
U Maung Maung Kha, Prime Minister (10000042)
U Tha Kyaw, member of the Council of State (10000047)
Dr Maung Maung, member of the Council of State (10000060)
General Min Gaung (10000086)
U Kyaw Nyein, Minister of Education (10000128)
U Sein Lwin, Minister for Home and Religious Affairs (10000137)
U Tha Tin, Minister for Mining (10000138)
UTint Swe, Minister for Industry (10000139)
General *Thura* Kyaw Htin, Deputy Prime Minister and Minister for Defence (10000141)
U Zaw Win, Secretary of the Council of State (10000142)
Thura U Saw Hpyu, Minister for Transport and Communications (10000147)
U Tun Tin, Deputy Prime Minister and Minister for Planning and Finance (10000159)
U Ba Thaw, member of the Council of State (10000165)
U Ban Ku, member off the Council of State (10000169)
The other 25 members of the Central Committee in 1981 with membership numbers below 200 were serving in leading positions in the Party organisation and members of various state organisations.

5.5. BSPP Central Committee Membership (1981) by Year of Birth, Ethnicity and Military/Civilian Career Pattern.

Year of birth	Army Burman serving		Army Bruman retired		Army non-Bruman serving		Army non-Burman retired		Civilian Burman		Civilian non-Burman		Total	
	No.	%	No.	%	No.	%	No.	%	No.	%	No.	%	No.	%
1911–19	0	0.0	4	1.5	0	0.0	1	0.4	0	0.0	0	0.0	5	1.9
1920–4	5	1.9	23	8.9	0	0.0	7	2.7	5	1.9	4	1.5	44	16.9
1925–9	24	9.3	49	18.9	6	2.3	12	4.6	10	3.9	1	0.4	102	39.9
1930–4	15	5.8	19	7.3	2	0.8	7	2.7	4	1.5	7	2.7	54	20.8
1935–40	4	1.5	1	0.4	0	0.0	2	0.8	17	6.5	20	7.7	44	16.9
1940+	1	0.8	0	0.0	0	0.0	0	0.0	6	2.3	4	1.5	11	4.2
Total	49	48.8	96	36.9	8	3.1	29	11.2	42	16.2	36	13.9	260	100.0

Wiant, 'Loosing Up on the Tiger's Tail'

the Central Committee were also greater among minority group members. Whereas 65 per cent of the Burman Central Committee members in 1981 were apparently retired or serving army officers and 35 per cent were civilians, these proportions are nearly reversed for minority representatives: 37 per cent and 63 per cent respectively. Minority group members, not surprisingly, were somewhat younger than the Burman members. While 41 per cent of the Burman members were more than fifty-five years old in 1981, only 26.5 per cent of the minority group members were. Nine per cent of the Burmans were under the age of 45 whereas this applied to 22 per cent of the minority group members. Burmans were a larger proportion of the 50-54 age category, 37 per cent as against 22 per cent of the minority group members, but minorities formed a larger proportion than Burmans of the 45-49 age category, 30 per cent to 12 per cent.[52]

With the passage of time and the greater penetration of the Party into civilian society, the leadership became more broadly based not only in terms of ethnicity but also in terms of background. Whereas 75.5 per cent of the Central Committee members in 1972 were from the armed forces,[53] 22 per cent were serving officers in 1981, though if retired officers are taken into account, the proportion from the military still reached 70 per cent. Many senior Party leaders had followed the example of the Party Chairman and of twenty other officers who left the army in 1972 as the Revolutionary Council prepared to inaugurate the 1974 constitution. Of the 280 mem-

---

52   See table 5.5. Non-Burmans included 10 Arakanese, 9 Mon, 1 Mon-Burman, 1 Mon-Shan, 3 Kayah, 12 Chin, 12 Karen, 1 Paku Karen, 6 Kachin, 1 Mayu, 1 Yawan, 8 Shan, 1 Dan, 1 Shan-Burman, 1 Gun-Shan, 1 Palaung, 2 Pa-O, 1 Wa, 1 Laha, and 1 Naga.

53   Wiant, 'Loosening Up on the Tiger's Tail', p. 180.

bers of the Central Committee elected in 1985, 67, or 24 per cent, were currently serving in the army.

An indication of the growing institutional maturity of the Party was the nature of new persons added to the Central Committee as older members retired or died. Firm data are not available, but it would appear that of the 240 members who sat in the Central Committee selected in 1977, 193 were re-selected in 1981, but only 135 of the members in 1985 had been in place eight years earlier. This meant that nearly half the members of the Central Committee in 1985 had been promoted in the previous four years.

Changes were also made in the membership of the Party's senior committees between 1981 and 1985. Between meetings of the Central Committee, the Central Executive Committee was the most powerful body; if the Party led the state, the Central Executive Committee led the Party. The most powerful individual in the country was the Chairman of this Committee, as he was also Chairman of the Party. Between 1962 and July 1988 only one man held that post, U Ne Win. The Central Executive Committee included the General Secretary of the Party as well as the Joint General Secretary and, after 1985, a Vice-Chairman. The other members were all senior ministers and other high army and government officials. The Revolutionary Council itself was the initial Central Executive Committee, and its senior membership was remarkably stable over a 26-year period. Of the Committee's 23 members in 1977, 13 were re-elected in 1981, but only nine of the 23 serving in 1977 continued after 1985. The changes that had been taking place in the Party were more fully illustrated by the composition of the Party Disciplinary Committee. Of the 19 members serving on it in 1977, 12 continued after 1981 but only one member serving in 1977 was still sitting in 1985.

The building of the mass Party between 1962 and 1971 was conducted primarily under the auspices of army personnel. The first tier of the Party hierarchy below the Revolutionary Council was composed of six Divisional Supervision Committees corresponding with the six military regional commands. Below these were established 15 Sub-Divisional Supervision Committees which corresponded roughly with the states and divisions, with an organising committee for the army. The basic level of Party organisation was at the township level, which meant bypassing the district administrative level of the state apparatus. The township Party units fell under the supervision of the Divisional Supervision Committee and the Divisional Coordination Committee, placing effective supervision of township units just one level away from the highest central state authorities. Below the township level Party units were formed in village, ward and workplace groups and cells. Only at the township level and below was there room for any significant participation by civilians in the early formation of the Party.[54] This pattern was not significantly changed after the Party became a mass organisation, though civilians had a larger role in the management of regional committees which replaced the Division Supervision Committees and its Sub-Divisional affiliates. In 1985, of the 112 members of the state and divisional Party regional committees, 16 were serving officers. Of these, nine were committee chairmen or secretaries and doubtless other senior figures were retired military men.

Below the regional and township Party committees there were Party sections and cells. In 1981 the Party General Secretary reported that there were 17,940 Party sections and 113,409 Party cells. The number was reported to have decreased in 1985 when the General Secretary revealed that there 13,881 Party sections and 111,002 Party cells. Not all of Burma's 314 townships had a Party unit in 1985. In 1981 there were 281 Party units, but 27 townships had what were referred to as organising committees. Between 1981 and 1985 nine Party organising committees became Party units after holding elections, but five Party units were abolished and replaced by organising committees. This left 26 organisation committees in existence while four townships had only one person attempting to form a Party unit.[55] Although there is no clear evidence to explain the absence of Party units in some townships, it is probable that the areas without basic Party organisations were on the periphery of the state where the authority of the central state was being most severely challenged throughout the BSPP years by insurgents.

Despite the alleged relative equality of women in Burma's society,[56] the Party's membership remained dominated by men, though the proportion of female members did increase over time. Only eight of the 280 members of the Party Central Committee in 1985 were women and there were none on the major central management and policy committees. In 1981, among

54   Wiant, 'Burmese Revolutionary Council', p. 10.

55   *The Working People's Daily*, 4 Aug. 1981; ibid., 3 Aug. 1985.

56   Mi Mi Khaing, *The World of Burmese Women* (Singapore: Times Book International, 1984), p. 1.

the Party rank-and-file, women accounted for 15 per cent of members, increasing to around 17 per cent in 1985.[57]

While over 2.3 million people, or about 10 per cent of the population over the age of 15, were involved in fortnightly party cell meetings and other Party activities by the mid-1980s, a much larger proportion of the population was organised into the Party's subsidiary organisations. As the Party General Secretary said in his 1981 political report to the Fourth Party Conference, 'in connection with the organisation activities of the mass organisations, the Burma Socialist Programme Party is bringing together the dispersed forces under mass, class and social organisations and creating conditions to enable the entire people to take part in socialist construction work.'[58]

The largest and most important of the mass/class bodies, the Peasants' Asiayon and the Workers' Asiayon, were first mooted by the Revolutionary Council in 1963 and 1964. When the Revolutionary Council issued a thirteen-point statement on workers' affairs on 1 May 1963, it pledged to assist workers in setting up regional workplace-based organisations for the protection of their rights. At the 1964 Kabaung peasants' seminar, the idea of a Peasants' Council was also raised and was approved by a resolution at the 1965 Rangoon peasants' seminar.[59] However, progress in forming a central body to supervise these activities was slow, and not until April 1968 was a Central People's Workers' Council organised. The Central People's Peasants' Council had been set up in March of the previous year.[60] The two bodies were renamed Asiayon in 1977 when they held their first national conferences.

Although it is implied in various documents that these organisations grew from the spontaneous desire of the workers and peasants, the impetus behind their formation clearly came from the Revolutionary Council. They were to serve two purposes. One was as a medium for transmission of the state's policies in the hope of generating popular support for them, while obviating the problems that would arise from the organisation of genuinely spontaneous and independent peasants' and workers' unions. The other was to provide a means by which the state could more effectively control productive labour. This was what the Party Chairman meant when discussing shortfalls in rice and other exports in his final address to the Fourth

57 *The Working People's Daily*, 4 Aug. 1981; ibid., 3 Aug. 1985.
58 Ibid., 3 Aug. 1985.
59 *Party Seminar 1965*, pp. 57-9.
60 Sein Tin, *Myanma Akyaung hnit Kabama Akyaung* (Myanmar's Affairs and World Affairs) (Rangoon: Thidadimyaing, 1982), p. 32.

Party Seminar in November 1969: the problem lay in the inadequate organisation of labour through the peasants' and workers' bodies, and as a result, the state was 'not yet able to exactly forecast ... production and exports. ... In future, after the peasants' organisations have been systematically formed, we hope to be more specific' in forecasting production and thus meeting export contracts.[61]

When the third Workers' Asiayon conference was held in December 1985, it was reported that 1,845,182 individuals were members, and that they were under the supervision of 273 Township Workers' Asiayon and 24 Township Workers' Asiayon Organising Committees.[62] Almost all employees of state and cooperatively-owned enterprises were members, but a large proportion of the workers in the private sector, except in 'stable' enterprises, were not. According to government estimates, in 1985 there were about 1,475,000 workers in the state-owned sectors appropriate for organisation of Workers' Asiayon, and another 3,727,000 in the cooperative and private sectors.[63] Thus, about 36 per cent of the potential members were involved in these organisations. As a significant proportion of those not organised would be involved in petty trade and small scale production activities, a large proportion of the easily organised working population was at least formally affiliated with the Asiayon.

The Peasants' Asiayon was a much larger body, but as its potential membership was scattered throughout the country's 13,700 villages, gaining the adherence of the peasantry was a much more daunting task. By November 1985, 272 Township Peasants' Asiayons had been organised along with seven Township Organising Committees. Under these were 13,192 ward and village tract subordinate bodies; this suggests a reasonably complete coverage of the most important agricultural regions. In all, there were said to be 7,577,733 members. Only about 80,000 persons were involved in the state agricultural sector while the bulk of the labour force, 9,312,000 out of a total of 14,792,000, were in the private sector, with a few in cooperatives.[64] The official figures suggest that about 81 per cent of the peasantry was organised, but many of these memberships, like those in the Workers'

---

61   'Address ... by General Ne Win ... Fourth Party Seminar', pp. 5-6.

62   *The Working People's Daily*, 10 Dec. 1985.

63   In forestry, mining, processing and manufacturing, power, construction, transportation and communications, social services, administration and trade; *Report to the Pyithu Hluttaw for 1985/86* (Rangoon: Ministry of Planning and Finance, 1985), Table 4, p. 23.

64   Ibid.

Asiayon, were merely nominal. Nonetheless, by 1984/85, the organisation was said to be self-sufficient in expenditure (meaning that membership dues were sufficient to support the organisation).[65]

Both the Workers' and the Peasants' Asiayon were managed by central Executive Committees elected at quadrennial conferences. All the senior leaders came from ranking state and party positions and their chairmen have always been senior ministers and/or members of the Council of State. Since 1981 the Minister for Labour has been the Chairman of the workers' organisation and the Minister of Agriculture the Chairman of the peasants' organisation. The initial memberships of the Central Executive Committees changed little until the 1980s, but only five or six of the thirty-five members of each committee had served more than eight years in 1985.

The Lansin Youth Organisation by 1985 claimed 1,050,802 members over the age of eighteen, of whom 211,954 were party members.[66] Formed in 1971, it had organised in 297 townships and at thirty-four educational institutions by 1985. Below it were various subordinate bodies designed to raise young people in the spirit of the Party. Teza Youth (named after the Japanese *nom de guerre* of Aung San) was for children aged six to ten, and *Hse Hsaung* (Future Leader) Youth was for youths aged 10-15. Lansin Youth accepted individuals aged 15-20.[67] All the organisations had over a million members. It is difficult to know to what extent they affected the socialisation process of the young when they existed. They held frequent meetings at the local level and held annual meetings in Rangoon. The annual Lansin Youth conference, like many of the Party's activities, had a military character, and young people were taught to parade as well as being introduced to the ideology of the Party. In rural areas one could also observe youths engaging in military drills with their local organisations at the weekend; the movement was redolent of the Boy Scouts.[68]

---

65   *The Working People's Daily*, 26 Nov. 1985.

66   Ibid., 3 Aug. 1985.

67   Sein Tin, *Myanma Akyaung hnit Kabama Akyaung*, p. 35.

68   Political Science as it was taught at Burma's universities also reflected the military imprint on the Party. In the third year final examination political science paper at the Institutes of Economics in Rangoon and Mandalay in 1984, eight questions were set. Of these, one asked the student to explain how the army played a leading role in the attainment and defence of national independence; others asked how capitalism creates fascism and world wars, and asked about the nature of Burma's Second World War anti-fascist resistance.

The Party and its mass/class organisations served to educate and guide their members, and through them the remainder of society, to understand and accept the policies and programmes of the central state managers. Their function was largely in the nature of ongoing political socialisation and paralleled the state's activities in the printed media and radio and television, attempting to get its message across while preventing counter-messages being heard and understood. Such activities took up a good deal of Party activists' time, but for many people they played only a marginal role in daily life. However, the Party and its message could not be ignored, for it was seen and heard in almost all places. Even remote villages and settlements miles from a township headquarters would have signboards proclaiming the presence of a village Party unit, the village branch of the Peasants' Asiayon and perhaps a Lansin Youth or other organisation. Party publications, though far from saturating society, tended to be widely available. The activities of state and Party officials dominated the news in radio broadcasts and in the newspapers, though the latter are difficult to find outside of the major towns.[69] Various party campaigns to aid the state by increasing production, by providing labour for building projects or by cleaning the streets, tended to be episodic and involved only a portion of the community, not necessarily willingly. The same is true of the annual state ceremonies such as the trooping of a flag through each state which was then brought to Rangoon to mark Union Day every February.

Participation in state management. To seek the support of the population at more than a symbolic level, the Revolutionary Council developed a system of elections to administrative bodies at various levels, which served to engender a feeling of responsibility for the state and to involve some people in the management of affairs. The local government elected bodies were the village and ward People's Councils, the township People's Councils, the State and Division People's Councils, and, at the top of the state structure, the repository of state sovereignty on behalf of the people, the Pyithu Hluttaw. Direct popular participation in the Pyithu Hluttaw could only be achieved through the ritual of elections, though the obligation of members to report back to their constituents after each of its biannual sessions required a public meeting to be held by Pyithu Hluttaw members, further linking the individuals who attended with the formal centre of the state.

---

69   Television, introduced in Rangoon in the early 1980s, did not become widely available in the major cities until near the end of the socialist era.

In 1985 there was approximately one member of the Pyithu Hluttaw for every 77,500 people in the country. Each township had at least one member of the Pyithu Hluttaw, and the constitution provided for additional members for townships with large populations and mandated that states or divisions with fewer than one million residents or less than ten townships should be given compensatory representation. Thus, in 1985, additional representation was provided for the Kayah, Karen and Chin States and for Tenasserim Division. The states and divisions which were 'over-represented' in the Pyithu Hluttaw (in the sense that their proportion of total representation was larger than their proportion of total population) were Rangoon, Mandalay, Kachin, Kayah, Chin, and Sagaing. The Kayah State was over-represented by a factor of over three and the Chin State by over two, but the difference for the other states and divisions was marginal. In Kayah, each of the state's eight members represented 21,000 persons and in Chin each of the 21 members represented 28,400 persons.

Elections for the Pyithu Hluttaw took place every four years simultaneously with elections for the village, ward, township and state and divisional People's Councils. Only nationals of the country could be elected to those posts, and while it was not mandatory that a candidate must be a member of the BSPP, in practice most of them were, as the single candidate put up for each position was previously selected by the relevant level Party unit and approved by the Central Executive Committee. At the voting booth, the elector was faced with the choice of either accepting or rejecting the Party's nominee. There were instances when the voters turned down the official nominee and an immediate by-election had to be called to fill the vacancy with someone acceptable to both the Party and the local population.

The function of elections during the socialist era, especially to the Pyithu Hluttaw, was similar to that in the Soviet Union and other one-party states. They were 'not presented as a possible redistribution of power, but as an affirmation of the existing power.' But the elections were more than just legitimizing rituals. 'The nominations, the campaigning, and the voting serve[d] as an intensified period of recruitment into participation.' The socialisation process was heightened during the campaigns as information was forced to circulate through the system.[70] Like the process of mass public discussion and the referendum campaign that preceded the introduction of the 1974 constitution, or the intense public touring and discussion by state officials before the passage of the 1983 Citizenship Law,

70   Friedgut, *Political Participation in the USSR*, p. 72.

elections were means of socialising individuals into the norms of the state, of legitimising its activities, and of communicating policy and other data to the public.

Four elections were held under the 1974 constitution. The number of voters grew during this time from more than 14 million in 1974 to more than 19 million in 1985. The number of Pyithu Hluttaw representatives increased from 450 to 489, while the number of persons elected to the state or divisional People's Councils remained unchanged at 976. The number of township People's Council representatives varied between 21,600 and 22,850 at each poll, while the number elected to ward and village tract People's Councils steadily declined from 288,681 in 1974 to 166,763 in 1985.[71] Serving on these local bodies was often considered to be arduous and it became increasingly difficult to persuade people to accept office. The larger committees were also found to be unwieldy and were also reduced in size for the sake of efficiency. The total of 15,940 ward and village tract People's Councils had an average of over ten members each in 1985.

It has been suggested that one function of elections in one-party social-ist states is as a 'mobilisation tool to bring into active participation sections of the population that might otherwise maintain traditional parochialism and political apathy.'[72] Without data from detailed research into the mem-bership and background of members elected to the Pyithu Hluttaw and subordinate People's Councils, it is impossible to know how far this was true in Burma. Certainly it appears anecdotally and perceptually that the passage of time created a much more unified polity familiar with the same political vocabulary and methods of analysing political issues. However, during the socialist era, it seems that at the national level only a small pro-portion of individuals not otherwise previously involved in state activities were brought into public life. Given the dominance of the military in the management of the state since 1962, it was not surprising that 40 per cent of the members of the Pyithu Hluttaw elected in 1977 were either serv-ing or retired members of the armed forces. Of those from the military, a larger proportion represented central divisional constituencies, while a larger proportion of civilians came from the border states. This suggests that election to the Pyithu Hluttaw, like membership in the Party, served as a means of attempting to involve individuals on the geographical and

---

71   Sein Tin, *Myanmar Akyaung hnit Kabama Akyaung*, p. 10; *The Working People's Daily*, 5 Oct. 1985.

72   Friedgut, *Political Participation in the USSR*, p. 91.

political periphery of the state's core activities. For example, all eight of the members from the Kayah state were civilians and had no previous military career; members from the Karen State included two serving officers, two retired officers, and nine civilians. Although there was no requirement that members of the Pyithu Hluttaw had to be residents or natives of the state or division from which they were elected, evidence on the basis of names suggests that most of the civilians elected from the border states came from one of the resident ethno-linguistic groups of the region. In contrast, the 1977 Irrawaddy Division was represented by ten serving officers, 14 retired officers and 24 civilians, and Mandalay Division had 29 civilians as against 14 serving and eight retired officers.

One of the novel features of the 1974 constitution was that it required all members of the Pyithu Hluttaw and other state-elected bodies to report back to constituents on their activities during the previous year. For the President, the Prime Minister and other high ranking state officials these meetings, widely reported in the press, are staid formal affairs with only invited constituency representatives in attendance. Their set speeches did, however, serve as reports on the state of the economy and the government and the problems the leadership feels are most pressing. For less important individuals, including even cabinet ministers, the report-back meetings were described as being much more spontaneous and informal. Peasants came from miles around, and were known to have questioned ministers at some length as to why promises previously made had not been fulfilled. For members of the Pyithu Hluttaw without a great deal of influence with the government, these must have been uncomfortable occasions, and that may be the reason why some embarrassing questions were occasionally asked in the generally stage-managed meetings of the legislature. However, the lack of responsiveness by the government to public criticisms was one of the reasons given for the ultimate failure of the 1974 constitutional system.

Data on the nature of participation in the state and divisional level People's Councils are more difficult to assess and analyse. The chairmanships and leading positions of these councils were often occupied by regional Party chairmen. There continued to be a great deal of overlap between state, military and Party personnel at this level, suggesting that control rather than participation was the primary purpose of the state's structure. State and divisional People's Councils were responsible for passing on the directives of the central state to the subordinate structures and for coordinating the activities of the township People's Councils and state-owned economic enterprises and agencies within their areas. Rather than policy making bodies, they were essentially extensions of the central state's administration.

It is at the township and village levels that the People's Councils became more genuinely participatory bodies. Though far from being institutions through which all persons had equal access to influence or authority, they did provide a mechanism by which much of the state's activities directly affecting the lives of the people was conducted under the supervision of local residents. Antagonism towards the system of village administration introduced by the British was often expressed during the colonial period, and after independence the government tried to modify that system to permit a greater degree of democracy in local government, but the attempt was generally considered a failure. In the view of the Party, in the central regions the old system destroyed the village community by its use of bureaucratic institutions and by the direct appointment of headmen by the state. In the peripheral regions, on the other hand, the British had maintained 'feudalism' and kept the people there from participating in their own affairs, thus blocking their entry into the modern world.[73] One of the purposes of the SAC system was to prepare the way for the introduction of participatory government at the local level.

The local level People's Councils had three functions. One was to control the population: the mechanisms to do this were developed and elaborated during the SAC period. The second was organisation, and here the People's Council served to assist the activities of the Party and the mass/class organisations. The third was participation and the elective principle, with frequent meetings and campaigns serving as the main means of achieving this. The township and ward and village-tract People's Councils had no legislative powers and did not meet to deliberate policy. Rather, they were institutions intended to interpret and carry out the directives of the central state in a manner appropriate for local conditions. This was one of the intended meanings of 'democratic socialism', a key principle of the constitution. Thus, among the organs of state power, the lower organs were to carry out 'the collective decisions and directives of the higher organs which in turn respect the views submitted by the lower organs.'[74] However, in car-

73   Myanma Hsoshelit Lansin Parti, Pati Seyanyei Baho Kommiti Danachok (Burma Socialist Programme Party, Party Organisation Central Committee Headquarters)), *Myanma Hsoshelit Lansin Pati ei Pyei twinyei Ahmat I* (Myanmar Socialist Programme Party's Internal Affairs Number 1) (Rangoon: Sapei Biman, 1966), p. 47.

74   Article 15 of the constitution.

rying out the directives of the central state, the People's Councils were expected to adjust them as necessary to fit local conditions. While at the top
and centre the structure of the state appeared quite rigid and dogmatic, at
the lowest levels local knowledge and sensitivities were intended to be used
to obviate the more extreme and negative consequences of state policies.

The People's Councils chose people from among their members to
staff their Executive Committees, on which most of the work fell, and the
People's Courts, as well as their Inspection and Affairs Committees. Few
studies of the working of the People's Councils at the lowest levels were
made, though the author did experience the operation of the ward People's
Councils in Rangoon, and one or two studies of conditions in the villagers
did reveal aspects of their composition and activities. The Councils primarily devoted their time to implementing plans provided by the Township
People's Council. They, in turn, received instructions from the State or
Divisional People's Council, where the goals of the central state were divided into tasks and quotas to be achieved by each township. The village
authorities then had to 'take part in the economic planning of the village,
such as how many acres [were] to be brought under cultivation, how much
paddy [was] to be sold, etc.'[75]

The goal of increasing the participation of individuals in the management of the state at the local level was not fully achieved. Village People's
Council leaders in one village studied came from the same families as the
former headmen and other village elders, and these tended to be individuals 'who represent[ed] the "upper layer" of the village and who live[d] in
the "best" houses'. The same individuals also tended to dominate the leadership of other local branches of central organisations such as the BSPP, the
Lansin Youth and the cooperative society.[76] In fact, despite the changes in
the structure of the state introduced after 1962, by the mid-1970s many villages were still largely untouched by external changes. Although traditional
village authorities such as monks and elders appeared to be less influential
than in the past, their place was not necessarily being taken by agents of the
state. Outside influence was mediated through the same families as before
because it seemed that new social organisations with their own dynamics
had not emerged in the villages studied.[77] This picture did not, however,

---

75   Mya Than, 'A Burmese Village – Revisited', *The South East Asian Review*, II, 2
      (Feb. 1978), pp. 13-14.

76   Ibid., p. 14.

77   Khin Maung Kyi and Associates, 'Process of Communication in Modernisa-

seem to be universal. In villages in the dry zone where extensive but as yet unpublished surveys have been conducted on the effects of change of the delivery of health care, researchers have indicated a great degree of state penetration. The author's observations in Rangoon and in central Burma would tend to confirm this latter view, as have interviews undertaken and research published since 1988.[78]

The manner in which the state delegated administrative responsibilities to village tracts and wards can be illustrated by the provisions of the 1975 Profit Tax Law. Under this legislation, every ward or village-tract People's Council Executive Committee was obliged to form a committee of three members to prepare a list of persons in their area who were required to pay the tax, and to submit this list to the township People's Council Executive Committee. It was then the township committee's task to organise a three-member assessment and collection committee which actually collected the tax under the supervision of the state or divisional People's Council Executive Committee. Appeals could be made, if the tax assessed was over Kt 500, to the above mentioned three-member committee, and from there, if the tax owed was more than Kt 10,000, to a central appeals body composed of three members of the Pyithu Hluttaw appointed by the Council of Ministers.

The activities of the township committee were aided by a Township Tax Officer who was responsible to the Ministry of Planning and Finance. He was required to advise the township committee as to who had to pay from the list submitted to the village and ward committee. He also had the power to add names to the list of assessable individuals. His activities were supervised by the state or divisional tax officers who advised the relevant appeals bodies. The Minister of Finance and Planning, with the approval of the cabinet, could overrule any assessment order. The assessing body also had the power to impose fines for non-payment of taxes. The system was quite complex, and the legislation establishing it not only spelt out the procedures to be followed, but concluded by reiterating the responsibility of the relevant level People's Councils to supervise the functioning of their respective assessment and collection committees, as well as reporting what steps were taken to the full People's Council. Not only did state and divi-

---

tion of Rural Society: A Survey Report on Two Burmese Villages', *The Malayan Economic Review*, XVIII, no. 1 (April, 1973), pp. 58, 73.

78   See, for example, Ardeth Maung Thawnghmung, *Behind the Teak Curtain: Authoritarianism, Agricultural Policies ad Political Legitimacy in Rural Burma/Myanmar.* London: Kegan Paul, 2004.

sional People's Councils have to follow these instructions, they had also to report on their activities directly to the Minister for Planning and Finance. At many points in these elaborate procedures opportunities for lowering or being excused taxation might be available through the application of influence, either political or monetary.

The state's desire to develop means of participation by local people in administration was clearly tempered by an equal desire to supervise affairs so as to ensure that decisions were not made which ran contrary to central requirements. From time to time, leading state officials expressed concern that some People's Councils did not follow directives but developed too much local initiative. Like the previous district SACs, the state and divisional People's Councils were charged with checking local initiatives. Also, the Pyithu Hluttaw possessed the power to dismiss elected People's Councils for a variety of misdemeanours, including 'inefficient discharge of duties'. This gave the Home Minister the power of veto over all local government bodies.[79]

The central state managers' concern about excessive local imitative was similar to that shown in the former Soviet Union over what was known as 'localism'. There the authorities also developed a highly complex system of bureaucratic control which made 'sense in terms of administrative functions only when viewed as an attempt to maintain centrally controlled administration together with a measure of local participation.'[80] The duplication of efforts at social control, planning and information which resulted at the local level from the existence not only of the People's Councils but also of the Party and its mass and class organisation provided a powerful set of cross-cutting controls upon the population, while also permitting local administration to take place. What it did not provide for, however, was efficiency in production and distribution, while distortion of information in order to appear to meet central targets led to the ultimate failure of this system of socialist democratic administration in Burma, just as it did in the Soviet Union.

The functions of the state

State security and public order. As a result of the Revolutionary Council's efforts to develop non-coercive forms of social control, reliance on force for

79   *Forward,* Nov. 1984.

80   Friedgut, *Political Participation in the USSR,* p. 39.

the maintenance of the state in its core areas did not increase after 1962, despite the deteriorating economic condition of much of the population. In the peripheral areas where separatist, Communist and smuggling forces developed in the late 1950s, the military did increase its control after initially losing ground and brought the state's civilian institutions in to dominate more territory. There was little evidence of efforts to organise peasant rebellions, and despite the desire of the Communist Party and other insurgent groups to gain mass support among the majority of the population in the core areas of the state, they were unsuccessful except among some disaffected urban youth.

This is not to argue, however, that there was no significant armed opposition to the state's policies and programmes during the socialist era. Distinct areas of discontent and protest existed in Burma's society before the major uprising that overthrew the regime in 1988. The Communist Party, with an armed forced estimated in 1985 to contain 12,000 regulars and 8,000 militiamen, controlled an area along the border with China, but lost its foothold in the Pegu Yoma in central Burma in the mid-1970s as it faced increasing military opposition and declining peasant support. The Karen National Liberation Army, the armed force of the Karen National Union, had an estimated 4,000 troops in 1985, though its resources had shrunk over several years owing to greater army pressure against its strongholds along the border with Thailand. Various separatist and smuggling bands in Shan State could field perhaps 10,000 anti-state forces and the Kachin Independence Army had an estimated 5,000 troops. Other smaller bands had no more than a few hundred troops each.[81]

As all of these groups existed on the periphery of the state and were unable to agree among themselves on a single course of action, they posed no major threat. But as long as they existed, they contained the seeds of a challenge to the state's perpetuation, and therefore the state devoted considerable attention to attempting to defeat them military as well as by other means. These included arming loyal villagers and extending the political and administrative system of the state into areas which had been recaptured by the army. The fact that four townships had only one party organiser in 1985 and 26 had organising committees rather than fully functioning party units suggests that the state did not have firm control of 30 of its 314 townships. As the average township had a population of 112,500, this

---

81   International Institute for Strategic Studies, *The Military Balance, 1985-86* (London, 1985), p. 122.

would suggest that about 3.5 million persons, or slightly less than 10 per cent of the total population of Burma, was not under the state's hegemony forty years after independence. However, as the population density of the four peripheral states where insurgency had been most prevalent, Shan, Kachin, Kayah and Karen, was much lower than in the core divisions (see table 5.1., pp. 307-308), the proportion of the total population outside of state control was probably significantly less. The average population of the 83 townships of these states was 44,807, and if 30 were assumed to be under the partial control of anti-state forces, then 1,344,210 persons, or 3.81 per cent of the total population, were outside the control of the state. This would seem to be a reasonable maximum estimate.

More immediately threatening to public order was the danger of unrest and protest in the cities. Here the activities of students and workers were of particular concern. Given the tumultuous nature of Burma's urban politics in the 1930s and 1940s, it was quite remarkable how free of political turmoil the cities were from 1962 until 1988. However, there were expressions of public discontent which led to the use of violence and the threat of future violence against protesters. Students were the most important group in this regard. Just four months after the 1962 coup, the army occupied Rangoon University and blew up the student's union building, killing at least 16 and perhaps as many as 60-100 students protesting against the Revolutionary Council's moves to close independent political organisations within the student body.[82] In 1967 there were brief riots in Rangoon, ostensibly over the involvement of the government of China in exporting the Cultural Revolution to the Chinese community resident in Burma, but in large part because of food shortages than then existed. In December 1969 student unrest at the university occurred again, forcing the government to remove at least 6,000 students from the campus during the South East Asian Games.[83]

The greatest urban challenge to the socialist state before 1988 came in 1974, when workers and students in Rangoon combined to protest against inflation and food shortages after changes in economic policy which favoured the rural sector were introduced in 1973. The protest began with strikes in state-owned factories and workshops and soon spread to other towns. Violence occurred after the arrest of some strike leaders. At the same time, to avoid students becoming involved, schools and universities were

82   Badgley, 'Burma: The Nexus', p. 90.
83   *New York Times*, 11 Dec. 1969.

closed. The two months of protests ended only with the use of force: at least 22 persons were killed and 73 wounded before order was restored on 8 June. Trouble erupted once more in December when students protested at the state's funeral arrangements for the former United Nations Secretary-General, U Thant. Students, joined by monks, seized U Thant's corpse and took it to the site of the former students' union. Martial law was declared and the military recovered the body, though only after the students had attacked police stations and offices of the BSPP. Student sources say that over 100 of their number were killed in the demonstrations.[84] Students demonstrated again a year later when 500 marched from the university to the centre of the city. In a protest which in style was reminiscent of student demonstrations against the British more than fifty years earlier, the students camped at the Shwedagon Pagoda. But the indigenous government did not hesitate to clear the pagoda and arrested 213 students.[85]

The military's response to these protests indicates its reliance upon minimal manpower and maximum firepower to demonstrate, as rapidly as possible, its determination to keep unrest from spreading and to serve as a deterrent. However, the Party and mass and class organisations were also used to try to stem dissatisfaction. During the 1974 workers' strike, People's and Workers' Council officials were sent to negotiate with the workers, and the Lansin Youth workers at the university were continually alert to signs of student discontent.

The armed forces after 1962 grew in size and expense, but not disproportionately to population growth or the expansion of the economy and government expenditure generally. However, by comparison with other non-Communist states in South East Asia, the proportion of the population in the armed forces was relatively high. It stood at 6.8 per thousand in 1973, but declined to 5.9 per thousand in 1983, compared with 2.4 and 1.7 for these respective years in Indonesia and 5.8 and 4.9 in Thailand. Only Malaysia and Singapore had a higher ratio in 1983.[86] In 1985, it was estimated that Burma had 186,000 men and women in the armed forces, of whom 170,000 were

---

84   Raja Segaran Arumugan, 'Burma: A Political and Economic Background', Institute of Southeast Asian Studies, *Southeast Asian Affairs 1975* (Singapore: Heinemann, 1976), pp. 42-3.

85   Raja Segaran Arumugam, 'Burma: Political Unrest and Economic Stagnation', Institute of Southeast Asian Studies, *Southeast Asian Affairs 1976* (Singapore: Heinemann, 1977), p. 168.

86   United States Arms Control and Disarmament Agency, *World Military Expenditure and Arms Transfers 1985* (Washington, DC, Aug. 1985).

in the army. Another 73,000 served in the People's Police Force and there were 35,000 members of the People's Militia.[87] This compares with an armed forces strength of about 125,000 in 1968.[88]

The military was essentially an infantry force and possessed none of the technologically sophisticated equipment considered by many to be essential for internal and external security. No significant amounts of foreign military assistance were received after the termination of a United States aid agreement at the end of the 1960s. The total assistance offered over a period of more than 12 years was only US$85.5 million, and not all the credits available were used on time.[89] Consequently, the army was a relatively inexpensive force per man. Expenditure on each soldier was only about US$1,100 per year in 1982. compared with a cost of US$6,575 per man per year for Thailand and US$10,498 for Indonesia. Annual expenditure per square kilometre of territory was also lower than that of other South East Asian countries, estimated at only US$295 per year in 1982 compared to US$2,980 for Thailand and US$1,481 for Indonesia. The ratio of personnel per square kilometre was also low at 265.5 compared with 453.3 men per square kilometre in Thailand, though Indonesia had a lower ratio at 141.2.[90]

As a proportion of total government expenditure, official defence spending declined fairly consistently from 1954 until 1988. At the time of the army's expansion at the end of the most intense phases of the civil war, in 1954, defence spending accounted for 40 per cent of total spending.[91] On average, during the years 1950/51 to 1954/55, defence accounted for 33.6 per cent of all government expenditure; it fell to an average of 32 per cent between 1955/56 and 1960/61. One official foreign agency estimated that military expenditure in 1973 accounted for 33.4 per cent of the government budget; this fell to 25.5 per cent in 1977.[92] An analysis of the government's published budgets from 1982/83 to 1986/87 revealed that defence expenditure as a proportion of total government expenditure declined from 29.1 per cent to a planned 20.7 per cent in 1986/87. Of course, some may

87   *The Military Balance, 1985-86*, pp. 121-2.

88   Ibid., 1968-69, p. 47.

89   *New York Times*, 25 Aug. 1970; 18 Aug. 1971.

90   See Robert H. Taylor, "Burma: Defence Expenditure and Threat Perceptions" in Chin Khin Wah, ed., *Defence Expenditure in Southeast Asia*. (Singapore: Institute of Southeast Asian Studies, 1987), pp. 252-80.

91   David I. Steinberg, *Burma's Road Toward Development: Growth and Ideology under Military Rule* (Boulder, CO: Westview Press, 1981), p. 165.

92   Ibid., p. 166.

have been hidden in other departmental expenditures; for example, military officers posted to civilian duties were paid by the departments to which they were assigned. Burma imported a small amount of military equipment each year, only US$5 million in 1973, US$30 million in 1979 and US$20 million in 1983, compared with figures in the latter years for Thailand of US$110, US$350 and US$320 million. However, as a proportion of total imports, these represented from 3.4 to 9.4 per cent of imports, while the Thai figure in these years did not exceed 5.3 per cent.[93] As a proportion of gross domestic product, military expenditure has been steadily declining from a high of 6.7 per cent to 6.3 per cent in 1962. By 1982, it was estimated to have fallen to 4.0 per cent, having reached a low of 3.9 per cent in 1975 and 1976.[94] In financial terms, the army had become by the mid-1980s less the centre of the state than it had been under the civilian governments of the 1950s.

Courts and the law. Accepting the argument that the previous legal system had worked only to the advantage of 'the bourgeoisie, the landed gentry and the capitalists', and was distinctly prejudicial to the interests of the 'working people', the Revolutionary Council set about changing the judicial system and its relationship with the public. In the process, the courts lost what independence they had enjoyed under the civilian administration. On 30 March 1962 the two highest courts, the Supreme Court and the High Court, were abolished and replaced by a new Chief Court. A new procedure was also followed of establishing People's Courts (not normally composed of lawyers or judicial officers) when the Revolutionary Council thought necessary, for the trial of special criminal cases.[95] However, all existing laws continued to remain valid and the subordinate courts functioned as before.[96]

Not until 7 August 1972 were the most radical changes made in the working of the court system. At the time of the abolition of the districts the role of district officers as judicial officers disappeared, and village tract, ward, township, and state or divisional Security and Administration Committees were

---

93   *World Military Expenditures and Arms Transfers, 1985.*

94   Stockholm International Peace Research Institute, *World Armaments and Disarmaments 1976* (Stockholm: Almqvist and Wiksell, 1976), pp. 160-1; ibid., 1977, p. 234; ibid., 1984 (London: Taylor and Francis, 1985), pp. 280-4.

95   Alan Gledhill, 'Burma', in John Gilissen (ed.), *Bibliographical Introduction to Legal History and Ethnology*, vol. E., no. 7. (Brussels: Editions de l'Institut de Sociologie, Université Libre de Bruxelles, 1970), p. 11.

96   *Party Seminar, 1965*, pp. 33-4.

given judicial powers. With the inclusion of local residents in the SACs, the latter were instructed to institute a system of People's Courts.[97] This system continued under the 1974 socialist constitution.

The purpose of the People's Court system, as explained by the drafts of the constitution, was to replace the single judge system instituted by the British with a panel of judges chosen from the people. Emphasis in these courts was to be placed on 'reforming the moral habits of transgressors' and on educating people on the nature of the law, as well as defending life and property and achieving justice. The new judicial system made it possible to abolish the former Justice Department; it was replaced by a Council of People's Justices chosen from among members of the Pyithu Hluttaw to supervise and administer the judicial system. The similarly chosen Council of People's Attorneys supervised the work of the state's law officers and prosecutors.[98] Ultimate appeal on the meaning of law and its correct implementation could be made to the fifteen-member Council of State, which was also appointed from members of the Pyithu Hluttaw and whose chairman was the state president.

The People's Court system was highly complex and, like the administrative system, combined features of participation with close supervision from the centre. However, the laws passed after 1962 were relatively simple and easy to understand, though sometimes open to contrary interpretations. Drafting simplified laws was consciously pursued in order to make them understandable to non-lawyers. According to the leading lawyer involved in the drafting of the constitution and the new legal system, 'the people's judicial system [was] a system in accord with Burma's heritage and is modern'.[99] It combined the traditional practice of arbitration and the search for norms of justice with the use of rules of evidence and procedure taken from Western legal traditions. After the rotating judges chosen from the People's Council made their decision in a case, the enforcement of their judgement was carried out by full time judicial officers. The latter also served as advisers and guides to the judges in explaining the law and procedures of the court.

At the village and ward level, the working of the courts appeared to be in the hands of local individuals, often from quite humble positions in society. In Rangoon it was said that wealthy persons had to face judgement from their

97   *Towhlanyei Kaungsi ei Hluthsaungchet Thamaing Akyinchut*, p. 192.

98   *Pyi Htuangsu Hsoshelit Thammata Myanma Nainngan Hpwetsinpun Akhyeihkan Upadei nhit Patthet taw Adipape Shinlinhkyetmya*, pp. 63-7.

99   Maung Maung, *Taya Upadei Ahtweidewei Bahuthua* (General Law Knowledge) (Rangoon: Win Maung U, 1975), p. 5.

own servants in minor trials. According to critics familiar with the working of the previous judicial system, these courts did not place much reliance on rules of evidence and procedure and were sometimes highly informal. Others have suggested that their very informality and local personnel made the courts seem accessible and no longer shrouded in mystery. However, bribery of panels of judges was easily possible, though more expensive than in the old system where one had to bribe only one judge.

In the township, state and divisional courts, closer adherence to procedure and a more formal atmosphere were apparently maintained, though this assessment must be taken with more than the usual degree of scepticism as data on their working were very difficult to collect and analyse. Certainly, in the Pyithu Hluttaw and in the press, there was an unusual amount of criticism of the courts, especially of their inability to produce justice with speed.[100] The courts faced an increased workload and the appeals rate was very high. Each year the number of cases accepted for trial increased and the number of cases remaining pending for over a year also grew. The appeal court at the regional level, composed of People's Judges who were also serving on other council committees with various duties to perform in the management of economic, political and social affairs, were particularly overloaded.[101]

In particular, by 1984 a significant backlog of cases waiting for final appeal had developed in the offices of the Council of State. As the members of this organisation were all busy with other duties, including the presidency, the prime ministership and ministerial and party posts, they had little time to settle cases. Similarly, as the Council of People's Justices members had many administrative tasks to perform, they had little time to sit as a court and decide appeals. One solution to this problem reached in 1985 was to expand the membership of the Council of People's Justices from five to eight. Another, far more important solution was to exclude a number of more important cases from the appeals procedure above the state and divisional level. However, the inefficiency of the courts system under the 1974 socialist constitution was an indication of inadequacy of the entire state and evidence of its inability to attempt to manage the entirety of society's production and consumptive needs.

---

100   See, for example, *The Guardian* (Rangoon), 5 Oct. 1983 and 6 Oct. 1983; *The Working People's Daily*, 17 Sept. 1984.

101   See the summary of the report of the Council of People's Justices in *The Working People's Daily*, 11 March 1986. A similar account was provided in earlier years; see, for example, *The Guardian* (Rangoon), 5 Oct. 1983.

The right to agricultural land is the most important legal issue for most of Burma's population. The tradition of resort to the courts to settle land disputes goes back to before the British period, but during the colonial era it became very frequent. Under the 1974 constitution, cases of disputed land use were to be settled in the first instance at the level of Township People's Council Executive Committee. Until March 1984 a Committee's decision could be appealed through the system to the Council of People's Justices, which resulted in long delays in final decisions being reached. To attempt to solve this problem, the Law on the Duties and Rights of People's Councils at Different Levels and Executive Committees at Different Levels was amended by the Pyithu Hluttaw so that no appeals could be made from the decision of the state or divisional People's Council.[102] But as with so many efforts made by the state to adapt the socialist system it had created to meet the requirements of efficiency and common sense, the attempted solution merely put off the day of ultimate reckoning.

Economic and financial. Despite the intentions of the ruling group, the socialist economic policies of the state after 1962 did not significantly change the structure of the economy or patterns of employment. However, the nationalisation of external and internal trade and of large sectors of manufacturing, together with the introduction of quantitative physical planning as the basic mechanism of economic control, did have other significant consequences. First, and most immediately obvious, the nationalisation of trade forced most of the remaining Indian population out of the economy as their enterprises were taken over by various Trading Corporations. It was estimated that between 125,000 and 300,000 Indians and Pakistanis left the country in 1963, 1964 and 1965.[103] The egalitarian intentions of the state also worked to keep income and wealth disparities from becoming too great. While adequate data on income distribution are difficult to find, a World Bank team estimated that income disparities in Burma in the mid-1970s were less than in neighbouring countries and that in urban areas the lowest 40 per cent of the population received 21 per cent of total income, compared with 15 per cent in India and 12 per cent in Malaysia.[104]

102   *The Working People's Daily*, 18 March 1984; 29 March 1984.

103   John Badgley, 'Burma's Zealot Wungyis: Maoists or St. Simonists', *Asian Survey*, V, 1 (Jan., 1965), p. 55; Steinberg, 'Burma Under Military Rule', p. 260.

104   The World Bank, *Development in Burma: Issues and Prospects*, Report no. 1024-BA, 27 July 1976, South Asia Regional Office, p. 12.

Moreover, the state's radical economic policies had two other significant consequences: one was to concentrate economic control and management in the hands of the state; the other was to decrease the involvement
in Burma's economy in the world economy. Both these consequences are
among the causes of Burma's relatively slow economic growth during the
socialist era relative to its South East Asian neighbours, and of the great
incentives for black market economic activity on the part of large segments
of the population, in particular the insurgent groups along the Thai border.
Nonetheless, the state's policies also enhanced the control of the state over
the population by making illegal, and therefore potentially punishable, a
wide range of economic activities, thus limiting the development of private
centres of wealth which could have spawned independent political power.

5.6.   Gross Domestic Product (GDP) at Constant 1969/70 Prices, Rate of GDP
        Growth, Investment at Constant 1969/70 Prices, and Rate of Growth of In-
        vestment, 1961/2 to 1985/6

	GDP (Kyat m.)	% change	Investment (Kyat m.)	% change
1961/2	7,798		806	
1965/6	8,715		912	
1966/7	8,355	− 4.1	985	8.0
1967/8	9,200	10.1	1,015	3.0
1968/9	9,503	3.3	1,098	8.2
1969/70	9,976	5.0	1,153	5.0
1970/1	10,388	4.1	1,019	− 11.6
1971/2	10,641	2.4	1,091	7.1
1972/3	10,538	− 1.0	895	− 18.0
1973/4	10,812	2.6	773	− 13.6
1974/5	11,101	2.7	780	0.9
1975/6	11,562	4.2	808	3.6
1976/7	12,265	6.1	965	19.4
1977/8	12,996	6.0	1,430	48.2
1978/9	13,843	6.5	1,852	29.5
1979/80	14,562	5.2	2,206	19.1
1980/1	15,718	7.9	2,158	− 2.2
1981/2	16,717	6.4	2,454	13.7
1982/3	17,654	5.6	2,787	13.6
1983/4	18,429	4.4	2,503	− 10.3
1984/5	19,464*	5.6*	2,335*	− 6.7*
1985/6	20,675*	6.2*	2,689*	15.2*

*Provisional figures

Source: Report to the Pyithu Hluttaw on the Financial, Economic and Social Conditions of the Socialist
Republic of the Union of Burma for 1977–8 (Rangoon: Ministry of Planning and Finance, 1977); ibid.,
1986–7 (1986).

5.7.   Origins of Gross Domestic Product, 1961/62 and 1985/86

	1961/2 % of total	1985/6 % of total
Agriculture	26.0	28.1
Livestock & fishing	5.6	6.8
Forestry	2.9	2.1
Mining	1.3	1.5
Manufacturing	10.5	10.5
Utilities	0.5	1.7
Construction	1.9	2.7
Transport & communications	6.1	5.9
Banking and finance	1.1	4.0
Wholesale & retail trade	29.3	20.6
Other services	14.8	16.1
GDP at factor cost	100.0	100.0

Source: *Report to the Pyithu Hluttaw, 1986–7*, pp. 46–7.

Having elected to avoid the involvement of foreign multinational corporations and large-scale foreign aid, as well as avoiding significant foreign borrowing in the first decade after the 1962 coup, the state had to rely largely on domestic sources of investment. Understandably, given the state's goal of keeping prices low and avoiding 'excess' profits being made at the expense of consumers, as well as the state's inability to accumulate domestic savings through taxation, the rate of investment in the economy throughout the 1960s remained low and contributed to a slow rate of growth of the gross domestic product.[105] Details are provided in table 5.6. By borrowing, usually from multilateral sources and at concessionary rates, more funds for investment became available from the mid-1970s to the early 1980s before debt repayment became a concern. There followed a significant increase in growth as a result of the state's borrowing as well as economic reforms, with real growth peaking in 1980/81 at 7.9 per cent.

Except for the late 1970s when the expansion of the economy was led by grain and other primary product exports, the state generally assumed that investment in agriculture was to be left to the private sector, and the bulk of official investment funds were channelled into import substitution manufacturing, power production, and transport and communications infrastructure. Following the nationalisation of the 1960s and the falling rate of investment, the state slowly began to encourage expansion of the private sector, including legislation to protect private investments in certain sec-

---

105   Ibid., pp. 39-40.

5.8.   Distribution of Labour Force, 1931 and 1984/85

	1931%	1984/5%
Agriculture	66.4	63.5
Livestock & fishery	2.3	1.3
Forestry	0.9	1.2
Mining	0.6	0.6
Manufacturing	9 1	8.3
Power	n.a.	0.1
Construction	1.6	1.6
Transport & communications	3.5	3.3
Social services	3.9	2.1
Administration	0.8	3.9
Trade	9.0	9.8
Others	1.9	4.3
Total	100.0	100.0

Sources: Louis J. Walinsky, *Economic Development in Burma 1951–1960* (New York: Twentieth Century Fund, 1962), p. 33; *Report to the Pyithu Hluttaw, 1986–7*, p. 28.

tors, but the prevailing tax regime and other conditions under which entrepreneurs had to operate meant that there was little response to the state's appeals for private sector investment.[106]

As table 5.7. shows, in macro-terms the economic structure of the country has changed little except for an increase in the proportion of GDP derived from agriculture, including livestock and fisheries, as well as from construction and power. Meanwhile, trade has declined and manufacturing has remained constant. The decline in trade is paralleled by the fall in the import and export of goods and services as a proportion of total GDP. Legal imports represented 19 per cent of GDP in 1960 but had declined to 2 per cent in 1981, and exports declined from 20 per cent to 9 per cent in the same period.[107] If it is accepted that illegal imports equal something between one-third and two-thirds of legal imports,[108] imports account for less than 3.5 per cent of GDP.

The structure of the labour force had, by the mid-1980s, changed remarkably little since the colonial period. Although the sources on which the per-

106   See the comments of the BSPP General Secretary in his 1981 Political Report, *The Working People's Daily*, 3 Aug., 1981.

107   The World Bank, *The World Development Report 1984* (New York: Oxford University Press, 1984), p. 226.

108   As a World Bank team did in 1976; *Development in Burma: Issues and Prospects*, p. 8.

centages provided in table 5.8 are based are not consistent in their use of labour categories, the similarity of the two groups of figures is quite striking. The proportion of the labour force in the state sector had reached only 10.6 per cent by 1985, and only in the relatively small construction, mining, forestry, power, social services and administration sectors did direct state employees outnumber those in the combined private and cooperative sectors. However, these figures belie the control the state had over private sector activities. After 1962, firms which were not nationalised were placed under strict supervision, and the state maintained a tight rein over the allocation of foreign exchange for imports of capital equipment as well as of raw materials. While there were still 39,239 private manufacturing establishments in 1985, compared with 719 cooperatively owned and 1,763 state owned, 34,596 of the private sector enterprises employed ten or fewer individuals. Only six private plants employed more than 100 workers.[109] The small proportion involved in the state sector of the workforce, however, was responsible for producing over 39 per cent of all output and services, compared with 55.5 per cent for the private sector and 5.4 per cent for the cooperatives. In agriculture, 94.0 per cent of all production was in the private sector, with state farms producing less than one per cent.[110]

Financing the state. A commonly used indicator of a state's ability to control the economy and an indirect indicator of its strength vis-à-vis civil society is the proportion of total current revenue as a percentage of gross national product (GNP) or gross domestic product (GDP). Among the industrial market economies of the West, this percentage in GNP terms ranged in 1982 from 18.4 per cent for Switzerland to 44.8 per cent for Belgium.[111] Such figures are of limited comparability, as they measure only central government revenue and ignore regional and local taxation authorities. As a general rule, however, low income countries tend to have centralised taxation systems and central government revenue accounts for nearly all taxation and government expenditure.

This was the case for Burma during the socialist period. By 1982, current state revenue from all sources as a proportion of GDP was 17.3 per cent, compared, in GNP terms, with Thailand's 14.4 per cent, Indonesia's 26.4 per cent, the Philippines' 11.7 per cent, and Tanzania's 19.6 per cent.

109 *Report to the Pyithu Hluttaw, 1986/87* (Rangoon: Ministry of Planning and Finance, 1986), p. 176.
110 Ibid., pp. 54-5.
111 *World Development Report 1984*, Table 27, pp. 270-1.

The 1982 figure for Burma is basically the same as that for 1958, when total government receipts were 17.1 per cent of GNP.[112] But in the case of Burma the proportion must have fallen dramatically in the 1960s, for current revenue as a proportion of GDP was only 10.6 per cent in 1974 and 9.9 per cent in 1975. Subsequently, it increased steadily to 17.7 per cent in 1981 before declining marginally in 1982. The trend suggests that the Revolutionary Council's initial nationalisation policies and administrative reorganisation significantly hampered the state's ability to tax and raise revenue in other ways. However, the reassertion of the state's capacity returned these rates to something near a 'normal' ratio for comparable states if the data are to be believed.

Between 1974 and 1982, foreign grants (aid) as a proportion of total revenue averaged 5.1 per cent, varying, with no clear pattern, from 2 per cent in 1977 to 8.1 per cent in 1982. Import duties as a proportion of total state revenue in the nine years between 1974 and 1983 also changed little, averaging 15.3 per cent a year and ranging from 12.8 per cent in 1976 to 20.4 per cent in 1975. By comparison, customs revenue accounted for 24.7 per cent of receipts in 1958. Where the state has clearly strengthened its taxing ability is through what amounts to indirect taxation, while direct taxation as a proportion of receipts, but not in relation to GDP growth, fell back towards the 1958 rate of 39.9 per cent. Total tax revenue, primarily composed of domestic taxes on goods and services, mainly as a sales tax, declined as a proportion of total revenue from 72.1 per cent in 1974 and a peak of 80.1 per cent in 1975 to a low of 56.0 per cent in 1981 and 56.8 per cent in 1982.[113] On the other hand, non-tax revenue entirely in the form of income from state-owned financial institutions and non-financial enterprises increased from 21.4 per cent in 1974 and a low of 13.3 per cent in 1975 to a peak of 40.2 per cent in 1981 and 35.1 per cent in 1982. Non-tax revenue in 1958 amounted to 35.7 per cent of the total. State-owned institutions enterprises are the easiest for the state to tap, and the

---

112   Ibid., which gives the figure for Burma as 17.1 per cent; calculations for Burma made from the *Report to the Pyithu Hluttaw, 1985/86* for GDP at current prices and the International Monetary Fund's *Government Finance Statistics Yearbook 1985* for consolidated central government total revenue. Calculations for 1958 are based on data from Walinsky, *Economic Development in Burma*, p. 114 and p. 422.

113   Calculated from IMF *Government Finance Statistics Yearbook 1985*, calculations from the official *Report to the Pyithu Hluttaw* for various years show a much more consistent pattern with tax revenues equalling around 60 per cent of total revenue and state economic enterprises providing 30 per cent or less.

government's decisions, taken at the First BSPP Congress in 1971, to limit subsidies to loss-making organisations and to require that they be run on a business basis made them much more useful as a source of revenue. Or, to put it another way, running the socialist state on business principles proved to be profitable.

To summarise, the capacity of the state to tax the economy directly increased after 1974 regardless of the declining proportion of total revenue coming from this source. In every year after 1974, with the slight exceptions of 1978, 1979 and 1982, the rate of domestic revenue increase has been greater than the growth of GDP in current terms.

Concentrating purely on the income of the central government reveals only part of the state's financial relations. Before 1971 the economy remained remarkably free from foreign capital inputs, and in several years there were capital outflows as debt repayment exceeded new funds. It is estimated that between 1962 and 1972 Burma received on average only US$28 million per year in foreign assistance; after 1972, aid and borrowing increased rapidly, and in 1979, for example, US$350 million was received.[114] As a consequence, debt rose rapidly and there developed problems of debt service in the mid-1980s. In 1970 Burma's long-term public and publicly guaranteed debt stood at only US$100.7 million. Eight years later this had increased by 759 per cent to US$864.4 million, and by 1984 it had grown another 157 per cent to US$2,311.2 million. By 1984 Burma's debt service ratio (gross external liabilities/gross national product [%]) had reached 36.3 per cent and was expected to increase for one or two more years more before beginning to decline.[115] The problem of debt repayment was compounded by a fall in commodity prices, especially for rice, in the mid-1980s, and by the fact that since 1962 the economy has diversified away from its reliance on primary product exports for its major foreign exchange earnings.

Because of the state's inability to change the structure of the economy, agriculture was still the principle source of livelihood for the bulk of the population and for the state. There remains a basic contradiction between the interests of the average peasant and the state: each claims a share of the produce of the country's fields and any increase in the state's share must

---

114   Research Institute for Peace and Security, *Asian Security 1980* (Tokyo, 1980), p. 160.

115   *World Debt Tables* (Washington, DC: International Monetary Fund, 1985), pp. 414-17.

be at the expense of the peasant, especially as the role of any putatively exploiting middleman has been removed by the government's nationalisation policies. The peasants makes their claim for the predominant share of the nation's agricultural surplus on the basis that if it were not for their labour, buffaloes, and tools used in the cultivation of the fields, there would be no annual crop. The state, on the other hand, claims that the land belongs to it, and that the farmers are merely using the land with its permission; they must therefore share the fruits of their mutual agricultural endeavour. Furthermore, the state claims that it has removed most of the insecurity of tenure and high cost of credit that plagued peasant farmers in the colonial and early post-colonial years, and therefore has eased the position of the peasant family. It not only makes available inexpensive credit, it also buys the peasant's crop through an advanced purchase scheme, provides him with highly subsidised fertiliser, undertakes the cost of marketing the crop, and provides an extensive planning system for determining what should be planted and in what quantities. Therefore the peasant has a moral obligation to fulfil his production and sales quotas.

The number of peasant families at the time of the Revolutionary Council's coming to power was 2.78 million, but because of land redistribution, population growth and the resultant division of family farms when the original cultivator died, the number had grown to 4.35 million in 1974. After 1974, however, the number of farm families began to decline, and in 1982 there were 64,237 fewer farming households than eight years earlier. The 4.28 million farm families in 1982 farmed over 24.21 million acres. One of the state's key agricultural goals after 1962 was the expansion of worked land, and by 1982 there had been an increase in tilled acreage of almost 5 million acres since 1961.[116]

But because of farm population growth, there was a significant reduction in the size of farms. In 1961/62, 84 per cent of farmers cultivated 10 or fewer acres; by 1982/83, 86 per cent of farmers cultivated 10 or fewer acres, but 25 per cent cultivated 5 or fewer acres. There was a significant disparity in the size of holdings, as 2.7 per cent of farm families cultivated 15 per cent of land and 12 per cent of farm families tilled 29 per cent of all planted acreage with holdings between 10 and 20 acres.[117] While farms of over 20 acres were probably not wet rice farms but upland and dry zone land capable of supporting fewer individuals per acre, such a dispar-

---

116   *Report to the Pyithu Hluttaw 1984/85*, pp. 46-7.
117   Ibid., 1977/78, p. 30; *ibid., 1985/86*, p. 46.

ity probably did not result in significant income inequalities. However, if farmers possessed more than 16 acres of wet rice land they probably had a greater income than their neighbours with fewer acres.

After 1962, the state implemented significant changes in its relationship with the peasant population, which appear to have been intended to achieve incompatible goals. The first change was to ensure that the peasantry remained loyal and did not engage in rebellion or give support to the Communist Party and other anti-government forces; the second was to increase the resources the state could extract from agriculture in order to finance the strengthening of the state both domestically and internationally by increasing its military and industrial capabilities. The efforts to implement these goals have led to compromises which made it impossible for the state to reform agrarian relations; for when faced with a choice between antagonising the peasant majority and increasing agricultural production, the state normally chose the former course. Also, as much of the lower level apparatus for organising the peasantry including the village Party units and People's Councils was in the hands of those peasants who benefited most from the existing situation, the state had limited ability to impose change against the interests of powerful local individuals.

This situation had come about as a result not only of the political and administrative structures introduced after 1962, but also of the state's policies towards agrarian taxation, land control, and rice purchasing. In keeping with the practice introduced by the government immediately after independence, land tax was not resorted to as a means of state revenue. Tax varied with the assessed quality of the land from 1.75 Kt to 5 Kt. per acre per year, a nominal sum.[118] The state exacted resources from the peasantry through the delivery system, under which as the sole legal purchaser of crops it controlled prices and kept them artificially low.[119] In exchange for this, the state attempted to guarantee the security of tenure for the cultivator and to keep his production costs low. The system provided the peasant with few incentives for investment, and until the state began making

---

118 Teruko Saito, 'Farm Household Economy under Paddy Delivery System in Contemporary Burma', *The Developing Economies*, XIX, 4 (Dec. 1981), p. 391.

119 The Revolutionary Council replaced the State Agricultural Marketing Board (SAMB) with the Union of Burma Agricultural Products Marketing Board (UBAM). The latter then became part of Trade Corporation No. 1 of the Ministry of Trade and then became the Agriculture and Farm Produce Trade Corporation; ibid., fn. 11, p. 370.

significant investment in agricultural technology in the mid-1970s, rice production stagnated. In the mid-1960s, Burma ceased to be one of the world's major rice exporting nations, and even faced rice shortages in urban areas and in rural areas unable to provide for their own subsistence.[120]

The basis of the agrarian system was the 1953 Land Nationalisation Act and the Revolutionary Council's Tenancy Act of 1963. The Land Nationalisation Act established the principle that land redistributed to peasants was not owned by them, but remained the property of the state as set forth in principle in the constitution. The state allowed them to cultivate the land with the authorisation of the village Land Committee, and in most instances each year these committees recognised the rights of existing peasant families to continue to work the same fields. This land could not be mortgaged, sold or rented legally, but only tilled by the approved peasant. However, by 1962 only 17 per cent of all land was held in this manner and the remaining 83 per cent was held in the name of private owners, either landlords or sitting farmers. The 1963 Tenancy Act was intended to change the condition of the remaining tenants and cultivating owners whose land had not been nationalised. Its provisions meant that landlords no longer had the right to determine who their tenants would be; this was now to be decided by the village Land Committee. The payment of tenancy rents in kind was prohibited, which gave the tenant control over his own produce, allowing him to sell it at the most propitious time or, when required, to sell it to the state, and an upper limit to tenancy rents was fixed. At the same time, a Peasants' Rights Protection Act was promulgated which made it impossible for creditors to seize the land and other assets of peasants or to seek their punishment for non-payment through the civil courts. In 1965 a further step was taken with an amendment to the Tenancy Act which made tenancy rents illegal. As a result, the selling, renting or collecting of farm rent was prohibited and the state, through the village Land Committees, became the sole arbiter of land use.[121] Initially, the determination of each peasant's obligatory annual crop was made by the local SAC as it estimated

---

120   The complications in assessing all of the problems involved in explaining this situation is set forth in H.V. Richter, *Burma's Rice Surpluses: Accounting for the Decline* (Canberra: Australian National University Development Studies Centre Working Paper), no. 3, 1976.

121   Saito, 'Farm Household Economy', pp. 368-9; John S. Ambler, 'Burma's Rice Economy Under Military Rule: The Evolution of Socialist Agricultural Programs and Their Impact on Paddy Farmers' (unpubl. paper, Cornell University, Oct. 1983), p. 31.

how to meet its quota as established by the central planners. After 1974, this responsibility was passed to the relevant People's Council.

Despite these measures to destroy the legal underpinnings of agricultural tenancy, the number of tenants in the country continued to increase up to 1970/71, the last year for which there were published figures. However, a proportion of the total number of cultivator tenants had declined slightly from 43.9 per cent in 1961/62 to 41.8 per cent in 1970/71.[122] In non-paddy land, it seems that tenancy legislation only affected land control marginally, and the control of paddy land was far from complete. While the transfer of upland non-paddy land was conducted quite openly in the village studied by Saito in the mid-1970s, paddy land transfers were controlled, but only *ex post facto*. The Land Committee, and after 1976 the People's Council, had 'almost been reduced to a land registry office'.[123] What the legislation had done was to drive tenancy underground and to make it extremely unlikely that paddy fields could be rented on more than a temporary basis[124] and on more flexible terms than in the past, though with kinship arrangements perhaps playing a larger role.[125] Complaints about irregularities in the management of the Land Committees and People's Councils had been a recurrent theme appearing in the government press in 1969 and 1970 and alluded to in Pyithu Hluttaw discussions subsequently.[126]

After the nationalisation of internal and external trade in rice and other major products, a paddy procurement scheme was implemented. 'It was a system which controlled the distribution of farm products by means of price controls on paddy and other major farm products by farmers to the government.'[127] As Saito argues in her study of one village in southern Burma, it was the combination of the land tenure systems and the paddy procurement system that provided the means for the state to control the economic life of the peasantry. As the state had never been able to implement complete land reform, it was only the paddy procurement scheme that kept a form of free trade in land and a return to something like the pre-1962 agrarian conditions from re-emerging. The land tenure system

---

122   Ambler, 'Burma's Rice Economy', p. 31.

123   Saito, 'Farm Household Economy', p. 394.

124   Ibid., p. 391.

125   Ambler, 'Burma's Rice Economy', p. 34.

126   Henderson et al., *Area Handbook for Burma*, p. 67; see, for example, *The Guardian*, 5 Oct. 1983.

127   Saito, 'Farm Household Economy', p. 368.

and the paddy procurement system 'seem to originate in the same idea of controlling distribution relations of farm rent between the state and the producers.'[128]

Under the procurement system, each cultivator was obliged to deliver a quota of paddy, as much as a third of the crop, to a paddy purchase centre at the end of the harvest. The size of the peasant's quota was calculated on the basis of a national average yield per acre and the number of acres cultivated. A massive annual effort by officials of the relevant state ministries, the Party, the Peasants' Asiayon and the military was involved in making the system work. Peasants were encouraged, cajoled, or perhaps threatened into meeting their quotas. Failure to meet quotas could lead to loss of the right to access to land and to limitations on state provided credit. The reason why the peasants did not wish to sell to the state, of course, was that there still existed a free market for rice in which a higher price could be obtained.[129] In some cases, farmers might have made illegal loan arrangements with moneylenders and incurred obligations to repay in paddy at or near the official procurement price.[130] The state attempted to control this by making the movement of paddy from one area to another illegal without the permission of the local township People's Council, except in certain rice deficit areas.

'The basic idea underlying the delivery system,' according to Saito, seems to have been 'that the state [would] absorb the differential rents into its own hands.' Thus, there was 'no room for private rent so long as the delivery system absorb[ed] nearly all of the marketable surplus of paddy.'[131] In fact, the system did this for farmers with fewer than 16 acres of land, and some were actually forced to buy paddy on the open market to meet their quota obligations and have food and seed left for themselves. However, for farmers with 16 or more acres of land, there was a surplus left over which could be sold at the free market price; the income of those families was significantly greater that those of the neighbours.[132] Thus having access to land was the key to wealth in the village, and land was controlled by the local People's Council. Membership of the Council, despite the extra burdens it

---

128   Ibid.
129   Ibid., pp. 370-1.
130   World Bank, *Agriculture Sector Review*, vol. 1, p. 20.
131   Saito, 'Farm Household Economy', p. 395.
132   Ibid., pp. 395-6.

imposed on individuals, also served as a means of protecting and enhancing the value of members' property.

Despite the inefficiencies and iniquities of the agrarian system, there was little incentive for the state to alter it. There were two possibilities routes of change. One was to introduce large-scale cooperatisation or, more radically, collective agriculture; this would probably have provoked widespread resistance. The other was to return to the conditions of the free sale of land and farm produce; this would have been politically undesirable, as it would have raised the spectre of large-scale peasant insecurity, even greater income disparities in the countryside, and a loss of control over the peasantry by the state. The paddy procurement scheme not only allowed the state to gain direct access to agricultural surpluses, but also ensured that a free market in land did not re-emerge on a large scale and thus restore capitalist agriculture. There was thus a political as well as an economic incentive to keep paddy procurement prices low. If the margin of profitability of agricultural investment had increased to near free market prices, the land control system would have collapsed under the pressure of the wealthier farmers increasing their holdings or moneylenders reclaiming land for debts.[133]

However, the state did seek to increase production through the provision of new technology, the appointment of village agricultural managers, and the establishment of producers' cooperatives. The cooperative movement was weak and was not accepted by the bulk of the peasantry. Although over 1,000 agricultural producers' cooperatives with over 90,000 members were established up to 1979/80, according to the General Secretary of the BSPP in 1981, 'these societies were not in a position to function in accord with the aims of the agriculture producers' cooperatives' as defined by the state.[134] The situation did not change subsequently. In the agricultural sector, as in much of the rest of the economy, the state has developed power 'sufficient to inhibit initiative, but insufficient to impel developments on the planned lines.'[135] Under the system which prevailed during the socialist era, 'those persons in positions of influence in the local communities ... benefited most',[136] and any attempt to consolidate small holdings either

---

133   As implied by Saito, ibid., p. 395.

134   *The Working People's Daily*, 4 Aug. 1981.

135   Richter, 'Development and Equality in Burma', p. 35.

136   Harvey Demaine, 'Current Problems of Agricultural Development Planning in Burma', in Institute of Southeast Asian Studies, *Southeast Asia Affairs 1979* (Singapore: Heinneman, 1979), p. 102.

'privately or collectively, [would have] create[d] tensions in the agrarian system that [might] even shake the very foundations of the existing social structure.'[137] Only powerful and autonomous states are willing to take such a risk.

External relations. As the state's personnel turned their attention to its reassertion on the basis of autarkic policies, international political activities and attempts to involve the country in general international issues became less important than in the 1950s. This was made possible by the Revolutionary Council continuing its predecessor's policy of neutrality and non-alignment, and extending its military implications to economic, cultural and educational policy as well. There was little deviation from that policy until 1974, although during certain periods particular aspects of international issues were more emphasised. Special attention was given to relations with the state's immediate neighbours, and conscious efforts were made to ensure that disputes with these states could not be used to allow outside powers to interfere in domestic politics. When such events occurred, however, as in 1967 when the Chinese Cultural Revolution led to anti-Ne Win demonstrations in Rangoon and to increased Chinese Communist support for the Kachin Independence Army and the Burma Communist Party,[138] or when the influx of Muslim refugees from Bangladesh threatened to lead to a border war in 1979, the state stood firmly by the five principles of peaceful coexistence including non-interference in the internal affairs of another state, and implicitly appealed to the United Nations and its member states for support.[139] The only major foreign policy document socialist Burma issued after the 1962 coup came in 1968 when it sought to demonstrate its international probity in the face of China's provocations.[140] On matters of international conflict such as the question of

---

137   Khin Maung Kyi, 'Problems of Agricultural Policy in Some Trade Dependent Small Countries: A Comparative Study of Burma and Thailand', *Kajian Ekonomi Malaysia*, XVI, nos. 1 and 2 (June/Dec. 1979), p. 350.

138   The most complete account is the declassified United States Central Intelligence Agency Directorate of Intelligence Report, 'Peking and the Burmese Communists: The Perils and Profits of Insurgency' (RSS no. 0052/71, July 1971; declassified 5 Dec. 1989).

139   See Albert D. Moscotti, 'Current Burmese and Southeast Asian Affairs', in Institute of Southeast Asian Studies, *Southeast Asian Affairs 1978* (Singapore: Heinneman, 1979), pp. 83-94; and Robert H. Taylor, 'Burma's Foreign Relations Since the Third Indochina Conflict', in ibid., 1983 (Aldershot: Gower, 1983) pp. 102-12.

140   Burma Socialist Programme Party, Central Organising Committee, *Foreign Policy of the Revolutionary Council Government of the Union of Burma* (Rangoon:

the Vietnamese invasion of Cambodia in 1979, the government urged all states to follow these same principles.

The Revolutionary Council strove to ensure that conflicts between neighbouring states did not expand so as to involve Burma. Burma was active in both the 1962 Geneva Conference on the neutralisation of Laos and the 1962 Colombo Conference of African and Asian nations which discussed the Chinese-Indian border conflict of that year.[141] Subsequently, Burma was less active in such multilateral diplomacy and tended to eschew opportunities to involve itself in other conflicts. However, the government did offer to make facilities for a negotiated settlement of the Vietnam war in the mid-1960s and for the Kampuchea question in 1980, although to no avail.

The state's radically autarkic economic policies and its nationalisation of foreign-owned enterprises placed strains on its relations with India and Britain, but did not lead to serious conflict. The nations of Eastern Europe and the former Soviet Union initially looked on developments in Burma with some favour and believed that Burma had partly joined the socialist camp.[142] While there was some greater openness shown to the socialist bloc in terms of the receiving of advisers and the despatch of Burmese students to Eastern Europe and the Soviet Union, the state was careful to balance this with ties to other countries. The United States military aid agreement, for example, was not ended until 1970, and Burma continued to receive significant amounts of Japanese assistance in the form of war reparations throughout the 1960s, as well as aid from West Germany, other European countries, and China both before and after the Cultural Revolution.

Despite Burma's less obvious involvement in international politics after 1962, the country received a variety of official visitors including heads of state and government, and some of the state's leading personnel travelled widely. During the 12 years between the coup and the inauguration of the 1974 constitution, heads of state or government visited Burma from Romania (1962), China (1962, 1964, 1965, 1966), North Korea (1964), In-

---

Sarpay Beikman for the BSPP, 1968).

141 *Party Seminar 1965*, p. 43.

142 *Pravda* noted that Burma was pursuing the 'correct path' to socialism in January 1965 (Steinberg, 'Burma Under Military Rule', p. 259), but subsequent Soviet analytical writings on Burma expressed greater scepticism and noted the 'reactionary' nature of the new ideology of the BSPP. See Rostislav Ulyanonvsky, *National Liberation*, 'The New Burma' with P.P. Anikeyev (Moscow: Progress Publishers, 1978), pp. 265-304.

dia (1965, 1969), Thailand (1966), Japan (1967), West Germany (1967), Hungary (1972), Malaysia (1972), Indonesia (1972), and Zaire (1973); and the Chairman of the Revolutionary Council visited Sri Lanka (1962, 1966), Thailand (1962, 1966, 1973), India (1965, 1970), Pakistan (1965, 1966, 1969), China (1965, 1971), the Soviet Union (1965), Czechoslovakia (1966), Romania (1966), the United States (1966), Japan (1966, 1970, 1973), Nepal (1966), Singapore (1968), Malaysia (1968, 1973), the Philippines (1970), Hungary (1972) and Indonesia (1973).[143] A similar pattern was maintained subsequently, revealing a conscious effort to balance visits between opposing states, especially China and India.

As Burma's armed forces did not possess the ability to project military power any appreciable distance beyond the state's borders, it posed no threat to any of its neighbours. Only if Burma became a base for the operations of a more powerful state, such as the United States or the Soviet Union, would India or China have seen Burma as threatening. For this reason, and because of the absence of any desire to have larger states affecting either domestic politics and society or foreign policy direction, neutrality was a convenient policy for the state during the Cold War. Burma's withdrawal from the Non-Aligned Movement in 1979 because of the aggressively interventionist programme advocated by some of its more vocal members, as well as their actual alignments with the great powers, reiterated the state's determination not to become embroiled in external affairs which did not directly and immediately affect the security of Burma. Since then, trade and aid relations have been the dominant concerns of the state in the international sphere.

Legitimacy and the state. The Revolutionary Council chose to maintain only part of the legacy of the previous state managers in its search for legitimacy. While maintaining the slogans and promises of egalitarian socialism and the creation of an affluent society along welfare state lines, it eschewed the use of religion as a basis for legitimacy. Rather, it argued that U Nu's use of religion had not only created greater dissatisfaction with the state by raising fears in the minds of non-Buddhists, but also encouraged politicisation of the monkhood and thus diverted it from its religious duties. Furthermore, the state had increasingly ignored its obligations to create a socialist society because of its concentration on religion, and had abandoned the secular goals of the pre-independence nationalist movement. The state's leading

---

143   *Towhlanyei Kaungsi ei Hluthsaungchet Thamaing Akyichut*, pp. 218-23.

personnel saw the utility of a state ideology in the form of the ideology of the ruling party as a means of creating a potentially non-divisive set of ideals and concepts around which state-society relations could be rebuilt.

Among the first actions of the Revolutionary Council was an order to cease state support for Buddhism. The directors of government joint venture firms were immediately ordered to halt payments for the reconstruction of the Mahazedi pagoda in Pegu.[144] In May the Buddha Sasana Council was dissolved.[145] Two years later, at the same time as the dissolution of political parties other than the BSPP, all Buddhist and other religious organisations were ordered to register with their local SACs and to refrain henceforth from political activities, but in May the order had to be rescinded after a monk immolated himself in protest.[146] The state attempted again in 1965 to bring the *sangha* under its control, but failed to do so because of continuing factionalism in the *sangha* and opposition to demands that monks had to be registered and carry documents. This opposition led to the arrest in April of 92 monks for political and economic activities, and forced the Revolutionary Council to defend itself repeatedly against charges that it was anti-religious and therefore no different from the Communist Party.[147] The Revolutionary Council, for its part, attributed the protests by the monks to collusion with illegal political parties.[148]

During this period the Revolutionary Council was also implementing restrictions on foreign missionaries and nationalising religious schools and hospitals usually run by Christian orders. It maintained, however, that the right to freedom of religion was preserved, and justified its actions in the name of economic policy and the need to develop an egalitarian educational system. Missionaries of long standing in the country were allowed to continue to function as before, and while contacts with outside religious bodies became increasingly difficult, this was the result of the general closure of foreign contacts with indigenous institutions, and not of religious discrimination as such.

---

144 Donald Eugene Smith, *Religion and Politics in Burma* (Princeton University Press, 1965), p. 170.
145 Steinberg, 'Burma Under the Military', p. 250.
146 Badgeley, 'Burma's Zealot Wungyi', p. 57.
147 Silverstein, 'Burma: Ne Win's Revolution', p. 101; Maung Maung, *Burma and General Ne Win* (New York: Asia Publishing House, 1969), p. ix.
148 *Party Seminar 1965*, pp. 62-3.

Large-scale involvement of Buddhist monks in overt political activity did not occur after 1965 until the 1974 demonstrations over the burial of U Thant. However, state managers were always concerned about the possibility of development of opposition to the state through the monkhood, a body to which individuals could retreat and gain immunity from the state's laws. The monkhood existed in a sort of legal limbo in relation with the state, and the presence within it of many factions made it a loose organisation, highly penetrable by individuals with a variety of intentions. Having dissolved the politicised self-governing institutions through which Nu had unsuccessfully tried to control the monkhood, for 15 years the state was unwilling to assault its independence directly.

Then, in May 1980, the relationship between the state and the *sangha* was fundamentally altered. The details of how this change was implemented have not become available, but at that time there was held in Rangoon the First Congregation of the Sangha of All Orders for the Purification, Perpetuation, and Propagation of the Sasana. This meeting adopted a constitution and other rules for the removal of individuals who did not fulfil the requirements of proper monks, according to the terms of the organisation, controlled by senior monks cooperating with the state. The meeting had been carefully prepared in advance by the Ministry of Home and Religious Affairs. The constitution adopted was essentially identical in structure to that of the state. Committees of leading monks were organised from the village tract and ward level upwards to a state central working committee which managed the sects in its area and which, through its executive committee, ensured that monks behaved according to the *Vinaya*, the Buddhist code of behaviour.[149] Failure to do so resulted in the relevant executive committee of the monkhood reporting violations to the township People's Council, which was empowered to take action against an individual or an entire monastery found to be misbehaving.[150]

From the state's perspective, the successful conclusion of the 1980 meeting of the *sangha* and of a second congregational meeting in mid-1985 indicated greater control by the state over the Buddhist monkhood than for

---

149   Thathanatow Thanshin Tetanpyanpwayei Gaingpaungsu Thaya Asiaweipwekyi Hpyitmyaukyei Thaya wanhsnaukhpwet, *Pyihtuangsu Hsoshelit Thammata Myanma Naingngan Thaya Ahpweasin Akhyeihkansinmyin (Mukyan)* (Rangoon: Kaba Ei Thathanayei Usi Dana Press), 1980.

150   Law on Solution of Cases and Conflicts in Accordance with the Rules of the Order (Pyithu Hluttaw Law no. 3, 1980), *The Working People's Daily*, 4 July 1980. See also Aung Kin, 'Burma in 1980'.

many years previously. The purpose of the organisation of the *sangha* body was clearly to strengthen the authority of the state over the monkhood. This was one of the goals of the state throughout Myanmar's history.[151]

Having denied the use of religion as a legitimizing ideology for the state, the state's managers chose to follow a secular socialist argument which stressed the state's obligation to create prosperity for the population. However, the impecunious condition of the state made that goal elusive. The stagnant economic conditions of the 1960s made it especially difficult to obtain capital for investment in human resources. Nonetheless, in macro terms, between 1962 and 1989 significant advances were made in the development of educational, health and other services designed to raise living standards. Burma's population increased from approximately 22.7 million in 1962 to 35.3 million in 1983, a rise of 55.5 per cent, and it grew at an estimated average of over 2 per cent per year for more than twenty years.[152]

Education received a significant amount of state expenditure, equal to 15 per cent of total government budgeted expenditure in the first half of the 1980s. Between 1962 and 1985 the number of primary, middle and secondary school teachers nearly tripled, and the number of vocational teachers and university teachers nearly quadrupled. These increases, however, barely kept pace with the growth in student numbers as the proportion of students from each relevant age category attending school also rose. By 1981 an estimated 81 per cent of all those of primary school age were attending school, while 20 per cent of those of secondary school age and 4 per cent of tertiary age were doing so. This compared with 56 per cent, 10 per cent and one per cent respectively in 1960. The government's efforts resulted in an increase in literacy from 57 per cent in 1963 to 81 per cent in 1985.[153]

Expansion of health care was also significant. Expenditure on health remained at less than 10 per cent of government after 1962 until the mid-1980s. Life expectancy for men increased from 45 in 1964 to 61 in 1983, and for women from 48 to 65.[154] After 1960, infant mortality dropped by

---

151   E. Michael Mendelson, *Sangha and State in Burma* (edited by John P. Ferguson; Ithaca: Cornell University Press, 1975), p. 118.

152   *Report to the Pyithu Hluttaw 1986/87* (Rangoon: Ministry of Planning and Finance, 1986, in Burmese), p. 25.

153   *The Working People's Daily*, 7 Aug. 1985.

154   Ibid.

more than one-third to 96 per 1,000 live births and the child death rate was halved to 12 per 1,000 live births by 1980. The provision of doctors rose from one for every 15,560 people in 1950 to one for every 4,660 people in 1980, and the number of nurses grew from one for every 8,520 persons to one for every 4,750 people.[155]

However, it was not possible to know to what extent the population credited the state with these improvements. School classes remained very large and equipment, if available, was poor. Hospitals, like schools, were not completely free, and individuals sought to use private medicine and education facilities where possible. The state thus devoted a good deal of attention to attempts to limit the activities of private schools and of doctors, who, working privately, could earn larger incomes. Particularly for the urban population, about a quarter of the total, the promise of improvement must have seemed hollow. While unemployment and underemployment rates were not available, they were thought to be high, even among the better educated. Expenditure on social welfare measures remained minuscule. The state had, to a certain extent, been able through its mass organisations to lower costs for itself by using 'volunteer' labour for certain projects such as sanitation and the construction of schools and other public buildings. How far these activities were genuinely voluntary was difficult to gauge, but where such activities were seen to be of direct benefit to residents, such as the construction of a village school or a water tank in a dry zone, cooperation would be more forthcoming. Whatever the case of a given individual, the ability of the state's organisations to persuade the population to provide such free labour demonstrated a degree of control over their lives which a weaker state could not generate.

The ideology of the state as developed by the Revolutionary Council, and promulgated through the organisations and publications of the state and Party, were sufficiently vague and general to appeal to a large proportion of the population without tying the state to specific policies other than general goals such as socialism and affluence. The ideology was grounded in Buddhist epistemology but gained its analytical language from Marxism and, to a certain extent, its political ideas from Leninism. The ideology combined classical Buddhist notions of the origin and purpose of the state with twentieth-century notions of political organisation and state practice. It thus served as a rationale for the socialist state without providing a justification for social and economic demands upon the state. Just as

---

155　*World Development Report 1984*, pp. 264, 266.

the ideological justifications of other states explain the need for obedience and sacrifice, so the ideology of the BSPP served to control and to mobilise its believers in the interests of the state and to obviate the desire to seek an alternative ideology.

The state ideology was not perceived by its formulators as a set of firmly held and immutable principles. Rather, it served as a basis and viewpoint from which Party and government policies and programmes were to be analysed and implemented in the light of experience. It was intended to provide a perceptual lens for its followers which would allow them to see conditions as they were from the position of the state. The ideology itself could be altered with changing circumstances.[156] At the heart of the ideology lay the concept of correlation. Dialectic, interaction, correlation, and cause and effect were seen as essentially the same phenomenon, and all these terms in various forms are key philosophical concepts in Theravada Buddhism.[157] When it is realised that in the ideology of the BSPP 'correlation' meant several different ideas in European philosophical traditions, the remainder of the Party's doctrines and the philosophy that underlay them, as delineated in the *System of Correlation of Man and Hen Environment* and derivative Party publications, become comprehensible and internally consistent.

The ideology began by making certain assumptions about the nature of man and of nature derived from Buddhist thought. Man, like all matter, is mutable, and within man there exists in correlation a mind and a body. It is man's mind that distinguishes him from other animals and makes his social existence possible. It is man's social existence that gives rise to politics and ultimately the state, because man 'is an egocentric animal' who 'instinctively seeks freedom in which to live and act' but, secondly, man 'is also an altruistic social animal' who lives in a society which 'is but an institution of human beings organised by them under their codes of law and behaviour.' Through society man strives to achieve both his personal and social needs for mind and body, and thus there is a correlation between his needs and the needs of society. Man's egotistical and altruistic characteristics have to be balanced.

---

156   *System of Correlation of Man and His Environment*, p. 38.

157   See Shwe Zan Aung and Rhys Davids, *Compendium of Philosophy* (a translation from Pali of *Abhidhammatttha-Sangaha*, translated by Shwe Zan Aung, veried and edited by Mrs. Rhys Davids) (London: Pali Text Society, 1910), Part VIII, Compendium of Relations, especially Section 7, The System of Correlation.

The theory is nearly identical to that used in the time of the kings to justify the functions of the state, but its contemporary purpose was in keeping with modern political expectations. Rather than seeking to create order to allow for man's religious salvation or the achievement of *nirvana*, the modern state must establish order so as to mobilise man's resources for the economic and cultural advancement of the society on which he is dependent. But in bending to the requirements of the larger society and the state which guides it, man's egotism, 'his instinctive spirit of freedom incites him to rise and shake off his fetters and clear his path of obstacles.'[158] Thus there exists in the relationship between man and society another 'correlated relationship' or 'dialectic' which is potentially antagonistic.

Within society there exists a dialectic or correlation between the material life and the spiritual life. The spiritual life, caused by man's thinking, interacts with society's need for material progress and is thus the engine of history. In the historical process, certain classes and social groups arise from time to time and these create social antagonism and conflicts between progressive and reactionary forces. As the currently dominant institution in human society, the state exists, by implication, to regulate this conflict.

The role of the Party as the leading institution of the state arises from the historical role of the working people. Since man is selfish and only enters into society for selfish purposes, because he cannot live alone and fulfil either his spiritual or his material needs, social constraints which check man's nature must exist to keep 'within bounds' man's 'self-aggrandisement and desire for freedom.' Society is capable of doing this to a certain extent through institutions such as marriage. It is at this point, however, that the ideology implicitly justifies the role of socialism as an economic system to control man's egotism; this is the basis of his greed. *Correlation* states that '(o)ur socialist economy shall be based on the dialectical unity of the individual and social interests of the citizens of the Union of Burma. Our socialist system is a system which will achieve a harmony between the individual and the social interests of the people.'[159] Socialism is seen as the means to regulate man's natural acquisitiveness, which if allowed full reign would not be either to his own or to society's long term advantage. It is at this point that the case for justification and legitimisation of the modern authoritarian state begins to emerge.

---

158   *System of Correlation*, pp. 6-7. All quotations are from the official translation.
159   Ibid., p. 25.

In both Buddhist thought and the ideology of the Party there is nothing inevitable about human progress as assumed in Marxism and most other Western ideologies. Rather, because of man's nature, either human improvement or degeneration are possible. In order to ensure that it is progress or good which takes place, society needs a guide. In historical Burmese thought the king provided the basis of good by preserving order in society to allow Buddhism to flourish. Under the BSPP, the Party and the state provided good by creating a cadre of superior people to lead society by a 'reorientation of views' to eradicate 'fraudulent practices, profit motive, easy living, parasitism, shirking and selfishness.'[160] Eradication of these evils, however, was a difficult goal to achieve, and in reality the Party was willing merely to regulate and limit the consequences of man's inherent greed.

The ideology condemned both capitalism and communism on moral grounds. Both were erroneously based upon materialism. Capitalism sought the solution to man's problems through his greed, operationalised as the profit motive, while communism tended to over-restrict man's egotism and killed his creative powers, perhaps achieving a spurious equity but not achieving spiritual happiness. Through the practice of socialist democracy in the Party and the state, the extreme errors of capitalism and communism were to be avoided because:

Socialist democracy includes the unity of will and initiative of the individual man and group on the one hand and the centralised guidance of the society on the other. In a society which aspires for progress two features are necessary, viz., centralism resting with the State and the freedom of initiative resting with individuals or the majority. Without centralism society will tend towards anarchism. Again without freedom of initiative of individuals society becomes mechanical and its progress is retarded.[161]

In this understanding, the Party replaced the king in ensuring that the correct balance between order and initiative was maintained.

The ideology, like Buddhist teachings, had an essentially moral and hortatory function. The Party and its cadres, who were trained in a manner of withdrawal from society like both Buddhist monks and modern soldiers, existed to ensure that the purpose of the state was successfully carried out by moral men and women who were able to provide the remainder of society with proper leadership. As the Party Member's Handbook stated:

---

160   Ibid., pp. 18-19.

161   Ibid., p. 31. Italics in the original.

Only if there is an organisation and leadership for all the working people which leads to the economic advantage of man, which is able to judge each man as a man, which is able to have just relations of man with man, which does not have great greed [*lawba*], hatred [*dawtha*] or conceit [*mana*], which is of good mind, will the socialist economic system be successful.

Socialist ideology is an important matter to be able correctly to lead the people. Socialist ideology is an important matter for not retreating [i e , turning back, corrupting—*mahpauk mapyan*].

Man is able to retreat (be corrupted). Therefore it is necessary to establish a socialist democratic living relations society which is able to analyse and control constantly the misconduct which causes retreat in humans.[162]

Throughout the ideology there was a clear perception of the need for order to be created and to be maintained by the state. Only in this way could greed be suppressed and equity achieved. The ideology did not posit the eventual creation of a classless or conflict free society; the nature of man would not allow for this. Rather, the goal of the Party was to create a balanced society which was able to understand and control the dialectics of extremes between anarchy and repression.

The plausibility of the ideology stemmed not only from its philosophical basis in classical Burmese Buddhist thought, but also from the recent history of Burma which provided it with meaning. Burma had experienced capitalism and colonialism, depression, poverty, rebellion and anarchy during the lifetime of the generation that came to power after independence. Personal experience had convinced many Burmese that balance and authority were required to create social harmony.

Politics under the socialist state

The consequences of the reassertion of the state between 1962 and 1988 for the practice of politics were significant. Largely hidden were the arguments about the nature and future of the state that dominated politics in the 1930s and the 1950s. The press reported nothing of the daily life of the leaders of the state other than their public appearances. The rumour and innuendo that were once at the heart of so much of Rangoon's politics, when ministers were made and broken on the basis of votes bought or cajoled

---

162   Myanma Hsoshelit Lansin Pati Baho Komitti Danachok (Burma Socialist Programme Party Central Committee Headquarters), *Myanmar Hsoshelit Lansin Patiwinmya Letswe* (Myanmar Socialist Programme Party Member's Handbook) (Rangoon: Myanmar Socialist Programme Party, 1978, repr. 1980), pp. 19-20.

in the House of Representatives, could not be found in print. Bribery and corruption were driven underground. Also missing were the local bosses who wielded influence through their private armies or henchmen over local electorates and upon whom central politicians depended for support. Other political types largely disappeared from view also, including student politicians assiduously labouring to bring down the government through street demonstrations, and union or party organisers ready to start new bodies in order to apply political pressure or to foment a 'genuine' revolution. Gone also was the political rhetoric which promised the voters all that they desired at little personal cost.

In place of these political types, viewed from the capital, Burma's politics became dull and tedious, a mere annual round of public meetings, guidance offered, and calls for unity and sacrifice interlayed with reams of statistics. But underneath there was a current of rumour and plot. The press reported the endless series of meetings to coordinate plans and to give awards attended by state and party officials from various levels of the administration. The tea shops, meanwhile, provided explanations of what was 'really' going on which often had the makings of a fine political novel, but which rarely approximated the dull tedium of day to day government. Rather, significant political events, including the sudden arrest and replacement of leading state personnel and announcements of significant changes in government policy, were largely unpredicted and equally unpredictable.

On closer analysis, there appeared to be three different kinds of politics present under the socialist state. There was, first, the politics of the central Party and state organisations, including the Party Central Committee, the Council of State, the cabinet, and that which surrounded the Party Chairman. Involved here were questions of state policy in terms of the direction of economic affairs, the control of personnel, and the question of political succession to the top leadership. The second level of politics concerned the institutions and personnel which provided the means by which central state policy was relayed to the populace. Here, at the level of the state and divisional People's Councils and Party units, regional military commands, administrators in the judicial services, and central ministries which serviced and guided regional and local administrations and the managers of state owned factories, there existed a form of administrative politics; this attempted to satisfy the requirements of the centre by encouraging, cajoling, ordering, demanding, and threatening subordinates in their respective political and administrative organisations to fulfil production targets while maintaining political order. At the township and village level, but perhaps somewhat less at the urban ward level, a third kind of politics was practised. There state officials came directly into contact with the population and were faced with the task of balancing the demands of the centre, as relayed to them through regional intermediaries, against the unwillingness of the population to abandon their time, produce or labour to the state.

Politics at the top or central level had about it something of the aura of court politics. One man, Party Chairman Ne Win, had so long dominated the state that he had developed a degree of loyalty and respect from his associates that no other political figure had achieved. He was the only member of the political leadership who had taken a leading role in the state's life since 1942. Involved in the displacement of the state as one of the Thirty Comrades, Ne Win had worked for the state since he was an officer in forces dominated by the Japanese and by the British, as the chief of the armed forces from 1948 through the civil war and the KMT intrusion, as Deputy Prime Minister and Minister of Defence when the Socialists and others abandoned power between 1948 and 1950, and as Prime Minister between 1958 and 1960 when the army intervened to 'clean up the mess' the civilian politicians had made of the first ten years of independence. As Chairman of the Revolutionary Council from 1962 to 1974, President of the state from 1974 to 1981, and Chairman of the Burma Socialist Programme Party from its inception until July 1988, Ne Win achieved the status of a founding father of modern Burma, equal only to the assassinated Aung San, to whom Ne Win was linked by comradeship in arms.

During the initial years of the Revolutionary Council, Ne Win's position was rather that of *primus inter pares*. The council had the potential of becoming just another military junta living off the state in a blatantly corrupt relationship. In 1964, however, a Revolutionary Council member was given a life sentence for benefiting financially from the order demonetising large denomination *kyat* notes.[163] Such action, taken early and publicly to punish an obvious misuse of public responsibility, served the state in its object of attempting to avoid being or looking excessively corrupt, despite occasional lapses and widespread low-level financial exchanges between Party and state officials and private businesses to finance state activities.[164]

---

163   Silverstein, 'Burma: Ne Win's Revolution Reconsidered', p. 100.

164   Kyaw Yin Hlaing, " Reconsidering the Failure of the Burma Socialist Programme Party to Eradicate Internal Economic Impediments", *South East Asia Research*, 11, 1 (March 2003), pp. 5-58.

Unlike what has occurred in many other states which created social-ist one-party regimes in the political lifetime of one leader, there was no obvious and conscious plan to create a cult of personality around Ne Win. He was a most unlikely charismatic figure, and compared with the public persona of Aung San and Nu before him, he appeared to be self-effacing. He affected no public pose and launched no personal crusades; his was a political style of gradual and cautious organisation. Nonetheless, a kind of charisma did grow around him, not so much a personal charisma but more a reflected charisma derived from his position in the state. Ne Win's per-sonal power came from the charisma of office, though it must be acknowl-edged that in the 1950s his position within the armed forces was developed through his personal relations with hundreds of men, most of whom re-mained personally loyal to him to the end of his period in power.[165]

Ne Win's treatment of his political 'equals' illustrated the manner in which his particular charisma developed. After the 1962 coup he not only held negotiations with the leaders of the legal political parties in Rangoon, but summoned to the capital leaders of the illegal groups, including the various Communist factions and the separatists. When these talks failed to produce a solution satisfactory to both the Revolutionary Council and the opposition groups, the leaders of the illegal parties were permitted to return to their base areas and to resume armed conflict with the government. Many leaders of the formerly legal parties were arrested and placed under deten-tion. Two or three years later they were released, and following the disorder that occurred during the food shortages of 1967-8 and the adoption of a hostile stance toward Burma by China during the Cultural Revolution, Ne Win invited them to discuss with him and the Revolutionary Council the nature and future of the state. For six months, thirty-three leading figures in the politics of the 1950s, including the former Prime Minister Nu and the former Deputy Prime Ministers Ba Swe and Kyaw Nyein, met under state auspices and prepared a majority report which essentially called for abandonment of the direction the Revolutionary Council had been taking the state for the past seven years, and restoration of the pre-coup political

---

165   On kinds of charisma and their relationship society, see the useful discussion by William H. Swatos, Jr., 'Revolutions and Charisma in a Rationalised World: Max Weber Revisited and Extended', in Ronald M. Glassman and Vatro Mur-var (eds), *Max Weber's Political Sociology: A Pessimistic Vision of a Rationalised World* (Westport, Conn.: Greenwood Press, 1984), pp. 203-5.

system. These demands were unacceptable to the Revolutionary Council and the discussions were terminated.[166]

Nu then left Burma, and together with other political leaders of the 1940s and 1950s began to plan to oust the Revolutionary Council by leading a resistance organisation from Thailand. The government-controlled press in Burma reported these activities for a few weeks in October 1970 much as they were presented in the world press at the time.[167] Nu's call for rebellion evoked little response from the public eight years after his fall, and despite his personal charisma in the 1950s, he posed no political threat to the Revolutionary Council. The publicity that the Revolutionary Council press gave to the rebels was a way of demonstrating their impotence when confronted with the new state structures.

The final act to demonstrate Ne Win's power over his rivals of the 1960s came in 1980 when the state offered an amnesty for all political offenders, including insurgents who surrendered within 90 days. At the same time, the state gave remission to other convicted criminals. The amnesty was announced by the Council of State 'as a token of joyously honouring the successful conclusion of the First Congregation of the Sangha of All Orders for the Purification, Perpetuation, and Propagation of the Sasana and thereby to promote unity and peace.'[168] The same day the Council of State, over the signature of its Chairman, Ne Win, announced an order instituting a title known as the 'Naing-Ngant Gon-Yi' to honour persons who had served the state. Adding also legislation passed later in the year providing for pensions for all the leading figures in Burmese politics and administration since the Hsaya San rebellion, the state declared that, regardless of their political opposition, the state that Ne Win headed was willing to take them back and to look after them in their final years.[169] Although it was unknown at that time, Ne Win's creation itself had only eight more years to live.

---

166   *Pyihtaungsu Myanma Naingngan Towhlanyei Kaungsi tho Tinthwin thaw Pyihtaungsu Myanma Naingngan Pyin twin Nyinyatyei Akyanpei ei Asiyinhkana* (Union of Myanmar Internal Unity Conference's Report Which Was Submitted to the Union of Myanmar Revolutionary Council) (n. p. [Rangoon]: n. d. [1969]).

167   Wiant, 'Burma's Revolutionary Council', pp. 27-8; *The New York Times*, 19 Oct. 1970, 27 Nov. 1970.

168   *The Working People's Daily*, 28 May 1980.

169   Details are provided in Aung Kin, 'Burma in 1980: Pouring Balm on Sore Spots', in Institute of Southeast Asian Studies, *Southeast Asian Affairs 1981* (Singapore: Institute of Southeast Asian Studies, 1982), pp. 106-110.

While a few of the then active Communist and separatist insurgents accepted the amnesty, the majority did not. However, large numbers of people who had joined Nu in his 1970 effort to overthrow Ne Win returned to Burma, as did the former Prime Minister himself. On 11 August 1980, Ne Win hosted a lunch for the leading recipients of his benevolence. In the film and photographs of the event released to the public and widely distributed throughout the country the Party Chairman was seated in a slightly raised chair surrounded by his previous opponents. Not only were all of the leading legal political figures of the 1950s seated to his right, along with former senior army officers from the same decade who had previously been dismissed, but the major dialectician and theorist of Burmese radical thought, the former Communist leader Thakin Soe, sat on his left. It was as if all the major mobilisers of mass action against the state between 1942 and 1980 had come to recognise the reassertion of the state and to acknowledge its current legitimacy.

The general recognition of the *de facto* legitimacy of the socialist state structure and Ne Win's supremacy within it made more conspicuous another political phenomenon at the centre. Gaining access to, and the trust of, the Party Chairman were the only ways of ensuring that objectives could be achieved, and his approval of a project was the key to its successful implementation. The central political position in the state was then focused on the person of the Party Chairman. Rivalries within the army and the Party posed the greatest challenges to Ne Win and those closest to him until the crisis of 1988. While in the mid-1960s anti-party organisations within the Party arose in the form of alleged Communist cells within the army, as had occurred in the 1940s, during the 1970s more formidable challenges emerged.

Following the worker and student protests of 1974 and 1975, the Minister of Defence and Chief of Staff of the Armed Forces, General Tin U, was forced to resign from his posts. These were then divided between two men, the Prime Minister, U Sein Lwin, and the Deputy Chief of Staff, General Kyaw Htin. Tin U left office, it was rumoured at the time, because of the corrupt activities of his wife—a common allegation in Rangoon about most leading figures' wives. It was also rumoured that a split had developed within the armed forces between a pro-Tin U faction of field commanders who had been facing the brunt of the fighting against the insurgents and the officers who had taken a leading part in the development of the Party and the state in Rangoon. Then, on 21 July 1976, seven military officers were arrested and tried for allegedly plotting to assassinate Ne Win and other top leaders, including the Party General Secretary and State Council Secretary, U San Yu, and the chief of the National Intelligence Bureau, Colonel Tin U.[170] By the time the seven officers came to trial in September, General Tin U, whom some had seen as a likely successor to Ne Win, was charged with knowledge of the assassination plot and placed on trial with a total of 14 officers. He was found guilty and imprisoned.

Less than a year later another plot to assassinate Ne Win and the cabinet was alleged, and two former officials of the BSPP were arrested and tried. As the main defendants were described as a Karen and an Arakanese (Rakhine), the motive for their action was rumoured to be disagreement with the Party over the rights of ethnic minorities. In September 1977, two ministers who had been appointed the previous March were dismissed and arrested, while more than 50 other top officials were removed from office in what was described as a 'purge' of the BSPP. This followed the second BSPP Congress at which Ne Win was rumoured to have come second or third in the balloting for position. The implication that Ne Win was no longer the most popular figure in the party was a great blow to his pride. The dominant rumour at that time to explain the removal of leading figures from the political scene was that they disagreed with the partial liberalisation of economic policy, including a guarantee of private investments against eventual nationalisation. Those dismissed were said to be leading members of the Party's alleged 'pro-Soviet' faction to which San Yu was thought to belong.[171] Others explained the conflict as the army reasserting its position over the Party within the state's guiding institutions.[172]

After this flurry of removals, there ensued a six-year period of remarkable calm at the centre of the state. The routine of meetings and speeches ground on, highlighted only by the departure of Ne Win as President and his replacement by San Yu, who, at the same time, gave up the apparently more influential position of General Secretary of the Party. Then, in June 1983, retired Brigadier General (formerly Colonel) Tin U, at that time serving as General Secretary of the Party, and formerly head of government intelligence services, was dismissed from office along with the Home

---

170   *New York Times*, 21 July 1976.

171   *Far Eastern Economic Review*, 7 Oct. 1977.

172   *The Burma Committee Information Quarterly*, vol. 3, no. 4 (Fall, 1977); this was an anti-government publication issued from Montreal by Burmese exiles.

Minister, Colonel Bo Ni. This General Tin U had risen rapidly through the ranks following the dismissal of the Chief of Staff Tin U in 1976. At the time of his dismissal, Tin U had replaced San Yu as the likely heir to Ne Win's position. Tin U was tried and convicted on charges of misappropriating public funds, and Bo Ni was convicted of abetting corruption on the part of his wife and son and of illegally using state property.[173] With Tin U eliminated, San Yu was once more seen as Ne Win's likely successor and he was made Vice Chairman at the 1985 Party Conference. At the same time many leading officials appointed by Tin U during his tenure as the Director of the National Intelligence Bureau were removed, and legislation was passed placing intelligence operations under a committee controlled by the Prime Minister and the Ministers for Defence and Foreign Affairs.[174]

This litany of personnel shifts and the commonly accepted explanations for them reveal no pattern and little consistency, other than to suggest that at the top of state there existed strong rivalries centred on control of the Party apparatus and the position of the Party Chairman. These manoeuvrings echoed the politics of the old Soviet Politburo or the Chinese Communist Party Central Committee. These episodes illustrate that capturing the top post in the Party had become the route to political power. None of the leading rivals for office ever indicated that they wished to see the state system replaced; they wished to control it.

The most ambitious participants in the middle level of politics, were they regional army commanders, Party officers, or technicians and managers, realised that the route to power was through impressing their superiors at the centre with their abilities to produce the goods and services required by the state's plans. These individuals were continually attempting to extract more from the peasants and workers who lived and worked in their areas of responsibility. Like the institutions to which they were responsible, the political actors at the intermediate level were all part of the state machinery, and wished to use it to further their own power and that of the state they served and depended upon.

It was at the village and township level that politics became crucial for the survival of the state for persons could decide to withhold their labour and produce from the state and thus drain away its resources. The responsi-

---

173   Details in Tin Maung Maung Than, 'Burma in 1983: From Recovery to Growth?', in Institute of Southeast Asian Studies, *Southeast Asian Affairs 1984* (Singapore: Institute of Southeast Asian Studies, 1984), pp. 116-118.

174   *The Working People's Daily*, 13 Oct. 1983.

bility given by the state to Party or mass and class organisations at township and village tract or urban ward was that of convincing people at the local level that it was in their interest to support the state voluntarily. Here, as in comparable political systems, it was the state's intention to draw people into participation in administration which 'may [have] serve[d] as an informational mechanism, may [have] aid[ed] in legitimizing the regime in the citizen's eyes and may [have] be[en] used to augment an inadequate administrative apparatus in distributional and supervisory activities in society.'[175] However, it was difficult to know to what extent the state had been able to legitimate itself in the eyes of the bulk of the population and thus ensure its dominance and perpetuation. Personal observations made in the 1970s and 1980s, and research by others, suggested that the language of the state was almost universally accepted and its symbols and ceremonies were widely followed.[176] The all-encompassing ideology of the Party appeared to be reflected in public and private discourse and, at least at the verbal level, its message was accepted. People seemed also to have developed a capacity to accept with resignation the gap that existed between the ideals and gaols of the state and the actual behaviour of its institutions and personnel. Most people had contact with the Party and the People's Councils in their daily lives, and the local agents of the state who lived in the community were recognised and used as intermediaries with the authorities at the middle and top levels of the state. For better or worse, the state was accepted as inevitable and it dominated other institutions. Its form and management, however, was to be severely tested in 1988.

---

175   Friedgut, *Political Participation in the USSR*, p. 29.

176   Supported by the research of Khin Maung Kyi, 'Indians in Burma: Problems of an Alien Subculture in a Highly Integrating Society', in K. Sandhu and S. Mani (eds), *Indians in Southeast Asia* (Singapore: Times Academic Press, 1993), pp. 625-66.

6

THE STATE REDUX, 1988-2008

The bankruptcy of socialist Burma

If, as it appeared, the modern state was re-established by the mid-1980s in a new guise on the foundations of its monarchical and colonial predecessors, its ability to govern Myanmar effectively, as opposed to merely presiding over it, remained in doubt, particularly in the more remote and inaccessible border areas where Communist and ethnically-designated insurgents maintained control. While the army persisted slowly and deliberately to wrest control from its armed opponents who had the advantage of sanctuaries and supporters in neighbouring countries, the state faced two other challenges that soon threatened to overwhelm it as Myanmar entered a second quarter century of socialist autarky. One was the challenge of financing itself while managing the economy to achieve economic growth. The other was the challenge of renewing its leadership in order to adapt to new domestic and international economic, social, and political challenges. Constructed in a period of ideological optimism to steer a command economy largely unaffected by international trends, the state found itself caught in a dilemma of its own making. Having attempted largely to opt out of international economy, it eventually discovered that it was almost as susceptible to global forces as states that had thoroughly integrated into international capitalist networks. The urgent necessity of reforming the economy, while preserving the political institutions built over the previous quarter century, was realised too late for the state's ageing managers to take effective action. Events would soon do that for them unbidden, and the state's crisis in 1988 proved to be another watershed in its evolution.

It was public disorder that ultimately created that crisis, but the process of change in the state began with the culmination of one of the fundamental dilemmas of socialist autarky. The financial position of the regime, always precarious, was dire by the mid-1980s. The attempt to generate the economic surplus expected to flow to the state by nationalisation of the remaining foreign and privately owned businesses and investment in the 1960s failed, and then an alternative source of investment capital attempted from the mid-1970s, acceptance foreign assistance and international loans, also proved an inadequate strategy. A decade later, when the repayment of international loans was due to commence and the rewards for previous investment received, there was little to show except US$5.679mn of foreign debt and increasing difficulties in finding the means to repay international creditors.[1] Having practised financial and fiscal prudence and austerity for 26 years, the regime had no reserves or resources on which to draw in a time of crisis.

While the government kept this information secret and failed to take timely action to correct the situation, the social and economic condition of many people, never much above subsistence at the best of times, deteriorated, especially in urban areas. Food prices increased while wages remained stagnant and unemployment and under-employment grew. As table 6.1 shows, the official consumer price index, essentially based on Yangon market prices, had been relatively stable until about 1985, but nearly doubled in the final three years of the decade, with no compensating increases in wages or earnings. Even members of the military, political, and economic elite, living in an official economy that had been marked by abstemiousness and frugality for most of the post-war era, managed to survive only by trading on the black market the few benefits they received from army and Party special stores and outlets. By the mid-1980s, the state itself was unable to function without recourse to petty illegal trading and frequent 'donations' from its supporters and clients.[2] Ironically, given the military origins of the socialist state, the army undermined the last prop of the economy, the black market, by hindering the smuggling of medicines and manufactured goods from Thailand in exchange for Myanmar's timber,

---

1   As of 31 March 1989. Ministry of Finance and Planning, *Economic and Social Indicators (Restricted)*, [Yangon:] March 1990, p. 21. The debt service ratio rose from 27.19 per cent in 1982-83 to 58.25 per cent in 1986-87. Ibid., p. 22.

2   Kyaw Yin Hlaing, "Reconsidering the Failure of the Burma Socialist Programme Party Government to Eradicate Internal Economic Impediments", *South East Asian Research*, 11, 1 (March 2003), pp. 5-58.

6.1.   Consumer Price Index, 1979-1989

(Base year 1985/86=100)

	Consumer Price Index	Annual Increase (%)
1979	73.33	6.1
1980	74.07	1.0
1981	74.28	0.3
1982	77.12	4.2
1983	81.77	5.6
1984	85.73	4.8
1985	91.57	6.8
1986	100.00	9.2
1987	123.94	23.9
1988	144.78	16.8
1989	184.15	27.2

Source: Table 9.1 Consumer Price Index, in Ministry of Planning and Finance, *Economic and Social Indicators (Restricted)*, (Yangon: March 1990), p. 25.

cattle, and minerals. A major consequence of the army's rejuvenated efforts in the mid-1980s to capture and close the cross-border trading points ('gates'), through which the Karen [Kayin] National Union (KNU) and other anti-regime armies generated much of their revenue, was to deny the population essential consumer goods.[3]

In the straitened financial circumstances of a state unable to purchase internationally spare parts and raw materials for Myanmar's few functioning industries, the military solution to one of the remaining political problems merely generated a new and more complex set of issues because of their interrelated characteristics. Near total state control was leading to near total state collapse. The government destroyed its financial credibility with the public as it sought to constrain the inflationary forces by attempting to control the money supply. However, as Myanmar did not have a sophisticated banking and financial sector, the only way of doing that was to demonetise the currency, as had been last done in 1964. On 3 November 1985 approximately 25 per cent of all currency in circulation, in the form

3   The army launched new offensives against the KNU and other insurgent groups in the mid-1980s. The KNU, consequently, was weakened financially and military at this time. Amnesty International received allegations about human rights abuses in Myanmar from 1984 from supporters of insurgent armies who fled into neighbouring states, particularly Thailand. See Amnesty International ASA a6/03.87: "Allegations of Extraterritorial Executions, Torture and Ill Treatment in the Socialist Republic of the Union of Burma.", September 1987. As noted in this report, during the 12 months between March 1986 and March 1987, the army was involved in 32 major battles among more than 3000 encounters with insurgent groups.

of 20, 50 and 100 kyat notes, became worthless, and only partial compensation was provided those whose capital was abolished.[4]

From about 1983, the official Gross Domestic Product (GDP) growth rate barely kept pace with the population increase and became negative by 1986-87. GDP per capita in constant prices fell from Kt 1,510 in 1985/86 to Kt 1,198 in 1988/89, a fall of more than 20 per cent.[5] Agricultural production stagnated as the government could no longer afford to import fertiliser and pesticides. Contributing to the country's international financial dilemmas was the fact that Myanmar, for the first time in its history, became a net importer of petroleum products in the last years of the 1970s, and the government's inability to purchase adequate petrol and other fuels contributed to the general run-down of the economy as the 1980s progressed. Official foreign exchange reserves by the third quarter of 1987 had fallen to a mere $23.8 mn, barely enough to cover one month's trading.[6]

Faced with the inability of the state adequately to compensate its own staff, employees in the government bureaucracy, party, and army created coping mechanisms that protected their incomes and, they hoped, their pensions. This behaviour by the political elite compounded the problems of the state. 'Triple grazing', a favoured device whereby an army officer would get himself posted to a civilian government role in his region and also to a position in a state-owned economic enterprise regardless of competence or training, became common. With three incomes, he and his family could survive, but if he lost his post, degradation loomed. As a consequence, an additional practice flourished, known in Myanmar as *ma lok, ma shot, ma pyot*—'don't do any work, don't get implicated—and don't get fired'. The state bureaucracy and its extended economic decision networks essentially became paralysed with even the minor decisions being passed up to 'higher

---

4   Tin Maung Maung Than, *State Dominance in Myanmar: The Political Economy of Industrialisation* (Singapore: Institute of Southeast Asian Studies, 2007), p. 193, fn.136, and p. 239.

5   Ministry of Finance and Planning, *Economic and Social Indicators*, p. 2. These figures are subject to dispute and are, at best, approximations. Underlying the collapse of the economy was a collapse in the capacity of the government to gather reliable economic data from which to extrapolate a realistic understanding of actual conditions.

6   Economist Intelligence Unit, *Thailand, Burma: Country Report*, no. 4, 1989 (London), p. 31; according to government figures, reserves stood approximately a year later at Kyat 346.6 mn or US$53.2mn at the official exchange rate. Ministry of Planning and Finance, *Economic and Social Indicators*, tables 8.6 and 8.7, pp. 23 and 24.

authority'. Faced with a serious economic crisis, the state machinery failed. This was blamed on the allegedly prevailing cultural notion of *ana de*,[7] but it was the structure of the state rather a unique Myanmar folk manifestation that explained state failure.

The political upheaval of 1988 resulted from a combination of these systemic problems coupled with several specific ones. As noted, the trigger was an international financial crisis, the inability of the state to service its international debt, but inflation and economic stagnation, fuelled by the inability of the state to import essential consumer goods and raw materials for industry, brought the people out into the streets. Unemployment grew as factories closed, and, as table 6.2 reveals, a further reversal in Myanmar's terms of trade in the 1980s compounded these problems as the international price for Myanmar's agricultural and timber exports further declined. The value of official imports fell 54.2 per cent between 1981 and 1987 while official exports fell 67.5 per cent in the same period.[8] Myanmar's major providers of credit, particularly Japan, were aware of the country's increasingly perilous financial position. In March 1987 the Japanese government, the source of nearly half of Myanmar's international credit, threatened to terminate its aid programme if major economic reforms were not implemented.[9] As a badge of failure of the socialist path chosen in 1962, in 1987 the United Nations, in a move designed to achieve debt relief, designated the country a Least Developed Country or LDC. The bracketing of Myanmar with the poorest African nations was deeply humiliating for many Myanmar citizens. The state that had sought financial independence from 1948 onwards learned the lesson that in the modern world foreign capital and trade are essential for maintaining viability, if at the cost of some degree of autonomy.[10]

The generation that had taken Myanmar to independence after the Second World War, had led the country during the civil war and then through the travails of socialism, realised in 1987 that it had little time remaining to

---

7   To be restrained from acting for fear of offending.

8   Economist Intelligence Unit, *Country Profile: Thailand, Burma, 1988-1989* (London, 1988), p. 59.

9   David I. Steinberg, 'Democracy, Power, and the Economy in Myanmar: Donor Dilemmas', *Asian Survey*, Vol. 31, 8 (August 1991), pp. 729-42; see also David I. Steinberg, 'Japanese Economic Assistance to Burma: Aid in the 'Tarengashi' Manner?' *Crossroads*, 5:2 (1990).

10   For a fuller discussion of the basis of the 1988 financial collapse of the state, see Tin, *State Dominance*, pp. 284-336.

6.2.   Terms of Trade, 1974 to 1989

	Export Unit Price Index	Import Unit Price Index	Terms of Trade
1974/75	84.6	57.4	147.4
1975/76	82.0	67.7	121.1
1976/77	85.1	78.5	108.4
1977/78	92.6	81.2	114.0
1978/79	100.1	88.7	112.9
1979/80	107.8	89.9	119.0
1980/81	125.1	92.6	135.1
1981/82	135.2	97.7	138.4
1982/83	109.8	98.2	111.8
1983/84	110.8	98.8	112.2
1984/85	115.7	99.5	116.3
1985/86	100.0	100.0	100.0
1986/87	82.5	100.6	82.0
1987/88	68.1	103.6	65.7
1988/89	83.4	112.2	74.3

(1985/86 = 100)

Source: Table 7.4 Terms of Trade, in *Economic and Social Indicators (Restricted)* (Yangon: March, 1990), p. 17.

attempt to reverse the decline of the state and nation before revolutionary pressures overwhelmed them. A generational shift was about to take place in which none of the major actors in the development of the state since independence would survive in any significant role. Chairman Ne Win unwittingly proclaimed the end of the old order on 10 August 1987. He called a joint meeting of the Central Committee of the Burmese Socialist Programme Party (BSPP) and the central organs of state power, the various People's Councils, and instructed them to develop plans for economic and political reform within one year. U Ne Win underscored the need for change to keep abreast of new conditions, but the leisurely timetable he set suggests he did not fully appreciate the imminence of the peril the state faced.[11] Having brought no younger and more dynamic individuals into his inner circle, despite intentions to bring educated technocrats into the party leadership, U Ne Win continued to surround himself with his elderly former military associates who were unable or unwilling to question

---

11   Tin Maung Maung Than, 'Burma in 1987: Twenty-Five Years after the Revolution', in Mohammed Ayoob and Ng Chee Yuen, eds., *Southeast Asian Affairs 1988* (Singapore: Institute of Southeast Asian Studies, 1988), p. 90; Min Maung Maung, *The Tatmadaw and Its Leadership Role in National Politics* (Yangon: Ministry of Information, News and Periodicals Enterprises, 1993), p. 270.

his edicts. When he was not available, as in April 1988 when he took his customary European holiday, little was done.

The economic success that China had begun to achieve under the leadership of Deng Xiaoping, and the beginnings of serious economic reform in Vietnam and other socialist countries, may have provided a broad, if imprecise, guide to the steps that U Ne Win and his colleagues saw as necessary for economic renewal and political preservation. Decisions made in the second half of 1987 would suggest this was the case, but the inconsistent and haphazard manner of their application demonstrated that the capacity to develop and implement effective policies was lacking. The domination of the decision making process by the 78-year-old Chairman Ne Win perhaps made this inevitable. The government's credibility with the public was as low as its confidence in its own ability to continue effectively to govern while reforming the economy.

For the next twelve months after the Party Chairman's call for reforms, the normal tedium of annual meetings and public celebrations of previous achievements, real and illusory, was lost in a rush of unexpected developments, many prompted by the government itself. U Ne Win's call for reforms resulted in economic speculation, driving up the prices of everyday necessities. Inflation, fuelled by uncertainty, was thus exacerbated. Rumours spread that the government was about to declare a third demonetisation of bank notes. On 29 August 1987, the official media denied this. In the first step in what many hoped would be further liberalisation of the economy, the formal state monopoly of trade of seven key items was ended three days later, effectively, but temporarily, decontrolling the price of rice and other basic commodities. This in turn further encouraged inflation as private traders began buying ever scarcer goods, hoping to create windfall profits in the future.

The government then undercut what little public confidence remained when, on 5 September, it announced the overnight demonetisation of larger denomination banknotes. Unlike the demonetisation in 1985, on this occasion no partial compensation was offered to cushion the effective confiscation of the people's liquid assets. Even smaller denomination banknotes such as 25 and 35 kyat were liquidated. While many believed that the primary reason for both demonetisations was a crude attempt to control inflation, or to confiscate the profits of black marketeers and commodity speculators, there were apparently other factors considered. One was the alleged imminent entry into circulation of thousands of counterfeit kyat notes by the KNU in an attempt to undermine the currency.[12] Whether caused by the civil war impinging again on the economy or other reasons, the effect of the second demonetisation, following the official pledge that it would not happen, was devastating. The next day students, apparently spontaneously as they were unable to pay new term fees and expenses, demonstrated and schools and universities across the country closed for several weeks.[13]

Chairman Ne Win announced further liberalisation measures on 9 October when he called on the BSPP Central Committee to speed economic reforms, including the legalisation of private business concerns. By the end of the month, schools and universities had reopened, and there were small student demonstrations again. However, stability seemed to have been re-established, but the underlying national malaise was underscored by the United Nations declaration on 11 December of the country's LDC status. The government was unable to improve the economic position of its increasingly demoralised and dwindling ranks of supporters, but merely resorted to the then hollow exhortations to work harder and sacrifice more for the development of the state. It was obvious that even the government did not believe its own words and statistics. The disaster created by the *htan-ta-bin sa-nit* (one palm tree system), the alleged practice of climbing one palm tree to survey an entire township to estimate the level of agricultural production, could no longer be hidden. This expression symbolised the fabricated statistics that passed through government and Party reporting chains, resulting in unreliable national accounts and a government that was unaware of the full dimensions of economic decline.

March of the year 1988, the year that marked the golden jubilee of the 1300 (1938) *ayeidawpun* (uprising) when students and workers forced the parliamentary collapse of the government of Dr Ba Maw, marked the next step in the termination of the old regime. Whereas the last five months of 1987 convincingly demonstrated the floundering economic management of the government, events between March and September 1988 showed that it was incapable of maintaining public order without resort to extreme physical coercion. On 12 March, a brawl broke out in a tea shop near the Yangon Institute of Technology (YIT) between Institute students and local youths. This sort of incident in previous years would have remained unreported and little noticed but now became a major *cause célèbre* because of the govern-

12 Tin Maung Maung Than, 'Burma in 1987', p. 91; Min Maung Maung, *Tatmadaw and Its Leadership Role*, p. 271.
13 Tin Maung Maung Than, 'Burma in 1987', p. 92.

ment's incompetent handling of its consequences as well as the disbelieving mood of the public. One student was injured in the incident and the police initially arrested and then released an alleged culprit related to a local government official. The next day students protested at the release and the police responded with gunfire, killing one student. Institute students, soon joined by colleagues from other tertiary institutions in the capital, demonstrated against the government and the police. Two days later riot police, known as *Lon Htein*, surrounded YIT and stormed the campus.[14] During the three intervening days between the tea shop brawl and the campus raid, the government claimed that there were

... 15 cases of arson, 2 of attempted arson, 86 of vandalism of peoples' [i. e., government] property and 15 of looting of co-operative stores[,] occur[rences] involving a loss to the State of K3,775,000. Out of 127 cognizable cases reported to the Police were cases under [the] arms Act and of causing grievous hurt (sic).[15]

---

14   The events of March to September 1988 are described in a number of sources. See Vince Boudreau, *Resisting Dictatorship: Repression and Protest in Southeast Asia* (New York: Cambridge University Press, 2004), pp. 84-102 and 190-214; Bertil Lintner, *Outrage: Burma's Struggle for Democracy* (Hong Kong: Review Publishing Company, 1989); Kyaw Yin Hlaing, 'Burma: Civil Society Skirting Regime Rules', in Muthiah Alagappa, ed., *Civil Society and Political Change in Asia: Expanding and Contracting Democratic Space* (Stanford: Stanford University Press, 2004), pp. 389-418; Maung Maung, *The 1988 Uprising in Burma* (New Haven: Yale Southeast Asia Studies Monograph No. 49, 1999); Martin Smith, *Burma: Insurgency and the Politics of Ethnicity* (London: Zed Press, revised edition 1999), Chapter 17, pp. 355-73; Min Maung Maung, *Tatmadaw Amyotha Nainghgnanyei Uhsaunghmu Ahkan Kana* (Min Maung Maung, *The Army's National Political Leadership Role*) (Yangon: News and Periodicals Enterprises, July 1995), Chapter 44, pp. 292-300); James F. Guyot, 'Burma in 1988: Perestroika with a Military Face', in Ng Chee Yuen, ed., *Southeast Asian Affairs 1989* (Singapore: Institute of Southeast Asian Studies, 1989), pp. 107-33; and Mary P. Callahan, 'When Soldiers Kill Civilians: Burma's Crackdown in 1988 in Comparative Perspective' in James T. Siegel and Audrey R. Kahin, eds, *Southeast Asian over Three Generations: Essays Presented to Benedict R. O'G. Anderson* (Ithaca, New York: Cornell University Southeast Asia Program, 2003), pp. 331-46. Regardless of the degree to which various authors attribute the cause of the demonstrations to economic, political, or ideological (i.e. 'pro-democracy') motives, there is little dispute among all sources about the events which took place between March and September. Estimates of casualties widely differ, however, as does acceptance of alleged first hand accounts subsequently retold to journalists. Discussions with persons living in Myanmar during the events can lead to very differing accounts. Some by both government and political leaders and former student sources are radically disparate and scarcely creditable.

15   Min Maung Maung, *Tatmadaw and Its Leadership Role*, pp. 272-3.

The protests spread across the city and the police and army responded with force in a number of locations, most famously at the so-called White Bridge in Inya Lake near the main campus of Yangon Arts and Sciences University. Retired Brigadier Aung Gyi subsequently claimed in an open letter to U Ne Win that 283 persons were killed and several female students raped, though no corroborating evidence was ever presented. After several months' delay, a government appointed commission confirmed that 41 persons died, having been arrested and then locked in a police van where they suffocated.[16]

The return of army rule

The following six months culminated in a nearly complete breakdown of public order as the institutions of the state in many regions and at all levels ceased to function. This period also saw the final collapse of the official economy. The result was that the army once more seized power and created the political, administrative, and economic structures that were to guide the state for the following two decades, if not longer. While the March teashop incident and subsequent demonstrations and violence appeared to have been contained, in Yangon and other cities during the following months there was a series of expressions of public disaffection. These grew increasingly violent, testing the capacity of the state to maintain social order. In Yangon, Mandalay, Pyi, Taunggyi, and other towns and cities in central and northern Myanmar, there were increasing signs of the collapse of public order as economic necessity, petty complaints, and religious tensions exploded in June and early July into demonstrations and riots.

The lassitude of the state was an expression of the disaffection of its own employees and agents. After purging of members of the BSPP who genuinely believed in socialism, the leadership of the party and the state came from persons who felt they were working for an ideological illusion. Having been unable to support themselves and their families at a satisfactory level without resort to petty corruption or 'triple grazing', the belief that public action would lead to both public and private benefits dissipated. When called upon to make decisions and seize the initiative in solving local problems, village and township officials in various parts of the administra-

---

16   Aung Gyi letter 8. 6. 88. He based his claims on a number of sources, especially the comments of the British, American and German ambassadors. The British ambassador gave the figure of 42 total dead including the initial fatality, a figure later confirmed in a government commissioned report issued in June.

tion took no action. Avoiding decisions, blaming higher authorities, and doing nothing became the norm in many areas. The internal life of the BSPP reflected the lassitude of government agents and agencies. While others waited for Chairman Ne Win to tell them what to do and how to do it, the decrepit social conditions of the people remained unaddressed, and the public began to take their revenge on the state, its agents, and eventually each other.

Finally, Ne Win acted on 23 July. He announced that he and other senior party and government leaders were resigning from office, leaving the party he had led for 26 years. The crisis of the state would have to be resolved without him. His unexpected departure speech at an Extraordinary BSPP Congress called to deal with the growing social unrest changed the nature of the informal public debate that had seized the country since his announcement the previous August of the need to consider economic and political reforms. Until then, public protests had been geared to specific issues such as student rights, economic grievances, or Buddhist-Muslim religious tensions. A proposal by U Ne Win, rejected by the BSPP Congress, for a referendum on whether the public wished to revert to a multi-party political system raised political change and the demand for restoration of multi-party politics to the centre of political attention. The unwillingness of the BSPP Extraordinary Congress to consider conceding power in an orderly process, or propose a viable means of resolving the current crisis, resulted in growing public disorder that only the eventual military takeover ended nearly two months later.

The evolution of the public protests from essentially specific student or local grievances to broader and more fundamental political and constitutional demands took place simultaneously with the growth of new or reactivated political forms and institutions in Myanmar. Initially these centred on the underground and largely informal urban 'reading groups' or 'discussion groups', some loosely affiliated with Communists or disgruntled socialists, who felt that the BSPP under U Ne Win's military-dominated leadership could never create the socialist order that they sought. Soon there emerged a number of other, more overt efforts at political organisation in the form of nascent student unions and trade unions, growing in time to include strike centres and neighbourhood protection committees, as the protests escalated, public order deteriorated, and violence grew. It was only late in the process of demonstration and suppression that formal political parties emerged, and then it was in incoherent and often discredited forms that owed more to Myanmar's political past than to the new issues and personalities of the country in the late 1980s.

The events of late July to 18 September when the army conducted a putsch against moribund remnants of the BSPP government and the anarchic forces in the streets are complex and their meaning much disputed. In outline, there were increasing public protests and demonstrations, eventually bringing civil servants and former supporters of the regime into the ranks of the protesters. A general strike was announced for 8 August over the Burmese Service of the BBC and via other international radio stations and a burgeoning domestic independent print media. The administration essentially collapsed with government shops, offices, and factories looted. The government—despite the efforts of the initial successor of Chairman Ne Win and President San Yu, U Sein Lwin, to reassert the authority of the state by force, including indiscriminate shootings as well as more targeted arrests of erstwhile leaders—proved incapable of stemming the initially largely peaceful and orderly demonstrations. Looting and plunder grew and individuals became caught up in local vendettas with accusations leading to decapitations and other violence as public institutions such as prisons, psychiatric hospitals, and the police ceased to function, and markets and shops closed or emptied.

After the failure of U Sein Lwin to re-establish order, following a brief hiatus the only nominal civilian in the old regime, Dr Maung Maung, was appointed by the Party to replace him. Maung Maung's government reversed the strategy of force chosen by U Sein Lwin's administration and attempted to regain public trust in the government by making measured concessions to political demands, including the release a number of prominent individuals. However, those concessions, including an eventual decision that a referendum on the one party system was unnecessary and a pledge to hold multi-party elections within three months of 11 September, did not satisfy the spokespersons who had emerged during August to attempt to lead the protests. By then, feeling the strength of public opinion and Western embassies behind them, incipient public leaders were demanding the formation of a new, interim government, though in unspecified terms. However, the inability of the various former political leaders and would-be political leaders to present a united front created both an opportunity for the government and a problem. Had they wished to negotiate an end to the protests with the ostensible leaders, as it is claimed they did, it was difficult to believe that such an agreement could have been made to work, given the discordant relations among the various actors and their lack of an organisational relationship with the public. When the army eventually did move against them, suppressing the anti-government movement was made easier by its lack of effective organisation or resources.

The absence of effective organisations and their lack of resources encouraged a degree of factionalism among the student political leaders as well as among older and experienced politicians. The financial and other assistance they received from Western embassies, and the publicity that leaders received via the international media, provided incentives for escalating demands and avoiding compromises of the kind that Dr Maung Maung extended. The lack of government credibility also meant that ending the demonstrations peacefully was becoming increasingly unlikely as the army's reserves of money, petrol, and other supplies were running very low and had to be replenished if anarchy was to be avoided. Moreover, markets were largely denuded of stocks and the population of Yangon and other cities were facing the prospect of an extreme food shortage and the collapse of public services.[17] The situation prompted the Minister of Defence, General Saw Maung, and the Director of the Directorate Defence Services (Intelligence) (DDS[I]), Colonel Khin Nyunt, to report to former General Ne Win that order could not be restored by the civilian government. Given the former Party Chairman's personal authority, despite his departure from formal office, his stewardship was still sought from his former subordinates. Following the report from top two military men, Dr Maung Maung and others were summoned to a meeting at the former President's residence and the decision was made by U Ne Win for the army to take power and the BSPP to be dissolved. U Ne Win remained a reference point for the military after the putsch, but slowly his influence and contact with events waned as he entered his eighties.

The seizure of power by the army, accompanied by renewed coercive measures, quickly ended the popular protests. Pledging that it would maintain Dr Maung Maung's promise to hold multi-party elections eventually, the army removed the barricades that had sprung up across Yangon and other cities, reopened markets, ordered civil servants to return to work, and told residents to clear up their neighbourhoods. The new military government assumed the title of the *Naingngantaw Nyein Wut Pi Phya Hmu Te*

---

17 Workers had seized control of the country's only oil refinery and production had been halted. The army also did not have cash with which to pay its troops or purchase supplies by the middle of September.

Hsauk Yei Konsi. This translates literally as the 'Council to Build/Make a Composed/Calm and Tranquil/Peaceful[18] State/Nation', but it was officially translated as the State Law and Order Restoration Council, creating an acronym seized upon for its Orwellian overtones by the foreign press and Western diplomats, SLORC.

The weeks leading up to the establishment of the SLORC government marked the most violent period in the urban history of Myanmar since the Second World War and the post-independence civil war. It is impossible to know how many were killed by the army and the police or by the enraged public and various political and criminal groups and individuals. One can find lurid descriptions of bloody massacres but it is very difficult to establish firm evidence for fatalities. Estimates range from 10,000 or more to the government's claim that the army shot 516 while denying that 3,000 or 4,000 died.[19] As happened several times between March and September 1988, an unknown number of persons were arrested following the putsch, most to be released reasonably promptly but some, accused of being leaders, remaining in detention for several years. A number of students and other young activists, perceiving that their colleagues' efforts to change the government would fail, or that they themselves were facing arrest, began leaving Yangon and other cities for the camps of various insurgent groups, mainly along the border with Thailand. Some had gone several months before the putsch. By 12 November 1988, the government claimed at least 11,455 had done so.[20]

While the patterns of urban political behaviour that had persisted throughout the years of Revolutionary Council and BSPP rule were ended and new political institutions and expectations were being formed, the fun-

18   According to *Judson's Burmese-English Dictionary*, the latter phrase implies that such a state is one that succeeds a period of anarchy and disorder (Rangoon: Baptist Board of Publications, 2nd printing, 1966). More modern dictionaries than Judson's, which was compiled in the early 19th century, make no reference to this implication. One source recalls the SLORC called initially the State Peace and Tranquillity Council on government radio.

19   'General Saw Maung: 'I Saved Burma'', *Asiaweek*, 17 January 1989, reprinted in *State Law and Order Restoration Council Chairman Commander in Chief of the Defence Services General Saw Maung's Addresses* (Yangon: News and Periodicals Enterprises, 7 January 1991), pp. 47-50. Dr Callahan suggests that 'several thousand', 'at least ten thousand' and 'at least three thousand probably died in Rangoon alone, and hundreds (maybe thousands) died in … other cities'. Callahan, "When Soldiers Kill Civilians", pp. 332; 333; fn. 4 and fn. 5, p. 333.

20   Min Maung Maung, *Tatmadaw Amyotha Nainghgnanyei Uhsaunghmu Ahkan Kana*, p. 311.

damental problem that had challenged the state since independence, Communist and ethnically-labelled insurgent movements, remained ongoing. Fortunately for the state managers, the Mon New State Party (MNSP) and the KNU, though nominal allies in the National Democratic Front (NDF), were fighting each other for control of the smuggling gate at Myawati on the Thai border during the height of the urban turmoil. Similarly, the Burma Communist Party (BCP) seemed initially to be taken unawares by the developments in the cities until very near the establishment of the SLORC. In mid-September, the BCP began to probe army positions in the eastern Shan State and fighting continued in that area until the end of the month.[21] Earlier, in the midst of the urban unrest, the army had also been involved in fighting in the South Eastern region against KNU and MNSP insurgents as well as small groups of BCP in the southern Tanintharyi area. Between 5 August and 5 September, according to the army, there were 24 military engagements resulting in the death of 47 insurgents and 8 soldiers plus another 16 government casualties.[22]

Those involved in the urban events of 1988, from octogenarians who had participated in the independence campaigns of the 1940s to the students who appeared on the scene for the first time in the wake of the 1987 demonetisation and 1988 tea shop fracas, had created a new political situation. However, neither they nor the army that unilaterally assumed power with the acquiescence, if not the encouragement, of the old regime were certain as to how to respond to the opportunities and challenges they faced. All of the nominally civilian political groups and leaders realised that they had to deal with an army they did not trust. The military leadership drew a number of lessons from the events of 1988, the most fundamental of which was that the army was the saviour of the nation and the only institution that stood in the way of anarchy and national disintegration. This became and remained their justification for seizing and holding power, claiming that while other political actors were motivated by partisan interests, only they represented a supra-political 'national politics'. All others were practicing a lesser, 'party' or 'liberal', politics that, for the sake of the state, had to be subordinated to 'national politics'. For the Communist and

---

21   Ibid., p. 312; also Bertil Lintner, *The Rise and Fall of the Communist Party of Burma (BCP)*, (Ithaca, NY: Southeast Asia Program, Cornell University, 1990), pp. 44-6.

22   Min Maung Maung, *Tatmadaw Amyotha Nainghgnanyei Uhsaunghmu Ahkan Kana*, p. 304.

ethnically-designated insurgent groups, the events of 1988 also created new and equally uncertain circumstances.

The state and its supporters, as well as those who wished to capture or change it, had entered into uncharted territory for which they were little prepared. The chaos which occurred on the streets of Yangon in 1988 was soon replaced by less overtly violent but no less complex politics, as it soon appeared to be a situation in which the blind fought the blind to define how the state and its institutions would be reshaped. High, often unrealistic expectations and suspicions of low cunning and conspiratorial plotting clashed repeatedly in the years to come. The conflict which emerged, and received the most international attention, saw an asymmetrical political contest in which possession of the state and its most crucial institution, the army, confronted softer and ultimately feebler political forces, albeit ones with powerful external allies. Other, more deeply rooted and long-standing conflicts began to be resolved as compromise and cooperation replaced armed conflict in the country's more remote regions.

Explanations for the occurrences of 1987-88 have been few. Most have attributed the events to the incompetence or the alleged brutality of the last years of the Ne Win-BSPP regime. However, as the regime had been displaying signs of growing dysfunctionalism for a number of years and predictions that its end was nigh were heard prior to 1988, this does not explain why that year saw the end of the socialist dream. Historians in the future will be able to study in detail the underlying forces at work. They will have to examine among others the thesis advanced above about the importance of state finance that triggered U Ne Win's call for revisions to the prevailing order. The admission in August 1987 that the regime needed to reform itself may have been as important as the economic crisis itself in emboldening students and others to challenge it.[23] Conceding that the regime had lost its way destroyed the last shreds of BSPP's credibility as its socialist élan, never strong, dissipated. The top of the party, captured initially by purblind ideologues and subsequently by the army, rather than led by civilians closer to the economic reality of the society that they governed as in China or Vietnam, had stifled internal party debate until it was too late.

Historians looking at the near collapse of the state in 1987-8 from the perspective of social change and historical contingency may highlight other

---

23   Crane Brinton, echoing Alex de Tocqueville, suggests in *Anatomy of Revolution* (New York: Random House, revised edition, 1965) that one of the first stages of a revolutionary process is the admission by the old order that they had lost faith in themselves and in their policies.

aspects of the events of those years. Marxist historians might draw attention to the fact that one of the consequences of the incompetence of management of the Burmese Road to Socialism was that such economic activity as took place during the latter years of the regime went underground into the black market. As the official economy unwound for a variety of reasons related to the army's success in the civil war and the loss of the country's energy self-sufficiency, the blackmarketeers, who were essentially a formally illegal but increasingly indispensable bourgeoisie, rose up to demand the legalisation of their position and given security to their operations. Myanmar had reached its Cromwellian moment. Interests in neighbouring Thailand and elsewhere assisted as they wished to open up the Myanmar economy in order to develop trade and gain access to raw materials. The speed with which Thailand and other regional governments endorsed the political change that occurred in Yangon lends credence to such a claim, despite the ultimately domestic nature of the crisis of the state in 1988.

The internal structures of the state and the party themselves may also help explain the events of 1988. When the history of the Myanmar Socialist Programme Party is eventually written, its relationship with the army that called for its creation, and the role of General Ne Win, will be an obvious theme to explore. How the party functioned, how it related to the economy and the state bureaucracy, especially the army, created the dynamics of the state between 1962 and 1988. With the benefit of hindsight, one can see how these dynamics were dysfunctional. In outline, one can understand why, but more detailed analysis is needed to develop the full story. The penchant of populist writers and politically constrained journalists is to blame one man; but powerful as he was, it is hard to believe that the crisis of the state in 1988 was the consequence merely of the decisions of General Ne Win.

The renewed contest for state power

The contest for state power which the Second World War had ushered in, and which the army, and those socialists ideologues who joined with it in forming the BSPP, had attempted to end in 1962, was renewed in September 1988 with old and new elements. The old forces were the army (but under renewed leadership), a few former political leaders, some BCP remnants, and multiple ethnically-designated armed insurgents. New elements emerged from efforts to revert to Myanmar's more open and turbulent political past and included students and political parties as well as a variety of exiled individuals and post-Cold War international institutions and actors. The Cold War had permitted the army and the BSPP to isolate domestic political conflicts as long as the Ne Win era governments ensured that Myanmar's politics did not result in a breakup of the state or a radical change in its foreign policy orientation. While all sides in the Cold War were happy to impinge occasionally on Myanmar's domestic politics,[24] neutralist Myanmar was for the major powers and interests a viable proposition in an otherwise complex, potentially dangerous, and politically quiescent region. Myanmar's new domestic political situation roughly coincided with the end of the Cold War, and thus the constraints on outside actors were removed in a way that had not happened since the 1940s and was not anticipated before the fall of the Berlin Wall. Each of the contestants for state power drew its own lessons from the Myanmar's political history and the altered, and often confusing international situation. More important, each drew lessons from the most recent developments, including the causes and consequences of the 1988 crisis of the state. The second post-colonial contest for state power, while marked by a number of arrests and public demonstrations, often violently suppressed, was however much less bloody and destructive than the events of 1948-52.

The looming state crisis and the consequent renewal of the contest for the state was heralded in small but, in retrospect, politically significant ways. Political activity among the former non-Communist civilian political classes displaced by the Revolutionary Council in 1962, and unable to respond following the introduction of the 1974 constitution, was renewed. This time, however, it was conducted from abroad, rather than inside the country—an initial and then unnoticed sign that a new dimension was developing in Myanmar's political life. Some former members of U Nu's defunct Parliamentary Democracy Party established the Committee for the Restoration of Democracy in Burma (CRDB) in the United States on 4 January 1987.[25] That year also saw the publication of the first Amnesty International report criticising the government for the consequences for

---

24   'Troubling the water in order to fish in them,' as Professor John Cady said in his
       lectures in the early 1960s.
25   Martin Smith, *Burma*, 1999, p. 402. See Maung Pyi Thu, *Si Aye Di Bi thomah-
       hut Pyipyei Tit Kyawpyan* (CRDD, Expatriate Return Again) (Yangon: News
       and Periodicals Enterprise, Ministry of Information, 2nd printing, 12 March
       1990) for a government account of the CRDB.

human rights of Myanmar's then 39-year-old civil war.[26] At about the same time, in Yangon, former Brigadier Aung Gyi began circulating open letters to Chairman U Ne Win comparing the economic progress and development of Thailand and Singapore with the backward and stagnant conditions of Myanmar.[27]

The SLORC and the State Peace and Development Council (SPDC). Having initially promised to transfer power to an elected civilian government, the army government began to qualify that offer during the 21 months between assuming power and the holding of elections in May 1990. During that time, the naivety of the proposal advanced by U Ne Win, and maintained by Dr Maung Maung, that a multi-party political system could be restored nearly as easily as the 1962 coup had been conducted became apparent. The tempestuous antagonism towards the old regime expressed by the student and other political leaders after the army putsch, as well as that of Western governments and media, and increasing antagonism towards the army itself as the inheritor and alleged proxy for U Ne Win, became palpable. The *tatmadaw,* or army, previously hailed as the selfless defender of the nation, became described as the oppressor of its population. Increasingly strong allegations were made on the veracity and character of senior state managers, which led eventually to the arrest of a number of civilian political figures in July 1989 that, seen retrospectively, could have been expected. The fact that many political leaders believed, whether erroneously or not, that the army never intended to honour its pledge to open up the political process resulted in their allegations becoming reality.

Abandoning socialist autarky at the same time as attempting political reform, unfettered by the constraints of the BSPP, required the army government to deal with a multiplicity of new forces for which it was little prepared. While the army accepted the new economic policies that the old regime had outlined in its final year, it retained little else from the BSPP era except an underlying ethos of organisational and rhetorical tools. The SLORC assumed all executive, legislative, and judicial powers when it abrogated the 1974 constitution. The courts were reorganised together with the attorney-general's department, the auditor-general's department, and

---

26 Amnesty International ASA a6/03.87: 'Allegations of Extraterritorial Executions, Torture and Ill-treatment in the Socialist Republic of the Union of Burma', September 1987.

27 U Aung Gyi's letters in mimeographed form were widely circulated in Yangon at the time and subsequently, and were eventually translated into English.

state or divisional, township, and ward and people's tract governments, staffed with mainly military officers and trusted civil servants. After the coup, SLORC dismissed many public officials including teachers because of their allegedly doubtful reliability and possible complicity in the August/September demonstrations.[28] For several years martial law was applied, with military courts replacing civilian courts for politically sensitive cases. The idea of a people's administration in contrast to the bureaucratic regime of the colonial state—an idea that had formed part of the underlying rationale of the BSPP order—was abandoned, and the administrative state that had characterised pre-1974 regimes was re-established to the extent possible.

Having concluded that it was the economic lethargy of the BSPP regime, as well as its inability to reach and implement decisions expeditiously, that underlay the crisis the army faced as it assumed state power,[29] the new regime acted initially with a dynamism that no government had demonstrated since the army Caretaker regime thirty years before. The State Law and Order Restoration Council, formed by nineteen senior officers, was chaired by General Saw Maung. Nine of the original SLORC members were regional commanders while the remainder were senior figures in the central command, including the Director of Defence Services Intelligence (DDS[I] or Military Intelligence [MI]) Colonel Khin Nyunt. He assumed the position of First Secretary to the SLORC, from which he developed an extensive range of responsibilities and became the most publicly visible SLORC leader until his removal in 2004. From ten of their number they created a small cabinet of 12, adding a colonel, the Quartermaster General, to manage the economy and foreign investment policy, while placing health and education under a civilian doctor who assumed the title of colonel. The new cabinet distinguished itself from its predecessor not only by its small size but also by the independence, initiative, and relative accessibility that ministers demonstrated in undertaking their responsibilities. That characteristic lasted until 1997 when a much more hierarchical set of relations was created between the top leadership of the government,

---

28   All were required to fill in forms outlining their political views on recent events and most were sent to civil service training camps to be informed of the situation of the country as perceived by the new army rulers.

29   *Tatmataw Thamaing, Part Seven, 1988-1994* (History of the Army, Part 7, 1988-1994) (Yangon: Thatin hnin sanezin lutnan, August 2000) (Yangon: News and Periodicals Enterprises, August 2000), Introduction, pp. hka 1-12.

renamed at that time the State Peace and Development Council (SPDC),[30] and newly appointed, relatively junior ministers.

A number of recommendations for action that the old regime had ignored, or lacked the capacity or political will to implement, such as the relocation of thousands of migrant squatters who had settled in the cemeteries, monasteries and parks of Yangon to new suburbs located miles from the centre of the city, were quickly carried out. There were also massive urban development, clean up and beautification campaigns that entailed significant public works including building walkways and bridges over major thoroughfares, widening and redirecting a number of roads, and building new markets and revitalising public spaces. As the country prepared itself for opening to international tourism, similar schemes were implemented across the country. As many of these projects were carried out with unpaid labour provided by local communities, as had been practiced in Myanmar for many years previously, complaints about the use of forced labour soon were advanced by some of the political activists who had fled to the Thai border. While economic reform and modernisation were primary features of public policy, state and regime security was, and remained, the top government priority. The building of a new brick wall around army headquarters located in the old British military cantonment in central Yangon captured the mood of the period. Similar walls were constructed around other military bases, replacing simple bamboo and wire fences of earlier eras.

The regime's political opponents interpreted these actions as signs of a malicious intention to cling to power indefinitely. What the army explained as prudent preparations for a possible repeat of the assault on the state that occurred in 1988, its critics saw, at best, as signs of panic and overreaction, and at worse, as signs of nefarious intent. Having nearly lost control of the state in 1988, it did not intend facing a second severe challenge to its capacity to defend the state and the state's major institutions and personnel. As the leading personnel explained their interpretation of their situation, the state was under siege from both the political right and the political left, at home and abroad. In a series of speeches, press conferences, and publications for several years after the putsch, SLORC spokesmen reiterated this view. The accounts that received the most publicity were those advanced by Secretary 1, Brigadier General Khin Nyunt, in two lengthy press confer-

---

30   *Naingngan Ayekyan thayayei: hnit hpwanhpyo:yei: Kaungsi*, literally the State/ Nation peaceful pleasant and prosperous developed matter council, was more aptly translated than had been its predecessor.

THE STATE IN MYANMAR

ences and several other presentations. In these, he explained a conspiratorial thesis that the events of 1988 had been orchestrated, exploiting the public's genuine economic distress, by Communist and externally-funded and motivated neo-imperialist foreign forces with the intention of breaking up and subjugating the state that the army was sworn to defend.[31]

Arrogating to themselves a position above party politics, the army insisted its role was by definition apolitical and therefore 'national'. Foreign observers and domestic critics of the regime contended that the army's view that it was facing pressure simultaneously from its old foes, particularly the Communist Party and ethnic insurgents, as well as expatriates in league with Western governments (particularly the United States and the United Kingdom), was obviously an internally inconsistent view. In the official army version of its and Myanmar's history since independence, however, that experience merely confirmed the multiplicity and duplicity of the current enemies they were facing. The senior officer corps repeatedly advanced the thesis that the army was the saviour of the nation and the only institution willing to defend the nationalist cause by defending the territorial integrity, sovereignty, and unity of the state.

The army's view of itself as the saviour of the nation has certain corollaries. One is that politicians are by their nature potentially anti-national as their purpose is to present a partial and partisan view of the national interest that only a supra-political organisation such as the tatmadaw can understand and defend. Striving for power for themselves and their followers, civilian politicians are allegedly willing to accept support from, and therefore obligations to, anti-national interests such as foreign governments that have their own separate ambitions and interests to pursue in opposition to the national interest. Thus the advancing of pro-democracy, anti-army arguments by Myanmar politicians during the 1988 events and subsequently, and the support they received and continued to receive from foreign

---

31   See *The Conspiracy of Treasonous Minions with the Myanmar Naing-ngan and Traitorous Cohorts Abroad* (Yangon: News and Periodicals Enterprise, Ministry of Information, 2nd printing, 7 November 1989) and *Burma Communist Party's Conspiracy to Take Over State Power* (Yangon: News and Periodicals Enterprise, Ministry of Information, 5th printing, 28 November 1989) supplemented by *Web of Conspiracy: Complicated Stories of Treacherous Machinations and Intrigues of BCP UG, DAB, and Some NLD Leaders to Seize State Power* (Yangon: News and Periodicals Enterprise, Ministry of Information, June, 1991) and *Scheming and Activities of the Burma Communist Party Politburo to Seize State Power* (Yangon: News and Periodicals Enterprise, Ministry of Information, 2nd printing, February 1990).

governments after the SLORC took power, demonstrated to the army the unreliability of the politicians who were seeking to overthrow their government and establish a civilian regime. Moreover, to be conciliatory toward one's rivals merely led to additional and unreasonable demands. As an official historian of the events of 1988 wrote,

Government made all concessions short of surrendering power. Protesters never thought of making any concessions once they realised that the government was weak; they began to demand a provisional government. Foreign machinations emerged openly. The worst was for the administrative machinery to have been paralyzed across the whole country and a proliferation of lawlessness and violence.[32]

It is impossible to know to what degree this self-perception of standing above the political fray as an idealistic, unselfish, and sacrificing institution was, and is, believed by the top leadership. Political party leaders and domestic and foreign critics took the view that this was at best self-deception, but more likely an illusion perpetrated in order to cover less worthy motives such as avarice, domination, and fear of punishment for real or alleged human rights violations. Allusions to the holding of Nuremburg type trials for senior army officers,[33] the subsequent development of the International Criminal Court (ICC), and the judicial pursuit of other former military rulers such as Generals Pinochet and Suharto, as human rights replaced security in Western foreign policies, perhaps made the fear of punishment seem real. It helped maintain army unity and obedience to the line of command, so that other sources of rivalry and conflict among senior officers were unable to emerge. Even rank-and-file soldiers came to fear possible conviction because of claims of systematic rape and other human rights violations by the army made by expatriate groups, prominent foreign individuals, and international human rights advocacy organisations.

The SLORC received strong criticism for the army's actions in suppressing the public protests in August and September 1988, especially from the US and British ambassadors. Human rights advocacy organisations and the Western media echoed their condemnation of the violence that occurred as being primarily the responsibility of the regime. Allegations of human rights

---

32   Min Maung Maung, *Tatmadaw and Its Leadership Role*, pp. 277-8.

33   As suggested by former Colonel turned politician U Kyi Maung in 1990 in *AsiaWeek*, 13 July 1990. The allusion to punishment for members of the army after the establishment of a civilian regime was not denied by the most prominent anti-regime politician subsequently. See Daw Aung San Suu Kyi in interviews published in 1997 in *Aung San Suu Kyi, The Voice of Hope (conversations with Alan Clements)* (London: Penguin, 1997), pp. 12, 37.

abuses resulting from the army's increasingly successful military campaigns against the Karen National Union and other ethnic insurgent organisations had grown in volume and frequency from the mid-1980s onwards. After the crisis of 1988, international human rights advocacy groups and Western media focused on these allegations and the imprisonment, often without a public trial by martial law courts, of civilian political activists. Reports based on specific cases of forced labour, rape, theft, and forced relocation that occurred in the midst of military campaigns in conflict zones were published in a way to suggest that these things were occurring in all parts of the country routinely. Moreover, it was implied that such human rights abuses were authorised by the SLORC as an aspect of public policy. The repression of political activists and their campaigns of defiance was depicted as integral to a 'brutal regime'. Some claims were doubtlessly exaggerated, and they were difficult to refute, but there was enough truth to them to cause concern to the army. Events were often retold in multiple reports, swelling their alleged magnitude, and making the distinguishing of truth from fiction became increasingly difficult.

Rather than condemning individual instances of human rights violations as violations of military law and acts that would not be condoned, the government, unused to having its views publicly questioned, often denied they had taken place, or insisted they were a purely internal matter. Thus, there was no plausible defence advanced by the government against widespread claims that human rights violations were integral to state policy. Incapable of getting its side of events understood and accepted by Western media outlets and human rights advocacy organisations, the SLORC concentrated on building its own security. In time, its image became so tarnished that when it did begin to slowly comprehend the public relations aspects of modern government, few critics were willing to listen to or credit their explanations amidst the barrage of condemnation. The army's position came to parallel that of the king's government in the 1880s, as '[e]xplanations would be weakness, and moreover useless to an enemy determined to see only the worst', as Fielding-Hall wrote a century earlier.[34]

---

34   H. Fielding [-Hall], *Thibaw's Queen* (New York and London: Harper and Brothers, 1899), p. 7. Fielding-Hall was describing the newspaper campaigns that preceded the third Anglo-Burmese War and the deposition of King Thibaw. Noting that the government was autocratic and hence likely to have many enemies, Fielding-Hall explained that Britain's newspapers were consequently full of 'the tales of spies whose only concern was to speak evilly.' While Thibaw's supporters remained distant and uncommunicative with his foreign opponents

National security and regime security became and remained the army's first priority after 1988. If the new brick wall around the old Ministry of Defence compound first symbolised these priorities, the move of the administrative capital to the new but unfinished city of Naypyitaw (prosaically named The Capital) in 2006 underscored the continuity of the point.[35] Total armed forces manpower grew rapidly in the first decade of SLORC rule, from approximately 186,000 to 370,000.[36] Growth then halted, and the security forces' total strength was estimated at 428,000 in 2005, of which 350,000 were in the army.[37] The number of regional military commands increased from nine in 1988 to thirteen in 2006 plus ten Light Infantry Divisions.[38] The navy expanded to gain some small capacity for patrolling Myanmar's territorial waters with six bases along Myanmar's extensive coastlines. The air force, which previously had been noteworthy for the antiquity and unreliability of its aircraft, acquired eight MiG 29s from Russia and 50 MiG 21s and other aircraft from China after 1988.[39]

In parallel with the expansion of army manpower and the enhancement of its weapons capability, through the purchase of guns and artillery from a number of countries, the army undertook a major expansion and upgrading of its officer corps. The Defence Services Academy expanded with annual enrolments increasing three or four times and new defence training

and even potential friends, their 'enemies were only too ready to pour their grievances and scandals into our, as they hoped, sympathetic ears, hoping thereby to obtain vengeance on those who had injured them.'

35   See Aung Myoe, *The Road to Naypyitaw: Making Sense of the Myanmar Government's Decision to Move Its Capital.* (Singapore: Asia Research Institute Working Paper Series No. 79, November, 2007).

36   Andrew Selth, *Transforming the Tatmadaw: The Burmese Armed Forces since 1988* (Canberra: Strategic and Defence Studies Centre, Australian National University, 1996).

37   Divided between 350,000 army, 13,000 navy, 12,000 air force, 800 naval infantry, and 107,250 paramilitary troops. The latter were divided between riot police (72,000), militia (35,000), and Pearl and Fishery Ministry police (250). Approximately 100,000 infantry were normally employed as labour gangs for military and state construction projects: International Institute for Strategic Studies, *The Military Balance 2005-2006*, (London: Routledge, October 2005), p. 291. In its annual estimates published for 2008, the IISS stated that the army had taken on an additional 25,000 troops in the intervening three years: *The Military Balance 2008* (London: Routledge, 2008), pp. 396-7. No rationale for the increased estimate is given and discussions in Myanmar suggest that, if anything, the army has reduced its manpower slightly in the intervening years.

38   Ibid. Naypyitaw Command was created in 2006.

39   Ibid., pp. 291-2.

institutions created and old ones revamped.[40] While small numbers of officers had previously been sent for training in the United States, the United Kingdom, West Germany and Australia, after 1988, and the withdrawal of places in those countries, the army sent larger numbers for training in Malaysia, Singapore, India, Pakistan, Russia, the former Yugoslavia, and China. Not only did the officer corps grow in size, there was also a vast increase in senior ranks. Promotions above the rank of colonel were rare in the Burma army before 1988 but now became increasingly common, with most officers aspiring for the rank of Brigadier or Major General, if not higher. The rapid expansion of the officer corps eventually resulted in a glut and several thousand were retired and given civilian positions or dismissed in 2007 with the introduction of strict promotion or dismissal criteria for the senior ranks.

In contrast to the socialist regime where expenditure on the military tended to be commensurate with the capacity of the state to fund requirements,[41] the post-1988 army abandoned fiscal prudence in favour of achieving its goals at the cost of inflation and other state requirements. Expenditure on the army grew from an estimated 2.1 per cent of gross domestic product in 1988 to as high as 3.7 per cent in 1995 before declining to a more modest 1.3 per cent in 2002, the last year for which the Stockholm International Peace Research Institute was willing to make a calculation. As shown in table 6.3, other analysts reach different conclusions. In historic terms, however, these percentages, if reasonably accurate, are relatively modest in comparison with the civil war years or the early 1960s. Similarly, the percentage of the annual government budget spent directly on the military, as shown in table 6.4, was historically in line with pre-1988 budgets going back to the 1950s.[42] There were probably a number of off-budget income and expenditure items for the army, and army personnel seconded to other ministries may have taken their emoluments from non-military sources. Despite the resources the state devoted to the army, many units were essentially self-reliant in terms of growing their own food and tending their own herds and flocks. The army also began developing its own income sources separate from the government

---

40   See Aung Myoe, *Officer Education and Leadership Training in the Tatmadaw: A Survey*. (Canberra: Strategic and Defence Studies Centre, Australian National University, Working Paper No. 346, May 2000.)

41   See R.H. Taylor, 'Burma: Defence Expenditure and Threat Perceptions' in Chin Khin Wah, ed., *Defence Expenditure in Southeast Asia*. (Singapore: Institute of Southeast Asian Studies, 1987), pp. 252-80.

42   See above, p. 254.

6.3.   Estimates of Military Expenditure as a Proportion of GDP, 1988 to 2005

	Percent GDP(a)	Percent GDP(b)	Percent GDP(d)	Percent GDP(e)	Percent GDP(f)	Percent GDP(g)	Percent GDP(h)
1988	2.1						
1989	3.0			3.5			
1990	3.4		4.1	3.6			3.6
1991	3.2		3.9	4.3	7.2		3.6
1992	3.4		4.5	3.7	8.3		2.9
1993	3.5		5.1	4.0	8.8		2.4
1994	3.5		4.6	4.1	7.6		2.6
1995	3.7		4.7	3.9	9.1	6.2	2.7
1996	3.5		4.0		7.6		2.3
1997	2.7		3.6		7.8		1.7
1998	2.3		3.1		7.8		1.5
1999	2.0				7.8		1.5
2000	2.3	2.5					1.2
2001	1.8	1.8					1.1
2002	1.3	1.4					0.9
2003		2.3					0.9
2004		1.9(c)					0.9
2005		1.4(c)					

Sources and notes:

a Stockholm International Peace Research Institute, 2006, online data base, accessed 2006.
b Both current and capital expenditure. International Monetary Fund, *Myanmar: Staff Consultation Report for the 2006 Article IV Consultation.* 20 September 2006. Table 22. Union Government Expenditure by Functional Classification, 2000/01-2006/07, (in percent of GDP), p. 24. Based on data provided by the Myanmar authorities and IMF staff estimates.
c Preliminary
d Stockholm International Peace Research Institute, *SIPRI Yearbook 2000: Armaments, Disarmament and International Security* (Oxford: Oxford University Press, 2000), p. 273, in Andre Selth, *Burma's Armed Forces: Power without Glory* (Norwalk, Conn.: EastBridge, 2002), p. 314.
e *World Military Expenditure and Arms Transfers 1996* (Washington, D. C.: US Arms Control and Disarmament Agency, 1997), p. 63, in Selth, *Burma's Armed Forces*, p. 315.
f *World Military Expenditure and Arms Transfers 1998* (Washington, D. C.: Bureau of Verification and Compliance, State Department, 2000), p. 75, in Selth, *Burma's Armed Forces*, p. 315, and Bureau of Verification and Compliance, State Department website.

budget by establishing a number of companies and joint venture institutions after the abandonment of socialism.[43]

---

43   The most complete study is Aung Myoe, *Building the Tatmadaw: Myanmar Armed*

6.4.   Percentage of Government Expenditure by Function, 1989 TO 2006

Year	1989-90	1990-91	1991-92	1992-93	1993-94	1994-95	1995-96	1996-97
Social Control[1]	46.84	35.11	45.84	42.21	35.33	24.22	18.53	24.14
Administration[2]	8.94	5.37	6.5	6.09	5.92	8.70	5.12	4.55
Defence[3]	26.24	43.47	31.37	31.28	39.82	37.54	32.04	32.10
Economic[4]	9.72	7.84	5.63	11.58	9.35	10.05	14.74	10.71
Infrastructure and Communications[5]	8.27	8.21	10.67	8.85	9.58	19.50	29.57	28.50
Total	100.0	100.0	100.0	100.0	100.0	100.0	100.0	100.0

1997-98	1998-99	1999-2000	2000-2001	2001-2002	2002-2003	2003-2004	2004-2005	2005-2006
22.12	22.12	21.07	30.93	28.15	31.68	25.59	27.11	25.17
4.60	5.24	5.89	6.29	4.67	3.93	6.12	14.95	5.39
31.34	30.77	33.58	32.76	30.45	26.41	27.82	24.14	27.24
15.54	16.40	15.99	14.88	13.22	15.48	15.54	14.44	19.06
26.39	25.47	23.47	15.15	23.53	22.50	24.94	19.37	23.15
100.0	100.0	100.0	100.0	100.0	100.0	100.0	100.0	100.0

Source: Author's calculations based on annual and supplementary state budget laws. Based on government data and IMF staff estimates, military expenditure as a proportion of all state expenditure was smaller, viz:

2000   28.79%

[1] Includes Chief Justice, Attorney-General, Progress of Border Areas and National Races and Development, Home Affairs, Immigration and Population, Religious Affairs, Social Welfare, Relief and Resettlement, Information, Culture, Education, Health, Sports, and Labour

[2] Includes State Law and Order Restoration Council/State Peace and Development Council, Multi-Party Democracy Election Commission, Government, Auditor-General, Foreign Affairs, National Planning and Economic Development, Finance and Revenue, Pensions and Gratuities, and Gratuities and Commuted Pensions.

[3] Includes Defence, Tatmadaw Affairs, and Municipal Cantonments under the Ministry of Defence.

[4] Includes Forestry, Agriculture and Irrigation, Livestock Breeding and Fisheries, Mines, Industry I, Industry 2, Science and Technology, Energy, Electric Power, Commerce, Hotels and Tourism Service, and Co-operatives

[5] Includes Construction, Transport, Rail Transportation, and Communications, Posts and Telegraphs

In the contest for state power after 1988, the army began from a much stronger position than its rivals. Despite its decrepit condition, inheriting the state and its apparatus gave it a distinct advantage over all other challengers. Throughout the more than two decades when it ruled alone, the power of the army and the state it controlled grew ever greater. Military rule in Myanmar had become the default position that it is for states persisting in the face of great political and social challenges. For reasons that

Forces since 1948 (Singapore: Institute of Southeast Asian Studies, forthcoming).

will become apparent from studying the state's behaviour and the attempts by the army's opponents to wrest power from it during the years following 1988, the army was in danger of becoming the state. Had that happened, and the distinction between the state and the army been completely lost, the prospects for significant political change in Myanmar, short of war, could have dissipated. The army's continual reiteration that its goal was to return the country to civilian rule after a period of reconstruction, 'reconsolidation' in its terms, created the conditions that may allow it to eventually attempt to share power with its rivals and critics.

The National League for Democracy (NLD). The NLD was the most successful organisation party to emerge from the *dirigiste* restoration of multi-party politics after 1988. Following the army putsch and the renewal of the promise of a multi-party general election, politicians and activists withdrew from the streets in order to begin to organise their parties and movements and leaders began to compete for prominence in formal organisations. The NLD, formed by the three most prominent figures after an abortive attempt by U Nu to reclaim power—former Brigadier Aung Gyi, former General Tin U, and Daw Aung San Suu Kyi, the daughter of the General Aung San—attracted many activists, young and old. They were joined by youths from the ranks of the disgruntled students who had discovered power during the previous months of demonstrations, and experienced older persons, mainly former members of the army who had been disgruntled with General Ne Win and his governments, some for over thirty years. Primarily on account of the growing national and international profile of its most prominent member, Daw Aung San Suu Kyi, especially after her first major public speech on 24 August 1988, and its eventual victory in the elections that were held in May 1990, the NLD was the best known and most popular rival to the army for state power after 1988.

It was only after the call for a national strike in August 1988 that efforts began to form political parties to provide leadership and organisation to the public beyond the anti-government demonstrations. The previous 26 years of socialist one-party rule had sapped most of the political institutions created and the skills honed in the 1920s and 1930s prior to the armed contest for state power in the late 1940s and 1950s. But gradually and haltingly, independent political activities began, though often reflecting the experience of the socialist years rather than Myanmar's colonial and parliamentary political history. It was not until 15 August, when Daw Aung San Suu Kyi and U Htwe Myint, a supporter of U Nu's failed bid for power in

1969, with others established a putative People's Consultative Committee that party-like organisational efforts commenced. This was a precursor to an abortive bid to establish an interim government.

Soon afterwards, a meeting between Daw Aung San Suu Kyi and 23 veteran *Thakin*, writers, lawyers, and former government officials and army officers marked the re-emergence of organised independent party politics in Myanmar.[44] Daw Aung San Suu Kyi had moved to India in 1960 with her mother, who served as Prime Minister U Nu's and subsequently the Revolutionary Council's Ambassador in Delhi until 1967. Leaving India, she studied at Oxford University and subsequently married a British scholar. She returned to Yangon from England in March 1988, to nurse her ailing mother, and emerged five months later as the most powerful symbol of political protest in the country, and perhaps more important, internationally. From her first major public address at the Shwedagon Pagoda when she called the prevailing demonstrations part of a 'second struggle for independence', creating a spurious analogy between the foreign rule of the British and the rule of the tatmadaw, she emerged as the fulcrum of protest politics in Myanmar.

Older politicians, veterans of the 1940s and 1950s, initially challenged her pivotal position in anti-Ne Win, anti-BSPP and anti-tatmadaw politics. Leading them was the former Prime Minister U Nu, who claimed to have re-established a legitimate government under the banner of a League for Democracy and Peace (LDP). The octogenarian's presumption that his claim to office, based on the 1960 election results, would lead others to follow him soon dissolved, however, when a number of persons he announced as ministers in his government refused to join him. Nonetheless, he briefly emerged as one of the figures identified, along with Daw Aung San Suu Kyi and former Brigadier Aung Gyi, as the major spokespersons for the public. Former General Tin U[45] soon joined their number; he began addressing public meetings in late August, also demanding the formation of

---

44   *Speech Delivered by State Law and Order Restoration Council Secretary (1) Major General Khin Nyunt at the Special 110ᵗʰ Press Conference, 14 May 1991.* (Yangon: News and Periodicals Enterprises, Ministry of Information, August 1991), p. 16; Aung San Suu Kyi, 'The First Initiative', in Michael Aris, ed., *Freedom from Fear and Other Writings* (London: Viking, 1991), pp. 192-7.

45   Former General Tin U, after 1988 often transliterated as Tin Oo, had been General Ne Win's heir apparent as Minister of Defence and Chief of Staff of the Army until his arrest in 1976. See above, p. 370.

an interim government. A group of veteran politicians and former soldiers known as the Patriotic Old Comrades League echoed that call.

Attempts to internationalise Myanmar's domestic political crisis commenced in early September when United States Congressman Stephen Solarz made an unexpected visit to Yangon to meet President Maung Maung as well as the emerging party leaders. Solarz, then Chairman of the House of Representatives International Affairs Committee Subcommittee on Asia and the Pacific, urged the establishment of an interim government, implying that President Maung Maung should share power with the most prominent persons who had emerged during the previous month. This the President refused, instead announcing that the BSPP had accepted his proposal that multi-party elections should be held without the necessity of a referendum on the political system first, and immediately appointing an election commission composed of five senior former officials and nationalist politicians to supervise the forthcoming ballot.[46] As there was no trust between the political leaders and the President, whom many portrayed as the puppet of General Ne Win, the public ignored this announcement, if it was heard in the din of the ongoing demonstrations, and renewed demands for an interim government continued until the 18 September putsch.

Dr Maung Maung's government, while exercising restraint in constraining the demonstrators and exuberant politicians who felt that power soon would be theirs by default, made plans for holding multi-party elections. On 16 September the army severed its formal ties with the BSPP with the abolition of the Tatmadaw Party Organising Committee, and Dr Maung Maung ordered all civil servants to avoid partisan politics and resign from the still ruling party. Thus matters rested until the late afternoon of the 18th when the army seized state power in its own name; it forcibly began the next morning to clear the streets of demonstrators. Within a few days, order was restored and a sort of calm returned. The events of the previous 12 months, and the heightened emotions and mistrust that had burgeoned during the demonstrations, created such rancour that the promises advanced by the new army government, especially that they would transfer

---

46   Two different translations of the speeches announcing these plans are available. See *The Working Peoples Daily,* 11 and 12 September, 1988, reprinted in Robert Taylor, compiler, *Dr. Maung Maung: Gentleman, Scholar, Patriot* (Singapore: Institute of Southeast Asian Studies, 2008), pp. 555-65, and Maung Maung, *1988 Uprising in Burma,* pp. 184-8 and 197-203. Before that he had appointed a commission to study public opinion, but its work was quickly foreclosed by the chaotic circumstances in which it operated.

power to the victors in elections they promised to hold in the indefinite future were disbelieved. Nonetheless, the institutions that the military government established anew or carried over from the previous regime, such as the Election Commission, were accepted as legitimate and the political parties formed accepted its rules and regulations, if under protest. The call for an interim government was heard no more after the putsch, though some more radical student activists criticised the NLD for abandoning the demand.[47]

Five days after the establishment of the army government, the most prominent names among the demonstrators, other than U Nu, formed the NLD. Its draft constitution owed much to that of the AFPFL and other leftist inspired parties with real power lying with the Central Executive Committee (CEC) and its officers, especially the General Secretary. The first CEC appointed former Brigadier Aung Gyi as Chairman, former General Tin U as Vice Chairman, and Daw Aung San Suu Kyi as General Secretary. Supporters quickly rallied to the party, a broad coalition of those who for diverse reasons had become disenchanted with U Ne Win and the army and the ruling party under his leadership. Dominated by General Secretary Daw Aung San Suu Kyi, it gained legal corporate form when it registered with the Election Commission from which it was fortunate to receive the widely recognised *khamauk,* a peasant's hat, in the lottery for party symbols. The new organisation soon appeared to be the largest, best organised, and most widely recognised of the 235 registered. Individuals who had worked in the former BSPP regime dominated the NLD CEC, unsurprisingly given Myanmar's political history. Only three of the ten members of the CEC who remained in office eight years after its foundation had not served in General Ne Win's post-1962 governments, and two of the other three had served in the army prior to the 1962 coup, leaving only Daw Aung San Suu Kyi with no formal role in the old regime. A number of younger, less well-known members, who advocated confrontational tactics, had been arrested in the interim.

Daw Aung San Suu Kyi, as the newest and least politically experienced and known—but, because of her father and her lack of a political history, most acknowledged—of the top NLD leaders, was the key figure in the party. She reiterated a doctrine of non-violent resistance to the military

---

47   Statement by Moe Thee Zun, Chairman, Leading Political Committee, New Society Democracy Party, Headquarters, Yangon, reprinted in *A Concise History of Myanmar and the Tatmadaw's Role 1948-1988.* (Yangon: News and Periodicals Enterprises, 1991), p. 39.

6.5.   27 May 1990 Election Results by State or Division and Party

State/Division	Party				
	National League for Democracy (NLD)	National Unity Party (NUP)	Independent	Ethnic or Regional or Minor Party	Total
Kachin	14	2		3[1]	19
Kayah	1	2	·	2[2]	8
Kayin	10			4[3]	14
Chin	4	1	2	6[4]	13
Sagaing	52	1	2	3[5]	58
Tanintharyi	13				13
Bago	47	1		3[6]	51
Magway	39				39
Mandalay	55		1		56
Mon	16			4[7]	20
Rakhine	9			17[8]	26
Yangon	59			2[9]	61
Shan	22	1		33[10]	56
Ayeyarwady	48	2	1		51

[1] Kachin State National Congress for Democracy (KSNCD)
[2] Kayah State Nationalities League for Democracy (KSNLD)
[3] Patriotic Old Comrades League (POCL) 1, and Karen State National Organisation (KSNO) 1, Mon National Democratic Front (MNDF) 1, Democratic Organisation for Kayan National Unity (DOKNU) 1
[4] Chin National League for Democracy (CNLD) 3, Mara People's Party (MPP) 1, Zomi National Congress (ZNC), 2
[5] Naga Hills Regional Progressive Party (NHRPP) 2, United Nationalities League for Democracy (UNLD) 1
[6] Party for National Democracy (PND)
[7] Mon National Democratic Front (MNDF)
[8] National Democratic Party for Human Rights (NDPHR) 4, Rahkine Democracy League (RDL) 11, Mro of Khami National Solidarity Organisation (M/KNSO) 1, Kamans National League for Democracy (KNLD) 1
[9] Democracy Party (DP) 1, Graduates and Old Students Democratic Association (GOSDA) 1
[10] Union National Democracy Party (UNDP) 1, Shan Nationalities League for Democracy (SNLP) 23, Union Paoh National Organisation 3, Union Danu League for Democracy Party (UDLDP) 1, Shan State Kokang Democratic Party (SSKDP) 1, Tayang (Palaung) National League for Democracy 2, Lahu National Development Party (LNDP) 1, Democratic Organisation for Kayan National Unity (DOKNU) 1

Source: *Working People's Daily*, 28 May to 3 July 1990.

government and commenced to tour the country, drawing significant crowds in defiance of government orders limiting public meetings to no more than five persons unless permitted by the local authorities or held within party premises. The party, though appearing as a united front, was divided by factionalism from the start. Supporters of the individual leaders eventually coalesced in the so-called intellectuals' or students' faction of the General Secretary and the old soldiers' faction of former members of the army led by former General Tin U. Former Brigadier Aung Gyi, who had a number of business associates among his supporters, drew attention to what he believed to be excessive influence within the party of current and former Communists. He wrote to Daw Aung San Suu Kyi on 25 November 1988, calling for the removal of the alleged Communists, and when the Party CEC rejected his demands, he resigned and formed a separate party, the Union National Democracy Party (UNDP), of which he became Patron.

Among the former army officers and civilian employees of General Ne Win's regimes in the CEC of the NLD, one of the three secretaries working with General Secretary Daw Aung San Suu Kyi was instrumental in shaping her evolving approach to politics. U Win Tin, a former editor of the BSPP-era government Burmese-language newspaper *Hanthawaddy,* allegedly introduced Daw Aung San Suu Kyi to the writings on non-violence by the 19th-century American author Henry David Thoreau, and was the architect of the confrontational policy that the NLD pursued from December 1988. That policy called upon party members and the wider public to disobey SLORC laws, orders, and regulations that the NLD leadership considered illegitimate, thus casting doubt on the legitimacy and disparaging the power of the army government. During the first months of 1989, following the state funeral of her mother on 2 January 1989, Daw Aung San Suu Kyi increased her attacks on the government, eventually accusing it of being 'fascist' and under the control of former General Ne Win. As she toured widely, drawing significant crowds, her increasingly strident criticism of the SLORC leadership was finally halted on 20 July 1989 when she, U Win Tin, former Brigadier Tin U, and many other senior NLD leaders were placed under house arrest or imprisoned. This followed plans by the NLD to conduct an unauthorised march and a parallel ceremony to that the government held annually at the tomb of General Aung San and others on the anniversary of their assassinations, Martyrs' Day, which could have led to violence between NLD supporters and the police and army.[48] Most of those arrested were released after about five years, though some core leaders were detained for up to 15 or more years. U Win Tin, given a twenty-year sentence, remained in custody nineteen years later.

---

48   For Daw Aung San Suu Kyi's views and the events leading to her first arrest, see Aris, 'Introduction', in Aris, ed., *Freedom from Fear,* p. xxi.

6.6.　27 May 1990 Election by Number of Candidates and Percentage of Valid Votes Won by Party

Parties	Seats Won	Seats Contested	Percentage of Valid Votes
National Parties			
National League for Democracy	392	447	59.87
National Unity Party[1]	10	482	23.12
Patriotic Old Comrades League	1	3	0.02
Party for National Democracy	3	3	0.48
Democracy Party	1	105	0.48
Graduates and Old Students Democratic Association	1	10	0.08
Union Nationals Democracy Party	1	247	1.48
Regional and Ethnically Designated Parties			
Kachin State National Congress for Democracy	3	9	0.11
Kayah State Nationalities League for Democracy	2	8	0.08
Karen State National Organisation	1	3	0.05
Mon National Democratic Front	5	19	1.05
Democratic Organisation for Kayan National Unity	2	3	0.11
Chin National League for Democracy	3	13	0.38
Mara Peoples Party	1	4	0.04
Zomi National Congress	2	4	0.14
Naga Hills Regional Progressive Party	2	6	0.08
United Nationalities League for Democracy	1	4	0.07
National Democratic Party for Human Rights	4	8	0.97
Rahkine Democracy League	11	25	1.21
Mro (or) Khami National Solidarity Organisation	1	4	0.17
Kamans National League for Democracy	1	3	0.08
Shan Nationalities League for Democracy	23	58	1.68
Union Paoh National Organisation	3	15	0.27
Union Danu League for Democracy Party	1	4	0.17
Shan State Kokang Democracy Party	1	2	0.05
Ta-aung (Paluang) National League for Democracy	2	9	0.18
Lahu National Development Party	1	7	0.12
Independents	12	82	6.75
Total	485	1587	100.00

[1] Includes NUP affiliates Peasants Unity Organisation, Youth Unity Organisation, and Workers Unity Organisation.

Source: *Working People's Daily*, 1, 2, 3 July 1990.

A year and a half after the putsch, and ten months after the arrest of much of the top NLD leadership, elections were held. Despite, or perhaps because of, the house arrest of Daw Aung San Suu Kyi and others, the NLD received 59.87 per cent of the valid vote, gaining 392 or 80.82 per cent of constituencies contested, in the 27 May 1990 ballot.[49] With a turnout of more than 72 per cent of the 20,818,313 eligible voters, this election had the highest participation rate of any in Myanmar's then seventy years of electoral history.[50] Although 93 different parties fielded one or more candidates, and another 82 individuals ran as independents, only 27 parties won one or more seats. Fifteen women were elected among the 485 victors, all standing for the NLD. As shown in tables 6.5 and 6.6, the second most successful party was the NLD-affiliated Shan Nationalities League for Democracy (SNLD) which won 23 constituencies, but the successor organisation to the former BSPP, the National Unity Party (NUP), gained only ten seats despite winning just over 25 per cent of the popular vote. The NUP was able to gain a plurality mainly in constituencies where the NLD ran candidates in competition with allied parties. The parties led by U Nu and former Brigadier Aung Gyi won only three seats and one seat respectively.[51]

Daw Aung San Suu Kyi led a political party that declared as its primary goal was the establishment of a multi-party parliamentary democratic state in Myanmar. She apparently felt, however, that her party was also a movement or a crusade to transform the 'Burmese mentality'.[52] Before returning

---

49 All election data come from the *Working People's Daily*, 28 May to 3 July 1990. No election took place in four constituencies because of the absence of adequate security, i.e. they were in areas controlled by insurgents.

50 See R.H. Taylor, 'Elections in Burma/Myanmar: For Whom and Why?' in R.H. Taylor, ed., *The Politics of Elections in Southeast Asia* (New York, Washington and Cambridge University Press and Woodrow Wilson Center Press, 1996), pp. 164-83.

51 For a fuller analysis of the election results, see R.H. Taylor, 'Myanmar 1990: New Era or Old?', in Sharon Siddique and Ng Chee Yuen, eds, *Southeast Asian Affairs 1991* (Singapore: Institute of Southeast Asian Studies, 1991), pp. 200-6. Also Taylor, "External Dimensions of the Myanmar Situation", in Rohana Mahmood and Hans-Joachim Esderts, eds, *Myanmar and the Wider Southeast Asia*. (Kuala Lumpur: Institute of Strategic and International Studies Malaysia, 1991), pp. 23-32.

52 Which she argued that the British had not understood when creating the colonial government in the 19th century. Aung San Suu Kyi, *Burma and India: Some Aspects of Intellectual Life Under Colonialism* (Shimla: Indian Institute of Advanced Study, 1990), p. 62. This is reprinted in Aris, ed., *Freedom from Fear*,

to Myanmar, she developed this idea in a series of essays, most particularly *Burma and India: Some Aspects of Intellectual Life under Colonialism*. In these, she articulated a thesis that the population of Myanmar was largely incapable of understanding and working a democratic political system. According to her, Myanmar had not experienced fully the political change that neighbouring India had during the colonial period. Her reliance on the concept of national, folk or ethnic 'mentalities' was also reflected in her attitude towards Myanmar's many ethnic minorities.[53] The alleged Myanmar or Bamar 'mentality', rooted in an authoritarian past, had made it easy for 'men without integrity and wisdom' to rule the country[54] and thus reinforced this alleged national thought pattern or political culture. Therefore, from 1988 onward, through her example, she sought to demonstrate to 'her people' how they should resist the military government and abandon the alleged fearful condition they were in to achieve a democratic society.

The heart of Daw Aung San Suu Kyi's thesis is that the country suffers from a form of 'political immaturity' despite inheriting a 'sound social system'. From monarchical times, the people 'had bred in them a tendency to live their own lives and keep away from the central administration as far as possible.'[55] Nothing in 'traditional Burmese education' encouraged 'speculation'. 'That was largely due to the view, so universally accepted that it appears to be part of the racial psyche of the Burmese, that Buddhism represents the perfected [sic] philosophy.'[56] The loss of national independence with the deposition of King Thibaw caused 'some Burmese to rail against their own impotence and foibles, but there was no serious attempt to analyse the causes of the deficiencies.'[57]

---

as 'Intellectual Life in Burma and India under Colonialism', pp. 82-139. Her speeches in Burmese in 1995 and 1996 are collected Ino Kenji, *Philosophy and Action of Aung San Suu Kyi* (Kita Kyushu: Kenkyu Forum of Asian Women, 2001 [in Japanese]), pp. 121-266.

53   'What does Suu Kyi have to say about the ethnic groups? "I have not studied the culture of the other ethnic peoples of Burma deeply enough to comment," she told an interviewed in 1999, "apart from the fact that my mother always taught me to think of them as very close to us, emphasising how loyal they were."' Cathy Scott-Clark and Adrian Levy, 'Portrait: Aung San Suu Kyi', *Prospect Magazine*, July 2001, p. 49.

54   Aung San Suu Kyi, 'In Quest of Democracy', in Aris, ed., *Freedom from Fear*, p. 169.

55   Aung San Suu Kyi, *Burma and India*, p. 22

56   Ibid., p. 27.

57   Ibid., p. 29.

Unlike in India, where she argues that English people were involved in the founding of Indian nationalism and therefore helped it develop a modernist cast that the Indian population readily accepted, in Myanmar the people allegedly rejected foreign ideas unless they could be made to fit into a pre-existing indigenous mould.[58] Consequently, whereas in India a 'synthesis of East and West, of theory and practice' created an Indian renaissance, Myanmar remained mired in the past and there developed 'a gulf between the earlier educated elite and the mainstream of Burmese aspirations.'[59] Early Myanmar nationalist organisations such as the YMBA failed to create 'the true synthesis of traditional and modern, Burmese and western'[60] and the nearest anyone in Myanmar came to her prerequisite for a democratic society were the *Khitsan* (modern literature) writers of the 1930s. An end to this putative impasse in the development of Myanmar's 'political maturity' was, she believed, emerging with her father's generation of student politicians in the Do Bama Asiayon in the late 1930s. However, the Second World War cut short that possibility and 'looking from the Indian situation to that of the Burmese there is almost a surreal impression of time warp' that is largely the result of 'the distinct cultural and historical background of Burma.'[61]

Through her speeches and behaviour Daw Aung San Suu Kyi appeared to challenge not only the military regime but also the commonly accepted patterns of deference and respect allegedly characterising much of Myanmar social exchange. Her direct manner of speaking and expression was very appealing to her younger, more radical supporters, but was often considered rude and undignified, especially for a woman and the daughter of General Aung San, by older, more conservative people. In support of her thesis and behaviour, U Tin U explained, '. . . Daw Aung San Suu Kyi feels the need to deepen people's understanding of democracy.'[62] He went on to explain that the party leadership 'represent the people and in so doing we want to educate them to also represent themselves.' Theirs was 'a mass democracy movement, a people's struggle.'[63] The hortatory activities of the

---

58   Ibid., pp. 35-6.

59   Ibid., p. 41.

60   Ibid., p. 49.

61   Ibid., p. 74.

62   Appendix 2, in *Aung San Suu Kyi, The Voice of Hope (conversations with Alan Clements)*, 'A Conversation with U Tin Oo', p. 207.

63   Ibid., p. 208.

NLD were part, therefore, of an effort to change Myanmar's putatively undemocratic 'political culture'.

After June 1990, the NLD and its supporters in Myanmar and abroad sought to assert that the party was the legitimate government of Myanmar, on the basis of its overwhelming electoral success in the first multi-party elections held since 1960. That these elections were 'free and fair', despite the limitations placed on campaigning and the absence of a free press, was widely accepted. The NLD's claim to power was rejected by the army government because of the failure of the party to first fulfil the conditions for a transfer to a civilian government established before the election. In June 1989, a SLORC spokesman stated that they would not '. . . transfer power as soon as the elections are held.' Rather, following the election, the 'elected representatives [were] to draw up the constitution. If the people approve the constitution, [they would] transfer power as soon as possible to the government which emerged according to that constitution.' Repeating Dr Maung Maung's concerns about observing constitutional norms during August and September of the previous year, the spokesman insisted that they were 'ever ready to transfer power', but that they were 'just stressing systematic transfer of power according to the law.'[64]

The requirement to draft, and ratify by popular referendum, a new constitution prior to any transfer of power was perceived by the NLD leadership as a scheme designed by U Ne Win to cling to power. Daw Aung San Suu Kyi and her advisers also assumed that Ne Win was dictating the SLORC's refusal to begin a 'dialogue' with any political party prior to the election. As the SLORC refused to meet with any political parties, the issue of what would happen after the ballot remained unresolved, according to the NLD. The consequences of the election, as expressed by Daw Aung San Suu Kyi in an interview prior to her first arrest, was a '. . . problem. Whoever [was] elected [would] first have to draw up a constitution that would have to be adopted before the transfer of power. [SLORC hadn't] said how the constitution [would] be adopted. It could be through a referendum, but [that] could mean months and months, if not years.'[65]

---

64 BBC SWB FE/0489 B/2, 22 June 1989. The most complete study of the controversy surrounding the 1990 election is Derek Tonkin, 'The 1990 Elections in Myanmar: Broken Promises or a Failure of Communication?', *Contemporary Southeast Asia*, Vol. 29, No. 1 (2007), pp. 33-54. See also, Bertil Lintner, "The Election Charade", *Far Eastern Economic Review*, 18 January 1990, p.15.

65 Reprinted from *Asiaweek*, as 'The People Want Freedom', in Aris, ed., *Freedom from Fear*, p. 233.

As the Election Commission published the results of the election in the daily press constituency by constituency from late May, 1990, Western governmental pressure grew on the SLORC to transfer power to the NLD. The army government, however, reiterated that it would not give up power in a manner that did not meet its predetermined criteria. Initially, the acting NLD Central Executive Committee, composed of cautious former officers, accepted that it would have to abide the army's terms and commence drafting a constitution. However, rank and file members of the party refused to comply with the SLORC's prerequisites and insisted on taking power immediately, causing a split in the party.[66] On 27 July, the SLORC issued Declaration No. 1/90 that restated the policy on the transfer of power only to a constitutionally formed government. In the meantime, it would continue to wield all legislative, judicial, and executive power. Two days later, the NLD convened a meeting of its unconfirmed but apparently successful candidates and demanded that a Pyithu Hluttaw be called before the end of September. The Gandhi Hall Declaration of the NLD, as the resolution of their meeting was named, failed, like many subsequent NLD ultimata over the next two decades, to specify what the NLD would do if its demands were not met. While moral certainty prevailed within the NLD, power continued to reside with the army.

The NLD strategy vis-à-vis the military from before the 1990 election had several strands to it. In addition to Daw Aung San Suu Kyi's own efforts to educate the population about civil rights and democratic action, and its electoral intentions and eventual results, a third strand of strategy was to attempt to weaken the government by obstructing its efforts to revive and development the economy, thus undercutting its fiscal base and the acquiescence of the public. Prior to the election, Daw Aung San Suu Kyi insisted that the people should not be 'sidetracked' from the struggle for democracy by economic issues. Rather, the achievement of democracy had to precede economic growth.[67] Her calls for tourists to avoid Myanmar before the establishment of a civilian government, for foreign investors equally to eschew the country for the interim, and for foreign governments to apply economic sanctions intensified after her

66   Kyaw Yin Hlaing, 'The State of the Pro-Democracy Movement in Authoritarian Myanmar/Burma' in Xialon Gue, ed., *Myanmar/Burma: Challenges and Perspective* (Stockholm: Institute for Security and Development Studies, 2008), pp. 97-8. See also, *Far Eastern Economic Review*, 11 October 1990, p.14.

67   Aung San Suu Kyi, "The Need for Solidarity among Ethnic Groups,', Aris, ed., *Freedom from Fear,* p. 228.

release from house arrest in July 1995. Related to these arguments was a hope that some members of the armed forces would eventually turn against their commanders and a split in the officer corps or a mutiny in the ranks would create the conditions for the NLD to come to power. No such event occurred but the threat of one led many in the senior ranks to be suspicious of the intentions of other officers who advocated coopera- tion or compromise with civilian groups.

The weakness of the NLD's strategy to wrest control of the state from the army led it to seek to internationalise Myanmar's domestic politics. The party sought support in an effort to isolate Myanmar internationally and force the army to concede power because of the failure of the economy. In late February 1989, to implement an idea of U Win Tin, a parallel party to the NLD known as the Party for National Democracy and led by Daw Aung San Suu Kyi's cousin, Dr Sein Win, was formed. He subsequently successfully stood in the Bahan constituency of Yangon that Daw Aung San Suu Kyi had been denied the right to contest because of her residence in Oxford and family connections with the United Kingdom. When, fol- lowing the unwillingness of the SLORC to concede power to the NLD prior to the approval of a new constitution, and after the post-election arrest of a number of other NLD leaders including the Chairman, former Colonel Kyi Maung, a number of successful candidates met in November 1990 in Mandalay. There they decided to form a parallel or provisional government in exile, and eleven of their number made their way to the KNU headquarters at Manerplaw on the Thai border to form the National Coalition Government of the Union of Burma (NCGUB).[68] The NCGUB joined with armed non-Communist ethnically-designated insurgent groups to form the National Council of the Union of Burma (NCUB), thus un- dermining its claim to be a government and opening it to claims that it collaborated with longstanding enemies of the state. The NCGUB, located first in Washington and then in Rockville, Maryland, was not recognised by any government but lobbied in Washington and other capitals, and at the United Nations, for international pressure on the SLORC/SPDC. Perhaps because of the personalisation of the campaign for democracy in Myanmar through the persona of Daw Aung San Suu Kyi, institutions such as the NLD and the NCGUB tended to lose visibility both inside and

---

68   Josef Silverstein, 'Aung San Suu Kyi: Is She Burma's Woman of Destiny?', in Aris, *Freedom from Fear,* pp. 277-8; reprinted from *Asian Survey*, xxx, 10, (1990), pp. 1007-1019. Two of the nine NLD members resigned a few days after the formation of the NCGUB, declaring that they had been duped.

outside Myanmar.[69] As the government arrested a number of NLD leaders and applied various pressures to encourage the regular members to resign 'of their own volition', the party organisation, never highly articulated, atrophied. Almost all the party's offices were closed and its ability to assist its members greatly reduced.

Outside Myanmar, the NLD's campaign of confrontation with the government found willing supporters, especially in the United States Congress and on university campuses where consumer boycott campaigns eventually discouraged multinational firms from investing in or remaining in Myanmar, thus increasing the antagonism of the SLORC/SPDC towards Daw Aung San Suu Kyi and her party. This occasionally descended to the level of character defamation of an indecorous nature as the government controlled press published scabrous cartoons and articles attacking her as well as holding mass rallies at which she and her party were denounced.[70] The criticism of Daw Aung San Suu Kyi expressed in the official press was matched by adulation on the part of American and European politicians, especially after she was awarded the Nobel Peace Prize less than two years after her first arrest; subsequently she received many other prestigious international human rights honours and much admiration from Western political leaders.[71]

Efforts to reach a *modus vivendi* between the NLD and the government failed following talks between senior members of the SLORC and Daw Aung San Suu Kyi in 1994. When released from house arrest in July 1995, she recommenced her political activities in a manner that antagonised the military government. The day after her release, the *New York Times* reported[72]:

She compared the situation in Myanmar to that of South Africa. "Once bitter enemies in South Africa are now working together for the betterment of their peo-

---

69   See Lisa Brooten, 'Feminization of Democracy under Siege: The Media, 'the Lady' of Burma, and U.S. Foreign Policy', *NWSA Journal*, Vol. 17, No. 3 (2005), pp. 134-56.

70   See, for example, *Sentiments of the Myanmar People (1998)* (Yangon: Committee to hold Yangon Division Mass Meeting Expressing Sentiments of the People, December, 1998).

71   See the honours page of the Daw Aung San Suu Kyi website, www.dassk.com. Examples of political comment can be found in Madeleine Albright, *Madam Secretary: A Memoir* (New York: Hyperion, 2003), pp. 200-2; and Gordon Brown, *Courage: Eight Portraits* (London: Bloomsbury, 2007), pp. 207-35.

72   Philip Shenon, *New York Times*, 12 July 1995.

ple," she said. "Why can't we look forward to a similar process? We have to choose between dialogue and utter devastation."

When she was reinstated as General Secretary of the NLD in October, a move declared illegal by the SLORC, confrontation and advocacy of international isolation, interpreted by most as calls for economic sanctions and a tourist boycott of Myanmar, became the leitmotif of the NLD. The NLD, which had agreed while Daw Aung San Suu Kyi was under house arrest to participate in a national convention to draft a new constitution that the SLORC convened in 1993, withdrew its delegates at the end of 1995, after she criticised the convention as being undemocratic in its procedures, composition, and conclusions. She made several thwarted attempts to travel beyond Yangon to visit NLD supporters and was turned back on each occasion by the police and army. Her implacable opposition to tourism and investment in Myanmar extended to human rights training for Myanmar civil servants provided by the Australian government, which she considered to be 'ill-advised'.[73] Several dissenting members of the NLD were expelled for writing to the government proposing low-level negotiations to attempt to break the impasse that had been reached, and several other senior party figures, including former chairman U Kyi Maung, resigned in 1997 as a result of dissatisfaction with her leadership and behaviour.

In 1998, the NLD again called on the SPDC to convene a Pyithu Hluttaw based on the 1990 election results and transfer power to it by 21 August despite the absence of an approved constitution. When the government ignored that demand, a Committee to Represent the People's Parliament (CRPP) was formed to act as an interim legislative body, leading to the arrest of many elected NLD members. The establishment of the CRPP, which was declared an illegal body by the government, contributed to a series of confrontational incidents that resulted in the government once more placing her under house arrest in 2000. In the face of strong international pressure, and factional conflict within the military regime, she was released again after 19 months in May, 2002. An agreement had then been reached, through the good offices of the United Nations Secretary General's Special Envoy to Myanmar, that she would tour the country under official escort, visit government development projects, and moderate her political activities and policies. In exchange, the government would reopen a dialogue

---

73   Tom Wingfield, 'Myanmar: Political Stasis and a Precarious Economy', in Daljit
      Singh, ed., *Southeast Asian Affairs 2000* (Singapore: Institute of Southeast Asian
      Studies, 2000), p. 211.

with her that she and NLD colleagues had long demanded. That dialogue, despite four meetings between senior NLD leaders including the General Secretary and the senior leadership of the SPDC, and 20 others between Daw Aung Suu Kyi and government ministers, proved to be unproductive. Following increasingly demonstrative evidence of political support for her among sections of the public, she was rearrested following a late night assault on her motorcade in May 2003 at the village of Dipeyin. As the party did not renew its leadership, and by the 2000s its CEC members averaged more than eighty years of age, many middle level district and township level leaders became disaffected with the absence of party initiatives when Daw Aung San Suu Kyi was unavailable to lead the party.[74]

Despite demands by many Western and other governments and international organisations, as well as occasional public demonstrations in Yangon and elsewhere in Myanmar, calling for her release, Daw Aung San Suu Kyi remained under house arrest subsequently. In October 2007, following more than a month of protests eventually led by politicised Buddhist monks, another Special Envoy of the United Nations Secretary General encouraged the government to renew talks with her on the country's constitutional future. The government responded by being willing to do so, but with conditions. She and her party would have to renounce their strong criticisms and demonstrations of opposition to the regime, her call for 'utter devastation', and abandon their call for the application of economic sanctions. In response, she issued a statement via the United Nations Special Envoy in English in Singapore, establishing her own conditions for a dialogue with the government and ignoring its previous conditional offer. Despite several meetings with a government minister appointed to liaise with her, as with previous meetings over the past 15 years, no agreement was reached. The substance of these discussions was never revealed but apparently the gap between the NLD's ideas about the nature of democracy and national reconciliation, as opposed to the army's ideas concerning stability, security, and national reconsolidation, remained unbridged, and apparently unbridgeable. Twenty years after its formation in a period of

---

74   For further discussion, see Robert H. Taylor, "One Day, One Fathom, Bagan Won't Move': On the Myanmar Road to a Constitution', in Trevor Wilson, *Myanmar's Long Road to National Reconciliation* (Singapore: Institute of Southeast Asian Studies, 2006), pp. 3-28; and Kyaw Yin Hlaing, 'Myanmar in 2004: Why Military Rule Continues,' in Chin Kin Wah and Daljit Singh, eds, *Southeast Asian Affairs 2004* (Singapore: Institute of Southeast Asian Studies, 2004), pp. 231-56.

revolutionary optimism, the NLD remained unable to wrest control of the state from the army.

Other political parties

Few independent political institutions created in the explosion of political activity that occurred between 1988 and 1990 endured. Although a plethora of political parties were formed, unless they had an established ethnic constituency they soon dissipated with the exception of the NUP and the NLD. The NUP, formally organised on 28 September 1988, was the successor in terms of organisation and bureaucratic connections of the Myanmar Socialist Programme Party. Twenty years after its re-formation, it claimed to have more than two million members in more than 300 branches across the country.[75] Occasionally issuing statements both supportive and critical of the army government, it generally kept a low profile, but claimed that it provided a number of services for its members and potential supporters, especially assistance in dealing with the authorities and resolving local disputes.

At the time of the elections in 1990, and subsequently, observers often suggested that the army government favoured the NUP. The fact that the party inherited resources, as well as personnel, from the BSPP, and the army had been the original creator of that party, lent credence to this notion. Apart from its dropping socialism from its ideological programme and substituting market economics, the NUP looked like the BSPP reborn.[76] However, at the time of the putsch and even earlier, the army's leadership was relieved to be no longer constrained by the policies and interests of the party that it believed was responsible for the nation's lack of economic and social development, and political stability.[77] The army made it clear at the time of the 1990 election it did not favour any party. It has shown no favouritism subsequently, but because the NUP accepted the constraints imposed on political activities without public demur, its distance from the SLORC and SPDC was not readily apparent.

---

75   Xinhua, 11 February 2008.

76   Taingyintha Silongnyinyuntyei Pati, Siyunyei Baho Komiti Danachok, *Taingyintha Silonnyinyatyei Pati Lanyunt Thabawtaya* (National Unity Party, Organisation Central Committee, *National Unity Party's Policy Direction*) (November 1995).

77   See Maung Maung, *1988 Uprising in Burma*, pp. 191, 262.

THE STATE IN MYANMAR

After the election, most of the political parties dissolved either for lack of public support or because of pressure by the government. Eventually, only ten parties remained formally registered with the Election Commission. In addition to the NLD and the NUP, both of which claimed 'national' coverage, the other eight represented specific ethnic or minority communities. The Shan Nationalities League for Democracy (SNLD), the largest of these, was placed under great pressure to refrain from political activities, especially after the arrest of its chairman, Hkun Htun Oo, and other party leaders in 2005 for allegedly conspiring with armed and illegal Shan separatist forces as well as some ceasefire groups to undermine state stability and security.[78] The other parties were the Union Pa-O National Organisation, the Shan State Kokang Democratic Party, the Lahu National Development Party, the Myo (or) Khamo National Solidarity Organisation, the Wa National Development and Unity Party, the Kokang Democracy and Unity Party, and the Union Kayin League.

The new political conditions created by the army's pledge eventually to return Myanmar to a multiparty constitutional political system allowed a relatively small degree of organisational opportunities. The confrontational atmosphere created between the army and the NLD, and the threat or reality of political demonstrations at critical times, contributed to a politically repressive atmosphere. Censorship of the press prevailed and exiled opposition internet sites were blocked. Despite the establishment of a number of private publishing houses with weekly newspapers and journals, and more relaxed public media in terms of non-political content, the generation of genuine political discussions, other than those of the teashop variety that survived on rumours, did not emerge, except in tiny pockets, under army rule.

The revival of student politics and other political movements

The 12 March 1988 teashop incident that became the starting point of seven months of anti-BSPP activities had no real political content in itself. The apparently spontaneous organisation of students on the university campuses echoed the tales of student heroism in the 1930s taught to succeeding generations through the school curriculum and the mobilisation activities of the Lansin Youth organisation, and celebrated on key national holidays. They were initially unorganised and uncoordinated, but a number of indi-

---

78   Information Committee of the State Peace and Development Council, Press Conference, 15 March 2005, pp. 26-9, 32-5.

viduals tried in 1988 to lead the students to articulate their demands for the right to organise independently of the governing party. These individuals, reflecting both the danger they faced from the authorities and their own romantic association with the 1930s and 1940s, assumed a number of *noms de guerre*. At one time, for example, there were three or more student leaders calling themselves *Min Ko Naing* (conqueror of the king), a name that eventually became identified with one totemic activist, Paw Oo Tun.

During 1988, as the students grew in confidence, and the authorities further revealed their incompetence, demands of a political and economic nature were made. The role of a number of the previously underground reading groups, formed to exchange views on current developments in theory and practice, some affiliated with Communist or other political groups, led the authorities to see the hand of more nefarious political forces at work among the student population. When the universities were eventually reopened in May 1988, Military Intelligence identified a 'whispering campaign' and other forms of agitation that, it claimed, led to further student demonstrations in June and July before the adult political leaders joined the students in demanding political change and repeated the call for the end of the one-party system.[79] The strike committee became the organisational form the renewed student movement took initially and several students, arrested in March but released in May, became the focal points for student activism. However, their ability to control the situation was limited and violence increasingly came to mark demonstrations and events.[80] Students remained in the forefront of the massive demonstrations of August and September and many volunteered to provide protection and advice to the older politicians. The success of these organisations, and the apparent lack of coordination among them, are reflected in the claim that the government spoke with leaders of 279 such bodies in August-September 1988.[81]

The centre of student politics was Yangon Arts and Sciences University (YASU or RASU) though students at other institutions were also active. At RASU, three factions of students emerged. While they all worked against the government, leadership rivalries among them were too strong to allow them to form a firm coalition. These groups were led by Paw Oo Tun and

---

79   *Speech Delivered by State Law and Order Restoration Council Secretary (1) Major General Khin Nyunt at the Special 110th Press Conference, 14 May 1991*, pp. 5-6, 15; Min Maung Maung, *Tatmadaw and It's Leadership Role*, p. 273.

80   Boudrea, *Resisting Dictatorship*, pp. 198-9.

81   Min Maung Maung, *Tatmadaw and It's Leadership Role*, p. 276.

Moe Thee Zun, both of whom had Communist affiliations, and Min Zaya and Than Win. By criticising the government strongly and publicly for the corrupt and incompetent behaviour of its officials, they began to overcome the inertia that had kept students from publicly opposing the regime since the U Thant affair in 1974. Optimism about their eventual success grew as the government released students arrested following the March demonstrations and conceded the death of the 42 persons at that time. That optimism was bolstered after Chairman Ne Win's resignation. When they received financial and other support from Western embassies, they began to feel that the BSPP would have to concede to them. After the BBC and VOA Burmese language broadcasting services began reporting on the students' activities, including the call for a general strike on 8 August 1988, the students' movement became nationwide. When foreign radio stations reported that members of the United States Senate had passed a resolution supporting their movement and criticising the government, the students' numbers swelled as powerful foreign forces appeared ready to assist them in changing the state's managers.

After the putsch, students organised as many as ten political parties, the most prominent of which was the Democratic Party for New Society (DPNS), led by Moe Thee Zun.[82] However, many students did not believe that participating in open politics would lead to effective change, and from earlier in 1988 some had begun leaving central and southern Myanmar cities to go to the border where they met with Communist or ethnic insurgent groups. Criticising Daw Aung San Suu Kyi and others for accepting the army's proposal to hold national elections, after abandoning the demand for an interim government,[83] many believed that, in imitation of the heroism of Bogyoke Aung San and the Thirty Comrades, they would be able to raise support for a successful armed attack on the government. The SLORC responded to the large numbers leaving the cities to trek to the borders with an invitation to the students to return home, enunciated a week after the putsch by the Vice-Chairman, General Than Shwe.[84] Eventually, more than 10,000 returned after the opening of resettlement camps in cooperation with the Thai government. To these urban youth, conditions on the border were very inhospitable, especially as the foreign assistance they were expecting to receive did not materialise.

82   Smith, *Burma: Insurgency and the Politics of Insurgency,* p. 407.
83   See footnote 47 above.
84   Min Maung Maung, *Tatmawdaw and Its Leadership Role,* p. 288.

After the election and the refusal of the SLORC to transfer power until after a constitution had been enacted, the student movement maintained linkages with other groups with which it had become loosely allied in 1988. These included factions of the monkhood and other pockets of society that maintained strong opposition to the military regime. From time to time through the 1990s, they managed to organise student demonstrations, as when Daw Aung San Suu Kyi received the Nobel Peace Prize and in the months following her release from house arrest in 1995. Because of student activism, universities were closed for three years after 1991 and intermittently throughout the 1990s in order to foreclose opportunities for protests to develop. After they were reopened in 1994, the students were given greatly shortened courses of instruction and the standards of higher education were further lowered. Established city campuses such as that of RASU were devoted only to teaching postgraduate students and undergraduate studies were relocated to more distant campuses and institutions in the new suburbs of the cities. While student numbers grew dramatically in subsequent years, there was no overt renewal of student politics. Educational staff closely monitored their students to ensure that incipient demonstrations did not occur. Moreover, the new economic and social situation turned most students away from politics towards other pursuits such as making money, mastering new technologies, going abroad to work, or global music fads and dress styles.[85]

Some activist students, however, kept the movement alive by establishing communication links with colleagues in exile. They attempted to isolate and pressure the regime by generating stories designed to encourage the international action against the military. Thus, when events of political interest occurred, such as when the NLD organised the CRPP, small demonstrations organised by students and former students received international publicity. However, the decline in student activism after the turn of the millennium was demonstrated by the failure of students in significant numbers to join in protests organised in Yangon and other cities in August and September 2007. Initially called and led by student activists arrested in 1988 and 1989 and released in 2005 or earlier, known as the 88 Generation, nominally headed by Min Ko Naing (Paw Oo Tun), they attracted relatively little public support. Many members of the 1988 Generation were rearrested for their organisational activities after the 2007 demonstrations,

---

85   Kyaw Yin Hlaing, "Myanmar in 2004: Why Military Rule Continues," *Southeast Asian Affairs 2004*, pp. 231-56.

though they were accused of other civil or criminal offences. There were said to be about 1,700 political prisoners in 2008, after the number had previously fallen to about 1,100, according to organisations such as Amnesty International and the UN Commission on Human Rights.

Buddhist monks participated in the events of 1988, but did not take a prominent role in the leadership. The senior abbots who composed the State Sangha Nayaka Committee, the top governing body of the monkhood, merely issued appeals for moderation and restraint during the demonstrations, while monks joined lay members of their communities to form neighbourhood security committees and provide other public services. However, following the army putsch, a number of monks in Mandalay, Sagaing and other areas of monastic concentration threatened to defy the new military authorities and withdraw the acceptance of alms from army personnel. These public demonstrations to show the alleged illegitimacy of the authorities, and the moral repugnance of the monkhood at the force that the army had used in suppressing the demonstrations, were highly damaging for military and regime morale and esteem. Affected were not only the officer corps but also their families as well as regular members of the army. The SLORC Chairman General Saw Maung was then reminded by the head of the monkhood of the obligation of a king to maintain the purity of the monkhood, the *sangha*. As the rules of the monkhood forbade its members from participating in secular political affairs, he and his government were thus authorised by the highest monastic authorities to defrock and arrest monks who refused to obey the senior monks and cease their avowedly political activity. Following these events in 1990-91, the monkhood largely refrained from overt political activity until 2007, except briefly in 1996 in Mandalay. However, a number of senior monks did continue to comment, often subtly and wittily, on the behaviour of both the military government and its political opponents.

Unexpectedly, in September 2007, after nineteen years of military rule, the largest public demonstrations of opposition to the state's managers since 1988 occurred with monks providing political leadership. Coinciding with unexplained reductions in state subsidies to petrol prices and a five-fold increase in the price of the compressed natural gas (CNG) in August, effectively doubling bus fares, and general economic discontent in Yangon, as noted above, members of the 88 Generation of Students attempted but failed to organise widespread public demonstrations against the regime. In early September, however, conflicts occurred between local authorities and

Buddhist monks in Pakokku, Sittwe, and other towns, leading to demonstrations in other cities, initially by monks alone demanding an apology from the authorities for their behaviour. After about a week, joined by members of the NLD and other political groups, their demands escalated to what was tantamount to regime change. Eventually, more than 10,000 monks and perhaps three times as many laypersons joined in daily demonstrations in Yangon and elsewhere. The army responded by raiding several monasteries where activist monks were known to be organising, and firing on demonstrators who refused to disperse. Several of the most prominent organisers of the monks' demonstrations had been student activists in 1988.[86] Those not arrested fled to the Thai border area.

The loose groupings of students, former students, and monks that have been politically active after 1990 were joined by members of the older generation, usually calling themselves the Veteran Politicians Organisation. Especially active in the late 1990s, when they tried to broker political discussions between the government and the NLD, these senior political figures continued to try to influence all sides in the nation's continuing political stalemate. Their organisational strength, however, was skeletal and, like so many other organisations that emerged after 1990, it was an organisation composed primarily of its own officers. Given the political atmosphere that prevailed in the country, they could be little else. By 2008, what little activity remained of the student and monastic political movements of the 1980s and 1990s was largely confined to the politics of exiled political groups. The unwillingness of state managers to allow overt political activity prior to the inauguration of a new constitution ensured that remained the case.

The emergence of exile politics

As the inability of the NLD, and other political parties and protest groups, effectively to organise to dislodge the control of the state by the army became more apparent in the early 1990s, exiled anti-SPDC politics seemed for many political activists the most viable strategy available. The state and the army were impervious to domestic political pressures, many activists

---

86   According to the United States Special Rapporteur for Human Rights in Myanmar, at least 31 persons were killed and several thousand arrested, most released after investigation. There were unsubstantiated claims that at least one of those killed was a monk. For details, see Robert H. Taylor, 'Growing Pressure for Change but the Regime Remains Obdurate', in Daljit Singh and Tin Maung Maung Than, eds, *Southeast Asian Affairs 2008* (Singapore: Institute of Southeast Asian Studies, 2008), pp. 247-273.

believed. Therefore, they argued, foreign support was essential if the contest for the state was to lead to regime change. However, individuals who went into exile rarely had faith in the efficacy of the existing expatriate political organisations, each of which, like the CRDB, had its own lineage back into events in Myanmar. Consequently, the number of such organisations grew substantially. In the international atmosphere that prevailed in the post-Cold War era, where human rights replaced anti-Communism as the ideological goal of Western politicians and governments—particularly the United States and its ally the United Kingdom—exiled political groups arguing their cause was that of democracy found a ready audience on university campuses, and in Western media and capitals. They also found ample funding relatively easy to acquire, not only from government sponsored organisations such as the Congressionally-funded National Endowment for Democracy (NED), the Open Society Foundation of Mr George Soros, German political party-affiliated foundations, and trade unions and other groups which prior to 1988 had ignored Myanmar. In Europe the European Union, and particularly Scandinavian governments, and non-governmental organisations, became a source of funding for the exile community.[87]

Thus the issues of human rights in Myanmar became a minor issue in the domestic politics of other, more powerful and wealthier countries. Aided by the growth of the internet and the worldwide web, the claims of anti-regime activists were widely received and their veracity rarely challenged by previously uninformed foreign audiences. The ability of state officials to explain and justify their actions was undermined by their inability to master sophisticated communications media in a foreign language or to understand the social and political changes that Western societies had undergone. Moreover, they had little knowledge of how Western democracies functioned. This was one of the consequences of Myanmar's previous twenty-six years of international isolation. In a mirror image of the siege mentality of the army government, some in the United States saw the cam-

---

87   The website of one source, the National Endowment for Democracy (www.ned.org.grants), showed grants amounting to $US3 million in 2006. USAID allocated US$10,890,000 for Burma in the same year, more than half of which was for political activities outside Myanmar. See www.usaid.gov/about_usaid/. There may be overlap in these funding sources. Groups such as Earth Rights International (www.earthrights.org) showed expenditure of over one million dollars in 2006. Income for the activities of exile groups is often hidden in the expenses of various groups and organisations that sponsor their activities in third countries. Examples are the Canadian Friends of Burma or Association Suisse-Birmanie, etc.

paign against the SLORC/SPDC as a form of low intensity warfare or an 'unarmed insurrection'.[88]

The most prominent exile groups were the National Council of the Union of Burma (NCUB), the Coalition Government of the Union of Burma (NCGUB), the All Burma Students' Democratic Front (ABSDF), the National League for Democracy (Liberated Area) (NLD-[LA]), the Forum for Democracy in Burma (FDB), the Federation of Trade Unions (Burma) (FTU[B]), and the Ethnic Nationalities Solidarity and Cooperation Committee (ENSCC).[89] These organisations took similar positions on a number of strategic and tactical issues in the anti-military campaign, though their origins differed according to whether they were rooted in Myanmar's urban or ethnic political issues. All shared the avowed general goals of removing the army government and establishing a federal system of government that would provide a greater degree of autonomy to people living in the border areas. Several of them, such as the NCUB and the FTU(B), shared officers. For example, Maung Maung (a.k.a. Pyithit Nyunt Wai), accused by the government of being a thief and an absconder, became particularly prominent for his role as Secretary-General of several exile organisations.

Most of the exile political groups shared the NLD's adherence to non-violence, but not all. Calling for revolution, on 5 November 1988, the All Burma Students Democratic Front (ABDSF) was formed at the KNU base at Kawmoorah near the Thai border.[90] Echoing Bogyoke Aung San six decades earlier, it hoped to defeat the government by military means. Although the ABDSF was able to raise several armed groups and militarily engaged the tatmadaw in some skirmishes, it was soon riven by violent internal disputes and accusations of infiltration by government agents.[91] A number were subsequently killed or 'executed'. The group split into two exile political groups, with some joining the Democratic Party for a New Society (DPNS) in exile and others forming the Network for Democracy and De-

---

88   Lisa Brooten, "Human Rights Discourse and the Development of Democracy in a Multi-ethnic State', *Asian Journal of Communications*, Vol. 14, No. 2, September, 2004), p. 178. See also Dr Brooten's 'Global Communications, Local Conceptions: Human Rights and the Politics of Communications among the Burmese Opposition-in-Exile' (PhD, Ohio University, Athens, Ohio), and Kurt Schock, *Unarmed Insurrections: People Power Movements in Nondemocracies* (Minneapolis: University of Minnesota Press, 2005), pp. 91-119 and *passim*.

89   Renamed in 2001 the Ethnic Nationalities Council.

90   Smith, *Burma: Insurgency and the Politics of Ethnicity*, p. 407.

91   Kyaw Zwa Moe, Naw Seng and Ko Thet, 'It's a Jungle Out There', *Irrawaddy*, June 2002.

velopment (NDD), while a hard core remained engaged in armed struggle. The factionalism of the ABDSF, like the factionalism that afflicted other exile organisations, often reflected leadership rivalries that had emerged in the events of 1988 within Myanmar itself.[92] Although the ABSDF failed in its initial military efforts, it persisted as a lobbying organisation in Thailand. Students and former students, some perhaps affiliated with the organisation, continued in a number of ways to try to effect the political situation in Myanmar by, for example, hijacking a Myanmar aeroplane flying from Bangkok in 1990, taking hostages in the Myanmar embassy in Bangkok in 1999, and calling for a renewal of mass anti-government demonstrations on symbolic dates such as 9-9-99.[93] Groups taking the name of students, such as the Vigorous Burmese Student Warriors, occasionally claimed, or were said by the government, to have perpetrated various terrorist bombings within Myanmar.[94]

A tenuous alliance between urban political activists and ethnic non-Communist insurgent groups was formed in 1988. Two months after the army putsch, a meeting was held at the KNU base at Klerday, near the Thai border, to form the Democratic Alliance of Burma (DAB). Members of 22 political parties and other organisations, including the CRDB and the ABSDF, met. Key leadership roles in the DAB were assumed by longstanding anti-government insurgent leaders from the NDF, such as Bo Mya from the Karen National Union, Brang Seng from the Kachin Independence Organisation, and Nai Shwe Kyin from the New Mon State Party.[95] The alliance of urban political dissidents with veteran armed contestants for state power allowed the regime to accuse the urban political activists and their affiliated parties of collaborating with terrorists and traitors. The DAB was joined in 1990 by the NCGUB as a subsidiary member, but its achievements remained nugatory. After a number of its initial members entered into ceasefire agreements with the SLORC, it was absorbed into the National Council of the Union of Burma (NCUB) in the mid-1990s.[96]

The capacity of exile activists to articulate anti-regime sentiments, widely shared among the audiences of Western media via the internet and news-

92 See Kyaw Yin Hlaing, 'Burma: Civil Society Skirting Regime Rules', pp. 408-12.

93 Wingfield, 'Myanmar: Political Stasis and a Precarious Economy', p. 212.

94 For example, *The New Light of Myanmar*, 23 May 2008.

95 Smith, *Burma: Insurgency and the Politics of Ethnicity*, p. 307.

96 The last of its leaders, Bo Mya, died in 2006.

THE STATE REDUX, 1988-2008

papers and television, magnified the political power of such groups in the
eyes of political activists inside the country. This is alleged to have encouraged political quiescence as it generated a belief that external forces would
resolve Myanmar's political and other issues without the need for domestic
activity. While exile media campaigns initially concentrated on issues surrounding the 1988 uprising and the abortive 1990 election, as the military
power of the KNU and other ethnically designated armed groups waned,
they also began to use international media to generate political support.[97]
Groups such as the Karen Human Rights Group (KHRG) and the Shan
Women's Action Network (SWAN) were developed to publicise alleged
human rights violations. Exile politics, especially in Thailand, thus came to
be driven by two imperatives, one to organise political activities designed
to strengthen anti-regime political forces inside and outside the country
and the other to document alleged human rights abuses against the ethnic
minorities in order to generate international pressure to isolate the military
government. Groups, however, had to orient their activities to the priorities of the foreign funding organisations, ensuring that gender, environmental, and equality issues entered into exile political discourse along with
the original political or ethnic demands heard within domestic Myanmar
politics. Conflict resolution seminars, media training programmes, and internet awareness campaigns became conditions of funding for exile activists
as Western political concerns and techniques were disseminated to exile activists. The government publicised in particular the training given by Gene
Sharp and the Einstein Institute in techniques of non-violent resistance to
bring down an authoritarian regime.[98] The heterogeneity of the exile political community reflected not only its ethnic and political diversity, and conflicting strategies and rivalries of the political actors, but also the funding
agencies' origins. Certain groups, such as the Federation of Trade Unions
(Burma), that achieved recognition from international labour movements

---

97   For the use of refugees and the issue of refugees in the internationalisation
      of internal conflicts see Daniel Byman et al., eds, *Trends in Outside Support
      for Insurgent Movements* (Santa Monica, CA: RAND Corporation, 2001), and
      Fiona Terry, *Condemned to Repeat: The Paradox of Humanitarian Action* (Ithaca,
      NY: Cornell University Press, 2002). For an example of a refugee organisations
      lobbying activities, see Burma Border Consortium, *Reclaiming the Right to Rice:
      Food Security and Internal Displacement in Eastern Burma* (Bangkok: Burma
      Border Consortium, October 2003).

98   Gene Sharp, *From Dictatorship to Democracy: A Conceptual Framework for Lib-
      eration* (Boston: Einstein Institute, 1993, reprint of first edition published in
      Bangkok: Committee for the Restoration of Democracy in Burma, 1993).

6.7.   Exile Political Organisations circa 2005

Organisation	Member of NCUB	Attended ENC Congress
National Coalition of the Union of Burma (NCUB)		
National Democratic Front (NDF)	*	*
Arakan Liberation Party (ALP)		*
Lahu Democratic Front (LDF)		
Pa-Laung State Liberation Front (PSLF)		
Pa-O People's Liberation Organisation (PPLO)		*
Wa National Organisation (WNO)		
New Mon State Party (NMSP)		
Kayan New Land Party (KNLP)		*
Karen National Union (KNU)		*
Democratic Alliance of Burma (DAB)	*	
Chin National Front (CNF)		*
All Burma Students Democratic Front (ABSDF)		
Overseas Burmese Liberation Front (OBLF)		
Overseas Karen Organisation		
All Burma Young Monks Union (ABYMU)		
Committee for Restoration of Democracy Burma (CRDB)		
Democratic Party for New Society (DPNS)		
People's Liberation Front (PLF)		
People's Progressive Front (PPF)		
People's Defence Force (PDF)		
Muslim Liberation Organisation Burma (MLOB)		
All Burma Muslim Union (ABMU)		
Democratic Party of Arakan (DPA)		
Arakan League for Democracy (ALD)		*
Naga National League for Democracy (NNLD)		
Myeik Dawei United Front (MDUF)		
Network for Democracy and Development (NDD)		
Federation of Trade Unions Burma (FTUB)		
Members of Parliament Union (MPU)	*	
National League for Democracy (Liberated Area) (NLD[LA])	*	
National Coalition Government of the Union of Burma (NCGUB)	*	
Free Burma Coalition (FBC)		
Association to Assist Political Prisoners (AAPP)		

Forum for Democracy in Burma (FDB)
All Federation of of Students Unions
Foreign Affairs Committee (ABSUF-
FAC)
Burmese Women's Union (1995)
Yaung Chi Oo Workers Association
**Ethnic Nationalities Council (Union of
Burma) (ENC)**
Arakan National Council (ANC) *
Chin National League for Democracy *
(Exile) (CNLD)
Kachin National Organisation *
Kachin Women's Association in *
Thailand
Karen Women's Association *
Karen Youth Organisation *
Karenni National Progressive Party *
Karenni National Youth Organisation *
Karenni Women's Organisation *
Lahu National Development Party *
Mon National Democratic Front *
Mon Unity League *
Mra People's Party *
Nationalities Youth Forum *
Political Affairs Committee of Chinland *
Shan Women's Action Network *
United Nationalities League for *
Democracy (Liberated Area)
Women's League of Chinland *
Democratic Organisation of Kayan
Unity
Zomi National Congress
Kachin National Congress for
Democracy
Union Karen League
Mara People's Party
Kayah State All Nationalities League for
Democracy
Euro-Burma Office
Vigorous Burmese Student Warriors

Sources: www.ncus.org, old.ncub.net.mpu, www.democraticforumburma.org,
www.encburma.org

over the issue of unpaid labour, and Earth Rights International, which led
in the litigation against an American oil and gas company for its investment
in constructing a gas pipeline, became particularly prominent in the campaign to make Myanmar's domestic politics an international issue.

Exile activists in the United States and other advanced capitalist countries were able to use the stories publicised by the media to bolster their
anti-investment campaigns. Organisations such as the Free Burma Coa-

lition (FBC) quickly developed the media skills of a single issue political movement in contemporary America. These skills were employed in mounting effective disinvestment and consumer boycott campaigns which by the late 1990s had made the reputational costs of doing business in Myanmar disproportion to the potential profits.[99] United States sanctions legislation in 1997 and a 2003 trade ban were largely symbolic, except for the textile trade, given the effectiveness of the consumer boycott campaigns that assisted their passage.[100] The Burma Campaign UK echoed its American counterpart in the United Kingdom.

Activist news agencies such as Mizzima and internet and magazine outlets such as *Irrawaddy* became increasingly plausible in purveying their interpretation of developments in Myanmar. An exile radio station, the Democratic Voice of Burma, added a Burmese voice to the foreign radio stations that broadcast anti-regime messages into the country. Human rights 'documentation' groups, such as the KHRG, often served as proxies or information outlets for more avowedly political and military organisations such as the KNU.[101]

The intention of leading participants in exile politics was either to terminate the military regime or to establish political autonomy for their groups. However, unexpectedly two other ends were achieved. One was to limit the range of politically acceptable issues that could be debated in shaping Western government politics towards Myanmar. Issues came to be seen in black or white and those who, for example, argued that sanctions were probably counterproductive were accused of being traitors, if Myanmar citizens, or military regime apologists, if foreign observers. The greater the distance from the Myanmar, it seemed, the greater the intensity of these views.[102] More important for politics within the country, international radio, primarily via the British Broadcasting Corporation's, Radio Free Asia's, and the

99   The founder of the Free Burma Coalition, Dr Zarni, subsequently concluded that confrontation and sanctions would not achieve political change in Myanmar. See Zarni and May Oo, *Common Problems, Shared Responsibilities: Citizens' Quest for National Reconciliation in Burma/Myanmar* (NP: Free Burma Coalition, October, 2004).

100   Kyaw Yin Hlaing, 'Burma: Civil Society Skirting Regime Rules', pp. 412-14.

101   These were sometimes retold by non-Myanmar cause organisations such as Christian Solidarity Worldwide and related evangelical and political movements, so that reports reached multiple media outlets.

102   See the observations of Michael Aung-Thwin, 'Parochial Universalism, Democracy Jihad and the Orientalist Image of Burma: The New Evangelism', *Pacific Affairs*, Vol. 74, No. 4, Winter 2001-2, pp. 483-505.

Voice of America's Burmese-language broadcasts, and the exile Democratic Voice of Burma, allowed the views of exile political actors to be heard. While the Myanmar government claimed these broadcasts were evidence of an international conspiracy to subjugate the state and its managers, the impact of exile or foreign media politics on domestic opinion is difficult to assess. Politically aware audiences listened to their broadcasts regularly, but whether they believed what they heard or acted upon it is unknown. On balance, it would appear that exile politics had a greater impact outside Myanmar than inside.[103]

Ceasefire agreements and new ethnic political relations

The major political, economic and social changes that have occurred in Myanmar since 1988 are as much the result of the new ethnic politics arising from a series of ceasefire agreements between the government and the ethnically designated insurgent groups as of the end of socialism or the promise of revival of multi-party politics—if not more. Amidst the welter of events that engulfed the state and challenged its incumbent personnel in 1988, largely unanticipated was the imminent change in relationships between the government and a majority of the political and ethnic groups that had been militarily contesting the state for control of territory for most of the four decades since independence. Most of these groups eventually became officially recognised semi-autonomous 'sub-contractors' of the state or were allowed to establish legitimate business interests in the larger national economy. Having been locked into low-level but seemingly endless armed conflict for more than 40 years, these groups had little to show for their efforts except poverty and death.[104] Villagers had been the subject of predatory armed groups that moved through upper elevations of the hills and mountains, descending into the valleys to contest with the government for temporary control. The smuggling of opium, timber, cattle, gemstones

---

103   On the failure of the exile political movement to achieve its goals and its condition by 2008, see Kyaw Yin Hlaing, 'The State of the Pro-Democracy Movement in Authoritarian Myanmar/Burma' in Xialon Gue, ed., *Myanmar/Burma: Challenges and Perspective*, pp. 67-105.

104   General Saw Maung discussed the death toll for all sides in the civil war in an address lamenting the destruction that Myanmar had experienced as a result of ideological and ethnic conflict on 9 January 1990 to the members of the SLORC; see *State Law and Order Restoration Council Chairman Commander-in-Chief of the Defence Services General Saw Maung's Addresses* (Yangon: News and Periodicals Enterprises, 7 January 1991), pp. 327-8.

and other products, and illicit taxation or theft from villagers in contested zones, had been their primary means of support.

The achievement of a tenuous peace in large parts of the country previously under the control of mutually antagonistic armed groups resulted from a series of ceasefire agreements with ethnically designated armies towards which the government had previously pursued a policy of military suppression. The limited resources the socialist state provided the army, arrayed against the myriad sources of supply available to the ethnic armies, plus the inhospitable terrain they occupied, and their foreign supporters and domestic allies, made military victory over them difficult. The Four Cuts policy that proved effective against the BCP in the Bago Yoma and the KNU in the Delta did not apply to the border areas.[105] The inability of any group to claim regional domination was perhaps the major, but unspoken, factor in the events of the early 1990s that evolved into a twenty-year process of learning to live, if not in harmony, at least in peace. The northern and all but the most extreme and remote eastern border areas of Myanmar once more became open for relatively easy access by both agents of the state and international and domestic institutions that shared its developmental goals and obeyed the government's laws and regulations.

The decision that began this transformation was made in 1979 when the Chinese Communist Party terminated support for the BCP. Five months after the 1988 putsch, the consequences of that decision began to be felt. Before then, the government denied that a change in policy toward its armed opponents was imminent,[106] despite the cordial relations that had developed between the government of Myanmar and the two neighbouring countries that had provided sanctuary and sustenance to its armed opponents in the past. Even before 1988, China and Myanmar had signed several border trade agreements and the re-demarcation of the border had commenced in 1987, with the Myanmar members of joint survey teams forced to approach the border from the Chinese side as the government did not have access via its own side.[107] The Thai Deputy Prime Minister

---

105   The Four Cuts policy, whereby insurgents were denied recruits, intelligence, food and weaponry, was inappropriate in border areas as opponents fled into China or Thailand where they received those requisites as well as shelter from pursuing troops.

106   *State Law and Order Restoration Council Chairman Commander-in-Chief of the Defence Services General Saw Maung's Addresses*, p. 56, reprinting an interview in *Asiaweek* given on 17 January 1990.

107   Economic Intelligence Unit, *Country Report: Thailand, Burma*, No. 1, 1987, p.

Chavalit Yongchaiyudh, the first senior government minister to visit Yangon after the putsch, made it clear that his government no longer regarded the existence of an armed border buffer zone as an aspect of the Kingdom's defence policy. Trade gradually replaced politics as the top priority in both relationships.

In March 1989, while the NLD was implementing its confrontation policy towards the SLORC, along the China-Myanmar border events occurred that ultimately proved advantageous to the government. In the middle of that month, in the northern Shan State, ethnic Kokang troops under the control of the Communist Party turned against their ageing leaders and ousted the party from their territories.[108] Expelling the ideologue guides of the workers' revolution after 20 years, they formed the Myanmar National Democratic Alliance (MNDA) and declared autonomy. Having received little assistance from the Chinese Communist Party for nearly a decade, the Kokang group, and others, had to rely increasingly on the illicit opium trade to support themselves and their families. During the 1980s, the Burma Communist Party had become one of the largest drug smuggling organisations in South East Asia. One month later, further north along the China-Myanmar border, ethnic Wa troops of the BCP similarly mutinied and formed the Myanmar Pyi (Country) National Solidarity Party, normally known as the Wa State Army. Both groups eventually entered into unwritten ceasefire agreements with the government, pledging not to secede from the Union. A former drug 'warlord', knowledgeable about the area, helped facilitate the negotiation of these agreements with officers of DDSI.[109] The Kokang and Wa areas were officially recognised as Shan State (North) Special Regions 1 and 2 respectively.

Seven months after the initial defections from the BCP, a third group, then not affiliated with the party but a member of the National Democratic Front (NDF) of non-Communist anti-central state groups, also agreed to 'rejoin the legal fold', as the government described the ceasefire agreements. The Shan State Army agreement was followed a month later by a third BCP

31.

108   Min Maung Maung, *Tatmadaw's Leadership Role*, p. 290; Lintner, *The Rise and Fall of the Communist Party*, pp. 39-46.

109   Min Maung Maung, *Tatmadaw's Leadership Role*, p. 290. See also the essays in Martin Jelsma, Tom Kramer and Pietje Vervest, eds, *Trouble in the Triangle: Opium and Conflict in Burma* (Chiang Mai, Thailand: Silkworm, 2005), especially that of Adrian Cowell, 'Opium Anarchy in the Shan State of Burma', pp. 1-22.

group of mixed Lahu, Akha and Shan ethnicities in eastern Shan State, the two becoming Shan State (North) and Shan State (East) Special Regions 3 and 4 respectively. The final mutinies of the Communist armies came in mid-January, 1990, when the New Democratic Army, the former BCP Unit 101, also abandoned the revolutionary cause to cooperate with the government, becoming officially recognised as Kachin State Special Region 1. The termination of Myanmar's post-independence civil war then fell into abeyance for one year, but as the army turned its resources away from the immediate China border area, other groups came under greater military pressure and they soon entered into ceasefire talks. In January 1991, the 4th Brigade of the non-Communist Kachin Independence Army left the NDF and DAB and reached a ceasefire agreement with the government, becoming Kachin State Special Region 2. The Pa O National Organisation agreed a ceasefire in April 1991, followed by the Palaung State Liberation Army in May 1991, but from then until early 1994 there was another hiatus and intense armed conflict continued in several areas. Following a ceasefire agreement between the KIO/KIA and the government in February 1994, conditions in northern Myanmar were radically altered. Given the size, strength, and prominence of the KIO among the non-Communist insurgent DAB, and the success of mutually acceptable intermediaries in negotiating the only written ceasefire agreement, the complete termination of insurgency looked possible.[110] Negotiations were then underway, with the assistance of mutually acceptable intermediaries from the Kayin community, between the government and KNU. On the cusp of agreement, the KNU leadership broke off discussions, which led to a split in the organisation as the Democratic Kayin Buddhist Army (DKBA) returned to government-controlled territory and turned against the predominantly Christian leadership of the organisation. Soon other, smaller KNU factions followed including a group led by the former KNU Timber Minister and Treasurer, Padoh Aung San, himself a Christian. Under mounting military pressure, the largest group then operating in the Shan State, the Mong Tai Army, led by Khun Sa, infamous as the largest drug warlord in the area,

---

110   Agreements were concluded with the Karenni State Nationalities Liberation Front (KSNLF), the Kayah New Land Party (KNLP), the Shan State Nationalities Liberation Organisation (SSNLO), the Karenni National Progressive Party (KNPP), and the New Mon State Party (NMSP) during the succeeding 12 months.

6.8.   Major Ceasefire Agreements, 1989-1997

	Name of Group	Date	Headquarters	Ethnicity/Designation
1	Northern Shan State Special Region 1	31 March 1989	Laukkai	Kokang
2	Northern Shan State Special Region 2	9 May 1989	Panhsan	Wa
3	Eastern Shan State Special Region 4	30 June 1989	Mongla	Shan/Akha/Lisu
4	Kachin State Special Region 1	15 December 1989	Panwa	National Democratic Army
5	Northern Shan State Special Region 3	24 September 1989	Seinkyawt	Shan State Army
6	Northern Shan State Special Region 5	11 January 1991	Kaungkha	Kachin Democratic Army
7	Southern Shan State Special Region 6	18 March 1991	Kyauktalon	Pa-O (White)
8	Northern Shan State Special Region 7	21 April 1991	Namtu	Palaung
9	Kayah State Special Region 1	27 February 1992	Mobye/Pekhon	Kayah National Group
10	Kachin State Special Region 2	24 February 1994	Laisin	Kachin Independence Organisation
11	Kayah State Special Region 3	26 July 1994	Pyinhsaung	Kayan Pyithit
12	Kayah State Special Region 2	5 September 1994	Hoya/Biya	Kayinni National People's Liberation Front
13	Shan State Nationalities People's Liberation Organisation	9 October 1994	Naungtaw	Pa-O (Red)
14	Kayinni National Progressive Party	21 March 1995	Dawtamagyi/Hit pokalo	Kayinni
15	New Mon State Party	29 June 1995	Yechaungphya	New Mon State Party
16	Shan State Army	5 January 1996	Homein/Lwelan	Mong Tai Army (Khun Sa)
17	Burma Communist Party (Rakhine)	4 June 1997	Buthidaung/Mau ngtaw	

surrendered with the bulk of his forces, handing over their arms to government troops in early 1996.[111]

This litany of ceasefire agreements should not be taken as summarising either a smooth or a certain process. Each of the groups controlled different regions with contrasting assets and resources, variable military capacities, dissimilar linkages with political and economic interests inside and outside Myanmar, and contrasting degrees of political sophistication. The former BCP groups had strong ties with China. The encouragement the Chinese government tacitly provided the ceasefire agreements helped ensure their viability despite a number of tensions between the central state's personnel and very suspicious and isolated ethnic leaders. The KIO/KIA ceasefire was

---

111   Maung Pho Shoke, *Why Did U Khun Sa's MTA Exchange Arms for Peace* (Yangon: Aung Zaw, nd [199?]).

facilitated by indigenous non-governmental organisations (NGOs) affiliated with the Christian churches in the Kachin State. Armed groups along the Thai border, given their links with foreign, often Christian evangelical groups, refugee assistance organisations, and foreign government agencies in the context of the more open political system of Thailand, meant that ceasefire negotiations in that area faced a number of countervailing pressures that made it more difficult to reach, and keep, agreements. The existence of large communities of refugees and ethnically similar groups to the ceasefire and non-ceasefire groups along the Thai border made for a much more fraught transitional process, still incomplete, than that which occurred in the north.

The oldest and once most powerful ethnically identified insurgent army, the KNLA, and its parent organisation, the KNU, having been on the verge of ceasefire agreements at least twice if not more frequently between 1994 and 2004, by 2008 had withered to a mere shadow of its former self. Capable of arming probably fewer than 2,000 men if required, it controlled little if any territory within Myanmar. Its leaders who had died natural deaths or been assassinated by former allies left their successors an organisation which could occasionally harass government forces, thus generating government efforts to find KNU supporters in border villages. The Thai police organised raids on all the remaining KNU leaders in Maesot and other border towns in 2008, underlining the point that the Kayin independence battle was over. Many KNU supporters who had lived in refugee camps in Thailand, a number for twenty years or more moved to third countries and their places in the camps were taken by Kachins and Chins fleeing not war, but poverty.

As shown in table 6.8, in all 17 different large armed groups and a number of smaller organisations entered into ceasefire agreements in the 1990s. Perhaps as many as 50,000 troops ceased their attacks on government forces,[112] but while a few small groups eventually surrendered their arms, most insisted they would never do so. Part of the unwritten ceasefire agreements was said to be an understanding that when a constitutional settlement was reached between all the parties involved, the groups were be disarmed. Reduced in size, most appear to have been converted into police forces and local militias, and would continue to operate for the foreseeable

---

112   The International Institute for Strategic and International Studies estimated that there were approximately 66,000 insurgent troops in Myanmar in 1987-88. IISS, *The Military Balance, 1987-88*, (London, 1987), pp. 121-22.

future. However, relieved of the necessity of defending their regions from government attacks, the ceasefire groups turned their attention to economic development. The autonomy they were granted over their diverse areas allowed them initially to pursue their previous economic activities unfettered, the result being an initial increase in opium production in the Northern and Eastern Shan State. By 1993, it was estimated that as many of 160,000 hectares were under opium poppy cultivation with a potential yield of 1,791 metric tons. However, because of international and domestic pressure, and an apparent desire to end the poverty that forced farmers in their areas to survive by growing opium, production began to decline as crop substitution and population relocation programmes were implemented. In 2005, Shan State (North) Special Region 2 was declared drug free, as two townships in Shan State (North) Special Region 1 had been in 2003. Therefore, in 2007 it was estimated that 27,700 hectares were devoted to poppy growing, producing a potential yield of 460 metric tons.[113] What is unknown is whether the ending of opium production will be sustainable in the absence of significant external support such as that provided by the United Nations Office on Drugs and Crime, various European NGOs, and the World Food Programme. The latter was providing food assistance for several hundreds of thousands of persons in Myanmar in the first decade of the 21st century. Despite efforts to develop the economy of the Special Regions and build roads and bridges within them, they remain remote and among the poorest regions of Asia.

The ability of the government to maintain most of the ceasefire agreements involved a number of different strategies. One was to give the leadership of the groups nominal internal governmental autonomy in the areas they controlled. This in some cases included control of international as well as local borders and, of course, the right to remain armed. However, there was no uniformity in these agreements and each group worked out its own *modus vivendi* with local tatmadaw commanders and intelligence officers. There were, from time to time, strains in relations because of personnel changes as well as differing understandings of the implications of verbal agreements. In addition to degrees of autonomy, the government also offered to assist in the economic development of the ceasefire regions. This included the construction of schools, hospitals, roads, bridges, dams, hydroelectric plants and communications infrastructure, as well as Chris-

---

113   United Nations Office on Drugs and Crime, *Opium Poppy Cultivation in Southeast Asia*, October 2007, pp. 50-2.

6.9.   Status of Ethnic Parties, 2004

1.   Main ceasefire groups that attended the National Convention

Name in state media	Usual name
Burma Communist Party (Rakine Group)	Communist Party of Burma (Arakan)*
Kachin State Special Region 1	New Democratic Party (Kachin)*
Kachin State Special Region 2	Kachin Independence Organisation**
Kayah State Special Region 1	Kayan National Army* ** ***
Kayah State Special Region 2	Karenni Nationalities Peoples Liberation Front*
Kayah State Special Region 3	Kayan New Land Party* **
New Mon State Party	New Mon State Party**
Shan State (North) Special Region 1	Myanmar National Democratic Alliance Army (Kokang)*
Shan State (North) Special Region 2	United Wa State Party*
Shan State (North) Special Region 3	Shan State Army, formerly Shan State Progress Party**
Shan State (East) Special Region 4	National Democratic Alliance Army*
Shan State (North) Special Region 5	Kachin Defence Army****
Shan State (South) Special Region 6	Pa-O National Organisation**
Shan State (North) Special Region 7	Palaung State Liberation Army**
Shan State National Army	Shan State National Army*****
Shan State Nationalities People's Liberation Organisation	Shan State Nationalities Liberation Organisation*

*Former ally or breakaway group from the Burma Communist Party.
**Former National Democratic Front member
***Breakaway group from the Kayan New Land Party
****Breakaway group from the Kachin Independence Organisation
*****Breakaway group from Mong Tai Army

1.   Breakaway factions from non-ceasefire groups that attended the National Convention

Name in State Media	Usual Name
From Karen National Union:	
Democratic Kayin Buddhist Association	Democratic Kayin Buddhist Army
Haungthayaw Special Region Group	Karen Peace Force
Phayagon Special Region Group	Padoh Aung San's group
From Karenni National Progressive Party	
Kayinni National Development Party	
Dragon Group	
Kayinni National Progressive Party	Hoya group
Kayinni National Unity and Solidarity Organisation	
From former Mong Tai Army	
Homein Regional Welfare and Development Group	
Shwepyi Aye Group	
Manpan Regional Militia Group	
From National United Party of Arakan	
Arakanese Army (AA)	
From New Mon State Party (preceasefire)	
Mon Armed Peace Group (Chaungchi Region)	Mon Army Myeik District
Mon Splinter Nai Sai Chan Group	

THE STATE REDUX, 1988-2008

1. Political Parties with Ethnic Designations from the 1990 Election that attended the National Convention

Kokang Democracy and Unity Party
Lahu National Development Party
Mro-Khami National Solidarity Organisation
Union Kayin League
Union Pao National Organisation
Wa National Development Party

2. Political Parties with Ethnic Designations from the 1990 Election that did not attend the National Convention and joined in the United Nationalities Alliance

Arakan League for Democracy
Chin National League for Democracy
Kachin State National Congress for Democracy
Kayah State All Nationalities League for Democracy
Kayin National Congress for Democracy
Mara People's Party
Mon National Democratic Front
Shan Nationalities League for Democracy
Zomi National Congress

3. Non-Ceasefire Groups

Arakan Liberation Party**
Arakan Rohingya National Organisation
Chin National Front**
Hongsawatoi Restoration Party***
Karen National Union**
Karenni National Progressive Party**
Lahu Democratic Front**
Mergui-Tavoy United Front*
National Socialist Council of Nagaland (Khaplang faction)
National United Party of Arakan
Rohingya Solidarity Organisation
Shan State Army (South)****
Wa National Organisation**

*Ex-Burma Communist Party affiliate
**Member or former member of the National Democratic Front
***Ex-New Mon State Party faction
****Ex-Mong Tai Army

Adapted from Martin T. Smith, "Ethnic Politics and Regional Development in Myanmar: The Need for New Approaches", in Kyaw Yin Hlaing, Robert H. Taylor and Tin Maung Maung Than, eds., *Myanmar: Beyound Politics to Societal Imperatives.* Singapore: Institute of Southeast Asian Studies, 2005, Appendix, pp. 78-80.

tian churches and Buddhist pagodas and rudimentary industries. In the most remote border areas, this led to the first ever significant penetration of non-coercive central state agents and institutions, including the Home and Immigration Ministries, the judiciary, and schools and hospitals.

In order to integrate the ceasefire groups into the larger national and regional economy, the government encouraged and facilitated their entry into various legitimate businesses beyond their own regions, such as transport, tourism, hotels, timber extraction, and mining. To oversee the government's assistance to these groups, a 'Master Plan for the Development of the Border Areas and National Races' was prepared in 1989. In 1994, the government established a new Ministry for the Development of Border Areas and the Progress of National Races and Development Affairs (DBANRDA), to coordinate the efforts of the army and other government ministries in the ceasefire and related areas.

As a result of the ceasefire agreements, and the slow but cumulatively effective economic development of the predominantly ethnic minority regions, there was a gradual transformation in the political and administrative relations within these areas and between them and the central government and army. As none of the ceasefire groups were internally democratic organisations, decisions to enter into agreements and the distribution of rewards and benefits were in the control of narrow, self-perpetuating groups. This sometimes led to conflict and jealousy, causing in some instances attempted leadership coups and factional splits. As they were essentially armed organisations encouraged to turn to politics and business, customary methods of conflict resolution were occasionally employed in extreme cases. With notable exceptions, most of the ceasefire group leaders were uneducated, and the government had to negotiate at length in order to achieve programmes and policies that it wished to undertake in their areas.

As opium production had been for many years an economic necessity for a number of the poorest villages in the Shan and Kachin State ceasefire areas, developing alternative crops and markets to generate incomes for them required both persuasion and coercion. As many as fifty thousand people were relocated from the northern Wa areas into southern Shan State, generating new conflict fault lines. In addition to the economic and military consequences of the ceasefire agreements, the cultural autonomy of the ethnic minority groups in the border areas remained an ongoing issue. The state's homogenising and centralising tendencies were often interpreted, as they had been in the past, as an attack on local cultures. To obviate such claims, the post-1988 military regime continued and enhanced the policies it inherited from the BSPP. The Institute for National Races was reorganised as the University for the Development of the National Races of the Union in 1991 and its enrolment enlarged. The government also per-

6.10.   Estimates of Numbers of Armed Groups Contesting for State Power, 1988 to 2008

	1987-1988[1]	2005-2006[2]	2008[3]
Burma Communist Party Peoples Army	8,000 active; 8-10,000 militia		
Shan State Nationalities Liberation Organisation (Pa-O)	Ca. 250		
Kayan New Land Army	Ca.100		
Karenni Peoples Liberation Organisation	Ca. 50		
Arakan Communist Party	Ca. 50		
Kachin Independence Army	ca. 4,000 active; 24,000 militia		
Kachin National Liberation Army		2-4,000	
Shan State Progress Army	2,500 plus 4,000 reserves		
Palaung State Liberation Army	400		
Wa National Army	Ca. 600		
Pa-O National Army	Ca. 350		
Karenni or Kayinni National Liberation Army	Ca. 400	800-2,000	800-2,000
Karen National Liberation Army/Karen National Union	Ca. 3,600	Ca. 5,000	2-4,000 plus 5,000
New Mon State National Liberation Army	300		
Arakan State Liberation Army	Ca. 60		

---

[1] International Institute for Strategic Studies, *The Military Balance 1987-1988* (London: IISS, 1987), cited in Economist Intelligence Unit, *Counntry Report: Thailand, Burma*, No. 1, 1988, p. 32.

[2] Selected Non-State Armed Groups in International Institute for Strategic Studies, *The Military Balance 2005-2006* (London: Routledge, October, 2005), pp. 427, 430.

[3] Selected Non-State Groups and Affiliates in International Institute for Strategic Studies, *The Military Balance2008* (London: Routledge, February 2008), pp. 481-482.

mitted, but did not pay for, minority groups to promote the teaching and studying of their own languages, unless they were suspected of using such teaching as a pretext for separatist or anti-state political movements.[114]

Although the ceasefire agreements did not establish a permanent *modus vivendi* with the ethnically designated armed political groups in Myanmar's border areas, peace became the norm in these areas. Small remnants and factions of the largest groups persisted in their military activities on a much reduced scale, but no major group decided that returning to war would be more advantageous to them than remaining militarily acquiescent. That this armed peace had been achieved without external assistance, except in providing development and food assistance in the opium growing areas, was a source of great pride to the state's leading personnel. Ironically, that this achievement was largely ignored, or denigrated, by the army's critics and civilian opponents perhaps helped ensure their success in maintaining the understandings the army reached with its former enemies. All sides found reasons to continue to compromise. Paradoxically, granting these groups autonomy created over time greater state control than any previous government had ever achieved.

Nearly two decades after the putsch the International Institute for Strategic Studies (IISS) estimated that there were between 10,000 and 15,000 armed troops still contesting for control of some regions of Myanmar. This was almost certainly a major exaggeration. As table 6.10 reveals, in 1987, the IISS estimated the KNLA was smaller than claimed in 2005 or 2008, despite multiple mutinies, splits, natural deaths and assassinations, and loss of supporters and territory to the government, in the intervening years. While there are still areas of armed conflict, particularly in northern Rakhine, southern Shan, and extreme eastern Kayin, Kayah and Mon States, the areas now controlled by armed groups are much smaller than those they had previously controlled. Most survive on the border with the assistance of sympathetic foreign group and perhaps unwitting refugee relief agencies. None pose a significant threat to the state's stability or security. However, as a result of occasional armed clashes, and a number of landmines scattered about the border areas, these conflicts still take a toll in lives and casualties. About many of the groups listed in section 5 of table 6.9, little is accurately known of their strength or even of their existence other than as websites and letterheads. Claims on their

---

114   Kyaw Yin Hlaing, 'The Politics of Language Policy in Myanmar: Imagining Togetherness, Practising Difference?', in Lee Hock Guan and Leo Suryadinata, eds, *Language, Nation and Development in Southeast Asia* (Singapore: Institute of Southeast Asian Studies, 2007), pp. 150-80.

behalf are occasionally heard and the existence of continuing armed conflict justifies, at least to the army, its continuing control of state security policy. As table 6.9 also reveals, the overwhelming majority of former insurgent groups participated in the national convention the government reconvened in 2004 to confirm the principles of a new state constitution.

Change and continuity in state-society relations

The abolition of the one-party political system in 1988 allowed revival of both officially sponsored and privately organised clubs, societies, foundations, and other civic organisations in the towns and cities of Myanmar. The promise of development of a thriving civil society held out by the end of the BSPP was not, however, achieved. This promise was encapsulated in the SLORC's sixth legislative act, the Law Relating to Forming Organisations (6/88) enacted ten days after the putsch. It gave such organisations legal form separate from overtly political institutions, thus ensuring that their potential political roles were emasculated at birth. The state thus remained the main organiser of society through its sponsorship of the largest and most prominent associations. However, small non-governmental organisations (NGOs) established by private individuals and groups to achieve peace, maintain the environment, or assist in economic and social development also flourished. Many had indirect or informal connections with the government, in some cases receiving help and assistance from state personnel, for the provision of reciprocal services. Others sought to remain as independent of the state as possible. While organisational life in Myanmar had not disappeared completely during the BSPP era, it was little visible and largely unnoticed except by individuals directly involved.[115] Voluntary organisations of all types became much more visible after 1988. The 2008 Yangon telephone directory, for example, listed 120 such organisations in 2008 plus another 34 sports clubs and associations. An incomplete list of non-governmental organisations circulated in 2007 in Yangon provided information on 67 different voluntary non-profit organisations including orphanages, child welfare, literary, medical, and environmental associations, and groups from the Buddhist, Christian, Muslim and Hindu communities, as well as from business. One study estimated there might be

---

115   See Kyaw Yin Hlaing, 'Associational Life in Myanmar: Past and Present,' in N. Ganesan and Kyaw Yin Hlaing, eds, *Myanmar: State, Society and Ethnicity* (Singapore: Institute of Southeast Asian Studies, 2007), pp. 143-71.

as many as 270 such organisations in Myanmar in the middle of the first decade of this century.[116]

The absence of an organic link between the state and the population following the effective annulment of the 1990 elections led to formation of the Union Solidarity and Development Association (USDA) in 1993. The chairman of the SLORC was its patron and senior ministers became in parallel its top officials.[117] The largest and most active of several government sponsored groups, by 2005 it claimed a membership of nearly 23 million persons, of whom 35 per cent were junior members and 65 per cent senior members. Every township had a branch of the USDA, as did nearly every ward and village tract.[118] Membership was essentially compulsory for civil servants and those who sought to do business with or receive services from the state. State and divisional officers of the Association were often prominent regional businessmen as well as military personnel and civil servants. Government ministers became identified with particular areas of USDA work. As a mass organisation, it was modelled on the BSPP but it also had parallels with the National Solidarity Association formed under the 1958-60 Caretaker government. When government ministers and other top state officials toured the country, as they frequently did, local USDA officials were normally present at meetings and other public discussions. The USDA became a prime articulator of the state's message down to the lowest levels of society. The organisation was formally barred from becoming a political party because of the ban on civil servants being party members after 1988, but some expected that, perhaps after being subdivided, it would be partially converted into a state-sponsored political party before electoral politics recommenced.

Also formed by government initiative were the Myanmar Maternal and Child Welfare Association, the Myanmar Women's Affairs Federation, and the War Veterans Organisation, as well as the Red Cross Society and various auxiliary fire brigades. The latter had existed under the old regime but were revitalised after 1988. All were involved, as was the USDA, in providing social services and organising community affairs as well as participating

---

116   Brian Heidel, *The Growth of Civil Society in Myanmar* (Np: np, nd), p. 16.

117   See Union Solidarity and Development Association in Union of Myanmar, *Historic Records of Endeavours Made by the State Law and Order Restoration Council (From 1 April 1995 to 14 November 1997)* (Yangon: Ministry of Information, News and Periodicals Enterprises, July 1999), pp. 31-34.

118   *Union Solidarity and Development Association in Brief* (Yangon: USDA, September, 2005).

in pro-regime rallies and demonstrations. Their voluntary activities only partially compensated for the absence or inadequacy of publicly funded social welfare and health facilities, though in certain areas, they achieved notable success. The Women's Affairs Federation, for example, received praise for its work in protecting women from abuse by their husbands and others. At times the mass organisations appeared to compete for public attention with the activities of United Nations agencies such as UNICEF and international NGOs such as the International Committee for the Red Cross (ICRC). Referred to in the official media as NGOs, they would more appropriately be categorised as GONGOs (acronym for the oxymoron term Government Organised Non Governmental Organisations). Each of the organisations had its own distinctive uniforms. The national leaders are normally the wives of prominent member of the SPDC, such as the prime minister's wife. The Women's Affairs Federation, for example, had to be reorganised and re-launched after the change of prime minister in 2004.

Often moribund except for the organisation of special events on national holidays and the organisation of campaigns on health or nutritional issues for example, the GONGOs and related organisations have been mobilised at various times in order to register support for the regime and express opposition to its opponents, especially the NLD and Daw Aung San Suu Kyi. For example, following the announcement by the government of a seven-step road map to constitutional government in August 2003, 263,000 persons attended 18 mass rallies in every state and division to support the plan. Present at all of these rallies were members from all of the GONGOs plus a number of smaller, often occupationally specific organisations such as the Myanmar Bankers Association, the Myanmar Medical Association, the Rice Merchants Association and cultural groups such as the Kayin Literature and Cultural Promotion Association.[119] Similarly, when relations became tense between Thailand and Myanmar, or after the demonstrations of monks and others in September 2007, mass rallies of GONGOs and related organisations were held throughout the country condemning the opponents of the state or the allies of the regime's political foes. These rallies are extensively reported in the national media and imply a degree of corporate solidarity otherwise not apparent.

The USDA, with its extensive membership base and close government support, engages in social and economic research as well as its organisational activities. Some of its members have been accused of involvement

---

119   *Mass Rallies in Support of the Seven-Point Road Map* (Np: No publisher, nd).

in attacks on opposition politicians and demonstrators. It is seen primarily by the state's managers as an organisation by which to control and direct public opinion in support of regime goals, but it is difficult to know to what extent it succeeds in that task. However, given the absence of alternative interpretations of political and other affairs, other than that provided by foreign radio broadcasts, and given the paucity of printed information, including newspapers, available outside major urban areas, GONGOs such as the USDA may be effective as transmitters of regime messages to the least politicised elements of the population. They may also develop a degree of solidarity among their members and a sense of linkage with national affairs as the BSPP once did. When they also provide services that their members and the public genuinely want, they may be effective in generating regime support in a general way. At the local level, they may encourage social solidarity and community support by organising public events in their neighbourhoods on holidays and other special occasions, and providing local social services.

Some smaller, more specialist GONGOs, such as the Union of Myanmar Federation of Chambers of Commerce (UMFCCI) and the Myanmar Fisheries Federation (MFF), serve as a two-way means of communication, both from and to the state. The UMFCCI, originally organised in 1988 as a revival of the old Union of Burma Chamber of Commerce and Industry (BCCI) by private entrepreneurs, was quickly reorganised and brought under the control of the Ministry of Trade, now the Ministry of Commerce. Linking the industry specific chambers of commerce in various states and divisions, it attempts to speak to the government about the concerns of the general business community as well as providing informational and training programmes for its members. Organisations representing specific industries tend to develop a relationship with the relevant ministry. Their success in this regard depends very much on the receptivity of the appropriate minister as well as the need for cooperation among their members. The relationship between the Minister for Livestock and Fisheries and the Myanmar Fisheries Federation served as something of a model in this regard. Despite the efforts of some NGOs to develop separately from the government, they remain very much beholden to the state for their existence and operate as its agents. Independent organisation among the business community remains very limited because of the *dirigiste* nature of political activities and economic policy. Independent trade unions and students' union have yet to be permitted.

448

Much smaller than the GONGOs are organisations such as the Metta Foundation and Shalom Foundation, or the Renewable Energy Association and the Myanmar Business Coalition on HIV/Aids. Operated by leaders with close ties with the people they serve, they have been involved, often with foreign and domestic partners, in providing developmental, health, and educational assistance to local communities. [120] Given the paucity of foreign assistance to Myanmar for humanitarian activities, and their desire not to attract negative attention from the authorities, their small sizes ensure that their overhead costs remain minimal, so that the maximum assistance gets to those who require it. Their ability to operate and innovate has often been a function of the prevailing political climate. Their leaders have to work constantly to inform and explain the nature of their work to sceptical regional commanders and other military officers and civil servants. Maintaining a strictly non-political posture has been essential for their success. Working in partnership within government planning expectations is often necessary. For example, there were 18 international NGOs and 17 Myanmar NGOs working with the United Nations and the Ministry of Health in 2008 under the National Health Plan to suppress the spread of HIV/Aids and other sexually transmitted diseases. The community of genuine NGOs remains small but organisational life is much more vibrant than before 1988. Developing a more overtly political role, however, has yet to occur.

The functions of the state

The capacity of the state to perform its primary functions of creating public order and security of persons and property, providing economic infrastructure and the conditions for the economic wellbeing of its population, managing collective public services such as education and health care, and collecting the taxes necessary to pay for these services was demonstrably inadequate in 1988. Never strong since 1942, the state had accomplished little in terms of lasting reforms or the development of viable institutions other than the army. In the political science language that has become popular in recent years, Myanmar had both a weak state and a weak society. The weak state had to rely on the coercive power of the army in order to

---

120   International NGOs have some impact on the organisational life of the country. In 2006 there were 50 operating in Myanmar. See *INGO Directory 2006: The Directory of International Non-Governmental Organisations (INGOs) and Red Cross Movement Organisations in Myanmar* (np: 2006).

maintain itself for nearly half a century, and that had the effect of sapping the vitality of the society and its ability to negotiate a lasting settlement with the state. Both the state and society were the losers.

State managers responsible for public finance and services were aware of this situation, and that in part inspired the reforms they attempted to implement from 1987 onwards. However, their resources were limited and there was no agreement on the necessity of fundamental change. Moreover, immediate defence and security concerns took priority in planning and resource allocation. Projects in support of change required a strong justification if change implied loss of control or the creation of uncertainty. Creating a viable strong state and a strong society in these circumstances was a challenge that defeated the BSPP state managers. In the absence of the party, it fell to the civilian civil service, sometimes reinforced and sometimes undermined by the army, to attempt that challenge after 1988. The state bureaucracy did not begin reconstruction from a position of strength. As one scholar of the subject has written,

The civil service has been crippled by repeated purges, politicisation, absurdly low wages, and unchecked corruption. These problems are so severe that the bureaucracy has difficulty accomplishing even basic tasks necessary to maintain the regime, such as collecting revenue and supplying the army.[121]

His description of the civil service could equally be applied to the judiciary, the police and other public functionaries. The elimination of systemic weaknesses of the state bureaucracy that were revealed in 1987-8 has yet to be achieved. As a result, some previous or poorly provided state functions are informally subcontracted to sectors of society including the GONGOs, so-called 'crony capitalists', and ceasefire groups acting as agents of the formal state.

State security and public order. The state and its military managers apply a relatively narrow definition of security. Human security has received relatively little attention despite a continual call for improving Myanmar's human resources.[122] The military managers' security concerns are shaped both by Myanmar's international position and by the memory of the events of

---

121   Neil A. Englehart, 'Is Regime Change Enough for Burma? The Problem of State Capacity', *Asian Survey*, vol 45, no. 4 (July/August 2005), p. 623.

122   Tin Maung Maung Than, 'Mapping the Contours of Human Security Challenges in Myanmar', in N. Ganesan and Kyaw Yin Hlaing, *Myanmar: State, Society and Ethnicity* (Singapore: Institute of Southeast Asian Studies, 2007), pp. 172-218.

1988. In addition to enhanced conventional defence and the expansion of the armed forces after 1988, a number of steps were taken to intensify the state's control of local and regional affairs. The ceasefire agreements, in particular, created a number of new opportunities. The Home Ministry became, in parallel with the Ministry of Defence, the key means by which the state increased its administrative capacity, while the Ministry for the Development of Border Areas and the Progress of National Races was central to extending the states reach into the border areas in the wake of the army. Latterly the Immigration and Population Ministry, which is responsible for issuing citizenship registration cards, conducting censuses and drawing up voter rolls, became involved in the expanding web of state regulation.

The revitalisation of the General Administration Department (GAD) of the Home Ministry was the beginning of the rebirth of Leviathan's bureaucracy. Soon after the putsch, the district level of administration, a layer between township government and the state and divisional authorities, was re-established, having been abolished in 1974 but having often maintained a shadow existence. The township, district, and state and divisional Law and Order Restoration Councils (LORCs), later Peace and Development Councils (PDCs), which provided sub-state level administrative services were, like the top ruling body upon which they were modelled, dominated by military personnel. Their chairmen and secretaries were military officers assisted by both civilians from the GAD and other ministries and local military personnel. However, members of the GAD were assigned at all levels, from the 14 states and divisions down through 64 district offices, 325 township offices, and finally 16,236 ward and village tract offices as of 1997.[123] From about 2005 onwards, increasingly power was handed to civilian officials, many recently retired from the army. Secretarial posts at township and district level were civilianised in 2005 and chairmanships in 2007. This was part of the army government's plan to establish a civilian government under a constitution in the future.

In addition to restoration of the former administrative system, a number of revisions were carried out reflecting concerns about ability to control particularly politically sensitive areas and take advantage of new opportunities. The politically turbulent and rapidly growing Yangon Division was divided into four sub-divisions and Mandalay Division into two,

---

123   *Ahtwehtwe Okchok Yeihyuhkin: (General Administration Affairs)*, (Yangon: Ministry of Home Affairs, General Administration Department, January 1997), p. 60.

with the military dominated city of Pwin Oo Lwin (formerly Maymyo) becoming a separate sub-division. Townships where border trade was conducted, Myawati, Tamu, Maungdaw, and Tachilek, were recognised as special districts and five townships controlled by ceasefire groups on the Chinese border were also recognised as special townships. The Shan State was also subdivided into three separate administrative areas, North, South and East,[124] and in 1997 Bago Division was similarly subdivided, into East and West Bago.[125]

The Myanmar Police Force, previously known as the People's Police Force, was considered by large segments of the public before the events of 1988 to be particularly corrupt, officious, and exploitative. This may explain in part the violence that was inflicted upon officers caught by the crowds during the anarchic events of August and September as well as the near collapse of the police during the same period. Reform of the police, therefore, was one of the goals the SLORC established early in its administration. Acknowledging the difficulties in changing the habits and corrupt customs which had developed in an under-resourced law enforcement agency, Secretary 1 noted 14 years after the SLORC took power that some police were still using torture and beatings in lieu of proper interrogation methods when preparing cases to go to court.[126] Further reforms were called for not only in that area but in other areas such drug law enforcement and human rights training of police and other law enforcement officials.[127]

Courts and the law

With the abolition of the 1974 socialist constitution, the state formally reverted to the judicial structures of the colonial and initial postcolonial order. The second legislative act of the SLORC was the Judiciary Law (2/88) which re-established the Supreme Court as the highest court in the land, replacing the Council of People's Justices. Created under the Supreme Court, and nominally appointed by it, were state and divisional, district, and township courts. In most instances, the law officers who had served as

---

124   Pyihteyei Wunkyidana, *Naingngan Ayehkanthawayei hnin Hhohpyoyei Kaungsi Ochokyei Sanit Pyaunglehmu*. (Ministry of Home Affairs, *Administrative Reform of State Peace and Development* Council 2004?), p. 33.

125   Ibid., p. 47.

126   *New Light of Myanmar*, 3 August 2002.

127   Pyihteyei Wunkyidana, *Naingngan Ayehkanthawayei hnin Hphohpyoyei Kaungsi Ochokyei Sanit Pyaunglehmu., passim.*

advisers to the People's Courts at various levels assumed the role of judges or magistrates in the restored system. The abolition of the 1974 constitution also resulted in reform of the Attorney General's office and the Auditor General's office. In the its first four months of power, SLORC enacted seventeen laws, rules and orders abolishing the institutions of the socialist era and restoring the old order to the extent feasible.

This penchant for legislative activity by ukase carried on into 1989 with 29 new laws, rules, and orders followed by a further 22 in 1990 and 13 in 1991. From then on, however, with the exception of 1993, legislative activity was largely confined to about ten acts and orders per year legalising government decisions. Much of the earliest SLORC legislation concerned economic reforms, including the reactivation of old British legislation such as the 1914 Companies Act (India Act VII, 1913) as the basis for the revived market economic system. Further reforms in the judicial system were carried out in 2000 with the enactment by the SPDC of a new basic Judiciary Law (5/2000) recognising also special juvenile courts, municipal offences courts, and traffic offences courts in Mandalay and Yangon Divisions.

Whereas under the socialist regime the untrained 'people's judges' tended to take their guidance from local party leaders and trained judicial officers from the Home Ministry, after 1988 judges were rather more constrained in their behaviour. Both the police Special Branch and Military Intelligence officers became more active and informed about proceeding and procedures, and in view of the priority given by the military government to security issues, police and army interests often came to guide the judges in their decisions. On occasion, judges were implicitly threatened with dismissal or relocation if an unfavourable decision resulted.

Economic and financial

Owing to the negative reactions of Western governments to the events of 1988 and the elections of 1990, international financial institutions such as the World Bank, the International Monetary Fund (IMF) and the Asian Development Bank (ADB) did not extend loans and other development assistance to Myanmar after the putsch.[128] When the government subsequently ceased making repayments on loans outstanding, the state

---

128 In contrast to the international response to the cancellation of election results by the Algerian army and government at about the same time. See Martin Evans and John Phillips, *Algeria: Anger of the Dispossessed* (New Haven and London: Yale University Press, 2007).

was technically in default to these institutions. As noted above, following the success of American and other consumer boycott campaigns and the NLD's call for economic sanctions, the United States government banned all new investment after 1997, the same year as a major financial crisis in Asia greatly slowed investment throughout the region. In the case of Myanmar, major investment flows did not resume except in the energy sector after economic growth returned to the rest of South East Asia. The European Union member countries did not ban investment, but they abolished the favourable tariff rate regime normally extended to developing economies, thus placing Myanmar's exports at a disadvantage. Moreover, the political atmosphere that prevailed in many capitals, particularly London, and the apparent political uncertainty and policy confusion within Myanmar had the same effect as an investment ban. American and European sanctions were tightened in 2003 and 2007.

The sanctions regimes, as they expanded, significantly added to the opportunity costs of doing business in Myanmar. While they did not directly impinge on the army or the state, they markedly slowed the rate of economic development and hence the growth of public finances. While neighbouring countries such as Vietnam and China received significant capital inflows during the two decades after 1988, Myanmar received comparatively little. The bulk of foreign investment was in the natural gas and hydroelectric power sectors, which meant that it created relatively few new employment opportunities. The little foreign aid received was for humanitarian purposes such as food support for former opium farmers and health assistance for coping with major diseases such as tuberculosis, malaria and HIV/Aids. This assistance had little impact on the bulk of the population, and rarely reached more than a US dollar or two per capita per year, compared to US 23 to 50 dollars per capita for comparatively developed societies in South East Asia.[129]

Agreed and reliable statistics on the economy and many other issues in Myanmar are rare. At best, most statistics can be seen as indicating trends and possibilities. Particularly disputable are estimates of the size of the gross domestic economy or product (GDP) and its rate of growth. The government has claimed double-digit growth varying from 10 to nearly 14 per cent since 2000. As shown in table 6.11, in contrast, the Economist Intelligence Unit provides much less optimistic estimates, even suggesting growth was negative

129   See United Nations Development Programme, *Human Development Report 2007/2008* (Basingstoke: Palgrave, 2007), see especially pp. 264 and 282.

in a year when the government claimed 13.8 per cent growth. Thanks to the sale of natural gas to Thailand, Myanmar's balance of payments became positive in 2002 for the first time in decades, and the agriculture and construction sectors appear stronger than previously. However, the government's estimates of the growth rate seem to be exaggerated, as do those of the EIU, though in opposite directions. There appears to have been real growth that was ongoing , but until more reliable statistics become available, all estimates are largely in the range of more or less well educated guesses.

The data provided in table 6.12 on the origins of GDP indicate the statistical problems that exist when attempting to assess the recent success of the state in managing the economy. Because of the incompatible systems used for collecting data between the previous system and the post-1988 administration, it is only possible to estimate any change in the structure of the economy resulting from the adoption of a constrained market economic system. Although the language and goals of the socialist era have been abandoned, economic management remains *dirigiste*. On balance, it appears that there has been relatively little change as agriculture continues to dominate the economy and manufacturing remains at about the same level as in 1961 and 1985. Unfortunately, there has been no labour force survey since 1990, so attempting to understand the structure of the economy from employment data is not possible.

In terms of ownership, there has been a significant shift caused by government policy. The previous state ideal of trying to achieve a distribution of ownership divided one third each between the state, the cooperative sector, and the private sector was abandoned, and as shown in table 6.13, the state now owns less than 7 per cent of economic activity, compared with more than 20 per cent twenty years before. The cooperative sector remains as insignificant as previously but the state still dominates in capital-intensive areas such as energy, communications and financial institutions. Most privately owned concerns are small and medium sized industries employing fewer than 100, and usually less than 25, employees, whereas the state manufacturing sector has a number of large installations.[130] The government has encouraged a few businessmen to develop significant holdings in fields such as construction, transport, timber extract and processing, and the like. This has led to allegations of development of 'crony capitalism'.

After 20 years of military rule, the state in Myanmar appears to be as emaciated financially as it was during the socialist period. The state domi-

---

130   See Tin Maung Maung Than, *State Dominance in Myanmar*, pp. 380-4.

6.11. Estimates of GDP Growth Rates, 1988 to 2008

Year	Government Estimate(a)	Economist Intelligence Unit Estimate (b)	IMF Estimate(c)
1988	-11.4		
1989	3.7		
1990	2.8		
1991	-0.6		
1992	9.7		
1993	6.0		
1994	7.5		
1995	6.9		
1996	6.4		
1997	5.7		
1998	5.8		
1999	10.9		
2000	13.7		
2001	11.3	5.3	
2002	12.0	5.3	
2003	13.8	-2.5	
2004	13.6	0.2	
2005	13.2	5.2	
2006		3.0	12.7
2007		3.5	5.5
2008			4.0

(a) Various issues of Central Statistical Organisation, *Statistical Yearbook* (Yangon and Naypyitaw: Ministry of National Planning and Economic Development, various).
(b) *Country Report: Myanmar (Burma)*, London: Economist Intelligence Unit, May, 2006, p. 5; November 2007, p. 5.
(c) IMF World Economic Report Data Base, October 2007.

nates, but it has relatively little capacity or resources to guide or develop the larger society or even its own institutions and agents. The state appeared to be weaker financially vis-à-vis the society in 2002 than it was in 1982, though again the unreliability of data from either period makes any comparison conjectural. As table 6.14 reveals, the state spent less than 9 per cent of GDP in 2005/6. In revenue terms, the state is also apparently as impecunious as at any time since independence. Whereas the state garnered 17.1 per cent, 10.6 per cent and 9.9 per cent of GDP in 1958, 1974 and 1985 respectively, as shown in table 6.15, in 2005 it could only muster 6.1 per cent. However, the percentage is possibly higher as a good deal of taxation and other payments, often known euphemistically as contributions or donations for services and favours, never enter into central government statistics. Thus, for example, much of the assistance provided for rehabilitation in areas damaged by a ma-

6.12. Origins of Gross Domestic Product, 1961, 1985, 2000, and 2005

Percent of Total

	1961	1985	2000	2005
Agriculture	26.0	28.1	48.8	38.5
Livestock & fisheries	5.6	6.8	7.9	7.7
Forestry	2.9	2.1	0.6	0.6
Mining	1.3	1.5	0.4	0.5
Manufacturing (&processing)	10.5	10.5	7.2	12.8
Utilities (power & energy)	0.5	1.7	0.3	0.4
Construction	1.9	2.7	1.8	3.7
Transport & communications	6.1	5.9	6.0	11.5
Banking & finance (financial institutions)	1.1	4.0	0.1	0.1
Wholesale & retail trade	29.3	20.6	24.0	21.7
Other services (social & administrative services; rentals & other services)	14.8	16.1	2.9	2.5
GDP at factor cost	100	100.0	100.0	100.0

Sources: *Report to the Pyithu Hluttaw, 1986-87*, pp. 46-7; International Monetary Fund, *Myanmar: Staff Consultation Report for the 2006 Article IV Consultation*. 20 September 2006, Table 6. Myanmar: Gross Domestic Product by Sector, 2000/01-2005/06, p. 8.

jor cyclone which killed more than 80,000 persons in 2008 was provided by so-called 'crony construction companies' as well as private citizens.

Much of this weakness stems from the state's inability to generate revenue through formal taxation. After the abandonment of a number of the socialist state income schemes, such as the compulsory purchase of rice from 2004, little has been done to develop new revenue sources, as demonstrated by the data in table 6.16. The inability of the state to generate greater revenues for itself, and its security and priorities, has ensured that annual expenditure on health and education has remained half or less of that of many comparable developing countries in South and South East Asia.[131] Despite reforms in the tax system to accommodate the return to market economics, tax avoidance remains rife. Under-remunerated customs and revenue officials, for example, remain easily open, despite occasional efforts to correct the situation, such as the prosecution of the entire central cus-

---

131   There are a number of United Nations reports that highlight the relevant information. See, for example, United Nations Development Programme, *Human Development Report 2007/2008*, especially pp. 264 and 282.

toms administration in 2006, to inducements to assist those with allergies to taxation.

The consistently negative revenue accounts have meant a substantial cost to the population as well as to the state. That cost is the inflation that is the government's solution to its revenue shortfall. As shown in table 6.17, the annual public expenditure deficit ran at an estimated 4.7 per cent of GDP per annum during the first six years of the 21st century. The result has been an official annual consumer price index increase, inflation rate, averaging more than 25 per cent per year (See table 6.18). Food, fuel and other prices rise regularly, but unlike in the 1980s, government and private sector employees were given occasional, but significant salary increases. These often severely lagged behind inflation, however, thus encouraging corruption and malfeasance. As the government pledged never again to demonetise bank notes, but failed to develop sophisticated banking and other financial institutions, 20 to 30 per cent inflation per annum has become the norm. The result has been a steady deterioration in the market value of the kyat. The open market kyat rate has declined from approximately 35 to the United States dollar in 1989 to nearly 1,300 in late 2007. Myanmar remains one of the world's poorest countries with a per capita income estimated at around US$200 per year. In terms of purchasing power parity, however, that equates to perhaps about US$2000 per year.[132] Reliable information on income distribution is unavailable, but the termination of socialism has allowed a visible middle class to begin to emerge along with a few very wealthy individuals and families.

As one review of the state's efforts at managing the economy since 1988 concluded, '. . . if current trends in Myanmar's political economy continue … the state will prevail rather than whither away under the onslaught of market forces, civil society, and globalization.'[133] Whether the state can develop itself in order to address society's needs effectively is unknown. The record to date is not encouraging.[134] Given the state's domination over the modern sector of the economy, the continuing reliance on agricultural and related sectors, and the tradition of economic policy making that the army

---

132   IMF World Economic Outlook Database, October 2007, from the Annual World Economic Report, posted on NetworkMyanmar.org website.

133   Tin Maung Maung Than, *State Dominance in Myanmar*, p. 397.

134   Toshihiro Kudo and Fumiharu Mieno, *Trade, Foreign Investment and Myanmar's Economic Development during the Transition to an Open Economy* (Chiba, Japan: Institute of Developing Economies Discussion Paper No. 116, August 2007).

6.13. GDP by Ownership, 2005/2006, in Percent of Sector Output

	State	Cooperative	Private
Agriculture	0.1	2.5	97.4
Livestock & fisheries	0.2	0.7	99.1
Forestry	30.9	1.0	68.1
Energy	81.3	12.6	6.1
Mining	3.9	0.1	95.7
Manufacturing & processing	9.4	0.3	90.3
Power	79.4	0.7	19.9
Construction	48.6	0.1	51.3
Transportation	2.4	0.3	97.3
Communications	100.0	0.0	0.0
Financial institutions	71.0	4.4	24.6
Social & administrative services	76.8	0.3	22.9
Rentals & other services	1.6	0.8	97.6
Trade	7.0	2.6	90.4
Gross domestic product	6.8	1.8	91.4

International Monetary Fund, *Myanmar: Staff Consultation Report for the 2006 Article IV Consultation.* 20 September 2006, Table 3, Gross Domestic Product by Form of Ownership, 2004/05 and 2005/06, p. 5.

6.14. Total State Expenditure by Percentage of GDP, 2000 to 2005

	2000	2001	2002	2003	2004	2005
Total expenditure	8.7	7.6	6.3	8.4	8.4	8.1
Current expenditure	5.2	4.8	3.4	3.1	3.6	2.8
Capital expenditure	3.4	2.8	2.9	5.4	4.8	5.3
Administration (a)	0.6	0.4	0.3	0.4	1.4	2.2
Defence	2.5	1.8	1.4	2.3	1.9	1.4
Economic Services(b)	2.7	2.3	2.0	2.6	2.7	3.0
Education	1.2	1.0	0.9	1.8	1.2	0.5
Health	0.3	0.3	0.3	1.0	0.3	0.2
Other social services(c)	0.2	0.1	0.1	0.1	0.1	0.0
Other(d)	1.2	1.7	1.1	0.8	1.0	0.8

a SPDC, Home Ministry, others including representative bodies
b Agriculture, Forestry, Public Works, Housing
c Pensions, gratuities, labour, social welfare
d Interest payments and other

International Monetary Fund, *Myanmar: Staff Consultation Report for the 2006 Article IV Consultation.* 20 September 2006, Official data and IMF staff estimates, Table 22, p. 24

6.15.   Taxation as Percent of GDP, 2000 to 2006

Union Government Revenues, 2000/01-2005/6 in percent of GDP

	2000/2001	2001/2002	2002/2003	2003/2004	2004/2005(a)	2005/2006(a)
Total revenue and grants	5.3	4.7	5.0	5.0	6.5	6.1
Tax revenue	2.7	2.1	1.9	2.1	3.2	3.4
Taxes on income	1.0	0.8	0.8	1.2	1.5	1.4
Income Tax	0.8	0.6	0.6	0.9	1.1	1.0
Profit Tax	0.2	0.2	0.2	0.3	0.5	0.4
Commercial Tax	1.3	0.9	0.8	0.8	1.2	1.8
Tax on property use	0.1	0.1	0.0	0.1	0.1	0.0
Customs duties(c)	0.2	0.2	0.1	0.1	0.2	0.1
Nontax revenue	2.5	2.5	3.1	2.9	3.3	2.6
Transfers from SEEs	1.6	1.5	1.3	2.2	2.3	2.1
Other	0.9	1.0	1.7	0.7	1.0	0.5
Foreign grants(b)	0.0	0.0	0.0	0.0	0.0	0.0

*Preliminary
**Valued at the official exchange rate
***Including excise duties

International Monetary Fund, *Myanmar: Staff Consultation Report for the 2006 Article IV Consultation.* 20 September 2006, Table 21. Union Government Revenues, 2001/2002 – 2006/07, p. 22.

6.16.   Sources of State Income, 1980 to 2000

	1980-81	1985-86	1990-91	1995-96	1997-98	1998-99	1999-2000
Taxes on Production and Expenditure	41.5	40.1	28.0	24.6	27.5	25.0	26.6
Commodities and Service Tax	39.1	37.1	1.4	0	2.9	0	0
Import License Fees	1.2	1.1	1.2	0.6	0.2	0.2	0.1
State Lottery	0.9	1.4	3.0	3.9	4.2	3.6	4.2
Stamps	0	0.3	0.7	1.3	1.3	0.7	0.6
Transportation Tax	0.1	0.1	0.3	0.3	0.9	0.8	0.9
Excise	0.1	0.1	0.1	0.3	0.2	0.2	0.2
Commercial Taxes	0.1	0	21.3	18.1	20.7	19.5	20.6
Customs Duties	14.1	15.4	14.4	11.4	9.8	4.5	4.7
Taxes on Income and Profit	3.0	5.0	20.0	19.9	17.5	17.6	13.9
Taxes on the use of state property	3.0	2.3	4.5	2.0	1.8	1.6	1.5
Receipts from Ministries and Departments	6.7	6.7	6.7	13.0	10.7	13.2	11.2
Earnings from State Economic Enterprises	28.4	26.3	24.4	26.9	30.8	37.6	41.6
Interest receipts	1.8	3.4	1.8	0.5	0.1	0.1	0.1
Foreign aid and grants	1.5	0.8	0.2	1.7	1.8	0.4	0.4
Total	100	100	100	100	100	100	100

government has perpetuated,[135] financial weakness and slow economic growth are a legacy that the state has yet to discover how to shed.

The switch from socialism to the market eventually began to have a positive effect on production primarily in agriculture and related sectors. State managers soon concluded that the market liberalisation commenced in 1987 with the abolition of the compulsory paddy scheme had been an overly radical step, and they sought partially to undo it. The inflationary effects of complete market liberalisation without making other adjustments in production and marketing systems impinged on the living standards of government employees and the military in particular, and in 1989 the paddy procurement scheme was reintroduced. However, the government reduced the amount it purchased from about 30 per cent of the crop on average to around 10 per cent and very little rice was exported for more than a decade. The effect was to artificially depress rice prices and make the basic daily commodity of all Myanmar citizens relatively inexpensive at the cost of increased productivity through market forces.

In order to maintain low urban food prices and generate a surplus for export again, non-market measures were taken to increase production. Fallow land was cleared and sown, irrigation schemes including dams and river water pumping stations were built, and double and, in some instances, triple crops of rice annually were encouraged. Increasing amounts of fertilizer and pesticides were imported and rice production gradually began to increase. Thus, in April 2003, a second step was taken to liberalise the rice market. The rice ration for government employees and the military was abolished, along with the last of the paddy procurement system. Initially it was believed that exports of rice would also be restored to the private sector, but steps in that direction were not fully implemented until 2007, and even then they were implemented in a manner that implied a government fear that rice prices would escalate too rapidly if rice was completely under the control of the free market. Various restrictions on where rice could be purchased for export and how it could be exported, thwarting the market with overregulation, were introduced.

A number of steps remain to be taken to return Myanmar's rice economy to the levels of international productivity that it experienced before the Second World War. Land remains in theory owned by the government and

---

135   See David I. Steinberg, 'Myanmar: The Roots of Economic Malaise', in Kyaw Yin Hlaing, Robert H. Taylor and Tin Maung Maung Than, eds, *Myanmar: Beyond Politics to Societal Imperatives* (Singapore: Institute of Southeast Asian Studies, 2005), pp. 86-116.

6.17.   Annual Public Expenditure Deficit as Percent of GDP, 2001-2007

Year	Percent
2001/02	-5.8
2002/03	-3.6
2003/04	-5.4
2004/05	-4.7
2005/06 (budget)	-1.9
2005/06 (estimate)	-3.8
2006/07 (budget)	-1.4
2006/07 (projected)	-4.9

Source: International Monetary Fund, *Myanmar: Staff Consultation Report for the 2006 Article IV Consultation.* 20 September 2006, Table 2. Myanmar: Summary of Operations of Nonfinancial Public Sector, 20001/02-2006/07. Based Myanmar government data and IMF staff estimates and projections.

6.18.   Estimates of Annual Consumer Price Inflation at Yangon, 1988-2008

Year	Percentage
1988	16.8
1989	27.2
1990	17.6
1991	32.3
1992	21.9
1993	33.6
1994	22.5
1995	21.8
1996	20.0
1997	33.9
1998	30.9
1999	15.7
2000	-1.7
2001	34.5
2002	58.1
2003	24.9
2004	3.8
2005	10.7
2006	25.7
2007	36.9
2008	27.5

Sources: Central Statistical Organisation, *Statistic Yearbook*, various years (Yangon and Naypyitaw: Central Statistical Organisation); for 2006 to 2008, IMF World Economic Report Data Base estimates.

6.19. Paddy Production, 1985 to 2004

Year	Paddy in tons ('000s)	Sown acres ('000s)	Harvested acres ('000s)
1985	14091	12114	11517
1990	13748	12720	11762
1995	17670	15166	14907
1998	16808	14230	13488
1999	19808	15528	15347
2000	20987	15713	15573
2001	21569	15940	15845
2002	21461	16032	15757
2003	22770	16168	16130
2004	24361	16946	16822

Source: Table 5.05. Sown Acreage, Harvester Acreage, and Production of Selected Crops in Central Statistical Organisation, *Statistical Yearbook 2005*. (Naypyitaw: 2007), p. 88.

while usufruct rights exist, farmers are unable to capitalise their land, which inhibits the develop of a viable legitimate rural credit system. Myanmar's rudimentary banking system is incapable of providing enough capital to assist the farmers to increase investment and productivity. Myanmar's rice milling capacity also remains undercapitalised, and its antiquated equipment produces inferior quality rice for world markets. Larger mills date back to the British period and during the past two decades the rice market has become localised around small mills. Despite reforms in production and marketing, two decades after the first liberalisation measures the full impact of establishing a free market in rice has yet to be achieved.

External relations

Having previously practiced a neutralist foreign policy, at times to the point of near isolation, during the Cold War, after 1988 the state's managers rapidly embraced globalisation and, initially, an outward looking foreign policy.[136] Ministries and departments joined, or in some cases rejoined, a number of international organisations and institutions beyond the immediate United Nations institutions that had become the primary means employed by Myanmar before 1988 to conduct international relations. The intention to rejoin the international community through a number of multilateral fora was driven by a sense that the state had fallen behind its peers during the 1970s and 1980s, and a strong effort had to be made to 'catch

136   N. Ganesan, 'Myanmar's Foreign Relations: Reaching out to the World', in Kyaw Yin Hlaing et al., eds, *Myanmar: Beyond Politics to Societal Imperatives*, pp. 30-55.

up'. As an indication of the new foreign policy orientation, Myanmar rejoined the Non-Aligned Movement in September 1992.[137]

However, this positive and outward foreign policy perspective was undermined by Western reactions to Myanmar's domestic politics and foreign policy became primarily geared to defending the state from the consequences of the political pressure and economic sanctions that came to be directed against its managers.[138] As Myanmar's human rights situation became the focus of exiled activists' anti-military campaigns, and the perception that Daw Aung San Suu Kyi and the National League for Democracy had been denied victory in the 1990 election became a 'fact', Myanmar foreign policy managers were forced to concentrate their efforts on defending their government from an unexpected onslaught of Western criticism.[139] Their primary means of doing so were to insist on the principle of non-interference in domestic affairs and to seek allies through joining international organisations and groupings of likeminded states. The initial outward reach was replaced with a withdrawal into regional Asian politics, with occasional forays out to other developing nations as Western economic, political and cultural influence in Myanmar failed to materialise. Having become isolated from the West to which the state's managers had initially intended to re-link, they were forced to rely increasingly on their immediate neighbours, none of whom, for historical reasons, they trusted.[140]

Trade and economic relations very much followed in the same patterns as political relations and as Myanmar was denied international financial assistance or Western investment and trade, it became increasingly dependent upon Asian markets. By 2005, international trade was overwhelmingly with other Asian economies and these economies, particularly China, India and Thailand, became the source of what little foreign direct investment entered

---

137   Details of this and other foreign policy movements are summarised in Ministry of Foreign Affairs, *History and Activities* (Yangon: Ministry of Foreign Affairs, 2005).

138   For a review of policies toward Myanmar during the first decade of army rule, see the essays collected in Institute for Democracy and Electoral Assistance, *Challenges to Democratization in Burma: Perspectives on Multilateral and Bilateral Responses* (Stockholm, 2001).

139   On the development of human rights as an aspect of post-Cold War foreign policy see David P. Forsythe, *Human Rights and Comparative Foreign Policy* (Tokyo: United Nations University Press, 2000).

140   The most complete review is Jurgen Haacke, *Myanmar's Foreign Relations: Domestic Influence and International Implications*. (London: Routledge for the International Institute for Strategic Studies, June 2006).

6.20. Total Foreign Investment by Country of Origin to 31 March 2005

Country	Number of Projects	Total in US$ Mn
Thailand	58	7,375.623
Singapore	75	1,733.526
UK/Virgin Islands/Bermuda	44	1,671.691
Malaysia	33	660.747
Hong Kong	31	504.218
China	27	475.441
France	3	470.370
United States	15	243.565
Indonesia	12	241.497
South Korea	36	240.521
Netherlands	5	238.835
Japan	23	215.283
India	6	172.075
Philippines	2	146.667
Australia	14	82.080
Austria	2	72.500
Canada	17	61.231
Russia	1	33.000
Panama	1	29.101
Germany	1	15.000
Denmark	1	13.370
Cyprus	1	5.250
Macau	1	4.400
Switzerland	1	3.382
Bangladesh	2	2.957
Israel	1	2.400
Brunei Darussalam	1	2.040
Sri Lanka	1	1.000
Total	394	14722.558

Sources: Table 12.03 Foreign Investment of Permitted Enterprises by Country of Origin, Central Statistical Organisation, *Statistical Yearbook 2005* (Naypyitaw, 2007), p. 258; Table 25. Foreign Investment of Permitted Enterprises by Country of Origin, Central Statistical Organisation, *Selected Monthly Economic Indicators* (Naypyitaw September 2007), pp. 54-58.

the country, especially after 1997, as tables 6.20 and 6.21 show. The dramatic fall in exports to the United States in 2005/6 was a consequent of the trade ban imposed in 2004 by the Bush administration, which ended the textile trade developed through investment in Myanmar by Hong Kong, Taiwanese, and other Asian garment manufacturers. The significant United Kingdom investment total came largely from funds from Asian investors channelled through British Virgin Islands and Bermudan companies. As table 20 demonstrates, Myanmar's export trade has shifted from about 68 per cent with Asia in 1985/86 to 85 and 89 per cent in 1995/96 and 2004/5 respectively.

6.21. Direction of Exports, 1985-86, 1995-96 and 2004/05

Region/Country	1985/86	1995/96	2004/05
South East Asia	742.40	2105.57	9128.64
Singapore	353.30	986.80	807.28
Malaysia	92.91	147.48	620.54
Indonesia	0.20	299.57	308.86
Philippines	0.24	133.10	69.89
Thailand	134.67	534.97	7219.17
East and South Asia	1058.61	2126.12	5762.02
China	165.28	195.14	1658.80
Hong Kong	329.41	359.41	656.05
India	188.90	1036.78	1956.32
Japan	198.84	256.31	737.26
Pakistan	30.49	126.01	148.31
Korea, Republic of	17.33	71.78	210.16
Americas	50.51	260.50	79.77
United States	20.77	216.22	1.52
Canada	1.96	9.25	14.37
North West Europe	301.46	139.16	612.50
France	2.31	32.31	95.15
Germany	141.65	36.85	3.46
United Kingdom	45.03	38.50	316.18
Southern Europe	4.69	17.31	701.28
Other Regions	797.69	395.12	413.10
Total	2653.90	5043.78	16697.31

Source: Central Statistical Organisation, *Statistical Yearbook 2005* (Naypyitaw, 2007), Table 10.07. All exports by country, pp. 204-206.

As noted above, the Western investment and trade sanctions were not imposed immediately after the 1988 events or the 1990 election, but came into place primarily after 1995 because of the successful lobbying and campaigning of exiled activists and their single-issue associates in the United States and other countries, particularly the United Kingdom. Although a ban on weapons sales and assistance from international financial institutions came into effect immediately after 1988, neither Western governments nor their foreign policy advisers believed in the efficacy of sanctions to effect positive political change in a country such as Myanmar. As foreign trade composed such a small proportion of total economic activity in the 1980s, perhaps 3.5 per cent of GDP then (and two decades later still probably less than 8 per cent), Myanmar's economy was largely impervious to sanctions. The army and state managers had survived on minimal foreign resources for years and

6.22. Major Trading Partners, 2000/01 and 2005/06

	2000/01 exports	2000/01 imports	2005/06 exports	2005/06 imports
Asia (excluding Japan)	57.7	80.9	86.5	85.0
China	8.9	12.3	10.3	15.0
India	13.4	3.6	13.7	4.0
South Korea	1.1	12.4	1.1	4.0
Malaysia	3.7	5.3	2.6	7.0
Singapore	5.8	24.2	7.4	28.0
Thailand	14.4	13.1	38.3	12.0
Industrialised countries	25.7	16.4	10.5	13.0
United States	12.5	1.0	0.0	4.0
Europe Union countries	7.1	16.4	10.5	13.0
Japan	4.3	8.7	3.8	5.0
Rest of the world	16.6	2.7	3.0	2.0

Source: International Monetary Fund, *Myanmar: Staff Consultation Report for the 2006 Article IV Consultation.* 20 September 2006, Table 35. Myanmar: Direction of Trade, 2000/01-2005/06, p. 37.

could continue to do so relatively easily at the same low level of development. While sanctions would have a negative impact on the economy in terms of limiting the rates of growth and investment, the impact on the state-*qua*-state would be minimal, and, some argued, would lead to a further entrenchment of army power.

However, after the release of Daw Aung San Suu Kyi in 1995 and her call for sanctions, exiled activists had a powerful political argument to advance. In liberal US states such as Massachusetts and California, where cities passed selective purchasing legislation denying contracts to companies with investments in Myanmar, political pressure mounted. The withdrawal of Pepsi Cola from a joint venture investment in 1996 was a harbinger of the end of new Western economic involvement in Myanmar, but some well-known brands had withdrawn earlier. When powerful Senators such as Jesse Helms, Alfonso D'Amato, Daniel Patrick Moynihan, Mitchell McConnell and John Leahy began pushing for legislation to ban new investment in Myanmar, the President was forced to act.[141] With a penchant

---

141   See Senator McConnell's speech, 'Status Quo or Sanctions? Laissez-Faire or Liberty? Policy Options in Burma', in *Burma/Myanmar Today and American Policy* (Washington, DC: Johns Hopkins University, International Republic Institute and National Democratic Institute for International Affairs, 14 May 1996), pp. 12-17, where he described Myanmar as a battlefield between democracy and dictatorship.

for personalised issues, and not understanding the nature of the American political system, the Myanmar foreign policy elite believed that the departure of President Clinton and his Secretary of State Madeleine Albright, who had met Daw Aung San Suu Kyi in 1995, would lead to a change in American policy. However, the second Bush administration came under the same domestic political pressures as had the Clinton regime. Moreover, towards the end of President Bush's second term, he and his wife took up the cause of regime change in Myanmar in a visible manner.[142] Similarly, in Europe, Myanmar was never a major political issued after 1988 but when specific events occurred that highlighted human rights issues and the continuing role of the military in the management of the state, particular politicians made Myanmar a momentarily personal cause. Policy makers were forced to respond, knowing their political leaders' actions would probably be counterproductive.

Myanmar's beleaguered status under the military was greatly eased, however, by developments in Asia. The original members of the Association of South East Asian Nations (ASEAN) at the end of the Cold War wished to incorporate all of the ten countries of the region. Myanmar became a member in July 1997, despite opposition from the United States and EU member countries. For the ensuing decade, most ASEAN governments rallied to Myanmar's defence in international fora such as the International Labour Organisation (ILO), the United Nations General Assembly and the UN High Commission for Human Rights (UNHCHR) and rebuffed European efforts to exclude Myanmar from joint EU-ASEAN meetings. However, as some of the members of ASEAN came under increasing Western pressure to modify their position, their willingness to defend the military regime began to dissipate after 2003 and effectively ended in 2006. None, however, endorsed Western calls for economic sanctions, arguing that they would be counterproductive. Myanmar also joined the Bangladesh-India-Myanmar-Sri Lanka-Thailand Economic Community (BIMSTEC) in 1997 and the Asia-Europe Meeting (ASEM) summit process in 2004, and applied to join the South Asian Association for Regional Cooperation (SAARC) in 2008.

Among the members of ASEAN Thailand, with a long shared border with Myanmar, posed the greatest potential military challenge. Despite ef-

---

142   For a demi-official Myanmar view of American relations with Myanmar, see Lei'la thutit u, *Myanmar-Ayemeiyikan Hsethsanyei: thamaing: (Akyaung:akyo: akaung:ahso: pakatihpyitsinmya* (An Observer, *Myanmar-American Relations* [*Cause-effect, good-bad, normal/natural*]), (Yangon: Digast Media Bank, May 2007).

forts by both sides to maintain cordial relations, a number of problems arose from time to time that led to strained relations, including border closures and exaggerated claims and counterclaims. Tensions, such as occurred in 2001/02, were the result of a number of factors largely emanating from the pro-American foreign policy orientation of Thailand, its more open political system than that of Myanmar, the existence of KNU and other insurgent refugee camps in Thai territory, and Thailand's desire to access timber and energy from Myanmar. More minor irritants relating to fishing rights and border demarcation also persisted.[143] The fact that Myanmar sometimes claimed that anti-state groups such as the Shan State Army (South) were primarily drug smuggling armies receiving protection from Thai authorities created antipathy from time to time. However, the advantages to both sides of containing the degree of animosity expressed meant that relations remained mainly cordial, if wary.

Like Thailand, India and China, Myanmar's other important neighbours, also refused to endorse sanctions and both pursued policies of trying to gain influence in and access to the country's politics and markets. China from 1988 made it clear that it would not directly involve itself in Myanmar's domestic affairs. It sold on 'friendship terms', or provided as military assistance, weapons and other resources to bolster the army. Chinese trade began to grow as China sought to develop economically Yunnan province in its far southwest. Similarly, India, after initially condemning the military regime for its human rights record and abrogation of the 1990 election, began to see the economic and political potential of cooperating with the Yangon/Naypyitaw regime. India wanted assistance from Myanmar in its attempts to suppress militarily Naga and other ethnic insurgents in India's northeast which used Myanmar's north-western Sagaing Division as a refuge. In addition, like China, India wanted access to Myanmar's growing reserves of natural gas.

Stymied by the opposition of Myanmar's neighbours to imposing of economic sanctions on the regime, Western governments put increasing pressure on the United Nations and its Secretary General to become involved in Myanmar's politics. Initially this took the form of annual General Assembly and Third Committee resolutions leading to the appointment of special rapporteurs for human rights and designation of top UN officials or retired diplomats as special envoys to try to broker a deal between the military regime

---

143   The most complete study is Aung Myoe, *Neither Friend nor Foe: Myanmar's Relations with Thailand since 1988* (Singapore: IDSS Monograph 1, 2002).

and Daw Aung San Suu Kyi. Little came of such efforts. In 2005 and 2006, however, US attempts to argue that Myanmar's internal affairs were a threat to Asia's peace and security, a claim denied by Myanmar's neighbours, by putting the country on the agenda of the United Nations Security Council, eventually succeeded. When the Security Council voted on a joint US/UK draft resolution in January 2007, it was vetoed by both Russia and China, the first double veto in more than 20 years. South Africa also voted 'No'. Nine members voted in favour[144] and three others abstained, including ASEAN member Indonesia.[145] After 20 years of attempting to internationalise the state's domestic politics, every attempt had failed.

However, the intentions of Myanmar's policy makers to open the society and the economy to Western interests had also been thwarted. The legacy of mistrust that exists between Myanmar and Thailand, a legacy of Thailand's aid to anti-state insurgents such as the KNU; between Myanmar and India, a legacy of colonialism and leftist politics; and between Myanmar and China, a legacy of Chinese support for forty years of the BCP; as well as between Myanmar and the West encouraged a high degree of suspicion toward all international actors. Still largely unencumbered by major international connections, the state under the SPDC/SLORC has remained largely impervious to foreign economic and political pressure except in extreme and unusual circumstances. Tactical adjustments to policy succeeded in obviating the need to abandon regime goals.

Despite appearing impervious, the state's managers had constantly to defend against the onslaught of international pressure that they faced. As the Foreign Minister of Myanmar said in his annual address to the UN General Assembly on 1 October 2007, they felt they were on the cusp of war:

We are greatly disturbed that neo-colonialism has reared its ugly head in recent years. The strategies they employ are obvious. At a first step, they conduct media campaigns against the targeted country and spread disinformation that the country concerned is committing gross human rights violations. They portray these campaigns as a fight for democracy. Secondly, they impose sanctions that hinder economic development and cause poverty for the people. Here, I would like to stress that economic sanctions are counterproductive and can only delay the path to democracy. As a third step, they provide political, financial and other material support to create unrest in the country. Finally, under the pretext that a country

---

144   Belgium, France, Italy, Ghana, Panama, Peru, Slovakia, the United Kingdom and the United States.

145   Also Qatar and Republic of the Congo. *Irrawaddy*, 15 January 2007 and *New York Times*, 13 January 2007.

is undemocratic, unstable, and that it poses a threat to international peace and security, they intervene directly and invade the country. The current events clearly show that such a course of action can only result in conflict and untold sufferings for the people of the country.

Mr. President My country is currently subjected to such courses of action.

State security became the focus of foreign policy as it was the centre of domestic concerns. Even when faced with a major natural disaster, Cyclone Nargis in May 2008 that killed at least 85,000 persons and possibly as many as 135,000, the state in Myanmar resisted Western efforts to intervene in the name of humanitarian assistance.

The issue of state and regime legitimacy

The search for political legitimacy has vexed state managers in Myanmar since it became a political issue with the rise of nationalism and the republican state. The most fundamental political clash of values during the two decades after 1988 has been over the basis of the state's legitimacy and the right and ability of its military managers to structure social and political relationships under it. The army state managers constructed their claim to state legitimacy on their capacity to maintain and protect a number of values held dear by themselves and the state-*qua*-state, including sovereignty and territorial integrity. They believed the majority of the population tacitly accepted this proposition. In terms of content, these claims included appeals to nationalism, national defence, economic development, and the preservation of vaguely defined indigenous cultural, religious and social institutions. Opponents advanced the argument, made familiar with the rise of republicanism, that legitimacy comes primarily, if not solely, from the periodic consent of the people as expressed freely through the ballot box. The abrogation of the 1990 election denied that option, at least temporarily. The compromise that stable constitutional republics achieve between the ideal of representative government while maintaining security, sovereignty, territorial integrity, and other state goals between elections has yet to be achieved in Myanmar. Following every crisis of the state, there has been another attempt made to do so.

Conceding the point that the state after 1988 was not based on the consent of the citizenry via the ballot box, the army government advanced the argument that they were holding the state power in trust for the people until conditions were created such that a return to a representative civilian govern-

471

THE STATE IN MYANMAR

ment would be possible and permanent. To their critics and opponents, this was merely an excuse for not transferring power to the NLD before agreeing a constitution in 1990. The criticism that the regime received from its domestic and exiled political opponents, interpreted through the army's version of Myanmar's history, has provided state managers with the argument that they have used to justify themselves. At the heart of that argument is the thesis that in Myanmar's post-colonial history, only the army acted selflessly during state crises in 1948, 1958, 1962 and 1988. All other political actors, and especially politicians and political parties, acted selfishly or threatened to undermine the independence and sovereignty of the state.

Initially the army claimed it would govern for a brief period, until law and order, the economy and transportation system, were restored following the destruction of 1988. However, given inability of the NLD and the army to find a *modus vivendi* after the 1990 elections, the army began to see the process of returning the state to a civilian government as a much longer period of institution building. An implicit argument began to emerge in government statements that the society had to be rebuilt, that a middle class had to be created, and the nation 'reconsolidated' after the civil war. Only then would the conditions exist for transferring power to an elected government. Each of the previous state crises was attributed to the absence of the conditions for sustaining a representative state. The army government's policies from 1992 onwards took this long-term view. An outline of what was required was set forth in a volume commissioned by the SLORC and written by two army officers.[146] The national convention that convened in 1993 was a step in the process, but when it was adjourned in 1996, the process was extended into the 21st century.

The SLORC/SPDC's 12 political, economic and social objectives were printed in every issue of the country's half million daily newspapers and in all books and periodicals, as well as broadcast daily on radio and television. The four political objectives were essentially political stability, national reconsolidation, and the emergence of a new constitutional government. Every day, for years, at the bottom of the front page of all newspapers there ran a banner stating: 'Emergence of the State Constitution is the duty of all citizens of Myanmar Naing-Ngan.' The four economic objectives related to development of the country and its modernisation while ensuring that

---

146   Sethu Aung hnin. Maung Hma', *Shwe Pyitaw hmjo mawei: pyimo'* (Sethu Aung and Maung Hma, *The Golden Country Soon to be Expected)*. Yangon: Ministry of Information, October 1993.

ultimate control of the economy remains in indigenous private or state ownership. The notion of creating a middle class in Myanmar, implicit in the political and economic objectives as understood by the SLORC/SPDC, led to the creation of what critics of the regime called 'crony capitalism'. The social objectives centred on maintaining national unity and patriotism while improving educational and health standards as well as preserving the nation's cultural heritage and 'national character'. A theme that runs throughout all of these objectives is an appeal to nationalism, and that has been one of the strongest arguments advanced by the regime in its appeal for legitimacy. Casting their rivals such as the NLD and Daw Aung San Suu Kyi, because of their links with foreign governments and anti-state insurgent groups, as enemies of the nation, state managers argued that only the army stands above partisan politics and speaks for the nation.

While it is acknowledged that the economy since 1988 has not grown as fast those of other countries such Vietnam, this is blamed on Western economic sanctions requested by the NLD. Much credit is taken for the state's post-1988 record of constructing dams, bridges, highways, schools, hospitals, and other infrastructure projects, including the new capital at Naypyitaw, without reliance on foreign assistance. That record is set forth in table 6.23. The record of achievement in terms of human resource development has been far less impressive and many new school and university buildings remain largely empty shells with few material resources to assist in teaching and learning. However, in other ways, the public does experience the transformation that has taken place under the military regime in terms of opening up of communications and integration of the country's transport networks.

Two other aspects of the state's claim to legitimacy have grown out of the political challenges it has faced since 1988. The ceasefire agreements with ethnically-designated groups provided an opportunity to restate the argument as to what it meant to be a Myanmar citizen. The country's multi-ethnic identity was championed and celebrating Kayin and Kachin new year anniversaries and other cultural events, for example, received renewed emphasis. Traditional sports and competitions such as boat races and music contests were revived or invented and non-traditional activities, such as beauty contests and body-building competitions, banned under the socialist regime, were organised. No clear definition of Myanmar-ness was provided, other that it meant participation in Myanmar events and implied loyalty to the state irrespective of ethnicity or religion. Myanmar history as the history

6.23. Infrastructure Development 1988 Compared with End 2007

	1988	2007	Change
Arable land in acres, mn	23.8	53.78	29.98
Vacant land in acres, mn	26.1	10.4	-15.7
Dams	138	344	206
Dams under construction		40	
River pumping stations	0	305	305
River pumping stations under construction		298	
Reserved forests, square miles	38,839	47,668	8,829
Protected public forests	0	14,702	14,702
Railway track miles	2,793.86	4,230	1436.14
Road miles	13,635	19,020	5,385
Airports	21	38	17
Bridges longer than 180 feet	198	407	209
Post offices	1,114	1,356	242
Telegraph offices	310	504	194
Telephone exchanges	245	891	646
Microwave stations	71	232	161
Hydropower plants	14	50	36
State owned factories	624	794	170
Privately owned factories	26.690	43.506	16,816
Basic education schools	33,747	40,533	6,806
Universities and colleges	27	64	37
Technological universities and colleges	1	34	33
Computer studies universities and colleges	1	26	25
Hospitals	631	839	208

Source: *The New Light of Myanmar*, 12 February 2008, Union Day Supplement; 23 March 2008.

of Myanmar kings and a heroic struggle against British colonialism was extolled in the school curriculum. An effort was made to re-conceptualise that history from the colonial version of kings oppressing the indigenous peoples to one of kings as military state builders working harmoniously with all the peoples for an aeon. As the ceasefire agreements proved to be viable, this argument was advanced with increasing self-confidence, distorting the variety and diversity of Myanmar's historical relations.

While the multi-ethnic nature of the society was extolled, state institutions shed legacy labels of ethnicity created by the colonial state and continued after independence. For example, in 1989, the title of the Burma (Bamar) Rifles was abolished and the unit renamed No. 301 Infantry

Regiment. Similarly, the Kachin, Chin and Shan Rifles were re-designated as other three digit regiments commencing with the number three. This change recognised that the army had given up recruiting on a 'class basis', as the British referred to the organisation of the army by ethnic group. Ethnicity had no bearing on what unit in the armed forces a person might be assigned. That had been the situation since the expansion of the army in the mid-1970s, but not recognised in terms of labels. Like the University for the Development of National Races, nationwide radio and television broadcasting, and football, the army had become an institution for homogenising state and nation.

Given the linkage between ethnicity and religion among several of the smaller ethnic minorities, particularly the Kachins and Chins, as well as by the Bamar and the Shans, and given that there are significant religious minorities in all parts of the country, making Buddhism the state religion was a very contentious matter, as demonstrated in the 1950s and 1960s. However, because of the ceasefire agreements and growing integration of society, religion appears to have become much less contentious. Both the civil war and post-1988 economic and cultural trends that encouraged the emergence of a form of Myanmar-specific globalised tastes in popular music, dress and cuisine have resulted in a lessening of ethnic tensions and encouraged greater religious tolerance.[147] Unlike the socialist state that sought to isolate Myanmar's cultural life, by allowing global tastes to develop the state since 1988 has rarely attempted to interfere with cultural change.

The military managers of the state, realising that the religious beliefs of their former armed opponents have to be balanced with the necessity to appeal for support from the Buddhist monkhood and the Buddhist majority, have sought to accommodate both necessities. The leadership of the state have lavishly venerated the *sangha*, especially senior monks and abbots, as well as building many new pagodas and temples and renovated many old ones. The state has been involved in a number of highly visible public displays such as the circulation of a Buddha's tooth relic on loan from China in the mid-1990s, placing a new finial on the Shwedagon Pagoda in 1999, and hosting a World Buddhist summit in 2004. These major events, however, do not reveal the daily displays of religious devotion which top army officers are seen to make on television and in public.

---

147   R.H. Taylor, 'Do States Make Nations? The Politics of Identity in Myanmar Revisited', *South East Asian Research*, 13, 3 (November 2005), pp. 261-85.

Similarly, the participation of senior government officials in the religious festivals of other faiths demonstrates their tolerance and acceptance of religious diversity under the state. This display of religious tolerance, however, was belied by a policy of denying promotion to non-Buddhists in the armed forces.

The state under army management has tried to legitimise itself in such a way that the army's custody of state power can be accepted without question. In that the army has played such a large role in state management throughout the past 60 years, to a certain extent it seems to be part of the natural order. Many people have no problem in dealing with the army officers as legitimate state actors in non-military spheres and are more concerned about how well they perform as administrators than about whence they derive their authority.[148] While the army as an abstract institution may be condemned as an arbitrary ruler, many people rely on individual members of it for the connections and advantages their power brings. To the army's opponents, the '. . . SLORC[/SPDC]'s goal is to legitimize the military as a constitutional but extra political institution with the power to define the bounds of politics – in other words, the right to delegitimize politics, to depoliticize the political.'[149] Alternatively expressed, the army has sought to legitimise a role for itself in politics alongside, and in cooperation with, other claimants to state legitimacy. The immediate future of the state and its quest for legitimacy are integral to that solution.

Politics within the SLORC/SPDC

The internal dynamics of the SLORC initially were significantly different from the working of earlier military governments in Myanmar. General Ne Win dominated the Revolutionary Council and the subsequent BSPP regime because of his standing as one of the founders of the BIA and his apparent indispensability to every government from 1945 until 1988, if not beyond.

---

148   See the discussions in Ardeth Maung Thawnghmung, *Behind the Teak Curtain: Authoritarianism, Agricultural Policies and Political Legitimacy in Rural Burma/ Myanmar* (London: Kegan Paul, 2004); Kyaw Yin Hlaing, 'Myanmar in 2004: Why Military Rule Continues'; and Mary P. Callahan, 'Cracks in the Edifice? Changes in Military-Society Relations in Burma since 1988', in Morten B. Pedersen et al., eds, *Burma/Myanmar: Strong Regime, Weak State* (Adelaide: Crawford House, 2002), pp. 31-2.

149   Chao-Tzang Yawnghwe, 'Burma: The Depoliticization of the Political', in Muthiah Alagappa, ed., *Political Legitimacy in Southeast Asia: The Quest for Moral Authority*. (Stanford: Stanford University Press, 1995), p. 189.

Even after he resigned, many thought he was still managing the state via his chosen agents. During the initial months of the SLORC his views were doubtless sought, but over time his influence waned, and he died in December 2002 under virtual house arrest following an alleged plot by his son-in-law and grandsons to seize power in the name of a 'Ne Win dynasty' earlier the same year.[150] The SLORC putooh elevated a new generation of officers to power, none of whom could claim that their authority stemmed from the founding of the independent state and its army. All were career soldiers who had not joined the army because of revolutionary political ambitions as many of their predecessors had done. Rather, they were products of the post-colonial army. With little or no international training or experience, they were graduates of the Officers Training School (OTS) and the Defence Services Academy (DSA) where they were taught that their first loyalty was to the army, its chain of command and its collective responsibility.[151]

Because of the near equality in terms of age and experience of the major members of the SLORC, a new title, Senior General, had to be devised to distinguish its chairman from his colleagues. The first Chairman, General Saw Maung, never dominated his colleagues, many of whom also served as cabinet ministers, giving them independent resources and power bases outside the army. Throughout his period in office, members of the SLORC often operated on their own initiative with little reference back to the collective body or its leader. General Saw Maung was appointed Commander-in-Chief of the army in 1985 and became Minister of Defence in the midst of the 1988 state crisis. He was removed in April 1992, having, it was reported, suffered a nervous breakdown caused by overwork. His frequent rambling but revealing speeches and press conferences as head of state were unlike any given by his predecessors or his extremely reticent successor, Senior General Than Shwe.

When Senior General Than Shwe became chairman of the SLORC as Supreme Commander of the Armed Forces and Prime Minister, like his predecessor he also assumed the positions of Minister of Defence and Minister of Foreign Affairs.[152] He eventually assigned the Foreign Min-

150   Special Press Conference, 12 March 2002. Myanmar Information Committee.
151   Aung Myoe, *Officer Training and Leadership Training in the Tatmadaw: A Survey*, pp. 5-6.
152   The Senior General joined the Army in 1952 and served in operations in Karen, Kachin, and Shan states. From 1962 to 1967 he was lecturer at the BSPP's Central University of Political Science north of Yangon. In 1981 he became a BSPP Central Committee member and in July 1988 was appointed to the BSPP's

6.24. Members of the State Law and Order Restoration Council, September 1988

No.	Name	Command
1	General Saw Maung (Chairman)	Commander-in-Chief of the Armed Forces
2	Lt. General Than Shwe	Commander-in-Chief (Army)
3	Rear Admiral Maung Maung Khin	Commander-in-Chief (Navy)
4	Maj. General Tin Tun	Commander-in-Chief (Air Force)
5	Brig. General Ye Kyaw	Adjutant General
6	Maj. General Phone Myint	Quarter Master General
7	Maj. General Sein Aung	Bureau of Special Operations 1
8	Maj. General Chit Swe	Bureau of Special Operations 2
9	Brig. General Kyaw Ba	Northern Command
10	Colonel Maung Thint	North East Command
11	Brig. General Maung Aye	Eastern Command
12	Brig. General Nyan Lin	South East Command
13	Brig. General Myint Aung	South West Command
14	Brig. General Mya Thin	Western Command
15	Brig. General Tun Kyi	North West Command
16	Brig. General Aye Thaung	Central Command
17	Brig. General Myo Nyunt	Yangon Command
18	Brig. General Khin Nyunt (Secretary 1)	Director Directorate Military Intelligence
19	Colonel Tin Oo (Secretary 2)	Colonel General Staff

ister's role to the civilian permanent secretary of the Ministry but gave up the post of Prime Minister only in 2003, in a largely cosmetic move temporarily to bolster the authority of the then number three officer in the SPDC hierarchy, the head of Military Intelligence and Secretary 1, General Khin Nyunt. An undemonstrative figure who had served as a BSPP training officer in the 1960s as well as teaching in the psychologi-

Central Executive Committee and made Deputy Minister of Defence. Anon., *Letters to a Dictator*, pp. 9-10. He is married to an ethnic Pa-0, Daw Kyaing Kyaing.

cal war department at the OTS at Hwambi, Than Shwe held a relatively low BSPP membership number as a junior officer, number 1001489. His longevity in office suggests a strategic vision and tactical capacity unexpected by his critics and rivals. Throughout his time as Senior General his deputy, or Vice Chairman, was Brigadier General, eventually Vice-Senior General Maung Aye, a member of the first DSA course, and a regional commander in 1988.

Despite the outward appearance of continuity during the first two decades of SLORC/SPDC rule, the internal power dynamics of the ruling group changed significantly during that time. This evolution is demonstrated most clearly through the personnel changes in the top body. Only two men, the Chairman and the Vice-Chairman, from among the original 19 were still in office twenty years after the formation of the SLORC. While there were minor changes in the composition of the Council and an enlargement of the cabinet between 1988 and 1997, all of the original members remained in place. As ministries divided, a number of former regional commanders were transferred to Yangon to assume cabinet positions but not membership of the SLORC. Several of the ministers allegedly became involved in corrupt practices, in some instances to an unusual degree, during the brief period of significant foreign investment in the economy in the mid-1990s. This inspired both jealously and anger among some of the more puritanical officers and those without access to such largesse.

Unexpected was the purge of all of the members of the SPDC except four on 15 November 1997, at which time the SLORC became the SPDC. Only the Chairman, the Vice Chairman and the two Secretaries remained. To have accomplished such a power play so easily, the four remaining men had to use their positions as leaders and holders of intelligence information to effect. However, the line of command was respected and there is no evidence of any counterplot to remove the top four. From then on the structure of the ruling group became hierarchical, as the senior four members were recognised as the top figures in the regime, having been present from the creation. The most visible of these four was Secretary 1 whose intelligence organisation, and its think tank the Office of Strategic Services (OSS), progressively appeared to be a government within the government, usurping the power of ministers particularly in areas such as law and order, drug eradication, border and ethnic minority affairs, and foreign affairs. Lt General Khin Nyunt's appointees increasingly occupied top government posts, and although he was not a formal member of the cabinet, he often chaired its meetings in the absence of the Senior General. Persons who sought to do business with the government or needed official action taken, and were stymied by official inaction, would ask the Secretary 1's staff to circumvent normal procedures and force a decision.

Two of the 1997 appointees to the SPDC were new commanders of the navy and air force, with Lt General Maung Aye remaining Commander in Chief of the infantry. The other new members were the 12 regional commanders. A new cabinet was appointed composed of other serving and retired officers and a few civilians in portfolios such as foreign affairs, education, and health. The twelve regional commanders were, some analysts perceived, the real powers in the land as they allegedly ruled their regions as personal satrapies.[153] As the heads of the administration in their territories, and no longer fettered by the need to coordinate their activities with local party officials as before 1988, that perception appeared to be realistic. However, it overstated their independence from the central command and their dependence on their army position as the basis of their authority. It was not personal command but the authority that came with rank and the collective nature of the army that gave them power.

In November 2001, the army replaced all of the regional commanders and posted them to Yangon with appointments in the Ministry of Defence. Many retained their membership of the SPDC, though six members were dismissed, retired or died at about that time. Appointed to various positions such as adjutant general, director of training, or heads of bureaux of special operations with territorial responsibilities, the power they yielded in the regions was conferred on others newly promoted in rank. Only Senior General Than Shwe formally retained a seat in the cabinet as Prime Minister and Minister of Defence. Often, however, he delegated responsibility to General Khin Nyunt who increasingly appeared to operate outside the confines of the SPDC. The November 2001 reshuffle of Council and cabinet posts followed the death of Secretary 2 in a helicopter accident and included the removal of Secretary 3 on charges of corruption. Now there were only three original members of the SLORC/SPDC remaining.

The structure of the SPDC from late 2001 until October 2004 appeared increasingly to be one in which only the top three had effective power.

---

153 Mary P. Callahan, 'Junta Dreams or Nightmares? Observations of Burma's Military since 1988', *Bulletin of Concerned Asian Scholars*, Vol. 31, No. 3 (1999), pp. 52-8.

There developed a strong rivalry between Lt General Khin Nyunt and General Maung Aye. Tension between the intelligence service and the infantry within armies is common as their conflicting roles and resource requirements push them in different directions.[154] In this competition, the Senior General's role appeared to be primarily that of arbitrating or deciding the outcome of conflicts between Generals Khin Nyunt and Maung Aye. Both were promoted in September 2002, with Khin Nyunt becoming a full General and Maung Aye made Vice Senior General. At the same time, the ten regional commanders who had been called to Yangon the previous year were promoted to Lt General.

The different roles that Generals Khin Nyunt and Maung Aye had developed in the SPDC and the government meant that each had different strategies and methods to cope with issues that arose. Vice Senior General Maung Aye relied on the power of command and the structures of the army. From the time that he was responsible for reaching the ceasefire agreements with the ethnically-designated insurgents and former Communist armies in the early 1990s, General Khin Nyunt had not only been a negotiator and compromiser, but a man who needed allies in bolster his authority and utility with the SPDC. Lacking respect from the rank and file because of his reputation of being a weak battlefield commander, he created his own group of intelligence officers around him, many of whom were also resented for their arrogance and independence. Allies provided General Khin Nyunt power that his formal role in the most disliked section of the army did not provide. After the death of General Ne Win in late 2002, some speculated that Khin Nyunt's power would wane, but there are other explanations for his fall from power in October 2004.

Foreign policy became embroiled in domestic political issues and SPDC rivalries in the early years of the new millennium. The election of George Bush as President of the United States was thought, by those close to General Khin Nyunt, to provide a new opening for the SPDC in its relations with the West. The effectiveness of the Secretary General of the United Nations Special Envoy to Myanmar, at that time, Ambassador Razali Ismail, in brokering an understanding between the regime and Daw Aung San Suu Kyi also opened an opportunity for resolving the biggest domestic issue that effected foreign relations. If Khin Nyunt and his appointees could have ne-

---

154   See Alfred Stephan, *Rethinking Military Politics: Brazil and the Southern Cone* (Princeton University Press, 1988).

6.25. Members of the State Peace and development Council, November 1997 to June 2008.

No.	Name and rank 1997	Command 1997	Command 2008	Rank 2008	No
1	Senior General Than Shwe (Chairman)	Commander-in-Chief (Armed Forces)	Commander-in-Chief (Armed Forces)	Senior General (Chairman)	1
2	General Maung Aye (Vice Chairman)	Commander-in-Chief (Army)	Commander-in-Chief (Army)	Vice Senior General (Vice Chairman)	2
3	Lt. General Khin Nyunt (Secretary 1)	Director of Defence Services Intelligence/ Office of Strategic Studies		Arrested 2004 (General)	
4	Lt. General Tin Oo (Secretary 2)	Chief of Staff/Bureau of Special Operations		Deceased 2001	
5	Lt. General Win Myint (Secretary 3)	Adjutant General		Dismissed 2001	
6	Vice Admiral Nyunt Thein	Commander in Chief (Navy)		Retired 2000	
7	Lt. General Kyaw Than	Commander in Chief (Air Force)		Retired 2001	
8	Maj. General Aung Htwe	Western Command	Chief of Armed Forces Training	Lt. General	3
9	Maj. General Ye Myint	Central Command	Chief of Bureau of Special Operations 1	Lt. General	4	Kachin, Chin, Sagaing, Magway, Mandalay
10	Maj. General Khin Maung Than	Yangon Command	Chief of Bureau of Special Operations 3	Lt. General	5	Bago, Yangon, Ayeyarwady, Rakhine
11	Maj. General Kyaw Win	Northern Command	Chief of Bureau of Special Operations 2	Lt. General	6	Kayah, Shan
12	Maj. General Thiha Thura Sitt Maung	Coastal Command		Deceased 2001	
13	Maj. General Thein Sein	Triangle Region Command	Prime Minister	General	7	Formerly Adjutant General
14	Brig. General Maung Bo	Eastern Command	Chief of Special Operations 4	Lt. General	8	Kayin, Mon, Tanintharyi
15	Brig. General Thiha Thura Tin Aung Myint Oo	North East Command	Quarter- Master General (Secretary 1)	Lt. General	9
16	Brig. General Myint Aung	South East Command		Retired in 2000	

gotiated a *modus vivendi* between the SPDC and both the NLD leader and the West, his power within the regime would have been assured.

Daw Aung San Suu Kyi, having been once more placed under house arrest in 1999, began secret talks with members of the regime in 2000 and 2001. Razali also met her and apparently convinced her of the need to compromise with Khin Nyunt and others in the SPDC in order to break the impasse that they had reached. She was released from house arrest in May 2002. She then began touring the country, in the company of military intelligence personnel, to view government development projects. Meetings were also held between her and government ministers. A second prong of the strategy that General Khin Nyunt and his colleagues had developed was to get recognition for the efforts the regime had made with the cease-fire groups in reducing and eventually eliminating opium production in the Shan State. If the United States government would recognise (certify in the language of US legislation) that Myanmar was acting positively to achieve drug eradication, then the United States would provide economic assistance for the anti-drug activities and relations between Washington and Yangon would begin to normalise. As a step in improving relations, Myanmar gave the United States Air Force overfly permission for bombers based in Thailand in the initial bombing of Afghanistan after the attack on the World Trade Center and other American targets in September 2001.

Other aspects of General Khin Nyunt's strategy included a plan to co-operate with the International Labour Organisation to help end allegations of forced labour in government construction projects, and an invitation to Amnesty International and the UN Special Rapporteur for Human Rights to visit Myanmar. However, in January 2003 the President denied certification of Myanmar's anti-drug programme for political reasons, ignoring the U S Drug Enforcement Agency's own findings on the decline in opium production in their most recent joint survey with Myanmar intelligence officers. One key initiative of General Khin Nyunt's offensive was thus blocked. The following April, the European Union reconfirmed the sanctions and visa bans it had previously imposed on Myanmar, though noting the improved political situation in the country.

As the talks between Daw Aung San Suu Kyi and government ministers failed to find common ground, and she became increasingly lionised by the public as she travelled the country with a large and boisterous youthful entourage, the agreement reached between the SPDC and her appeared to be collapsing. At the end of May 2003, apparently unknown to Khin Nyunt and his military intelligence colleagues, an attack was made on the convey of Daw Aung San Suu Kyi at the village of Dipeyen between Monwya and Mandalay and she was placed once more under house arrest. Khin Nyunt then had to regroup as his efforts to reach cooperative agreements with the regime's strongest opponents had ended in failure. The rearrest of Daw San Suu Kyi caused even some of the government's supporters until then, including a number of ASEAN governments, to begin voicing criticism of the SPDC. Though many viewed the regime as a monolithic entity, it was not so at that time.

Relations among the top three in the regime were under strain as they jockeyed for power in the wake of these events. In February 2003 Lt General Soe Win, former Northwest Regional Commander and Adjutant General, was appointed as Secretary 2 of the SPDC. At the end of August, a further shuffle took place with General Khin Nyunt made Prime Minister, Lt General Soe Win Secretary 1, and Lt. General Thein Sein Secretary 2. There were a number of minor changes in the cabinet at the same time. The Prime Minister General Khin Nyunt announced a seven-step road map to a new constitution also at the end of August. This was an attempt by SPDC to fill the political vacuum created by the failure of any of the General Khin Nyunt's efforts to improve relations with the US government or Daw Aung San Suu Kyi.

Fourteen months later, on 19 October 2004, General Khin Nyunt and the foreign minister, U Win Aung, a former intelligence officer, were removed from office. Win Aung was tried and received a lengthy jail sentence. Khin Nyunt was placed under house arrest after being charged with insubordination, corruption and dereliction of duty, and allowed to retire on the grounds of ill health. A number of foreign commentators then declared that the head of Military Intelligence had been a secret liberal all along. General Khin Nyunt was tried and convicted, and remained under house arrest. The entire Military Intelligence organisation was abolished and a number of its members were tried and jailed for a number of offences. The ostensible cause of the purge of General Khin Nyunt and his entourage was the discovery of a sizeable illegal holding of gold and other valuables at the checkpoint on the Chinese border at Muse. However, the rivalry that had developed between General Khin Nyunt and his intelligence colleagues on one side, and the infantry under Vice Senior General Maung Aye on the other, underlay these events. The superior power of the regular army was victorious after General Khin Nyunt no longer appeared to be indispensable.

The ensuing cabinet reshuffles saw the removal of a number of ministers who had worked closely with the Military Intelligence chief. Secretary 1, General Soe Win, succeeded as Prime Minister, and Secretary 2, Lt. General Thein Sein, became Secretary 1. When General Soe Win died of natural causes at the age of 59 in 2007, Lt General Thein Sein succeeded as Prime Minister. Within the SPDC, the Senior General and the Vice Senior General were all that remained of the initial group. The two of them had after 20 years created a joint management in which all major strategic decisions were passed up to them for determination. The relatively open and accessible government that Myanmar had gained in 1988 had been gradually replaced by the closed circuit of power very similar to the final days of the BSPP era under General Ne Win. Esconced in Naypyitaw, the head of state and his deputy appeared on special state occasions, received foreign diplomats, and issued official statements.

General Thura Shwe Mann, Joint Chief of Staff (Army, Navy and Air Force), was considered the most likely person to succeed to the chairmanship of the SPDC on the eventual retirement of the top two men. Below him and the top two commanders, members of the SPDC were either assigned army functional responsibilities or sent as emissaries to various regions of the country to be responsible for overseeing regional commanders and state and divisional governments. At critical moments in negotiations between the state and ceasefire groups, they appeared as envoys of the SPDC to ensure that agreements and understandings were maintained. As the regime has become increasingly civilianised and often less effective, they intervened as crisis managers. Crisis management has become routine and is a role the army has defined as its duty in the maintenance of the state in Myanmar. Having begun as a very different government from that of General Ne Win and the BSPP, after 20 years in power the SLORC/SPDC looked very much like it. A third major resuffle of junior SPDC members and regional commanders in June 2008 confirmed that. Whether the aging managers of the state had learned, unlike their predecessors, the necessity of renewing its personnel and policies in order to perpetuate itself was a question yet to be answered.

ADDENDUM

THE THIRD CONSTITUTION OF
THE STATE IN MYANMAR

Background to the 2008 Constitutional Referendum

The third constitution of the state in Myanmar was approved in a nation-wide referendum of the adult population in May 2008.[1] Unlike the first constitution, which was a hastily drafted set of incompatible political compromises designed to ensure that independence was achieved speedily, and the second, an essay in one-party socialist statecraft, the third confirms the political compromises made and administrative structures created after the army took power in 1988. Rather than a document to create a new and idealistic order, it endorses the past and holds out the promise of sharing power with those who currently monopolise state authority. The major promise for the future is the possibility of the army sharing some power with civilian political parties. The new constitution creates marginal space for political parties to have an impact on legislation and policy, via a new bicameral

---

1   The referendum was held on two separate days following the destruction wrought by Cyclone Nargis and the subsequent tidal wave that killed from 85,000 to 135,000 people in the lower Ayeyawady Delta and Yangon. In the directly affected areas the vote was postponed for two weeks until 24 May, whereas in the remainder of the country the referendum was held on the initially announced date of 10 May. On the first day of polling, it was reported that 99.07 per cent of the electorate in 278 townships voted, with 92.4 per cent voting in favour of the draft constitution. In the second poll, held in 40 townships in Yangon Divison and seven in Ayeyawady Division, it was officially reported that 93.44 per cent of eligible voters cast their ballot, with 92.93 per cent in favour. Overall, 98.12 voted, 82.74 per cent on the day and 17.26 per cent in advance as absentee ballots; of those voting, 92.12 voted yes, 6.1 per cent voted no, and 1.42 per cent of ballot papers were spoilt. In all, 27,288,827 persons were eligible to vote, approximately half of the total estimated population.

national legislature and 14 state and regional single chamber assemblies, and potentially on the formation of government cabinets at all levels. In addition, minor legislative powers are granted to six ethnic minority self-governing autonomous zones, several controlled by ceasefire groups.

The new constitution is a complex document that attempts to address the major issues that have been at the heart of Myanmar's politics since independence was regained in 1948, particularly the demand for ethnic autonomy against the centralising impulse of the state. While ethnically-designated groups and ideologically-focused political parties will have a role in the future governance of the country, the army has secured for itself internal autonomy and administrative authority to override civilian power. Much as in the constitutions of Turkey, Pakistan, Bangladesh and Thailand, the army remains central to the new order. In the language of comparative military politics, the 2008 constitution, if it succeeds, will change the role of the army in Myanmar from that of a 'Ruler Military' to that of a 'Parent-Guardian Military', having abandoned its earlier role as an 'Arbitrator Military'.[2] However, for that to happen, there will have to be further, perhaps unacknowledged, constitutional adjustments and compromises, for as the document is written the army, perhaps in mufti, will continue to govern even if in partnership with others.

On 9 February 2008, the State Peace and Development Council (SPDC) announced that the referendum on a draft state constitution then nearing completion would be held in May. The date of the referendum was confirmed on 9 April, just before a ten-day period of public holidays to mark the annual Theravada Buddhist New Year. Also on 9 February, it was announced that, subsequent to approval of the constitution by a majority of more than 50 per cent of the total electorate, elections would be held some time in 2010 to form a national or union legislature (Pyihtaungsu Hluttaw) of two houses, 14 state and regional single chamber hluttaw, and the governments of six special autonomous administrative zones or divisions. That, the fifth step in the government's seven-step road map to constitutional government announced in August 2003, would lead to the formation of a new government in which civilians would share power with the military. Twenty years after the uprising of 1988, an end to the monopoly of state power by the military appeared to be in sight. Moreover, for almost

---

2   See the discussion in Ayesha Siddiqa, *Military Inc.: Inside Pakistan's Military Economy* (London: Pluto Press, 2007), especially chapter 1, pp. 30-57.

the first time in two decades, the government had given an indication of its plans in advance.

During the previous five months, following the conclusion of the national convention on 3 September where the fundamental principles and basic rules of a new constitution were confirmed, the government had come under intense international pressure, especially in the United Nations and ASEAN. The President of the United States and Western European political leaders demanded that the constitution drafting process should be reopened to allow Daw Aung San Suu Kyi and other representatives of the NLD and unnamed, and presumably exiled or insurgent, ethnic minority persons to participate. The Western demands placed emphasis on the support that the government received from China, India and some of the ASEAN countries. The SPDC's Asian neighbours may have sought to alleviate the pressure they were under by encouraging a timely advance to the process of reintroducing constitutional government to Myanmar. However, the government had foreseen 2008 as a year of change as early as 2006.[3]

The national convention to draft the fundamental principles and basic principles of the draft constitution took place over a 16-year period, commencing in 1992 when the government convened meetings with political party leaders and persons elected in 1990. U Aung Shwe, the Chairman of the NLD, and others participated in these meetings but those who had been arrested in 1989 and excluded from the election, such as Daw Aung San Suu Kyi, were not involved. At these meetings it was agreed to call a national convention to include other elements of society. Also accepted were the six fundamental objectives of the convention and the eventual constitution that the SLORC insisted upon.[4] The first five were the army's oft-repeated pledges about maintaining sovereignty and national unity, the establishment of a multi-party political system, and basic human values such as justice and equality. The sixth was the most controversial for those demanding the creation of a liberal state with the army under civilian control. The tatmadaw insisted that it would ' ... be able to participate in the national political leadership of the future State' and those who attended the preliminary convention meetings conceded the point, however unwillingly.

---

3   See Soe Mya Kyaw, *The Structure, Legislative Structure and Essence of Future State* (Yangon: Printing and Publishing Enterprise, Ministry of Information, August 2006).

4   SLORC Order No. 13/92.

Addendum 1. Delegate Categories and numbers, first and second sittings of the national convention.

Categories of delegates	1993-1996	2004-2007
Political parties chosen by the parties	49	29
Persons elected in 1990	107	13
Ethnic minority representatives	215	633
Peasants	93	93
Workers	48	48
Intellectuals and academics	41	56
Government employees	92	109
Other invited persons (after 2004 included ceasefire groups)	57	105
Total	702	1086

The first three years of the convention process included six sessions with 702 delegates drawn from eight different categories of persons. As shown in Addendum table 1, those categories were derived from Myanmar's socialist heritage. During the second three-year period, from 2004 to 2007, the convention met for five sessions with a total of 1,086 delegates. A majority of the delegates were chosen or approved by the government, and a minority came from political parties and other political, mainly ethnic minority, organisations. As also shown in Addendum table 1, the proportion of ethnic minority delegates increased significantly when the convention was reconvened in 2004.

During the first three-year period, 104 basic principles were agreed. A number of departures from earlier Myanmar constitutions were made in these principles. The most important was recognition of self-administered zones establishing the self-governing rights of particular ethnic minorities and ceasefire groups. Though federalism was an unacceptable word in the official constitutional lexicon of Myanmar—as it has always been advanced as a demand based on an assumption of the non-organic nature of the state, by the main ethnically designated opponents of the central state— the constitutional principles suggested a more elaborate form of attenuated federalism than had been promised previously.

At the end of 1995, the NLD delegates to the national convention withdrew in protest at what Daw Aung San Suu Kyi described as its undemocratic methods and conclusions. The convention met in closed sessions of the various delegate categories where they drew up papers establishing agreed positions on various issues and chapters of the draft principles. These papers were then compared and refined by a panel of chairmen drawn from the delegate groups. Their conclusions, heavily influenced by the government officials guiding the process, were eventually presented to plenary sessions of the convention for ratification. This, and the participation of the army in the national political leadership as a pre-convention agreed principle, drew the ire of Daw Aung San Suu Kyi when she was eventually released from house arrest in 1995. Towards the end of the year, the NLD delegates ceased to attend and were, under the rules of the convention, consequently expelled.[5] The government used the NLD's withdrawal as a pretext to adjourn the convention for eight years while consolidating the ceasefire agreements with the ethnic designated insurgents.

Following the Dipeyin incident in May 2003, the government resolved to fill the political vacuum created by the termination of the process of seeking a political rapprochement with Daw Aung San Suu Kyi, by announcing in August a seven-step road map to a constitutional government. The seven steps were:

1. reconvening the national convention
2. 'after the successful holding of the National Convention, step-by-step implementation of the process for the emergence of a genuine and disciplined democratic system'
3. drafting a constitution
4. adopting the constitution via a referendum
5. holding legislative elections according to the constitution
6. convening the legislatures
7. forming a government and other constitutional bodies.

No timetable was established for the roadmap and the ambiguity implied in step two suggested that the process might be very long, if not in-

5   The government often claimed that the withdrawal of the NLD from the convention was a decision made at the behest of Dr Madeleine Albright, who while serving as United States Ambassador to the United Nations visited Daw Aung San Suu Kyi prior to the decision. Dr Albright does not give the content of her meeting with the NLD leader in her published account in *Madam Secretary: A Memoir* (New York: Hyperion, 2003), pp. 200-2. For the NLD version of these events, see Anon., *Letters to a Dictator: Correspondence from NLD Chairman Aung Shwe to SLORC's Senior General Than Shwe.* (Bangkok: All Burma Students' Democratic Front, 1997).

definite. When the convention resumed, individual members of the NLD, the Shan Nationalities League for Democracy, and the Shan State Kokang Democracy and Unity Party who had walked out of the convention in 1995 were invited to resume membership, but following negotiations between the NLD leadership and the government over the terms of their participation, no agreement was reached before the convention reconvened on 17 May 2004. The NLD had made the release of Daw Aung San Suu Kyi and other NLD leaders and the reopening of party offices a condition of their participation. This the SPDC refused.

A final attempt to reopen the constitution drafting process occurred in August, September and October 2007. Following the suppression of demonstrations lead by Buddhist monks,[6] internationally there was a loud protest by many Western governments and extreme disquiet expressed by fellow ASEAN governments. Pressure mounted in the United Nations for the Secretary General to intervene and his Special Adviser on Myanmar, Ambassador Ibrahim Gambari, was sent to attempt to broker an understanding between the SPDC and Daw Aung San Suu Kyi. The government responded by allowing Professor Gambari to return to Myanmar for a third time and also by organising mass rallies denouncing the demonstrations and in support of the constitutional convention and its recently completed work.

Professor Gambari was able to meet Senior General Than Shwe and senior members of the SPDC as well as Daw Aung San Suu Kyi and other NLD leaders. However, his proposal that he become an interlocutor in meetings involving the SPDC and the NLD was rejected. As Ambassador Gambari left the country, the government did, however, announce that the Senior General would be willing to meet with Daw Aung San Suu Kyi if she stopped 'exerting efforts for Confrontation, Utter Devastation, and Imposing All Kinds of Sanctions including Economic Sanctions against Myanmar.'[7] This she failed to do in subsequent meetings with a representative from the government, Liaison Minister U Aung Kyi, or in a statement she released through Ambassador Gambari after his second visit to Myanmar in November.

---

6   See chapter 6 above.

7   As she had mentioned on the day after her released from house arrest in July 1995. Announcement Number 1/2007, 4 October 2007, *New Light of Myanmar*, 5 October 2007.

On 19 February 2008, less than six months after the last session of the convention, the 54-member drafting commission finished its work in two and a half months and on 26 February a 45-member referendum commission was appointed. On the same day, the referendum election law was promulgated. Changes in voting procedures were introduced with the new law. Unlike the procedures in earlier elections or the 1973 referendum on the socialist constitution, only one ballot box would be used. Previously there was a ballot box for each candidate, or in the 1973 referendum, one each for yes or no votes. Now a single ballot box would be placed at each polling station and ballots marked 'yes' or 'no'. Secrecy was thus assured, the authorities insisted.[8]

In a final attempt to internationalise the contest for the state in Myanmar before the May referendum, the United Nations Secretary-General's Special Adviser on Myanmar again visited Yangon in March 2008. In advance, the Secretary General had written to Senior General Than Shwe, setting forth five proposals. These were:[9]

1. That his Special Adviser's visits to Myanmar should be regularised so that he could enter when he wished, meet with whom he wished, and have a permanent representative office in the country.

---

8   Persons legally away from the polling place on the day of the referendum were to be provided with ballot papers in advance (absentee) and their names removed from the voting lists. Votes were to be counted at the polling station in front of at least ten witnesses in each village or ward by local referendum commission officials, rather than being sent to be consolidated at township or district level as in the past. In all other ways the election law was similar to previous Myanmar elections, including the franchise for all 18-year-old citizens and the exclusion of members of religious orders from the voting list. Interfering with the referendum process by destroying voting lists or election commission notices was punishable by imprisonment for up to three years or a fine not to exceed K 100,000 or both. Included among the crimes of interfering with the referendum was 'lecturing, distributing papers, using posters or disturbing the voting in any such manner in the polling booth or on the premises of polling booth or at the public or private place to destroy the referendum.' (Section 24. h. of Law No. 1/2008) This was interpreted in some international press reports before the referendum as meaning that campaigning for a 'no' vote would be illegal. A novel feature of the election law was that it required 50 per cent of eligible voters, not 50 per cent of actual voters, to ratify the constitution. Thus refraining from voting had the same effect as voting no.

9   The text of the letter, dated 19 February 2008, was not released and this list is based on the implications of the remarks of the Minister for Information, Brig. Gen. Kyaw Hsan, when meeting with Ambassador Gambari on 7 March, reprinted in *The New Light of Myanmar* on 8 March 2008.

2. That the constitution drafting process should be reopened to include groups, including the NLD and unnamed ethnically designated politicians, that were excluded for various reasons in 2004.
3. That there should be discussions between Daw Aung San Suu Kyi and the government with a definite time frame.
4. That Daw Aung San Suu Kyi and all other political prisoners should be released.
5. That a National Economic Forum should be established for addressing economic and social issues and the appropriation of humanitarian assistance.

On receipt of these proposals, the SPDC at first did nothing and stupefied the United Nations. Then the Minister for Information rebutted each of its proposals in a lengthy response.

On the first point, the Minister said that the Special Adviser would always be received when it was possible to do so, and that there was no need for him to open an office in Yangon as there were already many UN agencies there and he could also communicate via the Ministry of Foreign Affairs. In regard to the major political point, the reopening of the drafting procedure for a new constitution to include those who had not participated in the previous process, the minister explained at length the history of the national convention. The departure of the NLD in 1995 and its unwillingness to rejoin the convention in 2004 except on its own terms was said to be their decision and it would be unfair to those who had participated in the process to undo their work. Moreover,

Those who agree with the draft and those who object [to] it can vote freely at the referendum in accordance with law. When the Constitution has been approved, those in favour of it or those against it will have rights to establish political parties, organise and enter elections in accordance with laws concerned at appropriate time.

The minister also insisted that not only had the convention process been inclusive, but it had also been transparent as developments, including the conclusions of the national convention, were published or broadcast in the government media as they occurred.

In regard to the point concerning a dialogue between the government and Daw Aung San Suu Kyi, he indicated that a government Liaison Minister had been appointed to that effect and that several meetings had taken place between him and the NLD leader. However, as she had refused to renounce her call for economic sanctions and defiance of the government, and had, disingenuously, he suggested, implied that she had not advocated sanctions, the talks had been inconclusive as the government's conditions for progress had not been met. Disingenuously on his part, the minister said, in addressing the fourth point, that there were no political prisoners, but merely persons serving sentences for violating the law. As for Daw Aung San Suu Kyi's detention, he said

... she was restricted at home for the first time as her political defiance stance posed danger to the state.[10] During the restricted period, mutual understanding was built up and the first restriction was lifted. However, the next day the restriction was lifted, Daw Aung San Suu Kyi held a press conference and stuck to confrontation and utter devastation policies by shouting that the Government had to choose either dialogue or utter devastation.[11] Consequently, she slandered the national convention and asked NLD to walk out of the National Convention.[12] Moreover, she demanded for summoning Hluttaw using it as an attack and attempted to convene [the] Hluttaw by herself.[13] Finally as her activities posed a grave danger and became uncontrollable, she was restricted a second time.[14]

During the second restriction, the party led by the Head of State met and discussed with her for four times and the group comprising ministers for 20 times. Then, with some mutual agreements, the restriction was lifted. She was shown round the achievements in nation building work. At the beginning, she stood properly as agreed but later she tried to turn back to the former old track.

On the fifth point, the minister indicated that the United Nations had approached the question from the wrong end. Rather than finding ways to use humanitarian assistance to pressure the government, the United Nations should assist in removing the economic sanctions that were applied to Myanmar, thus obviating the need for humanitarian assistance which was caused by the slow pace of economic development. While the UN Special Adviser met for several more days with government officials and representatives of political groups, including Daw Aung San Suu Kyi, there was no change in the government's position as a result. Nor was he invited to Naypyitaw to meet senior officials.

The contest for the state that resumed in 1988 had resulted twenty years later in the isolation of the political party which demonstrated in 1990 its opposition to a continued role for the army in government. The inability of the party and the army to find a *modus vivendi* was perhaps inevitable given

10   The July 1989 Martyrs Day march.
11   July 1995.
12   December 1995.
13   August/September 1998.
14   May 2003

the history of animosity that existed between some of the leading participants in that conflict. However, some might argue that it was the methods
the two sides, and their various allies, resorted to which made agreement
impossible. The number of variables involved in that conflict and international context in which it took place make an easy analysis impossible. At
the end of two decades, the army appeared to have confirmed its position
as the default government of Myanmar.

The 2008 constitution

The 2008 constitution contains a number of points that attempt to address issues that had emerged in Myanmar's post-colonial history. Among
these, most prominently and controversially, in addition to the power and
autonomy of the armed forces and the complex issue of political autonomy
for ethnically-designated groups, was the distribution of power between
the executive, legislature and judiciary at various levels of government. The
constitution is the army government's attempt to cast these issues in terms
that will be politically resolvable and will avoid in the future both the severe
conflicts of the civil war and the popular upheaval of 1988. Whether the
constitution proves to be more durable and adaptable than its two predecessors, of course, is a question that future historians will answer.

The constitution is long and detailed. It contains 457 clauses in 15 chapters plus five appendices. After reiterating the basic principles that were
confirmed during the 1990s sessions, the chapters follow the order of the
discussions in the national convention. The formal name of the state in
the 2008 constitution is Pyihtaungsu Thamada Myanmar Naingngandaw.
'Hsoshelit' (socialist) was dropped but 'Thamada' (republic) was retained
from the changes introduced in 1974. In English, it is rendered as the Republic of the Union of Myanmar. Like its predecessors, the state assumes .
responsibilities for economic development as well as health, education,
and culture. Acknowledging the failure of socialism, the constitution calls
for a market oriented economic system and forswears the nationalisation
of property or the demonetarisation of the currency. Freedom of religion
is guaranteed as long as the practice of religion does not cause political
conflict. The constitution avers that equality prevails under the law in all
matters except two: certain occupations can be recognised in law as being
specifically for men, and Buddhism, as the religious of the majority, has a
special place in the state.

In regard to the political system, it is described as a 'discipline flourishing genuine multi-party democracy', thus seeking to combine the need for order with the desire to avoid the consequences of one-party rule as had occurred in the past. Eschewing the term federalism, the state is described as employing the 'union system', meaning that the administrative power of the state is divided among the central government, seven states named after ethnic groups, seven regions (formerly divisions), a union territory (Naypyitaw, the capital), five self-administered ethnically designated zones, and one self-administered ethnically designated division.[15] Legislative power, though predominantly remaining with the central government, is distributed also to the states and regions and the self-administered zones. The national legislature, known as the Pyihtaungsu Hluttaw, is composed of two chambers, but meets as a single chamber for purposes of electing the president, adopting the annual budget, and amending the constitution. Each state or region has a single house legislature and minor legislative powers are given to the leading bodies or governments of the self-administered zones.

The constitution created a strong presidency that has powers of appointment and removal, not only of the central government, but also of subsidiary governments. Certain cabinet positions are reserved to active military personnel. These concern defence, home affairs, security, and border administration. The army is also fiscally and administratively autonomous and exists not only for national defence but also for the protection and maintenance of the constitution. Under the control of the Commander-in-Chief of Defence Services, the army has arrogated a number of responsibilities and powers unto itself. For example, 25 per cent of the members of the Pyihtaungsu Hluttaw and its two chambers must be serving army officers appointed by the Commander-in-Chief as must one-third of the members of state or regional hluttaw. Thus, the army has a great deal of autonomous power and, like the civil service, is to be above partisan party politics and will practice 'national' politics as the SLORC/SPDC claimed to do.

The power of the army in the constitution is justified, in the minds of the SPDC, on at least two grounds. One is historical. As numerous articles and books during the two decades after 1988 argue, the army has frequently had to act to save the state from disintegration, lost of sovereignty, and other calamities. The origin of the army in 1942 as the BIA prior to independence is described as in the patriotic tradition of the pre-colonial kings

---

15   The names of the states and regions are the same as those of the current states and divisions.

and their armies, especially those of the founders of dynasties, rather than in that of student nationalists as argued during the socialist era. The role of the BIA and its successors in gaining independence under the leadership of Bogyoke Aung San is extolled at the expense of historical accuracy or consideration of other political actors in the 1940s. The army's role in the post-independence civil war, the 1958 Caretaker Government, the 1962 Revolutionary Council coup, and the events of 1988 are all cited as proof of the indispensability of the army in defence of the state and nation. The other justification is that the constitution requires a stabilising element in order to ensure that the politicians who will be pursuing their partisan interests in the elected governments to come do not destabilise the state or threaten its independence and sovereignty.[16] Unlike in the 1974 constitution where the Party took the role of the king in stabilising and guiding the state and nation, in the 2008 constitution that role is assumed by the army.

Thus, if a state of emergency is declared in any region, state or area of the country, the President has the right to assume all power and the army has an obligation to prevent danger and provide protection. The army can also act independently to protect the sovereignty of the state and compliance with the terms of the constitution. This supererogatory role is justified by the claim that the army stands above politics as a 'national' institution and therefore acts selflessly for the good of the state and nation. The validity of that claim is, of course, highly disputed by those who contest for state power, as are the qualifications for serving as President of the Republic.

The President must be at least 45 years of age and born of parents who were both citizens, a condition stipulated in the 1947 constitution, and must be acquainted with the political, administrative, economic, and military affairs of the state. He or she must also have no allegiance to, citizenship of, or rights and privileges availed by a foreign power; nor can his or her parents, spouse and children, or their spouses. Thus, the exclusionary requirements for election as President are expanded from previous constitutions. In addition, like members of the Pyihtaungsu Hluttaw, he or she has to have lived in Myanmar for the previous 20 years unless abroad with government permission, and must be free from criminal conviction, of sound mind, not destitute, and not in receipt of support from foreign governments or religious organisations. The requirement that he and his

---

16   As argued that the constitution requires a 'balancing weight' or a system of checks and balances. See Si Thu Aung, 'To service (sic) as balancing weight', *New Light of Myanmar*, 21 March 2008.

family have no allegiance or connection with foreign governments is normally interpreted as excluding Daw Aung San Suu Kyi from being elected President. The terms in the 1947 and the 1974 constitutions grew out of a distrust of the loyalty of Anglo-Burmese and other immigrant or 'mixed race' persons by nationalist politicians. The two Vice-Presidents who are also elected in the same manner as the President have to meet the same eligibility requirements.

The President is elected by the Pyihtaungsu Hluttaw meeting in plenary session after three candidates have been nominated by the two chambers and the army members meeting separately. Their qualifications are then scrutinised by the leaders and deputy leaders of the two houses of the Hluttaw. The expectation, given the composition of the three nominating groups, is that one will come from the ethnic minorities, one from a major political party, and one from the ranks of the armed forces. The presidential term of office is five years and he or she may serve for only two terms. If the President is a civil servant, army officer, or member of the Hluttaw at the time of her or his appointment, he or she will resign from that post; if a member of a political party, she or he will abstain from political activities while in office. The President must declare his or her assets as a protection against corruption and can be impeached if charged by 25 per cent of either house of the Pyihtaungsu Hluttaw. The charge will then be investigated by the other chamber and after receiving their report, the two houses will meet together to determine the case. For his removal, a two thirds vote is required. Should the presidency fall vacant, one of the two Vice-Presidents will succeed.

The Pyihtaungsu Hluttaw is composed of the Pyithu (People's) Hluttaw with 440 members and the Amyotha (Nationalities) Hluttaw with 224 members. Of the members of the Pyithu Hluttaw, 330 are elected on the basis of one per township plus others for more highly populated townships, and 110 appointed from the army. Each state or region elects 12 members of the Amyotha Hluttaw for a total of 168 with another 56 appointed by the army. Both Hluttaw have five year terms expected to be coterminous with that of the President, and each has a number of standard parliamentary committees such as those for public accounts and Hluttaw rights, and others for national races, economic, financial, social, foreign and other affairs. Only the membership of the Defence and Security Committee is specified; it must be composed of members of the armed forces with others co-opted if required. The two bodies have the power to establish joint committees

Addendum 2. Self-Administered Zones by Township

State or Region	Ethnic Group	Townships
Sagaing Region	Naga	Leshi, Lahe, Namyun
Shan State	Danu	Ywangna, Pindaya
	Pa-O	Hopong, Hsiheng, Pinlaung
	Palaung	Namhsan, Manton
	Kokang	Konkyan, Laukkai
	Wa	Hopang, Mongmao, Panwai, Nahpam, Pangsang (Pankham), Metman

and commissions with investigative powers. The Pyihtaungsu Hluttaw can be called into special session on the demand of 25 per cent of its members. The President has no ultimate veto power as vetoes can be overridden.

Regional and state hluttaw are formed on the basis of two persons per township plus one from each ethnic group with 0.1 per cent members in the state, unless they already have assigned to their group a self-administered area. As noted, one third of the membership will be from the armed forces. Qualifications for membership are basically the same as those noted for the President, other than age and the experience qualifications, and less stringent requirements relative to familial or external ties. Members of the Pyithu Hluttaw and state or regional hluttaw have to be at least 25 years of age, members of the Amyotha Hlutttaw have to be at least 30.

Legislative action in regard to defence, security, foreign affairs, and judicial affairs are solely within the power of the two chambers of the Pyihtaungsu Hluttaw. Financial powers primarily lie with the Pyihtaungsu Hluttaw, including currency and coinage, the central bank, and all taxation except land revenue and excise duties. As Union law takes precedent over state and regional law, all powers at that level and within the self-administered zones can be regulated by the central government. Many of the powers devolved to the states, regions and zones are essentially regulatory. For the self-administered zones, they include markets, pastures, forest protection, environmental protection, electricity and water supply, fire prevention and other matters such as local roads and bridges already administered at that level. If 25 per cent of the members agree, they can demand a special session of the Pyihtaungsu Hluttaw.

The budgetary process is highly centralised with much of the state and regional budget being provided by the central government. The central budget is prepared by a Finance Commission composed of the President, the two Vice-Presidents, the Attorney General, the Auditor General, the 14 chief ministers of states and regions, the Naypyitaw City Council Chairman, and the Minister for Finance. Pay and emoluments at all levels are to be set by the Finance Commission from the centre.

The President, under the effective supervision of the Commander-in-Chief of the Armed Forces, who however appoints him, is the most powerful individual in the governmental structure. He is to act as if he were responsible to the Pyihtaungsu Hluttaw. He appoints members of the cabinet who must be over forty years of age, and possess the qualifications to sit in the Pyihtaungsu Hluttaw, but do not have to be elected members. Deputy ministers have to be at least 35 years old. As noted, ministers responsible for defence, security, home affairs and border affairs must be appointed from a list provided by the Commander-in-Chief of the Armed Forces. The Hluttaw has no right, as the constitution is currently written, to reject a cabinet appointee or to question how many ministerial portfolios there shall be.

The President under his prerogative also makes other central government appointments. These are the Attorney General and the Auditor General and their deputies and the Chairman of the Union Civil Service Board. They must be at least 45 years of age (50 for the Civil Service Board chairman) and possess necessary qualifications for their posts. Again, the nominees advanced by the President cannot be refused or rejected by the Hluttaw.

The President also appoints the chief ministers, ministers and advocates general of the state and regional governments. They may be members of the relevant hluttaw, from an army list, nominees of autonomous zones, or national race affairs specialists. The meaning of the last of these is not specified but people can be so designated by the election commission. The minimum age is 35 years, although in the case of chairmen of autonomous zones, that can be relaxed. State and regional security and border affairs ministers have to be from an army list. Chief ministers can be impeached by the relevant hluttaw by a two-thirds vote of members. Central supervision of subordinate governments is maintained by the appointment of the secretary to the government from the General Administration Department of the Home Ministry. There may not be much difference, in effect, in the management of state and regional governments or autonomous zones from the system that prevailed during final years of military government. State

THE STATE IN MYANMAR

and regional attorneys general and auditors general will be appointed by the chief minister.

In the autonomous zones, the government will be formed by a leading body composed of ten members including hluttaw representatives, army nominees for security and border affairs, and others. The chairman will be chosen from the state or regional hluttaw members from the relevant autonomous zone. At least 25 per cent of the members must be from the army and all ethnic groups with at least 10,000 members in the zone and not otherwise represented must be so. The Chairman is responsible to the President and the General Administration Department will provide the autonomous zone's government secretary. The Naypyitaw city council is appointed by the President.

The President is chairman of the National Defence and Security Council (NDSC). This body is responsible for executive responsibilities including pardons, honours, diplomatic relations, and the declaration of war, with or without reference to the Pyihtuangsu Hluttaw. Between Hluttaw sessions it can amend the budget, but it must call a Hluttaw meeting within 60 days to ratify the change. The NDSC is composed of eleven persons who are the President, the two Vice-Presidents, the speakers of the two chambers of the Pyihtaungsu Hluttaw, the Commander-in-Chief of the armed forces and his deputy, and the ministers for defence, foreign affairs, home affairs and border affairs. At a minimum, therefore, there will be at least six serving members of the armed forces on the body. The NDSC will join with the President in appointing the Commander-in-Chief of the armed forces. It would appear that a tight circle dominated by military and retired military personnel will remain responsible for defence and security matters as under previous regimes.

The President, should he declare a state of emergency in a particular state, region or zone, can assume all governmental powers in that area through the NDSC. Similarly, the President can rule through the NDSC in the entire country after consulting with its members and declaring a state of emergency. If the NDSC cannot meet because of the existing conditions, he can consult with military members to the same end. This will have the effect of dissolving the government and the NDSC will rule in its own name until such time as new elections can be held under the constitution. The implication of this is that should the necessity to conduct a coup occur, there would be no need to write a new constitution before a return to multi-party power sharing took place.

The judiciary under the new constitution will function essentially in the same manner as the current judicial organisation of the state. Innovations are that the Chief Justice will have to retire when he reaches 70 years of age and other Supreme Court members when they reach 65. Also, a Constitutional Tribunal is created composed of nine persons, three appointed by the President and three by the speakers of the two chambers of the Pyihtaungsu Hluttaw, from legally qualified persons over the age of 50. It will be their responsibility to interpret the constitution and ensure that legislative, judicial and executive action is in conformity with it.

Political parties will participate in elections organised by a Union Election Commission appointed by the President. Political parties will be permitted to organise freely and stand in elections as long as they are loyal to the constitution and its fundamental principles. Parties will be banned if they are declared illegal organisations or found to have 'connections with or provide support or assistance to insurgent groups waging an armed rebellion against the State, organisations or persons the State has announced as the one committing terrorist acts or organisations the state has declared unlawful.' Also, parties will be declared illegal if they receive support directly or indirectly from religious groups or foreign governments.

To amend the fundamental principles of the constitution, its overall structures, and the rules for forming the legislature and the judiciary or declaring a state of emergency, 75 per cent of the Pyithaungsu Hluttaw must concur. Then the question is put to the people in the form of a referendum where a simple majority of eligible votes must agree to the change. Other aspects of the constitution can be amended without resort to approval via referendum by the people.

The new constitution will come into effect from the first meeting of the Pyihtaungsu Hluttaw, which will presumably assemble following elections in 2010. In the meantime, the SPDC will remain in power. In an innovation from the basic principles agreed at the National Convention, the constitution also gives immunity from legal action to the SPDC, its agents and personnel, for their decisions and activities prior to the coming into effect of the constitution.

Attitudes toward the draft constitution and the referendum process

Not unexpectedly, exiled opposition groups and the United States government rejected the draft constitution before it was issued. The 1988 Generation of Students issued a statement on 14 March calling for a 'No' vote

503

because the draft constitution was designed by the military, in their words, as a 'license to oppress' and would ensure that the people would 'become the slaves of the military for generations'. Similarly, the National Coalition of the Union of Burma (NCUB) on the same day called for a 'No' vote because they were opposed to the entire roadmap as announced by the SPDC in 2003. A spokesperson for the NCUB secretariat said, 'We have to oppose it at every stage and this is the basis of our decision.' The United States government also condemned the draft constitution and the referendum as a 'sham', while the European Union's Special Envoy on Burma/Myanmar said that the referendum required the freeing of political prisoners including Daw Aung San Suu Kyi in order to be creditable.[17]

Inside Myanmar the reaction was more muted. Given the lack of publicity the SPDC gave to the announcements about the referendum and the eventual publishing of the constitution, many gave scant consideration to the implications of the referendum. For those few civilians who did, there were two reactions. One was to reject the draft constitution outright, seeing it in the same way as the exile community. For many in this camp, their anger towards the army was so great and generalised that there was nothing that the government had done in the past twenty years which could receive credit. There is no way of knowing what proportion of the population felt positively or negatively about the referendum and draft constitution. Some did see it as an opportunity to begin to dismantle the tight grip that the army had on the state. Viewing the process as a gradual, evolutionary one, these persons argued that allowing the army to maintain 25 per cent of the seats in the legislature was better than the current situation where the army had 100 per cent power. The autonomy of the army and the constitution's authorisation of what would effectively be a coup d'état in the case of an emergency, they argued, merely recognised what was reality whatever the constitution said. The dominant position of the President, and particularly his exclusive power to appoint the cabinet, was a point that many wished to amend, however, at the first opportunity.

Those who accepted the constitution also began to consider the implications of its ratification and the holding of elections in 2010. The formation of political parties by ethnic-designated political leaders, business persons, and professionals had major implications for the outcome of the future elections. Creating the political freedom to conduct meaningful elections,

---

17   European Union Press Release, 12 March 2008, Office of the European Union Special Envoy for Burma/Myanmar.

they argued, required a degree of compromise between the government's persistent concerns about security and the threat posed by exile and opposition political groups. The need for a relaxation of press censorship and control of political activity to allow a genuine degree of debate, within confined space, to take place was seen as a minimal requirement to make the new system work effectively.

Ceasefire groups responded in various ways to the referendum and the publishing of the draft constitution. Some groups, especially those granted their own autonomous zones, were content with the process and its outcome. Others, who saw the constitution as potentially undermining the political autonomy they had gained through the ceasefire process, were less positive and threatened to withhold support in the referendum. For those groups that were part of larger ethnic communities such as the Kachin and Shan, which had states named after them and were not granted autonomous zones under the constitution, the new settlement posed a number of dilemmas. These they pressed on the SPDC and the leadership of the national convention, but they received little if any response to their expressions of concern. As in the past, their demands sought to lessen the administratively centralising powers of the state by the creation of a 'federal' system of government as opposed to the 'union' system set forth in the constitution. This demand was in some sense rhetorical, but in other ways concerned the fundamental essence of origins of the state. Was the state unitary, creating subsidiary powers as it saw fit, or was the central state the creation of its various parts and therefore their creation? That was the issue at the heart of the civil war after demands for sovereignty were abandoned in the 1970s. Whether there was the desire or the ability to resume that conflict remained to be demonstrated.

The most detailed critique of the constitution, presented by the Central Committee of the Kachin Independence Organisation in mid-July 2007,[18] argued that a new constitution should create an ethnically based state, rather than a territorially based state. Therefore the seven regions or divisions should be grouped together as one Bamar (Burman) state existing parallel and equal with the seven ethnic minority-designated states. Furthermore, they argued that the states and divisions should have greater legislative and judicial autonomy than implied in the 2008 constitution, allowing for the

---

18   Unfortunately, the author has only seen a copy of an unofficial translation of the letter from the Central Committee of the KIO to the chairman of the National Convention Commission and cannot vouch for its accuracy.

particular laws and customs of specific ethnic minorities to be applied to them rather than Union law. The KIO Central Committee also argued that the heads and members of state governments should be elected by their respective hluttaw rather than appointed by the President. In a criticism which some might argue was undemocratic, they called for members of the Amyotha Hluttaw elected from each state to be only members of the ethnic minority after which the state was named. They also objected to the creation of a central ministry for border affairs and sought some degree of border control for the state governments. State citizenship and a number of economic and social powers bestowed on the central government were also sought. To have accepted these criticisms, the constitutional assembly would have had to revisit the fundamental principles which were accepted in 1992, and the lack of response from the SPDC to these criticisms demonstrated its unwillingness to revise the army's concept of the state.

A return to competitive politics within the state or against the state?

The constitution which the army created allowed the officer corps to do more than 'hold the ring', as the British saw themselves doing in the 1930s. The army will not only hold the ring; it will provide the referees, dictate the rules, and become a significant independent economic and political actor in its own right. More than 60 years of internal strife and political discord have created an army which, no matter what the constitution says, will probably prevail in any future political conflicts. The constitution recognises that fact and the army tries to justify it as a virtue. Whether the army can ever just 'hold the ring' and allow the remainder of Myanmar's diverse and fractious population to work out a political settlement on their own terms remains to be seen. If the past is a guide, then this is unlikely. Whether Western governments, pursuing their own ideological and strategic goals, will allow that to happen also remains to be seen. The state in Myanmar will, however, persist as long as Myanmar survives. Whether 'common sense', as defined by the army, can give way to 'human nature', and the constitution evolve to serve the creation of a just and open society, is a question beyond the scope of this volume.[19]

---

19   See the quotation from J. S. Furnivall that forms the frontispiece to this book.

BIBLIOGRAPHY (PRE-1988)

Note: References to Burma Office files (BOF) and India Office files (IOF) are located in the India Office Archives and Library, London. Numbers given are the original file numbers. The press of Burma, the United States and Great Britain has been cited but not listed here.

Books and monographs in English

Adas, Michael, *The Burma Delta: Economic Development and Social Change on an Asian Rice Frontier, 1852–1941*. Madison: University of Wisconsin Press, 1974.

Anderson, Benedict, *Imagined Communities: Reflections on the Origin and Spread of Nationalism*. London: Verso, 1983.

Andrew, E.J.L., *Indian Labour in Rangoon*. London: Oxford University Press, 1933.

Aung San, *Burma's Challenge 1946*. South Okkalapa: Tathetta Sapei, 1974.

Aung-Thwin, Michael, *Pagan: The Origins of Modern Burma*. Honolulu: University of Hawaii Press, 1985.

Ba Maw, *Breakthrough in Burma: Memoirs of a Revolution*. New Haven: Yale University Press, 1968.

Becka, Jan, *The National Liberation Movement in Burma during the Japanese Occupation Period (1941–1945)*. Prague: Oriental Institute, Dissertationes Orientales, vol. 42, 1983.

Bendix, Reinhard, *Max Weber: An Intellectual Portrait*. Garden City, NY: Doubleday, 1960.

Brown, Ian, *A Colonial Economy in Crisis: Burma's Rice Cultivators and the World Depression of the 1930s*. London: Routledge Curzon, 2005.

Butwell, Richard, *U Nu of Burma*. Stanford University Press, 2nd imp., 1969.

Cady, John F., *A History of Modern Burma*. Ithaca and London: Cornell University Press, 1958, supplement, 1960.

———— *Post-War Southeast Asia: Independence Problems*. Athens, Ohio: Ohio University Press, 1974.

———— *Contacts with Burma, 1935–1949: A Personal Account*. Athens, Ohio:

507

Ohio University Center for International Studies, 1983.

Callahan, Mary P., *Making Enemies: War and State Building in Burma*. Ithaca and London: Cornell University Press, 2003.

Callis, Helmut G., *Foreign Capital in Southeast Asia*. New York: International Secretariat, Institute of Pacific Relations, 1942.

Chakravarti, N.R., *The Indian Minority in Burma: The Rise and Decline of an Immigrant Community*. London: Oxford University Press for the Institute of Race Relations, London, 1971.

Cocks, S.W., *Burma Under British Rule*. Bombay: K. and J. Cooper, 2nd edn, n.d.

Colbert, Evelyn, *Southeast Asia in International Politics 1941–1956*. Ithaca: Cornell University Press, 1977.

Collis, Maurice, *Into Hidden Burma*. London: Faber and Faber, 1953.

Crosthwaite, Charles, *The Pacification of Burma*. First published 1912, repr. London: Frank Cass, 1968.

Donnison, F.S.V., *Public Administration in Burma: A Study of Development During the British Connexion*. London: Royal Institute of International Affairs, 1953.

——— *Burma*. New York: Praeger; London: Benn, 1970.

Fielding[-Hall], H., *Thibaw's Queen*. New York and London: Harper and Brothers, 1899.

Foucar, E.C.V., *I Lived in Burma*. London: Dennis Dobson, 1956.

Friedgut, Theodore H., *Political Participation in the USSR*. Princeton University Press, 1979.

Furnivall, J.S., *Colonial Policy and Practice: A Comparative Study of Burma and Netherlands India*. Cambridge University Press, 1948; New York University Press, 1956.

——— *An Introduction to the Political Economy of Burma*. Rangoon: People's Literature Committee and House, 3rd ed., 1957.

Glass, Leslie, *The Changing of Kings: Memories of Burma, 1934–1949*. London: Peter Owen, 1985.

Golay, Frank H., Ralph Anspach, M. Ruth Pfanner, and Eliezer B. Ayal, *Underdevelopment and Economic Nationalism in Southeast Asia*. Ithaca: Cornell University Press, 1969.

Grantham, S.G., *Studies in the History of Tharrawaddy*. Cambridge University Press (for private circulation), 1920.

Hall, D.G.E., *A History of South East Asia*. London: Macmillan, 3rd edn, 1968.

Harvey, G.E., *History of Burma*. London: Frank Cass, 1967 (orig. publ. 1925).

——— *British Rule in Burma 1824–1942*. London: Faber and Faber, 1946.

Henderson, John W., *et al.*, *Area Handbook for Burma*. Washington, DC: United States Government Printing Office, 1971.

Herbert, Patricia, *The Hsaya San Rebellion (1930–1932) Reappraised*. Melbourne: Monash University Centre of Southeast Asian Studies Working Paper No. 27, 1982.

Hla Pe, *Burma: Literature, Historiography, Scholarship, Language, Life and Buddhism*. Singapore: Institute of Southeast Asian Studies, 1985.

International Institute for Strategic Studies, *The Military Balance 1985–86*, London: 1985.

International Monetary Fund, *World Debt Tables*. Washington, DC: International Monetary Fund, 1985.

———— *Government Finance Statistics Yearbook 1985*, Washington, DC: International Monetary Fund, 1985.

Kelly, Desmond, *Kelly's Burma Campaign*. London: Tiddim Press, 2003.

Khin Maung Kyi and Tin Tin, *Administrative Patterns in Historical Burma*. Singapore: Institute of Southeast Asian Studies Southeast Asian Perspectives no. 1, 1973.

Krasner, Stephen D., *Structural Conflict: The Third World Against Global Liberalism*. Berkeley: University of California Press, 1985.

Kyaw Win, Mya Han and Thein Hlaing, translated by Ohn Gaing and Khin Su, *The 1947 Constitution and the Nationalities*. 2 vols., Yangon: Universities Historical Research Centre and Innwa Publishing House, 1999.

Lieberman, Victor B., *Burmese Administrative Cycles: Anarchy and Conquest. c. 1580–1760*. Princeton University Press, 1984.

Lu Pe Win, *History of the 1920 University Boycott*. (Rangoon?): The author, for the Organization for the Celebration of the Golden Jubilee of the National Day, Nov. 1970.

Mahajani, Usha, *The Role of the Indian Minorities in Burma and Malaya*. Bombay: Vora, 1960.

Marr, David G., *Vietnamese Anti-Colonialism, 1885–1925*. Berkeley: University of California Press, 1971.

Maung Maung, *Burma's Constitution*. The Hague: Martinus Nijhoff, 2nd edn, 1961.

———— *Burma and General Ne Win*. New York: Asia Publishing House, 1969.

Maung Maung, *From Sangha to Laity, Nationalist Movements of Burma, 1920–1940*. Australian National University Monographs on South Asia no. 4, New Delhi: Manohar, 1980.

Mendelson, E. Michael., *Sangha and State in Burma, A Study of Monastic Sectarianism and Leadership*, edited by John P. Ferguson. Ithaca: Cornell University Press, 1975.

Milne, Patricia M., trans., *Selected Short Stories of Thein Pe Myint*. Ithaca:

Cornell University Southeast Asia Program Data Paper no. 91, June, 1973.

Mi Mi Khaing, *The World of Burmese Women*. Singapore: Times International, 1985.

Montgomery, John D., *The Politics of Foreign Aid: American Experience in Southeast Asia*. New York: Praeger, 1962.

Moscotti, Albert D., *British Policy and the Nationalist Movement in Burma 1917–1937*. Honolulu: Asian Studies at Hawaii, no. 11, University of Hawaii Press, 1974.

—— *Burma's Constitution and the Elections of 1974*. Singapore: Institute of Southeast Asian Studies Research Notes and Discussions no. 5, Sept., 1977.

Mya Sein, *Administration in Burma: Sir Charles Crosthwaite and the Consolidation of Burma*. Rangoon: Zabu Meitswa Pitaka Press, 1938; repr. Kuala Lumpur: Oxford University Press, 1973.

Ni Ni Myint, *Burma's Struggle Against British Imperialism (1885–1895)*. Rangoon: The Universities Press, 1983.

North, Douglas C. and Robert Paul Thomas, *The Rise of the Western World. A New Economic History*. Cambridge University Press, 1973.

Nu, *U Nu—Saturday's Son*. Trans. by Law Yone, edited by Kyaw Win. New Haven: Yale University Press, 1975.

Pearn, B.R., *History of Rangoon*. Rangoon: A.B.M. Press, 1939.

People's Literature Committee, *Who's Who in Burma, 1961*. Rangoon: Sarpay Beikman, 1962.

Pollack, Oliver B., *Empires in Collision: Anglo-Burmese Relations in the Mid-Nineteenth Century*. Westport, Conn.: Greenwood Press, 1979.

Purcell, Victor, *The Chinese in Southeast Asia*. London: Oxford University Press, 2nd edn, 1966.

Rao, A. Narayan, *Indian Labour in Burma*. Madras: Keshari Press, 1944.

Research Institute for Peace and Security, *Asian Security 1980*. Tokyo: 1980.

Richards, C.J., *Burma Retrospect and Other Essays*. Winchester, England: Herbert Curnow Ltd., the Cathedral Press, 1951.

Richter, H.V., *Burma's Rice Surpluses: Accounting for the Decline*. Canberra: Development Studies Centre, Australian National University, 1976.

Robinson, M. and L.A. Shaw, *The Coins and Banknotes of Burma*. Manchester: The authors, 1980.

Saimong Mangrai, *The Shan States and the British Annexation*. Ithaca: Cornell University Southeast Asia Program Data Paper no. 57, 1965.

Scott, James C., *The Moral Economy of the Peasant: Rebellion and Subsistence in Southeast Asia*. New Haven: Yale University Press, 1976.

Scott, J. George and J.P. Hardiman, *Gazetteer of Upper Burma and the Shan*

States. Rangoon: Government Printing and Stationery, 1900.

Sen, N.C., *A Peep into Burma Politics (1917–1941)*. Allahabad: Kitabistan, 1945.

Sein Win, *The Split Story*. Rangoon: Guardian Press, 1959.

Shein, *Burma's Transport and Foreign Trade (1885–1914)* Rangoon. Dept of Economics, University of Rangoon, 1964.

Shwe Zan Aung and Rhys Davids, *Compendium of Philosophy*. London: Pali Text Society, 1910.

Silverstein, Josef, *Burma: Military Rule and the Politics of Stagnation*. Ithaca: Cornell University Press, 1977.

Singh, Ganga, *Burma Parliamentary Companion*. Rangoon: British Burma Press, 1940.

Smith, Donald Eugene, *Religion and Politics in Burma*. Princeton University Press, 1965.

Soe and Chit Hlaing, *Soe: Socialism and Chit Hlaing: Memories*. Passau, Germany: Myanmar Literature Project Working Paper No. 10, 2008.

Spiro, Melford E., *Buddhism and Society: A Great Tradition and Its Burmese Vicissitudes*. New York: Harper and Row, 1972.

Steinberg, David I., *Burma's Road Toward Development: Growth and Ideology Under Military Rule*. Boulder, Colo.: Westview Press, 1981.

Stockholm International Peace Research Institute, *SIPRI Yearbook of World Armaments and Disarmament, 1968/69*. Stockholm: Almqvist and Wiksell, 1969.

—— *SIPRI Yearbook of World Armaments and Disarmament, 1976*. Stockholm: Almqvist and Wiksell, 1977.

—— *SIPRI Yearbook of World Armaments and Disarmament, 1984*. London: Taylor and Francis, 1985.

Tambiah, S.J., *World Conqueror and World Renouncer: A Study of Buddhism and Polity in Thailand Against a Historical Background*. Cambridge University Press, 1976.

Taylor, Robert H., *Foreign and Domestic Consequences of the KMT Intervention in Burma*. Ithaca: Cornell University Southeast Asia Program Data Paper no. 93, 1973.

—— *An Undeveloped State: The Study of Modern Burma's Politics*. Melbourne: Monash University Centre of Southeast Asian Studies Working Paper no. 28, 1983.

—— *Marxism and Resistance in Burma, 1942–1945: Thein Pe Myint's 'Wartime Traveller'*. Athens, Ohio: Ohio University Press, 1984.

Thiha, *The Chindits and the Stars*. London: Regency Press, 1971.

Tinker, Hugh, *Foundations of Local Self-Government in India, Pakistan and Burma*. Bombay: Lalvani, 1967.

Trager, Frank N., *Building a Welfare State in Burma, 1948–1956.* New York: Institute of Pacific Relations, 1958.

——— *Burma: From Kingdom to Independence.* London: Pall Mall Press, 1966.

——— and William J. Koenig (eds), *Burmese Sit-tans 1764–1826: Records of Rural Life and Administration.* Tucson: University of Arizona Press for the Association for Asian Studies, 1979.

Tun Wai, *Burma's Currency and Credit.* Bombay: Orient Longmans (revised edn), 1962.

Ulyanovsky, Rostislav, *National Liberation.* Moscow: Progress Publishers, 1978.

United States Arms Control and Disarmament Agency, *World Military Expenditures and Arms Transfers 1985.* Washington, DC: 1985.

Walinsky, Louis J., *Economic Development in Burma, 1951–1960.* New York: Twentieth Century Fund, 1962.

Weber, Max, *Economy and Society.* Edited by Guenther Roth and Claus Wittich. New York: Bedminster Press, 1968, vols. I–III.

World Bank, *World Development Report 1984.* Oxford University Press, 1984.

Articles in English

Adas, Michael, 'Immigrant Asians and the Economic Impact of European Imperialism: The Role of South Indian Chettiars in British Burma', *Journal of Asian Studies*, XXXIII, 3 (May 1974), pp. 385–401.

——— 'From Avoidance to Confrontation: Peasant Protest in Precolonial and Colonial Southeast Asia', *Comparative Studies in Society and History*, 23, 2 (April 1981), pp. 217–47.

Anderson, Benedict R. O'G., 'Old State, New Society: Indonesia's New Order in Comparative Historical Perspective', *Journal of Asian Studies*, XLII, 3 (May 1983), pp. 477–96.

Arumugam, Raja Segaran, 'Burma: A Political and Economic Background', in Institute of Southeast Asian Studies, *Southeast Asian Affairs 1975.* Singapore: FEP International, 1976, pp. 41–8.

——— 'Burma: Political Unrest and Economic Stagnation', in Institute of Southeast Asian Studies, *Southeast Asian Affairs 1976.* Singapore: FEP International, 1977, pp. 167–75.

ASMI, 'The State of Arakan', *The Guardian* (Rangoon) 1/10 (Aug. 1954), pp. 28–9; 1/11 (Sept. 1954), pp. 21–3.

Aung Kin, 'Burma in 1980: Pouring Balm on Sore Spots', in Institute of Southeast Asian Studies, *Southeast Asian Affairs 1981.* Singapore: Heinemann, 1982, pp. 103–25.

Aung-Thwin, Michael, 'Kingship, the *Sangha*, and Society in Pagan', in

Kenneth R. Hall and John K. Whitmore (eds), *Explorations in Early Southeast Asian History: The Origins of Southeast Asian Statecraft*. Ann Arbor: Michigan Papers on South and Southeast Asia no. 11, 1976, pp. 205–56.

———— 'The Role of *Sasana* Reform in Burmese History: Economic Dimensions of a Religious Purification', *Journal of Asian Studies*, XXXVIII, 4 (Aug. 1979), pp. 671–88.

———— 'Jampudipa: Classical Burma's Camelot', in John P. Ferguson (ed.), 'Essays on Burma', *Contributions to Asian Studies*, vol. 16, Leiden: E.J. Brill, 1981, pp. 38–61.

———— 'Divinity, Spirit, and Human: Conceptions of Classical Burmese Kingship', in Lorraine Gesick (ed.), *Centers, Symbols, and Hierarchies: Essays on the Classical State of Southeast Asia*. New Haven: Yale University Southeast Asian Studies Series no. 26, 1983, pp. 45–86.

Aye Hlaing, 'Observations on Some Patterns of Economic Development', *Burma Research Society Fiftieth Anniversary Publications no. 1*. Rangoon: Burma Research Society, 1961, pp. 9–16.

Badgley, John H., 'Burma: The Nexus of Socialism and Two Political Traditions', *Asian Survey*, III, 2 (Feb. 1963), pp. 89–95.

———— 'Burma's Zealot Wungyis: Maoists or St. Simonists', *Asian Survey*, V, 1 (Jan. 1965), pp. 55–62.

Baldwin, J.W., 'The Karens in Burma', *Journal of the Royal Central Asian Society*, XXXVI (1949), pp. 102–13.

Callahan, Mary P., "The Sinking Schooner: Murder and the State in Independent Burma, 1948-1958", in Carl A. Trocki, ed., *Gangsters, Democracy, and the State in Southeast Asia*. Ithaca, New York: Cornell University Southeast Asia Program, 1998), pp. 17-38.

———— "On Time Warps and Warped Time: Lessons from Burma's 'Democratic' Era", in Robert I. Rotberg, eds., *Burma: Prospects for a Democratic Future*. Washington, D. C.: Brookings Institution Press, 1998), pp. 49-68.

Demaine, Harvey, 'Current Problems of Agricultural Development Planning in Burma', in Institute of Southeast Asian Studies, *Southeast Asian Affairs 1979*. Singapore: Heinemann, 1979, pp. 95–103.

Everton, John, 'The Ne Win Regime in Burma', *Asia*, 2 (Autumn 1964), pp. 1–17.

Finer, Samuel E., 'State and Nation-Building in Europe: The Role of the Military', in Charles Tilly (ed.), *The Formation of National States in Europe*. Princeton University Press, 1975, pp. 84–163.

Furnivall, J.S., 'The Fashioning of Leviathan', *The Journal of the Burma Research Society*, XXIX, 3 (1939), pp. 1–138.

———— 'South Asia in the World Today', in Phillips Talbot (ed.), *South Asia in the World Today*. University of Chicago Press, 1950, pp. 3–24.

Gledhill, Alan, 'Burma', in John Gilissen (ed.), *Bibliographical Introduction to Legal History and Ethnology*, vol. E, no. 7. Brussels: Éditions de l'Institut de Sociologie, Université Libre de Bruxelles, 1970.

Guyot, James F., 'Bureaucratic Transformation in Burma', in Ralph Braibanti (ed.), *Asian Bureaucratic Systems Emergent from the British Imperial Tradition*. Durham, NC: Duke University Press, 1966, pp. 354–443.

Heine-Geldern, Robert, 'Conceptions of State and Kingship in Southeast Asia', *The Far Eastern Quarterly*, 2 (Nov. 1942), pp. 15–30.

Hla Aung, 'The Effect of Anglo-Indian Legislation on Burmese Customary Law', in David C. Buxbaum (ed.), *Family Law and Customary Law in Asia: A Contemporary Legal Perspective*. The Hague: Martinus Nijhoff, 1968, pp. 67–88.

Khin Maung Kyi, et al., 'Process of Communication in Modernisation of Rural Society: A Survey Report on Two Burmese Villages', *The Malayan Economic Review*, XVIII, no. 1 (April 1973), pp. 55–73.

Khin Maung Kyi, 'Problems of Agricultural Policy in Some Trade Dependent Small Countries: A Comparative Study of Burma and Thailand', *Kajian Ekonomi Malaysia*. XVI, nos. 1 and 2 (June/Dec. 1979), pp. 344–52.

———— 'Modernization of Burmese Agriculture: Problems and Prospects', in Institute of Southeast Asian Studies, *Southeast Asian Affairs 1982*. Singapore: Institute of Southeast Asian Studies, 1983, pp. 115–31.

———— 'Indians in Burma: Problems of an Alien Subculture in a Highly Integrating Society', in K. Sandhu and S. Mani (eds), *Indians in Southeast Asia*. Singapore: Times Academic press, 1993, pp. 625-666.

King, Winston L., 'Contemporary Burmese Buddhism', in Heinrich Dumoulin (ed.), *Buddhism in the Modern World*. London: Collier-Macmillan, 1976, pp. 81–98.

Kyaw Yin Hlaing, "Reconsidering the Failure of the Burma Socialist Programme Party to Eradicate Internal Economic Impediments", *South East Asia Research*, 11, 1 (March 2003), pp. 5-58.

Laidlaw, Richard B., "The OSS and the Burma Road, 1942-1945", in Rhodri Jeffreys-Jones and Andrew Lownie, eds., *North American Spies: New Revisionist Eassays*. Lawrence, Kansas: University of Kansas Press, 1991, pp. 102-22.

Lieberman, Victor B., 'The Political Significance of Religious Wealth in Burmese History: Some Further Thoughts', *Journal of Asian Studies*, XXXIX, 4 (Aug. 1980), pp. 753–69.

———— 'Provincial Reforms in Taung-ngu Burma', *Bulletin of the School of Oriental and African Studies*, XLIII, 3 (1980), pp. 548–69.

Linter, Bertil, 'The Shans and the Shan State of Burma', *Contemporary Southeast Asia*, vol. 5, no. 4 (March 1984), pp. 401–50.

Lissak, Moshe, 'The Class Structure of Burma: Continuity and Change', *Journal of Southeast Asian Studies*, 1, 1 (March 1970), pp. 60–73.

—— 'Social Change, Mobilization and Exchange of Services between the Military Establishment and the Civil Society: The Burmese Case', *Economic Development and Cultural Change*, XIII, 1, pp. 1–19.

Mills, J.A., 'Burmese Peasant Response to British Provincial Rule 1852–1885', in D.B. Miller (ed.), *Peasants and Politics*. Melbourne: Edward Arnold (Australia), 1978, pp. 77–104.

Moscotti, Albert D., 'Current Burmese and Southeast Asian Relations', in *Southeast Asian Affairs 1978*. Singapore: FEP International, 1979, pp. 83–94.

Mya Maung, 'Socialism and Economic Development of Burma', *Asian Survey*, IV, 12 (Dec. 1964), pp. 1182–90.

Mya Than, 'A Burmese Village—Revisited', *The South East Asian Review*, II, 2 (Feb. 1978), pp. 1–15.

Perlin, Frank, 'State Formation Reconsidered', *Modern Asian Studies*, 19, 3 (July 1985), pp. 415–80.

Pfanner, David E., 'A Semisubsistence Village Economy in Lower Burma', in Clifton R. Wharton, Jr. (ed.), *Subsistence Agriculture and Economic Development*. Chicago: Aldine, 1969, pp. 47–60.

Richter, H.V., 'The Union of Burma', in R.T. Shand (ed.), *Agricultural Development in Asia*. Canberra: Australian National University Press, 1969, pp. 141–80.

—— 'The Impact of Socialism on Economic Activity in Burma', in T. Scarlett Epstein and David H. Penny (eds), *Opportunity and Response, Case Studies in Economic Development* (London: C. Hurst, 1972), pp. 216–39.

Rueschemeyer, Dietrich and Peter B. Evans, 'The State and Economic Transformation: Toward an Analysis of the Conditions Underlying Effective Intervention', in Peter B. Evans, Dietrich Rueschemeyer and Theda Skocpol (eds), *Bringing the State Back In*. Cambridge University Press, 1985, pp. 44–77.

Saito, Teruko, 'Farm Household Economy under Paddy Delivery System in Contemporary Burma', *The Developing Economies*, XIX, 4 (Dec. 1981), pp. 367–97.

Sarkisyanz, E., 'Buddhist Backgrounds of Burmese Socialism', in Bardwell L. Smith (ed.), *Religion and Legitimation of Power in Thailand, Laos and Burma*. Chambersburg, Pennsylvania: Anima, 1978.

Schmitt, Hans O., 'Decolonisation and Development in Burma', *Journal of Development Studies*, IV, 1 (Oct. 1967), pp. 97–108.

Shein, Myint Myint Thant and Tin Tin Sein, '"Provincial Contract System" of British Indian Empire, in Relation to Burma—A Case of Fiscal Exploitation', *Journal of the Burma Research Society*, LII, Part II (Dec., 1969), pp. 1–26.

Silverstein, Josef, 'Burma: Ne Win's Revolution Reconsidered', *Asian Survey*, VI, 2 (Feb. 1966), pp. 95–104.

Skocpol, Theda, 'Bringing the State Back In: Strategies of Analysis in Current Research', in Peter B. Evans, Dietrich Rueschemeyer and Theda Skocpol (eds), *Bringing the State Back In*. Cambridge University Press, 1985, pp. 3–43.

Stein, Burton, 'State Formation and Economy Reconsidered', *Modern Asian Studies*, 19, 3 (July 1985), pp. 387–414.

Steinberg, David I., 'Burma Under the Military: Towards a Chronology', *Contemporary Southeast Asia*, 3, 3 (Dec. 1981), pp. 244–85.

Sutton, Walter D., 'U Aung San of Burma', *The South Atlantic Quarterly*, vol. XLVII, 1 (Jan. 1948), pp. 1–16.

Swatos, William H., Jr., 'Revolution and Charisma in a Rationalized World: Weber Revisited and Extended', in Ronald M. Glassman and Vatro Murvar (eds), *Max Weber's Political Sociology: A Pessimistic Vision of a Rationalized World*. Westport, Conn. and London: Greenwood Press, 1984, pp. 201–16.

Taylor, Robert H., 'Politics in Late Colonial Burma: The Case of U Saw', *Modern Asian Studies*, 10, 2 (April 1976), pp. 161–94.

——— 'Burma in the Anti-Fascist War', in Alfred W. McCoy (ed.), *Southeast Asia under Japanese Occupation*. New Haven: Yale University Southeast Asian Studies no. 22, 1980, pp. 159–90.

——— 'Perceptions of Ethnicity in the Politics of Burma', *Southeast Asian Journal of Social Science*, 10, 1 (1982), pp. 7–22.

——— 'Burma's Foreign Relations since the Third Indochina Conflict', in Institute of Southeast Asian Studies, *Southeast Asian Affairs 1983*. Aldershot: Gower, 1983, pp. 102–14.

——— 'Burma', in Zakaria Ahmad and Harold Crouch (eds), *Military-Civilian Relations in South-East Asia*. Singapore: Oxford University Press, 1985, pp. 13–49.

——— 'Burma', in Haruhiro Fukui (ed.), *Political Parties of Asia and the Pacific*. Westport, Conn.: Greenwood Press, 1985, vol. I, pp. 99–154.

——— 'The Burmese Concepts of Revolution', in Mark Hobart and Robert H. Taylor (eds), *Context Meaning and Power in Southeast Asia*. Ithaca: Cornell University Southeast Asia Program, 1986, pp. 79–92.

——— "Burma: Defence Expenditure and Threat Perceptions", in Chin Khin Wah, ed., *Defence Expenditure in Southeast Asia*. Singapore: Institute of

Southeast Asian Studies, 1987, pp. 252-280.

—— "Disaster of Release? J. S. Furnivall and the Bankruptcy of Burma," *Modern Asian Studies*, vol. 29, part 1 (February 1995), pp. 45-63.

—— "Elections in Burma/Myanmar: For Whom and Why?", in R. H. Taylor, ed., *The Politics of Elections in Southeast Asia*. Cambridge and New York: Cambridge University Press, 1996, pp. 164-183.

Tilly, Charles, 'Reflections on the History of European State-Making', in Charles Tilly (ed.), *The Formation of National States in Western Europe*. Princeton University Press, 1975, pp. 3–83.

Tin Maung Maung Than, 'Burma in 1983: From Recovery to Growth?', in Institute of Southeast Asian Studies, *Southeast Asian Affairs 1984*. Singapore: Institute of Southeast Asian Studies, 1984, pp. 89–122.

Turton, Andrew, 'Limits of Ideological Domination and the Formation of Social Consciousness', in Andrew Turton and Shigeharu Tanabe (eds), *History and Peasant Consciousness in South East Asia*. Osaka: Senri Ethnological Studies no. 13, National Museum of Ethnology, 1984, pp. 19–74.

Wiant, Jon A., 'Burma: Loosening Up on the Tiger's Tail', *Asian Survey*, XIII, 2 (Feb., 1973), pp. 179–86.

—— 'Insurgency in the Shan State', in Lim Joo-Jock and S. Vani (eds), *Armed Separatism in Southeast Asia*. Singapore: Issues in Southeast Asian Security, Institute of Southeast Asian Studies, 1984, pp. 81–110.

Official publications in English

Address Delivered by General Ne Win at the Closing Session of the Fourth Party Seminar on 11th November 1969, Rangoon: Sarpay Beikman, 1969.

British Burma Political Department, *Report on the Administration of Hill Tracts, Northern Arakan, 1870–71*. Rangoon: Secretariat Press, 1872.

Burma, 1, 1. Rangoon: Foreign Affairs Association, Sept., 1944.

Burma Handbook, Simla: Government of India Press, 1944.

Burma Socialist Programme Party, *The System of the Correlation of Man and His Environment*. Rangoon: Burma Socialist Programme Party, 1963.

——, Party Central Organizing Committee, *Party Seminar 1965*. Rangoon: Sarpay Beikman, 1966.

——, *Foreign Policy of the Revolutionary Government of the Union of Burma*. Rangoon: Sarpay Beikman, 1968.

——, Central Committee Headquarters. *The Fourth Party Congress 1981*. Rangoon: Printing and Publishing Corporation, 1985.

Census of Burma, 1931, Volume XI of the *Census of India, 1931*. Rangoon: Government Printing and Stationery, 1933.

Correspondence for the Years 1825–26 to 1842–43 in the Office of the Commissioner Tenasserim Division, Rangoon: Government Printing and Stationery,

1929.

Economic Survey of Burma 1958, Rangoon: Government Printing and Stationery, 1958.

Final Report of the Administration Reorganization Committee, 1951, Rangoon: Government Printing and Stationery, 1951.

Fiscal Enquiry Committee Report, Second Report, Rangoon: Government Printing and Stationery, 1938.

Report of the Education Reconstruction Committee, Rangoon: Government Printing and Stationery, 1947.

Report of the Indian Statutory Commission, Cmd. 3568. London: H.M.S.O. 1930.

Report on Indian Immigration, Rangoon: Government Printing and Stationery, 1941.

Report of the Land and Agriculture Committee, Rangoon: Government Printing and Stationery, 1939.

Report on the Progress of Arakan Under British Rule from 1826 to 1875, Rangoon: Government Press, 1876.

Report to the Pyithu Hluttaw on the Financial, Economic and Social Conditions of the Socialist Republic of the Union of Burma for 1977–78, Rangoon: Ministry of Planning and Finance, 1977.

Report to the Pyithu Hluttaw on the Financial, Economic and Social Conditions of the Socialist Republic of the Union of Burma, 1985–86, Rangoon: Ministry of Planning and Finance, 1985.

Riot Inquiry Committee, *Interim Report*. Rangoon: Government Printing and Stationery, 1938.

Selected Correspondence of Letters Issued from and Received in the Office of the Commissioner Tenasserim Division from the Years 1825–26 to 1842–43, Rangoon: Government Printing and Stationery, 1928.

Shan States Manual, Rangoon: Government Printing and Stationery, 1933.

A Study of the Social and Economic History of Burma (The British Period), Rangoon: Economic and Social Board, Office of the Prime Minister, roneoed, 1957, Parts I–V.

Two-Year Plan of Economic Development for Burma, Rangoon: Government Printing and Stationery, 1948.

Unpublished sources in English

Abu Talib bin Ahmad, 'Collaboration, 1941–1945: An Aspect of the Japanese Occupation of Burma', PhD, Monash University, 1984.

Ambler, John S., 'Burma's Rice Economy under Military Rule: The Evolution of Socialist Agricultural Programmes and Their Impact on Paddy Farmers', Cornell University, Oct. 1983.

Ba Thann Win, 'Administration of Shan States from the Panglong Conference to the Cessation of the Powers of the Saophas 1947–1959', MA, Rangoon Arts and Sciences University, n.d.

Cady, John F., 'The Character and Program of the Communist Party in Burma', Rangoon: American Consulate General, 26 March 1946.

Central Intelligence Agency, Directorate of Intelligence, 'Peking and the Burmese Communists: The Perils and Profits of Insurgency', July 1971 (declassified 1980).

Guyot, Dorothy Hess, 'The Political Impact of the Japanese Occupation of Burma', PhD, Yale University, 1966.

Khin Maung Kyi, 'Patterns of Accommodation to Bureaucratic Authority in a Transitional Culture (A Sociological Analysis of Burmese Bureaucrats with Respect to Their Orientations Toward Authority)', PhD, Cornell University, 1966.

Khin Mya, 'The Impact of Traditional Culture and Environmental Forces on the Development of the Kachins, a Sub-Cultural Group of Burma', PhD, University of Maryland, 1961.

Koenig, William J., 'The Early Kon-baung Polity, 1752–1819: A Study of Politics, Adminstration and Social Organization in Burma', PhD, University of London, 1978.

Kozicki, R.J., 'India and Burma, 1937–1957: A Study in International Relations', PhD, University of Pennsylvania, 1959.

Lieberman, Victor B., 'Continuity and Change in Burmese History: Some Preliminary Observations', subsequently published as 'Reinterpreting Burmese History', *Comparative Studies in Society and History*, 29, 1 (January, 1987), pp. 162–94.

Listowel, 'Memoirs of Lord Listowel.' www.redrice.com/listowel

Maung Maung, 'Nationalist Movements in Burma, 1920–1940: Changing Patterns of Leadership: From Sangha to Laity', MA, Australian National University, 1976.

Myo Myint, 'The Politics of Survival in Burma: Diplomacy and Statecraft in the Reign of King Mindon, 1853-1878', PhD, Cornell University, 1987.

Richter, H.V., 'Development and Equality in Burma'. Canberra: Department of Economics, Research School of Pacific Studies, Australian National University, 1974.

Taylor, Robert H., 'The Relationship Between Burmese Social Classes and British-Indian Policy on the Behaviour of the Burmese Political Elite, 1937–1942', PhD, Cornell University, 1974.

Than Aung, Moses, 'A General Study in the Economic Development of Burma with Special Reference to Economic Planning (1948–1958)', MA, Rangoon Arts and Sciences University, 1973.

Wiant, Jon W., 'The Burmese Revolutionary Council: Military Government and Political Change', seminar paper, Department of Government, Cornell University, 1971.

World Bank, South Asia Regional Office, *Development in Burma: Issues and Prospects*, report no. 1024–BA, 27 July 1976.

———, South Asia Projects Department, Agriculture Division, *Burma: Agricultural Sector Review*, vol. I: 'The Main Report', 30 Aug. 1977.

———, South Asia Regional Office, 'Burma: Country Economic Memorandum', report no. 1700–BA, 19 Oct. 1977.

Books and monographs in Burmese

Hpa Hsa Pa La–Konmyunit Apyanahlan Peisa (AFPFL–Communist Correspondence). Rangoon: Pyithu Ana Punhnat Taik, 1947.

Hpo Kyaw San, *Paliman Dimokayeisi Sannit hnit Myanma Naingngan* (Parliamentary Democracy and Burma State). (Rangoon: San Pya, n. d.).

Lei Maung, *Myanman Naingnganyei Thamaing* (History of Burma's Politics). Rangoon: Sapei Biman, 1974, 2 vols.

Maung Maung, *Taya Ubadei Ahtweidwei Bahuthuta* (General Legal Knowledge). Rangoon: Win Maung U, 1975.

Nyi Nyi, *Myanma Naingngan Amyotha Mawkun (1975)* (Burma's National Record [1975]). Rangoon: Pagan, 1978.

Saw, *Gyapan Lan Nyunt* (Japan Points the Way). Rangoon: Thuriya, 1936.

Sein Myin, *Hnit 200 Myanma Naingngan Thamaing Abidan* (Dictionary of 200 Years of Burma History). Rangoon: Sapei Yatana, 1969.

Sein Tin (ed.), *Myanma Akyaung hnit Kabama Akyaung* (Burma Affairs and World Affairs) (Rangoon: 1982).

Than Htun, *Pyithu Sit Pyithu Ana* (People's War, People's Power). Rangoon: publisher unnamed.

Thein Pe Myint, *Ashei ka Neiwun Htwetthe Bama* (As sure as the sun rises in the east). (Rangoon: Myat Sapei, n.d.), 2 vols.

Tin Htun Aung, *Myanma Naingnganyei hnit Thakin Ba Thaung* (Burma's Politics and Thakin Ba Thaung). Rangoon: Sapeu Sapei Hpyanchiyei, 1980.

Articles in Burmese

Aung Hsan, 'Naingnganyei Amyomyo' (Kinds of Politics), *Dagun Maggazin*, no. 234 (Feb. 1940), pp. 61–70; no. 236 (April 1940), pp. 17–26.

Ono Toru, 'Konbaung hkit Kyeitow Ywa Ngweihkyei Sanit' (The village money lending system of the Konbaung era). *Myawati*, March 1976, pp. 37–42.

Official publications in Burmese

Myanma Hsoshelit Lansin Pati Baho Kommiti Danachok (Burma Socialist Programme Party Central Committee Headquarters), *Myanma Hsoshelit Lansin Pati Pati Winmya Letswe* (Burma Socialist Programme Party Party Members' Handbook). Rangoon: Burma Socialist Programme Party, 1978, repr. 1982.

Myanma Hsoshelit Lansin Pati, Pati Seyunyei Baho Kowmiti Danachok (Burma Socialist Programme Party, Party Organization Central Committee Headquarters), *Myanma Hsoshelit Lansin Pati ei Pyei twinyei ya Ahmat 1* (Burma Socialist Programme Party's Internal Affairs no. 1). Rangoon: Sapei Biman, 1966.

———*Myanma Hsoshelit Lansin Pati Pwesepun Achekhan Sinmyin* (Constitution of the Burma Socialist Programme Party). Rangoon: 1983.

Myanma Hsoshelit Lansin Pati (Burma Socialist Programme Party), *Lu hnit Patwunkyindo ei Anya Manya Thabawtaya* (The System of the Correlation of Man and His Environment). Rangoon: Jan. 1964.

Pyihtaungsu Myanma Naingngan Towhlanyei Kaungsi (Union of Burma Revolutionary Council). *Myanma Hsoshelit Lansin Pati ei Witheitha Latkangamya* (Specific Characteristics of the Burma Socialist Programme Party). Rangoon: Burma Socialist Programme Party Party Affairs Central Committee, 4 Sept. 1964.

Pyi Htaungsu Hsoshelit Thammata Myanma Naingngan Hpwetsinpun Ahkyeihkan Upadei (Constitution of the Socialist Republic of the Union of Burma). Rangoon: Burma Socialist Programme Party, Printing and Publishing Corporation, 1973.

Pyihtaungsu Myanma Naingnan Towhlanyei Kaungsi tho Tinthwin thaw Pyihtaungsu Myanma Naingnan Pyi twin Nyinyatyei Akyanpei Apwei ei Asiyinhkansa (Union of Burma Internal Unity Conference's Report Which Was Submitted to the Union of Burma Revolutionary Council). Rangoon, 1969.

Pyi Htaungsu Hsoshelit Thammata Myanma Naingngan Hpwetsinpun Akhyeihkan Upadei hnit Patthet thaw Adipape Shinlinhkyetmay. (Explanatory Points Regarding the Constitution of the Socialist Republic of the Union of Burma). Rangoon: Burma Socialist Programme Party, Printing and Publishing Corporation, Sept., 1973.

Pyi Htaungsu Hsoshelit Thammata Myanama Naingngan Hpwetsinpun Akhyeihkan Upadei hnit Patthem thaw Asiyinhkansa. (Report Concerning the Constitution of the Socialist Republic of the Union of Burma). Rangoon: Burma Socialist Programme Party, Printing and Publishing Corporation, 1973.

Thathanatow Thanshin Tetanpyanpwayei Gaingpaungsu Thaya Asiaweipwekyi

Hpyitmyaukyei Thaya Wanhsaukhpwet (Sangha Executive Body for the Purification, Perpetuation and Propagation of the Sasana Making the Union of Sects Meeting to Purify the Sangha). *Pyihtaungsu Hsoshelit Thammata Myanma Naingngantow Thaya Ahpweasin Akhyeihkansinmyin (Mukyan)* (Organization Rules of the Socialist Republic of the Union of Burma State Sangha Body [Draft]). Rangoon: Kaba Ei Thathanayei Usi Dana Press, 1980.

Towhlanyei Kaungsi ei Hluthsaungchet Thamaing Akyinchut (Concise History of the Actions of the Revolutionary Council), Rangoon: Printing and Publishing Corporation, 2 March 1974.

1986–87 Hkunit atwet Pyi Htaungsu Hsoshelit Thammata Myanma Naingngantaw Bankayei, Sipwayei, Luhmuyei Ahkyei Anei hnit pathetthe Pyithu Hluttaw tho Asiyinhkansa (Report to the Pyithu Hluttaw on the Financial, Economic and Social Conditions of the Socialist Republic of the Union of Burma 1986–87). Rangoon: Simankein hnit Bankayei Wunkyi Dana, 1986.

Unpublished works in Burmese

San San Myin, 'Hpa Hsa Pa La Hkit Myanma Naingnganyei Thamaing 1948–1958' (Political History of Burma in the AFPFL Era, 1948–1958). MA, Rangoon Arts and Sciences University, 1979.

BIBLIOGRAPHY (POST 1988)

In addition to the largely academic works and official and semi-official publications listed here, since 1988 there have been a plethora of publications about the political, economic and social conditions of the country. Many of these are polemical in nature, but they nonetheless sometimes contain information of value if critically handled. Others are advocacy documents that are careless in their use of allegations and claims about causality. Many focus on assertions of human rights violations and mistake the particular for the general. The reports of Amnesty International and the International Crisis Group appear to be the most careful in their reporting, but need to be read carefully and critically.

Many more news reports and commentaries on developments in Myanmar have appeared after 1988 than at any time in the previous 40 years. Especially after the development of the internet and the funding of anti-government media by foreign governments and foundations, a number of new information generating outlets were created. Prominent among them are Mizzima, *Irrawaddy*, the *Shan Herald for News*, and the Democratic Voice of Burma. Their reports and others from mainstream news services are usually reprinted by Burmanetnews and Rebound88 amongst other websites. Like exile news agencies, most mainline press coverage of Myanmar provides a negative interpretation of events regardless of alternative possibilities. Government and pro-government views and information are available in the official *The New Light of Myanmar* and other daily Burmese language newspapers.

Books and monographs in English

Albright, Madeleine, *Madam Secretary: A Memoir*. New York: Hyperion, 2003.

Allot, Anna J., *Inked Over, Ripped Out*. New York: PEN Center, 1993.

Anon., *Burma/Myanmar Today and American Policy*. Washington, DC: Johns Hopkins University, International Republic Institute, and National Democratic Institute for International Affairs, 14 May 1996.

Anon., *Letters to a Dictator: Correspondence from NLD Chairman Aung Shwe to SLORC's Senior General Than Shwe.* Bangkok: All Burma Students' Democratic Front, 1997.

Anon., ed., *The Study on Trade and Investment Policies in Developing Countries: Myanmar.* Tokyo: Institute of Developing Economies, Japan External Trade Organisation, two volumes, 1997 and 1999.

Anon., ed., *Strengthening Civil Society in Burma.* Chiang Mai: Silkworm for the Burma Centre Netherlands and Transnational Institute, 1999.

Anon., 'Drugs and Conflict in Burma (Myanmar): Dilemmas for Policy Responses', *Drugs and Conflict.* Amsterdam: Transnational Institute Debate Paper No. 9, December 2003.

Anon., *Active Citizens under Political Wraps: Experiences from Myanmar/Burma and Vietnam.* Chiang Mai, Thailand: Heinrich-Boell-Stiftung, 2006.

Aris, Michael, ed., *Freedom from Fear and Other Writings.* London: Viking, 1991.

Aung Myoe, *Building the Tatmadaw: The Organisational Development of the Armed Forces in Myanmar, 1948-1998.* Canberra: Strategic and Defence Studies Centre, Working Paper No. 327, Australian National University, 1998.

——— *Military Doctrine and Strategy in Myanmar: A Historical Perspective.* Canberra: Strategic and Defence Studies Centre, Working Paper No. 339, Australian National University, 1999.

——— *The Tatmadaw since 1988: An Interim Assessment.* Canberra: Strategic and Defence Studies Centre, Working Paper No. 342, Australian National University, 1999.

——— *Officer Education and Leadership Training in the Tatmadaw: A Survey.* Canberra: Strategic and Defence Studies Centre, Working Paper No. 346, Australian National University, 2000.

——— *Neither Friend Nor Foe: Myanmar's Relations with Thailand since 1988.* Singapore: IDSS Monograph 1, Institute of Defense and Strategic Studies, 2004.

——— *The Road to Naypyitaw: Making Sense of the Myanmar Government's Decision to Move Its Capital.* Singapore: Asia Research Institute Working Paper Series No. 79, November 2006.

——— *A Historical Overview of Political Transition in Myanmar since 1988.* Singapore: Asia Research Institute Working Paper Series No. 95, National University of Singapore, August 2007.

Aung San Suu Kyi, *Burma and India: Some Aspects of Intellectual Life Under Colonialism.* New Delhi: Allied Publishers, 1990.

——— *Letters from Burma.* London: Penguin, 1997.

Badgley, John H., ed., *Reconciling Burma/Myanmar: Essays on U.S. Relations with Burma.* Seattle, Washington: National Bureau of Asian Research, Vol 15, No. 1, March 2004.

Bais, Karolien and Mijind Huijser, *The Profit of Peace: Corporate Responsibility in Conflict Regions.* Sheffield, England: Greenleaf, 2005.

Ball, Desmond and Hazel Lang, *Factionalism and the Ethnic Insurgent Organisations.* Canberra: Australian National University Strategic and Defence Studies Centre Working Paper No. 356, March 2001.

Bamforth, Vicky, Steven Lanjouw and Graham Mortimer, *Conflict and Displacement in Karenni: The Need for Considered Responses.* Chieng Mai (?): Burma Ethnic Research Group, May 2000.

Boudreau, Vince, *Resisting Dictatorship: Repression and Protest in Southeast Asia.* New York: Cambridge University Press, 2004.

Brandon, John J., ed., *Burma/Myanmar: Towards the Twenty-First Century: Dynamics of Continuity and Change.* Bangkok: Thai Studies Section, Open Society Institute, nd (1997?).

Brinton, Crane, *Anatomy of Revolution.* New York: Random House, revised edition, 1965.

Brown, Gordon, *Courage: Eight Portraits.* London: Bloomsbury, 2007.

Brown, Ian, *A Colonial Economy in Crisis: Burma's Rice Cultivators and the World Depression of the 1930s.* London: Routledge Curzon, 2005.

Bryant, Raymond, *The Political Ecology of Forestry in Burma, 1824-1994.* London: Hurst, 1997.

Burma Border Consortium, *Reclaiming the Right to Rice: Food Security and Internal Displacement in Eastern Burma.* Bangkok: Burma Border Consortium, October 2003.

Byman, Daniel, et al., eds, *Trends in Outside Support for Insurgent Movements.* Santa Monica, California: RAND Corporation, 2001.

Callahan, Mary P., *Making Enemies: War and State Building in Burma.* Ithaca: Cornell University Press; Singapore University Press, 2004.

——— 'Political Authority in Burma's Ethnic Minority States: Devolution, Occupation, and Coexistence.' *Policy Studies* 31 (Southeast Asia). Washington: East-West Centre; Singapore: Institute of Southeast Asian Studies, 2007.

Carey, Peter, ed., *The Challenge of Change in a Divided Society.* Basingstoke: Macmillan, 1997.

Chachavalpongpun, Pavin, *A Plastic Nation: The Curse of Thainess in Thai-Burmese Relations.* Lanham, MD: University Press of America, 2005.

Chandler, David, *From Kosovo to Kabul: Human Rights and International Intervention.* London and Sterling, Virginia: Pluto Press, 2002.

Clements, Alan, *Burma: The Next Killing Fields?* Berkeley, CA: Odonian Press, 1992.

———— *Aung San Suu Kyi, The Voice of Hope (conversations with Alan Clements)*. London: Penguin, 1997.

Dudley, Sandra, *'External' Aspects of Self-Determination Movements in Burma*. Oxford: Queen Elizabeth House Working Paper Series Number 94, February 2003.

Egreteau, Renaud, *Wooing the Generals: India's New Burma Policy*. New Delhi: Centre de Sciences Humaines, 2003.

Evans, Martin and John Phillips, *Algeria: Anger of the Dispossessed*. New Haven, Conn.: Yale University Press, 2007.

Fallah, Jonathan, *True Love and Bartholomew: Rebels on the Burmese Border*. Cambridge and New York: Cambridge University Press, 1991.

Fink, Christina, *Living Silence: Burma Under Military Rule*. Bangkok: White Lotus; London, Zed Books, 2001.

Ganesan, N. and Kyaw Yin Hlaing, eds, *Myanmar: State, Society and Ethnicity*. Singapore: Institute of Southeast Asian Studies, 2007.

Gravers, Mikael, ed., *Exploring Ethnic Diversity in Burma*. Copenhagen: NIAS Press, 2007.

Gue, Xialon, ed., *Myanmar/Burma: Challenges and Perspective*, Stockholm: Institute for Development and Security Studies, 2008.

Haacke, Jurgen, *Myanmar's Foreign Relations: Domestic Influence and International Implications*. London: Routledge for the International Institute for Strategic Studies, June 2006.

'HIV/AIDS and Drug Use in Burma/Myanmar', *Drug Policy Briefing* No. 17, Transnational Institute and Burma Centrum, Netherlands, May 2006.

Institute for Democracy and Electoral Assistance, *Challenges to Democratization in Burma: Perspectives on Multilateral and Bilateral Responses*. Stockholm, 2001.

International Institute for Strategic Studies, *The Military Balance 2005-2006*. London: Routledge, October 2005.

Jelsma, Martin and Tom Kramer, *Downward Spiral: Banning Opium in Afghanistan and Burma*. Amsterdam: Transnational Institute, June 2005.

————, and Pietje Vervest, *Trouble in the Triangle: Opium and Conflict in Burma*. Chiang Mai, Thailand: Silkworm, 2005.

Kan Zaw, *National Integration and Regional Development in Myanmar*. Tokyo: Institute of Developing Economies No. 312, 1998.

Kenji, Ino, *Philosophy and Action of Aung San Suu Kyi*, Kita Kyushu: Kenkyu Forum of Asian Women, 2001 [in Japanese], pp. 121-266.

Khin Maung Kyi, Ronald Finlay, R.M. Sundrum, Mya Maung, Myo Nyunt, Zaw Oo, et al., *Economic Development of Burma: A Vision and a Strategy*. Stockholm: Olof Palme International Centre, 2000.

Khoo Thwe, *From the Land of Green Ghosts: A Burmese Odyssey*. London: Harper Collins, 2002.

Kiuyu, Minoru, *Industrial Development and Reform in Myanmar: ASEAN and Japanese Perspectives*. Bangkok: White Lotus, 1999.

Kramer, Tom, *The United Wa State Party: Narco-Army or Ethnic Nationalist Party? Policy Studies 38 (Southeast Asia)*. Washington: East-West Centre; Singapore: Institute of Southeast Asian Studies, 2007.

Kudo, Toshihiro and Fumihari Mieno, *Trade, Foreign Investment and Myanmar's Economic Development during the Transition to an Open Economy*. Chiba, Japan: Institute of Developing Economies Discussion Paper No. 116, August 2007.

Kyaw Yin Hlaing, Robert H. Taylor and Tin Maung Maung Than, eds, *Myanmar: Beyond Politics to Societal Imperatives*. Singapore: Institute of Southeast Asian Studies, 2005.

Lang, Hazel J., *Fear and Sanctuary: Burmese Refugees in Thailand. Ithaca: Southeast Asia Program Publications*, Cornell University, 2002.

Lintner, Bertil, *Outrage: Burma's Struggle for Democracy*. Hong Kong: Review Publishing Company, 1989.

——— *Land of Jade: A Journey Through Insurgent Burma*. Edinburgh: Kiscadale, 1990.

——— *The Rise and Fall of the Communist Party of Burma (CPB)*. Ithaca, New York: Southeast Asia Program, Cornell University, 1990.

——— *Burma in Revolt: Opium and Insurgency since 1948*. Chiang Mai: Silkworm, 2nd ed., 1999.

Loeschmann, Heike, ed., *Active Citizens under Political Wraps: Experiences from Myanmar/Burma and Vietnam*. Chiengmai: Heinrich Boell Stiftung, 2006.

Mahmood, Rohana and Hans-Joachim Esderts, *Myanmar and the Wider Southeast Asia*. Kuala Lumpur: Institute of Strategic and International Studies Malaysia and the Friedrich Ebert Stiftung, 1991.

Mathieson, David S. and R.J. May, eds, *The Illusion of Progress: The Political Economy of Reform in Burma/Myanmar*. Adelaide, South Australia: Crawford House, 2004.

Maung Maung, *The 1988 Uprising in Burma*. New Haven: Yale University Southeast Asian Studies Monograph No. 49, 1999.

Mya Maung, *Totalitarianism in Burma: Prospects for Economic Development*. New York: Paragon House, 1992.

Mya Than, *Myanmar's External Trade: An Overview in the Southeast Asian Context.* Singapore: Institute of Southeast Asian Studies, 1992.

——— and Joseph L.T. Than, *Myanmar Dilemmas and Options: The Challenge of Economic Transition in the 1990s.* Singapore: Institute of Southeast Asian Studies, 1990.

Mya Than and Myat Thein, *Financial Resources for Development in Myanmar.* Singapore: Institute of Southeast Asian Studies, 2000.

Myanmar Medical Association and World Vision International, *Report on Review of the Aids Awareness, Education, and Prevention Project in Kawthaung.* NP: NP, May 1995.

Myat Thein, *Economic Development of Myanmar.* Singapore: Institute of Southeast Asian Studies, 2004.

Naing Luu Aung, Aung Moe Htet and Sit Nyein Aung, translators and eds, *Letters to a Dictator: Correspondence from NLD Chairman Aung Shwe to the SLORC's Senior General Than Shwe.* Bangkok: All Burma Students Democratic Front, July 1997.

National Unity Party, *The Guiding Philosophy of the National Unity Party.* Yangon: October 2007.

Nyi Win Hman, *Health Research in Myanmar: A Review of Studies.* Yangon: UNICEF, 1990.

Pedersen, Morten B., Emily Rudland and R.J. May, eds, *Burma/Myanmar: Strong Regime-Weak State?* Bathurst: Crawford House, 2000.

Rabinowitz, Alan, *Beyond the Last Village: A Journey of Discovery in Asia's Forbidden Wilderness.* Washington and London: Island Press, 2001.

——— *Life in the Valley of Death: The Fight to Save Tigers in a Land of Guns, Gold and Greed.* Washington and London: Island Press, 2008.

Renard, Ronald D., *The Burmese Connection: Illegal Drugs and the Making of the Golden Triangle.* Boulder and London: Lynne Rienner, 1996.

Rotbert, Robert, I., ed., *Burma: Prospects for a Democratic Future.* Washington, DC: Brookings Institution Press, 1998.

Sakhong, Lian H., *In Search of Chin Identity: A Study in Religion, Politics and Ethnic Identity in Burma.* Copenhagen: NIAS Press, 2003.

Schock, Kurt, *Unarmed Insurrections: People Power Movements in Nondemocracies.* Minneapolis: University of Minnesota Press, 2005.

Seekins, Donald M., *The Disorder in Order: The Army-State in Burma Since 1962.* Bangkok: White Lotus, 2002.

——— *Burma and Japan Since 1940: From 'Co-Prosperity' to 'Quiet Dialogue'.* Copenhagen: NIAS Press, 2007.

Selth, Andrew, *Burma's Arms Procurement Programme Destruction.* Canberra: Strategic and Defence Studies Centre, Working Paper No. 289, Australian National University, 1995.

———— *Transforming the Tatmadaw: The Burmese Armed Forces since 1988.* Canberra: Canberra Papers on Strategy and Defence No. 113, 1996.
———— *Burma's Intelligence Apparatus.* Canberra: Strategic and Defence Studies Centre, Working Paper No. 308, Australian National University, 1997.
———— *Burma's Defence Expenditure and Arms Industries Dimension.* Canberra: Strategic and Defence Studies Centre, Working Paper No. 309, Australian National University, 1997.
———— *The Burma Navy Dimension.* Canberra: Strategic and Defence Studies Centre, Working Paper No. 313, Australian National University, 1997.
———— *The Burma Air Force Dimension.* Canberra: Strategic and Defence Studies Centre, Working Paper No. 315, Australian National University, 1997.
———— *Burma and Weapons of Mass Destruction.* Canberra: Strategic and Defence Studies Centre, Working Paper No. 334, Australian National University, 1999.
———— *Burma's Order of Battle: An Interim Assessment.* Canberra: Strategic and Defence Studies Centre, Working Paper No. 351, Australian National University, 2000.
———— *Landmines in Burma: The Military Dimension.* Canberra: Strategic and Defence Studies Centre, Working Paper No. 352, Australian National University, 2000.
———— *Burma's Secret Military Partners,* Canberra: Canberra Papers on Strategy and Defence No. 136, Australian National University, 2000.
———— *Burma's Armed Forces: Power without Glory.* Norwalk, Conn.: East Bridge, 2002.
Sharp, Gene, *From Dictatorship to Democracy: A Conceptual Framework for Liberation.* Boston: Einstein Institute, 1993, reprint of first edition published in Bangkok: Committee for the Restoration of Democracy in Burma, 1993.
Siddiqa, Ayesha, *Military Inc.: Inside Pakistan's Military Economy.* London: Pluto Press, 2007.
Skidmorth, Monique, ed., *Burma at the Turn of the 21st Century.* Honolulu: University of Hawaii Press, 2005.
Smith, Martin, *State of Fear: Censorship in Burma.* London: Article 19 Country Report, December, 1991.
———— *Burma: Insurgency and the Politics of Insurgency.* London: Zed Books, revised edition, 1999.
———— *Burma (Myanmar): The Time for Change.* London: Minority Rights Group, 2002.

———— *State of Strife: the Dynamics of Ethnic Conflict in Burma.* Policy Studies 36 (Southeast Asia). Washington: East-West Centre; Singapore: Institute of Southeast Asian Studies, 2007.

South, Ashley, *Mon Nationalism and Civil War in Burma: The Golden Sheldrake.* London: Routledge Curzon, 2003.

Steinberg, David I., *The Future of Burma: Crisis and Choice in Myanmar.* Lanham and New York: the Asia Society and University Press of America, 1990.

Stephan, Alfred, *Rethinking Military Politics: Brazil and the Southern Cone* (Princeton University Press, 1988).

Taylor, Robert H., ed., *Burma: Political Economy Under Military Rule.* London: C. Hurst and Co., 2001.

———— compiler, *Dr. Maung Maung: Gentleman, Scholar, Patriot.* Singapore: Institute of Southeast Asian Studies, 2008.

Terry, Fiona, *Condemned to Repeat: The Paradox of Humanitarian Action.* Ithaca, NY: Cornell University Press, 2002.

Thawnghmung, Ardeth Maung, *Behind the Teak Curtain: Authoritarianism, Agricultural Policies and Political Legitimacy in Rural Burma/Myanmar.* London: Kegan Paul, 2004.

———— *The Karen Revolution in Burma: Diverse Voices, Uncertain Ends.* Washington, DC: East-West Centre Policy Studies 45 (South East Asia), 2008.

Thornton, Phil, *Restless Souls: Rebels, Refugees, Medics and Misfits on the Thai-Burma Border.* Bangkok: Asia Books, 2006.

Tin Maung Maung Than, *State Dominance in Myanmar: The Political Economy of Industrialization.* Singapore: Institute of Southeast Asian Studies, 2007.

Weller, Marc, ed., *Democracy and Politics in Burma.* Manerplaw: National Coalition Government of the Union of Burma (printed in Thailand), 1993.

Wilson, Trevor, ed., *Myanmar's Long Road to National Reconciliation.* Singapore: Institute of Southeast Asian Studies and Canberra: Asia Pacific Press, 2006.

Wingfield, Tom, 'Myanmar: Political Stasis and a Precarious Economy' in Daljit Singh, ed., *Southeast Asian Affairs 2000.* Singapore: Institute of Southeast Asian Studies, 2000, pp. 203-18.

Articles in English

Aldridge, Richard J., 'Legacies of Secret Service: Renegade SOE and the Karen Struggle in Burma, 1948-50', in Richard J. Aldridge, Gary D. Rawnsley and Ming-Yeh T. Rawnsley, eds, *Clandestine Cold War in Asia,*

1945-65: Western Intelligence, Propaganda and Special Operations, London: Cass, 2000, pp. 130-48.

Aung-Thwin, Michael, 'Parochial Universalism, Democracy Jihad and the Orientalist Image of Burma: The New Evangelism', *Pacific Affairs*, Vol. 74, No. 4, Winter 2001-2002, pp. 483 505.

Badgley, John, 'The Burmese Road to Capitalism', in Ng Chee Yuen and Chandran Jeshurun, eds, *Southeast Asian Affairs 1990*. Singapore: Institute of Southeast Asian Studies, 1990.

Booth, Anne, 'The Burma Development Disaster in Comparative Historical Perspective', *South East Asia Research*, II, 2 (July 2003), pp. 141-72.

Brooten, Lisa B., 'Human Rights Discourse and the Development of Democracy in a Multi-Ethnic State', *Asian Journal of Communications*, Vol. 14, No. 2 (2004), pp. 174-91.

————— 'Feminization of Democracy under Siege: The Media, "the Lady" of Burma, and U. S. Foreign Policy', *NWSA Journal*, Vol. 17, No. 3 (2005), pp. 134-56.

Callahan, Mary P., 'Junta Dreams or Nightmares? Observations of Burma's Military since 1988', *Bulletin of Concerned Asian Scholars*, 31, 3 (July-September 1999), pp. 52-8.

————— 'Burma: Soldiers as State Builders', in Mutiah Alagappa, ed., *Coercion and Governance: The Declining Political Role of the Military in Asia*. Stanford: Stanford University Press, 2001, pp. 413-29.

————— 'Cracks in the Edifice? Changes in Military-Society Relations in Burma since 1988', in Morten B. Pedersen et al., eds., *Burma/Myanmar: Strong Regime, Weak State?* Adelaide: Crawford House, 2002, pp. 31-2.

————— 'When Soldiers Shoot Civilians: Burma's Crackdown in 1988 in Comparative Perspective', in James T. Seigel and Audrey R. Kahin, eds, *Southeast Asia Over Three Generations*. Ithaca: Cornell University Southeast Asia Program Publications, 2003, pp. 331-46.

Clymer, Megan, 'Min Ko Naing, "Conqueror of Kings": Burma's Student Prisoner', *Journal of Burma Studies*, Vol. 8 (2003), pp. 33-63.

Englehart, Neil A., 'Is Regime Change Enough for Burma?: The Problem of State Capacity', *Asian Survey*, Vol. 45, No. 4 (July/August 2005), pp. 622-44.

Esche, Annemarie, 'Ethnic Policy of the Union of Myanmar: The Kayin Case', in Thomas Engelbert and Hans Deiter Kubitscheck, eds, *Ethnic Minorities and Politics in Southeast Asia*, Frankfurt am Main: Peter Lang, 2004, pp. 87-110.

Ganesan, N., 'Myanmar's Foreign Relations: Reaching out to the World', in Kyaw Yin Hlaing, Robert H. Taylor and Tin Maung Maung Than, eds, *Myanmar: Beyond Politics to Societal Imperatives.* Singapore: Institute of Southeast Asian Studies, 2005, pp. 30-55.

Guyot, James F., 'Burma in 1988: Perestroika with a Military Face', in Ng Chee Yuen, ed., *Southeast Asian Affairs 1989.* Singapore: Institute of Southeast Asian Studies, 1989, pp.107-136.

————— 'Myanmar: Several Endings, No Clear Beginnings', in Daljit Singh and Liak Teng Kiat, eds, *Southeast Asian Affairs 1996.* Singapore: Institute of Southeast Asian Studies, 1996, pp. 259-84.

Guyot, James F. and John Badgley, 'Myanmar in 1989: Tatmadaw V', *Asian Survey*, February 1990, pp. 187-95.

Harridon, Jessica, '"Making a Name for Themselves": Karen Identity and the Politicization of Ethnicity in Burma', *The Journal of Burma Studies*, vol. 7, 2002, pp. 84-144.

Khin Maung Kyi, 'Indians in Burma: Problems of an Alien Subculture in a Highly Integrating Society', in K. Sandhu and S. Mani (eds), *Indians in Southeast Asia,* Singapore: Times Academic Press, 1993, pp. 625-66.

————— 'Will Forever Flow the Ayeywarwady?' in Daljit Singh, ed., *Southeast Asian Affairs 1994.* Singapore: Institute of Southeast Asian Studies, 1994, pp. 209-32.

Kiryu, Minoru, 'Performance and Prospects of the Myanmar Economy', in Daljit Singh, ed., *Southeast Asian Affairs 1992.* Singapore: Institute of Southeast Asian Studies, 1992, pp. 238-56.

Kurlantzick, Joshua, 'Can Burma Reform?', *Foreign Affairs*, Vol. 81, No. 6 (November-December 2002), pp. 133-46.

Kyaw Yin Hlaing, 'The Politics of Government-Business Relations in Myanmar', *Asian Journal of Political Science*, 10, 1 (June 2002).

————— 'Myanmar in 2004: Why Military Rule Continues', in Chin Kin Wah and Daljit Singh, eds, *Southeast Asian Affairs 2004.* Singapore: Institute of Southeast Asian Studies, 2004, pp. 231-56.

————— 'Burma: Civil Society Skirting Regime Rules', in Muthiah Alagappa, eds, *Civil Society and Political Change in Asia: Expanding and Contracting Democratic Space.* Stanford: Stanford University Press, 2004, pp. 389-418.

————— 'Aung San Suu Kyi of Myanmar: A Review of the Biographies', *Contemporary Southeast Asia* 29, 2 (August 2007), pp. 359-76.

————— 'The Politics of Language Policy in Myanmar: Imagining Togetherness, Practising Difference?', in Lee Hock Guan and Leo Suryadinata, eds, *Language, Nation and Development in Southeast Asia.* Singapore: Institute of Southeast Asian Studies, 2007, pp. 150-80.

Lall, Marie, 'The Geopolitics of Energy in Asia: Indo-Chinese Competition over Myanmar's Far Reserves', *Panorama*, 2/2007, pp. 35-48.

Lambrecht, Curtis W., 'Oxymoronic Development: The Military as Bene-factor in the Border Regions of Burma', in Christopher R. Duncan, ed., *Civilising the Margins: Southeast Asian Government Policies for the Development of Minorities.* Ithaca: Cornell University Press, 2004, pp. 150-81.

Lorch, Jasmin, 'Civil Society under Authoritarian Rule: The Case of Myanmar', *Sudostasien Aktuell,* 2, 2006, pp. 3-38.

———— 'Myanmar's Civil Society—A Patch for the National Education System?', *Sudostasien Aktuell,* 3, 2007, pp. 55-88.

Matthews, Bruce, 'Myanmar: Beyond the Reach of International Relief?', in Daljit Singh and Anthony Smith, eds, *Southeast Asian Affairs 2001.* Singapore: Institute of Southeast Asian Studies, 2001, pp. 229-50.

Mutebi, Alex M., '"Muddling Through" Past Legacies: Myanmar's Civil Bureaucracy and the Need for Reform', in Kyaw Yin Hlaing, Robert H. Taylor and Tin Maung Maung Than, eds, *Myanmar: Beyond Politics to Societal Imperatives.* Singapore: Institute of Southeast Asian Studies, 2005, pp. 140-60.

Pedersen, Morten B., 'The World According to Burma's Military Rulers', in David S. Mathieson and R.J. May, ed., *The Illusion of Progress: The Political Economy of Reform in Burma/Myanmar.* Belair, South Australia: Crawford House, 2004, pp. 85-136.

———— 'Myanmar: The Future Takes Form—But Little Change in Sight', in Daljit Singh and Lorraine C. Salazaar, eds, *Southeast Asian Affairs 2007.* Singapore: Institute of Southeast Asian Studies, 2007, pp. 217-41.

Rajah, Ananda, 'A "Nation of Intent" in Burma: Karen Ethno-Nationalism, Nationalism, and Narrations of Nation', *The Pacific Review,* Vol. 15, No. 4 (2002), pp. 517-37.

Scott-Clarke, Cathy and Adrian Levy, 'Portrait: Aung San Suu Kyi', *Prospect,* July 2001, pp. 46-50.

Seekins, Donald, 'The North Wind and the Sun: Japan's Response to the Political Crisis in Burma, 1988-1998', *The Journal of Burma Studies,* Vol. 4, 1999, pp. 1-34.

Sherman, Jake, 'Burma: Lessons from the Cease-Fires', in Karen Ballentine and Jake Sherman, eds, *The Political Economy of Armed Conflict: Beyond Greed and Grievance.* Boulder and London: Lynne Rienner, 2003, pp. 225-55.

Silverstein, Josef, 'Fifty Years of Failure in Burma', in M.E. Brown and S. Ganguly, eds, *Government, Politics and Ethnic Relations in Asia and the Pacific.* Cambridge, MA: MIT Press, 1997, pp. 157-96.

———— 'Burma's Struggle for Democracy: The Army Against the People', in R.J. May and Viberto Selochan, eds, *The Military and Democracy in Asia and the Pacific*. Bathurst: Crawford House, 1998.

Skidmore, Monique, 'Darker than Midnight: Fear, Vulnerability, and Terror Making in Urban Burma (Myanmar)', *American Ethnologist*, 30, 1 (February 2003), pp. 5-21.

Smith, Martin T., 'Ethnic Politics and Regional Development in Myanmar: The Need for New Approaches', in Kyaw Yin Hlaing, Robert H. Taylor and Tin Maung Maung Than, eds, *Myanmar: Beyond Politics to Societal Imperatives*. Singapore: Institute of Southeast Asian Studies, 2005, pp. 56-87.

South, Ashley, 'Karen Nationalist Communities: The "Problem" of Diversity', *Contemporary Southeast Asia*, Vol. 29, No. 1 (April 2007), pp. 55-74.

Steinberg, David I., 'International Rivalries in Burma: The Rise of Economic Competition', *Asian Survey*, Vol. 30, No. 6 (June 1990), pp. 587-601.

———— 'Japanese Economic Assistance to Burma: Aid in the "Tarengashii Manner?"', *Crossroads*, 5:2 (1990).

———— 'Democracy, Power, and the Economy in Myanmar: Donor Dilemmas', *Asian Survey*, Vol. 31, 8 (August 1991), pp. 729-42.

———— 'Myanmar 1991: Military Intransigence', in Daljit Singh, ed., *Southeast Asian Affairs 1992*. Singapore: Institute of Southeast Asian Studies, 1992, pp. 221-37.

———— 'Myanmar: Regional Relationships and Internal Concerns', in Derek de Cunha and John Funston, eds, *Southeast Asian Affairs 1998*. Singapore: Institute of Southeast Asian Studies, 1998, pp. 179-98.

———— 'Myanmar: Reconcilation—Progress in the Process?', in Daljit Singh and Chin Kin Wah, eds, Southeast Asian Affairs 2003. Singapore: Institute of Southeast Asian Studies, 2003, pp. 171-88.

———— 'Myanmar: The Roots of Economic Malaise', in Kyaw Yin Hlaing, Robert H. Taylor and Tin Maung Maung Than, eds, *Myanmar: Beyond Politics to Societal Imperatives*. Singapore: Institute of Southeast Asian Studies, 2005, pp. 86-116.

———— 'The United States and Its Allies: The Problem of Burma/Myanmar Policy', *Contemporary Southeast Asia* 29, 2 (August 2007), pp. 210-37.

Taylor, Robert H., 'Burma: Defence Expenditure and Threat Perceptions', in Chin Khin Wah, ed., *Defence Expenditure in Southeast Asia*. Singapore: Institute of Southeast Asian Studies, 1987, pp. 252-80.

———— 'Myanmar: 1990, New Era or Old?' in Sharon Siddique and Ng Chee Yuen, eds, *Southeast Asian Affairs 1991*. Singapore: Institute of Southeast Asian Studies, 1991, pp. 199-221.

———— 'The Military in Myanmar: What Scope for a New Role?', in Viberto Selochan, ed., *The Military, the State, and Development in Asia and the Pacific*. Boulder: Westview Press, 1991.

———— 'External Dimensions of the Myanmar Situation', in Rohana Mahmood and Hans-Joachim Esderts, eds, *Myanmar and the Wider Southeast Asia*. Kuala Lumpur: Institute of Strategic and International Studies Malaysia, 1991, pp. 23-32.

———— 'J S. Furnivall and the Bankruptcy of Burma: Disaster or Release?', *Modern Asian Studies*, 29, 1 (February 1995), pp. 45-63.

———— 'Myanmar: New, but Different?' in Daljit Singh and Liak Teng Kiat, eds, *Southeast Asian Affairs 1995*. Singapore: Institute of Southeast Asian Studies, 1995, pp. 241-57.

———— Elections in Burma/Myanmar: For Whom and Why?', in Robert H. Taylor, ed., *The Politics of Elections in Southeast Asia*. New York: Cambridge University Press, 1996, pp. 164-83.

———— 'Do States Make Nations? The Politics of Identity in Myanmar Revisited', *South East Asian Research*, 13, 3 (November 2005), pp. 261-85.

———— '"One Day, One Fathom, Bagan Won't Move": On the Myanmar Road to a Constitution", in Trevor Wilson, ed., *Myanmar's Long Road to National Reconciliation*. Singapore: Institute of Southeast Asian Studies, 2006, pp. 3-28.

———— 'Growing Pressure for Change but the Regime Remains Obdurate', in Daljit Singh and Tin Maung Maung Than, eds, *Southeast Asian Affairs 2008*. Singapore: Institute of Southeast Asian Studies, 2008), pp. 247-73.

Tin Maung Maung Than, 'Burma in 1987: Twenty-Five Years After the Revolution', in Mohammed Ayoob and Ng Chee Yuen, eds, *Southeast Asian Affairs 1988*. Singapore: Institute of Southeast Asian Affairs, 1988, pp. 73-96.

———— 'Burma's National Security and Defence Posture,' *Contemporary Southeast Asia*, Volume II, No. 1 (June 1989), pp. 40-60.

———— 'Myanmar Democratization: Punctuated Equilibrium or Retrograde Motion', in Anek Laothamatas, ed., *Democratisation in Southeast and East Asia*. Singapore: Institute of Southeast Asian Studies, 1997, pp. 167-214.

———— 'Myanmar and China: A Special Relationship?', in Daljit Singh and Chin Kin Wah, eds, *Southeast Asian Affairs 2003*. Singapore: Institute of Southeast Asian Studies, 2003, pp. 189-212.

———— 'Myanmar's Energy Sector: Banking on Natural Gas', in Chin Kin Wah and Daljit Singh, eds, *Southeast Asian Affairs 2004*. Singapore: Institute of Southeast Asian Studies, 2004, pp. 257-92.

———— 'The Essential Tension: Democratization and the Unitary State in Myanmar (Burma)', *South East Asia Research*, 12, 2 (July 2004), pp. 187-212.

———— 'Myanmar: Challenges Galore for Opposition Failed to Score', in Daljit Singh and Lorraine C. Salazar, ed., *Southeast Asian Affairs 2006*. Singapore: Institute of Southeast Asian Studies, 2006, pp. 183-207.

———— 'Myanmar's Foreign Trade under Military Rule: Patterns and Recent Trends', in Daljit Singh and Lorraine C. Salazaar, eds, *Southeast Asian Affairs 2007*. Singapore: Institute of Southeast Asian Studies, 2007, pp. 242-56.

Tonkin, Derek, 'The 1990 Elections in Myanmar: Broken Promises or a Failure of Communication?', *Contemporary Southeast Asia*, Vol. 29, No. 1 (2007), pp. 33-54.

United Nations Development Programme, *Human Development Report 2007/2008*. Basingstoke: Palgrave, 2007.

Warr, Peter G., 'The Failure of Myanmar's Agricultural Policies', in Daljit Singh, ed., *Southeast Asian Affairs 2000*. Singapore: Institute of Southeast Asian Studies, 2000, pp. 219-40.

Wingfield, Tom, 'Myanmar: Political Stasis and a Precarious Economy', in Daljit Singh, ed., *Southeast Asian Affairs 2006*. Singapore: Institute of Southeast Asian Studies, 2006, pp. 203-18.

Yawnghwe, Chao-Tzang, 'Burma: The Depoliticization of the Political', in Muthiah Alagappa, ed., *Political Legitimacy in Southeast Asia: The Quest for Moral Authority*. Stanford: Stanford University Press, 1995, pp. 170-92, 364-75.

Official Myanmar publications in English

Address Delivered by the Chairman of the National Convention Convening Commission Lt Gen Myo Nyunt at the National Convention Plenary Session on 18 January 1994. Yangon(?): 1994.

Address Delivered by the State Law and Order Restoration Council Chairman Defence Services Commander-in-Chief Senior General Saw Maung at the Closing Ceremony of Course No. 4 of the Command and General Staff College on May 24th 1991. Yangon: Ministry of Information, August, 1991.

Attitude of the Nationalities Peace Groups. Yangon: New Light of Myanmar, December 1998.

Brief Account on National Convention. Np: nd [2004?]. In Burmese and English.

Burma Communist Party's Conspiracy to Take Over State Power. Yangon: Ministry of Information, 12 September 1989. Burmese and English.

Central Committee for Drug Abuse Control, Ministry of Home Affairs, *Narcotics Bulletin*, January-June 1990.

——— *The 15 Year Narcotics Elimination Plan.* Np: Nd [1999?].

——— *Prevention of Amphetamine Type Stimulants (ATS) in Myanmar.* Nd; NP.

——— *Endeavours of Drug Elimination in Myanmar (1999-2000): First Phase of the 15 Year Plan.* NP, (2001?).

Central Statistical Organisation, *Statistics Yearbook 2005.* Naypyitaw: 2007.

A Concise History of Myanmar and the Tatmadaw's Role 1948-1988. Yangon: News and Periodicals Enterprises, 1991.

The Conspiracy of Treasonous Minions within the Myanmar Naing-ngan and Traitorous Cohorts Abroad. Yangon: Ministry of Information, 23 October 1989.

Daw Suu Kyi, NLD Party and Our Ray of Hope. Yangon: Ministry of Information, September, 2003.

For Whom Does the US Impose Economic Sanctions on Myanmar? and Other Articles. Yangon: Ministry of Information, December 2004.

'Foreign Investment Commission, Union of Burma, Types of Economic Activities Allowed for Foreign Investment.' Yangon: Notification No. 1/89, 30 May 1989.

Fundamental Principles and Detailed Basic Principles adopted by the National Convention in drafting the State Constitution. Bilingual edition. NP: Ministry of Information, September 2007.

'"Give Us a Chance": An Interview with Senior General Than Shwe, Chairman, State Peace and Development Council,' Union of Myanmar, *Leader Magazine*, Vol. 21, No. 2 (1998), reprinted in *Thakaung Taman* (Ministry of Foreign Affairs Annual Magazine, Yangon, 1999), pp. 142-7.

Hla Min, *Political Situation of the Union of Myanmar and Its Role in the Region.* NP: 28th edition, April 2004.

Historic Records of Endeavours Made by the State Law and Order Restoration Council (From 1 April 1995 to 14 November 1997). Yangon: Ministry of Information, News and Periodicals Enterprises, July, 1999.

International Committee of the Red Cross (ICRC) in Myanmar. NP: Ministry of Home Affairs, ND.

Mass Rallies in Support of the Seven-Point Road Map. Np: np, nd.

Maung Pho Shoke, *Why Did U Khun Sa's MTA Exchange Arms for Peace?* Yangon: Aung Zaw, 1999.

Min Maung Maung, *The Tatmadaw and Its Leadership Role in National Politics.* Yangon: Ministry of Information, 1993.

Ministry of Foreign Affairs, *History and Activities.* Yangon: 2005.

Ministry of Home and Religious Affairs, Central Committee for Drug Abuse Control, *Narcotics Bulletin*, January-June 1990.

Ministry of Home Affairs, Endeavours. NP: ND.

Ministry of Labour and United National Population Fund, *Handbook on Human Resources Development Indicators, 2002.* Yangon: May 2003.

Ministry of National Planning and Economic Development, *Economic Development of Myanmar.* Yangon, 1998.

—————— *Myanmar's Socio-economic Development (Up to the end of December 2004).* Restricted. January 2005.

Ministry of Planning and Finance, Government of the Union of Myanmar, *Economic and Social Indicators.* Restricted. Yangon: March 1990.

—————— *The Central Bank of Myanmar Rules.* Yangon: April 1991.

Nation Building Endeavours: Historic Record of Endeavours Made by the State Law and Order Restoration Council from 1 April 1995 to 14 November 1997. Volume III, Yangon: Ministry of Information, July 1999.

New Light of Myanmar, Attitude of the Nationalities Peace Groups. December 1998.

Office of the Attorney General, *Myanmar Laws (1988-89).* Yangon: March 1999.

——————, *Myanmar Laws (1990).* Yangon: June 2001.

——————, *Myanmar Laws (1991-1992).* Yangon: June 2001.

——————, *Myanmar Laws (1993-1994).* Yangon: June 2003.

——————, *Myanmar Laws (1995-1996).* Yangon: April 2002.

——————, *Myanmar Laws (1997).* Yangon: March 1999.

——————, *Myanmar Laws (1998-1999).* Yangon: July, 2000.

——————, *Myanmar Laws (2000).* Yangon: January 2001.

——————, *Myanmar Laws (2001).* Yangon: July 2002.

——————, *Myanmar Laws (2002).* Yangon: January 2003.

——————, *Myanmar Laws (2003).* Yangon: January 2004.

——————, *Myanmar Laws (2004).* Yangon: January 2005.

——————, *Myanmar Laws (2005).* Yangon: January 2006.

——————, *Myanmar Laws (2006).* Naypyitaw: March 2007.

Office of Strategic Studies, Ministry of Defence, *Human Resource Development and Nation Building in Myanmar.* Yangon: 1997.

Press Conferences on Yodaya Myanmar Border Issue. Yangon: News and Periodicals Enterprises, August 2002. In Burmese and English.

Scheming and Activities of the Burma Communist Party Politburo to Seize State Power. Yangon: Ministry of Information, January 1990. English and Burmese.

Seminar on Understanding Myanmar. Yangon: Myanmar Institute of Strategic and International Studies, 2004.

Sentiments of Myanmar People (1998). Yangon: Committee to Hold Yangon Division Mass Meeting Expressing Sentiments of the People, December 1998.

Skyful of Lies: BBC, VOA, Their Broadcasts and Rebuttals to Disinformation, August 1988. Yangon: News and Periodicals Enterprises, Ministry of Information, July 1990.

Soe Mya Kyaw, *The Structure, Legislative Structure and Essence of Future State*. Naypyitaw: Ministry of Information, August 2006.

Speech Delivered by State Law and Order Restoration Council Secretary (1) Major General Khin Nyunt at the Special 110th Press Conference, 14 May 1991. Yangon: News and Periodicals Enterprises, Ministry of Information, August 1991.

State Law and Order Restoration Council Chairman Commander in Chief of the Defence Services General Saw Maung's Addresses. Yangon: Ministry of Information, Volume I, 1991; Volume II, October 1990. In Burmese and English.

State Law and Order Restoration Council's Stand Clarified Regarding Myanmar Naing-Ngan's National Objectives. Yangon: Ministry of Information, November 1990. English and Burmese.

Supreme Court, *The Judicial System of the Union of Myanmar*. March, 2001.

Sustainable Development in Education Sector, Health Sector. Naypyitaw: Ministry of Information, 2005.

Tatmadaw Researcher, A Concise History of Myanmar and the Tatmadaw's Role, 1948-1988. Yangon: NP: ND.

Union Solidarity and Development Association in Brief. Yangon: USDA, 2005.

Union Solidarity and Development Association. 23 February 2007.

Universities Historical Research Centre, *The 1947 Constitution and the Nationalities.* Yangon: Innwa Publishing House, Volume I and II, 1999.

Web of Conspiracy: Complicated Stories of Treacherous Machinations and Intrigues of BCP UG, DAB, and Some NLD Leaders to Seize State Power. Yangon: Ministry of Information, June 1991.

Yan Nyein Aye, *Endeavours of the Myanmar Armed Forces for National Reconsolidation.* Yangon: Aung Zaw, 2000.

Other sources in English

Amnesty International ASA a6/03.87: 'Allegations of Extraterritorial Executions, Torture and Ill Treatment in the Socialist Republic of the Union of Burma'. September 1987.

Brooten, Lisa, *Global Communications, Local Conceptions: Human Rights and the Politics of Communications among the Burmese Opposition-in-Exile.* PhD, Ohio University, Athens, Ohio, 2003.

Heidel, Brian, *The Growth of Civil Society in Myanmar.* NP: ND, photocopy, 2003?.

International Monetary Fund, Myanmar: *Staff Consultation Report for the 2006 Article IV Consultation.* 20 September 2006.

INGO Directory 2006: The Directory of International Non-Governmental Organisations (INGOs) and Red Cross Movement Organisations in Myanmar, compiled by International NGOs. Yangon: np, 2006.

Pedersen, Morten B., *Sanctions or Engagement? A Critique of Western Human Rights Policy on Burma/Myanmar.* PhD, Australian National University, September 2005.

Zarni and May Oo, *Common Problems, Shared Responsibilities: Citizens' Quest for National Reconciliation in Burma/Myanmar.* NP: Free Burma Coalition, October 2004.

Books and monographs in Burmese

Che, Hsaya, *Taja:hmja.ta tho. Patisun Demokayeisi Atweidwei ywei: kaukpwe kyi: thou.* (Towards a Multiple Party General Election which is Fair). Yangon: Aung Sitthe, February 1990.

Leiíla thutit u, *Myanmar-Ayemeiyikan Hsethsanyei: thamaing: (Akyaung:akyo: akaung:ahso: pakatihpyitsinmya* (An Observer, Myanmar-American Relations (Cause-effect, good-bad, normal/natural). Yangon: Digast Media Bank, May 2007.

Taingyintha Silonnyinyuntyei Pati, Sisyunyei Baho Komiti Danachok, Taingyintha Silonnyinyatyei Pati Lannyunt Thabawtaya (National Unity Party, Organisation Central Committee, National Unity Party's Policy Direction, Yangon: November 1995.

Official Myanmar publications in Burmese

Amyo:tha nyilahkan hni' patttheithow ahkye'ale'mya: akyi:hkyuí (Brief Account on National Convention). Nd: np.

Ahtwehtwe Okchok Yeihyuhkin (General Administration Affairs). Yangon: Ministry of Home Affairs, General Administration Department, January 1997.

Bohku'hmu:kji' Saw Maung ei' Mein.hkun:mya: Datiya. Twei (Senior General Saw Maung's Speeches, Volume 3). Yangon: Ministry of Information, February 1991.

Bohku'kji' Than: Hswei ei. Mein.khan:mya: (General Than Shwe's Speeches). Yangon: Ministry of Information, volume 1, August 1991; volume 2, September 1991, volume 3, September 1991.

Kabama Budda Batha Htei'thi Nyilahkan Hmattan, 9-11 Dizinbala 2004 (World Buddhist Summit Souvenir Album, 9-11 December 2004). Yangon: Ministry of Religious Affairs, July 2006.

Min Maung Maung, *Tatmadaw Amyotha Nainghgnanyei Uhsaunghmu Ahkan Kana* (Min Maung Maung, *The Army's National Political Leadership Role*). Yangon: News and Periodicals Enterprises, July 1995.

Myanmar Naingngan Tain: Kjou Pjipju., Naingngantow Njeinwu'pja: Hmu Tehshau'yei: Ahpwei. ei Hsaunjweichei Thamain:win Hmatan, 1988 Hku.hni'hma. 1991 Hku.hni (State of Myanmar Increasing Measures, State Law and Order Restoration Council Historical Record from 1988 to 1991). Yangon: SLORC, December, 1991.

Myanmar Naingngan Tain: Kjou Pjipju., Naingngantow Njeinwu'pja: Hmu Tehshau'yei: Ahpwei. ei Hsaunjwe'che' Thamain:win Hmatan, 1991 Hku.hni'hma. 1995 Hku.hni (State of Myanmar Increasing Measures, State Law and Order Restoration Council Historical Record from 1991 to 1995). Yangon: SLORC, September 1995.

Myanmar Naingngan Tain: Kjou Pjipju., Naingngantow Njeinwu'pja: Hmu Tehshau'yei: Ahpwei. ei Hsaunjweichei Thamain:win Hmatan, November la 15 yenei. 1997pyihnii hma. December 31 yenei 2000 pyinhi' (State of Myanmar Increasing Measures, State Law and Order Restoration Council Historical Record from 1988 to 1991). Yangon: SLORC, December 2001.

Pyihtaungsu Myanmar Naingngantaw Naingtaw Njeinwu'pja: Hmu Tehshau'yei: Ahpwei.Okata Bohkyo'hmu:kyi: Than: Shwe ei. Lan:nyunihmakya:hkye'mya: (kauknuthkye) (1992 hku.hni'hma 1995 hku.hni'ahti). (Union of Myanmar State Law and Order Restoration Council Chairman Senior General Than Shwe's Guidance (Excerpts) (From 1992 to 1995). Np: nd.

Pyihtaungsu Myanmar Naingngantaw Naingtaw Njeinwu'pja: Hmu Tehshau'yei: Ahpwei.Okata Bohkyo'hmu:kyi: Than: Shwe ei. Lan:nyun'hmakya:hkye'mya: (kauknuthkye) (1996 hku.hni'hma 2000 hku.hni'ahti. Union of Myanmar State Law and Order Restoration Council Chairman Senior General Than Shwei's Guidance (Excerpts) (From 1996 to 2000). Np: SPDP Office, nd.

Pyihteyei Wunkyidana, Naingngan Ayehkanthawayei hnin Hpohpyoyei Kaungsi Ochokyei Sanit Pyaunglehmu (Ministry of Home Affairs, Administrative Reform of State Peace and Development Council). 2004 (?).

Sethu Aung hnin. Maung Hma', *Shwe Pyitaw hmjo mawei: pyimo' (Sethu Aung and Maung Mma, The Golden Country Soon to be Expected)*. Yangon: Ministry of Information, October, 1993.

Si A Di Bi thomahtoui Pyipyei: ti' kyaw.pyan (CRDB or Catching Again an Expatriate). Yangon: Ministry of Information, 1990.

Tatmataw Thamaing: thaitama. Twei 1988-1993 (History of the Army, Part Seven, 1988-1993). Yangon: Sit Thamaing: Pyataik hnin Tatmataw Mawkwuntaik Hmuyoun, 2000.

Ye:kaung Kyawswa, *U: Nu. Pyipyei Bawa.ka. Batwei hpyi'hke.thale Batwei louihke.thale* (Ye Gaung Kyaw Swa, *U Nu's Expatriate World: What They Did and How They Acted).* Yangon: Ministry of Information, July 1991.

———— *Pyi twin njein:gjan:yei: ko Naingnghanyei:ne: hnin. Hpyeishin:kyathe Hsoyawe' (Declaring to Resolve by Political Means for Internal Peace).* Yangon: Ministry of Information, volumes 1 and 2, August 1991.

INDEX

Montagu-Chelmsford reforms 120-2, 179
Moulmein 167-8, 170
Mountbatten, Admiral 238, 264
Muslims 129, 201, 279, 355
Mya, Henzada U 175
Myanmar Fisheries Federation 448
Myanmar National Democratic Alliance 435
Myanmar Pyi National Solidarity Party 435
Myanmar Women's Affairs Federation 446-7
myei-daing (assistant to *thu-gyi* with special responsibilities for property and taxation) 35
Myinzaing, prince 159
myo 35
Myo/Khamo National Solidarity Organisation 420
Myochit (Patriots) Party 174, 188, 201
myo-ok (British-appointed township officer) 82, 85, 198
myo-sa 27; *see also* appanage system
myo-thu-gyi 35-7, 39, 84-6, 162; *see also* gentry, *thugyi*
myo-wun 23, 27, 34, 45
Nagani Book Club 210
naingngan (taw) (state) 1–3, 306, 311
National Coalition Government of the Union of Burma (NCGUB) 415-16, 427, 428
National Council of the Union of Burma 427, 428, 504
National Defence and Security Council (NDSC) 502
National Endowment for Democracy 426
National Intelligence Bureau 371-2
National League for Democracy (Liberated Area) 427
National League for Democracy (NLD) 403-20, 423, 425, 454, 464, 471-2, 489-92, 494-5
National Literary Conference 298

National Party 186, 198
National Solidarity Associations 245, 270, 317
National United Front (NUF) 250, 299
National Unity Party 410, 419-20
nationalism 10-11, 117-18, 121, 151-4, 166, 286-8, *see also names of parties*
nats 56, 59, 291
Naw Seng 271
Naypyitaw 399, 473, 484, 502
Ne Win, Lt. Col./Gen., Chairman 238-40, 251, 254, 271, 293, 296-7, 301, 304, 309, 322, 324-5, 355, 367-72, 380-7, 390-1, 476, 481, 484
Network for Democracy and Development (NDD) 427-8
New Democratic Army 436
New Mon State Party 428, 437
New Order Plan 227, *see also* Japan: invasion and occupation
NGOs 445-9
Non-Aligned Movement 301, 357, 464
Nu, Thakin, U 208, 210, 217, 223, 246, 247, 248, 251-2, 264, 265-6, 272-3, 290-2, 293, 294, 357, 359, 368, 369, 370, 392, 403, 404, 406

Office of Strategic Services 479
Ohn Pe, U 167-8
Ohn, U 208
oil 133-4, 187, 215-16, 238
opium growing 439, 442, 481-3
Ottama, U, 121, 179, 180, 183-4, 196

Pa O National Organisation 436-7
pahtamabyan examination 30
Pakistan 264, 303
Palaung State Liberation Army 436-7
Panglong Agreement 288, 305
Parliamentary Democracy Party 392
Party for National Democracy 415
patron-client relations 8, 17, 26-8, 45, 83, 87, 154
Paw Oo Tun 421; *see also* Min Ko Naing